THE ART OF THE THEATRE

THE ART

OF THE THEATRE

A Critical Anthology of Drama

~~~~~~

Edited by ROBERT W. CORRIGAN
New York University

and JAMES L. ROSENBERG
Carnegie Institute of Technology

 CHANDLER PUBLISHING COMPANY · SAN FRANCISCO

ANTIGONE, by Sophocles, translated by Michael Townsend, copyright © 1962 by Chandler Publishing Company, is used with the permission of the translator. "The Criticism of Greek Tragedy," by William Arrowsmith, is reprinted with the permission of the author from *Tulane Drama Review*, III:3, March, 1959.

LYSISTRATA, by Aristophanes, translated by Donald Sutherland, is copyright © 1961 by Chandler Publishing Company. "The Mythos of Spring: Comedy," by Northrop Frye, is reprinted by permission of Princeton University Press from *The Anatomy of Criticism*, by Northrop Frye, copyright © 1957 by Princeton University Press.

"*Macbeth* as the Imitation of an Action," by Francis Fergusson, is reprinted by permission of Columbia University Press from *English Institute Essays: 1951*, New York, Columbia University Press, 1952, pp. 41-43.

TARTUFFE, by Molière, translated by James L. Rosenberg, is copyright © 1962 by Chandler Publishing Company. "On the Nature of the Dramatic Emotion," by Émile Faguet, is translated by Philip M. Hayden for *TDR Document Series* and here reprinted by permission of Brander Matthews Museum, Columbia University.

MISS JULIE, by August Strindberg, and the author's *Preface* to *Miss Julie*, translated by E. M. Sprinchorn, are copyright © 1961 by Chandler Publishing Company.

UNCLE VANYA, by Anton Chekhov, translated by R. W. Corrigan, copyright © 1962 by R. W. Corrigan, is reprinted by permission of the translator and the publisher, Holt, Rinehart and Winston, Inc. "Comedy," by Christopher Fry, is copyright © December 26, 1950, by Christopher Fry and is reprinted by permission of the author.

"A Play: Scenario or Poem," by William L. Sharp, is reprinted with the permission of the author from *Tulane Drama Review*, V:2, December, 1960.

"Fundamental Interpretations of the Tragic," by Karl Jaspers, is reprinted by permission of the publishers from *Tragedy Is Not Enough*, by Karl Jaspers, copyright © 1952 Beacon Press.

THE ROSE TATTOO and *The Timeless World of a Play*, by Tennessee Williams, copyright 1950, 1951 by Tennessee Williams, are reprinted by permission of New Directions, Publishers; all rights reserved. Notes are based on the anthology version from Stanley A. Clayes and David G. Spencer, *Contemporary Drama*, copyright © 1962 by Charles Scribner's Sons.

THE NEW TENANT, by Eugène Ionesco, is reprinted from Eugène Ionesco's *Amedée, The New Tenant and Victims of Duty*, translated by Donald Watson, copyright © 1958 by John Calder (Publishers), Limited, published by Grove Press, Inc. "The Theatre in Search of a Fix," by Robert W. Corrigan, is reprinted with the permission of the author from *Tulane Drama Review*, V:4, June, 1961.

CONTENTS

PREFACE

There are only two grounds on which an anthology can justify its existence—inclusiveness and novelty. Our format, limiting us to ten plays, tends to inhibit inclusiveness, and novelty—particularly in an anthology—can very quickly reach a point of diminishing returns (one can represent Shakespeare by *Timon of Athens* instead of *Hamlet*, but to what purpose?).

At best, we can only modestly claim to have combined these two elements to the best of our ability. Within a ten-play limit, we have tried to include the entire history of the dramatic form—an aim which is nothing if not inclusive. At the same time, and without sacrificing the representative values of the individual plays, we have sought to avoid a mere rehash of the inevitable eight or ten Masterpieces of World Drama. While none of the plays in this volume (with the possible exception of the last one) is exactly a stranger to anthologies, we have tried, where feasible, to sidestep some of the more obvious chestnuts. Sophocles, as a result, is represented here by *Antigone*, not *Oedipus Rex;* Chekhov, by *Uncle Vanya*, not *The Cherry Orchard;* Williams, by *The Rose Tattoo*, not *A Streetcar Named Desire;* Ionesco, by the little-known but delightful *The New Tenant*, rather than by one of his half-dozen or so more widely publicized pieces.

Mere avoidance of main-traveled roads, though, is not in itself a guarantee of quality, and we have sought further to add a dimension to the book by accompanying each play with a critical essay of some sort. These essays, and the relationship they bear to their accompanying plays, vary widely, and should, we believe, offer concomitantly wide possibilities of use to both teachers and students. Some, for example, bear a very obvious and close relationship to their play, as does Strindberg's famous Preface to *Miss Julie* or Tennessee Williams' introduction to *The Rose Tattoo*. Others, while not so immediate in reference, offer examples of objective criticism of a specific work by a major critic; note, for instance, Francis Fergusson's "*Macbeth* as the Imitation of an Action" or William Arrowsmith's study of Greek tragedy. A third group—and perhaps the most interesting of all—consists of essays which are not immediately directed toward the plays they accompany in this volume, but which, on closer examination, can be seen as commenting upon them obliquely, subtly, and often quite provocatively. Some readers, for example, may be a little surprised to see an essay by Christopher Fry on "Comedy" employed here to shed light upon *Uncle Vanya*. But read the play and the essay side by side, and with care, and we suspect you will discover that they have more to say to and about one another than might appear at first glance. Similarly, Émile Faguet, writing on the nature of dramatic emotion, does little to analyze Molière's *Tartuffe* specifically, but says a great deal generally about the problems we encounter in trying to come to grips with such odd, ambiguous, and downright contradictory works. In short, we believe this combination of plays and essays is as interesting as it is flexible. Both of us have taught introductory courses in drama and theatre for a number of years now, and we have never found a text-anthology that has met the complex needs of such a course. There are undoubtedly many other teachers who feel the same way and we hope this volume begins to correct this state of affairs. It provides a chronological survey of the drama; it includes a sufficient variety of dramatic types to make it suitable for a genre approach to the teaching of drama; and the essays were chosen to serve the needs of those who believe the best way to teach the drama is to study its component elements, that is, language, character, plot, theme, and the like. The book, obviously, cannot be all things to all people; but that it may be is the foolhardy aspiration of every anthologist, including ourselves.

Finally, no anthology is complete as it stands when it comes off the presses. It requires, more than most books, the willing and active collaboration of every teacher and student who subsequently makes use of it. In a very real sense, each reader who uses, analyzes, and reshapes the following collection of plays and essays becomes our co-author, and it is to you, our unseen collaborators and colleagues in the world of drama, that we not only present but dedicate this volume.

Robert W. Corrigan
James L. Rosenberg

Carnegie Institute of Technology
Pittsburgh, Pennsylvania

THE ART OF THE THEATRE

SOPHOCLES

Antigone

Translated by MICHAEL TOWNSEND

∿∿∿∿∿∿∿∿∿∿∿∿∿∿∿∿∿∿∿∿∿

WILLIAM ARROWSMITH

The Criticism of
Greek Tragedy

THE CHARACTERS IN *ANTIGONE*

ANTIGONE

ISMENE

CREON

GUARD

HAEMON

TEIRESIAS

BOY

MESSENGER

EURYDICE

SERVANT

CHORUS

ANTIGONE

ANTIGONE   My darling sister Ismene, we have had
  A fine inheritance from Oedipus.
  God has gone through the whole range of sufferings
  And piled them all on us,—grief upon grief,
  Humiliation upon humiliation.   5
  And now this latest thing that our dictator
  Has just decreed . . . you heard of it? Or perhaps
  You haven't noticed our enemies at work.

ISMENE   No news, either good or bad, has come
  To me, Antigone: nothing since the day   10
  We were bereaved of our two brothers. No,
  Since the withdrawal of the Argive army
  Last night, I've heard nothing about our loved ones
  To make me glad or sad.

ANTIGONE   I thought as much.
  That's why I brought you out, outside the gate,   15
  So we could have a talk here undisturbed.

ISMENE   You've something on your mind. What is it then?

ANTIGONE   Only that our friend Creon has decided
  To discriminate between our brothers' corpses.
  Eteocles he buried with full honors   20
  To light his way to hell in a blaze of glory.
  But poor dear Polynices,—his remains
  Are not allowed a decent burial.
  He must be left unmourned, without a grave,
  A happy hunting ground for birds   25
  To peck for tidbits. This ukase applies
  To you,—and me of course. What's more, friend Creon
  Is on his way here now to supervise
  Its circulation in person. And don't imagine
  He isn't serious,—the penalty   30
  For disobedience is to be stoned to death.
  So, there you have it. You're of noble blood.
  Soon you must show your mettle,—if you've any.

ISMENE   Oh my fire-eating sister, what am I
  Supposed to do about it, if this is the case?   35

ANTIGONE   Just think it over—if you'll give a hand . . .

ISMENE   In doing what? What do you have in mind?

3

ANTIGONE   Just helping me do something for the corpse.

ISMENE   You don't intend to bury him? It's forbidden.

ANTIGONE   He is my brother, and yours. My mind's made up.
You please yourself.

ISMENE   But Creon has forbidden. . . .

5 ANTIGONE   What Creon says is quite irrelevant.
He is my brother. I will bury him.

ISMENE   Oh God.
Have you forgotten how our father died,
Despised and hated? How he turned
10 Detective to discover his own crimes,
Then stabbed his own eyes out with his own hands?
And then Jocasta, who was both together
His mother and his wife,
Hanged herself with a rope? Next, our two brothers
15 Became each other's murderers. We are left,
We two. How terrible if we as well
Are executed for disobeying
The lawful orders of the head of state.
Oh please remember,—we are women, aren't we?
20 We shouldn't take on men. In times of crisis
It is the strongest men who take control.
We must obey their orders, however harsh.
So, while apologizing to the dead,
Regretting that I act under constraint,
25 I will comply with my superior's orders.
Sticking one's neck out would be merely foolish.

ANTIGONE   Don't think I'm forcing you. In fact, I wouldn't
Have your assistance if you offered it.
You've made your bed; lie on it. I intend
30 To give my brother burial. I'll be glad
To die in the attempt,—if it's a crime,
Then it's a crime that God commands. I then
Could face my brother as a friend and look
Him in the eyes. Why shouldn't I make sure
35 I get on with the dead rather than with
The living? There is all eternity
To while away below. And as for you,
By all means be an atheist if you wish.

ISMENE   I'm not. I'm simply powerless to act
Against this city's laws.

40 ANTIGONE   That's your excuse.
Good-bye. I'm going now to make a grave
For our brother, whom I love.

ISMENE   Oh, dear.
   I'm terribly afraid for you.

ANTIGONE   Don't make a fuss
   On my account,—look after your own skin.

ISMENE   At least then promise me that you will tell
   No one of this; and I'll keep quiet too.   5

ANTIGONE   For God's sake don't do that,—you're sure to be
   Far more unpopular if you keep quiet.
   No; blurt it out, please do.

ISMENE   You're very cheerful.

ANTIGONE   That is because I'm helping those I know
   That I should help.

ISMENE   I only hope you can,   10
   But it's impossible.

ANTIGONE   Must I hang back
   From trying, just because you say I can't?

ISMENE   If it's impossible, you shouldn't try
   At all.

ANTIGONE   If that's your line, you've earned my hatred
   And that of our dead brother too, by rights.   15
   Oh, kindly let me go my foolish way,
   And take the consequences. I will suffer
   Nothing worse than death in a good cause.

ISMENE   All right then, off you go. I'm bound to say
   You're being very loyal, but very silly.   20

CHORUS   At last it has dawned, the day that sees
   The force that rode from Argos driven
   Back upon its road again
   With headlong horses on a looser rein.

   Roused by Polynices to aid his claim,   25
   Like an eagle screaming,
   With snow-tipped wings and bloody claws
   And mouth agape, it wheeled about our fortress doors.

   But Thebes, a hissing snake, fought back.
   The god of fire could get no grip   30
   Upon our crown of walls. That bird of prey,
   Its beak balked of our blood, has turned away.

   God hates presumption. When he saw
   Those men in ostentatious force

And clash of gold advancing,
He singled out one man all set
To shout the victory cry upon the parapet,
And flung at him a lightning bolt, to curtail his prancing.

5   Covered in flame he dropped
Down like an empty balance and drummed the earth;
He who before had breathed
The winds of hate against us. In many a foray and rout,
War, a runaway horse, was hitting out.

10   Seven enemy kings at seven gates,
Fighting at equal odds,
Left their arms as trophies to Theban gods.

Elsewhere, the hated pair,
Sons of the same mother,
15   Crossed their swords in combat and killed each other.

But now that Victory has smiled on us,
Let us forget the war, and dance
At every temple all night long. And let
Bacchus be king in Thebes, until the strong earth reels.

20   Ah, here comes Creon, our ruler,—in haste.
Something new has developed.
He has something afoot . . .
Else why has he summoned us to council?

CREON   Well, friends, our city has passed through stormy weather.
25   But now God has restored an even keel.
Why have I summoned you? Because I know
That you were at all times loyal to Laius.
And afterwards, when Oedipus put things right,
Then ruined them again, you showed
30   Your steadiness throughout his sons' dispute.
Well, now they're dead; and so, by due succession,
The power of the crown passes to me.
You cannot possibly judge a ruler's worth
Until he exercises the power he's got.
35   I've no time for the man who has full powers
Yet doesn't use them to enact good measures,
But adopts a timid policy of "do nothing."
Those aren't my principles. I'm not the man
To sit quietly by and watch my country

Sliding towards the precipice of ruin.
Nor can I be a friend to my country's foes.
This I believe—and God may witness it—
Our safety is bound up with that of our country. Therefore
All other loyalties are subject to   5
Our country's interests.
By such measures I'll make this city great;—
Measures like those that I have just enacted
Concerning Oedipus' sons. That Eteocles
Who died while fighting in his country's service,   10
Is to be buried with ceremonial honors.
But Polynices,—whose intention was
To fight his way back from exile, burn to the ground
His mother city and the temples of
His family's gods, to slaughter out of hand   15
And to enslave his fellow citizens—
He's not to have a grave or any mourning.
His corpse is to be left, a grim warning,
Pecked at by birds and worried by the dogs.
That is my policy. A malefactor mustn't   20
Have the same treatment as the loyal man.
I intend to see our country's friends rewarded
When they are dead, as well as while they live.

CHORUS   We understand the attitude you take
         Towards these men. It's true your word is law,   25
         And you can legislate for living and dead. . . .

CREON   What do you think then of this new enactment?

CHORUS   If I were younger, I might criticize . . . .

CREON   No turning back. The guard is set on the corpse.

CHORUS   What are the penalties for disobeying?   30

CREON   The penalty is death. As simple as that.

CHORUS   That ought to stop them. Who'd be such a fool?

CREON   You'd be surprised. Men led astray by hopes
        Of gain will risk even their lives for money.

GUARD   Sir, here I am. I can't pretend I'm puffed   35
        From running here with all possible speed.
        I kept changing my mind on the way.
        One moment I was thinking, "What's the hurry?
        You're bound to catch it when you get there." Then:
        "What are you dithering for? You'll get it hot   40
        And strong if Creon finds out from someone else."

Torn by these doubts I seem to have taken my time.
So what should be a short journey has become
A long one. Anyway I have arrived.
And now I'm going to tell you what I came
5   To tell you, even if you've heard it. See,
I've made up my mind to expect the worst.
We can't avoid what's coming to us, can we?

CREON   Well then, what puts you in such deep despair?

GUARD   First I must make a statement—about myself.
10   I didn't do it, and didn't see who did it.
So I'm quite in the clear, you understand.

CREON   For God's sake tell me what it is, and then
Get out.

GUARD   All right, all right. It amounts to this.
Somebody's buried the body, thrown earth on it,
15   And done the necessary purifications.

CREON   Someone has been a damn fool. Who was it?

GUARD   Dunno. There were no spade-marks in the earth.
The ground was hard and dry, and so there was
No sign of the intruder.
20   See, when the man who had the first day watch
Told us about it, we had the shock of our lives.
The corpse had not been buried in a grave,
But enough dust was thrown on to avoid
The curse unburied bodies suffer from.
25   There wasn't even a sign of any dog
That might have come and scuffed the dust upon him.
Then everyone started shouting. Each man blamed
His mate. We very nearly came to blows.
Everyone claimed that one of the others had done it,
30   And tried to prove that he himself was blameless.
To prove their innocence, some said they were
Prepared to pick up red-hot coals or walk
Through fire. While others swore on oath,
By a catalog of gods, they didn't do it
35   And weren't accomplices in any form.
When our investigations made no progress,
In the end one man came out with a sobering speech.
We couldn't answer him, though what he said
Was none too pleasant.
40   He said we mustn't try to hush it up,
But tell you everything. His view prevailed.
Who was to bring the news? We tossed for it.

I was the lucky person. I can tell you,
I don't like being the bearer of bad news.

CHORUS   I think I see the hand of God in this,
Bringing about the body's burial.

CREON   Shut up, before I lose my temper.   5
You may be old, try not to be foolish as well.
How can you say God cares about this corpse?
Do you suppose God feels obliged to him
For coming to burn down his temples and
His statues, in defiance of his laws?   10
Ever noticed God being kind to evildoers?
No. Certain hostile elements in the city
Who don't like discipline and resent my rule,
Are in on this. They've worked upon the guards
By bribes. There is no human institution   15
As evil as money. Money ruins nations,
And makes men refugees. Money corrupts
The best of men into depravity.
The people who have done this thing for money
Will get what's coming to them. Listen here,   20
I swear to you by God who is my judge,
That if you and your friends do not divulge
The name of him who did the burying
One hell won't be enough for you. You'll all
Be hanged up and flogged until you tell.   25
That ought to teach you to be more selective
About what you get your money from.

GUARD   Am I dismissed?
Or may I speak?

CREON   I thought I made it plain
I couldn't stand your talk.

GUARD   Where does it hurt you,—
Your ears, or in your mind?

CREON   What do you mean?   30
What does it matter where you give me pain?

GUARD   The guilty party bothers you deep down.
But my offense is only at ear level.

CREON   My dear good man, you're much too talkative.

GUARD   I may be that, but I am not your culprit.   35

CREON   I think you are, and that you did it for money.

GUARD   Oh God! I tell you your suspicions are wrong.

CREON   Suspicion he calls it! Look here, if you
Don't tell me who the culprits are, you'll find
That ill-gotten gains are not without their drawbacks.

GUARD   Good luck to you, I hope you find the man.
5   In any case I won't be in a hurry
To come back here again. I thank my stars
That I have saved my skin. I didn't expect to.

CHORUS   Many amazing things exist, and the most amazing is man.
He's the one, when the gale-force winds
10   Blow and the big waves
Tower and topple on every side,
Cruises over the deep on the gray tide.

He's the one that to and fro
Over the clods year after year
15   Wends with his horses and ploughing gear,
Works to his will the untiring Earth, the greatest of gods.

He traps the nitwit birds, and the wild
Beasts in their lairs. The ocean's myriad clan
In woven nets he catches,—ingenious man.

20   He has devised himself shelter against
The rigors of frost and the pelting weather.
Speech and science he's taught himself,
And the city's political arts for living together.

For incurable diseases he has found a cure;
25   By his inventiveness defying
Every eventuality there can be,—except dying.

But the most brilliant gifts
Can be misapplied.
On his moral road
30   Man swerves from side to side.

God and the government ordain
Just laws; the citizen
Who rules his life by them
Is worthy of acclaim.

35   But he that presumes
To set the law at naught
Is like a stateless person,
Outlawed, beyond the pale.

With such a man I'd have
No dealings whatsoever.
In public and in private
He'd get the cold shoulder.

What's this? What on earth?   5
My God. Can it be? Yes, Antigone.
Your father before, now you!
Is it so, you were caught disobeying the law?
How could you have been so stupid?

GUARD   Here she is. She is the one,—the one that did it.   10
We caught her in the act. Where's Creon gone?

CHORUS   There, by good luck he's coming out right now.

CREON   Soon as I leave the house, some trouble starts.
What's happening?

GUARD   Well, well, I never thought
That I'd be coming back here again so soon,   15
Considering how you swore at me just now.
But here I am, in spite of what I said.
I'm bringing in this girl. I caught her tending
The grave. I caught her, no one else. And so
I hand her over to you to stand her trial.   20
And now I reckon I'm entitled to beat it.

CREON   Give me full details, with the circumstances.

GUARD   This girl was burying him. As simple as that.

CREON   I trust you understand what you are saying.

GUARD   I saw her burying the corpse you said   25
Was not permitted to be buried. Clear enough?

CREON   Tell me precisely how you saw and caught her.

GUARD   It was like this. When we got back,
With your threats still smarting in our ears,
We swept all the dust from off the corpse,   30
And laid the moldering thing completely bare.
Then we went and sat on the high ground to windward,
To avoid the smell. And everyone gave hell
To the man who was on duty, to keep him up
To scratch. We watched till midday, when the sun   35
Is hottest. Suddenly a squall came on,—
A whirlwind with a thunderstorm; it ripped
The leaves from every tree in all the plain.
The air was full of it; we had to keep
Our eyes tight shut against the wrath of heaven.   40

At last, when all was over, there we see
The girl,—crying like a bird that finds
Its nest empty of chicks,—her having seen
The corpse uncovered. Then she started cursing
5   Whoever did it. Next she goes and fetches
Dust in her hands; and from a jug she pours
A set of three libations on the corpse.
When we saw that of course we jumped straight up
And grabbed the girl. She took it very calmly.
10   We charged her with this crime and the previous one,
And she admitted them. So I'm half glad,
Half sorry. Glad that I am out of danger,
But sorry someone that I like's in trouble.
However, main thing is that I'm all right.

15 CREON You, with your eyes fixed on the ground.
Do you admit the charges or deny them?

ANTIGONE I don't deny the charges. I admit them.

CREON (*to* GUARD) All right, clear off. Consider yourself lucky
To be absolved of guilt.
(*to* ANTIGONE) Now tell me, briefly,—I don't want a speech.
20   You knew about my edict which forbade this?

ANTIGONE Of course I knew. You made it plain enough.

CREON You took it on yourself to disobey?

ANTIGONE Sorry, who made this edict? Was it God?
Isn't a man's right to burial decreed
25   By divine justice? I don't consider your
Pronouncements so important that they can
Just . . . overrule the unwritten laws of heaven.
You are a man, remember.
These divine laws are not just temporary measures.
30   They stand forever. I would have to face
Them when I died. And I will die, without
Your troubling to arrange it. So, what matter
If I must die before my time? I'd welcome
An early death, living as I do now.
35   What I can't stand is passively submitting
To my own brother's body being unburied.
I dare say you think I'm being silly.
Perhaps you're not so very wise yourself.

CHORUS She's difficult, just like her father was.
40   She doesn't realize when to give in.

CREON I know these rigid temperaments. They're the first
To break. The hardest-tempered steel

Will shatter at a blow. The highest-mettled
Horses are broken in with a small bit.
That's what is needed, discipline. This girl
Knew damned well she was kicking over the traces,
Breaking the law. And now when she has done it,   5
She boasts about it, positively gloats.
If she gets away with this behavior,
Call me a woman and call her a man.
I don't care if she is my sister's daughter.
I don't care if she's closer to me than all   10
My family. She and her sister won't get off.
I'll execute them.
    Oh yes, her as well.
She's in it too. Go get her. She's inside.
I saw her in there muttering, half-balmy.
It is her conscience. She can't hide her guilt.   15
At least she doesn't try to justify it.

ANTIGONE Won't my death be enough? Do you want more?

CREON No, that will do, as far as I'm concerned.

ANTIGONE Then why not do it now? Our wills conflict
Head-on. No chance of reconciliation.   20
I can't think of a finer reason for dying,—
Guilty of having buried my own brother.
These men are on my side. But they daren't say so.

CREON That's where you're wrong. You're quite alone in this.

ANTIGONE They're on my side. They're forced to cringe to you.   25

CREON These men obey. But you and you alone
Decide to disobey. Aren't you ashamed?

ANTIGONE Ashamed? Ashamed of what? Ashamed of being
Loyal to my own family, my own brother?   30

CREON Eteocles was also your own brother.

ANTIGONE Indeed he was. Of course he was my brother.

CREON Then why were you so disloyal to him?

ANTIGONE If he were living now, he'd back me up.

CREON For treating his brother no differently from him!

ANTIGONE It was his brother that died, not just some servant.   35

CREON Died while commanding an invading force!
But Eteocles died fighting for his country.

ANTIGONE That doesn't affect the laws of burial.

CREON You can't treat friend and enemy the same.

ANTIGONE   Who knows what the rules are among the dead?

CREON   Your enemy doesn't become your friend by dying.

ANTIGONE   If we must have these groupings, let me say
I'll join anyone in loving, but not in hating.

5   CREON   All right then, die, and love them both in hell.
I'm not here to be shoved around by a woman.

CHORUS   Oh, look, by the gate, here's Ismene.
She's crying because of her sister.
What a shame this heavy cloud of grief
10   Should spoil her attractive appearance.

CREON   And now for you. You who've been skulking quiet,
Injecting your slow poison like a viper.
Imagine my not noticing,—I've been rearing
Two furies in my house, ready to bite
15   The hand that fed them. Just you tell me now—
Will you confess you were party to this burial,
Or will you swear you had no knowledge of it?

ISMENE   I did it, if she did it. I'm involved.
I'm in with her and bear my share of blame.

20   ANTIGONE   That's quite unjustified. You didn't want
To help me, and I didn't let you join me.

ISMENE   You are in trouble. May I then not make
Myself your comrade in adversity?

ANTIGONE   The dead know who it was that did the deed.
25   You took no action. Your speeches don't impress me.

ISMENE   How can you, being my sister, deny my wish
To die with you for Polynices' sake?

ANTIGONE   Don't go and die as well as me, and don't
Lay claim to what you haven't done. I'm going
To die. One death's enough.

30   ISMENE   Will life be worth
Living to me, left all alone without you?

ANTIGONE   May I suggest an object of affection?
Creon. He is your uncle, after all.

ISMENE   Why do you try to hurt me? What's the point?

35   ANTIGONE   I may make fun of you, but I feel this deeply.

ISMENE   I only want to know how I can help you.

ANTIGONE   Well, save yourself then. I don't grudge you that.

ISMENE   I don't want that. I want to die with you.

ANTIGONE   You chose to live; I chose to die, remember?

ISMENE   I didn't express my innermost convictions.

ANTIGONE   You sounded pretty convinced at the time.

ISMENE   I still maintain that we two share the guilt.   5

ANTIGONE   Don't worry. You won't die. But I've already
  Sacrificed my life to help the dead.

CREON   These girls! One of them's been mad all her life.
  And now the other one's gone balmy too.

ISMENE   But, sir, however sensible one is,   10
  Adversity is bound to affect one's judgment.

CREON   Well, it has yours! You join this criminal,
  And identify yourself with her misdeeds . . .

ISMENE   There is no life left for me without her.

CREON   Forget about her. She's as good as dead.   15

ISMENE   So you would execute your own son's bride?

CREON   Plenty of other women in the world.

ISMENE   But they were so well suited to each other.

CREON   I won't have my son marrying a bitch.

ANTIGONE   Poor Haemon! See how much your father cares.   20

CREON   Oh, go to hell,—you and your marriage with you,

ISMENE   You really intend to take her from your son?

CREON   I won't stop the marriage. Death will stop it.

ISMENE   There's no way out? It is fixed that she dies?

CREON   Of course it's fixed. Stop wasting time.   25
  You servants, take her in. It's very important
  To keep women strictly disciplined.
  That's the deterrent. Even the bravest people
  Will step down quick when they see death loom up.

CHORUS   Happy the man whose life is uneventful.   30
  For once a family is cursed by God,
  Disasters come like earthquake tremors, worse
  With each succeeding generation.

  It's like when the sea is running rough
  Under stormy winds from Thrace.   35
  The black ooze is stirred up from the sea-bed,
  And louder and louder the waves crash on shore.

Look now at the last sunlight that sustains
The one surviving root of Oedipus' tree,—
The sword of death is drawn to hack it down.

And all through nothing more than intemperate language.
5   All through nothing more than hasty temper.

What power on earth can resist
Your strength, O God? You stand supreme,
Untouched by sleep that makes all else feel old,
Untired by the passing years that wear all else away.

10 I know one rule that has stood,
And will stand, forever.
That nothing in our life can be exempt
From the universal forces that make for ruin.

Hope, that tramps all roads, may help at times.
15 More often, it deludes weak-minded men.
They never notice, till they feel the fire.

It is a wise saying, that
When God is set against you,
You welcome the path to ruin,—but not for long.

20 Here comes Haemon, your youngest son.
I expect he's grieved about his bride,
And this sudden bar to his marriage.

CREON   There's one way of finding out for certain.
My son, you've heard about this public decree.
25 Have you come here in a spirit of indignation
About your bride, or are you going to be
Loyal to me whatever I'm involved in?

HAEMON   I am your son. So while your policies
Are just, you have my full obedience.
30 I certainly wouldn't consider any marriage
As important as the right leadership by you.

CREON   Good, good. Your heart is in the right place. Nothing
Should come before your loyalty to your father.
Why else do fathers pray for well-behaved sons?
35 They do things together. Work together against
Their common enemy. Vie with each
Other in being good friends to their friends.
As for the man who brings up useless sons,

He's got himself a load of trouble,—all
His enemies laugh at them, a bad team.
Never get carried away by a woman, son.
Sex isn't everything. If she's a bitch,
You'll feel a coldness as she lies beside you.   5
Can there be anything worse than giving your love
To a bitch that doesn't deserve it? No, reject her,
And let her go and find a husband in hell.
Now that I've caught her flagrantly disobeying
When everybody else has toed the line,   10
The eyes of the nation are on me. I must stay
True to my principles. I must execute her.
I don't give a damn for all her talk
About family ties. If I allow
My own relations to get out of control,   15
That gives the cue to everybody else.
People who are loyal members of their families
Will be good citizens too. But if a person
Sets himself up above the law and tries
To tell his rulers what they ought to do,—   20
You can't expect me to approve of that.
Once a man has authority, he must be obeyed,—
In big things and in small, in every act,
Whether just or not so just. I tell you this,
The well-disciplined man is good   25
At giving orders and at taking them too.
In war, in a crisis, he's the sort of man
You like to have beside you. On the other hand,
There's nothing so disastrous as anarchy.
Anarchy means an ill-disciplined army,   30
A rabble that will break into a panic rout.
What follows? Plundered cities, homeless people.
A disciplined army loses few men;
Discipline pulls them through to victory.
We can't go about kowtowing to women.   35
If I must lose my throne, let it be a man
That takes it from me. I can't have people saying
My will has been defeated by a woman.

CHORUS   I think your observations very just,
In general . . . though perhaps I'm old and silly.   40

HAEMON   Father, don't you agree,—
Of all God's gifts, good sense is far the best.
I'm sure I'd be the last person to deny
That what you said is true. Yet there may be
A lot of justice in the opposite view.   45

I've one advantage over you,—I know
Before you what the people think about you,
Especially criticism. You're so held in awe
That people dare not say things to your face.
5   But I am able to hear their secret talk.
The people feel sorry for Antigone.
They say it isn't equitable she must die
   A horrible death for such a noble action.
They say that she in fact deserves special
10   Honor for refusing to allow
The body of her brother to be left
Unburied for dogs and birds to pull to pieces.
That is their secret opinion, and it's gaining ground.
Of course I want your rule to be a success.
15   There's nothing more important to me than that.
Such feeling is mutual, between father and son,—
One's glad to see the other doing well.
Don't be too single-minded, then. Don't think
You have a complete monopoly of the truth.
20   Isn't it true that people who refuse
   To see any other point of view but theirs
Often get shown up and discredited?
However acute one is, there's no disgrace
In being able to learn, being flexible.
25   In winter, when the streams turn into torrents,
   You can see the trees that try to resist the water
Get rooted out and killed. But those that bend
A little, manage to survive the flood.
In a gale at sea if you cram on full sail,
30   You'll soon have the waves breaking aboard
And bowling over all the furniture.
Why not relax and change your mind for once?
Perhaps at my age I should not express
An opinion, but I would like to say this:—
35   Not everyone can be right on every issue,
But the next best thing is to take notice of
And learn from the judicious thoughts of others.

CHORUS   Yes, everyone can learn. You, sir, can learn
From him,—and he of course from you. There's much
40   Of substance in the arguments on both sides.

CREON   Am I to stand here and be lectured to
By a kid? A man of my experience!

HAEMON   I'm not suggesting anything illegal.
I may be young, but judge me by the facts.

CREON The facts are, you're encouraging my detractors.

HAEMON I'm not encouraging anything that's wrong.

CREON You seem to have caught Antigone's disease.

HAEMON The people of Thebes don't call it a disease.

CREON Must I ask their permission for everything? 5

HAEMON You're talking like an adolescent now.

CREON Am I the king of Thebes, or am I not?

HAEMON It takes more than one person to make a nation.

CREON But a nation is personified in its ruler.

HAEMON In that case Thebes has got no population. 10

CREON I take it you are siding with this woman.

HAEMON It is your interests I have at heart.

CREON You show it by arguing against me?

HAEMON Because I think you're making a mistake.

CREON Must I let my authority be undermined? 15

HAEMON Yes, rather your authority than God's.

CREON What character! Subservient to a woman.

HAEMON Subservient to what I think is right.

CREON You've done nothing but back Antigone up.

HAEMON Not only her, but God, and you as well. 20

CREON Don't try to butter me up, you ladies' man.

HAEMON You like to talk, but you're not prepared to listen.

CREON This woman will not live to marry you.

HAEMON Then she won't be the only one to die.

CREON Oh, oh. Threats is it now? You've got a nerve. 25

HAEMON I'm trying to show you that you're being perverse.

CREON You will regret you tried to schoolmaster me.

HAEMON If you weren't my father, I'd say you were deranged.

CREON What's that? I've had enough of your abuse.
By heaven, I swear I'll make you suffer for it. 30
Take that hell-cat away. You'll watch her die.
Ha, she will die in front of her bridegroom's nose.

HAEMON I won't give you that satisfaction.
I won't be around when she dies.

You must find other friends to condone your madness.
You will never set eyes on me again.

CHORUS   He's rushed off in a really furious temper.
He's young,—I fear he may do something rash.

5   CREON   Let him.
Who does he think he is, God almighty?
In any case, he won't save these girls from death.

CHORUS   You don't mean to execute them both?

CREON   No, no. You're right. Not her that wasn't involved.

10   CHORUS   What sort of execution do you intend?

CREON   I'll take her to a deserted spot
And bury her alive in a trench.
She'll have enough food to avoid the curse,—
The people mustn't suffer because of her.
15   There she can pray to the god she likes so much,—
The god of death. Perhaps he'll save her life.
Either that, or she'll find out too late
That corpses are more trouble than they're worth.

CHORUS   What is it that nestles in
20   The soft cheeks of a girl,
And pervades the deep sea and the teeming earth,
And persecutes god and man, a force
Irresistible? We call it Love.
A man possessed by Love loses control.
25   Love drives the law-abiding into crime;
And sets a family against itself.

So here a lovely girl's appealing glance
Has prevailed, and destroyed the bonds of blood.
For Love makes mock of time-honored laws
30   Ordaining loyalty from son to father.

And grief also is irresistible.
The tears come to my eyes,—I cannot stop them;
Seeing Antigone go to such a bed,
The bed that puts all mortal things to sleep.

35   ANTIGONE   Take a good look. With life still strong in me,
I'm going on my last journey, seeing
For the last time the bright rays of the sun.

Unmarried, never having heard my wedding song,
Death takes me to the dark riverbanks to be his bride.

CHORUS   You have one glorious consolation.
  By your own choice you go down to death
  Alive, not wasted by disease,
  Nor hacked by instruments of war.

ANTIGONE   I shall go to sleep like Niobe.   5
  I know her story well. On Mount Sipylus
  The rock grew, like ivy, round her and weighed her down.
  And now the rain and snow
  Make tears that run across her stony face.

CHORUS   There's no comparison. For she was born   10
  Of divine parentage. You would be lucky
  To share the fate of mythical heroines.

ANTIGONE   Are you getting at me? Wait till I'm dead.
  I'm going to die,—do I merit no respect?
  O my city, O my friends, rich householders,   15
  O river Dirce, with the sacred grove
  Of Thebes the Charioteer, I call you all
  To witness that I die with nobody
  To shed a tear for me, the victim
  Of an unjust law. Who'd like to go with me   20
  To an eerie heap of stones, a tomb that is no tomb,
  A no-man's land between the living and the dead?

CHORUS   You tried to do the right thing by your brother.
  You stepped boldly towards the altar of Justice,
  But somehow stumbled. I fear you must suffer   25
  For your father's sins.

ANTIGONE   Don't speak of it again. It's only too well known,—
  My father's fate. To think how much
  Our family was admired, in generations past.
  Then came successive strokes of doom. My mother's   30
  Marriage to her son, the union
  From which I came, to end like this.
  My brother, dishonored, drags me down with him.
  And so I go to join my stricken family in hell.

CHORUS   We respect what you did for your brother.   35
  But there's no question that the orders
  Of those in authority must be obeyed.
  You were self-willed. That has been your undoing.

ANTIGONE   I see I have no friends to say good-bye.
  No friends, no tears for me, no marriage to look back on.   40
  Never again to see the face of the sun.

CREON   If I don't stop this blubbering, we'll be here
  All night. Stop wasting time. Take her away.

As my instructions state, you are to place
Her in the vaulted trench, and brick it in.
It's up to her then,—either live or die.
My hands are clean in this. I've merely
5   Deprived her of all contact with the living.

ANTIGONE   This stone dugout, half tomb, half bridal-chamber,
Will house me now for good. By this road
I go below to Queen Persephone's kingdom,
To see again so many of my family.
10   As I am the latest recruit, so is my fate
By far the cruelest. And I've not used
My life's full span.
At least I can look forward to a warm
Welcome from my dear mother and father and
15   My brother Eteocles. When they were dead,
I washed them and prepared them for the grave
With my own hands, and poured libations over them.
But now, for doing the same to Polynices,
This is my reward. Because Creon thinks
20   I have committed an act of brazen defiance.
For this I'm being dragged off by force,
Deprived of my chance to marry and raise children.
I'm to be buried alive, not very pleasant. . . .
I just want to ask, what moral law
25   Have I disobeyed? But what's the point
Of appealing to God? Or asking
Help from my fellow humans? It appears
That virtue is to be repaid by malice.
If that is God's idea of what is right,
30   Then I apologize; I made a mistake.
But if Creon is wrong, I only hope
He isn't treated any better than me.

CHORUS   A hurricane of passionate conviction
Still sweeps her mind.

35   CREON   Don't stand about, you lot; or else . . .
Hurry, and off with her.

ANTIGONE   Oh, right before me now. Death.

CHORUS   If you had any hopes, I should forget them.
Your punishment is fixed. There's no appeal.

40   ANTIGONE   This is it. The time has come.
For doing what was right,
I'm dragged away to death.
And Thebes, city where I was born,

And you my friends, the rich people of Thebes,
Will you judge between us?
You might at least look and remember.

CHORUS   My poor child, what must be
   Must be. Console yourself,   5
   Such things have happened before.

   There's nothing that can win the fight
   Against the force of destiny;
   Not wealth, or military might,
   Or city walls, or ships that breast the sea.   10

   Lycurgus, king of Thrace, tried to stop
   The bacchanal women and their torchlit orgies.
   For his vindictive rage,
   He lost his liberty with his temper, locked
   By Bacchus in a mountain cave   15
   To let his anger simmer down.

   In Salmydessus on the Euxine Sea,
   The two sons of Phineus lost their eyes.
   In their stepmother's hand, a pointed shuttle . . .
   And their blood on her nails cried out for vengeance.   20

   But their mother was jailed in a cavern
   Under a steep mountain far away.
   She was Cleopatra, the North Wind's daughter.
   A god's daughter, but fate weighed her down.

[*Enter* TEIRESIAS, *led by a boy.*]

TEIRESIAS   Councillors of Thebes, I have come,—   25
   A man with four eyes, half of them blind . . .

CREON   It's old Teiresias. What's up, old fellow?

TEIRESIAS   Listen, and I will tell you. I'm no liar . . .

CREON   I've never suggested that. Quite the reverse.

TEIRESIAS   By doing so, you were able to save Thebes.   30

CREON   True, I have found what you have said most useful.

TEIRESIAS   Listen to me. You're on the razor's edge.

CREON   What's wrong? The way you talk gives me a turn.

TEIRESIAS   You may think nothing's wrong. But my skill
   Says differently.   35
   I went to my accustomed place

Of augury, where there's a wide view of
The sky, to observe the birds. There I heard
An unprecedented din of birds, barbarous,
Confused, as though some madness stung them into
5 Screaming. I heard them fighting with their claws;
The noise was unmistakable, their wings
Whirring . . . and I felt fear. Immediately
I tried the burnt sacrifices, but
They gave no flame. Only a damp vapor
10 Smoldered and spat. The gall burst in the fire,
Exposing the thighbones bare of fat.
The boy saw all this and told it me.
Thus I interpret. These signs portend evil
For Thebes; and the trouble stems from your policy.
15 Why? Because our altars are polluted
By flesh brought by dogs and birds, pickings
From Polynices' corpse. Small wonder that
The gods won't accept our sacrifices.
My son, I ask you to consider well
20 What you are doing. We all make mistakes.
The wise man, having made an error of judgment,
Will seek a remedy, not keep grinding on.
Obstinacy isn't far removed from folly.
The man is dead. No need to persecute him.
25 You can give way, with good grace, to a corpse.
He has died once, why try to kill him again?
I'm saying this because I wish you well.
A bit of sound advice is always welcome.

CREON   Money! Must everyone set their cap at me
30 Because of money? Even you augurers
Have formed a corporation to exploit me.
For years now I have been traded about
By your gang in the open market like
A piece of merchandise. All right, rake in
35 The cash, pile up the wealth of Lydia
And all the gold of India in bribes.
You'll never persuade me to bury that corpse.
Not even if the eagles of Zeus decide
To carry off its flesh in their claws
40 And place it right on their master's throne.
I refuse for the simple reason that
It's quite impossible for any man
To throw pollution on the gods. They are
Inviolate. But certain gifted men
45 That I could mention do not seem to mind

A little sharp practice, in the matter
Of telling a lie or two, strictly for cash.

TEIRESIAS   Well!
Can there exist a man who doesn't know . . .

CREON   Watch out, here comes another resounding cliché!   5

TEIRESIAS   . . . Good sense is a man's most precious attribute?

CREON   And bad judgment is a great encumbrance?

TEIRESIAS   It's an encumbrance you have plenty of.

CREON   . . . No.
You started it, but I won't insult a "seer."

TEIRESIAS   You've done that already,—accused me of lying.   10

CREON   The whole lot of you seers are on the make.

TEIRESIAS   Kings also have been known to make their pile.

CREON   Are you implying some reflection on me?

TEIRESIAS   You wouldn't be king now, but for me.

CREON   You're good at your job. But you've gone crooked.   15

TEIRESIAS   Much more of this, and you'll make me reveal . . .

CREON   Reveal away. But straight, and not for bribes.

TEIRESIAS   You'll wish you had bribed me not to speak . . .

CREON   Don't try to pull the wool over my eyes.

TEIRESIAS   The sun won't run its course for many days   20
Before you have to repay a corpse of your own,
One of your own children as recompense.
One body that belongs to this world
You have locked up in a tomb. Another body
That rightly should be in the underworld   25
You have forcibly retained here on earth.
Because of this, the Furies have been waiting
To pay you back in your own coin. And so
It won't be long before your house is full
Of grief; I can see men and women crying.   30
Make up your own mind whether I've been bribed
To say this. Yes, it hurts. But you provoked me.
My boy, take me home. I'm not so young,—
I dare not be around when he explodes.
I only hope he learns from this to show   35
A little sense and keep a civil tongue.

CHORUS   That was a horrible prophecy.
I'm bound to say I've never known him wrong
In any of his predictions.

CREON   Yes, I know,
I know. I can't pretend that I'm not worried.
The consequences of giving in are terrible.
But if I hold out, I court disaster.

5   CHORUS   The right decision now is vitally important.

CREON   What should I do then? Tell me what to do.

CHORUS   You'll have to go and set Antigone free,
And give the exposed corpse a burial.

CREON   Is that your real opinion? To give in?

10   CHORUS   And waste no time about it, for the wrath
Of God will not be slow to catch you up.

CREON   Can't fight against what's destined. It is hard,
But I'll change my mind. You servants,—
Pick-axes, hurry, and come with me. I must
15   Personally undo what I have done.
I shouldn't have tried being unorthodox.
I'll stick by the established laws in the future.

CHORUS   We call on Bacchus, god of many names,
And god of many places.
20   You were once a little child
In Thebes here, the darling of your mother's eye.
Your father was Zeus, lord of the thundering sky;
But your mother was Semele, a Theban girl.

Are you among the rich cities
25   Of Italy? Or presiding
Over the cosmopolitan crowds
That throng the Eleusinian Games?

Perhaps the firebrand lights your face
Between the twin peaks of Mount Parnassus,
30   Where the nymphs of Castaly
And Corycus walk free.

Perhaps you hear the songs of poets
Where the ivy wreathes the crags
On Nysa, looking over green
35   Vineyards clustering on the plain.

But this is your home,—the oil-like waters
Of Ismene River, and the fields
Where the dragon's teeth were sown.

This is your mother city, Thebes.
This is the city you honor most.
If ever you heard us before, come to us now.
Our nation is in the grip of a dread disease.
Hasten to help us, speed to doctor our pain   5
Over the slopes of Parnes Hill or over the roaring seas.

MESSENGER   Citizens of Thebes, who knows how long
   Their luck will last? Whether you're up or down,
   It's all pure chance. You can't predict what's coming.
   Take Creon now. I thought he was doing well,—   10
   The savior of his country, king of Thebes,
   And the proud father of a lovely family.
   He's lost the lot. Oh, yes, he's wealthy still;
   But wealth can't buy you happiness. What's the use
   Of money without the means of enjoying it?   15
   His wealth's no more to him than a puff of smoke.
   You can't say Creon lives; he's just a walking corpse.

CHORUS   About Creon's family, is there bad news then?

MESSENGER   They're dead. And those that live deserve to die.

CHORUS   How did they die? Who's dead? Why can't you tell me?   20

MESSENGER   Haemon is dead. Committed suicide.

CHORUS   He killed himself? His father didn't do it?

MESSENGER   Suicide, because Creon had murdered her.

CHORUS   Teiresias' prophecy was all too true.

MESSENGER   That's what has happened. Now it's up to you.   25

CHORUS   Here is Eurydice, Creon's wife, poor woman.
   Why is she coming out? Perhaps she's heard. . . .

EURYDICE   As I was going out, I heard you talking.
   I was opening the door when I heard it,
   Some more bad news about my children. I fainted,   30
   But my maids held me up. Tell me about it.
   I am quite used to suffering.

MESSENGER   I'll tell you everything, my dear mistress.
   I was there, you know. No sense in glossing things over;
   You've got to hear it sometime.   35
   I went with my master, your husband, to the place
   Where Polynices' corpse was exposed,
   Cruelly torn by dogs. We said prayers
   Placating Hecate and Pluto; then we washed
   The body to purify it, gathered branches   40

Of olive, and cremated him or what
Was left of him. We piled him up a mound
Of his mother-earth; then went to get
Antigone. While we were on the way,
5   Somebody heard a sound of crying coming
From the stone chamber. He went up to Creon
And told him of it. Creon hurried on.
As we got near, the sound was all around us,—
Impossible to tell whose it was.
10   But Creon, in a voice breaking with grief,
Said, "Dare I prophesy? These yards of ground
Will prove the bitterest journey of my life.
It's faint, but it's my son's voice. Hurry, men,
Get round the tomb, pull back the stones, and look
15   Inside. Is it Haemon's voice, or do the gods
Delude me?" At the far end of the tomb
We saw Antigone hanging by the neck
In a noose of linen. He was hugging her
And talking bitterly of their marriage and
20   His father's action. Creon saw him and
Cried out and ran in, shouting, "Oh my son,
What is this? What possessed you? Why are you trying
To kill yourself? Come out now, please, I beg you."
His son made no reply, just looked at him
25   Savagely with a look of deep contempt.
Then he suddenly drew his sword, evaded Creon,
Held it out, and plunged the blade into his ribs.
He collapsed against Antigone's arms which were
Still warm, and hugged her. Then his blood came coughing,
30   And covered all her white cheeks with scarlet.
So now he lies, one corpse upon another;
And thus their marriage is consummated,—in hell.
It only goes to show good sense is best,
When all this tragedy comes from one rash action.

35   CHORUS   What a strange thing. Eurydice has gone,
Without saying a word.

MESSENGER   It is surprising.
I dare say she's too well-bred to go
Showing her grief in public. I expect
She's gone to have a good cry inside.

40   CHORUS   Perhaps. Noisy grief is a bad thing.
But this extraordinary silence is ominous.

MESSENGER   You're right. Let's go in then, and find out.
She may have had her mind on something rash.

CHORUS   Who's coming? Creon with
  The body of his son.
  If truth be told, he is
  Himself the murderer.

CREON   Wrong! How could I have been so wrong?   5
  And these deaths I caused—you have seen them—
  In my own family by my stubbornness.
  Oh my son, so young, to die so young,
  And all because of me!

CHORUS   It's a bit late to find out you were wrong.   10

CREON   I know that. God has taken his revenge,
  Leapt on my head and beaten me
  And trampled on the only joy I had.
  And all the years that I have labored—wasted.

SERVANT   My lord, what you see before your eyes,—   15
  It isn't all. You'd better come inside.

CREON   What fresh disaster could I suffer now?

SERVANT   Your wife, the mother of this corpse is dead.
  Only a moment ago, she stabbed herself.

CREON   Oh death, can I never wash it away?   20
  Why are you destroying me? What
  Is your message now? Why stab me again?
  My wife dead too?

SERVANT   See for yourself. They've brought the body out.

CREON   Oh.   25
  Another blow. What else has fate in store?
  My wife, my son.

SERVANT   Stabbed herself by the altar, and so passed on.
  But first she bewailed Megareus' death,
  Her first son, that was; then Haemon's death.   30
  And her last words were curses on your head.

CREON   Now I'm afraid. Why wasn't I killed?
  Why didn't somebody kill me, stab me to death?

SERVANT   Before she died she made a point of planting
  The guilt of these two deaths squarely on you.   35

CREON   How did she die? How did she kill herself?

SERVANT   I told you. Stabbed herself. Under the heart.
  Soon as she heard about her son's death.

CREON   Nobody else to share the blame. Just me . . .
  I killed you. I killed you, my dear.   40

Servants, carry me in, away from all this.
I wish I weren't alive.

CHORUS   Try to forget it. It is the only way.

CREON   I invite Death. Do you only come uninvited?
5   Come and take me. I cannot bear to live.

CHORUS   No time for such thoughts now. You're still in charge.
You've got to see about these corpses, or
We'll all be polluted.

CREON   I meant what I said.

CHORUS   No use in such prayers. You'll get what's destined.

10   CREON   Lead me away, a wreck, a useless wreck.
I'll keep out of the way. I killed them both.
Everything has crumbled. I feel
A huge weight on my head.

CHORUS   Who wants happiness? The main
15   Requirement is to be sensible.
This means not rebelling against
God's law, for that is arrogance.
The greater your arrogance, the heavier God's revenge.
All old men have learned to be sensible;
20   But their juniors will not take the lesson as proved.

THE CRITICISM OF GREEK
TRAGEDY

My purpose here is to do a little superstitious rapping in the hope
of persuading into existence something a little different in the kind
of criticism we normally bring to bear upon Greek tragedy. If
this seems pretentious, blame the subject in part: Greek tragedy
requires, I think, a formidable apparition by way of an adequate
criticism and certainly a larger one than I can summon up, though
also a larger one than presently attends the scene. What I want
to do is to outline the nature of the job to be done, as I see it,
and to discuss what seems to me inadequate in both the traditional and contemporary ways of writing about Greek tragedy.
I think I see—though vaguely—the kind of criticism to which
Greek tragedy points, though I recognize that this may turn out
to be merely a mirage made up to answer imaginary needs, or an
old familiar ghost in a new murk, or even something that concerns no one but students of Greek tragedy. Whatever the results,
I am convinced that the need is real; that we have reached some
kind of impasse in the study of Greek tragedy in which neither
the older nor the newer criticism, nor any compromise between
them, is really adequate; and further, that the need is general.

Impasse is perhaps a strong word, and certainly an easy one.
Yet the diagnosis should surprise no one. The inadequacies of the
older historical and philological criticism are by now notorious,
and we can dispense with a parade of slogans that have more
than accomplished their purpose. At the moment, the New Criticism enjoys high academic repute; it has, for the most part, been
thoroughly institutionalized; it continues to do striking work in
the hands of competent critics, and wherever it has allied itself
with true scholarship, it has been an instrument of subtlety and
depth. But as a method it is liable to the same distortion as any
method; and it has everything to fear from the literalness of its
zealots. No one who reads much recent criticism can be unaware
of the carking restiveness among the pioneers of the New Critics
as they see their methods turned into formulae and the crucial
tact of the good critic expelled by the needs of schematic order.
"I want," says R. P. Blackmur in *The Lion and the Honeycomb,*
"to protect the methods [of the New Criticism] from its methodologies." I have the same hope here, and it is a hope which I
want as much as possible to put in positive terms. But because
the field I have in mind is Greek tragedy and classical studies
generally, and because the situation of the New Criticism is differ-

31

ent in respect to a dead language than what it is to a modern one, these matters deserve a context.

Roughly since the end of the war the traditional methods of classical scholarship as they affected literary criticism have been under attack in our graduate schools by the advocates of the New Criticism. As compared with studies in modern literatures, the attack on the classical front came late, delayed both by the addiction to cultural lag which is almost a point of pride among classicists, and by the extreme penetration of classical studies by the austere and quasi-scientific methodologies of the German *gymnasium*. Unlike scholars of English who never really wholly renounced criticism, classicists in America came to regard criticism as the perverse imp of the subjective in a field they fondly imagined was objective. This suspicion of criticism, it should be noted, was a peculiarly American thing, just as the reaction against it has been, for the most part, American also. If the stimulus to this dislike of criticism derived from Germany, it is also true that the formidable influence of such great scholars as Wilamowitz countered the current there, while elsewhere in Europe the long tradition of humane scholarship kept the activities of critic and scholar in more or less vital relation. One can point with pride, it is true, to American achievements in classical scholarship in the twentieth century, but the achievements occur in just those fields where the refinement of method, and especially scientific method, is crucial: archaeology, epigraphy, papyrology, numismatics, palaeography. Worse yet, all of these dubious sciences were devoted with an appalling single-mindedness to one end, the discovery of fact, in which fact was arbitrarily and with killing literalness reduced to historical or philological fact. Criticism itself was clearly confounded with the journalism of values and pushed to the fringes where it petered out either in limp impressionistic essays on the value of the classics or in the mellow *obiter dicta* of dying scholars. In short, American classical scholarship for forty years effectively renounced literary criticism as an honorable and rational habit of mind, and the results are apparent in the dreary waste of literary studies during those years; at least I can think of no first-rate, nor even second-rate, critical work on Greek tragedy by an American scholar from 1900 to 1940, though there is God's good plenty of works on the stage, conventions, Attic society, resolved *scenarii* and the like. But certainly one finds nothing comparable to the real criticism of such European scholars as Sheppard, Wilamowitz or even the much-maligned Gilbert Murray.

When the attack finally came, it came with the energy that attends any deep habit of mind that has for a long time been rigorously suppressed. It was slowed, not merely by the entrenchment of the Germanic spirit, but by a factor of considerable but neglected importance: unlike English, both Greek and Latin are dead languages, poorly preserved and poorly documented, lacking precisely that richness of information about language which is everywhere the essential condition of the newer criticism. But in the enthusiasm for a method that had the advantage of being at least literary, that honored the work for itself and not for its historical or informational uses, this crucial limitation was brushed aside. Real excesses, however, were prevented by the salutary insistence of the older generation that the fundamental responsibilities of the scholar be observed. This insistence, because defensive, was both surly and grumpy, but it had its effect: at least no classical critic, to my knowledge, has yet proclaimed that the *Oresteia* is a "hierarchy of epiphanies." Moreover, from the first, the impulse to the restoration of criticism to scholarship in America came as much from the humane tradition of European scholarship as from critics like Empson, Brooks, Ransom and Blackmur. Indeed, it was on the whole European scholars who first appreciated the refinement of verbal techniques offered by the New Criticism. Besides, no critic worth his salt, however belligerent, could honestly deny that the extreme poverty of fact which attends classical studies had long ago forced scholars to adopt in desperation something very like the New Criticism: one thinks of Jebb's monumental close-reading of Sophocles, with its susceptibility to shade and texture; Wilamowitz' great edition of the *Heracles,* and now of Fraenkel's *Agamemnon;* on still another level, verging toward the perverse or crankish, are the strange works of Verrall and Norwood on Euripides and such non-classical oddities as Samuel Butler's *The Authoress of the Odyssey.*

But in the last ten years it is abundantly clear that criticism has returned to classical scholarship; if the New Criticism as such is not yet, in classics, the heavy industry it has become in English studies, its pressure is clearly visible and especially among the younger generation. The direct influence of the critics themselves upon classical studies has mostly been oblique, and, more often than not, unfortunate: Francis Fergusson's able but unconvincing piece on the *Oedipus Rex* is some kind of exception, extraordinary in its perceptivity, but crippled in its too great reliance upon theories of the ritual origins of tragedy. And neither Kenneth Burke's strange essay on the *Oresteia* nor Edmund Wilson's perversion of the *Philoctetes* provides reliable models. But the New Criticism is writ large in Goheen's study of the imagery of the *Antigone,* diffused throughout Kitto's *Greek Tragedy* and Lattimore's superb introduction to his translation of the *Oresteia,* or Owen's fine commentary on the *Iliad,* and everywhere visible in the spate of dissertations which study single plays or single metaphors or the master-tropes of tragedy, and in the insistent emphasis upon the key terms of the New Critics: irony, ambiguity, symbol, tone, image, texture, formal structure and myth. And finally, even the classical journals and the professional societies have shown in the last few years a grudging willingness to admit the newer critics as at least junior partners in the firm.

From the point of view of the past, these are encouraging signs, and all the more so since critical activity has here been accompanied by extraordinary energy in the field of translation—the new translations of Homer, tragedy, Vergil, Ovid, Hesiod, Pindar and Greek lyric. Good translation is, of course, exemplary and creative criticism: to have an *Iliad* or an *Oresteia* as substantial and moving as we have in Lattimore's translations is to have a guarantee of the fresh and right response of feeling without which criticism is an empty exercise. In this sense translations and criticism work hand in hand, each sponsoring the other's vitality: just as criticism is crippled if it neglects scholarship, so the translator's task is vitiated without the act of criticism. In this connection the difference between Lattimore's *Oresteia* and Pound's *Trachiniae* is illuminating; for what makes Pound's translation incomparably the poorer of the two is the way in which, the scholarship suspended almost altogether, the critical sense is so impaired that it can no longer supervise the adjustment of language to the moral and emotional facts of the play. Talent here, tethered to nothing except Pound's extraordinary sense of music, has gone rogue and wild. By which I do not mean, of course, that Lattimore's scholarship makes him an acceptably tame poet; on the contrary, there is an immense turbulence in his translation, but it is a true and Aeschylean turbulence, not an imposed wildness. Good poetry guarantees good turbulence; the work of critic and scholar are required to make that turbulence Aeschylean and true.

Up to now the most conspicuous failure of both the traditional and the new critics in respect to Greek tragedy has been the failure to realize turbulence: turbulence of experience, turbulence of morality in the process of getting made, and the turbulence of ideas under dramatic test. If any one charge can be brought against the older criticism, it would be, I think, that it has seemed to ask too little of Greek tragedy, and asking so little, has rarely discovered much. Its crucial failure has come at the point where all criticism is finally tested: the ability to transfer complex experience from one period or language to another, and to get the substance of that experience—its turbulence as well as its final order—into language. This is, of course, in the end, impossible, but it is the ideal by which we measure the adequacy of any interpretative criticism. Where the older criticism failed was in the deeper skills of the very humanity it professed, the point where passion is used to make the experience from which any great image of humanity, like the Greek one, is made. Intensely obsessed with history and politics, the traditional criticism failed to show how history and politics got into tragedy and what they did there in relation to the humanity of the heroes; concerned with man and his destiny, it could never quite conjure up the complex reality of experience and suffering that in the Greek plays gives human passion its meaning; committed to the task of clarity, it failed on the whole to remove that dense patina of stiffness and strangeness and austerity that makes Greek tragedy so formidable to our first impressions, or translated it into sentimental commonplaces and limp passions.

Who, after all, is really stirred by the standard interpretations of the *Antigone*—that tidy passion of a perfect heroine caught up on the gods' errand and hindered by a brutal Creon, a conforming Ismene, and a dunderheaded chorus with an inexplicable gift of tongues? And who believes the fashionable reverse, with its stubborn and presumptuous Antigone, its tragic Creon and its misunderstood Ismene? These interpretations are, to my mind, not credible because they so clearly violate the emotional experience of the play or reduce its difficulties to the vanishing-point. What has not gotten into them is the play's real turbulence and complexity and what they express is rather the superficial order the play throws up as its terms or its field, not its subject or solution. What is missing is what, to my mind, the play insists upon in both action and character: the way in which Antigone, trying to uphold a principle beyond her own, or human, power to uphold, gradually empties that principle in action, and then, cut off from her humanity by her dreadful heroism, rediscovers herself and love in the loneliness of her death; not the opposition between Antigone and Creon, but the family resemblance which joins them in a common doom; not great heroism justified by great principles, but conduct in the fateful grip of principles, making out of courage and love a deeper principle altogether. And if you look to the *Oedipus Rex* or the *Agamemnon* or the *Bacchae,* it seems to me you find the same impoverishment: what is real or turbulent in the life of those plays is for the most part expelled, either because the critic has let his own principles of order usurp the play, or because his own experience is unequal to it, or because he refuses the act of criticism once it gets near the difficult edge of experience. How many interpretations of the *Oedipus Rex,* for instance, have come to grief on the fruitless quest for a tragic flaw that will justify the hero's suffering simply in order that Aristotle be justified. How commonly the cry of botching is raised against Euripides because his plays refuse to conform to the critic's expectations of proper organic structure. And how little of the full turbulence of the *Orestes* or *Bacchae*—those great pitiless mirrors of the terrible

political and social desperation of late fifth-century Hellas—does
our criticism get, largely because we ask so much less of tragedy
than it requires.

Thanks to the New Criticism, we can hope to see the turbulence of language and rhetoric restored to tragedy, for the New
Critics are nothing if not keen-nosed where verbal subtlety and
density are concerned. And we have, I think, everything to hope
for from the thorough examination of the rhetorical habits of Greek
tragedy. But I sometimes wonder whether a keen nose for metaphor, irony or ambiguity is much to the point when the spoor is
as old and crossed as that of Greek tragedy. It is, for instance,
extremely difficult in fifth-century literature to distinguish between
metaphor that is genuinely fresh and metaphor that has hardened
into idiom or *cliché;* we simply do not possess the linguistic evidence that might allow us to tell them apart. How fresh, for instance, are those yoke and ship images which run like master-
tropes through all three tragedians? Or are these simply the meta-
phorical idiom of an agricultural and seafaring people? The answer, of course, lies in a desperately difficult tact, but that tact
comes far harder in Greek and Latin than it does in a living literature like English where we understand stress and tone as we never
can in Greek. And the chances are high, of course, that tact will
disappear before the critic's drive for conceptual consistency: I
know of at least one treatment of the symbolism of the *Oresteia*
where the interpretation derived more from the itch for conceptual
rigor in the imagery than from the emotional experience of the
play. And this risk seems to me particularly high for the New
Criticism in its academic setting, where the old insistence upon
methodology and the student's necessary economies with complexity combine to harden method into mere formula.

I would not, of course, like the consciousness of risk to damage
the enterprise: we badly need in Greek tragedy just that refinement of rhetoric which has been the success of the New Criticism.
We need to know, for instance, just how those *sententiae* with
which Greek tragedy is so lavish and which so embarrass modern
producers of Greek plays, arise from the action; the structure of
stichomythia, that brisk staccato exchange of single lines for up to
a hundred lines at a time, is badly in need of work; I suspect that
the relation between metaphor and dance-figures is crucially important; we know very little about irony in tragedy, so little that
the tone of whole scenes and even whole plays is in question; the
language itself, with its curious alternation between stiff archaism
and colloquial speech, its habits of rhetorical movement, from the
big jaw-breaking, piled-up compounds of Aeschylus to the deceptive simpleness of Euripides, is still *terra incognita;* and I suspect
that we have barely started to do the work required by the choral

lyrics. Beyond these jobs, it is my personal conviction that the study of tragedy would enormously benefit from a shift in perspective; we need to question, that is, our tacit assumption that Greek tragedy is staged in a religious context or represents a kind of collective worship, for the assumption vitally affects interpretation. And it seems to me that nothing but chaos can come from the fashionable notion that because Greek tragedy begins in ritual, its structure is therefore ritual dramatized, its hero a ritual scapegoat, and its action a shadow play of the death of the *Eniautos-daimon* or god of the year. The more I read of Greek tragedy, that is, the more I am impressed with its very distance from its ritual origins and its stubborn refusal to behave as honest ritual should. And there is something violently improbable about an image of the Greek theatre which does the kind of damage done by Gilbert Murray's recanted theory of its ritual elements and more recently by Francis Fergusson in his study of the *Oedipus.*

If we require an idea of the Greek tragic theatre at all, it seems to me that the clue might best be taken from the very charge of rhetoric so peristently brought against tragedy, and against Euripides in particular ever since the time of Schlegel. Over and over again, that is, the late fifth-century tragedy seems to suggest as its informing image a theatre shaped more by the law-court than by the altar. In this theatre, the *agon* is viewed essentially as a trial, and the characters, with all the tricks of sophistic rhetoric, put their cases in opposed speeches—often of identical length, as though timed by the waterclock of the Athenian dikastery. The audience in this theatre sits as jurors, not merely a panel of five hundred jurors, but the full *Heliaea,* the sovereign judicial assembly (*ekklesia*). No appeal, no matter how emotional, is debarred, and each character in his plea speaks with the formal passion of a man whose life and fortunes hang upon his words. But it is a formal and rhetorical passion, below which we can glimpse, as the jury must, the personal passion and the real motives glozed by the rhetoric and often exposed in action. Such a theatre, of course, is most appropriate to Euripides, but in some degree, I think, to Sophocles also, especially in the later plays. I find tentative confirmation of this not merely in the number of Greek tragedies which openly stage formal trial scenes, but in the very structure of Euripidean drama: its persistent avoidance of the single hero in favor of the *agon* of two chief characters—Pentheus vs. Dionysus, Phaedra vs. Hippolytus, Orestes vs. Menelaus, Ion vs. Creusa—and the corresponding division of so many plays into two almost disparate actions; the flat assertion of the intention to make a formal plea; and, most important, the constant impression of the plays as problem plays in which the judgment is never asserted, but left, as it were, to the audience of jurors. If they understand the play, they make the right decision, or better, understand that no moral decision is relevant because the problems are beyond the reach of moral judgment, i.e. are both tragic and true. If this is correct, it is understandable why the constant imposition upon Euripides of Aristotelian structure and the notion of a religious theatre so regularly distort him. I throw this suggestion out, not as a developed thesis, but merely as a hint. For it seems to me that in the study of tragedy, as in almost any other human study, the discoveries come in that slight shift of perspective which we get when we examine those prejudices and assumptions which are so close to habit that we are almost unaware of them. And both our almost unconscious Aristotelianism and our deep assumption that Greek tragedy is finally religious tragedy are habits which I think need severe scrutiny by any serious critic of Greek drama.

The last charge which I should like to bring against the New Criticism is related to just this refusal to examine one's oldest habits. It is finally full interpretation of the plays and the tragedians that we want, and I find it puzzling that the newer criticism of Greek tragedy so seldom undertakes the full job. This may be modesty, but I suspect it is the old illusion of objectivity in fancy dress; and between *Quellenforschungen* and metaphor-snooping, both uprooted from the values they are intended to discover or reinforce, I can see very little difference. It is not merely that the New Critics have failed to take up the job of full interpretation, however, that I find distressing, but the fact that their analyses proceed more from the habit of old interpretation than the fresh act. I am not by this proposing that the New Critics should make their fortunes by systematically inverting all traditional criticism, but that analysis, wherever possible, should free itself from the immense authority of the standard interpretations. A book I admire, Goheen's analysis of the imagery of the *Antigone,* originally written as a dissertation and suffering the handicaps of that impossible genre, ably illustrates just how much the New Critics have to offer in enriching our criticism of tragedy. But unless I am mistaken, Goheen's close analysis is subtly hindered by the authority of the nineteenth-century *Antigone,* whose shape guides the analysis where it needs to go, but not where it might have gone were its destination a little less certain. This is not slyness, of course, but the necessarily blinkered gaze of good conviction: you look where you are going, not askance. But the one metaphor Mr. Goheen overlooks—the metaphor of alienation, Antigone as *metic* or peregrine—a casual sport so far as his theory is concerned, seems to me the one metaphor that most illuminates the key word of the play—*philia* or love. Habit is hard to shed, of course, but in the case of Greek tragedy where critical habit has hardened into cultural habit, I think it is crucial to any hope of a fresh and exacting criticism.

In this connection one point deserves mention. Greek tragedy is, *par excellence,* a sacred cow, even more sacred, I suspect, than Shakespeare, since it is seldom produced or else produced via the atrocious medium of Mr. Robinson Jeffers and Broadway; and most students get introduced to it in the killing atmosphere of reverential hush that attends the reading of any classic in our general humanities courses. Worse, fewer and fewer literary men read Greek nowadays or read it with sufficient security to challenge the scholars on their own ground, as Goethe challenged Schlegel and Matthew Arnold challenged Newman with enormously fruitful results. And in scholarship, as I suggested earlier, unconscious timidity in the face of the accumulated judgments of dead scholars is a deep critical habit. In evidence of this attitude of blind deference to Greek tragedy, let me cite the production not so long ago on Broadway of two Greek plays by a modern Greek repertory troupe: night after night, audiences and dramatic critics, unable to understand a word of the productions, but deeply impressed with the performance of their cultural duties, willfully applauded on the curious assumption that Greek tragedy is mostly gesture anyway, and that a modern Greek company, by virtue of being Greek, somehow must possess the secrets of ancient Greek tragedy. Against adulation like this, it may be beyond the power of criticism to help, and the critic himself may be insensibly drawn into the work of justification rather than criticism. But it needs to be pointed out that we are in real danger of taking over almost intact the canon of Greek tragedy which the nineteenth century established. Who, after all, except classical scholars, now reads any Aeschylus except the *Oresteia* and *Prometheus,* any Sophocles except the Theban plays, and what Euripides besides the *Alcestis, Medea, Hippolytus* and *Bacchae?* I am not, of course, suggesting that these are not great plays, but that the canonizing of them into a cultural monument damages the chosen eleven as much as the excluded tragedies.

Worse, the difficulty is not merely that we have adopted an old taste, but the habits that accompany that taste as well, and especially the nineteenth century habit of making Sophocles the norm, if not the ideal, of tragedy—a habit which has done great damage to Aeschylus and almost irreparable damage to Euripides. It is no accident, for instance, that the favored plays of Euripides are precisely those which appear to meet the standards of so-called Aristotelian structure, that is, the "organic structure" which critics think they find in Sophocles. Against this tendency, I can only argue that it botches Sophocles as badly as Euripides, and that it cuts off our access to a power in Euripides that meant very little to the nineteenth-century but everything to the twentieth—I mean that part of Euripides that is concerned with political desperation, the corruption of power, and the corrosion of the civilized virtues into a set of specious slogans for demagogic consumption. We need not only the *Bacchae,* but the *Hecuba,* the *Heracles,* the *Orestes, Electra, Supplices* and *Trojan Women*—all plays in which we should sense the full turbulence of one of the very greatest of dramatists in a context that very easily becomes our own. But this means production as well as criticism, since nothing hinders the critic's right perception of a play more than the perpetual unavailability of his material in living form. At the moment, I can think of no greater service to Greek tragedy than the regular production of those plays that lie outside the canon and are so commonly regarded as undramatic, and particularly the plays of Euripides whose structure is censured by critics who have never seen them performed. But such a service needs to be regular, a continuous repertory production, and not merely those sporadic productions which derive from a duty to the classics; but it is a service I hope some lively academic theatre may be encouraged to perform, since Broadway offers even less to Greek tragedy than it does to the modern playwright.

What, in the meantime, should criticism do? I spoke earlier of the turbulence traditional criticism missed, and, at its most general, the charge I have preferred against the criticism of tragedy is its incompleteness. What was incomplete in the older criticism was that it over-generalized experience and missed whatever was complex and particular in human passion; it took the particular turbulence for granted, that is, and thereby leached its own generalizations of what should have given them life. What the newer criticism missed was meant to be implied by what it got—turbulence of language; but the implications, trapped by the New Criticism's notorious penchant for the autonomy of the work and its deep embarrassment in the face of value, only rarely succeeded; experience got swamped in the generalizing drive of the symbolism or the technique of the dramatist's work. What I want to restore to the criticism of tragedy is a sense, a feel, a look of significantly lived experience, particular before being general, the turbulence of the actual disorder of experience as it moves on to make the dramatist's order. To restore depth and passion to the terms of experience—the notion of a personal fate, responsibility, purpose, the emotions before and after their moralizing, illusion, necessity and reality; to show how values burgeon out of structure and plot; to know again why the plot is the "soul of the play," not its skeleton; to see that any character in a play who lives and uses his passion is prior to anything he may stand for; to refresh the simplicity of reason through the complexity of passion, not the other way around: this is a part of what I mean by turbulence, the turbulence to which both the critic and the producer are responsible. Unless the criticism of tragedy can make itself big enough to talk about experience at the level it proposes, it is doomed to even greater inadequacy than even criticism must normally expect. To talk about literature at the level of experience implies a criticism large enough to contain what is chaotic in experience as well as what is orderly. And it is my conviction that criticism of Greek tragedy, too heavily committed to the criteria of orderly reason and the rhetoric of intelligence, has dehumanized its heroes by cutting them off from the condition in relation to which they win their meaning. The hero, cut off by an inadequate criticism from the actual power and anguish of the condition he can never quite escape without destroying himself, loses the terrible tension and redeeming dignity of his equivocal status.

Nothing comes easier than to ask criticism to become more complete and humane, and nothing is harder to do. Nor can we prescribe methods for doing it without sooner or later ramming our plays into categories which violate them. What we need at this point seems to me not more method, but a refreshment of perspective: and particularly we want perspectives which undercut our old methods as they harden into habit and prevent us from seeing more than they allow. It is by such refreshment of perspective that we are apt to enlarge our criticism. At least this is my hope in the following remarks.

II

I suggested earlier that one refreshment of perspective might be found in a shift in our traditional idea of the Greek theatre, at least as that idea affects Euripides. And I should like to suggest further that we need much more precision in dealing with the hero and a different purchase on that central and elusive concept. What is most urgently needed is some sense of flexibility and variety in the ways heroism is manifested, and more attention to the *dramatic* use of the hero. The difficulty is not merely that we fail to distinguish between generic kinds of heroism or between the heroism of one dramatist and another, but that discussion begs almost all of the questions that affect the *dramatic* status of the hero in relation to his own humanity and also skirts whatever experience is relevant to the earning of heroism. Attempts to meet this problem with a unitary concept, as in Whitman's recent book on Sophocles, have been Procrustean in result: it is, of course, a pleasure to be rid of the view that Sophocles was an enlightened bishop and his heroes Anglicans in trouble, but a Nietzschean Sophocles with a Zarathustrian Antigone hardly helps us much.

But most commonly heroism is treated in drastically abrogated moral terms, or made to satisfy the Aristotelian theory of the hero's tragic flaw, or reduced to the protagonist, or hypostatized and used as a critical *deus ex machina*. The crucial questions relevant to heroism, however, seem to me to be the following. First, how is heroism asserted in tragedy and how is it sustained, both morally and dramatically? What skills of experience or reality distinguish the hero from the other characters and from his former self? What is the relation between the achieved dramatic reality of the hero and his symbolic dignity? What is the cost of heroism to the hero in contrast to the values of what his heroism asserts? How does the hero's mortality affect his morality? What are the *legitimate* limits of the hero's responsibility for his nature or his acts? What is the relation between necessity and illusion in the hero's ability to rise to, and even surpass, the meaning of his own experience?

All of these questions are uprooted from the plays that propose them, but they are proposed by the plays at that level where criticism cannot refuse them without really refusing everything. As they affect the *Antigone*, for instance, they seem to me to illuminate the whole moral and experiential fabric of the play. Here if ever, for instance, the tension between the cost of heroism and the values of its assertion is both vivid and crucial. Half of the dynamic horror of Antigone's tragedy is precisely her equivocal status: torn between the cold heroism of her assertion of principle and her humanity, she almost loses her humanity in the fateful grip of her principle. What distinguishes her from Creon? Principle, of course, but look again, and the distinction is replaced by the family resemblance, a stubborn intractable loyalty to principle, and even a resemblance in principle, for both claim to act on behalf of love, *philia*. This principle, it is true, may be translated to another level and replaced by a struggle between family gods and state gods, but both protagonists claim at bottom to be agents of love: Antigone asserts that she was born to love (*sumphilein*) while Creon, in words that have been very strangely neglected, clearly states that he acts on behalf of the state because *philia*, love, can only exist within the context of a stable and orderly society. And this same *philia is*, of course, Ismene's principle too, without Antigone's courage, but *philia* for all that; and when Antigone refuses Ismene the right to die with her, she refuses her sister, her *philē*, both her own principle and the dignity of a personal fate. If, then, Antigone is the heroine of *philia*, we have to see, in action, what it means to act for *philia* in a conflict of *philiai;* how fate is here set against fate; how the family resemblance between Creon and Antigone is carried out in action up to the moment of heroism, and only then are they separated in a common doom. If we see these things, I think we cannot help seeing and reporting the turbulence also:

the real disorder (but also the tragic symmetry) of a world where the living of love involves the denial of love elsewhere; where morality unmakes itself in conflict and is refreshed by significant passion; where heroism in the end means not surpassing one's humanity but discovering and incarnating its dignity at the moment of agony, and where the hero, finding weakness he never suspected, finds also his greatest strength. The hero, says Plato in one of his wonderfully crazy etymologies, "is born of love [that is, *erōs*]"; or, to put it in other terms, the hero is reduced, but also raised, to the human condition. So, at least, it seems to me with Antigone.

What she first accepts as a fate, the principle of love that dooms her to death, is hardened by her desperate plight and her desperate courage and loneliness; and this in turn hardens her—"Great suffering makes a stone of the heart," as Yeats puts it—making her refuse Ismene the same dignity of fate she claims. As she hardens, so does Creon on behalf of the same principle, denying Haemon in order to hurt Antigone, just as Antigone dishonors Ismene in order to honor Polyneices. Still hardened, but increasingly tormented by a loss she does not understand and yet the fate she chose, Antigone is condemned to her symbolic death, walled alive in a tomb, and thus cut off alike from both the living and the dead, the human being still alive, like Niobe, beneath the cold rock of her heroism. And suddenly, as the chorus compares her to a goddess, she knows what has happened, and cries, "I am mocked, I am mocked!" and the rock falls away, leaving that final warm confusion that makes her so human and so lovely. In all this Creon is left far behind, though he suffers perhaps even worse; he never had Antigone's human skills to begin with; he knows only the horror, Antigone knows the horror and the glory. And that knowledge, or better, merely *being* that knowledge, the final knowledge of tragedy, is Antigone's heroism. Until you come to that point, however, the experience is troubled, criss-crossed with paradox, turbulent with lonely passion and isolated meaning; if simplicity supervenes with heroism, that simplicity owes all of its power to the turbulence it tries to resolve.

Alternatively, in dealing with Euripides, we need to observe how the whole context of heroism has altered; that we are dealing with a world where the senselessness of circumstance may deprive the hero of responsibility, or strike at a point where responsibility is no longer relevant, as in the *Hecuba* or *Heracles*. With such an alteration, the nature of heroism is also altered, since its necessities change. Thus in the *Heracles,* the hero declares his triumph over the amoral powers which afflict him by the simple act of enduring in a world which tells him to die. For Euripides preserves the disorder of actual experience, measuring its horror against the unrequited illusion of order which sustains human beings, and the final dignity of Heracles is that he asserts the human cry for order and meaning almost in the very teeth of his own experience of hideous disorder. And the whole motive of the play is to bring the hero to the point where he shares, for the first time, common ground with the other characters. He discovers, that is, his condition and its anguish, an anguish from which his great strength has hitherto exempted him; in the discovery of anguish comes the discovery of community and love in weakness before necessity. Love is the hope which finally permits Heracles to endure a hideous necessity he never made, and from his discovery of love and helplessness flow acceptance and courage, the courage which asserts the human demand for order in a world which annuls all hope of a *moral* order. So much may be immediately obvious, but the point I should like to make is precisely the profound relationship between the hero's progress and the structure of the play, the way in which the created or assumed reality of each part of the play exactly defines, as challenge and disorder, the growth of heroism and order, forcing Heracles steadily back upon his humanity in order to refresh his heroism. Yet the *Heracles* has been savagely censured for its dislocation of plot, its apparent division into two discrete actions bound together by nothing more than sequence. But unless I am mistaken, everything that seems strange about the play's structure can be explained in terms of its intent, the conversion of heroism via the conversion of reality and necessity. At least it seems to me that, far from being botched, the *Heracles* is one of the most wonderfully constructed plays of Greek tragedy, if we mean by good construction a plot exactly designed to force meaning into action. What hinders us here, however, is the deeply Aristotelian bias of our critical habits and especially the habit of imposing the example of the *Oedipus Rex* upon all other Greek plays. We expect unity to be of one kind, and missing it, we misread or condemn the play in order to salvage our own bad habits.

Heroism is, of course, more difficult to comprehend in those plays—far more common than we like to believe—where we have no central dominating hero in the manner of the *Oedipus Rex* and the *Heracles*. Indeed, in the case of Euripides, the single hero is a comparative rarity. We have, for instance, a group of plays on the order of the *Hippolytus* or the *Phoenissae,* in which heroism is diffused over several characters or the whole human cast, and others, like the *Orestes,* the *Hecuba* and—I believe—the *Bacchae,* where there are protagonists but no heroes, and no heroism either. What you get in the *Orestes* is really like what you get in Shakespeare's *Troilus and Cressida:* an image of heroism seen as botched, disfigured and sick, carried along by the slogans and machinery of heroic tragedy and then exposed in action. This is neither a satire of tragedy, however, nor a melodramatic perversion, but tragedy of total turbulence, without a principle of order in sight except that order implied in the observation that heroism has been botched and all order omitted. Consider the *Bacchae* in this respect. Attempts to make heroes out of Pentheus and even Dionysus have not succeeded for obvious reasons: at least I find it hard to see the stuff of heroism in Pentheus' irritable voyeurism and Dionysus has all the heroism of an earthquake. What we have, of course, is not heroic tragedy but a tragic contest between parties who all claim to act on behalf of the same principle—*sophia,* badly translated as "wisdom"—and who all alike deprave their principle in action. What alone can order the play and judge that depravity to which *sophia* is subjected is an understanding of right *sophia;* but it is important to see that the play omits by merely implying the only order appropriate to its instances of heroism failed.

My point, then, is the simple one that heroism is too complex a term to be handled loosely, and that, if mishandled, it generates trouble in other directions. We need a tact with our terms which can distinguish when a particular concept is demanded and when it is superfluous; so far as heroism is concerned, we particularly need precision when we attempt to relate it to *dramatic* movement, plot, genre, and a particular dramatist. Where our definitions tend to be static rather than dynamic, or uprooted from a single type, or abstracted from one dramatist and imposed upon others, we impoverish tragedy in the critical act.

Likewise, in reading Aeschylus, we need to observe how a shifting or evolving cosmology fundamentally conditions the nature and possibilities of heroism. For surely we cannot alter the basic laws of the world in which men live and suffer without thereby deeply affecting the moral quality of their conduct and the judgments relevant to it. And the *Oresteia* is, of course, just such an evolving cosmology: a dramatic image of the gradual evolution, according to the masterplan of Zeus, of the institution of civilized justice. The progress itself hardly needs documentation. No one can read or see the trilogy and miss those wonderful transfigurations that chart the progress of justice from primitive blood-vengeance to civilized trial by jury: the blood-red tapestries on which Agamemnon goes to his death, suddenly revealed as the holy red robes of the transfigured Furies, or the metamorphosis of Persuasion (*Peitho*) from the sinister abstraction that seduces Helen, to Clytemnestra's coiling rhetoric as she lures Agamemnon to his doom, and finally that patient, crucial argument by which Athena persuades the Furies to accept an honored place in the new dispensation of Zeus. We are witnessing nothing less than the conversion of a world *and,* as the Chorus tells us, the reconciliation of Zeus and the Fates. Throughout the trilogy, from murder to murder to murder, we have been promised a fulfillment, a dawn, a delivery out of this intolerable net of contradictory evils, and finally, after so many false dawns and illusory solutions, we are shown the manifest pattern of Zeus the Fulfiller, the silver strand in the tapestry of blood.

A parable, then, of tragic scope, a passion of men and gods struggling from darkness into the light: so much is obvious. But if no one misunderstands the nature of the light, what do we make of the darkness there in the *Agamemnon* where everything is chaos and contradiction, where men are apparently whirled helplessly from evil to worse evil, with no end in sight ever? What, in other words, is the relation of Zeus of the *Eumenides* to the darker Zeus of the *Agamemnon?* Is he an inscrutable god, secretly at work behind all the apparent contradictions, slowly forcing the whole action toward an inevitable conclusion? A kind of Greek Jehovah, that is, tempting men, out of his enormous bewildering mystery, to cramp him in the small boxes of their own petty theodicies? Or is he like the Zeus of the *Prometheus*-trilogy, an undeveloped god who once again undergoes a progress from callous indifference to a final moral wisdom tempered by compassion? Or is he a gradualist, a reforming Fabian demiurge, hampered by a whole host of discordant powers, the still potent heirs of an older dispensation, and by quarrels on Olympus too?

As I see it, the world of the *Agamemnon* is clearly one in which the possibility of moral action is obscured and prevented by a deep discord in the nature of things. We have a prospect of insuperable moral difficulty, a nightmare of justice in which the assertion of any right involves a further wrong, in which fate is set against fate in an intolerable, necessary sequence of violence. There is Zeus, of course, and Zeus is strong; but if the Chorus, in a famous ode, praises Zeus' power and wisdom, we are meant to read that prayer, I think, not as a factual description of a known Zeus, but as a last desperate act of faith, cried in the very teeth of experience: *sorrow, sorrow, but may good win out in the end.* In other words, the *Agamemnon* presents us with a world which is at all points essentially Homeric; nothing, in fact, in the entire *Agamemnon*, including the choral ode on Zeus, is incompatible with the cosmology of Homer. The life of men on earth, torn this way and that by conflict and irresponsibility in heaven, is a tragic hell; and if men and gods jointly share the responsibility for human actions, the choices are irreparably clouded by inconsistency and discord among the gods. In the *Iliad* and the *Odyssey* there is a double standard: divine adultery, for instance, is comic, but human adultery is terribly punished. So too the *Agamemnon* shows us, in conscious juxtaposition, the same double standard: Agamemnon himself is the fatally chosen instrument of Zeus to punish the adultery of Paris, but Apollo callously and with impunity seduces Cassandra and leads her to her death at Clytemnestra's hands. The contrast could hardly be more glaring. And though in the *Eumenides* Apollo may very well incarnate the ruthlessness of the male in a contest with the female Furies, it is an intentional anomaly in the *Agamemnon* that the same ruthlessness should be visited on a helpless human victim. And what are we to make of the fact that Artemis, "angered at the flying hounds of her father," should openly flout the will of Zeus and demand the sacrifice of Iphigeneia before allowing the Greeks to proceed on the Zeus-enjoined conquest of Troy? The only possible conclusion is surely that there is discord in heaven, just as in the *Iliad* we see god set against god in a perpetual attempt to slow or cross the will of Zeus. Anomaly, contradiction, moral irresponsibility on earth and in heaven: this is the world of the *Agamemnon,* and it is, I think, precisely what we should expect. How else, dramatically speaking, could Aeschylus have shown us his gradual progress toward the light? For the light requires a darkness to dispel, and the darkness of the *Agamemnon* is a deliberately constructed one, not the result of the dramatist's confusion or inconsistency.

A related problem: does Agamemnon enjoy freedom of action or was he compelled to sacrifice Iphigeneia? Once again the answer, I think, is the Homeric one, which is to say that Agamemnon freely chose but he was also compelled to choose. So in the *Iliad* we see Agamemnon freely confiscate Achilles' prize and so bring on the fatal wrath; later, however, he declares that it was not he who did it but Zeus and Ate, which is simply Homer's way of sustaining the crucial doubleness of all his action: Agamemnon chose an act which Zeus also chose him to do. To modern ears this may seem an evasion of difficulty by way of paradox, but the notion, I believe, is firmly classical and also commonsensical: we all think we act with freedom though upon reflection it frequently seems that we could not possibly have acted otherwise than we did. So in the *Agamemnon* we find the Chorus declaring that Agamemnon put on the yoke of necessity, but before that it asks: "What course without evils?" Which, at least to my ears, suggests choice, however small in fact that choice may have been. In short, Agamemnon chooses his necessity, but equally Zeus' necessity chose him; being the kind of man he is, he chooses as he does. Consider in this connection the famous Aeschylean fragment: "when Zeus wishes to destroy a man's house utterly, he puts an *aitia* [i.e. a cause or responsibility] in the man." What does this mean except that a man acts from the necessity of his nature *and* as god compels him? Similarly we later find Agamemnon asserting that he and the gods are jointly responsible [*metaitioi*] for the destruction of Troy, and Clytemnestra likewise declares to Orestes that she and Destiny are jointly responsible accomplices [*paraitioi*] in the murder of Agamemnon. And surely it is just this joint responsibility that the action everywhere exhibits and requires. Thus in the famous central scene of the red tapestries, we see Agamemnon, reluctant and wary but also deeply tempted and guilty, finally lured into Clytemnestra's net as his fatal vanity once drove him, with the connivance and foreknowledge of heaven, to sacrifice his daughter. So too we can detect in Clytemnestra's action itself both the deep sources of her own motivation *and* the hand of heaven. She too chooses her revenge, but she is also the instrument chosen of heaven to cut down Agamemnon.

Consider also the deliberate parallel with Orestes. At the opening of the *Choephoroe* we find Orestes suffering under almost the same necessity as Agamemnon earlier: just as Artemis ordered Agamemnon to kill his daughter, so Orestes is commanded by Apollo to murder his mother. Hideous punishment is threatened if he disobeys, and yet Orestes, I think, can be said to choose here because he so clearly acts for motives that are properly his own: vengeance for his father and the recovery of his patrimony. He too chooses, that is, the act he is also constrained to commit. But there is this time a crucial difference: the comparative purity of the motive. Unlike Agamemnon and Clytemnestra, Orestes undertakes his murder with the reluctance and misgiving of an innocent heart and also with the determination of justice. Even Electra explicitly questions the wisdom of a god who could command that a mother be murdered by her son. For the first time, that is, in the history of the house of Atreus, a murder is being undertaken in something like purity of heart, for Orestes' act is clouded neither by his father's fatal vanity nor by his mother's jealousy and guilty hatred. It is revenge pure and simple, reluctant and unhappy and uncertain, but the nearest thing to the spirit of true justice that an age of vendetta-justice can offer. For we must be careful to judge the hero by the standards of the age in which he lives, and this is a world whose only justice as yet is the simple and brutal *lex talionis*.

Great consequences flow from this, I think, for innocence in this play is crucial. Not only does it signify to Zeus that the moment is at last ripe for the institution of civilized justice, but it is because Orestes' heart was pure and his action productive of conscience and remorse that he can, without divine inconsistency, be purged and finally acquitted. But there is more to it than that: precisely because Orestes' innocence is deeply his own, the native reaction of his own heart to the callous command of a god who told him to cut down his father's murderers "in their own fashion, to turn to the bull's fury in the loss of his estates," mankind becomes, through Orestes, partner and accessory [*metaitios*] with Zeus in the great act of justice that closes the trilogy. Orestes' act releases Zeus, but because the act was undertaken in free innocence, men share with Zeus the glory of the new justice which we now see has been Zeus' intent from the beginning. But wisdom on earth *must* precede Zeus' revelation: the condition of justice is the free and rightly motivated collaboration of men, and this could only come about when men discovered both innocence and compassion before necessity. Orestes kills but first he hesitates, and the whole world and the fate of mankind hang in that act of hesitation. For the play is about nothing less than the discovery of wisdom [*sophia*] under the yoke of awful necessity. To us, the heirs of Orestes' act, it may seem a small wisdom that a man who must kill should, for pity's sake, hesitate, but this is the wisdom appropriate to the necessity in question. And it marks, I think, in Aeschylus' eyes, a great moment in the fortunes of mankind, since it is the indispensable prerequisite of civilized justice itself. God sends necessity upon man that he may learn, and learning, become the partner of god in the great drama of the making of a civilized world.

Look back now at the *Agamemnon* from this vantage-point. If I am right, what we see is a world of terrible disorder, fate set against fate, god against god, man against man and god, all entangled in the great net of a justiceless, impossible justice. For this confusion, man and god are jointly responsible, but even the mind of Zeus is hampered and restricted by the still potent necessities of an older and more barbaric world-order. In this world, tragedy can only work itself out through time and suffering, and Zeus himself is powerless to act until the heart of man happens on the beginnings of a truer justice. For justice without the wisdom to sustain it would have been a meaningless gift, and wisdom, as the Chorus tells us, is learned in suffering. And so we see Clytemnestra and Agamemnon caught in a necessity which their own natures as well as the conflicting purposes of heaven have made. But we should not judge them too harshly; true, they do what they do and suffer what they suffer because they are what they are, but unless I am mistaken, we can almost hear Aeschylus saying between the lines, how can we expect men to be better than gods? If Agamemnon has murdered Iphigeneia, how much more brutal is the conduct of Apollo towards Cassandra. We must judge, that is, by the standards appropriate to Agamemnon's world, and if we judge him rightly we shall be in a position to understand the true stature of Orestes' heroism, surpassing in moral skills the god who commanded him to kill. Agamemnon, however proud, however guilty of *hybris,* is a man torn between the necessity of his own nature and the necessities imposed upon him by a world of moral disorder. He is not, I think, a true tragic hero—for Orestes is the hero of the *Oresteia*—but the self-involved tragic victim of a world which is as flawed as he is. He is therefore a candidate for compassion as much as judgment, and so are Clytemnestra and her victim, Cassandra. Only a mind unreceptive to the meaning of Athena's justice can refuse to give these casualties of a great cosmology in the making the human justice of pity and compassion. This, it seems to me, is an essential part of the real complexity and enormous moral turbulence of the *Oresteia*.

III

Unless I am mistaken, tragedy is also in deep need of some new perspectives in the matter of its operative moral terms as well as in structure and plot. And particularly, I think, we need to question again the relevance of Aristotle on at least two points—the so-called tragic flaw and the putative Aristotelian theory of tragic structure, the structure that draws its sanction from the *Oedipus Rex* and is reinforced by our modern preference for the organic. Aristotle is, I know, a rough customer: he has of necessity immense authority, and one is never quite sure whether one is talking about Aristotle or about something that has borrowed the authority of his name. But I have never been able to satisfy myself that the *Poetics* is the purely inductive treatise that scholars claim it is: again and again, that is, what is inductive in the *Poetics* seems to me to be directed by what is not, the pervasive notion of a purposive and rational universe and all that such a notion implies for tragedy and for the structure of tragedy. Thus for Aristotle a tragic fall is grounded in a consistent and harmonious sense of a man's responsibility for his nature and his actions: when the hero falls, he falls for his own failure, and behind the rightness of his fall, working both pity and terror by the precise and relentless nature of its operations, stands the order which society and a god-informed world impose upon the individual. What the law requires, the world requires too, and so the Aristotelian play portrays, like an image of human life, the individual torn and suffering between his nature and an objective world-order.

The tragic fall is, of course, in the common reading of Aristotle, based upon the hero's possession of a tragic flaw; and whether as doctrine or habit, the attempt to find a tragic flaw in Greek plays seems to me a persistent stumbling-block. If you really look at the *Oedipus,* for instance, it is immediately clear that Oedipus' tragic flaw is hard to discover: one wants to know—if you begin with the Aristotelian habit—just what in the hero's nature or his acts makes him suffer as hideously as he does, and the obvious answers—his anger, his treatment of Creon and Teiresias, his attempt to avoid his fate—are all unsatisfactory, or if satisfactory, indict the gods that could afflict a man so grievously for such offense. One recent critic of the play, an Aristotelian by conviction as well as habit, recognized his dilemma immediately and proceeded to solve it by the suggestion that Sophocles in this play has generalized *hamartia* into something like original sin: Oedipus has no particular flaws but suffers in the very flaw of his humanity. I suspect that very few classicists, whatever their religious color, will be happy with this theory, and I hope that even Aristotelians might object. But I use it to illustrate the kind of trouble that the expectation of a tragic flaw can create even in the treatment of a play which Aristotle regarded as the paradigm of his theories.

I cannot myself pretend to understand that mysterious play, but I wonder if we are perhaps not the better off for proceeding from the play rather than from Aristotle. Freed from our own *a prioris,* the experience of the play may at least propose itself in different terms. Thus it has always seemed to me that the single most pertinent fact of the *Oedipus* was not the hero's flaw, but his refusal to accept a ready-made fate: he wants his own fate, not the gods', and though his personal fate may be cut short by his doom, Oedipus at the close of the play insists upon distinguishing his own responsibility by blinding himself. It is the magnificence of his own declaration of responsibility that makes him so heroic: his fate is *his* and no one else's. His anger is anger, neither more nor less; it is not the source of his doom, but the irritant that he exhibits on the road to doom; and if he has a *hamartia,* it is not sin or flaw but the ungovernable tragic ignorance of all men: we do not know who we are nor who fathered us but go, blinded by life and hope, toward a wisdom bitter as the gates of hell. The cost of action is suffering, and heroism is the anguished acceptance of our own identities and natures, forged in action and pain in a world we never made. Whatever the final merits of this suggestion, it at least, I think, preserves the dignity of human passion in the play without violating in the name of a crude automatic justice the mysterious destiny that rules the play.

But crude or vulgar Aristotelianism[1] has hurt all three drama-

---

[1] Much of contemporary dogmatizing about what Aristotle did or did not mean seems to me to rest squarely upon uninformed or unimaginative interpretation of what Aristotle actually said. I am encouraged in this opinion by Professor Gerald F. Else's magisterial *Aristotle's Poetics: The Argument* (Harvard University Press, 1957), surely the most important book on Aristotelian criticism in the twentieth century and one which will inevitably shape and alter the whole tenor of modern explication of Aristotle.

At my request, Professor Else has provided me with a brief statement of his views of what Aristotle actually said, and I quote him verbatim in the conviction of complete agreement. He writes: "There is no doubt that the root and center of Aristotle's theory of tragedy, indeed of all poetry, is the idea of an action (N.B. "*an* action," not simply "action"). It should be easy to say what he means by an action, since he talks about it so much; but there are obscurities and ambiguities. Perhaps the key is that an action is a *trans*action, the living out of a decisive turn of events by a significant human being. Aristotle seems to say that neither *people* nor *situations*—

tists, and Euripides in particular, and one of the most urgent tasks for the criticism of tragedy is the thorough re-examination of Euripidean structure; once we get Euripides straight, we may be in a position to see just where we have subtly distorted Aeschylus and Sophocles in the name of a misunderstood Aristotle. But here again, I think, criticism might best begin from the obvious—the long insistence of critics that Euripidean plays lack unity, fall into disparate actions or are merely episodes strung together. We start, that is, from the fact of dislocation and attempt to see whether dislocation might not be deliberate method rather than the hit-or-miss *ad hoc* work of a genius who consistently botched. What is immediately apparent if we start from this point is the real coherence of the plays so far as structure is concerned; what is most obvious in the *Heracles* or *Hecuba* is true also of the *Bacchae, Hippolytus* and *Medea:* all lack the kind of unity which the organic theory requires, all exhibit dislocation. If we ask why this is so, I think we find it mirrored by a curious doubleness in the action or in the given and created realities of the plays. Thus the *Heracles* shows two successive plateaus, the first a reality appropriate to legend and old convention, i.e. a world of mythical illusion, the second the full created tragic reality out of which heroism is born. If we look, say, at the *Orestes,* we discover a play which freely invents its own reality and then confronts the action so created with an epiphany of Apollo in which the whole motion of the play up to that point is flatly contradicted. We get a head-on collision, that is, between the action of the play and the traditionalizing impossible *deus ex machina,* and no attempt is made to modulate or explain these incompatible sequences. The same is true of the *Iphigeneia at Aulis,* and also, I think, of the *Medea* and *Electra:* their conclusions are simply at variance, as real events, from the whole tenor of the action. In the *Hippolytus* and *Bacchae* this doubleness is used in a different and less violent way:

---

suffering, hopelessness, demoniacal possession, or whatever—are tragic in themselves. Involvement in action is the sign-manual of our human condition and our passport to happiness; it is also the warrant of our possible ruin. Without action a man can be, but he can neither win nor lose; and the winning or losing (not having-lost or being-about-to-lose, or even being-such-as-to-lose) is the tragedy. What is tragic is neither the potentiality nor the actuality of suffering, but its actualization. Tragedy cannot be *displayed,* but only *enacted.* It would seem to follow that the tragic action, though involved with universals—character (type), characteristic acts, pattern of events—is irreducibly a particular. Whether or not Oedipus is a type, the hell into which he enters is his individually, for *only he has entered it through this action.* But it is not clear whether Aristotle is aware of this further corollary. What he does do, beyond any ambiguity, is to insist on the primacy of the action."

both plays dramatize the full incredibility of a traditional account of Olympian anthropomorphism—it is incredible that gods, real gods, should act as Dionysus and Aphrodite do. But once the familiar reality has been exposed and displaced, both plays proceed, in a symbolic manner, to hint at a deeper meaning and a different reality for these displaced gods. What I am trying to suggest is that again and again in Euripides, what makes the plays dislocated in structure is a deliberate juxtaposition of antithetical realities— the reality of the material which the play takes from legend and myth, and the new reality which the dramatist forces, as action, from his old material. We get the same kind of jar, that is, that our lives receive when they proceed upon inadequate conviction and are suddenly confronted with difficulty too great for the old conviction. But to my mind our understanding of Euripidean structure rests firmly upon our ability to understand the dramatic experience that bridges the two or even three plateaus of reality that most Euripidean plays exhibit. In the *Heracles,* for instance, we get between the two actions no *propter hoc* connection of the kind Aristotelians insist upon, and yet the connection seems to me, if not quite necessitous, at least valid with whatever validity the conversion of human experience possesses.

If heroism happens to arise from a fortuitous and accidental eruption of the irrational in the nature of things—as in the *Heracles* or the *Hippolytus*—the very fact that it is in the nature of things makes the eruption necessary or probable: we tend to disbar it only because our Aristotelian habits predispose us to a dramatic world like that of Sophocles, where the apparent irrationalities of experience are explained by a divine order we cannot comprehend. But as applied to Euripides, these habits and their corollary in a crude notion of the tragic flaw can only complicate chaos further. We need rather a theory of Euripidean structure which starts from dislocation and attempts to show the relation of this form to a world of moral disorder. Unless I am mistaken, such examination must also show the irrelevance of *propter hoc* structure to Euripides, whose sense of necessity in drama derives more from the motion of the human mind under stress and the patterns which men's convictions make when confronted by adventitious realities. A man's character may be his destiny, but for Euripides destiny is often dependent upon and defined by circumstances the hero never made, nor the gods either. Unless we can restore an understanding of the importance of the dramatist's assumed world for his form, Euripides must stand perpetually condemned or be explained with all the willful improbability of Verrall. At least the latest book on Euripidean structure—Gilbert Norwood's *Essays on Euripidean Drama*—makes the implicit claim that these dislocations of plot and internal inconsistencies in the plays are best explained as the work of fourth century redactors. This seems both unfortunate and unnecessary.

One final point. Nothing, I think, more effectively hinders our understanding of the experience of Greek tragedy than the inadequacy and crudity of meaning which critics and translators assign to the operative moral terms of Greek tragedy—*sophia, hybris, anankē, sōphrosunē, aristeia, timē, authadia* and the like. For in much criticism of tragedy these terms are used as though they possessed simple English equivalents, without, I think, adequate reference to the experience with which they were meant to cope. Alternatively, they are exposed to static definition without regard to the transformations which tragedy may force upon them as the hero moves from a situation of conventional morality and reality to an ordeal for which the traditional wisdom of the Chorus may be utterly inadequate. In such situations it is my conviction that the old moral terms are employed with a meaning so turbulent with fresh or restored experience that they are no longer the same terms, nor the hero to whom they apply the same man. *Timē,* for instance, is normally translated as *honor,* but its root meaning is price, or valuation, and in most tragedies where the concept is important—the *Antigone,* for instance—the word operates very much like the deep sense of our word "respect." Thus when Ismene claims that Antigone has not shown *timē* to her, and that Creon has not shown *timē* to Haemon, she means, not that she and Haemon have been dishonored, or insulted, but that they have not been respected: they have been disallowed the dignity of a fate and their dignity as individuals. They have, as it were, been priced all wrong, and this charge is, of course, central to the play, since Antigone claims to act for *philia* because she wishes to give *timē* to Polyneices. What, the play seems to suggest, is the assertion of *philia* worth without *timē* too? And what is a *philia* which, in order to respect one person, shows disrespect to another, both equally claiming the rights of *philia?*

Or consider the word *sophia,* which we badly translate as "wisdom," as it gets into the *Bacchae.* Among other things, *sophia* means a knowledge and acceptance of one's nature and therefore of one's place in the scheme of things. It presupposes, that is, self-knowledge, an acceptance of those necessities that compose the limits of human fate. It also means the consequent refinement of feelings by which a man recognizes and respects the sufferings of others before necessity: it issues in compassion.[2] *Sophia* is further contrasted with its opposite, *amathia,* a deep, brutal, unteachable,

[2] Cf. *Electra,* ll. 294-5, where Orestes states that pity *(to oiktos)* is never to be found among the *amatheis* but only among the *sophoi* i.e. compassion is a true component of "wisdom."

ungovernable self-ignorance which breaks out in violence and cruelty. If the *sophos* is by definition susceptible to the feelings of civilized humanity, a compassion learned in fellow-suffering, the *amathēs* is callous and merciless, a barbarian by nature. But it is these meanings which crowd into the *Bacchae* and everywhere provide, through dramatic action and testing, the play's missing principle of order. For in the course of the action, through the very brutality which they use to support their claims to *sophia,* both Pentheus and Dionysus utterly expose their own *amathia.*

But more than the self-indictment of Pentheus or Dionysus is involved here. For Euripides has taken elaborate pains to show in Pentheus something more than the man who does not know the deep Dionysiac necessity of his own nature: he is also the proud iconoclastic innovator, the rebel at war with tradition, standing outside of the community's *nomos* [custom as law] and as *theomachos,* disdainful of any power above man. Ranged against him are Cadmus, Teiresias and the chorus, who all alike appeal to the massive tyranny of tradition and folk-belief, and constantly invoke as the sanction of society against the rebellious or anti-traditional man the words *sōphrosunē* and *dikē.* Thus in flat opposition to Pentheus' lonely arrogance of the "exceptional" (*perissos*) man, defying the community's *nomos* in the name of his own self-will, is set the chorus' tyrannous tradition: "Beyond the old beliefs, no thought, no act shall go (891-2)." We have, that is, a head-on collision between the forces which represent a brutally depraved conservative tradition and the arrogant exemplar of the ruthlessly anti-traditional mind. Both positions are alike in the cruel and bigoted violence with which they meet opposition, and the *sophia* and *sōphrosunē* and *dikē* which they both claim mock their pretensions and condemn their conduct. If the conduct of the chorus and Dionysus outrage our sympathies and finally enlist them on Pentheus' behalf, it is because, in the nature of things, the *amathia* of a man is less heinous than that of a god. But both are *amatheis,* Pentheus no less than the chorus, and the play as a whole employs them and their struggle as a bitter image of both Athens and Hellas terribly divided between the forces that, in Euripides' mind, more than anything else destroyed them: on the one side, the conservative and aristocratic tradition in its extreme corruption, disguising avarice for wealth and power with the fair professions of the traditional *aretai,* meeting all attempts at change or moderation with the tyranny of popular piety, and disclosing in its actions the callousness and refined cruelty of civilized barbarism; on the other side, the exceptional individual, selfish and egotistical, impatient of public welfare and tradition alike, opportunistic, demagogic and equally brutal in action. In saying this, I do not intend to dispute the obvious religious concerns of the *Bac-chae*, but to stress what, to my knowledge, has not been emphasized, that the play is, like the *Heracles*, the *Electra* and the *Orestes*, a composite of discrete conversions, social and political as well as religious. And all of these concerns meet in the term *sophia* and its opposite, *amathia*, which at their widest enclose most of what we mean by "civilized" and "uncivilized," both morally and politically. Thus when Euripides has his chorus assert that *to sophon* is not the same as *sophia*, he means that the pretensions and conventions and habits of civilization are by no means equivalent to civilized practices.

But in my opinion the same widening and deepening of the operative moral terms of Greek culture is to be found everywhere in tragedy—*philia* in *Antigone*, *sōphrosunē* in *Hippolytus*, *eugeneia* in *Heracles*, *aristeia* in *Orestes*, etc.—and it would be surprising if it were not so. But upon our sense of the play off the traditional or lazy meanings of these words and the definitions which the tragic action makes lies, I think, much of the turbulence now missing from the criticism of tragedy.

Let me close with a brief note on necessity, for necessity seems to me the crucial center of Greek tragedy, just as Greek tragedy seems to me unique in the firmness and sharpness with which it follows necessity into human action. In its basic aspect, necessity (*anankē*) is that set of unalterable, irreducible, unmanageable facts which we call the human condition. Call it destiny, call it fate, call it the gods, it hardly matters. Necessity is, first of all, death; but it is also old age, sleep, the reversal of fortune and the dance of life; it is thereby the fact of suffering as well as pleasure, for if we must dance and sleep, we also suffer, age and die. It is also sex, the great figure of amoral Aphrodite who moves in the sea, land and air and as an undeniable power in the bodies of men, compelling and destroying those who, like Hippolytus, refuse to accept her. Or it is Dionysus, the terrible ambiguous force of the *Bacchae*, "the force that through the green fuse drives the flower," and who destroys Pentheus who lacks the *sophia* that accepts him. It is the great god-sprung trap of the *Oedipus* and also the nature of Oedipus himself, that stubborn human courage of pride that drives him relentlessly into the trap. It is the necessity of political power which, in corruption, destroys Hecuba and Iphigeneia and Cassandra and Polyxena. It is the inherent hostility of blind chance, the incalculable daemonic malice which in the Euripidean *Heracles* calls out to the hero to die and tells him that there is no hope and no moral order in the world at all. Suspend necessity in the form of the play, and you get such charming, romantic plays as *Iphigeneia at Tauris* and the *Helen*. Romantic, that is, because not tragic; and not tragic because necessity, the mainspring of

tragedy, has been, for fun, for entertainment and experiment, removed. Where men are freed from the yoke of necessity, their
lives cease to be tragic, and with the loss of suffering comes also
the loss of dignity and *sophia*.

For it is in the *struggle* with necessity that heroism is born, and
even the hero, if he is to retain his humanity, must accept necessity. Ripeness is all. And so we see Orestes discover purity and
compassion in the face of a necessity that threatens to deform him
as it has already deformed his father and mother and as it inevitably deforms the weak, the flawed, the average human nature. So
too Antigone accepts her necessity, the consequence of her own
act, humanity pushed to the extreme, and thereby comes again
upon her humanity in the very act of acceptance and recognition
of loss. So Oedipus by asserting his total utter responsibility for his
own fate, wins the victory over a necessity that would have destroyed a lesser man. And so Heracles claims a moral dignity forever out of reach of the amoral powers that persecute him. There
is a magnificence here in the power to rise, in the anguished acceptance that must always, in Greek tragedy, precede the winning
of dignity. For it is here before necessity that old morality is un-
made and then remade into a new thing. Thus Orestes, having
discovered at least that compassion that made him hesitate, enables justice to be born. And so too at the close of the *Hippolytus*
and *Bacchae* we see the suffering human survivors of the play discover, under the awful yoke of an intolerable necessity, the love
and *compassion,* the shared suffering that makes men endure with
love in a world which shrieks at them to die. Learn wisdom
through suffering, says Aeschylus, and if we are loyal to the turbulence of Greek tragedy, we can see what he means. For, stripped
to the bone, the essential *action* of the greatest of the Greek tragedies is an enactment of lives lived out under the double yoke of
man's own nature and a world he did not make; the weaker fail
or are deformed; the strong survive, and by surviving and enduring, liberate the dignity of significant suffering which gives man
the crucial victory over his own fate.

ARISTOPHANES

Lysistrata

Translated by DONALD SUTHERLAND

~~~~~~~~~~~~~~~~~~~~~~~~~~~~~~~~~~~~

NORTHROP FRYE

The Mythos
of Spring: Comedy

THE CHARACTERS IN *LYSISTRATA*

LYSISTRATA
KALONIKE   Athenian women
MYRRHINA

LAMPITO, a Spartan woman

CHORUS OF OLD MEN

CHORUS OF WOMEN

ATHENIAN COMMISSIONER

OLD MARKET-WOMEN

CINESIAS, an Athenian, husband of Myrrhina

SPARTAN HERALD

SPARTAN AMBASSADORS

ATHENIAN AMBASSADORS

Application for any performance of *Lysistrata* by Aristophanes, translated by Donald Sutherland, should be made to Literary Discoveries, Inc., 604 Mission Street, San Francisco 5, California. No performance may take place unless a license has been obtained.

LYSISTRATA

[*A street in Athens before daylight*]

LYSISTRATA   If anyone had asked them to a festival
of Aphrodite or of Bacchus or of Pan,
you couldn't get through Athens for the tambourines,
but now there's not one solitary woman here.
Except my next-door neighbor. Here she's coming out.   5
Hello, Kalonike.

KALONIKE   Hello, Lysistrata.
What are you so upset about? Don't scowl so, dear.
You're less attractive when you knit your brows and glare.

LYSISTRATA   I know, Kalonike, but I am smoldering
with indignation at the way we women act.   10
Men think we are so gifted for all sorts of crime
that we will stop at nothing—

KALONIKE   Well, we are, by Zeus!

LYSISTRATA   —but when it comes to an appointment here with me
to plot and plan for something really serious
they lie in bed and do not come.

KALONIKE   They'll come, my dear.   15
You know what trouble women have in going out:
one of us will be wrapped up in her husband still,
another waking up the maid, or with a child
to put to sleep, or give its bath, or feed its pap.

LYSISTRATA   But they had other more important things to do
than those.   20

KALONIKE   What ever is it, dear Lysistrata?
What have you called us women all together for?
How much of a thing is it?

LYSISTRATA   Very big.

KALONIKE   And thick?

LYSISTRATA   Oh very thick indeed.

KALONIKE   Then *how* can we be late?

LYSISTRATA   That's not the way it is. Or we would all be here.   25
But it is something I have figured out myself
and turned and tossed upon for many a sleepless night.

KALONIKE   It must be something slick you've turned and tossed
   upon!

LYSISTRATA   So slick that the survival of all Greece depends
upon the women.

61

KALONIKE   On the women? In that case
poor Greece has next to nothing to depend upon.

LYSISTRATA   Since now it's we who must decide affairs of state:
either there is to be no Spartan left alive—

5   KALONIKE   A very good thing too, if none were left, by Zeus!

LYSISTRATA   —and every living soul in Thebes to be destroyed—

KALONIKE   Except the eels! Spare the delicious eels of Thebes!

LYSISTRATA   —and as for Athens—I can't bring myself to say
the like of that for us. But just think what I mean!
10   Yet if the women meet here as I told them to
from Sparta, Thebes, and all of their allies,
and we of Athens, all together we'll save Greece.

KALONIKE   What reasonable thing could women ever do,
or glorious, we who sit around all prettied up
15   in flowers and scandalous saffron-yellow gowns,
groomed and draped to the ground in oriental stuffs
and fancy pumps?

LYSISTRATA   And those are just the very things
I count upon to save us—wicked saffron gowns,
perfumes and pumps and rouge and sheer transparent frocks.

KALONIKE   But what use can they be?

20   LYSISTRATA   So no man in our time
will raise a spear against another man again—

KALONIKE   I'll get a dress dyed saffron-yellow, come what may!

LYSISTRATA   —nor touch a shield—

KALONIKE   I'll slip into the sheerest gown!

LYSISTRATA   —nor so much as a dagger—

KALONIKE   I'll buy a pair of pumps!

25   LYSISTRATA   So don't you think the women should be here by now?

KALONIKE   I don't. They should have *flown* and got here long ago.

LYSISTRATA   You'll see, my dear. They will, like good Athenians,
do everything too late. But from the coastal towns
no woman is here either, nor from Salamis.

30   KALONIKE   I'm certain those from Salamis have crossed the strait:
they're always straddling *something* at this time of night.

LYSISTRATA   Not even those I was expecting would be first
to get here, from Acharnae, from so close to town,
not even they are here.

KALONIKE   But one of them, I know,

is under way, and three sheets to the wind, by now.
But look—some women are approaching over there.

LYSISTRATA   And over here are some, coming this way—

KALONIKE   Phew! Phew!
Where are they from?

LYSISTRATA   Down by the marshes.

KALONIKE   Yes, by Zeus!
It smells as if the bottoms had been all churned up!   5

[*Enter* MYRRHINA, *and others.*]

MYRRHINA   Hello Lysistrata. Are we a little late?
What's that? Why don't you speak?

LYSISTRATA   I don't think much of you,
Myrrhina, coming to this business only now.

MYRRHINA   Well, I could hardly find my girdle in the dark.
If it's so urgent, tell us what it is. We're here.   10

KALONIKE   Oh no. Let's wait for just a little while until
the delegates from Sparta and from Thebes arrive.

LYSISTRATA   You show much better judgment.

[*Enter* LAMPITO, *and others.*]

                                        Here comes Lampito!

LYSISTRATA   Well, darling Lampito! My dearest Spartan friend!
How very sweet, how beautiful you look! That fresh   15
complexion! How magnificent your figure is!
Enough to crush a bull!

LAMPITO   Ah shorely think Ah could.
Ah take mah exacise. Ah jump and thump mah butt.

KALONIKE   And really, what a handsome set of tits you have!

LAMPITO   You feel me ovah lahk a cow fo sacrafahce!   20

LYSISTRATA   And this other young thing—where ever is *she* from?

LAMPITO   She's prominent, Ah sweah, in Thebes—a delegate
ample enough.

LYSISTRATA   By Zeus, she represent Thebes well,
having so trim a ploughland.

KALONIKE   Yes, by Zeus, she does!
There's not a weed of all her field she hasn't plucked.   25

LYSISTRATA   And who's the other girl?

LAMPITO   Theah's nothing small, Ah sweah,
  or tahght about her folks in Corinth.

KALONIKE   No, by Zeus!—
  to judge by this side of her, nothing small or tight.

LAMPITO   But who has called togethah such a regiment
  of all us women?

LYSISTRATA   Here I am. I did.

5 LAMPITO   Speak up,
  just tell us what you want.

KALONIKE   Oh yes, by Zeus, my dear,
  do let us know what the important business is!

LYSISTRATA   Let me explain it, then. And yet . . . before I do . . .
  I have one little question.

KALONIKE   Anything you like.

10 LYSISTRATA   Don't you all miss the fathers of your little ones,
  your husbands who have gone away to war? I'm sure
  you all have husbands in the armies far from home.

KALONIKE   Mine's been away five months in Thrace—a general's
      guard,
  posted to see his general does not desert.

15 MYRRHINA   And mine has been away in Pylos seven whole months.

LAMPITO   And mahn, though he does get back home on leave
      sometahms,
  no soonah has he come than he is gone again.

LYSISTRATA   No lovers either. Not a sign of one is left.
  For since our eastern allies have deserted us
20 they haven't sent a single six-inch substitute
  to serve as leatherware replacement for our men.
  Would you be willing, then, if I thought out a scheme,
  to join with me to end the war?

KALONIKE   Indeed I would,
  even if I had to pawn this very wrap-around
25 and drink up all the money in one day, I would!

MYRRHINA   And so would I, even if I had to see myself
  split like a flounder, and give half of me away!

LAMPITO   And so would Ah! Ah'd climb up Mount Taÿgetos
  if Ah just had a chance of seeing peace from theah!

30 LYSISTRATA   Then I will tell you. I may now divulge my plan.
  Women of Greece!—if we intend to force the men
  to make a peace, we must abstain . . .

KALONIKE   From what? Speak out!

LYSISTRATA   But will you do it?

KALONIKE   We will, though death should be the price!

LYSISTRATA   Well then, we must abstain utterly from the prick.
   Why do you turn your backs? Where are you off to now?
   And you—why pout and make such faces, shake your heads?   5
   Why has your color changed? Why do you shed those tears?
   Will you do it or will you not? Why hesitate?

KALONIKE   I will not do it. Never. Let the war go on!

MYRRHINA   Neither will I. By Zeus, no! Let the war go on!

LYSISTRATA   How can you say so, Madam Flounder, when just
      now   10
   you were declaiming you would split yourself in half?

KALONIKE   Anything else you like, anything! If I must
   I'll gladly walk through fire. That, rather than the prick!
   Because there's nothing like it, dear Lysistrata.

LYSISTRATA   How about you?

MYRRHINA   I too would gladly walk through fire.   15

LYSISTRATA   Oh the complete depravity of our whole sex!
   It is no wonder tragedies are made of us,
   we have such unrelenting unity of mind!
   But you, my friend from Sparta, dear, if you alone
   stand by me, only you, we still might save the cause.   20
   Vote on my side!

LAMPITO   They'ah hahd conditions, mahty hahd,
   to sleep without so much as the fo'skin of one . . .
   but all the same . . . well . . . yes. We need peace just as bad.

LYSISTRATA   Oh dearest friend!—the one real woman of them all!

KALONIKE   And if we really should abstain from what you say—   25
   which Heaven forbid!—do you suppose on that account
   that peace might come to be?

LYSISTRATA   I'm absolutely sure.
   If we should sit around, rouged and with skins well creamed,
   with nothing on but a transparent negligé,
   and come up to them with our deltas plucked quite smooth,   30
   and, once our men get stiff and want to come to grips,
   we do not yield to them at all but just hold off,
   they'll make a truce in no time. There's no doubt of that.

LAMPITO   We say in Spahta that when Menelaos saw
   Helen's ba'e apples he just tossed away his swo'd.   35

KALONIKE   And what, please, if our husbands just toss *us* away?

LYSISTRATA   Well, you have heard the good old saying: Know
Thyself.

KALONIKE   It isn't worth the candle. I hate cheap substitutes.
But what if they should seize and drag us by brute force
into the bedroom?

LYSISTRATA   Hang onto the doors!

5 KALONIKE   And if—
they beat us?

LYSISTRATA   Then you must give in, but nastily,
and do it badly. There's no fun in it by force.
And then, just keep them straining. They will give it up
in no time—don't you worry. For never will a man
10   enjoy himself unless the woman coincides.

KALONIKE   If both of you are for this plan, then so are we.

LAMPITO   And we of Spahta shall persuade ouah men to keep
the peace sinceahly and with honah in all ways,
but how could anyone pe'suade the vulgah mob
15   of Athens not to deviate from discipline?

LYSISTRATA   Don't worry, we'll persuade our men. They'll keep
the peace.

LAMPITO   They won't, so long as they have battleships afloat
and endless money sto'ed up in the Pahthenon.

LYSISTRATA   But that too has been carefully provided for:
20   *we* shall take over the Acropolis today.
The oldest women have their orders to do that:
while *we* meet here, *they* go as if to sacrifice
up there, but really seizing the Acropolis.

LAMPITO   All should go well. What you say theah is very smaht.

25 LYSISTRATA   In that case, Lampito, what are we waiting for?
Let's take an oath, to bind us indissolubly.

LAMPITO   Well, just you show us what the oath is. Then we'll
sweah.

LYSISTRATA   You're right. Where is that lady cop?

[*To the armed* LADY COP *looking around for a* LADY COP]

                              What do you think
you're looking for? Put down your shield in front of us,
30   there, on its back, and someone get some scraps of gut.

KALONIKE   Lysistrata, what in the world do you intend
to make us take an oath on?

LYSISTRATA What? Why, on a shield,
just as they tell me some insurgents in a play
by Aeschylus once did, with a sheep's blood and guts.

KALONIKE Oh *don't*, Lysistrata, don't swear upon a *shield*,
not if the oath has anything to do with peace! 5

LYSISTRATA Well then, what *will* we swear on? Maybe we should get
a white horse somewhere, like the Amazons, and cut
some bits of gut from it.

KALONIKE *Where* would we get a horse?

LYSISTRATA But what kind of an oath *is* suitable for us?

KALONIKE By Zeus, I'll tell you if you like. First we put down 10
a big black drinking-cup, face up, and then we let
the neck of a good jug of wine bleed into it,
and take a solemn oath to—add no water in.

LAMPITO Bah Zeus, Ah jest can't tell you how Ah lahk that oath!

LYSISTRATA Someone go get a cup and winejug from inside. 15

[KALONIKE *goes and is back in a flash.*]

KALONIKE My dears, my dearest dears—how's *this* for pottery?
You feel good right away, just laying hold of it.

LYSISTRATA Well, set it down, and lay your right hand on this pig.
O goddess of Persuasion, and O Loving-cup,
accept this victim's blood! Be gracious unto us. 20

KALONIKE It's not anaemic, and flows clear. Those are good signs.

LAMPITO What an aroma, too! Bah Castah it *is* sweet!

KALONIKE My dears, if you don't mind—I'll be the first to swear.

LYSISTRATA By Aphrodite, no! If you had drawn first place
by lot—but now let all lay hands upon the cup. 25
Yes, Lampito—and now, let one of you repeat
for all of you what I shall say. You will be sworn
by every word she says, and bound to keep this oath:
No lover and no husband and no man on earth—

KALONIKE No lover and no husband and no man on earth— 30

LYSISTRATA *shall e'er approach me with his penis up.* Repeat.

KALONIKE shall e'er approach me with his penis up. Oh dear,
my knees are buckling under me, Lysistrata!

LYSISTRATA *and I shall lead an unlaid life alone at home,*

KALONIKE and I shall lead an unlaid life alone at home, 35

LYSISTRATA *wearing a saffron gown and groomed and beautified*

KALONIKE   wearing a saffron gown and groomed and beautified

LYSISTRATA   *so that my husband will be all on fire for me*

KALONIKE   so that my husband will be all on fire for me

LYSISTRATA   *but I will never willingly give in to him*

5 KALONIKE   but I will never willingly give in to him

LYSISTRATA   *and if he tries to force me to against my will*

KALONIKE   and if he tries to force me to against my will

LYSISTRATA   *I'll do it badly and not wiggle in response*

KALONIKE   I'll do it badly and not wiggle in response

10 LYSISTRATA   *nor toward the ceiling will I lift my Persian pumps*

KALONIKE   nor toward the ceiling will I lift my Persian pumps

LYSISTRATA   *nor crouch down as the lions on cheese-graters do*

KALONIKE   nor crouch down as the lions on cheese-graters do

LYSISTRATA   *and if I keep my promise, may I drink of this—*

15 KALONIKE   and if I keep my promise, may I drink of this—

LYSISTRATA   *but if I break it, then may water fill the cup!*

KALONIKE   but if I break it, then may water fill the cup!

LYSISTRATA   Do you all swear to this with her?

ALL   We do, by Zeus!

LYSISTRATA   I'll consecrate our oath now.

KALONIKE   Share alike, my dear,
20 so we'll be friendly to each other from the start.

LAMPITO   What was that screaming?

LYSISTRATA   That's what I was telling you:
the women have already seized the Parthenon
and the Acropolis. But now, dear Lampito,
return to Sparta and set things in order there—
25 but leave these friends of yours as hostages with us—
And let *us* join the others in the citadel
and help them bar the gates.

KALONIKE   But don't you think the men
will rally to the rescue of the citadel,
attacking us at once?

LYSISTRATA   They don't worry me much:
30 they'll never bring against us threats or fire enough
to force open the gates, except upon our terms.

KALONIKE   Never by Aphrodite! Or we'd lose our name
for being battle-axes and unbearable!

[Exeunt. The scene changes to the Propylaea of the Acropolis. A chorus of very old men struggles slowly in, carrying logs and firepots.]

ONE OLD MAN   Lead on! O Drakës, step by step, although your
        shoulder's aching
    and under this green olive log's great weight
        your back be breaking!

ANOTHER   Eh, life is long but always has   5
        more surprises for us!
    Now who'd have thought we'd live to hear
        this, O Strymodorus?—

    The wives we fed and looked upon
    as helpless liabilities   10
    now dare to occupy the Parthenon,
    our whole Acropolis, for once they seize
    the Propylaea, straightway
    they lock and bar the gateway.

CHORUS   Let's rush to the Acropolis with due precipitation   15
    and lay these logs down circlewise, till presently we turn them
    into one mighty pyre to make a general cremation
    of all the women up there—eh! with our own hands we'll burn
        them,
    the leaders and the followers, without discrimination!

AN OLD MAN   They'll never have the laugh on me!   20
        Though I may not look it,
    I rescued the Acropolis
        when the Spartans took it
    about a hundred years ago.
    We laid a siege that kept their king   25
    six years unwashed, so when I made him throw
    his armor off, for all his blustering,
    in nothing but his shirt he
    looked very very dirty.

CHORUS   How strictly I besieged the man! These gates were all
        invested   30
    with seventeen ranks of armored men all equally ferocious!
    Shall women—by Euripides and all the gods detested—
    not be restrained—with me on hand—from something so
        atrocious?
    They shall!—or may our trophies won at Marathon be bested!
        But we must go a long way yet   35
        up that steep and winding road

before we reach the fortress where we want to get.
How shall we ever drag this load,
lacking pack-mules, way up there?
I can tell you that my shoulder has caved in beyond repair!
Yet we must trudge ever higher,
ever blowing on the fire,
so its coals will still be glowing when we get where we are going
Fooh! Fooh!
Whoo! I choke!
What a smoke!

Lord Herakles! How fierce it flies
out against me from the pot!
and like a rabid bitch it bites me in the eyes!
It's female fire, or it would not
scratch my poor old eyes like this.
Yet undaunted we must onward, up the high Acropolis
where Athena's temple stands
fallen into hostile hands.
O my comrades! shall we ever have a greater need to save her?
Fooh! Fooh!
Whoo! I choke!
What a smoke!

FIRST OLD MAN Well, thank the gods, I see the fire is yet alive and waking!

SECOND OLD MAN Why don't we set our lumber down right here in handy batches,
then stick a branch of grape-vine in the pot until it catches

THIRD OLD MAN and hurl ourselves against the gate with battering and shaking?

FIRST OLD MAN and if the women won't unbar at such an ultimatum
we'll set the gate on fire and then the smoke will suffocate 'em.

SECOND OLD MAN Well, let's put down our load. Fooh fooh, what smoke! But blow as needed!

THIRD OLD MAN Your ablest generals *these* days would not carry wood like *we* did.

SECOND OLD MAN At last the lumber ceases grinding my poor back to pieces!

THIRD OLD MAN These are your orders, Colonel Pot: wake up
    the coals and bid them
report here and present to me a torch lit up and flaring.

FIRST OLD MAN O Victory, be with us! If you quell the women's
    daring
we'll raise a splendid trophy of how you and we undid them!

[*A* CHORUS *of middle-aged women appears in the offing.*]

A WOMAN I think that I perceive a smoke in which appears a
    flurry   5
of sparks as of a lighted fire. Women, we'll have to hurry!

CHORUS OF WOMEN
            Oh fleetly fly, oh swiftly flit,
            my dears, e'er Kalykë be lit
            and with Kritylla swallowed up alive
                    in flames which the gales dreadfully drive   10
                    and deadly old men fiercely inflate!
            Yet one thing I'm afraid of: will I not arrive too late?
            for filling up my water-jug has been no easy matter
            what with the crowd at the spring in the dusk and the
                    clamor and pottery clatter.   15
                    Pushed as I was, jostled by slave-
                    women and sluts marked with a brand
                    yet with my jug firmly in hand
                    here I have come, hoping to save
                        my burning friends and brave,   20

                    for certain windy, witless, old,
                    and wheezy fools, so I was told,
            with wood some tons in weight crept up this path,
                    not having in mind heating a bath
                    but uttering threats, vowing they will   25
            consume those nasty women into cinders on grill!
            But O Athena! never may I see my friends igniting!
            Nay!—let them save all the cities of Greece and their
                    people from folly and fighting!
                    Goddess whose crest flashes with gold,   30
                    they were so bold taking your shine
                    only for this—Goddess who hold
                    Athens—for *this* noble design,
                    braving the flames, calling on you
                        to carry water too!   35

[*One of the old men urinates noisily.*]

CHORUS OF WOMEN   Be still! What was that noise? Aha! Oh,
wicked and degraded!
Would any good religious men have ever done what *they* did?

CHORUS OF MEN   Just look! It's a surprise-attack! Oh, dear, we're
being raided
by swarms of them below us when we've got a swarm above us!

CHORUS OF WOMEN   Why panic at the sight of us? This is not
5   many of us.
We number tens of thousands but you've hardly seen a fraction.

CHORUS OF MEN   O Phaidrias, shall they talk so big and we not
take some action?
Oh, should we not be bashing them and splintering our lumber?

[*The old men begin to strip for combat.*]

CHORUS OF WOMEN   Let us, too, set our pitchers down, so they
will not encumber
10   our movements if these gentlemen should care to offer battle.

CHORUS OF MEN   Oh someone should have clipped their jaws—
twice, thrice, until they rattle—
(as once the poet put it)—then we wouldn't hear their prating.

CHORUS OF WOMEN   Well, here's your chance. Won't someone
hit me? Here I stand, just waiting!
No other bitch will ever grab your balls, the way I'll treat you!

CHORUS OF MEN   Shut up—or I will drub you so old age will never
15   reach you!

CHORUS OF WOMEN   Won't anyone step and lay one finger on
Stratyllis?

CHORUS OF MEN   And if we pulverize her with our knuckles, will
you kill us?

CHORUS OF WOMEN   No, only chew your lungs out and your in-
nards and your eyes, sir.

CHORUS OF MEN   How clever is Euripides! There is no poet wiser:
he says indeed that women are the worst of living creatures.

CHORUS OF WOMEN   Now is the time, Rhodippe: let us raise our
20   brimming pitchers.

CHORUS OF MEN   Why come up here with water, you, the gods'
abomination?

CHORUS OF WOMEN   And why come here with fire, you tomb? To
give yourself cremation?

CHORUS OF MEN   To set your friends alight upon a pyre erected
   for them.

CHORUS OF WOMEN   And so we brought our water-jugs. Upon
   your pyre we'll pour them.

CHORUS OF MEN   *You'll* put my fire out?

CHORUS OF WOMEN   Any time! You'll see there's nothing to it.

CHORUS OF MEN   I think I'll grill you right away, with just this
   torch to do it!

CHORUS OF WOMEN   Have you some dusting-powder? Here's your
   wedding-bath all ready.   5

CHORUS OF MEN   *You'll* bathe me, garbage that you are?

CHORUS OF WOMEN   Yes, bridegroom, just hold steady!

CHORUS OF MEN   Friends, you have heard her insolence—

CHORUS OF WOMEN   I'm free-born, not your slave, sir.

CHORUS OF MEN   I'll have this noise of yours restrained—

CHORUS OF WOMEN   Court's out—so be less grave, sir.

CHORUS OF MEN   Why don't you set her hair on fire?

CHORUS OF WOMEN   Oh, Water, be of service!

CHORUS OF MEN   Oh woe is me!

CHORUS OF WOMEN   Was it too hot?   10

CHORUS OF MEN   Oh, stop! What *is* this? Hot? Oh no!

CHORUS OF WOMEN   I'm watering you to make you grow.

CHORUS OF MEN   I'm withered from this chill I got!

CHORUS OF WOMEN   You've got a fire, so warm yourself. You're
   trembling: are you nervous?

[*Enter a* COMMISSIONER, *escorted by four Scythian policemen with
bows and quivers slung on their backs.*]

COMMISSIONER   Has the extravagance of women broken out   15
   into full fury, with their banging tambourines
   and constant wailings for their oriental gods,
   and on the roof-tops their Adonis festival,
   which I could hear myself from the Assembly once?
   For while Demostratos—that numbskull—had the floor,   20
   urging an expedition against Sicily,
   his wife was dancing and we heard her crying out
   "Weep for Adonis!"—so the expedition failed

with such an omen. When the same Demostratos
was urging that we levy troops from our allies
his wife was on the roof again, a little drunk:
"Weep for Adonis! Beat your breast!" says she. At that,

5   he gets more bellicose, that god-Damn-ox-tratos.
To this has the incontinence of women come!

CHORUS OF MEN   You haven't *yet* heard how outrageous they can
be!
With other acts of violence, these women here
have showered us from their jugs, so now we are reduced

10   to shaking out our shirts as if we'd pissed in them.

COMMISSIONER   Well, by the God of Waters, what do you expect?
When we ourselves conspire with them in waywardness
and give them good examples of perversity
such wicked notions naturally sprout in them.

15   We go into a shop and say something like this:
"Goldsmith, about that necklace you repaired: last night
my wife was dancing, when the peg that bolts the catch
fell from its hole. I have to sail for Salamis,
but if you have the time, by all means try to come

20   towards evening, and put in the peg she needs."
Another man says to a cobbler who is young
and has no child's-play of a prick, "Cobbler," he says,
"her sandal-strap is pinching my wife's little toe,
which is quite delicate. So please come by at noon

25   and stretch it for her so it has a wider play."
Such things as that result of course in things like this:
when I, as a Commissioner, have made a deal
to fit the fleet with oars and need the money now,
I'm locked out by these women from the very gates.

30   But it's no use just standing here. Bring on the bars,
so I can keep these women in their proper place.
What are *you* gaping at, you poor unfortunate?
Where are *you* looking? Only seeing if a bar
is open yet downtown? Come, drive these crowbars in

35   under the gates on that side, pry away, and I
will pry away on this.

[LYSISTRATA *comes out.*]

LYSISTRATA   No need to pry at all.
I'm coming out, of my own will. What use are bars?
It isn't bolts and bars we need so much as brains.

COMMISSIONER   Really, you dirty slut? Where is that officer?

40   Arrest her, and tie both her hands behind her back.

LYSISTRATA   By Artemis, just let him lift a hand at me
and, public officer or not, you'll hear him howl.

COMMISSIONER   You let her scare you? Grab her round the middle,
you.
Then *you* go help him and between you get her tied.

[KALONIKE *comes out.*]

KALONIKE   By Artemis, if you just lay one hand on her   5
I have a mind to trample the shit out of you.

COMMISSIONER   It's out already! Look! Now where's the other one?
Tie up *that* woman first. She babbles, with it all.

[*Myrrhina comes out.*]

MYRRHINA   By Hecatë, if you just lay a hand on her
you'll soon ask for a cup—to get your swellings down!   10

[*The policeman dashes behind the* COMMISSIONER *and clings to him
for protection.*]

COMMISSIONER   What happened? Where's that bowman, now? Hold
onto *her!*

[*He moves quickly away downhill.*]

I'll see that none of you can get away through here!

LYSISTRATA   By Artemis, you come near her and I'll bereave
your head of every hair! You'll weep for each one, too.

COMMISSIONER   What a calamity! This one has failed me too.   15
But never must we let ourselves be overcome
by women. All together now, O Scythians!—
let's march against them in formation!

LYSISTRATA   You'll find out
that inside there we have four companies
of fighting women perfectly equipped for war.   20

COMMISSIONER   Charge! Turn their flanks, O Scythians! and tie
their hands!

LYSISTRATA   O allies—comrades—women! Sally forth and fight!
O vegetable vendors, O green-grocery-
grain-garlic-bread-bean-dealers and inn-keepers all!

[*A group of fierce* OLD MARKET-WOMEN, *carrying baskets of vegetables, spindles, etc. emerges. There is a volley of vegetables. The
Scythians are soon routed.*]

Come pull them, push them, smite them, smash them into bits!
Rail and abuse them in the strongest words you know!
Halt, Halt! Retire in order! We'll forego the spoils!

COMMISSIONER [*tragically, like say Xerxes*] Oh what reverses have
my bowmen undergone!

5 LYSISTRATA But what did you imagine? Did you think you came
against a pack of slaves? Perhaps you didn't know
that women can be resolute?

COMMISSIONER I know they can—
above all when they spot a bar across the way.

CHORUS OF MEN Commissioner of Athens, you are spending
words unduly,
10 to argue with these animals, who only roar the louder,
or don't you know they showered us so coldly and so cruelly,
and in our undershirts at that, and furnished us no powder?

CHORUS OF WOMEN But beating up your neighbor is inevitably
bringing
a beating on yourself, sir, with your own eyes black and bloody.
15 I'd rather sit securely like a little girl demurely
not stirring up a single straw nor harming anybody,
So long as no one robs my hive and rouses me to stinging.

CHORUS OF MEN How shall we ever tame these brutes? We cannot
tolerate
the situation further, so we must investigate
20 this occurrence and find
with what purpose in mind
they profane the Acropolis, sieze it, and lock
the approach to this huge and prohibited rock,
to our holiest ground!

25 Cross-examine them! Never believe one word
they tell you—refute them, confound them!
We must get to the bottom of things like this
and the circumstances around them.

COMMISSIONER Yes indeed! and I want to know first one thing:
30 just *why* you committed this treason,
barricading the fortress with locks and bars—
I insist on knowing the reason.

LYSISTRATA To protect all the money up there from you—
you'll have nothing to fight for without it.

35 COMMISSIONER You think it is *money* we're fighting for?

LYSISTRATA All the troubles we have are about it.
It was so Peisander and those in power

of his kind could embezzle the treasure
that they cooked up emergencies all the time.
    Well, let them, if such is their pleasure,
but they'll never get into this money again,
    though you men should elect them to spend it.   5

COMMISSIONER And just what will *you* do with it?

LYSISTRATA   Can you ask?
    Of course we shall superintend it.

COMMISSIONER You will superintend the treasury, *you!?*

LYSISTRATA   And why should it strike you so funny?
    when we manage our houses in everything   10
    and it's we who look after your money.

COMMISSIONER But it's not the same thing!

LYSISTRATA   Why not?

COMMISSIONER   It's war,
    and *this* money must pay the expenses.

LYSISTRATA To begin with, you needn't be waging war.

COMMISSIONER   To survive, we don't need our defenses?   15

LYSISTRATA You'll survive: we shall save you.

COMMISSIONER   Who? You?

LYSISTRATA   Yes, we.

COMMISSIONER   You absolutely disgust me.

LYSISTRATA You may like it or not, but you *shall* be saved.

COMMISSIONER   I protest!

LYSISTRATA   If you care to, but, trust me,
    this has got to be done all the same.

COMMISSIONER   It has?   20
    It's illegal, unjust, and outrageous!

LYSISTRATA We must save you, sir.

COMMISSIONER   Yes? And if I refuse?

LYSISTRATA   You will much the more grimly engage us.

COMMISSIONER And whence does it happen that war and peace
    are fit matters for women to mention?   25

LYSISTRATA I will gladly explain—

COMMISSIONER   And be quick, or else
    you'll be howling!

LYSISTRATA   Now, just pay attention
    and keep your hands to yourself, if you can!

COMMISSIONER   But I can't. You can't think how I suffer
from holding them back in my anger!

AN OLD WOMAN   Sir—
if you don't you will have it much rougher.

COMMISSIONER   You may croak that remark to yourself, you hag!
      Will *you* do the explaining?

5 LYSISTRATA   I'll do it.
Heretofore we women in time of war
      have endured very patiently through it,
putting up with whatever you men might do,
      for never a peep would you let us
10 deliver on your unstatesmanly acts
      no matter how much they upset us,
but we knew very well, while we sat at home,
      when you'd handled a big issue poorly,
and we'd ask you then, with a pretty smile
15   though our heart would be grieving us sorely,
"And what were the terms for a truce, my dear,
      you drew up in assembly this morning?"
"And what's it to you?" says our husband, "Shut up!"
      —so, as ever, at this gentle warning
I of course would discreetly shut up.

20 KALONIKE   Not me!
      You can bet I would never be quiet!

COMMISSIONER   I'll bet, if you weren't, you were beaten up.

LYSISTRATA   *I'd* shut up, and I do not deny it,
but when plan after plan was decided on,
25   so bad we could scarcely believe it,
I would say "This last is so mindless, dear,
      I cannot think how you achieve it!"
And then he would say, with a dirty look,
      "Just you think what your spindle is for, dear,
30 or your head will be spinning for days on end—
      let the *men* attend to the war, dear."

COMMISSIONER   By Zeus, *he* had the right idea!

LYSISTRATA   You fool!
      Right ideas were quite out of the question,
when your reckless policies failed, and yet
35   we never could make a suggestion.
And lately we heard you say so yourselves:
      in the streets there'd be someone lamenting:
"There's not one man in the country now!"
      —and we heard many others assenting.

After that, we conferred through our deputies
      and agreed, having briefly debated,
to act in common to save all Greece
      at once—for why should we have waited?
So now, when we women are talking sense,   5
      if you'll only agree to be quiet
and to listen to us as we did to you,
      you'll be very much edified by it.

COMMISSIONER   *You* will edify *us!* I protest!

LYSISTRATA   Shut up!

COMMISSIONER   *I'm* to shut up and listen, you scum, you?!   10
Sooner death! And a veil on your head at that!

LYSISTRATA   We'll fix that. It may really become you:
do accept this veil as a present from me.
Drape it modestly—so—round your head, do you see?
And now—*not* a word more, sir.   15

KALONIKE   Do accept this dear little wool-basket, too!
Hitch your girdle and card! Here are beans you may chew
the way all of the nicest Athenians do—
and the *women* will see to the war, sir!

CHORUS OF WOMEN   Oh women, set your jugs aside and keep a
    closer distance: 20
our friends may need from us as well some resolute assistance.

      Since never shall I weary of the stepping of the dance
    nor will my knees of treading, for these ladies I'll advance
          anywhere they may lead,
          and they're daring indeed,   25
     they have wit, a fine figure, and boldness of heart,
       they are prudent and charming, efficient and smart,
       patriotic and brave!

But, O manliest grandmothers, onward now!
    And you matronly nettles, don't waver!   30
but continue to bristle and rage, my dears,
    for you've still got the wind in your favor!

[*The* CHORUS OF WOMEN *and the* OLD MARKET-WOMEN *join.*]

LYSISTRATA   But if only the spirit of tender Love
      and the power of sweet Aphrodite
were to breathe down over our breasts and thighs   35
      an attraction both melting and mighty,

and infuse a pleasanter rigor in men,
    raising only their cudgels of passion,
then I think we'd be known throughout all of Greece
    as makers of peace and good fashion.

COMMISSIONER   Having done just what?

5   LYSISTRATA   Well, first of all
    we shall certainly make it unlawful
    to go madly to market in armor.

AN OLD MARKET-WOMAN   Yes!
    By dear Aphrodite, it's awful!

10   LYSISTRATA   For now, in the midst of the pottery-stalls
    and the greens and the beans and the garlic,
    men go charging all over the market-place
    in full armor and beetling and warlike.

COMMISSIONER   They must do as their valor impels them to!

15   LYSISTRATA   But it makes a man only look funny
    to be wearing a shield with a Gorgon's head
    and be wanting sardines for less money.

OLD MARKET-WOMEN   Well, I saw a huge cavalry-captain once
    on a stallion that scarcely could hold him,
20   pouring into his helmet of bronze a pint
    of pea-soup an old women had sold him,
    and a Thracian who, brandishing shield and spear
    like some savage Euripides staged once,
    when he'd frightened a vendor of figs to death,
25   gobbled up all her ripest and aged ones.

COMMISSIONER   And how, on the international scale,
    can you straighten out the enormous
    confusion among all the states of Greece?

LYSISTRATA   Very easily.

COMMISSIONER   How? Do inform us.

30   LYSISTRATA   When our skein's in a tangle we take it thus
    on our spindles, or haven't you seen us?—
    one on this side and one on the other side,
    and we work out the tangles between us.
    And that is the way we'll undo this war,
35   by exchanging ambassadors, whether
    you like it or not, one from either side,
    and we'll work out the tangles together.

COMMISSIONER   Do you really think that with wools and skeins
    and just being able to spin you
40   can end these momentous affairs, you fools?

LYSISTRATA   With any intelligence in you
  you statesmen would govern as we work wool,
      and in everything Athens would profit.

COMMISSIONER   How so? Do tell.

LYSISTRATA   First, you take raw fleece
  and you wash the beshittedness off it: 5
  just so, you should first lay the city out
    on a washboard and beat out the rotters
  and pluck out the sharpers like burrs, and when
      you find tight knots of schemers and plotters
  who are out for key offices, card them loose,   10
      but best tear off their heads in addition.
  Then into one basket together card
      all those of a good disposition
  be they citizens, resident aliens, friends,
      an ally or an absolute stranger,   15
  even people in debt to the commonwealth,
      you can mix them all in with no danger.
  And the cities which Athens has colonized—
      by Zeus, you should try to conceive them
  as so many shreddings and tufts of wool   20
      that are scattered about and not leave them
  to lie around loose, but from all of them
      draw the threads in here, and collect them
  into one big ball and then weave a coat
      for the people, to warm and protect them.   25

COMMISSIONER   Now, isn't this awful? They treat the state
      like wool to be beaten and carded,
  who have nothing at all to do with war!

LYSISTRATA   Yes we do, you damnable hard-head!
  We have none of your honors but we have more   30
      then double your sufferings by it.
  First of all, we bear sons whom you send to war.

COMMISSIONER   Don't bring up our old sorrows! Be quiet!

LYSISTRATA   And now, when we ought to enjoy ourselves,
      making much of our prime and our beauty,   35
  we are sleeping alone because all the men
      are away on their soldierly duty.
  But never mind *us*—when young girls grow old
      in their bedrooms with no men to share them.

COMMISSIONER   You seem to forget that men, too, grow old.   40

LYSISTRATA   By Zeus, but you cannot compare them!
  When a man gets back, though he be quite gray,
      he can wed a young girl in a minute,

but the season of woman is very short:
   she must take what she can while she's in it.
And you know she must, for when it's past,
   although you're not awfully astute, you're
5 aware that no man will marry her then
   and she sits staring into the future.

COMMISSIONER   But he who can raise an erection still—

LYSISTRATA   Is there some good reason you don't drop dead?
   We'll sell you a coffin if you but will.
10 Here's a string of onions to crown your head
   and I'll make a honey-cake large and round
   you can feed to Cerberus underground!

FIRST OLD MARKET-WOMAN   Accept these few fillets of leek from
   me!

SECOND OLD MARKET-WOMAN   Let me offer you these for your
   garland, sir!

15 LYSISTRATA   What now? Do you want something else you see?
   Listen! Charon's calling his passenger—
   will you catch the ferry or still delay
   when his other dead want to sail away?

COMMISSIONER   Is it not downright monstrous to treat *me* like this?
20 By Zeus, I'll go right now to the Commissioners
   and show myself in evidence, just as I am!

[*He begins to withdraw with dignity and his four Scythian policemen.*]

LYSISTRATA   Will you accuse us of not giving you a wake?
   But your departed spirit will receive from us
   burnt offerings in due form, two days from now at dawn!

[LYSISTRATA *with the other women goes into the Acropolis. The*
COMMISSIONER *etc. have left. The male chorus and the mixed
female chorus are alone.*]

CHORUS OF MEN   No man now dare fall to drowsing, if he wishes
25   to stay free!
   Men, let's strip and gird ourselves for this eventuality!

      To me this all begins to have a smell
      of bigger things and larger things as well:
      most of all I sniff a tyranny afoot. I'm much afraid
30   certain secret agents of the Spartans may have come,
      meeting under cover here, in Cleisthenes's home,

instigating those damned women by deceit to make a raid
    upon our treasury and that great sum
    the city paid my pension from.

Sinister events already!—think of lecturing the state,
women as they are, and prattling on of things like shields of
    bronze,   5
even trying hard to get us reconciled to those we hate—
those of Sparta, to be trusted like a lean wolf when it yawns!
All of this is just a pretext, men, for a dictatorship—
but to me they shall not dictate! Watch and ward! A sword I'll
    hide
underneath a branch of myrtle; through the agora I'll slip,   10
following Aristogeiton, backing the tyrannicide!

[*The* OLD MEN *pair off to imitate the gestures of the famous group
statue of the tyrannicides Harmodius and Aristogeiton.*]

Thus I'll take my stand beside him! Now my rage is goaded raw
I'm as like as not to clip this damned old woman on the jaw!

CHORUS OF WOMEN Your own mother will not know you when
    you come home, if you do!
Let us first, though, lay our things down, O my dear old friends
    and true.   15

      For now, O fellow-citizens, we would
      consider what will do our city good.
Well I may, because it bred me up in wealth and elegance:
    letting me at seven help with the embroidering
    of Athena's mantle, and at ten with offering   20
cakes and flowers. When I was grown and beautiful I had my
    chance
      to bear her baskets, at my neck a string
      of figs, and proud as anything.

Must I not, then, give my city any good advice I can?
Need you hold the fact against me that I was not born a man,   25
when I offer better methods than the present ones, and when
I've a share in this economy, for I contribute men?
But, you sad old codgers, *yours* is forfeited on many scores:
you have drawn upon our treasure dating from the Persian wars,
what they call grampatrimony, and you've paid no taxes back.   30
Worse, you've run it nearly bankrupt, and the prospect's pretty
    black.
Have you anything to answer? Say you were within the law
and I'll take this rawhide boot and clip you one across the jaw!

CHORUS OF MEN   Greater insolence than ever!—
that's the method that she calls
"better"—if you would believe her.
But this threat must be prevented! Every man with both his balls
must make ready—take our shirts off, for a man must reek of
5   male
outright—not wrapped up in leafage like an omelet for sale!

       Forward and barefoot: we'll do it again
to the death, just as when we resisted
tyranny out at Leipsydrion, when
10   we really existed!

       Now or never we must grow
young again and, sprouting wings
over all our bodies, throw
off this heaviness age brings!

15   For if any of us give them even just a little hold
nothing will be safe from their tenacious grasp. They are so bold
they will soon build ships of war and, with exorbitant intent,
send such navies out against us as Queen Artemisia sent.
But if they attack with horse, our knights we might as well delete:
20   nothing rides so well as woman, with so marvelous a seat,
never slipping at the gallop. Just look at those Amazons
in that picture in the Stoa, from their horses bringing bronze
axes down on men. We'd better grab *these* members of the sex
one and all, arrest them, get some wooden collars on their necks!

25   CHORUS OF WOMEN   By the gods, if you chagrin me
or annoy me, if you dare,
I'll turn loose the sow that's in me
till you rouse the town to help you with the way I've done your
hair!
Let us too make ready, women, and our garments quickly doff
30   so we'll smell like women angered fit to bite our fingers off!

       Now I am ready: let one of the men
come against me, and *he'll* never hanker
after a black bean or garlic again:
no woman smells ranker!

35   Say a single unkind word,
I'll pursue you till you drop,
as the beetle did the bird.
My revenge will never stop!

Yet you will not worry me so long as Lampito's alive
and my noble friends in Thebes and other cities still survive.
You'll not overpower us, even passing seven decrees or eight,
you, poor brutes, whom everyone and everybody's neighbors hate.
Only yesterday I gave a party, honoring Hecatë,   5
but when I invited in the neighbor's child to come and play,
such a pretty thing from Thebes, as nice and quiet as you please,
just an eel, they said she couldn't, on account of your decrees.
You'll go on forever passing such decrees without a check
till somebody takes you firmly by the leg and breaks your neck!   10

[LYSISTRATA *comes out. The* CHORUS OF WOMEN *addresses her in
the manner of tragedy.*]

Oh Queen of this our enterprise and all our hopes,
wherefore in baleful brooding hast thou issued forth?

LYSISTRATA   The deeds of wicked women and the female mind
discourage me and set me pacing up and down.

CHORUS OF WOMEN   What's that? What's that you say?   15

LYSISTRATA   The truth, alas, the truth!

CHORUS OF WOMEN   What is it that's so dreadful? Tell it to your
friends.

LYSISTRATA   A shameful thing to tell and heavy not to tell.

CHORUS OF WOMEN   Oh, never hide from me misfortune that is
ours!

LYSISTRATA   To put it briefly as I can, we are in heat.   20

CHORUS OF WOMEN   Oh Zeus!

LYSISTRATA   Why call on Zeus? This is the way
things are.
At least it seems I am no longer capable
of keeping them from men. They are deserting me.
This morning I caught one of them digging away
to make a tunnel to Pan's grotto down the slope,   25
another letting herself down the parapet
with rope and pulley, and another climbing down
its sheerest face, and yesterday was one I found
sitting upon a sparrow with a mind to fly
down to some well-equipped whoremaster's place in town.   30
Just as she swooped I pulled her backward by the hair.
They think of every far-fetched excuse they can
for going home. And here comes one deserter now.
You there, where are you running?

FIRST WOMAN   I want to go home,

because I left some fine Milesian wools at home
that must be riddled now with moths.

LYSISTRATA   Oh, damn your moths!
Go back inside.

FIRST WOMAN   But I shall come back right away,
just time enough to stretch them out upon my bed.

5   LYSISTRATA   Stretch nothing out, and don't you go away at all.

FIRST WOMAN   But shall I let my wools be ruined?

LYSISTRATA   If you must.

SECOND WOMAN   Oh miserable me! I sorrow for the flax
I left at home unbeaten and unstripped!

LYSISTRATA   One more—
wanting to leave for stalks of flax she hasn't stripped.
Come back here!

10   SECOND WOMAN   But, by Artemis, I only want
to strip my flax. Then I'll come right back here again.

LYSISTRATA   Strip me no strippings! If you start this kind of thing
some other woman soon will want to do the same.

THIRD WOMAN   O lady Artemis, hold back this birth until
15   I can get safe to some unconsecrated place!

LYSISTRATA   What is this raving?

THIRD WOMAN   I'm about to have a child.

LYSISTRATA   But you weren't pregnant yesterday.

THIRD WOMAN   I am today.
Oh, send me home this instant, dear Lysistrata,
so I can find a midwife.

LYSISTRATA   What strange tale is this?
What is this hard thing you have here?

20   THIRD WOMAN   The child is male.

LYSISTRATA   By Aphrodite, no! You obviously have
some hollow thing of bronze. I'll find out what it is.
You silly thing!—you have Athena's helmet here—
and claiming to be pregnant!

THIRD WOMAN   So I am, by Zeus!

LYSISTRATA   In that case, what's the helmet for?

25   THIRD WOMAN   So if the pains
came on me while I'm still up here, I might give birth
inside the helmet, as I've seen the pigeons do.

LYSISTRATA   What an excuse! The case is obvious. Wait here.
  I want to show this bouncing baby helmet off.

[*She passes the huge helmet around the* CHORUS OF WOMEN.]

SECOND WOMAN   But I can't even sleep in the Acropolis,
  not for an instant since I saw the sacred snake!

FOURTH WOMAN   The owls are what are killing *me*. How can I
      sleep   5
  with their eternal whit-to-whoo-to-whit-to-whoo?

LYSISTRATA   You're crazy! Will you stop this hocus-pocus now?
  No doubt you miss your husbands: don't you think that they
  are missing us as much? I'm sure the nights they pass
  are just as hard. But, gallant comrades, do bear up,   10
  and face these gruelling hardships yet a little while.
  There is an oracle that says we'll win, if we
  only will stick together. Here's the oracle.

CHORUS OF WOMAN   Oh, read us what it says!

LYSISTRATA   Keep silence, then and hear:

  "Now when to one high place are gathered the fluttering swallows, 15
  Fleeing the Hawk and the Cock however hotly it follows,
  Then will their miseries end, and that which is over be under:
  Thundering Zeus will decide.

A WOMAN   Will *we* lie on top now, I wonder?

LYSISTRATA   *But if the Swallows go fighting each other and spring-*
      ing and winging
  Out of the holy and high sanctuary, then people will never   20
  Say there was any more dissolute bitch of a bird whatsoever.

A WOMAN   The oracle is clear, by Zeus!

LYSISTRATA   By *all* the gods!
  So let us not renounce the hardships we endure.
  But let us go back in. Indeed, my dearest friends,
  it would be shameful to betray the oracle.   25

[*Exeunt into the Acropolis.*]

CHORUS OF MEN   Let me tell you a story I heard one day
            when I was a child:
  There was once a young fellow Melanion by name

who refused to get married and ran away
   to the wild.
   To the mountains he came
   and inhabited there
5   in a grove
   and hunted the hare
   both early and late
   with nets that he wove
   and also a hound
10 and he never came home again, such was his hate,
   all women he found
   so nasty, and we
   quite wisely agree.

Let us kiss you, dear old dears!

15 CHORUS OF WOMEN   With no onions, you'll shed tears!

CHORUS OF MEN   I mean, lift my leg and *kick*.

CHORUS OF WOMEN   My, you wear your thicket thick!

CHORUS OF MEN   Great Myronides was rough
   at the front and black enough
20   in the ass to scare his foes.
    Just ask anyone who knows:
    it's with hair that wars are won—
    take for instance Phormion.

CHORUS OF WOMEN   Let me tell you a story in answer to
   Melanion's case.
25 There is now a man, Timon, who wanders around
in the wilderness, hiding his face from view
   in a place
   where the brambles abound
   so he looks like a chip
30   off a Fur-
   y, curling his lip.
   Now Timon retired
   in hatred and pure
   contempt of all men
35 and he cursed them in words that were truly inspired
   again and again
   but women he found
   delightful and sound.

Would you like your jaw repaired?

CHORUS OF MEN   Thank you, no. You've got me scared.

CHORUS OF WOMEN   Let me jump and kick it though.

CHORUS OF MEN   You will let your man-sack show.

CHORUS OF WOMEN   All the same you wouldn't see,
  old and gray as I may be,   5
  any superfluity
   of unbarbered hair on me;
   it is plucked and more, you scamp,
   since I singe it with a lamp!

[*Enter* LYSISTRATA *on the wall.*]

LYSISTRATA   Women, O women, come here quickly, here to me! 10

WOMEN   Whatever is it? Tell me! What's the shouting for?

LYSISTRATA   I see a man approaching, shaken and possessed,
  seized and inspired by Aphrodite's power.
  O thou, of Cyprus, Paphos, and Cythera, queen!
  continue straight along this way you have begun! 15

A WOMAN   Whoever he is, where is he?

LYSISTRATA   Near Demeter's shrine.

A WOMAN   Why yes, by Zeus, he is. Who ever can he be?

LYSISTRATA   Well, look at him. Do any of you know him?

MYRRHINA   Yes.
 I do. He's my own husband, too, Cinesias.

LYSISTRATA   Then it's your duty now to turn him on a spit, 20
  cajole him and make love to him and not make love,
  to offer everything, short of those things of which
  the wine-cup knows.

MYRRHINA   I'll do it, don't you fear.

LYSISTRATA   And I
  will help you tantalize him. I will stay up here
  and help you roast him slowly. But now, disappear! 25

[*Enter* CINESIAS.]

CINESIAS   Oh how unfortunate I am, gripped by what spasms,
  stretched tight like being tortured on a wheel!

LYSISTRATA   Who's there? Who has got this far past the sentries?

CINESIAS   I.

LYSISTRATA   A man?

CINESIAS   A man, for sure.

LYSISTRATA   Then clear away from here.

CINESIAS   Who're you, to throw me out?

LYSISTRATA   The look-out for the day.

CINESIAS   Then, for the gods' sake, call Myrrhina out for me.

LYSISTRATA   You don't say! Call Myrrhina out! And who are you?

5   CINESIAS   Her husband. I'm Cinesias Paionides.

LYSISTRATA   Well, my dear man, hello! Your name is not unknown
among us here and not without a certain fame,
because your wife has it forever on her lips.
She can't pick up an egg or quince but she must say:
Cinesias would enjoy it so!

10   CINESIAS   How wonderful!

LYSISTRATA   By Aphrodite, yes. And if we chance to talk
of husbands, your wife interrupts and says the rest
are nothing much compared to her Cinesias.

CINESIAS   Go call her.

LYSISTRATA   Will you give me something if I do?

15   CINESIAS   Indeed I will, by Zeus, if it is what you want.
I can but offer what I have, and I have this.

LYSISTRATA   Wait there. I will go down and call her.

CINESIAS   Hurry up!
because I find no charm whatever left in life
since she departed from the house. I get depressed
20   whenever I go into it, and everything
seems lonely to me now, and when I eat my food
I find no taste in it at all—because I'm stiff.

MYRRHINA [offstage]   I love him, how I love him! But he doesn't
want
my love! [on wall] So what's the use of calling me to him?

25   CINESIAS   My sweet little Myrrhina, why do you act like that?
Come down here.

MYRRHINA   There? By Zeus, I certainly will not.

CINESIAS   Won't you come down, Myrrhina, when I'm calling
you?

MYRRHINA   Not when you call me without needing anything.

CINESIAS   Not needing anything? I'm desperate with need.

MYRRHINA   I'm going now.

CINESIAS   Oh no! No, don't go yet! At least
you'll listen to the baby. Call your mammy, you.

BABY   Mammy mammy mammy!

CINESIAS   What's wrong with you? Have you no pity on your child
when it is six days now since he was washed or nursed?   5

MYRRHINA   Oh, *I* have pity. But his father takes no care
of him.

CINESIAS   Come down, you flighty creature, for the child.

MYRRHINA   Oh, what it is to be a mother! I'll come down,
for what else can I do?

[MYRRHINA *exits to reenter below.*]

CINESIAS   It seems to me she's grown
much younger, and her eyes have a more tender look.   10
Even her being angry with me and her scorn
are just the things that pain me with the more desire.

MYRRHINA   Come let me kiss you, dear sweet little baby mine,
with such a horrid father. Mammy loves you, though.

CINESIAS   But why are you so mean? Why do you listen to   15
those other women, giving me such pain?—And you,
you're suffering yourself.

MYRRHINA   Take your hands off of me!

CINESIAS   But everything we have at home, my things and yours,
you're letting go to pieces.

MYRRHINA   Little do I care!

CINESIAS   Little you care even if your weaving's pecked apart   20
and carried off by chickens?

MYRRHINA [*bravely*]   Little I care, by Zeus!

CINESIAS   You have neglected Aphrodite's rituals
for such a long time now. Won't you come back again?

MYRRHINA   Not I, unless you men negotiate a truce
and make an end of war.

CINESIAS   Well, if it's so decreed,   25
we will do even that.

MYRRHINA   Well, if it's so decreed,
I will come home again. Not now. I've sworn I won't.

CINESIAS   All right, all right. But now lie down with me once more.

MYRRHINA   No! No!—yet I don't say I'm not in love with you.

CINESIAS   You love me? Then why not lie down, Myrrhina dear?

MYRRHINA   Don't be ridiculous! Not right before the child!

CINESIAS   By Zeus, of course not. Manes, carry him back home.
5   There now. You see the baby isn't in your way.
       Won't you lie down?

MYRRHINA   But *where*, you rogue, just where
       is one to do it?

CINESIAS   Where? Pan's grotto's a fine place.

MYRRHINA   But how could I come back to the Acropolis
       in proper purity?

CINESIAS   Well, there's a spring below
10   the grotto—you can very nicely bathe in that.

[*Ekkyklema or inset-scene with grotto*]

MYRRHINA   And then I'm under oath. What if I break my vows?

CINESIAS   Let me bear all the blame. Don't worry about your oath.

MYRRHINA   Wait here, and I'll go get a cot for us.

CINESIAS   No no,
       the ground will do.

MYRRHINA   No, by Apollo! Though you *are*
15   so horrid, I can't have you lying on the ground. [*Leaves.*]

CINESIAS   You know, the woman loves me—*that's* as plain as day.

MYRRHINA   There. Get yourself in bed and I'll take off my clothes.
       Oh, what a nuisance! I must go and get a mat.

CINESIAS   What for? I don't need one.

MYRRHINA   Oh yes, by Artemis!
       On the bare cords? How ghastly!

20 CINESIAS   Let me kiss you now.

MYRRHINA   Oh, very well.

CINESIAS   Wow! Hurry, hurry and come back.

[MYRRHINA *leaves. A long wait.*]

MYRRHINA   Here is the mat. Lie down now, while I get undressed.
       Oh, what a nuisance! You don't have a pillow, dear.

CINESIAS   But I don't need one, not one bit!

MYRRHINA   By Zeus, *I* do! [*Leaves.*]

CINESIAS Poor prick, the service around here is terrible!

MYRRHINA Sit up, my dear, jump up! Now I've got everything.

CINESIAS Indeed you have. And now, my golden girl, come here.

MYRRHINA I'm just untying my brassiere. Now don't forget:
about that treaty—you won't disappoint me, dear? 5

CINESIAS By Zeus, no! On my life!

MYRRHINA   You have no blanket, dear.

CINESIAS By Zeus, I do not need one. I just want to screw.

MYRRHINA Don't worry, dear, you will. I'll be back right away.

[*Leaves.*]

CINESIAS This number, with her bedding, means to murder me.

MYRRHINA Now raise yourself upright.

CINESIAS   But *this* is upright now! 10

MYRRHINA Wouldn't you like some perfume?

CINESIAS   By Apollo, no!

MYRRHINA By Aphrodite, yes! You must—like it or not. [*Leaves.*]

CINESIAS Lord Zeus! Just let the perfume spill! That's all I ask!

MYRRHINA Hold out your hand. Take some of this and rub it on.

CINESIAS This perfume, by Apollo, isn't sweet at all. 15
It smells a bit of stalling—not of wedding nights!

MYRRHINA I brought the *Rhodian* perfume! How absurd of me!

CINESIAS It's fine! Let's keep it.

MYRRHINA   You *will* have your little joke.

[*Leaves.*]

CINESIAS Just let me at the man who first distilled perfumes!

MYRRHINA Try this, in the long vial.

CINESIAS   I've got one like it, dear. 20
But don't be tedious. Lie down. And please don't bring
anything more.

MYRRHINA [*going*] That's what I'll do, by Artemis!
I'm taking off my shoes. But dearest, don't forget
you're going to vote for peace.

CINESIAS   I will consider it.

She has destroyed me, murdered me, that woman has! 25
On top of which she's got me skinned and gone away!

What shall I do? Oh, whom shall I screw,
cheated of dear Myrrhina, the first
beauty of all, a creature divine?
How shall I tend this infant of mine?
5   Find me a pimp: it has to be nursed!

CHORUS OF MEN [*in tragic style, as if to Prometheus or An-
dromeda bound*]
In what dire woe, how heavy-hearted
I see thee languishing, outsmarted!
   I pity thee, alas I do.
What kidney could endure such pain,
10   what spirit could, what balls, what back,
what loins, what sacroiliac,
if they came under such a strain
and never had a morning screw?

CINESIAS   O Zeus! the twinges! Oh, the twitches!

15 CHORUS OF MEN   And this is what she did to you,
that vilest, hatefullest of bitches!

CINESIAS   Oh nay, by Zeus, she's dear and sweet!

CHORUS OF MEN   How can she be? She's vile, O Zeus, she's vile!
Oh treat her, Zeus, like so much wheat—
20   O God of Weather, hear my prayer—
and raise a whirlwind's mighty blast
to roll her up into a pile
and carry her into the sky
far up and up and then at last
25   drop her and land her suddenly
astride that pointed penis there!

[*The ekkyklema turns, closing the inset-scene. Enter, from opposite
sides, a SPARTAN and an Athenian official.*]

SPARTAN   Wheah is the Senate-house of the Athenians?
Ah wish to see the chaihman. Ah have news fo him.

ATHENIAN   And who are you? Are you a Satyr or a man?

30 SPARTAN   Ah am a herald, mah young friend, yes, by the gods,
and Ah have come from Sparta to negotiate.

ATHENIAN   And yet you come here with a spear under your arm?

SPARTAN   Not Ah, bah Zeus, not Ah!

ATHENIAN   Why do you turn around?

Why throw your cloak out so in front? Has the long trip
given you a swelling?

SPARTAN   Ah do think the man is queah!

ATHENIAN   But you have an erection, oh you reprobate!

SPARTAN   Bah Zeus, Ah've no sech thing! And don't you fool
around!

ATHENIAN   And what have you got there?

SPARTAN   A Spahtan scroll-stick, suh.   5

ATHENIAN   Well, if it is, *this* is a Spartan scroll-stick, too.
But look, I know what's up: you can tell *me* the truth.
Just how are things with you in Sparta: tell me that.

SPARTAN   Theah is uprising in all Spahta. Ouah allies
are all erect as well. We need ouah milkin'-pails.   10

ATHENIAN   From where has this great scourge of frenzy fallen on
you?
From Pan?

SPARTAN   No, Ah think Lampito began it all,
and then, the othah women throughout Spahta joined
togethah, just lahk at a signal fo a race,
and fought theah husbands off and drove them from theah cunts.   15

ATHENIAN   So, how're you getting on?

SPARTAN   We suffah. Through the town
we walk bent ovah as if we were carrying
lamps in the wind. The women will not let us touch
even theah berries, till we all with one acco'd
have made a peace among the cities of all Greece.   20

ATHENIAN   This is an international conspiracy
launched by the women! Now I comprehend it all!
Return at once to Sparta. Tell them they must send
ambassadors fully empowered to make peace.
And our Assembly will elect ambassadors   25
from our side, when I say so, showing them this prick.

SPARTAN   Ah'll run! Ah'll flah! Fo all you say is excellent!

CHORUS OF MEN   No wild beast is more impossible than woman is
to fight,
nor is fire, nor has the panther such unbridled appetite!

CHORUS OF WOMEN   Well you know it, yet you go on warring with
me without end,   30
when you might, you cross-grained creature, have me as a trusty
friend.

CHORUS OF MEN   Listen: I will never cease from hating women
till I die!

CHORUS OF WOMEN   Any time you like. But meanwhile is there
any reason why
I should let you stand there naked, looking so ridiculous?
I am only coming near you, now, to slip your coat on, thus.

CHORUS OF MEN   That was very civil of you, very kind to treat
5   me so,
when in such uncivil rage I took it off a while ago.

CHORUS OF WOMEN   Now you're looking like a man again, and
not ridiculous.
If you hadn't hurt my feelings, I would not have made a fuss,
I would even have removed that little beast that's in your eye.

CHORUS OF MEN   *That* is what was hurting me! Well, won't you
10   take my ring to pry
back my eyelid? Rake the beast out. When you have it, let me see,
for some time now it's been at my eye and irritating me.

CHORUS OF WOMEN   Very well, I will—though you were *born* an
irritable man.
What a monster of a gnat, by Zeus! Look at it if you can.
15   Don't you see it? It's a native of great marshes, can't you tell?

CHORUS OF MEN   Much obliged, by Zeus! The brute's been digging
at me like a well!
So that now you have removed it, streams of tears come welling
out.

CHORUS OF WOMEN   I will dry them. You're the meanest man alive,
beyond a doubt,
yet I will, and kiss you, too.

CHORUS OF MEN   Don't kiss me!

CHORUS OF WOMEN   If you will or not!

CHORUS OF MEN   Damn you! Oh, what wheedling flatterers you
20   all are, born and bred!
That old proverb is quite right and not inelegantly said:
"There's no living *with* the bitches and, without them, even *less*"—
so I might as well make peace with you, and from now on, I guess,
I'll do nothing mean to you and, from you, suffer nothing wrong.
25   So let's draw our ranks together now and start a little song:

For a change, we're not preparing
any mean remark or daring
aimed at any man in town,
but the very opposite: we plan to do and say
only good to everyone,   5
when the ills we have already are sufficient anyway.
    Any man or woman who
    wants a little money, oh
    say three minas, maybe two,
    kindly let us know.   10
    What we have is right in here.
    (Notice we have purses, too!)
    And if ever peace appear,
    he who takes our loan today
        never need repay.   15

    We are having guests for supper,
    allies asked in by our upper
    classes to improve the town.
There's pea-soup, and I had killed a sucking-pig of mine:
I shall see it is well done,   20
so you will be tasting something very succulent and fine.
    Come to see us, then, tonight
    early, just as soon as you
    have a bath and dress up right:
    bring your children, too.   25
    Enter boldly, never mind
    asking anyone in sight.
    Go straight in and you will find
    you are quite at home there, but
    all the doors are shut.   30

And here come the Spartan ambassadors,
        dragging beards that are really the biggest **I**
have ever beheld, and around their thighs
        they are wearing some sort of a pig-sty.

    Oh men of Sparta, let me bid you welcome first,   35
    and then you tell us how you are and why you come.

SPARTAN   What need is theah to speak to you in many words?
Fo you may see youahself in what a fix we come.

CHORUS OF MEN   Too bad! Your situation has become
    terribly hard and seems to be at fever-pitch.   40

SPARTAN Unutterably so! And what is theah to say?
Let someone bring us peace on any tuhms he will!

CHORUS OF MEN And here I see some natives of Athenian soil,
holding their cloaks far off their bellies, like the best
5   wrestlers, who sicken at the touch of cloth. It seems
that overtraining may bring on this strange disease.

ATHENIAN Will someone tell us where to find Lysistrata?
We're men, and here we are, in this capacity.

CHORUS OF MEN This symptom and that other one sound much
alike.
10   Toward morning I expect convulsions do occur?

ATHENIAN By Zeus, we are exhausted with just doing that,
so, if somebody doesn't reconcile us quick,
there's nothing for it: we'll be screwing Cleisthenes.

CHORUS OF MEN Be careful—put your cloaks on, or you might
be seen
15   by some young blade who knocks the phalluses off herms.

ATHENIAN By Zeus, an excellent idea!

SPARTAN [*having overheard*] Yes, bah the gods!
It altogethah is. Quick, let's put on our cloaks.

[*Both groups cover quick and then recognize each other with full
diplomatic pomp.*]

ATHENIAN Greetings, O men of Sparta! [*to his group*] We have
been disgraced!

SPARTAN [*to one of his group*] Mah dearest fellah, what a dreadful
20   thing fo *us*,
if these Athenians had seen ouah wo'st defeat!

ATHENIAN Come now, O Spartans: one must specify each point.
Why have you come here?

SPARTAN   To negotiate a peace.
We ah ambassadahs.

ATHENIAN   Well put. And so are we.
25   Therefore, why do we not call in Lysistrata,
she who alone might get us to agree on terms?

SPARTAN Call her or any man, even a Lysistratus!

CHORUS OF MEN   But you will have no need, it seems, to call her
    now,
  for here she is. She heard you and is coming out.

CHORUS OF MEN *and* CHORUS OF WOMEN   All hail, O manliest
    woman of all!
        It is time for you now to be turning
  into something still better, more dreadful, mean,   5
        unapproachable, charming, discerning,
  for here are the foremost nations of Greece,
        bewitched by your spells like a lover,
  who have come to you, bringing you all their claims,
        and to *you* turning everything over.   10

LYSISTRATA   The work's not difficult, if one can catch them now
  while they're excited and not making passes at
  each other. I will soon find out. Where's *HARMONY?*

[*A naked maid, perhaps wearing a large ribbon reading HAR-
MONY, appears from inside.*]

  Go take the Spartans first, and lead them over here,
  not with a rough hand nor an overbearing one,   15
  nor, as our husbands used to do this, clumsily,
  but like a woman, in our most familiar style:
  If he won't give his hand, then lead him by the prick.
  And now, go bring me those Athenians as well,
  leading them by whatever they will offer you.   20
  O men of Sparta, stand right here, close by my side,
  and *you* stand over there, and listen to my words.
  I am a woman, yes, but there is mind in me.
  In native judgment I am not so badly off,
  and, having heard my father and my elders talk   25
  often enough, I have some cultivation, too.
  And so, I want to take and scold you, on both sides,
  as you deserve, for though you use a lustral urn
  in common at the altars, like blood-relatives,
  when at Olympia, Delphi, or Thermopylae—   30
  how many others I might name if I took time!—
  yet, with barbarian hordes of enemies at hand,
  it is Greek men, it is Greek cities, you destroy.
  That is one argument so far, and it is done.

ATHENIAN   My prick is skinned alive—that's what's destroying *me*.   35

LYSISTRATA   Now, men of Sparta—for I shall address you first—
  do you not know that once one of your kings came here

and as a suppliant of the Athenians
sat by our altars, death-pale in his purple robe,
and begged us for an army? For Messenë then
oppressed you, and an earthquake from the gods as well.
5   Then Cimon went, taking four thousand infantry,
and saved the whole of Lacedaemon for your state.
That is the way Athenians once treated you;
you ravage their land now, which once received you well.

ATHENIAN   By Zeus, these men are in the wrong, Lysistrata!

SPARTAN [*with his eyes on* HARMONY]   We'ah wrong . . . What
10   an unutterably lovely ass!

LYSISTRATA   Do you suppose I'm letting you Athenians off?
Do you not know that once the Spartans in their turn,
when you were wearing the hide-skirts of slavery,
came with their spears and slew many Thessalians,
15   many companions and allies of Hippias?
They were the only ones who fought for you that day,
freed you from tyranny and, for the skirt of hide,
gave back your people the wool mantle of free men.

SPARTAN   Ah nevah saw a woman broadah—in her views.

20   ATHENIAN   And I have never seen a lovelier little nook.

LYSISTRATA   So why, when you have done each other so much
good,
go on fighting with no end of malevolence?
Why don't you make a peace? Tell me, what's in your way?

SPARTAN   Whab, *we* ah willin', if *they* will give up to us
that very temptin' cuhve.   [*of* HARMONY, *as hereafter*]

LYSISTRATA   What curve, my friend?

25   SPARTAN   The bay
of Pylos, which we've wanted and felt out so long.

ATHENIAN   No, by Poseidon, you will not get into that!

LYSISTRATA   Good friend, do let them have it.

ATHENIAN   No! What other town
can we manipulate so well?

LYSISTRATA   Ask them for one.

30   ATHENIAN   Damn, let me think! Now first suppose you cede to us
that bristling tip of land, Echinos, behind which
the gulf of Malia recedes, and those long walls,
the legs on which Megara reaches to the sea.

SPARTAN   No, mah deah man, not *everything*, bah Castah, no!

LYSISTRATA   Oh, give them up. Why quarrel for a pair of legs?

ATHENIAN   I'd like to strip and get to plowing right away.

SPARTAN   And *Ah* would lahk to push manuah, still earliah.

LYSISTRATA   When you have made a peace, then you will do all
    that.
  But if you want to do it, first deliberate,   5
  go and inform your allies and consult with them.

ATHENIAN   Oh, damn our allies, my good woman! We are stiff.
  Will all of our allies not stand resolved with us—
  namely, to screw?

SPARTAN   And so will ouahs, Ah'll guarantee.

ATHENIAN   Our mercenaries, even, will agree with us.   10

LYSISTRATA   Excellent. Now to get you washed and purified
  so you may enter the Acropolis, where we
  women will entertain you out of our supplies.
  You will exchange your pledges there and vows for peace.
  And after that each one of you will take his wife,   15
  departing then for home.

ATHENIAN   Let's go in right away.

SPARTAN   Lead on, ma'am, anywheah you lahk.

ATHENIAN   Yes, and be quick.

[*Exeunt into Acropolis*]

CHORUS OF MEN *and* CHORUS OF WOMEN
      All the rich embroideries, the
      scarves, the gold accessories, the
      trailing gowns, the robes I own   20
  I begrudge to no man: let him take what things he will
  for his children or a grown
  daughter who must dress for the procession up Athena's hill.
      Freely of my present stocks
      I invite you all to take.   25
      There are here no seals nor locks
      very hard to break.
      Search through every bag and box,
      look—you will find nothing there
      if your eyesight isn't fine—   30
      sharper far than mine!

      Are there any of you needing
      food for all the slaves you're feeding,
      all your little children, too?

I have wheat in tiny grains for you, the finest sort,
and I also offer you
plenty of the handsome strapping grains that slaves get by the
    quart.
    So let any of the poor
5   visit me with bag or sack
    which my slave will fill with more
    wheat than they can pack,
    giving each his ample share.
    Might I add that at my door
10   I have watch-dogs?—so beware.
    Come too close by day or night,
    you will find they bite.

[*Voice of drunken* ATHENIANS *from inside*]

FIRST ATHENIAN   Open the door! [*shoves the porter aside*]
                  And will you get out of my way?

[*A second drunken* ATHENIAN *follows. The first sees the chorus.*]

What are you sitting *there* for? Shall I, with this torch,
burn you alive? [*drops character*]
15   How vulgar! Oh, how commonplace!
I can not do it!

[*Starts back in. The second* ATHENIAN *stops him and remonstrates
with him in a whisper. The first turns and addresses the audience.*]

             Well, if it really must be done
to please you, we shall face it and go through with it.

CHORUS OF MEN *and* CHORUS OF WOMEN
    And *we* shall face it and go through with it with you.

FIRST ATHENIAN [*in character again, extravagantly*]
    Clear out of here! Or you'll be wailing for your hair!

[CHORUS OF WOMEN *scours away in mock terror.*]

20   Clear out of here! so that the Spartans can come out
and have no trouble leaving, after they have dined.

[CHORUS OF MEN *scours away in mock terror.*]

SECOND ATHENIAN   I never saw a drinking-party like this one:

even the Spartans were quite charming, and of course
we make the cleverest company, when in our cups.

FIRST ATHENIAN   You're right, because when sober we are **not**
    quite sane.

If I can only talk the Athenians into it,
we'll always go on any embassy quite drunk,   5
for now, going to Sparta sober, we're so quick
to look around and see what trouble we can make
that we don't listen to a single word they say—
instead we think we hear them say what they do not—
and none of our reports on anything agree.   10
But just now everything was pleasant. If a man
got singing words belonging to another song,
we all applauded and swore falsely it was fine!
But here are those same people coming back again
to the same spot! Go and be damned, the pack of you!   15

[*The* CHORUS, *having thrown off their masks, put on other cloaks,
and rushed back on stage, stays put.*]

SECOND ATHENIAN   Yes, damn them, Zeus! Just when the party's
    coming out!

[*The party comes rolling out.*]

A SPARTAN [*to another*]
    Mah very chahmin friend, will you take up youah flutes?
    Ah'll dance the dipody and sing a lovely song
    of us and the Athenians, of both at once!

FIRST ATHENIAN [*as pleasantly as he can*]
    Oh yes, take up your little reeds, by all the gods: 20
    I very much enjoy seeing you people dance.

SPARTAN   Memory, come,
            come inspiah thah young
            votaries to song,
            come inspiah theah dance!   25

[*other* SPARTANS *join*]
            Bring thah daughtah, bring the sweet
                Muse, fo well she knows
            us and the Athenians,
                how at Ahtemisium
            they in godlike onslaught rose   30
            hahd against the Puhsian fleet,
                drove it to defeat!

Well she knows the Spartan waws,
  how Leonidas
  in the deadly pass
  led us on lahk baws
5   whettin' shahp theah tusks, how sweat
on ouah cheeks in thick foam flowahed,
off ouah legs how thick it showahed,
  fo the Puhsian men were mo'
  than the sands along the sho'.
10   Goddess, huntress, Ahtemis,
slayeh of the beasts, descend:
vuhgin goddess, come to this
feast of truce to bind us fast
so ouah peace may nevah end.
15   Now let friendship, love, and wealth
come with ouah acco'd at last.
May we stop ouah villainous
wahly foxy stealth!
    Come, O huntress, heah to us,
20   heah, O vuhgin, neah to us!

LYSISTRATA   Come, now that all the rest has been so well arranged,
you Spartans take these women home; these others, you.
Let husband stand beside his wife, and let each wife
stand by her husband: then, when we have danced a dance
25   to thank the gods for our good fortune, let's take care
hereafter not to make the same mistakes again.

ATHENIAN   Bring on the chorus! Invite the three Graces to follow,
and then call on Artemis, call her twin brother,
the leader of choruses, healer Apollo!

CHORUS [*joins*]   Pray for their friendliest favor, the one and the
30   other.
Call Dionysus, his tender eyes casting
flame in the midst of his Maenads ecstatic with dancing.
  Call upon Zeus, the resplendent in fire,
  call on his wife, rich in honor and ire,
35   call on the powers who possess everlasting
memory, call them to aid,
call them to witness the kindly, entrancing
peace Aphrodite has made!
    Alalai!
40   Bound, and leap high! Alalai!
    Cry, as for victory, cry
    Alalai!

LYSISTRATA   Sing us a new song, Spartans, capping our new song.

SPARTANS   Leave thah favohed mountain's height,
  Spahtan Muse, come celebrate
  Amyclae's lord with us and great
  Athena housed in bronze;   5
  praise Tyndareus' paih of sons,
  gods who pass the days in spoht
  wheah the cold Eurotas runs.

[*general dancing*]

  Now to tread the dance,
  now to tread it light,   10
  praising Spahta, wheah you find
    love of singing quickened bah the pounding beat
      of dancing feet,
  when ouah guhls lahk foals cavoht
  wheah the cold Eurotas runs,   15
  when they fleetly bound and prance
    till theah haih unfilleted shakes in the wind,
  as of Maenads brandishin'
  ahvied wands and revelin',
    Leda's daughtah, puah and faiah,   20
  leads the holy dances theah.

FULL CHORUS [*as everyone leaves dancing*]

  So come bind up youah haih with youah hand,
          with youah feet make a bound
  lahk a deeah; fo the chorus clap out
          an encouragin' sound,   25
  singin' praise of the temple of bronze
          housin' her we adaw:
  sing the praise of Athena: the goddess unvanquished in waw!

THE MYTHOS OF SPRING: COMEDY

Dramatic comedy, from which fictional comedy is mainly descended, has been remarkably tenacious of its structural principles and character types. Bernard Shaw remarked that a comic dramatist could get a reputation for daring originality by stealing his method from Molière and his characters from Dickens: if we were to read Menander and Aristophanes for Molière and Dickens the statement would hardly be less true, at least as a general principle. The earliest extant European comedy, Aristophanes' *The Acharnians,* contains the *miles gloriosus* or military braggart who is still going strong in Chaplin's *Great Dictator;* the Joxer Daly of O'Casey's *Juno and the Paycock* has the same character and dramatic function as the parasites of twenty-five hundred years ago, and the audiences of vaudeville, comic strips, and television programs still laugh at the jokes that were declared to be outworn at the opening of *The Frogs.*

The plot structure of Greek New Comedy, as transmitted by Plautus and Terence, in itself less a form than a formula, has become the basis for most comedy, especially in its more highly conventionalized dramatic form, down to our own day. It will be most convenient to work out the theory of comic construction from drama, using illustrations from fiction only incidentally. What normally happens is that a young man wants a young woman, that his desire is resisted by some opposition, usually paternal, and that near the end of the play some twist of the plot enables the hero to have his will. In this simple pattern there are several complex elements. In the first place, the movement of comedy is usually a movement from one kind of society to another. At the beginning of the play the obstructing characters are in charge of the play's society, and the audience recognizes that they are usurpers. At the end of the play the device in the plot that brings hero and heroine together causes a new society to crystallize around the hero, and the moment when this crystallization occurs is the point of resolution in the action, the comic discovery, *anagnorisis* or *cognitio.*

The appearance of this new society is frequently signalized by some kind of party or festive ritual, which either appears at the end of the play or is assumed to take place immediately afterward. Weddings are most common, and sometimes so many of them occur, as in the quadruple wedding at the end of *As You Like It,* that they suggest also the wholesale pairing off that takes place in a dance, which is another common conclusion, and the normal one for the masque. The banquet at the end of the *Taming of the*

Shrew has an ancestry that goes back to Greek Middle Comedy; in Plautus the audience is sometimes jocosely invited to an imaginary banquet afterwards; Old Comedy, like the modern Christmas pantomime, was more generous, and occasionally threw bits of food to the audience. As the final society reached by comedy is the one that the audience has recognized all along to be the proper and desirable state of affairs, an act of communion with the audience is in order. Tragic actors expect to be applauded as well as comic ones, but nevertheless the word *"plaudite"* at the end of a Roman comedy, the invitation to the audience to form part of the comic society, would seem rather out of place at the end of a tragedy. The resolution of comedy comes, so to speak, from the audience's side of the stage; in a tragedy it comes from some mysterious world on the opposite side. In the movie, where darkness permits a more erotically oriented audience, the plot usually moves toward an act which, like death in Greek tragedy, takes place offstage, and is symbolized by a closing embrace.

The obstacles to the hero's desire, then, form the action of the comedy, and the overcoming of them the comic resolution. The obstacles are usually parental, hence comedy often turns on a clash between a son's and a father's will. Thus, the comic dramatist as a rule writes for the younger men in his audience, and the older members of almost any society are apt to feel that comedy has something subversive about it. This is certainly one element in the social persecution of drama, which is not peculiar to Puritans or even Christians, as Terence in pagan Rome met much the same kind of social opposition that Ben Jonson did. There is one scene in Plautus where a son and father are making love to the same courtesan, and the son asks his father pointedly if he really does love mother. One has to see this scene against the background of Roman family life to understand its importance as psychological release. Even in Shakespeare there are startling outbreaks of baiting older men, and in contemporary movies the triumph of youth is so relentless that the moviemakers find some difficulty in getting anyone over the age of seventeen into their audiences.

The opponent to the hero's wishes, when not the father, is generally someone who partakes of the father's closer relation to established society: that is, a rival with less youth and more money. In Plautus and Terence he is usually either the pimp who owns the girl, or a wandering soldier with a supply of ready cash. The fury with which these characters are baited and exploded from the stage shows that they are father-surrogates, and even if they were not, they would still be usurpers, and their claim to possess the girl must be shown up as somehow fraudulent. They are, in short, impostors, and the extent to which they have real power implies some criticism of the society that allows them their power.

In Plautus and Terence this criticism seldom goes beyond the immorality of brothels and professional harlots, but in Renaissance dramatists, including Jonson, there is some sharp observation of the rising power of money and the sort of ruling class it is building up.

The tendency of comedy is to include as many people as possible in its final society: the blocking characters are more often reconciled or converted than simply repudiated. Comedy often includes a scapegoat ritual of expulsion which gets rid of some irreconcilable character, but exposure and disgrace make for pathos, or even tragedy. *The Merchant of Venice* seems almost an experiment in coming as close as possible to upsetting the comic balance. If the dramatic role of Shylock is ever so slightly exaggerated, as it generally is when the leading actor of the company takes the part, it is upset, and the play becomes the tragedy of the Jew of Venice with a comic epilogue. *Volpone* ends with a great bustle of sentences to penal servitude and the galleys, and one feels that the deliverance of society hardly needs so much hard labor; but then *Volpone* is exceptional in being a kind of comic imitation of a tragedy, with the point of Volpone's *hybris* carefully marked.

The principle of conversion becomes clearer with characters whose chief function is the amusing of the audience. The original *miles gloriosus* in Plautus is a son of Jove and Venus who has killed an elephant with his fist and seven thousand men in one day's fighting. In other words, he is trying to put on a good show: the exuberance of his boasting helps to put the play over. The convention says that the braggart must be exposed, ridiculed, swindled, and beaten. But why should a professional dramatist, of all people, want so to harry a character who is putting on a good show—*his* show at that? When we find Falstaff invited to the final feast in *The Merry Wives,* Caliban reprieved, attempts made to molify Malvolio, and Angelo and Parolles allowed to live down their disgrace, we are seeing a fundamental principle of comedy at work. The tendency of the comic society to include rather than exclude is the reason for the traditional importance of the parasite, who has no business to be at the final festival but is nevertheless there. The word "grace" with all its Renaissance overtones from the graceful courtier to the gracious God of Christianity, is a most important thematic word in Shakespearean comedy.

The action of comedy in moving from one social center to another is not unlike the action of a lawsuit, in which plaintiff and defendant construct different versions of the same situation, one finally being judged as real and the other as illusory. This resemblance of the rhetoric of comedy to the rhetoric of jurisprudence has been recognized from earliest times. A little pamphlet called the *Tractatus Coislinianus,* closely related to Aristotle's *Poetics,* which sets down all the essential facts about comedy in about a page and a half, divides the *dianoia* of comedy into two parts, opinion (*pistis*) and proof (*gnosis*). These correspond roughly to the usurping and the desirable societies respectively. Proofs (i.e. the means of bringing about the happier society) are subdivided into oaths, compacts, witnesses, ordeals (or tortures), and laws—in other words the five forms of material proof in law cases listed in the *Rhetoric.* We notice how often the action of a Shakespearean comedy begins with some absurd, cruel, or irrational law: the law of killing Syracusans in the *Comedy of Errors,* the law of compulsory marriage in *A Midsummer Night's Dream,* the law that confirms Shylock's bond, the attempts of Angelo to legislate people into righteousness, and the like, which the action of the comedy then evades or breaks. Compacts are as a rule the conspiracies formed by the hero's society; witnesses, such as overhearers of conversations or people with special knowledge (like the hero's old nurse with her retentive memory for birthmarks), are the commonest devices for bringing about the comic discovery. Ordeals (*basanoi*) are usually tests or touchstones of the hero's character: the Greek word also means touchstones, and seems to be echoed in Shakespeare's Bassanio whose ordeal is to make a judgement on the worth of metals.

There are two ways of developing the form of comedy: one is to throw the main emphasis on the blocking characters; the other is to throw it forward on the scenes of discovery and reconciliation. One is the general tendency of comic irony, satire, realism, and studies of manners; the other is the tendency of Shakespearean and other types of romantic comedy. In the comedy of manners the main ethical interest falls as a rule on the blocking characters. The technical hero and heroine are not often very interesting people: the *adulescentes* of Plautus and Terence are all alike, as hard to tell apart in the dark as Demetrius and Lysander, who may be parodies of them. Generally the hero's character has the neutrality that enables him to represent a wish-fulfilment. It is very different with the miserly or ferocious parent, the boastful or foppish rival, or the other characters who stand in the way of the action. In Molière we have a simple but fully tested formula in which the ethical interest is focussed on a single blocking character, a heavy father, a miser, a misanthrope, a hypocrite, or a hypochondriac. These are the figures we remember, and the plays are usually named after them, but we can seldom remember all the Valentins and Angeliques who wriggle out of their clutches. In *The Merry Wives* the technical hero, a man named Fenton, has only a bit part, and this play has picked up a hint or two from

Plautus's *Casina,* where the hero and heroine are not even brought on the stage at all. Fictional comedy, especially Dickens, often follows the same practice of grouping its interesting characters around a somewhat dullish pair of technical leads. Even Tom Jones, though far more fully realized, is still deliberately associated, as his commonplace name indicates, with the conventional and typical.

Comedy usually moves toward a happy ending, and the normal response of the audience to a happy ending is "this should be," which sounds like a moral judgement. So it is, except that it is not moral in the restricted sense, but social. Its opposite is not the villainous but the absurd, and comedy finds the virtues of Malvolio as absurd as the vices of Angelo. Molière's misanthrope, being committed to sincerity, which is a virtue, is morally in a strong position, but the audience soon realizes that his friend Philinte, who is ready to lie quite cheerfully in order to enable other people to preserve their self-respect, is the more genuinely sincere of the two. It is of course quite possible to have a moral comedy, but the result is often the kind of melodrama that we have described as comedy without humor, and which achieves its happy ending with a self-righteous tone that most comedy avoids. It is hardly possible to imagine a drama without conflict, and it is hardly possible to imagine a conflict without some kind of enmity. But just as love, including sexual love, is a very different thing from lust, so enmity is a very different thing from hatred. In tragedy, of course, enmity almost always includes hatred; comedy is different, and one feels that the social judgement against the absurd is closer to the comic norm than the moral judgement against the wicked.

The question then arises of what makes the blocking character absurd. Ben Jonson explained this by his theory of the "humor," the character dominated by what Pope calls a ruling passion. The humor's dramatic function is to express a state of what might be called ritual bondage. He is obsessed by his humor, and his function in the play is primarily to repeat his obsession. A sick man is not a humor, but a hypochondriac is, because, *qua* hypochondriac, he can never admit to good health, and can never do anything inconsistent with the role that he has prescribed for himself. A miser can do and say nothing that is not connected with the hiding of gold or saving of money. In *The Silent Woman,* Jonson's nearest approach to Molière's type of construction, the whole action recedes from the humor of Morose, whose determination to eliminate noise from his life produces so loquacious a comic action.

The principle of the humor is the principle that unincremental repetition, the literary imitation of ritual bondage, is funny. In a tragedy—*Oedipus Tyrannus* is the stock example—repetition leads

logically to catastrophe. Repetition overdone or not going anywhere belongs to comedy, for laughter is partly a reflex, and like
other reflexes it can be conditioned by a simple repeated pattern.
In Synge's *Riders to the Sea* a mother, after losing her husband
and five sons at sea, finally loses her last son, and the result is a
very beautiful and moving play. But if it had been a full-length
tragedy plodding glumly through the seven drownings one after
another, the audience would have been helpless with unsympathetic laughter long before it was over. The principle of repetition
as the basis of humor both in Jonson's sense and in ours is well
known to the creators of comic strips, in which a character is established as a parasite, a glutton (often confined to one dish), or
a shrew, and who begins to be funny after the point has been
made every day for several months. Continuous comic radio programs, too, are much more amusing to habitués than to neophytes.
The girth of Falstaff and the hallucinations of Quixote are based
on much the same comic laws. Mr. E. M. Forster speaks with disdain of Dickens's Mrs. Micawber, who never says anything except
that she will never desert Mr. Micawber: a strong contrast is
marked here between the refined writer too finicky for popular
formulas, and the major one who exploits them ruthlessly.

The humor in comedy is usually someone with a good deal of
social prestige and power, who is able to force much of the play's
society into line with his obsession. Thus the humor is intimately
connected with the theme of the absurd or irrational law that the
action of comedy moves toward breaking. It is significant that the
central character of our earliest humor comedy, *The Wasps*, is obsessed by law cases: Shylock, too, unites a craving for the law
with the humor of revenge. Often the absurd law appears as a
whim of a bemused tyrant whose will is law, like Leontes or the
humorous Duke Frederick in Shakespeare, who makes some arbitrary decision or rash promise: here law is replaced by "oath,"
also mentioned in the *Tractatus*. Or it may take the form of a
sham Utopia, a society of ritual bondage constructed by an act
of humorous or pedantic will, like the academic retreat in *Love's
Labor's Lost*. This theme is also as old as Aristophanes, whose
parodies of Platonic social schemes in *The Birds* and *Ecclesiazusae* deal with it.

The society emerging at the conclusion of comedy represents,
by contrast, a kind of moral norm, or pragmatically free society.
Its ideals are seldom defined or formulated: definition and formu-
lation belong to the humors, who want predictable activity. We are
simply given to understand that the newly married couple will
live happily ever after, or that at any rate they will get along in
a relatively unhumorous and clear-sighted manner. That is one
reason why the character of the successful hero is so often left

undeveloped: his real life begins at the end of the play, and we have to believe him to be potentially a more interesting character than he appears to be. In Terence's *Adelphoi,* Demea, a harsh father, is contrasted with his brother Micio, who is indulgent. Micio being more liberal, he leads the way to the comic resolution, and converts Demea, but then Demea points out the indolence inspiring a good deal of Micio's liberality, and releases him from a complementary humorous bondage.

Thus the movement from *pistis* to *gnosis,* from a society controlled by habit, ritual bondage, arbitrary law and the older characters to a society controlled by youth and pragmatic freedom is fundamentally, as the Greek words suggest, a movement from illusion to reality. Illusion is whatever is fixed or definable, and reality is best understood as its negation: whatever reality is, it's not *that.* Hence the importance of the theme of creating and dispelling illusion in comedy: the illusions caused by disguise, obsession, hypocrisy, or unknown parentage.

The comic ending is generally manipulated by a twist in the plot. In Roman comedy the heroine, who is usually a slave or courtesan, turns out to be the daughter of somebody respectable, so that the hero can marry her without loss of face. The *cognitio* in comedy, in which the characters find out who their relatives are, and who is left of the opposite sex not a relative, and hence available for marriage, is one of the features of comedy that have never changed much: *The Confidential Clerk* indicates that it still holds the attention of dramatists. There is a brilliant parody of a *cognitio* at the end of *Major Barbara* (the fact that the hero of this play is a professor of Greek perhaps indicates an unusual affinity to the conventions of Euripides and Menander), where Undershaft is enabled to break the rule that he cannot appoint his son-in-law as successor by the fact that the son-in-law's own father married his deceased wife's sister in Australia, so that the son-in-law is his own first cousin as well as himself. It sounds complicated, but the plots of comedy often are complicated because there is something inherently absurd about complications. As the main character interest in comedy is often focussed on the defeated characters, comedy regularly illustrates a victory of arbitrary plot over consistency of character. Thus, in striking contrast to tragedy, there can hardly be such a thing as inevitable comedy, as far as the action of the individual play is concerned. That is, we may know that the convention of comedy will make some kind of happy ending inevitable, but still for each play the dramatist must produce a distinctive "gimmick" or "weenie," to use two disrespectful Hollywood synonyms for *anagnorisis.* Happy endings do not impress us as true, but as desirable, and they are brought about by manipulation. The watcher of death and tragedy has nothing to do but sit and wait for the inevitable end; but something gets born at the end of comedy, and the watcher of birth is a member of a busy society.

The manipulation of plot does not always involve metamorphosis of character, but there is no violation of comic decorum when it does. Unlikely conversions, miraculous transformations, and providential assistance are inseparable from comedy. Further, whatever emerges is supposed to be there for good: if the curmudgeon becomes lovable, we understand that he will not immediately relapse again into his ritual habit. Civilizations which stress the desirable rather than the real, and the religious as opposed to the scientific perspective, think of drama almost entirely in terms of comedy. In the classical drama of India, we are told, the tragic ending was regarded as bad taste, much as the manipulated endings of comedy are regarded as bad taste by novelists interested in ironic realism.

The total *mythos* of comedy, only a small part of which is ordinarily presented, has regularly what in music is called a ternary form: the hero's society rebels against the society of the *senex* and triumphs, but the hero's society is a Saturnalia, a reversal of social standards which recalls a golden age in the past before the main action of the play begins. Thus we have a stable and harmonious order disrupted by folly, obsession, forgetfulness, "pride and prejudice," or events not understood by the characters themselves, and then restored. Often there is a benevolent grandfather, so to speak, who overrules the action set up by the blocking humor and so links the first and third parts. An example is Mr. Burchell, the disguised uncle of the wicked squire, in *The Vicar of Wakefield*. A very long play, such as the Indian *Sakuntala*, may present all three phases; a very intricate one, such as many of Menander's evidently were, may indicate their outlines. But of course very often the first phase is not given at all: the audience simply understands an ideal state of affairs which it knows to be better than what is revealed in the play, and which it recognizes as like that to which the action leads. The ternary action is, ritually, like a contest of summer and winter in which winter occupies the middle action; psychologically, it is like the removal of a neurosis or blocking point and the restoring of an unbroken current of energy and memory. The Jonsonian masque, with the antimasque in the middle, gives a highly conventionalized or "abstract" version of it.

*　　*　　*　　*

We pass now to the typical characters of comedy. In drama, characterization depends on function; what a character is follows from what he has to do in the play. Dramatic function in its turn depends on the structure of the play; the character has certain things to do because the play has such and such a shape. The structure of the play in its turn depends on the category of the play; if it is a comedy, its structure will require a comic resolution and a prevailing comic mood. Hence when we speak of typical characters we are not trying to reduce lifelike characters to stock types, though we certainly are suggesting that the sentimental notion of an antithesis between the lifelike character and the stock type is a vulgar error. All lifelike characters, whether in drama or fiction, owe their consistency to the appropriateness of the stock type which belongs to their dramatic function. That stock type is not the character but it is as necessary to the character as a skeleton is to the actor who plays it.

With regard to the characterization of comedy, the *Tractatus* lists three types of comic characters: the *alazons* or impostors, the *eirons* or self-deprecators, and the buffoons (*bomolochoi*). This list is closely related to a passage in the *Ethics* which contrasts the first two, and then goes on to contrast the buffoon with a character whom Aristotle calls *agroikos* or churlish, literally rustic. We may reasonably accept the churl as a fourth character type, and so we have two opposed pairs. The contest of *eiron* and *alazon* forms the basis of the comic action, and the buffoon and the churl polarize the comic mood.

. . . The humorous blocking characters of comedy are nearly always impostors, though it is more frequently a lack of self-knowledge than simple hypocrisy that characterizes them. The multitudes of comic scenes in which one character complacently soliloquizes while another makes sarcastic asides to the audience show the contest of *eiron* and *alazon* in its purest form, and show too that the audience is sympathetic to the *eiron* side. Central to the *alazon* group is the *senex iratus* or heavy father, who with his rages and threats, his obsessions and his gullibility, seems closely related to some of the demonic characters of romance, such as Polyphemus. Occasionally a character may have the dramatic function of such a figure without his characteristics: an example is Squire Allworthy in *Tom Jones,* who as far as the plot is concerned behaves almost as stupidly as Squire Western. Of heavy-father surrogates, the *miles gloriosus* has been mentioned: his popularity is largely due to the fact that he is a man of words rather than deeds, and is consequently far more useful to a practising dramatist than any tight-lipped hero could ever be. The pedant, in Renaissance comedy often a student of the occult sciences, the fop or coxcomb, and similar humors, require no comment. The female *alazon* is rare: Katherina the shrew represents to some extent a female *miles gloriosus,* and the *précieuse ridicule* a female pedant, but the "menace" or siren who gets in the way of the true heroine is more often found as a sinister figure of melodrama or romance than as a ridiculous figure in comedy.

The *eiron* figures need a little more attention. Central to this group is the hero, who is an *eiron* figure because, as explained, the dramatist tends to play him down and make him rather neutral and unformed in character. Next in importance is the heroine, also often played down: in Old Comedy, when a girl accompanies a male hero in his triumph, she is generally a stage prop, a *muta persona* not previously introduced. A more difficult form of *cognitio* is achieved when the heroine disguises herself or through some other device brings about the comic resolution, so that the person whom the hero is seeking turns out to be the person who has sought him. The fondness of Shakespeare for this "she stoops to conquer" theme needs only to be mentioned here, as it belongs more naturally to the mythos of romance.

Another central *eiron* figure is the type entrusted with hatching the schemes which bring about the hero's victory. This character in Roman comedy is almost always a tricky slave (*dolosus servus*), and in Renaissance comedy he becomes a scheming valet who is so frequent in Continental plays, and in Spanish drama is called the *gracioso*. Modern audiences are most familiar with him in Figaro and the Leporello of *Don Giovanni*. Through such intermediate nineteenth-century figures as Micawber and the Touchwood of Scott's *St. Ronan's Well*, who, like the *gracioso*, have buffoon affiliations, he evolves into the amateur detective of modern fiction. The Jeeves of P. G. Wodehouse is a more direct descendant. Female confidants of the same general family are often brought in to oil the machinery of the well-made play. Elizabethan comedy had another type of trickster, represented by the Matthew Merrygreek of *Ralph Roister Doister*, who is generally said to be developed from the vice or iniquity of the morality plays: as usual, the analogy is sound enough, whatever historians decide about origins. The vice, to give him that name, is very useful to a comic dramatist because he acts from pure love of mischief, and can set a comic action going with the minimum of motivation. The vice may be as light-hearted as Puck or as malignant as Don John in *Much Ado*, but as a rule the vice's activity is, in spite of his name, benevolent. One of the tricky slaves in Plautus, in a soliloquy, boasts that he is the *architectus* of the comic action: such a character carries out the will of the author to reach a happy ending. He is in fact the spirit of comedy, and the two clearest examples of the type in Shakespeare, Puck and Ariel, are both spiritual beings. The tricky slave often has his own freedom in mind as the reward of his exertions: Ariel's longing for release is in the same tradition.

The role of the vice includes a great deal of disguising, and the type may often be recognized by disguise. A good example is the Brainworm of Jonson's *Every Man in His Humour,* who calls the action of the play the day of his metamorphoses. Similarly Ariel has to surmount the difficult stage direction of "Enter invisible." The vice is combined with the hero whenever the latter is a cheeky, improvident young man who hatches his own schemes and cheats his rich father or uncle into giving him his patrimony along with the girl.

Another *eiron* type has not been much noticed. This is a character, generally an older man, who begins the action of the play by withdrawing from it, and ends the play by returning. He is often a father with the motive of seeing what his son will do. The action of *Every Man in His Humour* is set going in this way by Knowell Senior. The disappearance and return of Lovewit, the owner of the house which is the scene of *The Alchemist,* has the same dramatic function, though the characterization is different. The clearest Shakespearean example is the Duke in *Measure for Measure,* but Shakespeare is more addicted to the type than might appear at first glance. In Shakespeare the vice is rarely the real *architectus:* Puck and Ariel both act under orders from an older man, if one may call Oberon a man for the moment. In *The Tempest* Shakespeare returns to a comic action established by Aristophanes, in which an older man, instead of retiring from the action, builds it up on the stage. When the heroine takes the vice role in Shakespeare, she is often significantly related to her father, even when the father is not in the play at all, like the father of Helena, who gives her his medical knowledge, or the father of Portia, who arranges the scheme of the caskets. A more conventionally treated example of the same benevolent Prospero figure turned up recently in the psychiatrist of *The Cocktail Party,* and one may compare the mysterious alchemist who is the father of the heroine of *The Lady's Not for Burning.* The formula is not confined to comedy: Polonius, who shows so many of the disadvantages of a literary education, attempts the role of a retreating paternal *eiron* three times, once too often. *Hamlet* and *King Lear* contain subplots which are ironic versions of stock comic themes, Gloucester's story being the regular comedy theme of the gullible *senex* swindled by a clever and unprincipled son.

We pass now to the buffoon types, those whose function it is to increase the mood of festivity rather than to contribute to the plot. Renaissance comedy, unlike Roman comedy, had a great variety of such characters, professional fools, clowns, pages, singers, and incidental characters with established comic habits like malapropism or foreign accents. The oldest buffoon of this incidental nature is the parasite, who may be given something to do, as Jonson gives Mosca the role of a vice in *Volpone,* but who, *qua* parasite, does nothing but entertain the audience by talking about his appetite. He derives chiefly from Greek Middle Comedy, which appears to have been very full of food, and where he was, not unnaturally, closely associated with another established buffoon type, the cook, a conventional figure who breaks into comedies to bustle and order about and make long speeches about the mysteries of cooking. In the role of cook the buffoon or entertainer appears, not simply as a gratuitous addition like the parasite, but as something more like a master of ceremonies, a center for the comic mood. There is no cook in Shakespeare, though there is a superb description of one in the *Comedy of Errors,* but a similar role is often attached to a jovial and loquacious host, like the "mad host" of *The Merry Wives* or the Simon Eyre of *The Shoemakers Holiday.* In Middleton's *A Trick to Catch the Old One* the mad host type is combined with the vice. In Falstaff and Sir Toby Belch we can see the affinities of the buffoon or entertainer type both with the parasite and with the master of revels. If we study this entertainer or host role carefully we shall soon realize that it is a development of what in Aristophanic comedy is represented by the chorus, and which in its turn goes back to the *komos* or revel from which comedy is said to be descended.

Finally, there is a fourth group to which we have assigned the word *agroikos,* and which usually means either churlish or rustic, depending on the context. This type may also be extended to cover the Elizabethan gull and what in vaudeville used to be called the straight man, the solemn or inarticulate character who allows the humor to bounce off him, so to speak. We find churls in the miserly, snobbish, or priggish characters whose role is that of the refuser of festivity, the killjoy who tries to stop the fun, or like Malvolio, locks up the food and drink instead of dispensing it. The melancholy Jaques of *As You Like It,* who walks out on the final festivities, is closely related. In the sulky and self-centered Bertram of *All's Well* there is a most unusual and ingenious combination of this type with the hero. More often, however, the churl belongs to the *alazon* group, all miserly old men in comedies, including Shylock, being churls. In *The Tempest* Caliban has much the same relation to the churlish type that Ariel has to the vice or tricky slave. But often, where the mood is more light-hearted, we may translate *agroikos* simply by rustic, as with the innumerable country squires and similar characters who provide amusement in the urban setting of drama. Such types do not refuse the mood of festivity, but they mark the extent of its range. In a pastoral comedy the idealized virtues of rural life may be represented by a simple man who speaks for the pastoral ideal, like Corin in *As You Like It.* Corin has the same *agroikos* role as the "rube" or "hayseed" of more citified comedies, but the moral attitude to the role is reversed. Again we notice the principle that dramatic structure is a permanent and moral attitude a variable factor in literature.

In a very ironic comedy a different type of character may play the role of the refuser of festivity. The more ironic the comedy, the more absurd the society, and an absurd society may be condemned by, or at least contrasted with, a character that we may call the plain dealer, an outspoken advocate of a kind of moral norm who has the sympathy of the audience. Wycherley's Manly, though he provides the name for the type, is not a particularly good example of it: a much better one is the Cléante of *Tartuffe*. Such a character is appropriate when the tone is ironic enough to get the audience confused about its sense of the social norm: he corresponds roughly to the chorus in a tragedy, which is there for a similar reason. When the tone deepens from the ironic to the bitter, the plain dealer may become a malcontent or a railer, who may be morally superior to his society, as he is to some extent in Marston's play of that name, but who may also be too motivated by envy to be much more than another aspect of his society's evil, like Thersites, or to some extent Apemantus.

In tragedy, pity and fear, the emotions of moral attraction and repulsion, are raised and cast out. Comedy seems to make a more functional use of the social, even the moral judgement, than tragedy, yet comedy seems to raise the corresponding emotions, which are sympathy and ridicule, and cast them out in the same way. Comedy ranges from the most savage irony to the most dreamy wish-fulfilment romance, but its structural patterns and characterization are much the same throughout its range. This principle of the uniformity of comic structure through a variety of attitudes is clear in Aristophanes. Aristophanes is the most personal of writers, and his opinions on every subject are written all over his plays. We know that he wanted peace with Sparta and that he hated Cleon, so when his comedy depicts the attaining of peace and the defeat of Cleon we know that he approved and wanted his audience to approve. But in *Ecclesiazusae* a band of women in disguise railroad a communistic scheme through the Assembly which is a horrid parody of a Platonic republic, and proceed to inaugurate its sexual communism with some astonishing improvements. Presumably Aristophanes did not altogether endorse this, yet the comedy follows the same pattern and the same resolution. In *The Birds* the Peisthetairos who defies Zeus and blocks out Olympus with his Cloud-Cuckoo-Land is accorded the same triumph that is given to the Trygaios of the *Peace* who flies to heaven and brings a golden age back to Athens.

Let us look now at a variety of comic structures between the extremes of irony and romance. As comedy blends into irony and satire at one end and into romance at the other, if there are different phases or types of comic structure, some of them will be closely parallel to some of the types of irony and of romance. A somewhat forbidding piece of symmetry turns up in our argument at this point, which seems to have some literary analogy to the circle of fifths in music. I recognize six phases of each *mythos,* three being parallel to the phases of a neighboring *mythos.* The first three phases of comedy are parallel to the first three phases of irony and satire, and the second three to the second three of romance. The distinction between an ironic comedy and a comic satire, or between a romantic comedy and a comic romance, is tenuous, but not quite a distinction without a difference.

The first or most ironic phase of comedy is, naturally, the one in which a humorous society triumphs or remains undefeated. A good example of a comedy of this type is *The Alchemist,* in which the returning *eiron* Lovewit joins the rascals, and the plain dealer Surly is made a fool of. In *The Beggar's Opera* there is a similar twist to the ending: the (projected) author feels that the hanging of the hero is a comic ending, but is informed by the manager that the audience's sense of comic decorum demands a reprieve, whatever Macheath's moral status. This phase of comedy presents what Renaissance critics called *speculum consuetudinis,* the way of the world, *cosi fan tutte.* A more intense irony is achieved when the humorous society simply disintegrates without anything taking its place, as in *Heartbreak House* and frequently in Chekhov.

We notice in ironic comedy that the demonic world is never far away. The rages of the *senex iratus* in Roman comedy are directed mainly at the tricky slave, who is threatened with the mill, with being flogged to death, with crucifixion, with having his head dipped in tar and set on fire, and the like, all penalties that could be and were exacted from slaves in life. An epilogue in Plautus informs us that the slave-actor who has blown up in his lines will now be flogged; in one of the Menander fragments a slave is tied up and burned with a torch on the stage. One sometimes gets the impression that the audience of Plautus and Terence would have guffawed uproariously all through the Passion. We may ascribe this to the brutality of a slave society, but then we remember that boiling oil and burying alive ("such a *stuffy* death") turn up in *The Mikado.* Two lively comedies of the modern stage are *The Cocktail Party* and *The Lady's Not for Burning,* but the cross appears in the background of the one and the stake in the background of the other. Shylock's knife and Angelo's gallows appear in Shakespeare: in *Measure for Measure* every male character is at one time or another threatened with death. The action of comedy moves toward a deliverance from something which, if absurd, is by no means invariably harmless. We notice too how frequently a comic dramatist tries to bring his action as close to a catastrophic overthrow of the hero as he can get it, and then reverses the action as quickly as possible. The evading or breaking of a cruel law is often a very narrow squeeze. The intervention of the king at the end of *Tartuffe* is deliberately arbitrary: there is nothing in the action of the play itself to prevent Tartuffe's triumph. Tom Jones in the final book, accused of murder, incest, debt, and double-dealing, cast off by friends, guardian, and sweetheart, is a woeful figure indeed before all these turn into illusions. Any reader can think of many comedies in which the fear of death, sometimes a hideous death, hangs over the central character to the end, and is dispelled so quickly that one has almost the sense of awakening from nightmare.

Sometimes the redeeming agent is actually divine, like Diana in *Pericles;* in *Tartuffe* it is the king, who is conceived as a part of the audience and the incarnation of its will. An extraordinary number of comic stories, both in drama and fiction, seem to approach a potentially tragic crisis near the end, a feature that I may call the "point of ritual death"—a clumsy expression that I would gladly surrender for a better one. It is a feature not often noticed by critics, but when it is present it is as unmistakably present as a stretto in a fugue, which it somewhat resembles. In Smollett's *Humphrey Clinker* (I select this because no one will suspect Smollett of deliberate mythopoeia but only of following convention, at least as far as his plot is concerned), the main characters are nearly drowned in an accident with an upset carriage; they are then taken to a nearby house to dry off, and a *cognitio* takes place, in the course of which their family relationships are regrouped, secrets of birth brought to light, and names changed. Similar points of ritual death may be marked in almost any story that imprisons the hero or gives the heroine a nearly mortal illness before an eventually happy ending.

Sometimes the point of ritual death is vestigial, not an element in the plot but a mere change of tone. Everyone will have noted in comic actions, even in very trivial movies and magazine stories, a point near the end at which the tone suddenly becomes serious, sentimental, or ominous of potential catastrophe. In Aldous Huxley's *Chrome Yellow,* the hero Denis comes to a point of self-evaluation in which suicide nearly suggests itself: in most of Huxley's later books some violent action, generally suicidal, occurs at the corresponding point. In *Mrs. Dalloway* the actual suicide of Septimus becomes a point of ritual death for the heroine in the middle of her party. There are also some interesting Shakespearean variations of the device: a clown, for instance, will make a speech near the end in which the buffoon's mask suddenly falls off and we look straight into the face of a beaten and ridiculed slave. Examples are the speech of Dromio of Ephesus beginning "I am an ass indeed" in the *Comedy of Errors,* and the speech of the Clown in *All's Well* beginning "I am a woodland fellow."

The second phase of comedy, in its simplest form, is a comedy in which the hero does not transform a humorous society but simply escapes or runs away from it, leaving its structure as it was before. A more complex irony in this phase is achieved when a society is constructed by or around a hero, but proves not sufficiently real or strong to impose itself. In this situation the hero is usually himself at least partly a comic humor or mental runaway, and we have either a hero's illusion thwarted by a superior reality or a clash of two illusions. This is the quixotic phase of comedy, a difficult phase for drama, though *The Wild Duck* is a fairly pure example of it, and in drama it usually appears as a subordinate theme of another phase. Thus in *The Alchemist* Sir Epicure Mammon's dream of what he will do with the philosopher's stone is, like Quixote's, a gigantic dream, and makes him an ironic parody of Faustus (who is mentioned in the play), in the same way that Quixote is an ironic parody of Amadis and Lancelot. When the tone is more light-hearted, the comic resolution may be strong enough to sweep over all quixotic illusions. In *Huckleberry Finn* the main theme is one of the oldest in comedy, the freeing of a slave, and the *cognitio* tells us that Jim had already been set free before his escape was bungled by Tom Sawyer's pedantries. Because of its unrivalled opportunities for double-edged irony, this phase is a favorite of Henry James: perhaps his most searching study of it is *The Sacred Fount,* where the hero is an ironic parody of a Prospero figure creating another society out of the one in front of him.

The third phase of comedy is the normal one that we have been discussing, in which a *senex iratus* or other humor gives way to a young man's desires. The sense of the comic norm is so strong that when Shakespeare, by way of experiment, tried to reverse the pattern in *All's Well,* in having two older people force Bertram to marry Helena, the result has been an unpopular "problem" play, with a suggestion of something sinister about it. We have noted that the *cognitio* of comedy is much concerned with straightening out the details of the new society, with distinguishing brides from sisters and parents from foster-parents. The fact that the son and father are so often in conflict means that they are frequently rivals for the same girl, and the psychological alliance of the hero's bride and the mother is often expressed or implied. The occasional "naughtiness" of comedy, as in the Restoration period, has much to do, not only with marital fidelity, but with a kind of comic Oedipus situation in which the hero replaces his father as a lover. In Congreve's *Love for Love* there are two Oedipus themes in counterpoint: the hero cheats his father out of the heroine, and his best friend violates the wife of an impotent old man who is the heroine's guardian. A theme which would be recognized in real life as a form of infantile regression, the hero pretending to be impotent in order to gain admission to the women's quarters, is employed in Wycherley's *Country Wife,* where it is taken from Terence's *Eunuchus.*

The possibilities of incestuous combinations form one of the minor themes of comedy. The repellent older woman offered to Figaro in marriage turns out to be his mother, and the fear of violating a mother also occurs in *Tom Jones.* When in *Ghosts* and *Little Eyolf* Ibsen employed the old chestnut about the object of the hero's affections being his sister (a theme as old as Menander), his startled hearers took it for a portent of social revolution. In Shakespeare the recurring and somewhat mysterious father-daughter relationship already alluded to appears in its incestuous form at the beginning of *Pericles,* where it forms the demonic antithesis of the hero's union with his wife and daughter at the end. The presiding genius of comedy is Eros, and Eros has to adapt himself to the moral facts of society: Oedipus and incest themes indicate that erotic attachments have in their undisplaced or mythical origin a much greater versatility.

Ambivalent attitudes naturally result, and ambivalence is apparently the main reason for the curious feature of doubled characters which runs all through the history of comedy. In Roman comedy there is often a pair of young men, and consequently a pair of young women, of which one is often related to one of the men and exogamous to the other. The doubling of the *senex* figure sometimes gives us a heavy father for both hero and heroine, as in *The Winter's Tale,* sometimes a heavy father and benevolent uncle, as in Terence's *Adelphoi* and in *Tartuffe,* and so on. The action of comedy, like the action of the Christian Bible, moves from law to liberty. In the law there is an element of ritual bondage which is abolished, and an element of habit or convention which is fulfilled. The intolerable qualities of the *senex* represent the former and comprise with him the latter in the evolution of the comic *nomos.*

With the fourth phase of comedy we begin to move out of the world of experience into the ideal world of innocence and romance. We said that normally the happier society established at the end of the comedy is left undefined, in contrast to the ritual bondage of the humors. But it is also possible for a comedy to present its action on two social planes, of which one is preferred and consequently in some measure idealized. At the beginning of Plato's *Republic* we have a sharp contest between the *alazon* Thrasymachus and the ironic Socrates. The dialogue could have stopped there, as several of Plato's dialogues do, with a negative victory over a humor and the kind of society he suggests. But in the *Republic* the rest of the company, including Thrasymachus, follow Socrates inside Socrates's head, so to speak, and contemplate there the pattern of the just state. In Aristophanes the comic action is often ironic, but in *The Acharnians* we have a comedy in which a hero with the significant name of Dicaeopolis (righteous city or citizen) makes a private peace with Sparta, celebrates the peaceful festival of Dionysos with his family, and sets up the pattern of a temperate social order on the stage, where it remains throughout the play, cranks, bigots, sharpers, and scoundrels all being beaten away from it. One of the typical comic actions is at least as clearly portrayed in our earliest comedy as it has ever been.

Shakespeare's type of romantic comedy follows a tradition established by Peele and developed by Greene and Lyly, which has affinities with the medieval tradition of the seasonal ritual-play. We may call it the drama of the green world, its plot being assimilated to the ritual theme of the triumph of life and love over the waste land. In *The Two Gentlemen of Verona* the hero Valentine becomes captain of a band of outlaws in a forest, and all the other characters are gathered into this forest and become converted. Thus the action of the comedy begins in a world represented as a normal world, moves into the green world, goes into a metamorphosis there in which the comic resolution is achieved, and returns to the normal world. The forest in this play is the embryonic form of the fairy world of *A Midsummer Night's Dream,* the Forest of Arden in *As You Like It,* Windsor Forest in *The Merry Wives,* and the pastoral world of the mythical sea-coasted Bohemia in *The Winter's Tale.* In all these comedies there is the same rhythmic movement from normal world to green world and back again. In *The Merchant of Venice* the second world takes the form of Portia's mysterious house in Belmont, with its magic caskets and the wonderful cosmological harmonies that proceed from it in the fifth act. We notice too that this second world is absent from the more ironic comedies *All's Well* and *Measure for Measure.*

The green world charges the comedies with the symbolism of the victory of summer over winter, as is explicit in *Love's Labor's Lost,* where the comic contest takes the form of the medieval debate of winter and spring at the end. In *The Merry Wives* there is an elaborate ritual of the defeat of winter known to folklorists as "carrying out Death," of which Falstaff is the victim; and Falstaff must have felt that, after being thrown into the water, dressed up as a witch and beaten out of a house with curses, and finally supplied with a beast's head and singed with candles, he had done about all that could reasonably be asked of any fertility spirit.

In the rituals and myths the earth that produces the rebirth is generally a female figure, and the death and revival, or disappearance and withdrawal, of human figures in romantic comedy generally involves the heroine. The fact that the heroine often brings about the comic resolution by disguising herself as a boy is familiar enough. The treatment of Hero in *Much Ado,* of Helena in *All's Well,* of Thaisa in *Pericles,* of Fidele in *Cymbeline,* of Hermione in *The Winter's Tale,* show the repetition of a device in which progressively less care is taken of plausibility and in which in consequence the mythical outline of a Proserpine figure becomes progressively clearer. These are Shakespearean examples of the comic theme of ritual assault on a central female figure, a theme which stretches from Menander to contemporary soap operas. Many of Menander's plays have titles which are feminine participles indicating the particular indignity the heroine suffers in them, and the working formula of the soap opera is said to be to "put the heroine behind the eight-ball and keep her there." Treatments of the theme may be as light-hearted as *The Rape of the Lock* or as doggedly persistent as *Pamela.* However, the theme of rebirth is not invariably feminine in context: the rejuvenation of the *senex* in Aristophanes' *The Knights,* and a similar theme in *All's Well* based on the folklore motif of the healing of the impotent king, come readily to mind.

The green world has analogies, not only to the fertile world of ritual, but to the dream world that we create out of our own desires. This dream world collides with the stumbling and blinded follies of the world of experience, of Theseus' Athens with its idiotic marriage law, of Duke Frederick and his melancholy tyranny, of Leontes and his mad jealousy, of the Court Party with their plots and intrigues, and yet proves strong enough to impose the form of desire on it. Thus Shakespearean comedy illustrates, as clearly as any *mythos* we have, the archetypal function of literature in visualizing the world of desire, not as an escape from "reality," but as the genuine form of the world that human life tries to imitate.

In the fifth phase of comedy, some of the themes of which we have already anticipated, we move into a world that is still more romantic, less Utopian and more Arcadian, less festive and more pensive, where the comic ending is less a matter of the way the plot turns out than of the perspective of the audience. When we compare the Shakespearean fourth-phase comedies with the late fifth-phase "romances," we notice how much more serious an action is appropriate to the latter: they do not avoid tragedies but contain them. The action seems to be not only a movement from a "winter's tale" to spring, but from a lower world of confusion to an upper world of order. The closing scene of *The Winter's Tale* makes us think, not simply of a cyclical movement from tragedy and absence to happiness and return, but of bodily metamorphosis and a transformation from one kind of life to another. The materials of the *cognitio* of *Pericles* or *The Winter's Tale* are so stock that they would be "hooted at like an old tale," yet they seem both far-fetched and inevitably right, outraging reality and at the same time introducing us to a world of childlike innocence which has always made more sense than reality.

In this phase the reader or audience feels raised above the action, in the situation of which Christopher Sly is an ironic parody. The plotting of Cleon and Dionyza in *Pericles,* or of the Court Party in *The Tempest,* we look down on as generic or typical human behavior: the action, or at least the tragic implication of the action, is presented as though it were a play within a play that we can see in all dimensions at once. We see the action, in short, from the point of view of a higher and better-ordered world. And as the forest in Shakespeare is the usual symbol for the dream world in conflict with and imposing its form on experience, so the usual symbol for the lower or chaotic world is the sea, from which the cast, or an important part of it, is saved. The group of "sea" comedies includes *A Comedy of Errors, Twelfth Night, Pericles,* and *The Tempest. A Comedy of Errors,* though based on a Plautine original, is much closer to the world of Apuleius than to that of Plautus in its imagery, and the main action, moving from shipwreck and separation to reunion in a temple in Ephesus, is repeated in the much later play of *Pericles.* And just as the second world is absent from the two "problem" comedies, so in two of the "sea" group, *Twelfth Night* and *The Tempest,* the entire action takes place in the second world. In *Measure for Measure* the Duke disappears from the action and returns at the end; *The Tempest* seems to present the same type of action inside out, as the entire cast follows Prospero into his retreat, and is shaped into a new social order there.

These five phases of comedy may be seen as a sequence of stages in the life of a redeemed society. Purely ironic comedy exhibits this society in its infancy, swaddled and smothered by the society it should replace. Quixotic comedy exhibits it in adolescence, still too ignorant of the ways of the world to impose itself. In the third phase it comes to maturity and triumphs; in the fourth it is already mature and established. In the fifth it is part of a settled order which has been there from the beginning, an order which takes on an increasingly religious cast and seems to be drawing away from human experience altogether. At this point the undisplaced *commedia,* the vision of Dante's *Paradiso,* moves out of our circle of *mythoi* into the apocalyptic or abstract mythical world above it. At this point we realize that the crudest Plautine comedy-formulas have much the same *structure* as the central Christian myth itself, with its divine son appeasing the wrath of a father and redeeming what is at once a society and a bride.

At this point too comedy proper enters its final or sixth phase, the phase of the collapse and disintegration of the comic society. In this phase the social units of comedy become small and esoteric, or even confined to a single individual. Secret and sheltered places, forests in moonlight, secluded valleys, and happy islands become more prominent, as does the *penseroso* mood of romance, the love of the occult and the marvellous, the sense of individual detachment from routine existence. In this kind of comedy we have finally left the world of wit and the awakened critical intelligence for the opposite pole, an oracular solemnity which, if we surrender uncritically to it, will provide a delightful *frisson*. This is the world of ghost stories, thrillers, and Gothic romances, and, on a more sophisticated level, the kind of imaginative withdrawal portrayed in Huysmans' *À Rebours*. The somberness of Des Esseintes' surroundings has nothing to do with tragedy: Des Esseintes is a dilettante trying to amuse himself. The comic society has run the full course from infancy to death, and in its last phase myths closely connected psychologically with a return to the womb are appropriate.

WILLIAM SHAKESPEARE

The Tragedy of Macbeth

~~~~~~~~~~~~~~~~~~~~~~~~~~~~~~~~~~~~~

FRANCIS FERGUSSON

Macbeth *as the*
Imitation of an Action

THE CHARACTERS IN *THE TRAGEDY OF MACBETH*

DUNCAN, King of Scotland

MALCOLM
DONALBAIN } his sons

MACBETH
BANQUO } Generals of the Scottish Army

MACDUFF
LENNOX
ROSS
MENTEITH } Noblemen of Scotland
ANGUS
CAITHNESS

FLEANCE, Son to Banquo

SIWARD, Earl of Northumberland, General of the English forces

YOUNG SIWARD, his son

SEYTON, an Officer attending on Macbeth

BOY, son to Macduff

A SERGEANT

A PORTER

AN OLD MAN

AN ENGLISH DOCTOR

A SCOTTISH DOCTOR

LADY MACBETH

LADY MACDUFF

A GENTLEWOMAN, attending on Lady Macbeth

THREE WITCHES

HECATE

THE GHOST OF BANQUO

APPARITIONS

LORDS, GENTLEMEN, OFFICERS, SOLDIERS, MURDERERS, MES-
SENGERS, ATTENDANTS

Scene: Scotland, England

THE TRAGEDY OF MACBETH

ACT ONE

Scene One

[*Scotland. An open place. Thunder and lightning. Enter three* WITCHES.]

FIRST WITCH   When shall we three meet again
  In thunder, lightning, or in rain?

SECOND WITCH   When the hurlyburly's done,
  When the battle's lost and won.

THIRD WITCH   That will be ere set of sun.   5

FIRST WITCH   Where the place?

SECOND WITCH   Upon the heath.

THIRD WITCH   There to meet with Macbeth.

FIRST WITCH   I come, Graymalkin!

SECOND WITCH   Paddock calls.

THIRD WITCH   Anon!

ALL   Fair is foul, and foul is fair.   10
  Hover through the fog and filthy air.

[*Exeunt.*]

Scene Two

[*A camp near Forres. Alarum within. Enter* KING DUNCAN, MAL-
COLM, DONALBAIN, LENNOX, *with* ATTENDANTS, *meeting a bleed-ing* SERGEANT.]

KING   What bloody man is that? He can report,
  As seemeth by his plight, of the revolt
  The newest state.

MALCOLM   This is the sergeant
  Who like a good and hardy soldier fought
  'Gainst my captivity. Hail, brave friend!   5
  Say to the King the knowledge of the broil
  As thou didst leave it.

SERGEANT   Doubtful it stood,
As two spent swimmers that do cling together
And choke their art. The merciless Macdonwald
10 (Worthy to be a rebel, for to that
The multiplying villanies of nature
Do swarm upon him) from the Western Isles
Of kerns and gallowglasses is supplied;
And Fortune, on his damned quarrel smiling,
15 Show'd like a rebel's whore. But all's too weak;
For brave Macbeth (well he deserves that name),
Disdaining Fortune, with his brandish'd steel,
Which smok'd with bloody execution
(Like valor's minion), carv'd out his passage
20 Till he fac'd the slave;
Which ne'er shook hands nor bade farewell to him
Till he unseam'd him from the nave to th' chaps
And fix'd his head upon our battlements.

KING   O valiant cousin! worthy gentleman!

25 SERGEANT   As whence the sun 'gins his reflection
Shipwracking storms and direful thunders break,
So from that spring whence comfort seem'd to come
Discomfort swells. Mark, King of Scotland, mark.
No sooner justice had, with valor arm'd,
30 Compell'd these skipping kerns to trust their heels
But the Norweyan lord, surveying vantage,
With furbish'd arms and new supplies of men,
Began a fresh assault.

KING   Dismay'd not this
Our captains, Macbeth and Banquo?

SERGEANT   Yes,
35 As sparrows eagles, or the hare the lion.
If I say sooth, I must report they were
As cannon's overcharg'd with double cracks, so they
Doubly redoubled strokes upon the foe.
Except they meant to bathe in reeking wounds,
40 Or memorize another Golgotha,
I cannot tell—
But I am faint; my gashes cry for help.

KING   So well thy words become thee as thy wounds;
They smack of honor both. Go get him surgeons.

Line 21. Which = Macbeth.

[*Exit* SERGEANT, *attended. Enter* ROSS.]

Who comes here?

MALCOLM   The worthy Thane of Ross.   45

LENNOX   What a haste looks through his eyes! So should he look
  That seems to speak things strange.

ROSS   God save the King!

KING   Whence cam'st thou, worthy thane?

ROSS   From Fife, great King,
  Where the Norweyan banners flout the sky
  And fan our people cold. Norway himself,   50
  With terrible numbers,
  Assisted by that most disloyal traitor
  The Thane of Cawdor, began a dismal conflict,
  Till that Bellona's bridegroom, lapp'd in proof,
  Confronted him with self-comparisons,   55
  Point against point, rebellious arm 'gainst arm,
  Curbing his lavish spirit; and to conclude,
  The victory fell on us.

KING   Great happiness!

ROSS   That now
  Sweno, the Norways' king, craves composition;
  Nor would we deign him burial of his men   60
  Till he disbursed, at Saint Colme's Inch,
  Ten thousand dollars to our general use.

KING   No more that Thane of Cawdor shall deceive
  Our bosom interest. Go pronounce his present death
  And with his former title greet Macbeth.   65

ROSS   I'll see it done.

KING   What he hath lost noble Macbeth hath won.

[*Exeunt.*]

Scene Three

[*A blasted heath. Thunder. Enter the three* WITCHES.]

FIRST WITCH   Where hast thou been, sister?

Line 50. Norway = the king of Norway.
Line 54. Bellona's bridegroom = Macbeth.

SECOND WITCH   Killing swine.

THIRD WITCH   Sister, where thou?

FIRST WITCH   A sailor's wife had chestnuts in her lap
5   And munch'd and munch'd and munch'd. 'Give me,' quoth I.
       'Aroint thee, witch!' the rump-fed ronyon cries.
       Her husband's to Aleppo gone, master o' th' Tiger;
       But in a sieve I'll thither sail
       And, like a rat without a tail,
10   I'll do, I'll do, and I'll do.

SECOND WITCH   I'll give thee a wind.

FIRST WITCH   Th' art kind.

THIRD WITCH   And I another.

FIRST WITCH   I myself have all the other,
15   And the very ports they blow,
       All the quarters that they know
       I' th' shipman's card.
       I will drain him dry as hay.
       Sleep shall neither night nor day
20   Hang upon his penthouse lid.
       He shall live a man forbid.
       Weary sev'nights, nine times nine,
       Shall he dwindle, peak, and pine.
       Though his bark cannot be lost,
25   Yet it shall be tempest-tost.
       Look what I have.

SECOND WITCH   Show me! show me!

THIRD WITCH   Here I have a pilot's thumb,
       Wrack'd as homeward he did come.

[*Drum within.*]

30 THIRD WITCH   A drum, a drum!
       Macbeth doth come.

ALL   The Weird Sisters, hand in hand,
       Posters of the sea and land,
       Thus do go about, about,
35   Thrice to thine, and thrice to mine,
       And thrice again, to make up nine.
       Peace! The charm's wound up.

[*Enter* MACBETH *and* BANQUO.]

MACBETH   So foul and fair a day I have not seen.

BANQUO   How far is't call'd to Forres? What are these,
So wither'd, and so wild in their attire,   40
That look not like th' inhabitants o' th' earth,
And yet are on't? Live you? or are you aught
That man may question? You seem to understand me,
By each at once her choppy finger laying
Upon her skinny lips. You should be women,   45
And yet your beards forbid me to interpret
That you are so.

MACBETH   Speak, if you can. What are you?

FIRST WITCH   All hail, Macbeth! Hail to thee, Thane of Glamis!

SECOND WITCH   All hail, Macbeth! Hail to thee, Thane of Cawdor!

THIRD WITCH   All hail, Macbeth, that shalt be King hereafter!   50

BANQUO   Good sir, why do you start and seem to fear
Things that do sound so fair? I' th' name of truth,
Are ye fantastical, or that indeed
Which outwardly ye show? My noble partner
You greet with present grace and great prediction   55
Of noble having and of royal hope,
That he seems rapt withal. To me you speak not.
If you can look into the seeds of time
And say which grain will grow and which will not,
Speak then to me, who neither beg nor fear   60
Your favors nor your hate.

FIRST WITCH   Hail!

SECOND WITCH   Hail!

THIRD WITCH   Hail!

FIRST WITCH   Lesser than Macbeth, and greater.   65

SECOND WITCH   Not so happy, yet much happier.

THIRD WITCH   Thou shalt get kings, though thou be none.
So all hail, Macbeth and Banquo!

FIRST WITCH   Banquo and Macbeth, all hail!

MACBETH   Stay, you imperfect speakers, tell me more!   70
By Sinel's death I know I am Thane of Glamis;
But how of Cawdor? The Thane of Cawdor lives,
A prosperous gentleman; and to be King
Stands not within the prospect of belief,

Line 71. MACBETH's father.

75 No more than to be Cawdor. Say from whence
You owe this strange intelligence, or why
Upon this blasted heath you stop our way
With such prophetic greeting. Speak, I charge you.

[WITCHES *vanish*.]

BANQUO   The earth hath bubbles, as the water has,
80   And these are of them. Whither are they vanish'd?

MACBETH   Into the air, and what seem'd corporal melted
As breath into the wind. Would they had stay'd!

BANQUO   Were such things here as we do speak about?
Or have we eaten on the insane root
85   That takes the reason prisoner?

MACBETH   Your children shall be kings.

BANQUO   You shall be King.

MACBETH   And Thane of Cawdor too. Went it not so?

BANQUO   To th' selfsame tune and words. Who's here?

[*Enter* ROSS *and* ANGUS.]

ROSS   The King hath happily receiv'd, Macbeth,
90   The news of thy success; and when he reads
Thy personal venture in the rebels' fight,
His wonders and his praises do contend
Which should be thine or his. Silenc'd with that,
In viewing o'er the rest o' the selfsame day,
95   He finds thee in the stout Norweyan ranks,
Nothing afeard of what thyself didst make,
Strange images of death. As thick as hail
Came post with post, and every one did bear
Thy praises in his kingdom's great defense
And pour'd them down before him.

100 ANGUS   We are sent
To give thee from our royal master thanks;
Only to herald thee into his sight,
Not pay thee.

ROSS   And for an earnest of a greater honor,
105   He bade me, from him, call thee Thane of Cawdor;
In which addition, hail, most worthy Thane!
For it is thine.

BANQUO   What, can the devil speak true?

MACBETH   The Thane of Cawdor lives. Why do you dress me
In borrowed robes?

ANGUS   Who was the Thane lives yet,
But under heavy judgment bears that life   110
Which he deserves to lose. Whether he was combin'd
With those of Norway, or did line the rebel
With hidden help and vantage, or that with both
He labor'd in his country's wrack, I know not;
But treasons capital, confess'd and prov'd,   115
Have overthrown him.

MACBETH [aside]   Glamis, and Thane of Cawdor!
The greatest is behind. [To ROSS and ANGUS] Thanks for your
     pains.
[Aside to BANQUO] Do you not hope your children shall be kings,
When those that gave the Thane of Cawdor to me
Promis'd no less to them?

BANQUO [aside to MACBETH] That, trusted home,   120
Might yet enkindle you unto the crown,
Besides the Thane of Cawdor. But 'tis strange!
And oftentimes, to win us to our harm,
The instruments of darkness tell us truths,
Win us with honest trifles, to betray 's   125
In deepest consequence.—
Cousins, a word, I pray you.

MACBETH [aside]   Two truths are told,
As happy prologues to the swelling act
Of the imperial theme.—I thank you, gentlemen.—
[Aside] This supernatural soliciting   130
Cannot be ill; cannot be good. If ill,
Why hath it given me earnest of success,
Commencing in a truth? I am Thane of Cawdor.
If good, why do I yield to that suggestion
Whose horrid image doth unfix my hair   135
And make my seated heart knock at my ribs
Against the use of nature? Present fears
Are less than horrible imaginings.
My thought, whose murder yet is but fantastical,
Shakes so my single state of man that function   140
Is smother'd in surmise and nothing is
But what is not.

BANQUO   Look how our partner's rapt.

Line 117. Has not arrived yet.
Line 120. If you believe all of that.

MACBETH [*aside*]   If chance will have me King, why, chance may
    crown me,
    Without my stir.

BANQUO   New honors come upon him,
145   Like our strange garments, cleave not to their mold
    But with the aid of use.

MACBETH [*aside*]   Come what come may,
    Time and the hour runs through the roughest day.

BANQUO   Worthy Macbeth, we stay upon your leisure.

MACBETH   Give me your favor. My dull brain was wrought
150   With things forgotten. Kind gentlemen, your pains
    Are regist'red where every day I turn
    The leaf to read them. Let us toward the King.
    [*Aside to* BANQUO] Think upon what hath chanc'd; and, at more
    time,
    The interim having weigh'd it, let us speak
    Our free hearts each to other.

155 BANQUO [*aside to* MACBETH]   Very gladly.

MACBETH [*aside to* BANQUO]   Till then, enough.—Come, friends.

[*Exeunt.*]

Scene Four

[*Forres. The palace. Flourish. Enter* KING DUNCAN, LENNOX, MAL-
COLM, DONALBAIN, *and* ATTENDANTS.]

KING   Is execution done on Cawdor? Are not
    Those in commission yet return'd?

MALCOLM   My liege,
    They are not yet come back. But I have spoke
    With one that saw him die; who did report
5   That very frankly he confess'd his treasons,
    Implor'd your Highness' pardon, and set forth
    A deep repentance. Nothing in his life
    Became him like the leaving it. He died
    As one that had been studied in his death
10   To throw away the dearest thing he ow'd
    As 'twere a careless trifle.

KING   There's no art

Lines 151-152. Are kept in my memory.

To find the mind's construction in the face.
He was a gentleman on whom I built
An absolute trust.

[*Enter* MACBETH, BANQUO, *and* ANGUS.]

                O worthiest cousin,
The sin of my ingratitude even now   15
Was heavy on me! Thou art so far before
That swiftest wing of recompense is slow
To overtake thee. Would thou hadst less deserv'd,
That the proportion both of thanks and payment
Might have been mine! Only I have left to say,   20
More is thy due than more than all can pay.

MACBETH   The service and the loyalty I owe,
In doing it pays itself. Your highness' part
Is to receive our duties; and our duties
Are to your throne and state children and servants,   25
Which do but what they should by doing everything
Safe toward your love and honor.

KING   Welcome hither.
I have begun to plant thee and will labor
To make thee full of growing. Noble Banquo,
That hast no less deserv'd, nor must be known   30
No less to have done so, let me infold thee
And hold thee to my heart.

BANQUO   There if I grow,
The harvest is your own.

KING   My plenteous joys,
Wanton in fulness, seek to hide themselves
In drops of sorrow. Sons, kinsmen, thanes,   35
And you whose places are the nearest, know
We will establish our estate upon
Our eldest, Malcolm, whom we name hereafter
The Prince of Cumberland; which honor must
Not unaccompanied invest him only,   40
But signs of nobleness, like stars, shall shine
On all deservers. From hence to Inverness,
And bind us further to you.

MACBETH   The rest is labor, which is not us'd for you!
I'll be myself the harbinger, and make joyful   45
The hearing of my wife with your approach;
So, humbly take my leave.

KING   My worthy Cawdor!

MACBETH [*aside*] The Prince of Cumberland! That is a step
On which I must fall down, or else o'erleap,
50 For in my way it lies. Stars, hide your fires!
Let not light see my black and deep desires.
The eye wink at the hand; yet let that be,
Which the eye fears, when it is done, to see. [*Exit.*]

KING True, worthy Banquo: he is full so valiant,
55 And in his commendations I am fed;
It is a banquet to me. Let's after him,
Whose care is gone before to bid us welcome.
It is a peerless kinsman.

[*Flourish. Exeunt.*]

Scene Five

[*Inverness.* MACBETH'S *castle. Enter* MACBETH'S WIFE, *alone with a letter.*]

LADY [*reads*] 'They met me in the day of success; and I have
learn'd by the perfect'st report they have more in them than
mortal knowledge. When I burn'd in desire to question them
further, they made themselves air, into which they vanish'd.
5 Whiles I stood rapt in the wonder of it, came missives from the
King, who all-hail'd me Thane of Cawdor, by which title, before,
these Weird Sisters saluted me, and referr'd me to the coming
on of time with "Hail, King that shalt be!" This have I thought
good to deliver thee, my dearest partner of greatness, that thou
10 mightst not lose the dues of rejoicing by being ignorant of what
greatness is promis'd thee. Lay it to thy heart, and farewell.'

Glamis thou art, and Cawdor, and shalt be—
What thou art promis'd. Yet do I fear thy nature.
It is too full o' th' milk of human kindness
15 To catch the nearest way. Thou wouldst be great;
Art not without ambition, but without
The illness should attend it. What thou wouldst highly,
That wouldst thou holily; wouldst not play false,
And yet wouldst wrongly win. Thou'ldst have, great Glamis,
20 That which cries 'Thus thou must do,' if thou have it;
And that which rather thou dost fear to do
Than wishest should be undone. Hie thee hither,
That I may pour my spirits in thine ear
And chastise with the valor of my tongue
25 All that impedes thee from the golden round

Which fate and metaphysical aid doth seem
To have thee crown'd withal.

[*Enter* MESSENGER.]
                              What is your tidings?

MESSENGER   The King comes here to-night.

LADY   Thou'rt mad to say it!
   Is not thy master with him? who, were't so,
   Would have inform'd for preparation.   30

MESSENGER   So please you, it is true. Our Thane is coming.
   One of my fellows had the speed of him,
   Who, almost dead for breath, had scarcely more
   Than would make up his message.

LADY   Give him tending;
   He brings great news.

[*Exit* MESSENGER.]
                        The raven himself is hoarse   35
   That croaks the fatal entrance of Duncan
   Under my battlements. Come, you spirits
   That tend on mortal thoughts, unsex me here,
   And fill me, from the crown to the toe, top-full
   Of direst cruelty! Make thick my blood;   40
   Stop up th' access and passage to remorse,
   That no compunctious visitings of nature
   Shake my fell purpose nor keep peace between
   Th' effect and it! Come to my woman's breasts
   And take my milk for gall, you murd'ring ministers,   45
   Wherever in your sightless substances
   You wait on nature's mischief! Come, thick night,
   And pall thee in the dunnest smoke of hell,
   That my keen knife see not the wound it makes,
   Nor heaven peep through the blanket of the dark   50
   To cry 'Hold, hold!'

[*Enter* MACBETH.]
                        Great Glamis! worthy Cawdor!
   Greater than both, by the all-hail hereafter!
   Thy letters have transported me beyond
   This ignorant present, and I feel now
   The future in the instant.

MACBETH   My dearest love,   55
   Duncan comes here to-night.

LADY   And when goes hence?

MACBETH   To-morrow, as he purposes.

LADY   O, never
    Shall sun that morrow see!
    Your face, my Thane, is as a book where men
60 May read strange matters. To beguile the time,
    Look like the time; bear welcome in your eye,
    Your hand, your tongue; look like the innocent flower,
    But be the serpent under't. He that's coming
    Must be provided for; and you shall put
65 This night's great business into my dispatch,
    Which shall to all our nights and days to come
    Give solely sovereign sway and masterdom.

MACBETH   We will speak further.

LADY   Only look up clear.
    To alter favor ever is to fear.
70 Leave all the rest to me.

    [*Exeunt.*]

Scene Six

    [*Inverness. Before* MACBETH'S *castle. Hautboys and torches. Enter*
    KING DUNCAN, MALCOLM, DONALBAIN, BANQUO, LENNOX,
    MACDUFF, ROSS, ANGUS, *and* ATTENDANTS.]

KING   This castle hath a pleasant seat. The air
    Nimbly and sweetly recommends itself
    Unto our gentle senses.

BANQUO   This guest of summer,
    The temple-haunting martlet, does approve
5   By his lov'd mansionry that the heaven's breath
    Smells wooingly here. No jutty, frieze,
    Buttress, nor coign of vantage, but this bird
    Hath made his pendent bed and procreant cradle.
    Where they most breed and haunt, I have observ'd
    The air is delicate.

    [*Enter* LADY MACBETH.]

10 KING   See, see, our honor'd hostess!

    The love that follows us sometime is our trouble,

    Lines 60-61. The time = the people around you.
    Lines 68-70. Just keep looking serene. To change expression is always
    dangerous.

Which still we thank as love. Herein I teach you
How you shall bid God ild us for your pains
And thank us for your trouble.

LADY   All our service
In every point twice done, and then done double,   15
Were poor and single business to contend
Against those honors deep and broad wherewith
Your Majesty loads our house. For those of old,
And the late dignities heap'd up to them,
We rest your hermits.

KING   Where's the Thane of Cawdor?   20
We cours'd him at the heels and had a purpose
To be his purveyor; but he rides well.
And his great love, sharp as his spur, hath holp him
To his home before us. Fair and noble hostess,
We are your guest to-night.

LADY   Your servants ever   25
Have theirs, themselves, and what is theirs, in compt,
To make their audit at your Highness' pleasure,
Still to return your own.

KING   Give me your hand;
Conduct me to mine host. We love him highly
And shall continue our graces towards him.   30
By your leave, hostess.

[*Exeunt.*]

Scene Seven

[*Inverness.* MACBETH'S *castle. Hautboys. Torches. Enter a* SEWER,
and divers SERVANTS *with dishes and service, and cross the stage.
Then enter* MACBETH.]

MACBETH   If it were done when 'tis done, then 'twere well
It were done quickly. If th' assassination
Could trammel up the consequence, and catch,
With his surcease, success; that but this blow

Line 13. Ild = yield, in the archaic sense of "reward."
Line 20. We are reverent toward you.
Line 22. Purveyor = forerunner.
Lines 25-28. We are ready to account to you for ourselves and for what
we hold.
Line 4. With his surcease = with Duncan's death.

5   Might be the be-all and the end-all here,
       But here, upon this bank and shoal of time,
       We'ld jump the life to come. But in these cases
       We still have judgment here, that we but teach
       Bloody instructions, which, being taught, return
10   To plague th' inventor. This even-handed justice
       Commends th' ingredients of our poison'd chalice
       To our own lips. He's here in double trust:
       First, as I am his kinsman and his subject—
       Strong both against the deed; then, as his host,
15   Who should against his murderer shut the door,
       Not bear the knife myself. Besides, this Duncan
       Hath borne his faculties so meek, hath been
       So clear in his great office, that his virtues
       Will plead like angels, trumpet-tongu'd, against
20   The deep damnation of his taking-off;
       And pity, like a naked new-born babe,
       Striding the blast, or heaven's cherubin, hors'd
       Upon the sightless couriers of the air,
       Shall blow the horrid deed in every eye,
25   That tears shall drown the wind. I have no spur
       To prick the sides of my intent, but only
       Vaulting ambition, which o'erleaps itself
       And falls on th' other side.

   [*Enter* LADY MACBETH.]
                                  How now? What news?

   LADY   He has almost supp'd. Why have you left the chamber?

   MACBETH   Hath he ask'd for me?

30 LADY   Know you not he has?

   MACBETH   We will proceed no further in this business.
       He hath honor'd me of late, and I have bought
       Golden opinions from all sorts of people,
       Which would be worn now in their newest gloss,
       Not cast aside so soon.

35 LADY   Was the hope drunk
       Wherein you dress'd yourself? Hath it slept since?
       And wakes it now to look so green and pale
       At what it did so freely? From this time
       Such I account thy love. Art thou afeard
40   To be the same in thine own act and valor
       As thou art in desire? Wouldst thou have that

   Line 7. Jump = contemptuously ignore.

Which thou esteem'st the ornament of life,
And live a coward in thine own esteem,
Letting 'I dare not' wait upon 'I would,'
Like the poor cat i' th' adage?

MACBETH   Prithee peace!   45
I dare do all that may become a man.
Who dares do more is none.

LADY   What beast was't then
That made you break this enterprise to me?
When you durst do it, then you were a man;
And to be more than what you were, you would   50
Be so much more the man. Nor time nor place
Did then adhere, and yet you would make both.
They have made themselves, and that their fitness now
Does unmake you. I have given suck, and I know
How tender 'tis to love the babe that milks me.   55
I would, while it was smiling in my face,
Have pluck'd my nipple from his boneless gums
And dash'd the brains out, had I so sworn as you
Have done to this.

MACBETH   If we should fail?

LADY   We fail?
But screw your courage to the sticking place,   60
And we'll not fail. When Duncan is asleep
(Whereto the rather shall his day's hard journey
Soundly invite him), his two chamberlains
Will I with wine and wassail so convince
That memory, the warder of the brain,   65
Shall be a fume, and the receipt of reason
A limbeck only. When in swinish sleep
Their drenched natures lie as in a death,
What cannot you and I perform upon
Th' unguarded Duncan? what not put upon   70
His spongy officers, who shall bear the guilt
Of our great quell?

MACBETH   Bring forth men-children only;
For thy undaunted mettle should compose
Nothing but males. Will it not be receiv'd,
When we have mark'd with blood those sleepy two   75
Of his own chamber and us'd their very daggers,
That they have done't?

Line 44. The cat which dares not damp her paw / Will catch no fish to
fill her maw.

LADY   Who dares receive it other,
     As we shall make our griefs and clamor roar
     Upon his death?

MACBETH   I am settled and bend up
80   Each corporal agent to this terrible feat.
     Away, and mock the time with fairest show;
     False face must hide what the false heart doth know.

[*Exeunt.*]

Line 81. Mock the time = mislead everyone.

ACT TWO

Scene One

[*Inverness. Court of* MACBETH'S *castle. Enter* BANQUO, *and* FLEANCE *with a torch before him.*]

BANQUO   How goes the night, boy?

FLEANCE   The moon is down; I have not heard the clock.

BANQUO   And she goes down at twelve.

FLEANCE   I take't, 'tis later, sir.

BANQUO   Hold, take my sword. There's husbandry in heaven;
Their candles are all out. Take thee that too.   5
A heavy summons lies like lead upon me,
And yet I would not sleep. Merciful powers,
Restrain in me the cursed thoughts that nature
Gives way to in repose!

[*Enter* MACBETH, *and a* SERVANT *with a torch.*]

                                    Give me my sword.
Who's there?   10

MACBETH   A friend.

BANQUO   What, sir, not yet at rest? The King's abed.
He hath been in unusual pleasure and
Sent forth great largess to your offices.
This diamond he greets your wife withal   15
By the name of most kind hostess, and shut up
In measureless content.

MACBETH   Being unprepar'd,
Our will became the servant to defect,
Which else should free have wrought.

BANQUO   All's well.
I dreamt last night of the three Weird Sisters.   20
To you they have show'd some truth.

MACBETH   I think not of them.
Yet when we can entreat an hour to serve,
We would spend it in some words upon that business,
If you would grant the time.

Lines 17-19. Our hospitality was inadequate, though we would have made it better had we been prepared.

145

BANQUO   At your kind'st leisure.

25 MACBETH   If you shall cleave to my consent, when 'tis,
It shall make honor for you.

BANQUO   So I lose none
In seeking to augment it but still keep
My bosom franchis'd and allegiance clear,
I shall be counsell'd.

MACBETH   Good repose the while!

30 BANQUO   Thanks, sir. The like to you!

[*Exeunt* BANQUO *and* FLEANCE.]

MACBETH   Go bid thy mistress, when my drink is ready,
She strike upon the bell. Get thee to bed.

[*Exit* SERVANT.]

Is this a dagger which I see before me,
The handle toward my hand? Come, let me clutch thee!
35 I have thee not, and yet I see thee still.
Art thou not, fatal vision, sensible
To feeling as to sight? or art thou but
A dagger of the mind, a false creation,
Proceeding from the heat-oppressed brain?
40 I see thee yet, in form as palpable
As this which now I draw.
Thou marshall'st me the way that I was going,
And such an instrument I was to use.
Mine eyes are made the fools o' th' other senses,
45 Or else worth all the rest. I see thee still;
And on thy blade and dudgeon gouts of blood,
Which was not so before. There's no such thing.
It is the bloody business which informs
Thus to mine eyes. Now o'er the one half-world
50 Nature seems dead, and wicked dreams abuse
The curtain'd sleep. Now witchcraft celebrates
Pale Hecate's offerings; and wither'd murder,
Alarum'd by his sentinel, the wolf,
Whose howl's his watch, thus with his stealthy pace,
55 With Tarquin's ravishing strides, towards his design
Moves like a ghost. Thou sure and firm-set earth,
Hear not my steps which way they walk, for fear
Thy very stones prate of my whereabout

Line 25. If you will support me when the time comes.
Line 28. Franchised = free (of guilt).

And take the present horror from the time,
Which now suits with it. Whiles I threat, he lives; 60
Words to the heat of deeds too cold breath gives.

[*A bell rings.*]

I go, and it is done. The bell invites me.
Hear it not, Duncan, for it is a knell
That summons thee to heaven, or to hell. [*Exit.*]

Scene Two

[*Inverness.* MACBETH'S *castle. Enter* LADY MACBETH.]

LADY That which hath made them drunk hath made me bold;
   What hath quench'd them hath given me fire. Hark! Peace!
   It was the owl that shriek'd, the fatal bellman
   Which gives the stern'st good-night. He is about it.
   The doors are open, and the surfeited grooms 5
   Do mock their charge with snores. I have drugg'd their possets,
   That death and nature do contend about them
   Whether they live or die.

MACBETH [*within.*]   Who's there? What, ho?

LADY Alack, I am afraid they have awak'd, 10
   And 'tis not done! Th' attempt, and not the deed,
   Confounds us. Hark! I laid their daggers ready;
   He could not miss 'em. Had he not resembled
   My father as he slept, I had done't.

[*Enter* MACBETH.]

                     My husband!

MACBETH I have done the deed. Didst thou not hear a noise? 15

LADY I heard the owl scream and the crickets cry.
   Did you not speak?

MACBETH   When?

LADY   Now.

MACBETH   As I descended?

LADY Ay.

MACBETH Hark!
   Who lies i' th' second chamber?

LADY   Donalbain. 20

MACBETH   This is a sorry sight. [*Looks on his hands.*]

LADY   A foolish thought, to say a sorry sight.

MACBETH   There's one did laugh in's sleep, and one cried 'Murder!'
That they did wake each other. I stood and heard them.
25   But they did say their prayers and address'd them
Again to sleep.

LADY   There are two lodg'd together.

MACBETH   One cried 'God bless us!' and 'Amen!' the other,
As they had seen me with these hangman's hands.
List'ning their fear, I could not say 'Amen!'
When they did say 'God bless us!'

30   LADY   Consider it not so deeply.

MACBETH   But wherefore could not I pronounce 'Amen'?
I had most need of blessing, and 'Amen'
Stuck in my throat.

LADY   These deeds must not be thought
After these ways. So, it will make us mad.

35   MACBETH   Methought I heard a voice cry 'Sleep no more!
Macbeth does murder sleep'—the innocent sleep,
Sleep that knits up the ravell'd sleave of care,
The death of each day's life, sore labor's bath,
Balm of hurt minds, great nature's second course,
Chief nourisher in life's feast.

40   LADY   What do you mean?

MACBETH   Still it cried 'Sleep no more!' to all the house;
'Glamis hath murder'd sleep, and therefore Cawdor
Shall sleep no more! Macbeth shall sleep no more!'

LADY   Who was it that thus cried? Why, worthy Thane,
45   You do unbend your noble strength to think
So brainsickly of things. Go get some water
And wash this filthy witness from your hand.
Why did you bring these daggers from the place?
They must lie there. Go carry them and smear
The sleepy grooms with blood.

50   MACBETH   I'll go no more.
I am afraid to think what I have done;
Look on't again I dare not.

LADY   Infirm of purpose!
Give me the daggers. The sleeping and the dead
Are but as pictures. 'Tis the eye of childhood
55   That fears a painted devil. If he do bleed,

I'll gild the faces of the grooms withal,
For it must seem their guilt. [*Exit.*]

[*Knocking within.*]

MACBETH   Whence is that knocking?
How is't with me when every noise appals me?
What hands are here? Ha! they pluck out mine eyes!
Will all great Neptune's ocean wash this blood.   60
Clean from my hand? No. This my hand will rather
The multitudinous seas incarnadine,
Making the green one red.

[*Enter* LADY MACBETH.]

LADY   My hands are of your color, but I shame
To wear a heart so white.

[*Knock.*]
                         I hear a knocking.   65
At the south entry. Retire we to our chamber.
A little water clears us of this deed.
How easy is it then! Your constancy
Hath left you unattended.

[*Knock.*]
                         Hark! more knocking.
Get on your nightgown, lest occasion call us   70
And show us to be watchers. Be not lost
So poorly in your thoughts.

MACBETH   To know my deed, 'twere best not know myself.

[*Knock.*]

Wake Duncan with thy knocking! I would thou couldst!

[*Exeunt.*]

Scene Three

[*Inverness.* MACBETH'S *castle. Enter a* PORTER. *Knocking within.*]

PORTER   Here's a knocking indeed! If a man were porter of hell
gate, he should have old turning the key.

[*Knock.*]

Knock, knock, knock! Who's there, i' th' name of Belzebub?
Here's a farmer that hang'd himself on th' expectation of plenty.

Line 62. Making all the green (sea) red.

5   Come in time! Have napkins enow about you; here you'll sweat
for 't.

[*Knock.*]

Knock, knock! Who's there, in th' other devil's name? Faith,
here's an equivocator, that could swear in both the scales against
either scale; who committed treason enough for God's sake, yet
10   could not equivocate to heaven. O, come in, equivocator!

[*Knock.*]

Knock, knock, knock! Who's there? Faith, here's an English
tailor come hither for stealing out of a French hose. Come in,
tailor. Here you may roast your goose.

[*Knock.*]

Knock, knock! Never at quiet! What are you? But this place is
15   too cold for hell. I'll devil-porter it no further. I had thought to
let in some of all professions that go the primrose way to th'
everlasting bonfire.

[*Knock.*]

Anon, anon! [*Opens the door.*] I pray you remember the porter.

[*Enter* MACDUFF *and* LENNOX.]

MACDUFF Was it so late, friend, ere you went to bed,
20   That you do lie so late?

PORTER Faith, sir, we were carousing till the second cock; and
drink, sir, is a great provoker of three things.

MACDUFF What three things does drink especially provoke?

PORTER Marry, sir, nose-painting, sleep, and urine. Lechery, sir, it
25   provokes, and unprovokes: it provokes the desire, but it takes
away the performance. Therefore much drink may be said to be
an equivocator with lechery: it makes him, and it mars him; it
sets him on, and it takes him off; it persuades him, and dis-
heartens him; makes him stand to, and not stand to; in conclu-
30   sion, equivocates him in a sleep, and, giving him the lie, leaves
him.

MACDUFF I believe drink gave thee the lie last night.

PORTER That it did, sir, i' the very throat on me; but I requited
him for his lie; and, I think, being too strong for him, though
35   he took up my legs sometime, yet I made a shift to cast him.

MACDUFF Is thy master stirring?

[*Enter* MACBETH.]
Our knocking has awak'd him; here he comes.

LENNOX   Good morrow, noble sir.

MACBETH   Good morrow, both.

MACDUFF   Is the King stirring, worthy Thane?

MACBETH   Not yet.

MACDUFF   He did command me to call timely on him;   40
I have almost slipp'd the hour.

MACBETH   I'll bring you to him.

MACDUFF   I know this is a joyful trouble to you;
But yet 'tis one.

MACBETH   The labor we delight in physics pain.
This is the door.

MACDUFF   I'll make so bold to call,   45
For 'tis my limited service. [*Exit*.]

LENNOX   Goes the King hence to-day?

MACBETH   He does; he did appoint so.

LENNOX   The night has been unruly. Where we lay,
Our chimneys were blown down; and, as they say,
Lamentings heard i' th' air, strange screams of death,   50
And prophesying, with accents terrible,
Of dire combustion and confus'd events
New hatch'd to th' woeful time. The obscure bird
Clamor'd the livelong night. Some say the earth
Was feverous and did shake.

MACBETH   'Twas a rough night.   55

LENNOX   My young remembrance cannot parallel
A fellow to it.

[*Enter* MACDUFF.]

MACDUFF   O horror, horror, horror! Tongue nor heart
Cannot conceive nor name thee!

MACBETH *and* LENNOX   What's the matter?

MACDUFF   Confusion now hath made his masterpiece!   60
Most sacrilegious murder hath broke ope
The Lord's anointed temple and stole thence
The life o' th' building!

MACBETH   What is't you say? the life?

LENNOX Mean you his Majesty?

65 MACDUFF Approach the chamber, and destroy your sight
With a new Gorgon. Do not bid me speak.
See, and then speak yourselves.

[*Exeunt* MACBETH *and* LENNOX.]

                              Awake, awake!
Ring the alarum bell. Murder and treason!
70 Banquo and Donalbain! Malcolm! awake!
Shake off this downy sleep, death's counterfeit,
And look on death itself! Up, up, and see
The great doom's image! Malcolm! Banquo!
As from your graves rise up and walk like sprites
75 To countenance this horror! Ring the bell!

[*Bell rings. Enter* LADY MACBETH.]

LADY What's the business,
That such a hideous trumpet calls to parley
The sleepers of the house? Speak, speak!

MACDUFF   O gentle lady,
'Tis not for you to hear what I can speak!
80 The repetition in a woman's ear
Would murder as it fell.

[*Enter* BANQUO.]

                              O Banquo, Banquo,
Our royal master's murder'd!

LADY   Woe, alas!
What, in our house?

BANQUO   Too cruel anywhere.
Dear Duff, I prithee contradict thyself
85 And say it is not so.

[*Enter* MACBETH, LENNOX, *and* ROSS.]

MACBETH Had I but died an hour before this chance,
I had liv'd a blessed time; for from this instant
There's nothing serious in mortality;
All is but toys; renown and grace is dead;
90 The wine of life is drawn, and the mere lees
Is left this vault to brag of.

[*Enter* MALCOLM *and* DONALBAIN.]

DONALBAIN   What is amiss?

MACBETH   You are, and do not know't.
  The spring, the head, the fountain of your blood
  Is stopp'd, the very source of it is stopp'd.

MACDUFF   Your royal father's murder'd.

MALCOLM   O, by whom?   95

LENNOX   Those of his chamber, as it seem'd, had done't.
  Their hands and faces were all badg'd with blood;
  So were their daggers, which unwip'd we found
  Upon their pillows.
  They star'd and were distracted. No man's life   100
  Was to be trusted with them.

MACBETH   O, yet I do repent me of my fury
  That I did kill them.

MACDUFF   Wherefore did you so?

MACBETH   Who can be wise, amazed, temperate, and furious,
  Loyal and neutral, in a moment?   No man.   105
  The expedition of my violent love
  Outrun the pauser, reason. Here lay Duncan,
  His silver skin laced with his golden blood,
  And his gash'd stabs look'd like a breach in nature
  For ruin's wasteful entrance; there, the murderers,   110
  Steep'd in the colors of their trade, their daggers
  Unmannerly breech'd with gore. Who could refrain
  That had a heart to love and in that heart
  Courage to make 's love known?

LADY   Help me hence, ho!

MACDUFF   Look to the lady.   115

MALCOLM [aside to DONALBAIN]   Why do we hold our tongues,
  That most may claim this argument for ours?

DONALBAIN [aside to MALCOLM]   What should be spoken here,
      where our fate,
  Hid in an auger hole, may rush and seize us?
  Let's away. Our tears are not yet brew'd.   120

MALCOLM [aside to DONALBAIN]   Nor our strong sorrow
  Upon the foot of motion.

BANQUO   Look to the lady.

[LADY MACBETH is carried out.]

  Line 112. Unmannerly breech'd = crudely covered.

And when we have our naked frailties hid,
125 That suffer in exposure, let us meet
And question this most bloody piece of work,
To know it further. Fears and scruples shake us.
In the great hand of God I stand, and thence
Against the undivulg'd pretense I fight
Of treasonous malice.

MACDUFF   And so do I.

130 ALL   So all.

MACBETH   Let's briefly put on manly readiness
And meet i' th' hall together.

ALL   Well contented.

[*Exeunt all but* MALCOLM *and* DONALBAIN.]

MALCOLM   What will you do? Let's not consort with them.
To show an unfelt sorrow is an office
135 Which the false man does easy. I'll to England.

DONALBAIN   To Ireland I. Our separated fortune
Shall keep us both the safer. Where we are,
There's daggers in men's smiles; the near in blood,
The nearer bloody.

MALCOLM   This murderous shaft that's shot
140 Hath not yet lighted, and our safest way
Is to avoid the aim. Therefore to horse!
And let us not be dainty of leave-taking
But shift away. There's warrant in that theft
Which steals itself when there's no mercy left.

[*Exeunt.*]

Scene Four

[*Inverness. Outside* MACBETH'S *castle.   Enter* ROSS *with an* OLD
MAN.]

OLD MAN   Threescore and ten I can remember well;
Within the volume of which time I have seen
Hours dreadful and things strange; but this sore night
Hath trifled former knowings.

Lines 161-162. The closer the kinship (to the king), the more imminent
the danger.

Ross   Ah, good father,
  Thou seest the heavens, as troubled with man's act,   5
  Threaten his bloody stage. By th' clock 'tis day,
  And yet dark night strangles the traveling lamp.
  Is 't night's predominance, or the day's shame,
  That darkness does the face of earth entomb
  When living light should kiss it?

Old Man   'Tis unnatural,   10
  Even like the deed that's done. On Tuesday last
  A falcon, tow'ring in her pride of place,
  Was by a mousing owl hawk'd at and kill'd.

Ross   And Duncan's horses [a thing most strange and certain],
  Beauteous and swift, the minions of their race,   15
  Turn'd wild in nature, broke their stalls, flung out,
  Contending 'gainst obedience, as they would make
  War with mankind.

Old Man   'Tis said they eat each other.

Ross   They did so, to th' amazement of mine eyes
  That look'd upon't.

[*Enter* Macduff.]

                      Here comes the good Macduff.   20
  How goes the world, sir, now?

Macduff   Why, see you not?

Ross   Is 't known who did this more than bloody deed?

Macduff   Those that Macbeth hath slain.

Ross   Alas, the day!
  What good could they pretend?

Macduff   They were suborn'd.
  Malcolm and Donalbain, the King's two sons,   25
  Are stol'n away and fled, which puts upon them
  Suspicion of the deed.

Ross   'Gainst nature still!
  Thriftless ambition, that wilt ravin up
  Thine own live's means! Then 'tis most like
  The sovereignty will fall upon Macbeth.   30

Macduff   He is already named, and gone to Scone
  To be invested.

Ross   Where is Duncan's body?

Macduff   Carried to Colmekill,

The sacred storehouse of his predecessors
And guardian of their bones.

35 ROSS   Will you to Scone?

MACDUFF   No, cousin, I'll to Fife.

ROSS   Well, I will thither.

MACDUFF   Well, may you see things well done there. Adieu!
Lest your old robes sit easier than our new!

ROSS   Farewell, father.

OLD MAN   God's benison go with you, and with those
That would make good of bad, and friends of foes!

[*Exeunt omnes.*]

ACT THREE

Scene One

[*Forres. The Palace. Enter* BANQUO.]

BANQUO   Thou hast it now—King, Cawdor, Glamis, all,
    As the weird women promis'd; and I fear
    Thou play'dst most foully for't. Yet it was said
    It should not stand in thy posterity,
    But that myself should be the root and father   5
    Of many kings. If there come truth from them
    (As upon thee, Macbeth, their speeches shine),
    Why, by the verities on thee made good,
    May they not be my oracles as well
    And set me up in hope? But, hush, no more!   10

[*Sennet sounded. Enter* MACBETH, *as King;* LADY MACBETH, *as Queen;* LENNOX, ROSS, LORDS, *and* ATTENDANTS.]

MACBETH   Here's our chief guest.

LADY   If he had been forgotten,
    It had been as a gap in our great feast,
    And all-thing unbecoming.

MACBETH   To-night we hold a solemn supper, sir,
    And I'll request your presence.

BANQUO   Let your Highness   15
    Command upon me, to the which my duties
    Are with a most indissoluble tie
    For ever knit.

MACBETH   Ride you this afternoon?

BANQUO   Ay, my good lord.   20

MACBETH   We should have else desir'd your good advice
    (Which still hath been both grave and prosperous)
    In this day's council; but we'll take to-morrow.
    Is 't far you ride?

BANQUO   As far, my lord, as will fill up the time   25
    'Twixt this and supper. Go not my horse the better,
    I must become a borrower of the night
    For a dark hour or twain.

MACBETH   Fail not our feast.

157

BANQUO   My lord, I will not.

30   MACBETH   We hear our bloody cousins are bestow'd
In England and in Ireland, not confessing
Their cruel parricide, filling their hearers
With strange invention. But of that to-morrow,
When therewithal we shall have cause of state
35   Craving us jointly. Hie you to horse. Adieu,
Till you return at night. Goes Fleance with you?

BANQUO   Ay, my good lord. Our time does call upon 's.

MACBETH   I wish your horses swift and sure of foot,
40   And so I do commend you to their backs.
Farewell.

[*Exit* BANQUO.]

Let every man be master of his time
Till seven at night. To make society
The sweeter welcome, we will keep ourself
Till supper time alone. While then, God be with you!

[*Exeunt all but* MACBETH *and a* SERVANT.]

45   Sirrah, a word with you. Attend those men
Our pleasure?

SERVANT   They are, my lord, without the palace gate.

MACBETH   Bring them before us.

[*Exit* SERVANT.]

To be thus is nothing,
But to be safely thus. Our fears in Banquo
50   Stick deep; and in his royalty of nature
Reigns that which would be fear'd. 'Tis much he dares,
And to that dauntless temper of his mind
He hath a wisdom that doth guide his valor
To act in safety. There is none but he
55   Whose being I do fear; and under him
My genius is rebuk'd, as it is said
Mark Antony's was by Cæsar. He chid the sisters
When first they put the name of King upon me,
And bade them speak to him. Then prophet-like,
60   They hail'd him father to a line of kings.
Upon my head they placed a fruitless crown
And put a barren sceptre in my gripe,
Thence to be wrench'd with an unlineal hand,
No son of mine succeeding. If 't be so,
65   For Banquo's issue have I filed my mind;

For them the gracious Duncan have I murder'd;
Put rancors in the vessel of my peace
Only for them, and mine eternal jewel
Given to the common enemy of man
To make them kings, the seed of Banquo kings!   70
Rather than so, come, Fate, into the list,
And champion me to th' utterance! Who's there?

[*Enter* SERVANT *and two* MURDERERS.]

Now go to the door and stay there till we call.

[*Exit* SERVANT.]

Was it not yesterday we spoke together?

MURDERERS   It was, so please your Highness.

MACBETH   Well then, now   75
Have you consider'd of my speeches? Know
That it was he, in the times past, which held you
So under fortune, which you thought had been
Our innocent self. This I made good to you
In our last conference, pass'd in probation with you   80
How you were borne in hand, how cross'd; the instruments;
Who wrought with them; and all things else that might
To half a soul and to a notion craz'd
Say "Thus did Banquo.'

FIRST MURDERER   You made it known to us.

MACBETH   I did so; and went further, which is now   85
Our point of second meeting. Do you find
Your patience so predominant in your nature
That you can let this go? Are you so gospell'd
To pray for this good man and for his issue,
Whose heavy hand hath bow'd you to the grave   90
And beggar'd yours for ever?

FIRST MURDERER   We are men, my liege.

MACBETH   Ay, in the catalogue ye go for men,
As hounds and greyhounds, mongrels, spaniels, curs,
Shoughs, water-rugs, and demi-wolves are clept
All by the name of dogs. The valued file   95
Distinguishes the swift, the slow, the subtle,
The housekeeper, the hunter, every one
According to the gift which bounteous nature
Hath in him closed; whereby he does receive

Line 83. Even to a halfwit and a crazy mind.

100   Particular addition, from the bill
That writes them all alike; and so of men.
Now, if you have a station in the file,
Not i' th' worst rank of manhood, say't;
And I will put that business in your bosoms
105   Whose execution takes your enemy off,
Grapples you to the heart and love of us,
Who wear our health but sickly in his life,
Which in his death were perfect.

SECOND MURDERER   I am one, my liege,
Whom the vile blows and buffets of the world
110   Have so incensed that I am reckless what
I do to spite the world.

FIRST MURDERER   And I another,
So weary with disasters, tugg'd with fortune,
That I would set my life on any chance,
To mend it or be rid on 't.

MACBETH   Both of you
Know Banquo was your enemy.

115 MURDERERS   True, my lord.

MACBETH   So is he mine; and in such bloody distance
That every minute of his being thrusts
Against my near'st of life; and though I could
With barefaced power sweep him from my sight
120   And bid my will avouch it, yet I must not,
For certain friends that are both his and mine,
Whose loves I may not drop, but wail his fall
Who I myself struck down. And thence it is
That I to your assistance do make love,
125   Masking the business from the common eye
For sundry weighty reasons.

SECOND MURDERER   We shall, my lord,
Perform what you command us.

FIRST MURDERER   Though our lives—

MACBETH   Your spirits shine through you.
                            Within this hour at most
I will advise you where to plant yourselves,
130   Acquaint you with the perfect spy o' th' time,
The moment on 't; for't must be done to-night,
And something from the palace; always thought
That I require a clearness; and with him,

Lines 132-133. At all times remembering that you must not involve me.

To leave no rubs nor botches in the work,
Fleance his son, that keeps him company,   135
Whose absence is no less material to me
Than is his father's, must embrace the fate
Of that dark hour. Resolve yourselves apart;
I'll come to you anon.

MURDERERS   We are resolv'd, my lord.

MACBETH   I'll call upon you straight. Abide within.   140

[*Exeunt* MURDERERS.]

It is concluded. Banquo, thy soul's flight,
If it find heaven, must find it out to-night. [*Exit.*]

Scene Two

[*Forres. The Palace. Enter* LADY MACBETH *and a* SERVANT.]

LADY   Is Banquo gone from court?

SERVANT   Ay, madam, but returns again to-night.

LADY   Say to the King I would attend his leisure
For a few words.

SERVANT   Madam, I will. [*Exit.*]

LADY   Naught's had, all's spent,
Where our desire is got without content.   5
'Tis safer to be that which we destroy
Than by destruction dwell in doubtful joy.

[*Enter* MACBETH.]

How now, my lord? Why do you keep alone,
Of sorriest fancies your companions making,
Using those thoughts which should indeed have died   10
With them they think on? Things without all remedy
Should be without regard. What's done is done.

MACBETH   We have scotch'd the snake, not kill'd it.
She'll close, and be herself, whilst our poor malice
Remains in danger of her former tooth.   15
But let the frame of things disjoint, both the worlds suffer,
Ere we will eat our meal in fear and sleep
In the affliction of these terrible dreams
That shake us nightly. Better be with the dead,

20   Whom we, to gain our peace, have sent to peace,
     Than on the torture of the mind to lie
     In restless ecstasy. Duncan is in his grave;
     After life's fitful fever he sleeps well.
     Treason has done his worst. Nor steel nor poison,
25   Malice domestic, foreign levy, nothing,
     Can touch him further.

LADY   Come on.
     Gentle my lord, sleek o'er your rugged looks;
     Be bright and jovial among your guests to-night.

MACBETH   So shall I, love; and so, I pray, be you.
30   Let your remembrance apply to Banquo;
     Present him eminence both with eye and tongue—
     Unsafe the while, that we
     Must lave our honors in these flattering streams
     And make our faces vizards to our hearts,
     Disguising what they are.

35 LADY   You must leave this.

MACBETH   O, full of scorpions is my mind, dear wife!
     Thou know'st that Banquo, and his Fleance, lives.

LADY   But in them Nature's copy's not eterne.

MACBETH   There's comfort yet! They are assailable.
40   Then be thou jocund. Ere the bat hath flown
     His cloister'd flight, ere to black Hecate's summons
     The shard-borne beetle with his drowsy hums
     Hath rung night's yawning peal, there shall be done
     A deed of dreadful note.

LADY   What's to be done?

45 MACBETH   Be innocent of the knowledge, dearest chuck,
     Till thou applaud the deed. Come, seeling night,
     Scarf up the tender eye of pitiful day,
     And with thy bloody and invisible hand
     Cancel and tear to pieces that great bond
50   Which keeps me pale! Light thickens, and the crow
     Makes wing to th' rooky wood.
     Good things of day begin to droop and drowse,
     Whiles night's black agents to their preys do rouse.
     Thou marvel'st at my words; but hold thee still:
55   Things bad begun make strong themselves by ill.
     So prithee go with me.

  [*Exeunt.*]

Scene Three

[Forres. A park near the palace. Enter three MURDERERS.*]*

FIRST MURDERER   But who did bid thee join with us?

THIRD MURDERER   Macbeth.

SECOND MURDERER   He needs not our mistrust, since he delivers
   Our offices, and what we have to do,
   To the direction just.

FIRST MURDERER   Then stand with us.
   The west yet glimmers with some streaks of day.   5
   Now spurs the lated traveller apace
   To gain the timely inn, and near approaches
   The subject of our watch.

THIRD MURDERER   Hark! I hear horses.

BANQUO *[within]*   Give us a light there, ho!

SECOND MURDERER   Then 'tis he! The rest
   That are within the note of expectation   10
   Already are i' th' court.

FIRST MURDERER   His horses go about.

THIRD MURDERER   Almost a mile; but he does usually,
   So all men do, from hence to th' palace gate
   Make it their walk.

[Enter BANQUO, *and* FLEANCE *with a torch.]*

SECOND MURDERER   A light, a light!

THIRD MURDERER   'Tis he.

FIRST MURDERER   Stand to't.   15

BANQUO   It will be rain to-night.

FIRST MURDERER   Let it come down!

[They fall upon BANQUO.*]*

BANQUO   O, treachery! Fly, good Fleance, fly, fly, fly!
   Thou mayst revenge. O slave! *[Dies.]*

*[*FLEANCE *escapes.]*

THIRD MURDERER   Who did strike out the light?

FIRST MURDERER   Was 't not the way?

THIRD MURDERER   There's but one down; the son is fled.

20 SECOND MURDERER   We have lost
      Best half of our affair.

FIRST MURDERER   Well, let's away, and say how much is done.

[*Exeunt.*]

Scene Four

[*Forres. Hall in the palace. Banquet prepared. Enter* MACBETH,
LADY MACBETH, ROSS, LENNOX, LORDS, *and* ATTENDANTS.]

MACBETH   You know your own degrees, sit down. At first
      And last the hearty welcome.

LORDS   Thanks to your Majesty.

MACBETH   Ourself will mingle with society
      And play the humble host.
5   Our hostess keeps her state, but in best time
      We will require her welcome.

LADY   Pronounce it for me, sir, to all our friends,
      For my heart speaks they are welcome.

[FIRST MURDERER *appears at the door.*]

MACBETH   See, they encounter thee with their hearts' thanks.
10   Both sides are even. Here I'll sit i' th' midst.
      Be large in mirth; anon we'll drink a measure
      The table round. [*Goes to the door.*] There's blood upon thy face.

MURDERER   'Tis Banquo's then.

MACBETH   'Tis better thee without than he within.
15   Is he dispatch'd?

MURDERER   My lord, his throat is cut. That I did for him.

MACBETH   Thou art the best o' th' cut-throats! Yet he's good
      That did the like for Fleance. If thou didst it,
      Thou art the nonpareil.

MURDERER   Most royal sir,
20   Fleance is scap'd.

MACBETH [*aside*]   Then comes my fit again. I had else been per-
          fect;
      Whole as the marble, founded as the rock,
      As broad and general as the casing air.

But now I am cabin'd, cribb'd, confin'd, bound in
To saucy doubts and fears.—But Banquo's safe?   25

MURDERER   Ay, my good lord. Safe in a ditch he bides,
With twenty trenched gashes on his head,
The least a death to nature.

MACBETH   Thanks for that!
There the grown serpent lies; the worm that's fled
Hath nature that in time will venom breed,   30
No teeth for th' present. Get thee gone. To-morrow
We'll hear ourselves again.

[*Exit* MURDERER.]

LADY   My royal lord,
You do not give the cheer. The feast is sold
That is not often vouch'd, while 'tis a-making,
'Tis given with welcome. To feed were best at home.   35
From thence, the sauce to meat is ceremony;
Meeting were bare without it.

[*Enter the* GHOST OF BANQUO, *and sits in* MACBETH'S *place.*]

MACBETH   Sweet remembrancer!
Now good digestion wait on appetite,
And health on both!

LENNOX   May't please your Highness sit.

MACBETH   Here had we now our country's honor, roof'd,   40
Were the graced person of our Banquo present;
Who may I rather challenge for unkindness
Than pity for mischance!

ROSS   His absence, sir,
Lays blame upon his promise. Please 't your Highness
To grace us with your royal company.   45

MACBETH   The table's full.

LENNOX   Here is a place reserved, sir.

MACBETH   Where?

LENNOX   Here, my good lord. What is't that moves your Highness?

MACBETH   Which of you have done this?

LORDS   What, my good lord?

MACBETH   Thou canst not say I did it. Never shake   50
Thy gory locks at me.

Line 32. Hear ourselves = talk with each other.

Ross Gentlemen, rise. His Highness is not well.

Lady Sit, worthy friends. My lord is often thus,
And hath been from his youth. Pray you keep seat.
55 The fit is momentary; upon a thought
He will again be well. If much you note him,
You shall offend him and extend his passion.
Feed, and regard him not.—Are you a man?

Macbeth Ay, and a bold one, that dare look on that
Which might appal the devil.

60 Lady   O proper stuff!
This is the very painting of your fear.
This is the air-drawn dagger which you said
Led you to Duncan. O, these flaws and starts
(Impostors to true fear) would well become
65 A woman's story at a winter's fire,
Authorized by her granddam. Shame itself!
Why do you make such faces? When all's done,
You look but on a stool.

Macbeth Prithee see there! behold! look! lo! How say you?
70 Why, what care I? If thou canst nod, speak too.
If charnel houses and our graves must send
Those that we bury back, our monuments
Shall be the maws of kites.

[Ghost *vanishes*.]

Lady What, quite unmann'd in folly?

Macbeth If I stand here, I saw him.

Lady   Fie, for shame!

75 Macbeth Blood hath been shed ere now, i' th' olden time,
Ere humane statute purg'd the gentle weal;
Ay, and since too, murders have been perform'd
Too terrible for the ear. The time has been
That, when the brains were out, the man would die,
80 And there an end! But now they rise again,
With twenty mortal murders on their crowns,
And push us from our stools. This is more strange
Than such a murder is.

Lady   My worthy lord,
Your noble friends do lack you.

Macbeth   I do forget.
85 Do not muse at me, my most worthy friends.
I have a strange infirmity, which is nothing

To those that know me. Come, love and health to all!
Then I'll sit down. Give me some wine, fill full.
I drink to th' general joy o' th' whole table,
And to our dear friend Banquo, whom we miss.   90
Would he were here! To all, and him, we thirst,
And all to all.

LORDS   Our duties, and the pledge.

[*Re-enter* GHOST.]

MACBETH   Avaunt, and quit my sight! Let the earth hide thee!
Thy bones are marrowless, thy blood is cold;
Thou has no speculation in those eyes   95
Which thou dost glare with!

LADY   Think of this, good peers,
But as a thing of custom. 'Tis no other.
Only it spoils the pleasure of the time.

MACBETH   What man dare, I dare.
Approach thou like the rugged Russian bear,   100
The arm'd rhinoceros, or th' Hyrcan tiger;
Take any shape but that, and my firm nerves
Shall never tremble. Or be alive again
And dare me to the desert with thy sword.
If trembling I inhabit then, protest me   105
The baby of a girl. Hence, horrible shadow!
Unreal mock'ry, hence!

[GHOST *vanishes*.]

                        Why, so! Being gone,
I am a man again. Pray you sit still.

LADY   You have displaced the mirth, broke the good meeting
With most admired disorder.

MACBETH   Can such things be,   110
And overcome us like a summer's cloud
Without our special wonder? You make me strange
Even to the disposition that I owe,
When now I think you can behold such sights
And keep the natural ruby of your cheeks   115
When mine is blanch'd with fear.

ROSS   What sights, my lord?

LADY   I pray you speak not. He grows worse and worse;
Question enrages him. At once, good night.
Stand not upon the order of your going,
But go at once.

120 LENNOX   Good night, and better health
    Attend his Majesty!

LADY   A kind good night to all!

[*Exeunt all but* MACBETH *and* LADY MACBETH.]

MACBETH   It will have blood, they say; blood will have blood.
    Stones have been known to move and trees to speak;
    Augurs and understood relations have
125   By maggot-pies and choughs and rooks brought forth
    The secret'st man of blood. What is the night?

LADY   Almost at odds with morning, which is which.

MACBETH   How say'st thou that Macduff denies his person
    At our great bidding?

LADY   Did you send to him, sir?

130 MACBETH   I hear it by the way; but I will send.
    There's not a one of them but in his house
    I keep a servant fee'd. I will to-morrow
    (And betimes I will) unto the Weird Sisters.
    More shall they speak; for now I am bent to know
135   By the worst means the worst. For mine own good
    All causes shall give way. I am in blood
    Stepp'd in so far that, should I wade no more,
    Returning were as tedious as go o'er.
    Strange things I have in head, that will to hand,
140   Which must be acted ere they may be scann'd.

LADY   You lack the season of all natures, sleep.

MACBETH   Come, we'll to sleep. My strange and self-abuse
    Is the initiate fear that wants hard use.
    We are yet but young in deed.

[*Exeunt.*]

Scene Five

[*A heath. Thunder. Enter the three* WITCHES, *meeting* HECATE.]

FIRST WITCH   Why, how now, Hecate? You look angerly.

HECATE   Have I not reason, beldams as you are,
    Saucy and overbold? How did you dare

Line 142. Self-abuse = self-delusion; the reference is to the vision of
Banquo's ghost.

To trade and traffic with Macbeth
In riddles and affairs of death;   5
And I, the mistress of your charms,
The close contriver of all harms,
Was never call'd to bear my part
Or show the glory of our art?
And, which is worse, all you have done   10
Hath been but for a wayward son,
Spiteful and wrathful, who, as others do,
Loves for his own ends, not for you.
But make amends now. Get you gone
And at the pit of Acheron   15
Meet me i' th' morning. Thither he
Will come to know his destiny.
Your vessels and your spells provide,
Your charms and everything beside.
I am for th' air. This night I'll spend   20
Unto a dismal and a fatal end.
Great business must be wrought ere noon.
Upon the corner of the moon
There hangs a vaporous drop profound.
I'll catch it ere it come to ground;   25
And that, distill'd by magic sleights,
Shall raise such artificial sprites
As by the strength of their illusion
Shall draw him on to his confusion.
He shall spurn fate, scorn death, and bear   30
His hopes 'bove wisdom, grace, and fear;
And you all know security
Is mortals' chiefest enemy.

[*Music and a song within.* 'Come away, come away,' &c.]

Hark! I am call'd. My little spirit, see,
Sits in a foggy cloud and stays for me. [*Exit.*]   35

FIRST WITCH   Come, let's make haste. She'll soon be back again.

[*Exeunt.*]

Scene Six

[*Forres. The palace. Enter* LENNOX *and another* LORD.]

LENNOX   My former speeches have but hit your thoughts,
Which can interpret farther. Only I say
Things have been strangely borne. The gracious Duncan

Was pitied of Macbeth. Marry, he was dead!
5 And the right valiant Banquo walk'd too late;
Whom, you may say (if 't please you) Fleance kill'd,
For Fleance fled. Men must not walk too late.
Who cannot want the thought how monstrous
It was for Malcolm and for Donalbain
10 To kill their gracious father? Damned fact!
How it did grieve Macbeth! Did he not straight,
In pious rage, the two delinquents tear,
That were the slaves of drink and thralls of sleep?
Was not that nobly done? Ay, and wisely too!
15 For 'twould have anger'd any heart alive
To hear the men deny't. So that I say
He has borne all things well; and I do think
That, had he Duncan's sons under his key
(As, an't please heaven, he shall not), they should find
20 What 'twere to kill a father. So should Fleance.
But peace! for from broad words, and 'cause he fail'd
His presence at the tyrant's feasts, I hear
Macduff lives in disgrace. Sir, can you tell
Where he bestows himself?

LORD   The son of Duncan,
25 From whom this tyrant holds the due of birth,
Lives in the English court, and is received
Of the most pious Edward with such grace
That the malevolence of fortune nothing
Takes from his high respect. Thither Macduff
30 Is gone to pray the holy King upon his aid
To wake Northumberland and warlike Siward;
That by the help of these (with Him above
To ratify the work) we may again
Give to our tables meat, sleep to our nights,
35 Free from our feasts and banquets bloody knives,
Do faithful homage and receive free honors—
All which we pine for now. And this report
Hath so exasperate the King that he
Prepares for some attempt of war.

LENNOX   Sent he to Macduff?

40 LORD He did; and with an absolute 'Sir, not I!'
The cloudy messenger turns me his back
And hums, as who should say, 'You'll rue the time
That clogs me with this answer.'

LENNOX   And that well might
Advise him to a caution t' hold what distance

His wisdom can provide. Some holy angel   45
Fly to the court of England and unfold
His message ere he come, that a swift blessing
May soon return to this our suffering country
Under a hand accursed!

LORD   I'll send my prayers with him.

[*Exeunt.*]

ACT FOUR

Scene One

[*A cavern. In the middle, a cauldron boiling. Thunder. Enter the three* WITCHES.]

FIRST WITCH   Thrice the brinded cat hath mew'd.

SECOND WITCH   Thrice and once the hedge-pig whin'd.

THIRD WITCH   Harpier cries: 'tis time, 'tis time.

FIRST WITCH   Round about the cauldron go;
5   In the poison'd entrails throw.
Toad, that under cold stone
Days and nights has thirty-one
Swelt'red venom sleeping got,
Boil thou first i' th' charmed pot.

10   ALL   Double, double, toil and trouble;
Fire burn, and cauldron bubble.

SECOND WITCH   Fillet of a fenny snake,
In the cauldron boil and bake;
Eye of newt, and toe of frog,
15   Wool of bat, and tongue of dog,
Adder's fork, and blindworm's sting,
Lizard's leg, and howlet's wing;
For a charm of powerful trouble
Like a hell-broth boil and bubble.

20   ALL   Double, double, toil and trouble;
Fire burn, and cauldron bubble.

THIRD WITCH   Scale of dragon, tooth of wolf,
Witch's mummy, maw and gulf
Of the ravin'd salt-sea shark,
25   Root of hemlock, digg'd i' th' dark;
Liver of blaspheming Jew,
Gall of goat, and slips of yew
Sliver'd in the moon's eclipse;
Nose of Turk and Tartar's lips;
30   Finger of birth-strangled babe
Ditch-deliver'd by a drab:
Make the gruel thick and slab.
Add thereto a tiger's chaudron
For th' ingredients of our cauldron.

172

ALL   Double, double, toil and trouble;   35
    Fire burn, and cauldron bubble.

SECOND WITCH   Cool it with a baboon's blood,
    Then the charm is firm and good.

[*Enter* HECATE.]

HECATE   O, well done! I commend your pains,
    And every one shall share i' th' gains.   40
    And now about the cauldron sing
    Like elves and fairies in a ring,
    Enchanting all that you put in.

[*Music and a song,* 'Black spirits,' &c. *Exit* HECATE.]

SECOND WITCH   By the pricking of my thumbs,
    Something wicked this way comes.   45
            Open locks,
            Whoever knocks!

[*Enter* MACBETH.]

MACBETH   How now, you secret, black, and midnight hags?
    What is 't you do?

ALL   A deed without a name.

MACBETH   I conjure you by that which you profess   50
    (Howe'er you come to know it), answer me.
    Though you untie the winds and let them fight
    Against the churches; though the yeasty waves
    Confound and swallow navigation up;
    Though bladed corn be lodged and trees blown down;   55
    Though castles topple on their warders' heads;
    Though palaces and pyramids do slope
    Their heads to their foundations; though the treasure
    Of nature's germens tumble all together,
    Even till destruction sicken—answer me   60
    To what I ask you.

FIRST WITCH   Speak.

SECOND WITCH   Demand.

THIRD WITCH   We'll answer.

FIRST WITCH   Say, if th' hadst rather hear it from our mouths
    Or from our masters.

MACBETH   Call 'em! Let me see 'em.

FIRST WITCH   Pour in sow's blood, that hath eaten
65   Her nine farrow; grease that's sweaten
From the murderer's gibbet throw
Into the flame.

ALL   Come, high or low;
Thyself and office deftly show!

[*Thunder.* FIRST APPARITION, *an* ARMED HEAD.]

MACBETH   Tell me, thou unknown power—

FIRST WITCH   He knows thy thought.
70   Hear his speech, but say thou naught.

FIRST APPARITION   Macbeth! Macbeth! Macbeth! Beware Macduff;
Beware the Thane of Fife. Dismiss me. Enough. [*He descends.*]

MACBETH   Whate'er thou art, for thy good caution thanks!
Thou hast harp'd my fear aright. But one word more—

75   FIRST WITCH   He will not be commanded. Here's another,
More potent than the first.

[*Thunder.* SECOND APPARITION, *a* BLOODY CHILD.]

SECOND APPARITION   Macbeth! Macbeth! Macbeth!

MACBETH   Had I three ears, I'd hear thee.

SECOND APPARITION   Be bloody, bold, and resolute; laugh to scorn
80   The power of man, for none of woman born
Shall harm Macbeth. [*Descends.*]

MACBETH   Then live, Macduff. What need I fear of thee?
But yet I'll make assurance double sure
And take a bond of fate. Thou shalt not live!
85   That I may tell pale-hearted fear it lies
And sleep in spite of thunder.

[*Thunder.* THIRD APPARITION, *a* CHILD CROWNED, *with a tree in
his hand.*]
                                What is this
That rises like the issue of a king
And wears upon his baby-brow the round
And top of sovereignty?

ALL   Listen, but speak not to't.

90   THIRD APPARITION   Be lion-mettled, proud, and take no care
Who chafes, who frets, or where conspirers are.
Macbeth shall never vanquish'd be until

Great Birnam Wood to high Dunsinane Hill
Shall come against him. [*Descends.*]

MACBETH   That will never be.
  Who can impress the forest, bid the tree   95
  Unfix his earth-bound root? Sweet bodements, good!
  Rebellion's head rise never till the Wood
  Of Birnam rise, and our high placed Macbeth'
  Shall live the lease of nature, pay his breath
  To time and mortal custom. Yet my heart   100
  Throbs to know one thing. Tell me, if your art
  Can tell so much—shall Banquo's issue ever
  Reign in this kingdom?

ALL   Seek to know no more.

MACBETH   I will be satisfied. Deny me this,
  And an eternal curse fall on you! Let me know.   105
  Why sinks that cauldron? and what noise is this?

[*Hautboys.*]

FIRST WITCH   Show!

SECOND WITCH   Show!

THIRD WITCH   Show!

ALL   Show his eyes, and grieve his heart!   110
  Come like shadows, so depart!

[*A show of eight* KINGS, *the last with a glass in his hand; and*
  BANQUO'S GHOST *following.*]

MACBETH   Thou are too like the spirit of Banquo. Down!
  Thy crown does sear mine eyeballs. And thy hair,
  Thou other gold-bound brow, is like the first.
  A third is like the former. Filthy hags!   115
  Why do you show me this? A fourth? Start, eyes!
  What, will the line stretch out to th' crack of doom?
  Another yet? A seventh? I'll see no more.
  And yet the eighth appears, who bears a glass
  Which shows me many more; and some I see   120
  That twofold balls and treble sceptres carry.
  Horrible sight! Now I see 'tis true;
  For the blood-bolter'd Banquo smiles upon me
  And points at them for his. [APPARITIONS *vanish.*] What? Is this
    so?

Line 119. Glass = mirror. Same in preceding stage direction.

125 FIRST WITCH Ay, sir, all this is so. But why
    Stands Macbeth thus amazedly?
    Come, sisters, cheer we up his sprites
    And show the best of our delights.
    I'll charm the air to give a sound
130   While you perform your antic round,
    That this great king may kindly say
    Our duties did his welcome pay.

[*Music. The* WITCHES *dance, and vanish.*]

MACBETH Where are they? Gone? Let this pernicious hour
    Stand aye accursed in the calendar!
    Come in, without there!

[*Enter* LENNOX.]

135 LENNOX   What's your Grace's will?

MACBETH Saw you the Weird Sisters?

LENNOX   No, my lord.

MACBETH Came they not by you?

LENNOX   No indeed, my lord.

MACBETH Infected be the air whereon they ride,
    And damn'd all those that trust them! I did hear
140   The galloping of horse. Who was't came by?

LENNOX 'Tis two or three, my lord, that bring you word
    Macduff is fled to England.

MACBETH   Fled to England?

LENNOX Ay, my good lord.

MACBETH [*aside*] Time, thou anticipat'st my dread exploits.
145   The flighty purpose never is o'ertook
    Unless the deed go with it. From this moment
    The very firstlings of my heart shall be
    The firstlings of my hand. And even now,
    To crown my thoughts with acts, be it thought and done!
150   The castle of Macduff I will surprise,
    Seize upon Fife, give to the edge o' th' sword
    His wife, his babes, and all unfortunate souls
    That trace him in his line. No boasting like a fool!
    This deed I'll do before this purpose cool.
155   But no more sights!—Where are these gentlemen?
    Come, bring me where they are.

[*Exeunt.*]

Scene Two

[*Fife.* MACDUFF'S *castle. Enter* MACDUFF'S WIFE, *her* SON, *and* ROSS.]

WIFE   What had he done to make him fly the land?

ROSS   You must have patience, madam.

WIFE   He had none.
 His flight was madness. When our actions do not,
 Our fears do make us traitors.

ROSS   You know not
 Whether it was his wisdom or his fear.   5

WIFE   Wisdom? To leave his wife, to leave his babes,
 His mansion, and his titles, in a place
 From whence himself does fly? He loves us not,
 He wants the natural touch. For the poor wren
 (The most diminutive of birds) will fight,   10
 Her young ones in her nest, against the owl.
 All is the fear, and nothing is the love,
 As little is the wisdom, where the flight
 So runs against all reason.

ROSS   My dearest coz,
 I pray you school yourself. But for your husband,   15
 He is noble, wise, judicious, and best knows
 The fits o' th' season. I dare not speak much further;
 But cruel are the times, when we are traitors
 And do not know ourselves; when we hold rumor
 From what we fear, yet know not what we fear,   20
 But float upon a wild and violent sea
 Each way and none. I take my leave of you.
 Shall not be long but I'll be here again.
 Things at the worst will cease, or else climb upward
 To what they were before.—My pretty cousin,   25
 Blessing upon you!

WIFE   Father'd he is, and yet he's fatherless.

ROSS   I am so much a fool, should I stay longer,
 It would be my disgrace and your discomfort.
 I take my leave at once. [*Exit.*]

WIFE   Sirrah, your father's dead;   30
 And what will you do now? How will you live?

SON   As birds do, mother.

WIFE   What, with worms and flies?

SON   With what I get, I mean; and so do they.

WIFE   Poor bird! thou'dst never fear the net nor lime,
35   The pitfall nor the gin.

SON   Why should I, mother? Poor birds they are not set for.
My father is not dead, for all your saying.

WIFE   Yes, he is dead. How wilt thou do for a father?

SON   Nay, how will you do for a husband?

40 WIFE   Why, I can buy me twenty at any market.

SON   Then you'll buy 'em to sell again.

WIFE   Thou speak'st with all thy wit; and yet, i' faith,
With wit enough for thee.

SON   Was my father a traitor, mother?

45 WIFE   Ay, that he was!

SON   What is a traitor?

WIFE   Why, one that swears, and lies.

SON   And be all traitors that do so?

WIFE   Every one that does so is a traitor and must be hanged.

50 SON   And must they all be hanged that swear and lie?

WIFE   Every one.

SON   Who must hang them?

WIFE   Why, the honest men.

SON   Then the liars and swearers are fools; for there are liars and
55   swearers enow to beat the honest men and hang up them.

WIFE   Now God help thee, poor monkey! But how wilt thou do
for a father?

SON   If he were dead, you'ld weep for him. If you would not, it
were a good sign that I should quickly have a new father.

60 WIFE   Poor prattler, how thou talk'st!

[*Enter a* MESSENGER.]

MESSENGER   Bless you, fair dame! I am not to you known,
Though in your state of honor I am perfect.
I doubt some danger does approach you nearly.
If you will take a homely man's advice,
65   Be not found here. Hence with your little ones!
To fright you thus methinks I am too savage;

To do worse to you were fell cruelty,
Which is too nigh your person. Heaven preserve you!
I dare abide no longer. [*Exit.*]

WIFE   Whither should I fly?
  I have done no harm. But I remember now   70
  I am in this earthly world, where to do harm
  Is often laudable, to do good sometime
  Accounted dangerous folly. Why then, alas,
  Do I put up that womanly defense
  To say I have done no harm?—What are these faces?   75

[*Enter* MURDERERS.]

MURDERER   Where is your husband?

WIFE   I hope, in no place so unsanctified
  Where such as thou mayst find him.

MURDERER   He's a traitor.

SON   Thou liest, thou shag-hair'd villain!

MURDERER   What, you egg!
  [*Stabs him.*] Young fry of treachery!

SON   He has kill'd me, mother.   80
  Run away, I pray you! [*Dies.*]

[*Exit* LADY MACDUFF, *crying 'Murder!' and pursued by the* MURDER-
ERS.]

Scene Three

[*England. Before* KING EDWARD'S *palace. Enter* MALCOLM *and*
MACDUFF.]

MALCOLM   Let us seek out some desolate shade, and there
  Weep our sad bosoms empty.

MACDUFF   Let us rather
  Hold fast the mortal sword and, like good men,
  Bestride our downfall'n birthdom. Each new morn
  New widows howl, new orphans cry, new sorrows   5
  Strike heaven on the face, that it resounds
  As if it felt with Scotland and yell'd out
  Like syllable of dolor.

MALCOLM   What I believe, I'll wail;
  What know, believe; and what I can redress,

10 As I shall find the time to friend, I will.
What you have spoke, it may be so perchance.
This tyrant, whose sole name blisters our tongues,
Was once thought honest; you have loved him well;
He hath not touched you yet. I am young; but something
15 You may deserve of him through me, and wisdom
To offer up a weak, poor, innocent lamb
T' appease an angry god.

MACDUFF   I am not treacherous.

MALCOLM   But Macbeth is.
A good and virtuous nature may recoil
20 In an imperial charge. But I shall crave your pardon.
That which you are, my thoughts cannot transpose.
Angels are bright still, though the brightest fell.
Though all things foul would wear the brows of grace,
Yet grace must still look so.

MACDUFF   I have lost my hopes.

25 MALCOLM   Perchance even there where I did find my doubts.
Why in that rawness left you wife and child,
Those precious motives, those strong knots of love,
Without leave-taking? I pray you,
Let not my jealousies be your dishonors,
30 But mine own safeties. You may be rightly just,
Whatever I shall think.

MACDUFF   Bleed, bleed, poor country!
Great tyranny, lay thou thy basis sure,
For goodness dare not check thee! Wear thou thy wrongs;
The title is affeer'd! Fare thee well, lord.
35 I would not be the villain that thou think'st
For the whole space that's in the tyrant's grasp
And the rich East to boot.

MALCOLM   Be not offended.
I speak not as in absolute fear of you.
I think our country sinks beneath the yoke,
40 It weeps, it bleeds, and each new day a gash
Is added to her wounds. I think withal
There would be hands uplifted in my right;
And here from gracious England have I offer
Of goodly thousands. But, for all this,
45 When I shall tread upon the tyrant's head
Or wear it on my sword, yet my poor country

Lines 14-15. But some reward might come to you through injuring me.
Line 34. Affeer'd = assured.

Shall have more vices than it had before,
More suffer and more sundry ways than ever,
By him that shall succeed.

MACDUFF   What should he be?

MALCOLM   It is myself I mean; in whom I know   50
   All the particulars of vice so grafted
   That, when they shall be open'd, black Macbeth
   Will seem as pure as snow, and the poor state
   Esteem him as a lamb, being compar'd
   With my confineless harms.

MACDUFF   Not in the legions   55
   Of horrid hell can come a devil more damn'd
   In evils to top Macbeth.

MALCOLM   I grant him bloody,
   Luxurious, avaricious, false, deceitful,
   Sudden, malicious, smacking of every sin
   That has a name. But there's no bottom, none,   60
   In my voluptuousness. Your wives, your daughters,
   Your matrons, and your maids could not fill up
   The cistern of my lust; and my desire
   All continent impediments would o'erbear
   That did oppose my will. Better Macbeth   65
   Than such an one to reign.

MACDUFF   Boundless intemperance
   In nature is a tyranny. It hath been
   Th' untimely emptying of the happy throne
   And fall of many kings. But fear not yet
   To take upon you what is yours. You may   70
   Convey your pleasures in a spacious plenty,
   And yet seem cold—the time you may so hoodwink.
   We have willing dames enough. There cannot be
   That vulture in you to devour so many
   As will to greatness dedicate themselves,   75
   Finding it so inclin'd.

MALCOLM   With this there grows
   In my most ill-composed affection such
   A stanchless avarice that, were I King,
   I should cut off the nobles for their lands,
   Desire his jewels, and this other's house,   80
   And my more-having would be as a sauce
   To make me hunger more, that I should forge
   Quarrels unjust against the good and loyal,
   Destroying them for wealth.

MACDUFF   This avarice
85   Sticks deeper, grows with more pernicious root
Than summer-seeming lust; and it hath been
The sword of our slain kings. Yet do not fear.
Scotland hath foisons to fill up your will
Of your mere own. All these are portable,
90   With other graces weigh'd.

MALCOLM   But I have none. The king-becoming graces,
As justice, verity, temperance, stableness,
Bounty, perseverance, mercy, lowliness,
Devotion, patience, courage, fortitude,
95   I have no relish of them, but abound
In the division of each several crime,
Acting it many ways. Nay, had I power, I should
Pour the sweet milk of concord into hell,
Uproar the universal peace, confound
All unity on earth.

100   MACDUFF   O Scotland, Scotland!

MALCOLM   If such a one be fit to govern, speak.
I am as I have spoken.

MACDUFF   Fit to govern?
No, not to live. O nation miserable,
With an untitled tyrant bloody-scepter'd,
105   When shalt thou see thy wholesome days again,
Since that the truest issue of thy throne
By his own interdiction stands accurs'd
And does blaspheme his breed? Thy royal father
Was a most sainted king; the queen that bore thee,
110   Oftener upon her knees than on her feet,
Died every day she lived. Fare thee well!
These evils thou repeat'st upon thyself
Have banish'd me from Scotland. O my breast,
Thy hope ends here!

MALCOLM   Macduff, this noble passion,
115   Child of integrity, hath from my soul
Wiped the black scruples, reconciled my thoughts
To thy good truth and honor. Devilish Macbeth
By many of these trains hath sought to win me
Into his power; and modest wisdom plucks me
120   From over-credulous haste; but God above
Deal between thee and me! for even now
I put myself to thy direction and
Unspeak mine own detraction, here abjure

The taints and blames I laid upon myself
For strangers to my nature. I am yet   125
Unknown to woman, never was forsworn,
Scarcely have coveted what was mine own,
At no time broke my faith, would not betray
The devil to his fellow, and delight
No less in truth than life. My first false speaking   130
Was this upon myself. What I am truly,
Is thine and my poor country's to command;
Whither indeed, before thy here-approach,
Old Siward with ten thousand warlike men
Already at a point was setting forth.   135
Now we'll together; and the chance of goodness
Be like our warranted quarrel! Why are you silent?

MACDUFF   Such welcome and unwelcome things at once
'Tis hard to reconcile.

[*Enter a* DOCTOR.]

MALCOLM   Well, more anon. Comes the King forth, I pray you?   140

DOCTOR   Ay, sir. There are a crew of wretched souls
That stay his cure. Their malady convinces
The great assay of art; but at his touch,
Such sanctity hath heaven given his hand,
They presently amend.

MALCOLM   I thank you, doctor.   145

[*Exit* DOCTOR.]

MACDUFF   What's the disease he means?

MALCOLM   'Tis call'd the evil:
A most miraculous work in this good king,
Which often since my here-remain in England
I have seen him do. How he solicits heaven
Himself best knows; but strangely-visited people,   150
All swol'n and ulcerous, pitiful to the eye,
The mere despair of surgery, he cures,
Hanging a golden stamp about their necks,
Put on with holy prayers; and 'tis spoken,
To the succeeding royalty he leaves   155
The healing benediction. With this strange virtue,
He hath a heavenly gift of prophecy,

Lines 142-143. Convinces the great assay of art = resists efforts at medical treatment.

And sundry blessings hang about his throne
That speak him full of grace.

[*Enter* Ross.]

MACDUFF   See who comes here.

160   MALCOLM   My countryman; but yet I know him not.

MACDUFF   My ever gentle cousin, welcome hither.

MALCOLM   I know him now. Good God betimes remove
The means that makes us strangers!

ROSS   Sir, amen.

MACDUFF   Stands Scotland where it did?

ROSS   Alas, poor country,
165   Almost afraid to know itself! It cannot
Be call'd our mother, but our grave; where nothing,
But who knows nothing, is once seen to smile;
Where sighs and groans, and shrieks that rent the air,
Are made, not mark'd; where violent sorrow seems
170   A modern ecstasy. The dead man's knell
Is there scarce ask'd for who; and good men's lives
Expire before the flowers in their caps,
Dying or ere they sicken.

MACDUFF   O, relation
Too nice, and yet too true!

MALCOLM   What's the newest grief?

175   ROSS   That of an hour's age doth hiss the speaker;
Each minute teems a new one.

MACDUFF   How does my wife?

ROSS   Why, well.

MACDUFF   And all my children?

ROSS   Well too.

MACDUFF   The tyrant has not batter'd at their peace?

ROSS   No; they were well at peace when I did leave 'em.

180   MACDUFF   Be not a niggard of your speech. How goes't?

ROSS   When I came hither to transport the tidings

    Line 163. What keeps us apart—that is, Macbeth.
    Line 166. Nothing = no one.
    Line 170. Modern ecstasy = an ordinary feeling.
    Lines 173-174. Relation too nice = report too accurate.

Which I have heavily borne, there ran a rumor
Of many worthy fellows that were out;
Which was to my belief witness'd the rather
For that I saw the tyrant's power afoot. 185
Now is the time of help. Your eye in Scotland
Would create soldiers, make our women fight
To doff their dire distresses.

MALCOLM   Be 't their comfort
We are coming thither. Gracious England hath
Lent us good Siward and ten thousand men. 190
An older and a better soldier none
That Christendom gives out.

ROSS   Would I could answer
This comfort with the like! But I have words
That would be howl'd out in the desert air,
Where hearing should not latch them.

MACDUFF   What concern they? 195
The general cause? or is it a fee-grief
Due to some single breast?

ROSS   No mind that's honest
But in it shares some woe, though the main part
Pertains to you alone.

MACDUFF   If it be mine,
Keep it not from me, quickly let me have it. 200

ROSS   Let not your ears despise my tongue for ever,
Which shall possess them with the heaviest sound
That ever yet they heard.

MACDUFF   Humh! I guess at it.

ROSS   Your castle is surprised; your wife and babes
Savagely slaughter'd. To relate the manner, 205
Were, on the quarry of these murder'd deer,
To add the death of you.

MALCOLM   Merciful heaven!
What, man! Ne'er pull your hat upon your brows.
Give sorrow words. The grief that does not speak
Whispers the o'erfraught heart and bids it break. 210

MACDUFF   My children too?

Line 183. Out = in rebellion; "out in the hills."
Line 184. Power afoot = army active.
Line 186. Eye = appearance, presence.
Line 196. Fee = private.

Ross   Wife, children, servants, all
  That could be found.

MACDUFF   And I must be from thence?
  My wife kill'd too?

Ross   I have said.

MALCOLM   Be comforted.
  Let's make us medicines of our great revenge
215 To cure this deadly grief.

MACDUFF   He has no children. All my pretty ones?
  Did you say all? O hell-kite! All?
  What, all my pretty chickens and their dam
  At one fell swoop?

MALCOLM   Dispute it like a man.

220 MACDUFF   I shall do so;
  But I must also feel it as a man.
  I cannot but remember such things were
  That were most precious to me. Did heaven look on
  And would not take their part? Sinful Macduff,
225 They were all struck for thee! Naught that I am,
  Not for their own demerits, but for mine,
  Fell slaughter on their souls. Heaven rest them now!

MALCOLM   Be this the whetstone of your sword. Let grief
  Convert to anger; blunt not the heart, enrage it.

230 MACDUFF   O, I could play the woman with mine eyes
  And braggart with my tongue! But, gentle heavens,
  Cut short all intermission. Front to front
  Bring thou this fiend of Scotland and myself.
  Within my sword's length set him. If he scape,
  Heaven forgive him too!

235 MALCOLM   This tune goes manly.
  Come, go we to the King. Our power is ready;
  Our lack is nothing but our leave. Macbeth
  Is ripe for shaking, and the powers above
  Put on their instruments. Receive what cheer you may.
240 The night is long that never finds the day.

  [*Exeunt.*]

ACT FIVE

Scene One

[*Dunsinane.* MACBETH'S *castle. Enter a* DOCTOR OF PHYSIC *and a* WAITING-GENTLEWOMAN.]

DOCTOR   I have two nights watched with you, but can perceive no truth in your report. When was it she last walked?

GENTLEWOMAN   Since his Majesty went into the field I have seen her rise from her bed, throw her nightgown upon her, unlock her closet, take forth paper, write upon 't, read it, afterwards seal   5
it, and again return to bed; yet all this while in a most fast sleep.

DOCTOR   A great perturbation in nature, to receive at once the benefit of sleep and do the effects of watching! In this slumb'ry agitation, besides her walking and other actual performances, what, at any time, have you heard her say?   10

GENTLEWOMAN   That, sir, which I will not report after her.

DOCTOR   You may to me, and 'tis most meet you should.

GENTLEWOMAN   Neither to you nor any one, having no witness to confirm my speech.

[*Enter* LADY MACBETH, *with a taper.*]

Lo you, here she comes! This is her very guise, and, upon my   15
life, fast asleep! Observe her; stand close.

DOCTOR   How came she by that light?

GENTLEWOMAN   Why, it stood by her. She has light by her continually. 'Tis her command.

DOCTOR   You see her eyes are open.   20

GENTLEWOMAN   Ay; but their sense is shut.

DOCTOR   What is it she does now? Look how she rubs her hands.

GENTLEWOMAN   It is an accustomed action with her, to seem thus washing her hands. I have known her continue in this a quarter of an hour.   25

LADY   Yet here's a spot.

DOCTOR   Hark, she speaks! I will set down what comes from her, to satisfy my remembrance the more strongly.

LADY   Out, damned spot! out, I say! One; two. Why then 'tis time

187

30 to do 't. Hell is murky. Fie, my lord, fie! a soldier, and afeard?
What need we fear who knows it, when none can call our power
to account? Yet who would have thought the old man to have
had so much blood in him?

DOCTOR   Do you mark that?

35 LADY   The Thane of Fife had a wife. Where is she now? What,
will these hands ne'er be clean? No more o' that, my lord, no
more o' that! You mar all with this starting.

DOCTOR   Go to, go to! You have known what you should not.

GENTLEWOMAN   She has spoke what she should not, I am sure of
40 that. Heaven knows what she has known.

LADY   Here's the smell of the blood still. All the perfumes of
Arabia will not sweeten this little hand. Oh, oh, oh!

DOCTOR   What a sigh is there! The heart is sorely charged.

GENTLEWOMAN   I would not have such a heart in my bosom for
45 the dignity of the whole body.

DOCTOR   Well, well, well.

GENTLEWOMAN   Pray God it be, sir.

DOCTOR   This disease is beyond my practice. Yet I have known
those which have walked in their sleep who have died holily in
50 their beds.

LADY   Wash your hands, put on your nightgown, look not so pale!
I tell you yet again, Banquo's buried. He cannot come out on 's
grave.

DOCTOR   Even so?

55 LADY   To bed, to bed! There's knocking at the gate. Come, come,
come, come, give me your hand! What's done cannot be undone.
To bed, to bed, to bed. [*Exit*.]

DOCTOR   Will she go now to bed?

GENTLEWOMAN   Directly.

60 DOCTOR   Foul whisperings are abroad. Unnatural deeds
Do breed unnatural troubles. Infected minds
To their deaf pillows will discharge their secrets.
More needs she the divine than the physician.
God, God forgive us all! Look after her;
65 Remove from her the means of all annoyance,
And still keep eyes upon her. So good night.
My mind she has mated, and amazed my sight.
I think, but dare not speak.

GENTLEWOMAN   Good night, good doctor.

[*Exeunt.*]

Scene Two

[*The country near Dunsinane. Drum and Colors. Enter* MENTEITH,
CAITHNESS, ANGUS, LENNOX, SOLDIERS.]

MENTEITH   The English power is near, led on by Malcolm,
His uncle Siward, and the good Macduff.
Revenges burn in them; for their dear causes
Would to the bleeding and the grim alarm
Excite the mortified man.

ANGUS   Near Birnam Wood   5
Shall we well meet them; that way are they coming.

CAITHNESS   Who knows if Donalbain be with his brother?

LENNOX   For certain, sir, he is not. I have a file
Of all the gentry. There is Siward's son
And many unrough youths that even now   10
Protest their first of manhood.

MENTEITH   What does the tyrant?

CAITHNESS   Great Dunsinane he strongly fortifies.
Some say he's mad; others, that lesser hate him,
Do call it valiant fury; but for certain
He cannot buckle his distemper'd cause   15
Within the belt of rule.

ANGUS   Now does he feel
His secret murders sticking on his hands.
Now minutely revolts upbraid his faith-breach.
Those he commands move only in command,
Nothing in love. Now does he feel his title   20
Hang loose about him, like a giant's robe
Upon a dwarfish thief.

MENTEITH   Who then shall blame
His pester'd senses to recoil and start,
When all that is within him does condemn
Itself for being there?

CAITHNESS   Well, march we on   25
To give obedience where 'tis truly owed.
Meet we the medicine of the sickly weal;

Line 27. Let us meet Malcolm, who will cure the sick kingdom.

And with him pour we in our country's purge
Each drop of us.

LENNOX   Or so much as it needs
5   To dew the sovereign flower and drown the weeds.
Make we our march towards Birnam.

[*Exeunt, marching.*]

Scene Three

[*Dunsinane. A room in the castle. Enter* MACBETH, DOCTOR, *and*
ATTENDANTS.]

MACBETH   Bring me no more reports. Let them fly all!
Till Birnam Wood remove to Dunsinane,
I cannot taint with fear. What's the boy Malcolm?
Was he not born of woman? The spirits that know
10   All mortal consequences have pronounced me thus:
'Fear not, Macbeth. No man that's born of woman
Shall e'er have power upon thee.' Then fly, false thanes,
And mingle with the English epicures.
The mind I sway by and the heart I bear
15   Shall never sag with doubt nor shake with fear.

[*Enter* SERVANT.]

The devil damn thee black, thou cream-faced loon!
Where got'st thou that goose look?

SERVANT   There is ten thousand—

MACBETH   Geese, villain?

SERVANT   Soldiers, sir.

MACBETH   Go prick thy face and over-red thy fear,
20   Thou lily-liver'd boy. What soldiers, patch?
Death of thy soul! Those linen cheeks of thine
Are counsellors to fear. What soldiers, whey-face?

SERVANT   The English force, so please you.

MACBETH   Take thy face hence.

[*Exit* SERVANT.]

                                 Seyton!—I am sick at heart,
30   When I behold—Seyton, I say!—This push
Will cheer me ever, or disseat me now.

I have lived long enough. My way of life
Is fallen into the sere, the yellow leaf;
And that which should accompany old age,
As honor, love, obedience, troops of friends,   25
I must not look to have; but, in their stead,
Curses not loud but deep, mouth-honor, breath,
Which the poor heart would fain deny, and dare not.
Seyton!

[*Enter* SEYTON.]

SEYTON   What's your gracious pleasure?

MACBETH   What news more?   30

SEYTON   All is confirmed, my lord, which was reported.

MACBETH   I'll fight, till from my bones my flesh be hacked.
Give me my armor.

SEYTON   'Tis not needed yet.

MACBETH   I'll put it on.
Send out more horses, skirr the country round;   35
Hang those that talk of fear. Give me mine armor.
How does your patient, doctor?

DOCTOR   Not so sick, my lord,
As she is troubled with thick-coming fancies
That keep her from her rest.

MACBETH   Cure her of that!
Canst thou not minister to a mind diseased,   40
Pluck from the memory a rooted sorrow,
Raze out the written troubles of the brain,
And with some sweet oblivious antidote
Cleanse the stuff'd bosom of that perilous stuff
Which weighs upon the heart?

DOCTOR   Therein the patient   45
Must minister to himself.

MACBETH   Throw physic to the dogs, I'll none of it!—
Come, put mine armor on. Give me my staff.—
Seyton, send out.—Doctor, the thanes fly from me.—
Come, sir, dispatch.—If thou couldst, doctor, cast   50
The water of my land, find her disease,
And purge it to a sound and pristine health,
I would applaud thee to the very echo,

That should applaud again.—Pull 't off, I say.—
\55   What rhubarb, senna, or what purgative drug,
Would scour these English hence? Hear'st thou of them?

DOCTOR   Ay, my good lord. Your royal preparation
Makes us hear something.

MACBETH   Bring it after me!
I will not be afraid of death and bane
60   Till Birnam Forest come to Dunsinane.

[*Exeunt all but the* DOCTOR.]

DOCTOR   Were I from Dunsinane away and clear,
Profit again should hardly draw me here. [*Exit.*]

Scene Four

[*The country near Birnam Wood. Drum and colors. Enter* MAL-
COLM, SIWARD, MACDUFF, SIWARD'S SON, MENTEITH, CAITHNESS,
ANGUS, LENNOX, ROSS, *and* SOLDIERS, *marching.*]

MALCOLM   Cousins, I hope the days are near at hand
That chambers will be safe.

MENTEITH   We doubt it nothing.

SIWARD   What wood is this before us?

MENTEITH   The Wood of Birnam.

MALCOLM   Let every soldier hew him down a bough
5   And bear't before him. Thereby shall we shadow
The numbers of our host and make discovery
Err in report of us.

SOLDIERS   It shall be done.

SIWARD   We learn no other but the confident tyrant
Keeps still in Dunsinane and will endure
Our setting down before't.

10 MALCOLM   'Tis his main hope;
For where there is advantage to be given,
Both more and less have given him the revolt;
And none serve with him but constrained things,
Whose hearts are absent too.

MACDUFF   Let our just censures

Lines 54 and 58. "It" is a piece of Macbeth's armor.

Attend the true event, and put we on 15
Industrious soldiership.

SIWARD   The time approaches
  That will with due decision make us know
  What we shall say we have, and what we owe.
  Thoughts speculative their unsure hopes relate,
  But certain issue strokes must arbitrate; 20
  Towards which advance the war.

[*Exeunt, marching.*]

Scene Five

[*Dunsinane. Within the castle. Enter* MACBETH, SEYTON, *and* SOL-
  DIERS, *with drum and colors.*]

MACBETH   Hang out our banners on the outward walls.
  The cry is still, 'They come!' Our castle's strength
  Will laugh a siege to scorn. Here let them lie
  Till famine and the ague eat them up.
  Were they not forced with those that should be ours, 5
  We might have met them dareful, beard to beard,
  And beat them backward home.

[*A cry within of women.*]
                          What is that noise?

SEYTON   It is the cry of women, my good lord. [*Exit.*]

MACBETH   I have almost forgot the taste of fears.
  The time has been, my senses would have cool'd 10
  To hear a night-shriek, and my fell of hair
  Would at a dismal treatise rouse and stir
  As life were in't. I have supp'd full with horrors.
  Direness, familiar to my slaughterous thoughts,
  Cannot once start me.

[*Enter* SEYTON.]
                          Wherefore was that cry? 15

SEYTON   The Queen, my lord, is dead.

MACBETH   She should have died hereafter;
  There would have been a time for such a word.
  To-morrow, and to-morrow, and to-morrow
  Creeps in this petty pace from day to day 20
  To the last syllable of recorded time;

And all our yesterdays have lighted fools
The way to dusty death. Out, out, brief candle!
Life's but a walking shadow, a poor player,
25 That struts and frets his hour upon the stage
And then is heard no more. It is a tale
Told by an idiot, full of sound and fury,
Signifying nothing.

[*Enter a* MESSENGER.]

Thou com'st to use thy tongue. Thy story quickly!

30 MESSENGER   Gracious my lord,
I should report that which I say I saw,
But know not how to do 't.

MACBETH   Well, say, sir!

MESSENGER   As I did stand my watch upon the hill,
I look'd toward Birnam, and anon methought
The wood began to move.

35 MACBETH   Liar and slave!

MESSENGER   Let me endure your wrath if 't be not so.
Within this three mile may you see it coming;
I say, a moving grove.

MACBETH   If thou speak'st false,
Upon the next tree shalt thou hang alive,
40 Till famine cling thee. If thy speech be sooth,
I care not if thou dost for me as much.
I pull in resolution, and begin
To doubt th' equivocation of the fiend,
That lies like truth. 'Fear not, till Birnam Wood
45 Do come to Dunsinane!' and now a wood
Comes toward Dunsinane. Arm, arm, and out!
If this which he avouches does appear,
There is nor flying hence nor tarrying here.
I 'gin to be aweary of the sun,
50 And wish th' estate o' th' world were now undone.
Ring the alarum bell! Blow wind, come wrack,
At least we'll die with harness on our back!

[*Exeunt.*]

Scene Six

[*Dunsinane. Before the castle. Enter* MALCOLM, SIWARD, MACDUFF, *and their* ARMY, *with boughs.*]

MALCOLM   Now near enough. Your leavy screens throw down
And show like those you are. You, worthy uncle,
Shall with my cousin, your right noble son,
Lead our first battle. Worthy Macduff and we
Shall take upon 's what else remains to do,   5
According to our order.

SIWARD   Fare you well.
Do we but find the tyrant's power to-night,
Let us be beaten if we cannot fight.

MACDUFF   Make all our trumpets speak, give them all breath,
Those clamorous harbingers of blood and death.   10

[*Exeunt. Alarums continued.*]

Scene Seven

[*Another part of the field. Enter* MACBETH.]

MACBETH   They have tied me to a stake. I cannot fly,
But bear-like I must fight the course. What's he
That was not born of woman? Such a one
Am I to fear, or none.

[*Enter* YOUNG SIWARD.]

YOUNG SIWARD   What is thy name?

MACBETH   Thou'lt be afraid to hear it.   5

YOUNG SIWARD   No; though thou call'st thyself a hotter name
Than any is in hell.

MACBETH   My name's Macbeth.

YOUNG SIWARD   The devil himself could not pronounce a title
More hateful to mine ear.

MACBETH   No, nor more fearful.

YOUNG SIWARD   Thou liest, abhorred tyrant! With my sword   10
I'll prove the lie thou speak'st.

[*Fight, and* YOUNG SIWARD *slain.*]

Thou wast born of woman.
But swords I smile at, weapons laugh to scorn,
Brandish'd by man that's of a woman born. [*Exit.*]

[*Alarums. Enter* MACDUFF.]

MACDUFF   That way the noise is. Tyrant, show thy face!
15   If thou be'st slain and with no stroke of mine,
My wife and children's ghosts will haunt me still.
I cannot strike at wretched kerns, whose arms
Are hired to bear their staves. Either thou, Macbeth,
Or else my sword with an unbattered edge
20   I sheathe again undeeded. There thou shouldst be.
By this great clatter one of greatest note
Seems bruited. Let me find him, Fortune!
And more I beg not. [*Exit.*]

[*Alarums. Enter* MALCOLM *and* SIWARD.]

SIWARD   This way, my lord. The castle's gently render'd:
25   The tyrant's people on both sides do fight;
The noble thanes do bravely in the war;
The day almost itself professes yours,
And little is to do.

MALCOLM   We have met with foes
30   That strike beside us.

SIWARD   Enter, sir, the castle.

[*Exeunt. Alarum.*]

Scene Eight

[*Another part of the field. Enter* MACBETH.]

MACBETH   Why should I play the Roman fool and die
On mine own sword? Whiles I see lives, the gashes
Do better upon them.

[*Enter* MACDUFF.]

MACDUFF   Turn, hellhound, turn!

5   MACBETH   Of all men else I have avoided thee.
But get thee back! My soul is too much charged
With blood of thine already.

MACDUFF   I have no words;
  My voice is in my sword, thou bloodier villain
  Than terms can give thee out!

[*Fight. Alarum.*]

MACBETH   Thou losest labor.
  As easy mayst thou the intrenchant air
  With thy keen sword impress as make me bleed.   10
  Let fall thy blade on vulnerable crests.
  I bear a charmed life, which must not yield
  To one of woman born.

MACDUFF   Despair thy charm!
  And let the angel whom thou still hast served
  Tell thee, Macduff was from his mother's womb   15
  Untimely ripp'd.

MACBETH   Accursed be that tongue that tells me so.
  For it hath cow'd my better part of man!
  And be these juggling fiends no more believed,
  That palter with us in a double sense,   20
  That keep the word of promise to our ear
  And break it to our hope! I'll not fight with thee!

MACDUFF   Then yield thee, coward,
  And live to be the show and gaze o' th' time!
  We'll have thee, as our rare monsters are,   25
  Painted upon a pole, and underwrit
  'Here may you see the tyrant.'

MACBETH   I will not yield,
  To kiss the ground before young Malcolm's feet
  And to be baited with the rabble's curse.
  Though Birnam Wood be come to Dunsinane,   30
  And thou opposed, being of no woman born,
  Yet I will try the last. Before my body
  I throw my warlike shield. Lay on, Macduff,
  And damn'd be him that first cries 'Hold, enough!'

[*Exeunt fighting. Alarums.*]

[*Retreat and flourish. Enter, with drum and colors,* MALCOLM,
  SIWARD, ROSS, THANES, *and* SOLDIERS.]

MALCOLM   I would the friends we miss were safe arrived.   35

SIWARD   Some must go off; and yet, by these I see,
  So great a day as this is cheaply bought.

MALCOLM   Macduff is missing, and your noble son.

Ross   Your son, my lord, has paid a soldier's debt.
40   He only lived but till he was a man,
        The which no sooner had his prowess confirm'd
        In the unshrinking station where he fought
        But like a man he died.

SIWARD   Then he is dead?

Ross   Ay, and brought off the field. Your cause of sorrow
45   Must not be measured by his worth, for then
        It hath no end.

SIWARD   Had he his hurts before?

Ross   Ay, on the front.

SIWARD   Why then, God's soldier be he!
        Had I as many sons as I have hairs,
        I would not wish them to a fairer death.
        And so his knell is knoll'd.

50 MALCOLM   He's worth more sorrow,
        And that I'll spend for him.

SIWARD   He's worth no more.
        They say he parted well and paid his score,
        And so, God be with him! Here comes newer comfort.

[*Enter* MACDUFF, *with* MACBETH's *head.*]

MACDUFF   Hail, King! for so thou art. Behold where stands
55   Th' usurper's cursed head. The time is free.
        I see thee compass'd with thy kingdom's pearl,
        That speak my salutation in their minds;
        Whose voices I desire aloud with mine—
        Hail, King of Scotland!

ALL   Hail, King of Scotland!

[*Flourish.*]

60 MALCOLM   We shall not spend a large expense of time
        Before we reckon with your several loves
        And make us even with you. My thanes and kinsmen,
        Henceforth be earls, the first that ever Scotland
        In such an honor named. What's more to do
65   Which would be planted newly with the time—
        As calling home our exiled friends abroad
        That fled the snares of watchful tyranny,
        Producing forth the cruel ministers

Line 61. Reward each of you for your loyalty.

Of this dead butcher and his fiend-like queen,
Who, as 'tis thought, by self and violent hands   70
Took off her life—this, and what needful else
That calls upon us, by the grace of Grace
We will perform in measure, time, and place.
So thanks to all at once and to each one,
Whom we invite to see us crown'd at Scone.   75

[*Flourish. Exeunt omnes.*]

"MACBETH" AS THE IMITATION
OF AN ACTION

I propose to attempt to illustrate the view that *Macbeth* may be understood as "the imitation of an action," in approximately Aristotle's sense of this phrase.

The word "action"—*praxis*—as Aristotle uses it in the *Poetics,* does not mean outward deeds or events, but something much more like "purpose" or "aim." Perhaps our word "motive" suggests most of its meaning. Dante (who in this respect is a sophisticated Aristotelian) uses the phrase *moto spiral,* spiritual movement, to indicate *praxis.* In Aristotle's own writings *praxis* is usually rational, a movement of the will in the light of the mind. But Dante's *moto spiral* refers to all modes of the spirit's life, all of its directions, or focuses, or motives, including those of childhood, dream, drunkenness, or passion, which are hardly rationalized at all. When using Aristotle's definition for the analysis of modern drama it is necessary to generalize his notion of action in this way, to include movements of the spirit in response to sensuous or emotionally charged images, as well as consciously willed purpose. But it seems to me a legitimate extension of the basic concept; and I do not think it does real violence to Aristotle's meaning.

Aristotle, in his *Psychology* and *Ethics,* as well as in the *Poetics,* and Dante in the *Divine Comedy,* seem to imagine the psyche much as an amoeba looks under the microscope: moving toward what attracts it, continually changing direction or aim, and taking its shape and color from the object to which it is attached at the moment. This movement is "action"; and so we see that while the psyche is alive it always has action; and that this changing action in pursuit of real or imagined objects defines its mode of being moment by moment.

When Aristotle says that a tragedy is the imitation of an action, he is thinking of an action, or motive which governs the psyche's life for a considerable length of time. Such an action is the quest for Laius's slayer in *Oedipus Rex,* which persists through the changing circumstances of the play. In this period of time, it has a beginning, a middle, and an end, which comes when the slayer is at last identified.

I remarked that action is not outward deeds or events; but on the other hand, there can be no action without resulting deeds. We guess at a man's action by way of what he does, his outward and visible deeds. We are aware that our own action, or motive, produces deeds of some sort as soon as it exists. Now the plot of a play is the arrangement of outward deeds or incidents, and the dramatist uses it, as Aristotle tells us, as the first means of imitating the action. He arranges a set of incidents which point to the action or motive from which they spring. You may say that the action is the spiritual content of the tragedy—the playwright's inspiration—and the plot defines its existence as an intelligible *play*. Thus, you can never have a play without both plot and action; yet the distinction between plot and action is as fundamental as that between form and matter. The action is the matter; the plot is the "first form," or, as Aristotle puts it, the "soul" of the tragedy.

The dramatist imitates the action he has in mind, first by means of the plot, then in the characters, and finally in the media of language, music, and spectacle. In a well-written play, if we understood it thoroughly, we should perceive that plot, character, diction, and the rest spring from the same source, or, in other words, realize the same action or motive in the forms appropriate to their various media.

You will notice that this is a diagrammatic description of the perfect play, perfectly understood. Therefore one cannot hope to illustrate it perfectly, even in the case of a play like *Macbeth*. *Macbeth*, however, does impress most of its readers as having a powerful and unmistakable unity of this kind: the plot, characters, and imagery all seem to spring from the one inspiration. It is that strong and immediately felt unity which I rely on—and upon your familiarity with the play. Not that I am so foolish as to suppose I grasp the play completely or that I could persuade you of my view of it in these few minutes. All I can attempt is to suggest the single action which seems to me to be the spiritual content of the play, and illustrate it, in only a few of its metaphors, plot devices, and characterizations.

The action of the play as a whole is best expressed in a phrase which Macbeth himself uses in Act II, scene 3, the aftermath of the murder. Macbeth is trying to appear innocent, but everything he says betrays his clear sense of his own evil motivation, or action. Trying to excuse his murder of Duncan's grooms, he says,

> The expedition of my violent love [*for Duncan, he means*]
> Outran the pauser, reason.

It is the phrase "to outrun the pauser, reason," which seems to me to describe the action, or motive, of the play as a whole. Macbeth, of course, literally means that his love for Duncan was so strong and swift that it got ahead of his reason, which would have counseled a pause. But in the same way we have seen his greed and ambition outrun his reason when he committed the murder; and in the same way all the characters, in the irrational darkness of Scotland's evil hour, are compelled in their action to strive beyond what they can see by reason alone. Even Malcolm and Macduff, as we shall see, are compelled to go beyond reason in the action which destroys Macbeth and ends the play.

But let me consider the phrase itself for a moment. To "outrun" reason suggests an impossible stunt, like lifting oneself by one's own bootstraps. It also suggests a competition or race, like those of a nightmare, which cannot be won. As for the word "reason," Shakespeare associates it with nature and nature's order, in the individual soul, in society, and in the cosmos. To outrun reason is thus to violate nature itself, to lose the bearings of common sense and of custom, and to move into a spiritual realm bounded by the irrational darkness of hell one way, and the superrational grace of faith the other way. As the play develops before us, all the modes of this absurd or evil or supernatural action are attempted, the last being Malcolm's and Macduff's acts of faith.

In the first part of the play Shakespeare, as is his custom, gives us the intimate feel of this paradoxical striving beyond reason in a series of echoing tropes and images. I remind you of some of them, as follows.

From the first Witches' scene:

> When the battle's lost and won.

> Fair is foul and foul is fair.

From the "bleeding-Sergeant" scene:

> Doubtful it stood;
> As two spent swimmers that do cling together
> And choke their art. . . .

> So from that spring whence comfort seem'd to come
> Discomfort swells.

> Confronted him with self-comparisons
> Point against point, rebellious arm 'gainst arm.

> What he hath lost noble Macbeth hath won.

From the second Witches' scene:

> So foul and fair a day.

> Lesser than Macbeth, and greater.

> His wonders and his praises do contend
> Which should be thine or his.

> This supernatural soliciting
> Cannot be ill; cannot be good.

> . . . nothing is, but what is not.

These are only a few of the figures which suggest the desperate and paradoxical struggle. They are, of course, not identical with each other or with outrunning reason, which seems to me the most general of all. But they all point to the "action" I mean, and I present them as examples of the imitation of action by means of the arts of language.

But notice that though these images themselves suggest the action, they also confirm the actions of the characters as these are shown in the story. The bleeding Sergeant, for instance, is striving beyond reason and nature in his effort to report the battle—itself a bewildering mixture of victory and defeat—in spite of his wounds. Even the old King Duncan, mild though he is, is caught in the race and sees his relation to Macbeth competitively. "Thou art so far before," he tells Macbeth in the next scene, "That swiftest wing of recompense is slow To overtake thee." He then races Macbeth to his castle, whither the Messenger has outrun them both; and when he arrives, he is at once involved in a hollow competition with Lady Macbeth, to outdo her in ceremony.

I do not need to remind you of the great scenes preceding the murder, in which Macbeth and his Lady pull themselves together for their desperate effort. If you think over these scenes, you will notice that the Macbeths understand the action which begins here as a competition and a stunt, against reason and nature. Lady Macbeth fears her husband's human nature, as well as her own female nature, and therefore she fears the light of reason and the common daylight world. As for Macbeth, he knows from the first and he is engaged in an irrational stunt: "I have no spur To prick the sides of my intent, but only Vaulting ambition, which o'erleaps itself And falls on th' other." In this sequence there is also the theme of outwitting or transcending time, an aspect of nature's order as we know it: catching up the consequences, jumping the life to come, and the like. But this must suffice to remind you of the Macbeths' actions, which they paradoxically understand so well.

The Porter scene has been less thoroughly studied as a variation on the play's main action. But it is, in fact, a farcical and terrible version of "outrunning reason," a witty and very concentrated epitome of this absurd movement of spirit. The Porter first teases the knockers at the gate with a set of paradoxes, all of which present attempts to outrun reason; and he sees them all as ways into Hell. Henry N. Paul[1] has explained the contemporary references: the

[1] See *The Royal Play of Macbeth,* New York, 1950.

farmer who hanged himself on the expectation of plenty, the equivocator who swore both ways to commit treason for God's sake.
When the Porter has admitted the knockers he ironically offers them
lewd physical analogies for outrunning reason: drink as tempting
lechery into a hopeless action; himself as wrestling with drink. The
relation of the Porter to the knockers is like that of the Witches to
Macbeth—he tempts them into Hell with ambiguities. And the
inebriation of drink and lust, lewd and laughable as it is, is closely
analogous to the more terrible and spiritual intoxication of the
Macbeths.

Thus, in the first part of the play both the imagery and the
actions of the various characters indicate or "imitate" the main
action. Aristotle says the characters are imitated "with a view to the
action"—and the Porter, who has little importance in the story—
is presented to reveal the action of the play as a whole in the un-
expected light of farcical analogies, contemporary or lewd and
physical.

Before I leave this part of the play I wish to point out that the
plot itself—"the arrangement or synthesis of the incidents"—also
imitates a desperate race. This is partly a matter of the speed with
which the main facts are presented, partly the effect of simultaneous
movements like those of a race: Lady Macbeth is reading the letter
at the same moment that her husband and Duncan are rushing
toward her. And the facts in this part of the play are ambiguous in
meaning and even as facts.

These few illustrations must serve to indicate how I understand
the imitation of action in language, character, and plot in the first
two acts of the play. Macbeth and his lady are embarked on a race
against reason itself; and all Scotland, the "many" whose lives depend upon the monarch, is precipitated into the same darkness and
desperate strife. Shakespeare's monarchs do usually color the
spiritual life of their realms. And we, who remember Hitlerite Germany, can understand that, I think. Even Hitler's exiles, like the
refugees from Russian or Spanish tyranny, brought the shadow to
this country with them.

I now wish to consider the action of the play at a later stage, in
Act IV, scene 3. This is the moment which I mentioned before, the
beginning of Malcolm's and Macduff's act of faith which will constitute the final variation on "outrunning reason." The scene is laid
in England, whither Malcolm and Macduff have fled, and it immediately follows the murder of Macduff's wife and child. Like the exiles
we have known in this country, Macduff and Malcolm, though in
England, have brought Scotland's darkness with them. They have
lost all faith in reason, human nature, and common sense, and can
therefore trust neither themselves nor each other. They are met in
the hope of forming an alliance, in order to get rid of Macbeth; and

yet under his shadow everything they do seems unreasonable, paradoxical, improbable.

In the first part of the scene, you remember, Malcolm and Macduff fail to find any basis for mutual trust. Malcolm mistrusts
Macduff because he has left his wife and child behind; Macduff
quickly learns to mistrust Malcolm, because he first protests that he
is unworthy of the crown, to test Macduff, and then suddenly reverses himself. The whole exchange is a tissue of falsity and paradox,
and it ends in a sort of nightmarish paralysis.

At this point there is the brief interlude with the Doctor. The
King's Evil and its cure and the graces which hang about the English throne are briefly described. Paul points out that this interlude
may have been introduced to flatter James I; but, however that may
be, it is appropriate in the build of the scene as a whole. It marks
the turning point, and it introduces the notion of the appeal by
faith to Divine Grace which will reverse the evil course of the action
when Malcolm and Macduff learn to outrun reason in that way,
instead of by responding to the Witches' supernatural solicitations
as Macbeth has done. Moreover, the Doctor in this scene, in whom
religious and medical healing are associated, foreshadows the Doctor
who will note Lady Macbeth's sleepwalking and describe it as a
perturbation in nature which requires a cure beyond nature.

But to return to the scene. After the Doctor's interlude, Ross
joins Malcolm and Macduff, bringing the latest news from Scotland.
To greet him, Malcolm clearly states the action, or motive, of the
scene as a whole: "Good God, betimes remove The means that
makes us strangers!" he says. Ross's chief news is, of course, Lady
Macduff's murder. When he has gradually revealed that, and Macduff and Malcolm have taken it in, accepting some of the guilt, they
find that the means that made them strangers has in fact been
removed. They recognize themselves and each other once more, in
a sober, but not nightmarish light. And at once they join faith in
their cause and prepare to hazard all upon the ordeal of battle,
itself an appeal beyond reason. The scene, which in its opening
sections moved very slowly, reflecting the demoralization of Malcolm and Macduff, ends hopefully, with brisk rhythms of speech
which prepare the marching scenes to follow.

> This tune goes manly . . .

> Receive what cheer you may.
> The night is long that never finds the day.

The whole scene is often omitted or drastically cut in production,
and many critics have objected to it. They complain of its slowness,
of the baroque overelaboration of Malcolm's protests, and of the
fact that it is too long for what it tells us about the story. All we

learn is that Malcolm and Macduff are joining the English army to attack Macbeth, and this information could have been conveyed much more quickly. In the first part of the play, and again after this scene, everything moves with the speed of a race; and one is tempted to say, at first, that in this scene Shakespeare lost the rhythm of his own play.

Now, one of the reasons I chose this scene to discuss is that it shows, as does the Porter scene, the necessity of distinguishing between plot and action. One cannot understand the function of the scene in the whole plot unless one remembers that the plot itself is there to imitate the action. It is then clear that this scene is the peripeteia, which is brought about by a series of recognitions. It starts with Malcolm and Macduff blind and impotent in Macbeth's shadow and ends when they have gradually learned to recognize themselves and each other even in that situation. "Outrunning reason" looks purely evil in the beginning, and at the end we see how it may be good, an act of faith beyond reason. The scene moves slowly at first because Shakespeare is imitating the action of groping in an atmosphere of the false and unnatural; yet we are aware all the while of continuing speed offstage, where

> Each new morn
> New widows howl, new orphans cry, new sorrows
> Strike heaven on the face . . .

The scene is thus (within the rhythmic scheme of the whole play) like a slow eddy on the edge of a swift current. After this turning, or peripeteia, the actions of Malcolm and Macduff join the rush of the main race, to win. I admit that these effects might be hard to achieve in production, but I believe that good actors could do it.

Shakespeare's tragedies usually have a peripeteia in the fourth act, with scenes of suffering and prophetic or symbolic recognitions and epiphanies. In the fourth act of *Macbeth* the Witches' scene reveals the coming end of the action in symbolic shows; and this scene also, in another way, foretells the end. The last act, then merely presents the literal facts, the wind-up of the plot, long felt as inevitable in principle. The fifth act of *Macbeth* shows the expected triumph of Malcolm's and Macduff's superrational faith. The wood does move; Macbeth does meet a man unborn of woman; and the paradoxical race against reason reaches its paradoxical end. The nightmare of Macbeth's evil version of the action is dissolved, and we are free to return to the familiar world, where reason, nature, and common sense still have their validity.

To sum up: my thesis is that *Macbeth* is the imitation of an action (or motive) which may be indicated by the phrase "to outrun the pauser, reason." I have tried to suggest how this action is presented in the metaphors, characters, and plot of the first two acts; and also in the peripeteia, with pathos and recognitions, the great scene between Malcolm, Macduff, and Ross.

I am painfully aware that these few illustrations are not enough to establish my thesis. Only a detailed analysis of the whole play might do that—and such an analysis would take hours of reading and discussion. But I think it would show that Aristotle was essentially right. He had never read *Macbeth,* and I suppose if he could he would find Shakespeare's Christian, or post-Christian, vision of evil hard to understand. But he saw that the art of drama is the art of imitating action; and this insight, confirmed and deepened by some of Aristotle's heirs, can still show us how to seek the unity of a play, even one which shows modes of the spirit's life undreamed of by Aristotle himself.

MOLIÈRE

Tartuffe

Done into English Verse by JAMES L. ROSENBERG

ÉMILE FAGUET

On the Nature of the Dramatic Emotion

Translated by PHILIP M. HAYDEN

THE CHARACTERS IN *TARTUFFE*

MADAME PERNELLE, mother of Orgon

ORGON

ELMIRE, Orgon's wife

DAMIS, son of Orgon, stepson of Elmire

MARIANE, daughter of Orgon and stepdaughter of Elmire

VALÈRE

CLÉANTE, brother-in-law of Orgon, brother of Elmire

TARTUFFE

DORINE, companion of Mariane

MONSIEUR LOYAL, bailiff

A POLICE OFFICER

FLIPOTE, Madame Pernelle's servant

The setting throughout is the salon of ORGON'S *house in Paris. The furnishings are those of a well-to-do bourgeois.*

Application for any performance of *Tartuffe* by Molière, translated by James L. Rosenberg, should be made to Literary Discoveries, Inc., 604 Mission Street, San Francisco 5, California. No performance may take place unless a license has been obtained.

TARTUFFE

ACT ONE

Scene One

[MADAME PERNELLE, FLIPOTE, ELMIRE, MARIANE, DORINE, DAMIS, and CLÉANTE]

MME. PERNELLE   Come on, Flipote, away from their mad chatter.

ELMIRE   Heavens, Madame! Now what can be the matter?

MME. PERNELLE   Enough, enough; spare me their smiling faces.
I can well dispense with certain airs and graces.

ELMIRE   Madame, no one has given you cause to grieve;   5
Why, I pray, are you so resolved to leave?

MME. PERNELLE   I cannot stand this place a minute more;
My every wish is trampled and spurned to the floor.
I leave your house no wiser, but much sadder,
And now—heigh ho!—you ask me what's the matter.   10
None honors age, all speak with impudence,
This house has become like a Court of Insolence.

DORINE   If . . .

MME. PERNELLE   You are, my girl, a humble maid, a minion,
And yet you talk and give us your free opinion
Like the veriest, blabbiest, gabbling hobbledehoy!   15

DAMIS   But . . .

MME. PERNELLE   In words of single syllables, my boy,
You are a fool. And that's all there is to that.
You've no more common sense than my old cat.
I've warned your father, not once, but a hundred times
That in the end you'd not be worth a dime.   20

MARIANE   I think . . .

MME. PERNELLE   And you, his sister, so demure and shy!
But I suspect that sparkle in your eye;
I note the adage about waters running deep
When I hear you sweetly sigh and softly weep.

ELMIRE   But, mother . . .

MME. PERNELLE   And you who should above all play the role   25
Of modesty and grace; upon the whole

211

I find your conduct shocking. Is it your place
To squander your husband's money, paint your face,
And boldly parade your charms before the world
30   Like a golden galleon with all her sails unfurled?
A woman who only seeks to attract her spouse
Does not so gaily decorate the house!

CLÉANTE   But, madame, after all . . .

MME. PERNELLE   And you, my lad,
I honor, love and respect you, need I add?
35   But if I were in my son her husband's place
I'd earnestly ask you not to show your face
Ever again in my house. It seems you preach
Tireless moral maxims, but what you teach
And what you live do not precisely agree.
40   Forgive my bluntness; my manner of speech is free.

DAMIS   I'm sure, madame, your Tartuffe is fortunate . . .

MME. PERNELLE   He is a man you might well imitate,
And it makes me furious through and through
To hear him maligned by a fool and a dolt like you.

45   DAMIS   What the devil? (Pardon the expression!)
Am I to live at the bigoted discretion
Of a puritanical tyrant and beg his consent
To live or breathe in my father's establishment?

DORINE   According to him and his maxims, we can't begin
50   To wiggle a toe without committing a sin.
He's got his nose in everything, sniffing out wrongs.

MME. PERNELLE   Wherever his nose is, there, I'm sure, it belongs.
He seeks to lead you with him on Heaven's path,
And you, like silly geese, just sit and laugh.

55   DAMIS   Neither the due respect I owe to my father
Nor anything else could make me go to the bother
Of trying to like that unctuous hypocrite,
And I cannot live at ease with myself and sit
At the table with him, smiling and wishing him well,
60   Or wishing, in short, he were anywhere else but in Hell!

DORINE   Indeed, I say it's a monstrous and scandalous thing
To see a stranger come and put a ring
In the master's nose and lead him around like a bull—
A penniless tramp whose belly was seldom full,
65   Whose shoes and coat were as holy as now he allows
His precious soul is—having the run of the house!

MME. PERNELLE   Ah! mercy on us! how happy we would be
If we all obeyed his wise and pious decrees.

DORINE   He's a shining saint in your imagination
    But a hypocrite in our frank estimation.   70

MME. PERNELLE   Hold your tongue!

DORINE   I wouldn't trust him, by the book,
    As far as I could throw a ten-ton rock.

MME. PERNELLE   All your malicious lies leave me unmoved.
    In my opinion, Tartuffe stands approved
    In every way. You hate him, you foolish things,   75
    Because he tells you of your faults and brings
    A message calling your souls away from sin.
    Heaven's all he's interested in.

DORINE   Oh, yes, indeed! But tell me why, I pray,
    He wants to drive all visitors away.   80
    When someone calls, is Heaven so offended
    That he must rave as though the world had ended?
    Do you know what I think of the affair? [*pointing to* ELMIRE]
    I think he's jealous of Madame—so there!

MME. PERNELLE   Hold your tongue and mind what you are say-
    ing.
    He's not alone in finding your giddy playing   85
    And all your social life a bit too much:
    These carriages and servants, crowds and such,
    Disturb the neighborhood with an uproar
    The like of which has not been heard before   90
    By decent folk. No doubt there's no harm done,
    But gossip breeds like flies in the summer sun.

CLÉANTE   Ah, madame, would you cure the human race
    Of gossiping or showing the double face?
    And what a sorry world now this would be   95
    If every little lie that touched on me
    Forced me to lose a friend. The fact
    Is, no one's ever legislated tact.
    No one's safe against the tongue of slander
    Or those malicious souls who long to pander   100
    To the mob's desire for scandal. No, each man
    Must merely live as wisely as he can.

DORINE   Isn't it old Daphne and that shrimp
    Of a husband of hers—the little pimp!—
    Who've been busy spreading their gossip and lies   105
    About us? We're sinners in their eyes,
    Or so they say. But why, pray, is it those
    Whose own inane behavior, Heaven knows,
    Is always most ridiculous or suspect
    Who seem to feel it's their duty to inflict   110

Their stupid opinions upon the rest of us?
Can it be these peccadilloes they discuss
Are exactly the things they're up to on the sly
And they think the insinuating lie
115   Of who was seen ascending someone's stairs
Will leave them free to conduct their own affairs?

MME. PERNELLE   All this chitchat's quite beside the point.
You all, I'm sure, know my dear friend Orante,
A good and saintly woman, full of grace;
120   *She's* not pleased with what goes on in this place.

DORINE   A fine example, and a most chaste wife!
It's true indeed she lives an austere life,
But age has waked that cold reforming zeal;
The fire dies down when one runs out of fuel.
125   Many a prude's born when youth's beauty dies
And looks perforce on life with saintly eyes.
Orante now hides beneath discretion's veil
Those fading charms that from henceforth must fail
To win esteem. These veteran coquettes
130   Revenge themselves on a world that soon forgets
Their fast-decaying beauty and retire
To rectitude, renouncing all desire;
Cheated of love, they turn to criticism
And make Morality their catechism;
135   They censure all who taste the joy of life
And concentrate on stirring endless strife.
Not principle, but envy, activates
Their tireless tongues and bitterly creates
That twisted malice which insanely drives them
140   To hate those pleasures of which age deprives them.

MME. PERNELLE [*to* ELMIRE]   These are the things that you de-
    light to hear,
And it seems this gracious lady has your ear
And is allowed to go on talking all the day
While I must keep my peace and go my way.
145   Alas, the sins of this world! Yet I'll be heard
And give you, will-you nill-you, this last word:
The wisest decision my son has ever made
Was in taking this holy man to be his guide;
God has sent him here to redeem your sins
150   And show you where the road to Heaven begins.
All those balls and dances, conversations,
Those goings to and fro, those visitations
Are surely inspired by the Evil One's decrees;
One never hears a pious word or sees

A modest action; all come in for their share 155
In the tide of malicious gossip running there.
In short, all sensible people lose their sense
In that sea of shallow frippery and pretense.
A thousand silly stories spread in a day,
And I heard a certain noted doctor say 160
This house has become a virtual Tower of Babel
Where everyone talks as fast and loud as he's able.
And to explain how this comment came to be . . . [*pointing to*
        CLÉANTE]
But I see yon gentleman secretly smiling at me.
Eh bien, go find the fools who make you gay. [*to* ELMIRE] 165
To you, my daughter, I've nothing more to say,
Except that I disapprove of your home and friends;
Good-bye. Farewell. Here our acquaintance ends. [*giving* FLIPOTE
        a box on the ear]
Come on, wake up, you silly gaping goose!
I'll fetch you a wallop will knock your senses loose! 170
Come on, away, away!

Scene Two

[CLÉANTE and DORINE]

CLÉANTE   I'll not go rushing
    After her, for fear of more tongue-lashing.
    That old battle-axe . . .

DORINE   Ah, it's a pity
    She can't hear you. What a lively ditty
    She would sing you now—she'd shout and scold 5
    To let you know she's not so awfully old!

CLÉANTE   How angry she was with us, and all for nothing!
    Tartuffe has got her poor old brain a-buzzing.

DORINE   All this is a minor situation
    Compared to the master's infatuation. 10
    If you could only see him, you'd say he's turned
    An utter fool. In recent years he'd earned
    The reputation of a man of sense,
    But since Tartuffe's bewitched him, all pretense
    Of plain intelligence has left his head. 15
    He calls him "brother" and has often said
    He loves him more than daughter, son, or wife.
    He makes him the director of his life
    And his secret soul's true confidant;

20 A mistress or a sweetheart couldn't want
 More tender demonstrations of his love;
 At the dining table, Tartuffe sits above
 In the place of honor, like a greedy glutton
 Devouring vast slabs of beef and mutton;
25 The choicest cuts are his, let him but "hic"
 The master cries "God bless you!" double quick.
 In short, he dotes upon him like a fool;
 Tartuffe's his hero, and he's the villain's tool.
 He quotes him with the wildest admiration
30 And praises him on every least occasion.
 Tartuffe, who knows a sucker when he sees him,
 Employs a hundred little arts to please him;
 He steals him blind, meanwhile, with pious maxims,
 While criticizing all the family's actions.
35 Even that sneering jackanapes of a boy
 Who serves him as a page seems to enjoy
 The freedom of the house and has the power
 To lecture and correct us hour by hour.
 A handkerchief of mine drew his complaints
40 Because he found it pressed in a Book of Saints.

Scene Three

[ELMIRE, MARIANE, DAMIS, CLÉANTE, *and* DORINE]

ELMIRE You're lucky, brother, your ears were not made sore
 By her haranguing all the way to the door.
 But I saw my husband as I was passing the stair;
 I'll be in my room, if he wishes to see me there.

5 CLÉANTE Thanks. I'll wait, despite your friendly warning,
 And try at least to wish him a "Good morning."

Scene Four

[CLÉANTE, DAMIS, *and* DORINE]

DAMIS Speak to him, if you will, about Mariane.
 You know I'm interested in her plan
 To marry Valère. I fear my father's delay
 Is based on Tartuffe's dislike of the wedding day.

If Valère and my sister marry, it may be   5
My own joy with his sister I may see
Quite soon . . .

CLÉANTE   Here he comes.

Scene Five

[ORGON, CLÉANTE, *and* DORINE]

ORGON   Ah, good morning, brother.

CLÉANTE   Dear Orgon, I am glad to have another
  Chance to speak to you. The fields are drying . . .

ORGON   Forgive me, brother, but I'm dying
  To hear the latest news about the household   5
  From the greatest drawing-room to the smallest mousehole. [*to*
    DORINE]
  Has all gone happily since yesterday?
  How's everybody's health? Tell me, I pray!

DORINE   Madame was feverish and had to take
  A medicine to cure a vile headache.   10

ORGON   And Tartuffe?

DORINE   Tartuffe? Healthy, stout and merry,
  Bright as paint and ruddy as a cherry.

ORGON   Poor man!

DORINE   Last night, her headache grew so bad
  She scarce could stir out of her bed
  And could not eat a bit of dinner.   15

ORGON   And Tartuffe?

DORINE   He ate—that well-fed sinner—
  A brace of good plump partridges, done brown,
  With a bottle of red wine to wash them down.

ORGON   Poor man!

DORINE   She passed a tortured, sleepless night
  In endless pain; the morning's cold gray light   20
  At last relieved her fever, but we sat
  Beside her all night long; just think of that!

ORGON   And Tartuffe?

DORINE   Replete and sleepy, satisfied,
  He drifted from the meal to his fireside,

25   Crept thence into his warm and cozy bed
        And snored till dawn, the comfy sleepy-head.

ORGON   Poor man!

DORINE   Madame, agreeing to our fond persuasions,
        Consented to the doctor's ministrations
        And, bled and physicked, felt somewhat relieved.

ORGON   And Tartuffe?

30 DORINE   Not, I must confess, unduly grieved
        By Madame's illness, but right valiantly
        Took arms against foul trouble's surging sea
        And drank some wine to replace the blood she'd lost.

ORGON   Poor man!

DORINE   I'm happy to report the danger's past,
35   And now I'll hasten to inform my mistress
        How pleased you are she's cured of her distress.

Scene Six

[ORGON *and* CLÉANTE]

CLÉANTE   Brother, she's laughing in your very face
        And, though I'm far from wishing you disgrace,
        I must say that she's right in her estimation.
        Who ever saw such a mad infatuation?
5   Is it possible this man has charmed you so
        That you can forget all else for him, and go
        Running about to do his commands? I swear
        I've never seen such nonsense . . .

ORGON   Stop right there;
        For you don't know the man of whom you speak.

10 CLÉANTE   All right, then. I don't know him, if you like,
        But I know various things that I have heard.

ORGON   To know him is to love him, take my word.
        I model myself on him whenever I can;
        He is a man who . . . well, in short, a man.
15   Whoever follows his precepts lives in peace
        And sees the rest of the world as so much dross.
        Yes, I have changed since he came into my life;
        He's taught me not to waste my love on my wife
        Or on any mortal thing; what's more,
20   I could see my children turned away from my door,

Thanks to him, without the least concern.

CLÉANTE   These are surely humane truths to learn!

ORGON   Ah, if you could have seen him when at first
 We met, in the days when my life was still accursed!
 Each day in church he came and, if you please,   25
 Fell with a crash before me to his knees.
 He drew the attention of everybody there
 With the ardency and loudness of his prayer.
 He sighed, stretched flatly forth on his abdomen,
 And kissed the floor with every passing moment.   30
 When I departed, he ran along before me
 And lightly sprinkled holy water o'er me.
 I made inquiries of his servant, and he
 Told me of who he was, and his poverty
 Described so movingly, I could not choose   35
 But offer gifts to him, which he'd refuse,
 Forever crying, "No, no, it's too much;
 I am unworthy, no, I dare not touch
 A penny of it!" And, if I persisted,
 He'd give it to the poor. Oh, he assisted   40
 Many a one that way. Chaste Heaven, at last,
 Moved me to take him in here as my guest.
 Since then, all prospers. Sternly he reproves
 All sinful and suspect behavior, moves
 Particularly to guard my sacred honor   45
 Where my wife's concerned. He keeps upon her
 A most strict watch, and is indeed more jealous
 Of all those coxcombs and conceited fellows
 Who hang around her than *I* am, I feel;
 You'd scarce believe the extent of his pious zeal. 50
 One day he killed a flea with too much pique,
 Then scourged himself and fasted for a week.

CLÉANTE   Brother, I swear, there's something wrong with your
 head.
 Are you laughing at me with all this that you've said?
 What does it mean? This madness worries me . . . 55

ORGON   Your language, brother, savors of heresy.
 Your thinking's somewhat tainted by that vice,
 And, as I've had to warn you once or twice,
 You're liable to a judgment on your head.

CLÉANTE   To think like you is worse than being dead. 60
 You voluntary blind men always call
 The rest of us "freethinkers," whereas all
 We're guilty of is scorning empty shows

And faithlessness. And now do you suppose
65 Your veiled denunciations frighten me?
My heart is open for all men to see.
I am no dupe of formalistic panders;
Religion, like the throne, has false pretenders.
And as the truly brave aren't always those
70 Who trumpet loudest or with gaudy shows
Paint their performance, so the true devout
Don't always pray the loudest or go about
With piously exaggerated gestures;
True worth does not reside in outward vestures,
75 Hypocrisy too often masks religion,
And men like you confuse life's true condition
By judging that the mask must be the face;
But don't you see such judgment's a disgrace?
The shadow, not the substance, is your God;
80 The false coin's what you worship, not the good.
Man must be, indeed, a curious creature
Who can't obey the simple laws of nature.
Reason seems to hem him in too tightly,
And so he never plays his part quite rightly.
85 He ruins every act by exaggeration
In trying to advance in estimation.
And, brother, by the way, a word to the wise . . .

ORGON   Well, you must be a scholar in disguise,
For clearly all the wisdom of the ages
90 Has found its home in you; the greatest sages
Are nothing unto you—you are a Cato,
A Socrates, a Zeno, or a Plato!

CLÉANTE   I'm not a doctor of philosophy,
And all life's wisdom doesn't reside in me.
95 My science lies in being able to see
Distinctions between truth and falsity.
And as I know of nothing more commendable
Than the honest piety of dependable
And devoted holy men, so too I find
100 Nothing's worse than those whose double mind
Betrays true holiness, those hypocrites
Upon whose subtle faces triumph sits
In smiling sacrilegious impudence,
Whose lives are nothing but one long pretense
105 Of piousness, the while they make a mock
Of all that's good, and while they fleece the flock
Of silly sheep by various devices
Designed to line their pockets; all their vices
Masquerade as virtue; on their way

To Heaven they contrive to jest and play 110
In secrecy, maintaining the disguise
Of holiness by lifting up their eyes
In pious, zealous ardor; who, in short,
While living in the luxury of Court,
Dryly preach abstinence, plain living, 115
And retirement; who, without misgiving,
Can reconcile their vices and their zeal;
Passionate, revengeful, they conceal
Their petty jealousies beneath the cloak
Of piety and goodness and invoke 120
God's name to consecrate their evils,
So bold and fearless are these subtle devils.
They place themselves upon the side of Heaven
And assassinate their foes with a sacred weapon.
This modern age, I fear, too rankly teems 125
With such pretenders, but although it seems
Hard to detect them, still true piety
Is never really difficult to see:
Look at Ariston, look at Périandre,
Oronte, Alcidamas, Polydore, and Clitandre. 130
No one would dare deny to them the title
Of honesty in any true recital
Of virtue's servants; never do they show
This ostentatious righteousness or go
Meddling into other folk's affairs 135
And giving themselves these smug and holy airs.
Their goodness is direct and free and simple
And only by their own benign example
Do they ever even so much as venture
To subject others unto moral censure. 140
They do not trust the face that evil shows
But are the first to think the best of those
Whom lying slander villainously attacks.
We find no intrigues or no secret pacts
Among them; virtue's what they're interested in; 145
They love the sinner, though they hate the sin.
Above all, they're embarrassed to disclose
Toward Heaven greater zeal than Heaven shows
Toward them. Such people truly share my heart.

ORGON   And have you finally spoken all your part? 150

CLÉANTE   Yes.

ORGON   Your servant, sir. I bid you a good day.

CLÉANTE   A moment, brother. Please don't run away.
Do you recall your promise to Valère?

ORGON   Yes.

CLÉANTE   And that you'd blessed the happy, loving pair?

ORGON   That's true.

155   CLÉANTE   Why, then, is there this great delay?

ORGON   I don't know.

CLÉANTE   You're planning for another day?

ORGON   Perhaps.

CLÉANTE   You mean you'd break your word?

ORGON   I don't say that.

CLÉANTE   From what I've heard,
You have no reason to delay things thus.

ORGON   That depends.

160   CLÉANTE   There certainly should be no fuss.

ORGON   I suppose not.

CLÉANTE   What shall I tell Valère?

ORGON   Whatever you please.

CLÉANTE   But don't you care
To make your wishes clear?

ORGON   I care
Only to do what Heaven wills.

CLÉANTE   Come, now,
165   You gave the lad your sacred vow.

ORGON   Farewell. [*Exits.*]

CLÉANTE   I fear the worst in this affair.
I must speak further quickly with Valére.

ACT TWO

Scene One

[ORGON *and* MARIANE]

ORGON Mariane.

MARIANE Father?

ORGON Come closer; let me speak
To you.

MARIANE [*to* ORGON, *who is peering off stage*] What is it there
that you seek?

ORGON I'm looking to see if anyone's eavesdropping.
This is a likely place for tricksy snooping.
There now. All's well. Now then, my dear,   5
There's something that I wish for you to hear;
You know I've always held you in my heart.

MARIANE You've always played a loving father's part.

ORGON Well said! And to deserve that love, my treasure,
You should think of nothing but your father's pleasure.   10

MARIANE I hope I never merit your reproof.

ORGON Splendid! Tell me, what do you think of Tartuffe?

MARIANE Who, I?

ORGON You. Take care with your answer, pray.

MARIANE Alas! I'll say whatever you wish me to say.

[DORINE *enters quietly and stands behind* ORGON *without his seeing
her.*]

Scene Two

[ORGON, MARIANE, *and* DORINE]

ORGON Ah, wisely spoken. Then say, my dearest dove,
He has inspired your heart with tender love
And that the crown of joy upon your life
Descends the day that you become his wife.

223

MARIANE   What?

ORGON   Eh?

MARIANE   What did you say?

ORGON   Me?

5 MARIANE   Heavens above!
Who is it that's inspired my heart with love?
Who'll place the crown of joy upon my life
The day that I agree to be his wife?

ORGON   Tartuffe.

MARIANE   But, father, I feel nothing of the sort.
10   Would you have me betray the truth of my true heart?

ORGON   But I *want* it to be true. It should suffice
That my wishes in this matter are precise.

MARIANE   What? You wish . . .?

ORGON   I intend, you see,
To firmly unite Tartuffe to my family
15   By marrying him to you. With that in view,
I'm resolved this marriage must . . . [*sees* DORINE] Ha! You!
Your curiosity must be a powerful passion
To make you come and eavesdrop in this fashion.

DORINE   I must say, sir, I don't know whether I can
20   Tell whether the rumor arose by careful plan
Or accident, but when somebody spoke
Of such a marriage, I treated it all as a joke.

ORGON   And what is so incredible, I pray?

DORINE   I'm sorry. I can't believe a word that you say.

25 ORGON   I know how to make you believe it, I'll tell you that.

DORINE   Ha! What a tale! You're talking through your hat!

OREGON   I'm telling you what will very soon prove true.

DORINE   Nonsense!

ORGON   Now, daughter, I mean what I say, I'm warning you.

30 DORINE   Ha, ha! Don't believe him! He's only laughing!

ORGON   I tell you . . .

DORINE   What stuff! Get out! You must be chaffing!

ORGON   I warn you now, take care; my anger's rising!

DORINE   Well, I must say, it's surely most surprising.
35   Are we to believe a man as wise as you
With that splendid beard and eyes of baby blue

Would be so big a fool . . .

ORGON   Now listen here!
 You're taking certain liberties, my dear,
 Which do not please me at all, I can't deny.

DORINE Come, let's speak calmly, sir, if we can, and try
 To understand each other. Of course, you're joking.   40
 Your daughter to marry a bigot, whose manner of speaking
 Would scarce melt butter? And explain, if you can,
 What such an alliance would bring to you, a man
 Of notable wealth—to corrupt your daughter's love
 By marrying her off to a beggar . . .

ORGON   That's enough!   45
 I tell you that's the reason I revere him.
 His poverty is honest. If you could hear him
 Spurning worldly wealth and vulgar rank
 As gross deceptions, then, my girl, you'd thank
 Your father for marrying you to a saint,   50
 A man who never has a word of complaint,
 Whatever his woes. But with my modest aid
 He'll soon regain the splendid role he played
 In happier days. He once owned property
 And was a landed squire in his home county.   55

DORINE Yes, so he says; I say his vanity
 Does not sort well with all his piety.
 When you set up in business as a saint,
 You shouldn't boast and brag without restraint.
 Humility and love and true devotion   60
 Are strange bedmates, indeed, for gross ambition.
 Why be so haughty? But I see that you
 Don't care at all for this. Then let's turn to
 His person, not his claims to noble rank;
 Doesn't it make you sometimes shudder or shrink   65
 To think of a hypocritical fool
 Like that corrupting the innocent soul
 Of a girl like this? Stop and consider
 The consequences, if you commit her
 To such a loathesome and revolting marriage.   70
 You'd better save your breath to cool your porridge
 Than try to lecture a young and ardent wife
 Who's bound by marriage to a hateful life.
 Those husbands who wear horns upon their heads
 Have driven their wives away from their weary beds   75
 By their stupidities; and woe to those fathers
 Who make such marriages for their poor daughters!
 Beware of driving her to be a wife.

ORGON   It's nice of you to tell me about life!

80   DORINE   You could do worse than follow my advice.

ORGON   I'm sure these learned strictures are very nice.
But, daughter, you will do what I command.
Obey your father: that's the law of the land.
At one time, true, I'd pledged you to Valère,
85   But now I'm much disturbed by what I hear
Of that young man: free-thinking, playing cards, and such.

DORINE   And next you'll say you don't see him in church
Like those who go for advertising's sake.

ORGON   May I remind you that I didn't make
90   A special request for *your* precise advice.
I don't intend to speak to you more than twice.
The other man of whom we speak, I say,
Has made his peace with Heaven. That's the way
To build a marriage rich in every blessing.
95   You'll love each other. There'll be no transgressing.
You'll coo and gurgle like two doting turtles
And grow to be the happiest of mortals.
You'll make of him whatever you wish to make.

DORINE   She'll furnish him with horns within a week.

ORGON   What? What's that?

100   DORINE   He's got the head for it,
And I fear the melancholy aspect of his planet,
Despite your daughter's virtue, will prove too strong.

ORGON   *I* say stop interrupting and hold your tongue!
Mind your business; stop this damnable meddling.

105   DORINE   I'm only trying to stop your foolish fiddling.

ORGON   That's very kind of you. Now please be silent.

DORINE   If I didn't love you, sir . . .

ORGON   I'm growing violent.

DORINE   I want to help you, sir, despite your ire.

ORGON   Ha!

DORINE   It's true. Believe me, I can't bear
110   All the mocking you'd be subject to.

ORGON   You won't shut up?

DORINE   Whatever else, I'm true,
True-blue, to my employer all the way.

ORGON   Serpent! Silence! The next word you say . . .!

DORINE   A holy man like you, in such a temper?

ORGON   You plague me so, I find I can't remember   115
   What I started to say. Not one more squawk!

DORINE   All right, but I can think, if I can't talk.

ORGON   Think, if you like, but see that you don't dare
   To utter a word. [*to* MARIANE] I'll grant you that Valère
   Is a handsome chap . . .

DORINE   It drives me simply crazy   120
   Not to be able to speak.

ORGON   Though no fop or daisy,
   Tartuffe has looks . . .

DORINE   Indeed! To stop a clock.

ORGON   And, too, he comes of very ancient stock.
   His other gifts . . .

DORINE   Oh, you fortunate girl!
   If I were forced to marry such a churl,   125
   I'd have my sweet revenge already planned
   And prove a woman always has at hand
   Those weapons that will give her the last hit.

ORGON   You won't obey my orders? Is that it?

DORINE   What's your trouble? I'm not talking to you.   130

ORGON   To whom, pray tell?

DORINE   Why, to myself, that's who.

ORGON [*aside*]   *Eh bien.* There's only one recourse in such a case
   And that's to give her a slap across the face.

[*Raises his hand to give her a blow, but whenever he looks at her,
she stands mute and motionless*]

ORGON   Daughter, you ought to think well of my scheme;
   Tartuffe's the answer to a maiden's dream. [*to* DORINE]   135
   Why don't you speak?

DORINE   I've nothing more to say.

ORGON   Go on. One little word.

DORINE   Thanks, not today.

ORGON   I'm all ready for you.

DORINE   I'm not *that* dumb.

ORGON [*to* MARIANE]   It's not that I want my daughter under my
   thumb,

140   But you must learn to accept a father's rule.

DORINE [*fleeing*]   I'd die before I'd marry that fat fool!

[ORGON *tries to slap her but misses and falls down as she runs out.*]

ORGON   I can't live any longer with that pest
    Or I'll suffer the sin of anger. I must rest.
    I'm not in any state to go on with our talk.
145   Excuse me while I go and take a walk.

[*Exit* ORGON. DORINE *re-enters cautiously.*]

Scene Three

[MARIANE *and* DORINE]

DORINE   Mariane—ye gods—have you nothing to say?
    And must I play the part that you should play?
    A proposition utterly absurd,
    And yet you don't defend yourself with a word!

5   MARIANE   His power is absolute. What can I do?

DORINE   Anything, except what he wants you to.

MARIANE   What?

DORINE   Tell him that a girl can't love by proxy,
    And when it comes to marrying a foxy
    And bigoted old hypocrite—*mon Dieu!*—
10   *Your* wishes ought to count for something, too.
    If he loves Tartuffe dearer than a brother,
    Then—Devil take it!—Let them marry each other!

MARIANE   I know, but father is so overbearing,
    I don't dare raise my voice within his hearing.

15   DORINE   Look here. Let's think this through. Valère, you know,
    Has offered you his hand. Is that not so?

MARIANE   Stop it, Dorine! Of course I love Valère
    More than words can tell, and I can't bear
    To think of looking at another lover;
20   But I've repeated all this ten times over.

DORINE   I'm sometimes doubtful of such a coy admission
    And wonder if you're merely feigning passion.

MARIANE   You do me wrong in doubting me, my dear.
    I'd thought that you believed I was sincere.

25   DORINE   In short, you love the boy?

MARIANE   Oh, yes, with passion!   25

DORINE   And it would seem he loves you in like fashion?

MARIANE   I think so.

DORINE   And the way to happiness
  For both of you is marriage?

MARIANE   Yes, oh, yes!

DORINE   And what about Tartuffe, love's adversary?

MARIANE   I'll kill myself, if that seems necessary.   30

DORINE   Oh, fine! "I'll kill myself," the maid replied.
  The answer to life's grief is suicide.
  A sovereign cure! It makes me mad clear through
  To hear that kind of crazy talk from you.

MARIANE   Good heavens, what a temper! There you go!   35
  You don't much sympathize with others' woe.

DORINE   I don't much sympathize with those who drivel,
  Like you; then, when the test comes, shrivel.

MARIANE   You know I've always been a timid sort.

DORINE   But love demands a strong, courageous heart.   40

MARIANE   Loyalty to Valère's my firm intent,
  But he must ask, and gain, Papa's consent.

DORINE   But if your father is an utter goof
  Who's so infatuated with Tartuffe
  He'll break the promise that he's pledged you to,   45
  What is there left for poor Valère to do?

MARIANE   If I confess my true scorn for Tartuffe,
  Won't I reveal unconsciously the truth
  Of my affections? Though I love Valère,
  Should I abandon modesty and dare   50
  To flaunt my love for all the world to see?

DORINE   Oh, never mind. At least it's clear to me
  You really want to be Madame Tartuffe,
  And I was wrong to offer my reproof.
  Why should I argue with two loving hearts?   55
  The match would be ideal on both your parts.
  Monsieur Tartuffe! a pretty pouter pigeon!
  Tartuffe the Great! A man of high position!
  A lucky girl she is who is his wife!
  She royally has fixed herself for life.   60
  Every day, each hour, you hear his praises
  Sung by choirs in half a dozen places;

His ears are red as is the richest rose,
Only surpassed in glory by his nose.

MARIANE   Oh, God!

65   DORINE   What ecstasy will fill your loving breast
When you go home to share his little nest.

MARIANE   Stop this agonizing talk! Not one more word!
I cannot stand it any more. I've heard
Enough. Tell me how I can escape his clutches.

70   DORINE   A daughter should obey her father's wishes,
Although he choose a monkey for her mate.
I'd like to help, but really, it's too late.
Just think, you'll have a splendid horse and carriage
To help you ease the boredom of your marriage.

75   You can go calling on aunts, uncles, cousins,
Whom you'll find round the city by the dozens.
You'll call upon the Lord High Mayoress
And on the tax-collector's wife, no less,
Who'll seat you on a stool, the place of honor,

80   And might invite you to stay on for dinner;
A round of balls—as much as once a year—
Two bagpipes for a band, some watery beer;
Perhaps a puppet show, complete with monkey.
However, if your husband . . .

MARIANE   Oh, that donkey!
85   Dorine, for heaven's sake, I need advice.

DORINE   You must excuse me.

MARIANE   Please, I've asked you twice.

DORINE   To punish you, this marriage must go through.

MARIANE   Dorine!

DORINE   No!

MARIANE   I'll speak to father, as you wish me to.

DORINE   You've made your choice. It's clear Tartuffe's your man.

90   MARIANE   No more, Dorine. I've done all that I can.
My tears and sighs don't even leave you ruffled.

DORINE   As far as I'm concerned, you'll be Tartuffled.

MARIANE   Since my unhappiness can't move your heart,
I must surrender to despair and start
95   To search out methods of escaping life:
A little vial of poison or a knife.

DORINE   Here, here, come back. I'll put aside my ire

And help you to attain your true desire.

MARIANE   Dorine, if they insist on martyring me,
   I'll simply die. I'll end my life. You'll see.   100

DORINE   Don't worry. We can find a way to spare
   Your life, I'm sure. But look, here comes Valère.

[*Enter* VALÈRE. *He speaks at first jestingly.*]

Scene Four

[VALÈRE, MARIANE, *and* DORINE]

VALÈRE   Mademoiselle, a story's reached my ears
   Confirming all my wildest doubts and fears.

MARIANE   What's that?

VALÈRE   You're marrying Tartuffe.

MARIANE   That's true.
   My father wishes . . . What else can I do?

VALÈRE   Your father, mademoiselle . . .

MARIANE   Has changed his mind.   5
   Tartuffe's the man for whom I am designed.

VALÈRE   Is he serious?

MARIANE   As serious as serious can be.
   He just was urging this affair to me.

VALÈRE   What's your opinion of this serious prank,
   Pray tell?

MARIANE   I just don't know.

VALÈRE   Well, at least, that's frank.   10
   You don't know?

MARIANE   No.

VALÈRE   No?

MARIANE   What's your advice?

VALÈRE   Accept this splendid husband. Don't think twice.

MARIANE   That's your advice?

VALÈRE   Yes.

MARIANE   Really?

VALÈRE   Absolutely.
   You must pursue this rare chance resolutely.

15 MARIANE I'm much obliged to you for this sage counsel.

VALÈRE No thanks are due. I scarcely strained a tonsil.

MARIANE I'll ponder your advisements at my leisure.

VALÈRE I gave the counsel but to give you pleasure.

DORINE [aside] I wonder how this all is going to end?

20 VALÈRE I owe you thanks for frankness, at least, my friend.
   When you . . .

MARIANE   I beg you not to talk like that.
   You told me in so many words I should accept
   The man my father chose to pledge me to;
   I'm saying that's what I intend to do;
25 I'm simply following your own advice.

VALÈRE Don't fob me off with that antique device.
   Before I ever spoke, your mind was fixed
   And now you're seizing on some frivolous pretext
   To justify your falsehood to my face.

MARIANE Well put! Quite true.

30 VALÈRE   The plain facts of the case
   Are that you've never loved me for a minute.

MARIANE Think what you will, if you take pleasure in it.

VALÈRE Pleasure? Ha! The hurt you've dealt my heart
   Is deep, but I'll learn to make a second start
35 And find more sympathy and warmth than I do here.

MARIANE I don't doubt that. What girl would not admire
   Your character?

VALÈRE   Forget my character.
   It's not so hot. I'm crooked as a barrister,
   Blind as a fool in love, yes, even blinder,
40 But there's a girl somewhere who may be kinder
   Than you. She'll take me on the rebound, if she must.

MARIANE The loss is not so great. Somehow, I trust,.
   I'll manage to sustain it stoically.

VALÈRE I'm sure you will comport yourself heroically.
45 And, as for me, it's never very pleasant
   To find oneself forgotten. For the present,
   I'll do my best to sigh, smile and forget,
   Or, if I can't forget, pretend. And yet
   There's something weak and pitiful and wilted
50 About a man who weeps when he's been jilted.

MARIANE A lofty sentiment, indeed, if true.

VALÈRE   More people should approve it, as you do.
  What! Would you have me keep within my heart
  My love for you unchanging from the start,
  See you go happy to another's arms   55
  And not seek solace in a lady's charms?

MARIANE   Why, not at all! That's what I most desire—
  A new romance to set your heart afire!

VALÈRE   You'd like that?

MARIANE   Yes.

VALÈRE   Enough of this detraction!
  I'll try to give you instant satisfaction. [*starts to leave and re-*
    turns through the next few speeches]   60

MARIANE   Good.

VALÈRE   Kindly remember that, for good or ill,
  I follow your example.

MARIANE   As you will.

VALÈRE   Your wishes are quite clear. I will comply.

MARIANE   Fine!

VALÈRE   Enough. You get no more of me. Good-by.   65

MARIANE   Excellent!

VALÈRE   Eh?

MARIANE   What?

VALÈRE   I thought I heard my name.

MARIANE   You must be hearing things.

VALÈRE   This game
  Begins to weary me. Farewell.

MARIANE   Adieu.

DORINE   May I
  Speak up now as a humble stander-by
  And say I think you both are addled   70
  And ought to have your backsides paddled?
  Monsieur Valère!

[*She takes him by the arm; he feigns resistance.*]

VALÈRE   What do you want, Dorine?

DORINE   Come here!

VALÈRE   No, no! I'm in a rage. You've seen
  I'm doing what she wants. Don't interfere.

DORINE   Stop!

75   VALÈRE   The matter is all settled, that's quite clear.

DORINE   Ha!

MARIANE   My presence here clearly annoys someone.
It's wiser if I leave him quite alone.

[DORINE *leaves* VALÈRE *and runs to* MARIANE.]

DORINE   Where are you going?

MARIANE   Let me alone!

DORINE   Come back!

MARIANE   No use, Dorine. You try another tack.

80   VALÈRE   It's clear it tortures her to look at me.
I'll just remove myself and set her free.

DORINE [*leaving* MARIANE *and running to* VALÈRE] What the
deuce? What's all this that I hear?
Now stop this nonsense! Both of you come here! [*She pulls at
them, one with each hand.*]

VALÈRE   What are you up to?

MARIANE   What do you think you're doing?

85   DORINE   Trying to get you two to billing and cooing.

VALÈRE   You must be crazy, as far as I can see.
Didn't you hear the way she talked to me?

DORINE [*to* MARIANE] You act as if you're going off your head.

MARIANE   Didn't you hear the awful things he said?

DORINE   You're crazy, both of you. [*to* VALÈRE] Now I am sure
90   The only thing she wants is to be yours.
[*to* MARIANE] He loves you only; I'm prepared to swear
That marriage—and to you—is his desire.

MARIANE [*to* VALÈRE] Why did you give me, then, your vile advice?

VALÈRE [*to* MARIANE] Your asking for it wasn't exactly nice.

95   DORINE   I said you both were crazy. Give me your hand.
Yours, now.

VALÈRE   Why give you my hand?

DORINE   You'll understand.

MARIANE   What *is* all this?

DORINE   Just this. You're both in love
  More than you're either of you conscious of.

VALÈRE   Well, there's no harm—at least once in a while—
  In giving a man a little friendly smile.   100

[MARIANE *looks at* VALÈRE *and smiles feebly*.]

DORINE   The fact is, lovers are completely daft.

VALÈRE   *I've* reason to complain, you know. You laughed
  At me and scorned me with reproof
  Because I thought you'd said "Yes" to Tartuffe.

MARIANE   But you yourself . . . it really is a shame . . .   105

DORINE   Let's leave this issue for another time.
  The thing we need now is a cunning plan.

MARIANE   Speak up, Dorine. We'll do all that we can.

DORINE   There are a lot of tricks that we can play.
  Your father's bluffing, surely, but the way   110
  For you to get around him is to feign
  Complete compliance with his mad design,
  So that, in case of crisis, you can manage
  To keep postponing this unwelcome marriage.
  Time has many virtues; it can heal   115
  Many a wound that seems beyond repeal.
  And there are many tricks. Say you fell ill;
  No one can force you then against your will.
  Or maybe some dire omen greets your eyes:
  A funeral in the street (a grim surprise),   120
  A broken mirror, auguring the worst,
  A black cat, which suggests your life is cursed—
  A dozen dodges. But I would much rather
  You two would not be seen like this together.
  [*to* VALÈRE] Now go and use the help of all your friends   125
  To win the girl that clearly Fate intends
  For you. [*to* MARIANE] I'm sure you'll get your brother
  To help you, not to mention your stepmother.
  Good-by!

VALÈRE [*to* MARIANE]   We all will do whatever we can do,
  But my best hope and love resides in you.   130

MARIANE   I don't know what my father may decide.
  I only know I'll not be Tartuffe's bride.

VALÈRE   You make me very happy. And if ever . . .

DORINE   Lovers are never tired. They talk forever.
Come on, get going!

VALÈRE   Farewell . . .

135 DORINE   Oh, talk, talk, talk!
You that way, and you this. Come on, now! Walk!

ACT THREE

Scene One

[DAMIS *and* DORINE]

DAMIS   Let Heaven strike me with a lightning bolt,
   Let all the world call me a rogue, a dolt;
   No talk of filial respect, no father's power
   Will hold me back; I'll act within the hour!

DORINE   For Heaven's sake, enough of this mad chatter;   5
   Your father's merely talked about the matter.
   Need I remind you that there's many a slip
   Betwixt the smooth cup and the slippery lip?

DAMIS   I'll stop that fat conspirator's career;
   I'll speak a word or two into his ear.   10

DORINE   Easy does it, boy; let your stepmother
   Handle him, the way she does your father.
   Tartuffe becomes like putty in her hands
   And easily agrees to her demands.
   I think he eyes her with a secret yen;   15
   Lord knows, I hope that that's the case, for then
   She'll come to interview him, for your sake,
   Learn what his feelings are and make
   Him understand what troubles will be brewing
   If he continues as he has been doing.   20
   His valet tells me that he's at his prayers;
   No one can see him; he's alone upstairs.
   But he'll be coming down in a minute or two,
   So beat it, please; I'll see what I can do.

DAMIS   I must be present when he talks to her.   25

DORINE   Never! Beat it!

DAMIS   I won't speak or stir.

DORINE   Nonsense! I know how you fly off the handle,
   And that's the surest way to snuff the candle.
   Go on!

DAMIS   I promise I won't rage or shout.

DORINE   Oh, what a pest you are! Look, here he comes! Get out!   30

[DORINE *pushes him out.* TARTUFFE *enters and, seeing* DORINE, *calls off stage.*]

Scene Two

[TARTUFFE *and* DORINE]

TARTUFFE [*calls off stage*]   Put away my hair shirt and my scourge
 And pray perpetually that Heaven may purge
 Our souls of sin. If someone asks for me,
 I've gone to bless the poor with charity.

5 DORINE [*aside*]   What hogwash! What a stupid thing to say!

TARTUFFE   What do you want?

DORINE   I . . .

TARTUFFE [*drawing out a kerchief*]   Wait! I pray,
 Take this handkerchief before you speak.

DORINE   Why?

TARTUFFE   Cover that bosom which demurely peeks
 Above your bodice. Such forbidden sights
10 May well give rise to slightly carnal thoughts.

DORINE   You must be quite concupiscently queasy
 If a little flesh can make you so uneasy.
 Of course, I don't know how you're stimulated
 But I'm not quite so easily elated.
15 Why, I could see you nude without a qualm;
 In fact, I think I'd stay supremely calm.

TARTUFFE   A bit more modesty in speech, my dear,
 Or I'll withdraw and leave you standing here.

DORINE   No, I will go and leave you here alone,
20 But first, there's something that you should have known;
 Madame Elmire will soon come into view.
 She'd like to have a word or two with you.

TARTUFFE   Delighted!

DORINE [*aside*]   He leaps and bleats just like a woolly lamb.
 I'm right, he has a hankering for madame.

TARTUFFE   She's coming soon?

25 DORINE   Yes, here she comes this way;
 I'll leave you two together, if I may. [*Exit.*]

Scene Three

[ELMIRE *and* TARTUFFE]

TARTUFFE   May Heaven's grace, madame, preserve you whole
  And sound in mind, in body, and in soul,
  And bless your days according to the prayers
  Of one who's much concerned with your affairs.

ELMIRE   I'm deeply grateful for your pieties.   5
  Let us sit down and chat more at our ease.

TARTUFFE   I trust, madame, your fever's not persisted?

ELMIRE   I'm feeling well; the fever's quite arrested.

TARTUFFE   My poor and humble prayers here in this place
  Seem all too small to have brought down such grace   10
  Upon you from on high; yet I confess
  My constant thoughts are of your happiness.

ELMIRE   Your pious zeal is rather overpowering.

TARTUFFE   Pray Heaven that the heavens keep on showering
  Blessings on you; I'd give my life for yours.   15

ELMIRE   There's no need for such drastic overtures.
  But I'm indebted to you for your prayers.

TARTUFFE   Dear lady, *anything* to ease your cares . . .

[DAMIS *enters unseen behind them.*]

ELMIRE   I wanted to speak privately to you.
  I'm glad we're here out of the public view.   20

TARTUFFE   And so am I! Dear Heaven, but it's sweet
  To be beside you, madame, on this seat.
  This is a chance for which I've often prayed;
  It seems a stroke of luck that Fate has made.

ELMIRE   I know, my friend, exactly what you mean.   25
  I've often longed for a chat like this, unseen.

TARTUFFE   Oh, how I've prayed that we could freely share
  Our thoughts and words, that I could boldly bare
  My soul unto you, that I might explain
  My distaste for the friends you entertain   30
  Springs not from my dislike of your devotion
  To them, but rather from my own profound emotion
  Which fairly chokes me . . .

ELMIRE   Well, your zeal
  Is something, sir, that you need not conceal.

TARTUFFE [*taking her hand and squeezing her fingers*]   How hard
35   I pray for you, and even harder . . .

ELMIRE   Ouch! You're hurting me!

TARTUFFE   Forgive my ardor!
  I had no idea of hurting you, I swear!
  It's just . . . [*puts his hand on her knee*]

ELMIRE   Your hand. What is it doing there?

TARTUFFE   Just feeling the material; it's nice!

40   ELMIRE   I'm ticklish. Please, don't make me ask you twice.

[*She moves her chair away;* TARTUFFE *brings his closer. This continues throughout the scene.*]

TARTUFFE   I am a great admirer of fine lace.
  The workmanship, the beauty, and the grace
  Of the design. What lovely decoration!

ELMIRE   Perhaps. But now, sir, to our conversation.
45   I hear my husband wants to marry you
  To Mariane. Pray tell me, is that true?

TARTUFFE   He's mentioned it. But, lady, need I say
  That's not the joy I dream of night and day?
  It's elsewhere that I see the lovely fire
50   Which blazes with the beauties I desire.

ELMIRE   You mean you don't love earthly things alone?

TARTUFFE   I mean, madame, my heart's not made of stone.

ELMIRE   I see. You mean your thoughts are turned to Heaven,
  Toward which your yearning spirit long has striven.

55   TARTUFFE   The love which draws us toward eternal beauty
  Does not release us from our earthly duty
  To love each other. Heaven often forms
  A vessel whose supernal beauty warms
  Our earthly blood. And such a one are you;
60   My spirit soars when you come into view.
  Heaven's glories shine within your face;
  Your form and figure testify to Grace.
  O perfect beauty, perfect in each feature!
  In you I worship great creating Nature.
65   Fair goddess! wondrous woman; in your eyes
  I see the will of Heaven and am wise.
  At first I trembled, lest my sacred passion
  For you prove false, a hindrance to salvation,
  Perhaps—who knows?—a horrid stratagem
70   Of the Evil One, a trap to catch me in.

I even thought to flee in foolish fashion,
But then I came to see that such a passion,
Inspired by Heaven as it is, undoubtedly,
Need not be inconsistent with true modesty.
And so I gave my eager heart full rein.   75
I know I should not hope that you will deign
To smile with condescension on my suit;
But still, when Heaven calls, dare man be mute?
In you is all my hope, my good, my peace;
In you rests my damnation or release.   80
I may taste bliss or be tormented still;
It all will be according to your will.

ELMIRE   This is indeed a gallant declaration.
I must confess, though, to some consternation.
You should have steeled your feelings somewhat better;   85
Why, what would happen if my husband ever
Heard words like this from such a pious man? . . .

TARTUFFE   Though I am pious, I am still a man,
An erring, mortal man, and when your beauties
Flame on my sight, all my religious duties   90
Grow somewhat blurred. I know such an appraisal
May shock you somewhat. Still, I'm not an angel.
And if you view my conduct with alarm,
You must accuse your own bewitching charm.
Since I first viewed your beauty's flawless art,   95
You've been the sovereign of my secret heart.
My poor soul struggled, but alas! in vain
Against your distant beauty and disdain;
In vain, in vain my fasting, prayers and tears.
Each soft breeze blew your sweet name to my ears.   100
How long I've sought to say this with my eyes;
Now hear it in my words and in my sighs.
And if you look with pity and compassion
Upon this poor unworthy slave of passion,
If you consent to bring me consolation   105
And bring about my yearning soul's salvation,
I'll swear to you with most profound emotion
Unending service and a true devotion.
And in my hands be sure a lady's honor
Is safe, no danger that there'll come upon her   110
The smallest breath of scandal. These young sparks
That ladies dote on are unsafe. Their larks,
Their jokes, their boasts about the wars of love
Leave ladies' reputations not above
Reproach, and many ladies have been tarnished   115
By faithless gallants whose careers have furnished

Examples of betrayal and deceit.
But fear me not, dear lady; I'm discreet.
The care a man like me takes of his name
120   Is guarantee that you need fear no shame;
You buy, if you accept my heart, my dear,
Love without scandal, pleasure without fear.

ELMIRE   I'm fascinated; and your rhetoric
Effectively removes all the inveterate
125   Fears I might have felt; but don't *you* fear
That I might speak a word in Orgon's ear
About your strange behavior here today?
If I did, what do you think he'd say?

TARTUFFE   I know you are too merciful and good
130   And that my love is not misunderstood.
Pity for human frailty will excuse
My over-ardent voicing of such views.
Although I yearn toward the True and Good,
Still I am human, merely flesh and blood.

135 ELMIRE   Another woman might, indeed, repeat
This story; but I too can be discreet.
I'll not tell Orgon of your strange behavior;
In turn I'll beg of you a certain favor:
I want you to speak boldly and declare
140   That you support the marriage of Valère
And Mariane, that you renounce the claim
By which you would usurp another's name,
And . . .

Scene Four

[ELMIRE, DAMIS *and* TARTUFFE]

DAMIS [*emerging*] No, madame, no! This news must come to
    light!
I've been this while concealed there, within sight
And hearing. Heaven's favor led me there
To trap this hypocrite in his own snare
5   And place within my hands at last the power
Of sweet revenge. Aha! Within the hour
I'll undeceive my father and he'll know
The gross sins of that fat Lothario!

ELMIRE   No, Damis, it's enough if he repents.
10   I'll count that a sufficient recompense

I've promised it; don't make me break a vow.
No nasty scenes; I'm willing to allow
The whole affair to pass and not displease
My husband's ears with such absurdities.

DAMIS You may have reason, madame, to be lenient,   15
But I do not consider it convenient
To lose this chance of pricking his fat bubble
And plunging him up to the ears in trouble.
His sanctimonious impudence too long
Has stirred up trouble in our home; too long   20
He's bilked my father, led him by the nose.
And now with vengeance sure, do you suppose
I'll overlook my opportunity?
It is a grace that Heaven's conferred on me.
Now and henceforth I am Heaven's debtor,   25
And Heaven knows when I will find a better
Chance to give this slippery fox a jolt.
If I passed up this chance, I'd be a dolt.

ELMIRE Damis . . .

DAMIS   I must do what I think is justified.
I've never felt so richly satisfied.   30
Please don't deter me. Try to understand
My joy in holding vengeance in my hand.
I'll have full satisfaction, I vow,
And see, here comes my opportunity, right now.

Scene Five

[ORGON, ELMIRE, DAMIS, *and* TARTUFFE]

DAMIS [*continuing, to* ORGON, *who enters*]   Father, I've got a bit
    of a surprise
For you; some news to open up your eyes.
Your kindnesses have here been well repaid;
This gentleman, behind your back, has made
Proposals to madame which cast upon her
A curious light and work to your dishonor.   5
In short, I've just surprised this monstrous beast
In making love to her and, sir, he ceased
Only when I spoke. Madame implored
I spare you this recital, but I've stored
A thirst for vengeance in my hungry heart,   10
And I don't choose to play a forgiving part.

ELMIRE   I think a wife ought never to annoy
    Her husband with such silly tales. My boy,
    A woman likes to handle such affairs
15   In her own way, so that nobody shares
    The knowledge of the circumstances. You'd be
    Silent now if you were ruled by me. [*Exit*.]

Scene Six

[ORGON, DAMIS, *and* TARTUFFE]

ORGON   Oh, gracious Heavens! Can I trust my ears?

TARTUFFE   Alas, the case is just as it appears:
    I am a sinner lost in deep iniquity,
    One who would let mere physical propinquity
5   Corrupt his holy purposes and stain
    His spotless shield of honor; don't refrain
    From heaping censure on me. I'm a beast.
    My life's a mass of crime; there's not the least
    Extenuation possible for me.
10   Heaven has contrived all this, I see,
    As punishment for my most rank misdeeds
    And Heaven has ordained that no one pleads
    For me. Let no man speak. Let me be driven
    Out of your house, out of the sight of Heaven.

15 ORGON [*to* DAMIS]   Traitor! How do you dare, with nasty lies,
    To bring the innocent tears into his eyes?

DAMIS   Don't tell me all this blubbering and bluster
    Is going to make you think . . .

ORGON   Be silent, monster!

TARTUFFE   Ah, let him speak! How wrongly you accuse him!
20   Believe his words! It's wrong if you refuse him
    Your trusting ears. Why put your faith in me?
    How do you know what sort of man I might be?
    Brother, how can you trust my outward seeming?
    Perhaps when you look at me you're merely dreaming.
25   No, no, my outward semblance may deceive;
    Within, I am far worse than you believe.
    Although I commonly pass for a man of virtue,
    You sadly let my outer surface cheat you. [*to* DAMIS]
    Speak, dear boy, call me a vile traitor,
30   Perfidious, a liar, a betrayer
    Of friendship's trust; call me the vilest term

You can imagine; I'm lower than a worm [*on his knees*]
Let me acknowledge here upon my knees
My horrid crimes. Condemn me, if you please.

ORGON Brother, this is too much! [*to* DAMIS] So—your heart   35
Remains unmoved?

DAMIS   He's merely playing a part!

ORGON Silence, scoundrel! [*to* TARTUFFE] My brother, I beg you,
stand! [*to* DAMIS]
Rascal!

DAMIS He can . . .

ORGON   Silence!

DAMIS   Don't you understand?

ORGON Just one more word, and I'll punch you in the nose!

TARTUFFE Do not be angry, brother. Do you suppose   40
I would not rather suffer indignity
Than have him suffer the slightest scratch for me?

ORGON [*to* DAMIS] Ingrate!

TARTUFFE   Leave him in peace! See, I'm kneeling
To ask you for his pardon.

ORGON Oh, what feeling! [*falling on his knees and embracing*
TARTUFFE]
Observe his goodness!

DAMIS   But . . .

ORGON   Peace!

DAMIS   But, I . . .

ORGON   Quiet!   45
I understand why you're raising all this riot.
You hate him, all of you: my faithful wife,
My children, servants—why, upon my life!
It's a conspiracy to drive this saint
Out of my house. And this absurd complaint   50
Against him doesn't move me, not a whit.
I'll stand with him forever; you can sit
And spin your lies; I'll hasten with my plan
To marry this wronged saint to Mariane.

DAMIS You think you'll force her into such a plight?   55

ORGON Yes, and, to spite you all, this very night!
Oh, I defy you! Defy you, do you hear?
I'll show you, mark my words, who's master here!

Take back your wicked words, you monster, and entreat
60   His pardon. I command you, fall at his feet!

DAMIS   What? Fall at the feet of this repulsive liar?

ORGON   Ah, you resist my will? You've roused my ire!
Give me a stick, a stick! Don't hold me back!
Out of my sight! I'll deal you such a crack
65   Your ears will ring! Out! Out of my place!

DAMIS   All right, I'll go, but . . .

ORGON   Don't let me see your face!
Reptile, I'll remove you from my will!
Take my curse, and go—wherever you will.

[*Exit* DAMIS.]

Scene Seven

[ORGON *and* TARTUFFE]

ORGON [*continuing, to* TARTUFFE]   Think of offering such insults
to you!

TARTUFFE   May Heaven pardon him, as I would do.
Ah, could you know how bitterly I suffer
To hear such words spoken to my brother . . .

ORGON   Alas!

5 TARTUFFE   Merely to think of such ingratitude
Makes my heart ache. Words so rough and crude
Fill my soul with a horror that's so deep
I can do nothing but beat my breast and weep!

ORGON [*runs to the door where he has driven* DAMIS]   Villain!
I'm sorry I didn't knock you down
10   When I had the chance! Liar! Monster! Clown!

TARTUFFE   Brother, compose yourself. Don't be distressed.
Let's have no more of this. I think it best
That I should leave your home, dear friend, right now.
I'll never return to bother you, I vow.

ORGON   You're jesting!

15 TARTUFFE   No, no, they all hate me here.
They'd even question my sincerity, I fear.

ORGON   Do you think I listen to anything they say?

TARTUFFE   But they'll go on with their tales, day after day.

These stories that today have left you grieved
Tomorrow may be readily believed.   20

ORGON   Oh, never, brother, never!

TARTUFFE   Brother, a wife
May sway a husband's mind and rule his life.

ORGON   You shall not go! Never! I will not hear it!

TARTUFFE   Well, I'll remain, to mortify my spirit.
Still, if you desired it . . .

ORGON   Oh!

TARTUFFE   Well, no more.   25
I'll not behave as I have done before.
Honor is delicate, and, like Caesar's wife,
I must be past suspicion. On my life,
I'll flee the presence of madame and call . . .

ORGON   No, you'll attend her, to defy them all.   30
My one desire now is to fully spite them;
You must be with her constantly—we'll fight them,
Fire with fire, slander with suspicion,
To keep their tongues a-wagging. In addition,
I'm firm resolved that you must be my heir.   35
I'll change my will today, and I'll declare
That all my wealth is yours by legal right.
I tell you, brother, I take more delight
In you, my heir, than in all my family.

TARTUFFE   May Heaven's will be done eternally.   40

ORGON   Come, let's change the document; meanwhile,
Let the jealous choke on their own bile!

ACT FOUR

Scene One

[CLÉANTE *and* TARTUFFE]

CLÉANTE   Everywhere I go I hear this story;
  It's one that doesn't add unto your glory;
  And I am glad, sir, I've run into you
  So I can tell you briefly what my view
5 Of the matter is. I won't weigh right and wrong;
  In any case, the evidence is strong.
  But let's assume the tale Damis propounded
  Was false, and the whole thing was unfounded.
  Should not a Christian pardon the mistake,
10 Turning the other cheek for charity's sake?
  Should such a quarrel, by purpose or by chance
  Be cause for Damis' disinheritance?
  In perfect frankness, sir, let me repeat:
  The story's spreading; everyone you meet
15 Is talking of it. Look at what you've done!
  It's not too late for father and for son
  To reconcile; if you promote this union,
  You'll bring yourself back into good opinion.

TARTUFFE   Alas, how happy I would be, if this could be!
20 God knows, my heart of rancor is quite free.
  I would not harm him, bless you, if I could;
  I long with all my heart to do him good.
  But Heaven's will doesn't always fit my heart;
  If he returns to the house, I must depart.
25 No, no, I couldn't stay with him in this place,
  Not without a sense of complete disgrace;
  It would be an intolerable situation;
  Why, people might accuse me of calculation.
  They'd say I was pretending, as a ruse, sir,
30 False charity to silence my accuser.
  They'd say I kept him here beneath surveillance
  Merely to ensure his guilty silence.

CLÉANTE   Your statements have some plausibility,
  But still it all sounds quite far-fetched to me.
35 Since when are you the self-appointed judge

248

Of who must cringe beneath great Heaven's scourge?
Let God decide on matters of election
And let him implement his own correction.
And he who's moved by Heaven, not his humors,
Should not be sensitive to idle rumors.   40
No need, I'm sure, for fearing idle tongues
When you act truly to correct great wrongs,
And he who would take justice in his hands
Should first be sure he's tuned to God's commands.

TARTUFFE   My one desire's to be obedient   45
To God, whenever it's expedient.
But, after Damis' recent rude behavior,
I'd not forgive him, no, were I the Savior.

CLÉANTE   And does God order you to punish him
By aiding and abetting Orgon's whim   50
To disinherit him? And does God know
How you will profit by his overthrow?

TARTUFFE   No one who's plumbed the true depths of my spirit
Could think a thing like that of me, or fear it.
The riches of this world are dross to me;   55
Their gleaming superficiality
Does not seduce me; and if I accept
Something of the wealth Orgon has kept
Hidden away, my motives are quite pure:
To keep it out of the hands of an evildoer,   60
Someone who might, alas! make evil use
Of it, or squander it without excuse;
How better, then, to give it to one who swore he
Would dedicate its use to Heaven's glory?

CLÉANTE   Your reasons are somewhat sophistical,   65
If not, indeed, a trifle egotistical.
Why not let Damis have his proper wealth,
As long as you have liberty and health?
Better, indeed, to let the lad misuse it
Than countenance the rumor you'd abuse it   70
For your own purposes. I'm amazed
You could have heard this plan and not have raised
Your voice in protest. As far as I'm aware,
God doesn't condone defrauding a son and heir.
And if God in truth your heart has steeled   75
Against Damis, then why not quit the field
As any honorable adversary should
And leave the house to him? I'm sure I would.
Believe me, sir, it does you no great credit
To have this story spread, and if you let it   80

Gain further credence, your basic piety
Will seem . . .

TARTUFFE Excuse me, sir, it's half-past three;
I must retire to prayers and meditations;
I leave you with my best felicitations. [*Exit.*]

Scene Two

[ELMIRE, MARIANE, CLÉANTE, *and* DORINE]

DORINE Sir, can't you help her soul gain some relief,
For she is suffering a most cruel grief?
This hateful marriage pledge her father's made
Has sickened her poor heart, and it's betrayed
5 Her fondest hopes. He's coming now. Let's try
To undermine this project on the sly,
And unite this poor maid and Valère.

[*Enter* ORGON.]

Scene Three

[ORGON, ELMIRE, MARIANE, CLÉANTE, *and* DORINE]

ORGON I'm glad to find you all assembled here. [*to* MARIANE]
There's something in this deed to make you smile,
And I'll reveal it in a little while.

MARIANE Father, I call on Heaven, which knows my grief!
5 Look in your heart and offer me relief
From this oppressive sorrow; oh, relax
The rights of fatherhood, I pray. Don't tax
My frail forbearance, so that I must cry
In bitter protest unto God on high.
10 Don't make a senseless tragedy
Out of that life which you have given me.
Though you forbid my wedding the one I love,
At least, I beg, by all the powers above,
Don't bring me to this miserable estate
15 By forcing me to marry one I hate.
Don't drive me to an act of blind despair
By bringing all your legal powers to bear.

ORGON [*aside*] Be strong, my heart! Don't yield to human frailty!

MARIANE I'm not distressed by your continued loyalty
   To him. Give him your wealth, if that's what you want to do   20
   And, if that's not enough, why, take mine too.
   Give him all that I have; it cannot worsen
   My grief. But don't consign to him my person!
   Just spare me that. Then, when the deed is done,
   Let me retire to spend my life as a nun.   25

ORGON You think, by waxing weepy and despondent,
   And talking crazily about a convent,
   You'll frighten me? Get up! I say, the more
   Your heart recoils, the more you'll answer for.
   So mortify your senses by your yielding   30
   Meekly to the power that I'm wielding.

DORINE But what . . . ?

ORGON   Be silent! Speak when you're spoken to!
   I don't want to hear a syllable out of you!

CLÉANTE If you'll permit me to offer some advice . . .

ORGON Your words, dear brother, always are quite nice,   35
   And your advice is always full of merit,
   So much so, I'd prefer just not to hear it.

ELMIRE [*to* ORGON] Seeing all this, I find myself struck dumb.
   I can't believe how blind you have become.
   You must be hypnotized, or else insane,   40
   To doubt our word about this recent scene.

ORGON I believe your words, dear, one by one,
   And I know how fond you are of my rascal son.
   Clearly you were afraid to disavow
   The fraud he tried to perpetrate just now.   45
   And you were, I must protest, a shade too calm;
   A woman in your place should have showed alarm.

ELMIRE Should a woman's honor be so stirred
   If someone offers her a wicked word?
   And does a mere suggestion then require   50
   Denunciations and a tongue of fire?
   Why, all I do is laugh at such advances;
   To me, they're unimportant circumstances.
   I try to wear my virtue modestly
   And not like some protesting prudes I see   55
   Whose virtue comes full-armed with teeth and claws
   Ready to scratch and bite at the slightest cause.
   Heaven preserve me from such purity!
   True Virtue needs no arms and need not be
   Masked by scowls. A firm and simple "No"   60
   Will tell unwelcome lovers where to go.

ORGON   You needn't try to make a dupe of me.

ELMIRE   I can't believe your gullibility!
    Could I shake your blind, unthinking faith
65 By making you witness to the truth?

ORGON   Witness?

ELMIRE   Yes.

ORGON   Nonsense!

ELMIRE   Suppose
    I show you the fact before your very eyes?

ORGON   Balderdash!

ELMIRE   Oh, what a man! It's too absurd!
    You obviously won't believe a word.
70 Suppose we could place you here concealed
    Where you could see what would be revealed,
    And you saw the truth? Then what would you do?

ORGON   I'd say in that case . . . well, I'd say "Pooh pooh!"
    For it cannot be.

ELMIRE   You've been too long unwise,
75 And you've accused me for too long of telling lies.
    Now, for my satisfaction and your proof,
    I'll make you witness to the living truth.

ORGON   I'll take you up on that! Let's see your scheme.
    The truth will be far stranger than you dream.

ELMIRE [to DORINE]   Send him in here.

80 DORINE   He's clever as a fox
    And he won't be easily trapped within a box.

ELMIRE   Some men are easily fooled by infatuation;
    Such blindness must be cured by illumination.
    Have him come down. [to CLÉANTE and MARIANE] And, you
    two, please go.

[Exeunt DORINE, CLÉANTE, and MARIANE.]

Scene Four

[ELMIRE and ORGON]

ELMIRE [continuing, to ORGON]   See that table? There's your
    place—below.

ORGON   What?

ELMIRE   You'll have to hide yourself, that's clear.

ORGON   But why beneath the table?

ELMIRE   Get under here!
I have my plan; You'll see how it works out;
Under the table, quick, and when you're set,   5
Not a whisper. Don't make any comments.

ORGON   I must say, I'm most patient with your nonsense.
Well, let me see you wiggle out of this one.

ELMIRE   Remember, there are one or two conditions:
Since this is a rather ticklish situation,   10
I must behave according to the occasion;
Pray don't be scandalized if I seem to behave
Quite forwardly; I do it for you, to save
Your sanity; some questions I may ask
Are merely traps to tempt him to unmask,   15
And if I smile upon his lewd desires
It's merely to arouse his amorous fires.
Remember: for your sake and his confusion
I have consented here in this seclusion
To meet with him. The action will subside   20
As soon as you feel fully satisfied.
Your task will be, concealed there as you are,
To call a halt if things have gone too far.
A husband, after all, should shield his wife
From the unpleasant perils of this life;   25
You are the master in the house, and your will
Should be obeyed . . . Sh! Here he comes! Be still!

Scene Five

[TARTUFFE, ELMIRE, and ORGON. ORGON is under the table]

TARTUFFE   They said, dear lady, you were waiting here.

ELMIRE   Yes. I've a secret for your private ear.
But close that door first, please, and peep
About the room. Let's not be caught asleep.

[TARTUFFE shuts the door and looks about.]

ELMIRE   We certainly don't want again, you know,   5
The sort of scene we had a while ago.
That was most disagreeable, it's true,
And I was in a panic because of you.
You saw I did my best to keep him quiet.

10   But he was clearly determined to raise a riot.
Of course, I was so alarmed—I was nearly dead!—
I didn't think to deny the things he'd said.
But, Heaven be praised, it all worked out ideally
And everything is understood—yes, really!
15   Your reputation's so strong, it cannot fall,
And my husband does not suspect you, not at all.
In fact, to still the voice of slander, he
Wants us to be together continually.
So now we're able to be sequestered here
20   Behind locked doors and free of blame or fear,
And I can reveal what my true feelings are
About you, sir—but perhaps I go too far.

    TARTUFFE   This talk is rather baffling, I'll admit;
    You've changed, madame, since the last time we met.

25   ELMIRE   Why, if you're angry at my earlier rebuff,
You don't know women's hearts quite well enough.
You don't know what our hearts are trying to speak
When our defense seems languid, slow, and weak.
And ever our modesty must make a show
30   Of struggling valiantly to overthrow
Our feelings, which, the while we're yielding,
We blush to find our words have been revealing.
At first we fight against them, but our tender
Sighs betray our swift complete surrender.
35   For honor's sake, we put our hearts on trial
And promise everything with a denial.
I fear I'm speaking much too honestly
And overlooking proper modesty.
But, since I'm speaking frankly, don't you see
40   Why I didn't struggle to restrain Damis?
And would I, pray, so graciously, so long,
Have listened to your offer, and so long
Have let you pour your heart out in full measure
If the affair did not afford me pleasure?
45   And when I argued with such force and courage
To get you to renounce your coming marriage
Why would my claims have been so strongly pressed
Except for my own selfish interest?
In short, I feared this marriage might divide
50   A heart I wanted whole, and near my side.

    TARTUFFE   Ah, madame, it gives me joy extreme
To hear such words from you. It's like a dream!
Their honey pours into my tortured brain;
Their liquid sweetness flows through every vein.

My aim's to please you, all things else above; 55
My heart's beatitude lies in your love.
And yet I hope you'll not think me suspicious
To dare to doubt my joys are so delicious.
I could almost suspect a sly arrangement
To get me to break off my late engagement. 60
And so, madame, to put the matter bluntly,
And much as I enjoy your lovely company,
I'll dare to doubt your tender words until
Some tangible favors indicate your will,
Implanting in my wavering soul a faith 65
That your dear bounty's not a vagrant wraith.

ELMIRE [*coughing to warn* ORGON]   What do you mean? Don't
    tell me that you think
You can rush love to its climax in a wink!
I've forced myself to make a rash admission,
But now you'd add, I see, another condition, 70
And you won't be satisfied until you win
Love's final favors almost before you begin.

TARTUFFE   The less one merits, the less one dares to hope;
    Where talk is cheap, each parish priest's a Pope.
One easily mistrusts a promised bliss 75
And can't believe it till it's really his.
Knowing how little I am worthy of you,
I doubt I'll ever be allowed to love you.
In short, madame, I'll not believe a word
Till facts confirm these promises I've heard. 80

ELMIRE   Dear me! Your love is really quite tyrannical.
    I'd hate to think I'm being puritanical,
But, mercy me! love drives men quite insane,
So powerful and violent is its reign;
Can I not raise my hands in weak defense? 85
Is there no way to curb your violence?
Take pity on a lady, sir, and send her
Reprieve. Complete, abject surrender
Is frightening, you know, and it may cost
You a regard you'd rather not have lost. 90

TARTUFFE   If you receive my homage with compassion,
    Then why withhold love's tangible expression?

ELMIRE   But, if I consent, won't Heaven be offended?
    This is your constant theme, and I commend it.

TARTUFFE   Pooh! If Heaven's all that's worrying you, 95
    I'll take care of that, and easily too;
I can remove such obstacles with ease.

ELMIRE   And yet they threaten us so with Heaven's decrees!

TARTUFFE   I can banish such superstitious fear.
100   There is an art, you know, in making clear
           Heaven's will, and though Heaven may proscribe
           Certain joys, a bit of a spiritual bribe
           Can clear the path sometimes. There is a science
           Of loosening the conscience so compliance
105   Is easy, and the evil of an action
           Is rectified to Heaven's satisfaction.
           I'll teach you all these secrets; you will see.
           But you must put your confidence in me.
           Content my longings, lady; do not fear.
110   The risk is mine; don't hesitate, my dear.

[ELMIRE coughs.]

TARTUFFE   You have a nasty cough . . .

ELMIRE   It's most distressing.

TARTUFFE   I have some cough drops. Try one, with my blessing.

ELMIRE   I've had this cough for weeks, would you believe it?
    I fear that all your cough drops can't relieve it.

TARTUFFE   Very annoying.

115   ELMIRE   Yes, it's quite severe.

TARTUFFE   Well, at least I can dispel your fear.
           Your secret is known to us alone,
           And evil's not evil until it's known
           To the world at large, and, as for sin,
120   To sin in silence is not to sin.

ELMIRE [coughs]   In short, I see that I shall have to yield
           And, fleeing, leave you master of the field
           Of my poor honor, for I can't convince
           A man who demands such tangible evidence.
125   I must admit I fear to go so far,
           But who cares what my foolish scruples are?
           And since I'm driven to it cruelly
           By one who seems to find my pleas unduly
           Quibbling and demands complete conviction
130   I must decide to render satisfaction
           Unto his claims. If there is any crime
           In such consent, it's clear the blame's not mine.
           Surely I am not responsible.

TARTUFFE   Of course not, lady! Why the thought's impossible!

ELMIRE   But first, please open the door—but not too wide—   135
   And see if my husband's lurking there outside.

TARTUFFE   Pooh! Why worry about dolts like those?
   He's the type you can lead around by the nose,
   The type to abet our little intimacies;
   Why, we can make him believe whatever we please.   140

ELMIRE   All the same, I'd feel much more secure
   If you'd take a look around just to be sure.

[*Exit* TARTUFFE.]

Scene Six

[ORGON *and* ELMIRE]

ORGON [*emerging from under the table*]   Such wickedness is in-
   conceivable!
   I'm thunderstruck! It's unbelievable!

ELMIRE   What, crawling out so soon? Don't be absurd!
   Creep in again and wait. You haven't heard
   A fraction yet. Wait, and you'll correct your   5
   Ideas further, and it won't be mere conjecture.

ORGON   Nothing more wicked has ever come out of hell!

ELMIRE   Don't be too quick to believe the tales they tell
   About him. Perhaps you are mistaken
   And you've let your faith be far too lightly shaken . . .   10

[*As* TARTUFFE *re-enters,* ELMIRE *quickly hides* ORGON *behind her.*]

Scene Seven

[TARTUFFE, ELMIRE, *and* ORGON]

TARTUFFE   Everything's working out, madame, for the best.
   The coast is clear. It seems that Heaven has blessed
   This moment. My senses are delighted . . .

[*As he advances to embrace* ELMIRE, *she steps aside, and he walks
into the arms of* ORGON.]

ORGON   Hold on a minute! Don't get so excited!
   Don't let your passions carry you away!   5

Aha! You pious soul, you thought to betray
Your benefactor by seducing his wife,
Wedding his daughter and fixing yourself for life!
I've long suspected that some day I would see
10   You're not all that you're cracked up to be.
But now I've seen enough, yes, and I've heard
More than enough. No, not another word.

ELMIRE [*to* TARTUFFE]   It's not my manner to tease and betray,
But I've been forced to treat you in this way.

TARTUFFE [*to* ORGON]   What, can you believe . . . ?

15   ORGON   Let no more be said.
Get out of here before I lose my head.

TARTUFFE   I only sought . . .

ORGON   To secretly seduce my spouse!
I know. This minute—get out of my house!

TARTUFFE   But, just a moment—*you* are the one to leave.
20   This house belongs to me, I do believe.
There's no use trying to pick a quarrel with me
On such a poor excuse. You wait! You'll see!
You're in a poor position to evict me,
When *you're* the one to pack and leave—and quickly!
25   I have the power to avenge offended Heaven;
Please be gone by quarter past eleven. [*Exit.*]

Scene Eight

[ELMIRE *and* ORGON]

ELMIRE   What's he talking about? It's all a bluff.

ORGON   I wish it were. I fear he's serious enough.

ELMIRE   What is it?

ORGON   This is a pretty mess, indeed.
I made a great mistake when I gave him that deed.

ELMIRE   A deed?

5   ORGON   Yes, and it's signed and sealed.
But there may be even more to be revealed.

ELMIRE   What's that?

ORGON   I'll tell you later; first, I want to see
If my strongbox still is where it used to be.

ACT FIVE

Scene One

[ORGON *and* CLÉANTE]

CLÉANTE   Where are you going?

ORGON   I don't know.

CLÉANTE   It's clear
   We need to talk about this dreadful affair.

ORGON   The strongbox mainly weighs upon my mind,
   More than all the other matters combined.

CLÉANTE   This strongbox is an important mystery?   5

ORGON   It has a most unusual history.
   My good friend Argas gave it to me in trust,
   Impressing on me, come what may, I must
   Keep it a secret; his life, his property
   Depended on that box he gave to me.   10

CLÉANTE   Then why, pray tell, did you give it to Tartuffe?

ORGON   I know, dear brother; I merit your reproof.
   I hoped to keep my conscience easy, though,
   And he persuaded me to let it go
   By telling me that, in case of investigation,   15
   I might deny then any imputation
   Of guilty knowledge and could take an oath
   That would not be contrary to the truth.

CLÉANTE   I must confess, I fear you're on the rocks.
   The deed of gift, the transfer of the box—   20
   I speak the truth, I cannot deal in lies—
   To put the matter gently, were most unwise.
   With these as evidence, it's clear he's got you
   Exactly where he wants you. You forgot you
   Were dealing with a man of many schemes;   25
   You never should have pushed him to extremes.

ORGON   Oh! Under such an outward show of piety
   To hide such wickedness and impropriety!
   To think I rescued him from sheer disgrace!
   From now on, I renounce the human race.   30

Henceforth I'll shun them utterly and call
Myself a fool if I don't hate them all!

CLÉANTE Now there you go, flying off the handle!
Won't you ever learn to burn the candle
35 At just one end? You waver wildly, brother,
From one grotesque extreme back to the other.
You see your error now and recognize
That you were taken in by pious lies,
But why correct your error and confusion
40 By falling into greater disillusion
And lump all mankind in one category
As though that told the full facts of the story?
Because a rascal cuts truth on the bias,
Pretending to be holy, good, and pious,
45 You would conclude that Chaos is upon us
And that the human race has turned dishonest.
Let the freethinkers think that, if they choose,
But learn to separate the external views
From the inner truth. And then don't rush away
50 Too hastily, but keep to the middle way.
Try not to be the dupe of charlatans,
But don't brand truly pious men as harlequins
And if you must make one or the other choice,
Then let excessive leniency be your vice.

Scene Two

[ORGON, CLÉANTE, and DAMIS]

DAMIS Father, is it true this brazen rogue,
Forgetting all the favors you've bestowed,
Has grown presumptuous and threatens
To use your benefits against you as his weapons?

5 ORGON My son, I'm sorry to say it's all too true.

DAMIS Give me the word, and I'll run him through and through
With a carving-knife. One should never waver
Before the impudence of that soul-saver!
I'll fix him so he'll never bother us again!

10 CLÉANTE Ah, that's the speech of youth. But now and then
It's necessary to be more composed.
We're men, not beasts; the course that you've proposed
Is surely no way to resolve the matter.

Scene Three

[MADAME PERNELLE, ORGON, ELMIRE, CLÉANTE, MARIANE, DAMIS, *and* DORINE]

MME. PERNELLE   Good Heavens, what's the meaning of all this chatter?

ORGON   Strange things indeed I've seen with my own eyes,
And a strange and most unpleasant kind of surprise!
I rescue a man from abject poverty,
Give him my home, my daughter, my property,   5
Treat him, in short, better than my brother,
Crown every benefit I give him with another,
And what is my reward, upon my life?
He seeks beneath my nose to seduce my wife,
And, still not fully satisfied with this,   10
He dares to use against me my own gifts,
Trying to bring me down by using the hold
I've given him by my kindness, and he's bold
Enough to kick me from under this roof that's covered him
And leave me in the gutter where I discovered him!   15

DORINE   The poor man!

MME. PERNELLE   My son, I can't imagine
He could behave in such a fashion.

ORGON   What!

MME. PERNELLE   People always envy pious men.

ORGON   Do I have to tell you all of this again?

MME. PERNELLE   I know that people here don't love him;   20
I know they're all quite jealous of him.

ORGON   And what's that got to do with this affair?

MME. PERNELLE   When you were a boy, I warned you to take care,
For virtue's always slandered by a lie;
Though envy perishes, the envious won't die.   25

ORGON   I don't see how any of this is apropos.

MME. PERNELLE   Liars will tirelessly spread their lies, you know.

ORGON   I tell you I saw it all with my very own eyes!

MME. PERNELLE   Ah, alas! that this world is so full of lies!

ORGON   You'll make me sin through anger. For the last time,   30
I tell you I *saw* his shameless attempt at crime!

MME. PERNELLE   This world is ever full of slanderous tongues
    Ready to make up tales of imagined wrongs.

ORGON   What you are saying is absolute nonsense!
35   I *saw* the man! He hasn't the slightest defense!
    I *saw* him try to do it! Do I have to yell
    The simple truth in your ear or ring a bell?

MME. PERNELLE   Mercy me! Appearances often deceive.
    Don't be overly rash in what you believe.

ORGON   You're driving me crazy!

40 MME. PERNELLE   False suspicion
    Is common to one in your condition.

ORGON   Then he piously sought to improve my life
    By making infamous love to my wife?

MME. PERNELLE   You need *facts* to support an accusation
45   Which might destroy a good man's reputation.

ORGON   *Facts?* How in the hell can I be more factual
    Than to catch the scoundrel in the actual
    Act of . . . no, you almost made me say it.

MME. PERNELLE   If there's evil in him, he doesn't betray it,
50   Not by the slightest glance or sneer;
    I just can't believe these stories I hear.

ORGON   Good Lord, I'm so mad I could jump on my hat!
    If you weren't my mother, I'd do worse than that!

DORINE [*to* ORGON]   You wouldn't believe a word we'd say;
55   Now turn about, I'm afraid, is fair play.

CLÉANTE   We're wasting time here babbling like silly sheep;
    When the wolf is on the prowl, one shouldn't sleep.
    How are we going to meet that scoundrel's scheme?

DAMIS   He wouldn't have the nerve! He wouldn't dream . . . !

60 ELMIRE   I really doubt if he'd take legal action
    Merely to obtain his satisfaction.

CLÉANTE   Don't be too sure. He's got tricks up his sleeve,
    And we know he's slyer than anyone dare believe.
    For less than this, men have served a spell
65   With bread and water in a prison cell.
    And I repeat, since we know what his weapons are,
    You made a mistake in pushing him so far.

ORGON   All right, all right, but what else could I do?
    His impudence simply angered me through and through.

CLÉANTE   I wish with all my heart we could arrange   70
  Some kind of fair and equitable exchange.

ELMIRE   If I had known he held such trumps in hand,
  I'd have thought twice about the trick I planned.

[M. LOYAL *appears at the door;* DORINE *goes to meet him.*]

Scene Four

[ORGON, MADAME PERNELLE, ELMIRE, MARIANE, CLÉANTE, DAMIS,
  DORINE, *and* MONSIEUR LOYAL]

ORGON   Who's that fellow? Tell him to go away.
  I'm in no state to deal with callers today.

M. LOYAL   Sister, good morning. Your master, pray, where is he?
  I must speak to him at once.

DORINE   He's busy.
  He can't see anyone, I fear.   5

M. LOYAL   I shouldn't like to intrude upon him here.
  But I don't think my business will upset him;
  He can hear my news, if you will let him.

DORINE   Your name?

M. LOYAL   Just say I've come to bring him proof
  Of the warm regard of Monsieur Tartuffe.   10

DORINE [*to* ORGON]   He is a messenger, and quite soft-spoken,
  From our old friend. He says he brings a token
  Of Tartuffe's regard.

CLÉANTE   You'd better see
  Who he is and what his news can be.

ORGON   Maybe he's coming to offer apologies.   15
  Should I greet him politely and put him at his ease?

CLÉANTE   Speak softly, but don't vouchsafe any admission.
  If he offers peace, though—better listen.

M. LOYAL   Greetings, good sir! May Heaven confound your foes
  And shower you with love and sweet repose!   20

ORGON [*to* CLÉANTE]   A most polite beginning! An indication
  He wants a reconciliation.

M. LOYAL   Your family's interests have long been mine.
  I served your worthy father many a time.

25 ORGON   I beg your pardon, sir, but to my shame
        I must confess I don't recall your name.

M. LOYAL   My name is Loyal. I too have a confession.
        I am a process server by profession.
        For forty years it's been my pride and joy
30   To hold that honorable office, man and boy.
        You asked my business here, sir? This is it:
        To serve upon you this judicial writ.

ORGON   What!

M. LOYAL   Now, please, let's talk without unseemly friction.
        It's just a little notice of eviction.
35   You and your family must get out,
        Remove your goods and furniture, and in about—
        Let's say, an hour—sooner, if you could.

ORGON   What, leave my house!

M. LOYAL   If you would be so good.
        This house belongs, as you are well aware,
40   To good Monsieur Tartuffe. A deed I bear
        Attests unto the fact beyond dispute,
        So please don't force him, good sir, to bring suit
        And call upon the law in his defense.

DAMIS   I'm simply staggered by such insolence!

45 M. LOYAL   Young man, my business here is not with you,
        But with your father, a good man and true,
        Who knows his legal duties, you may trust us,
        And wouldn't dream of contravening justice.

ORGON   But . . .

M. LOYAL   Yes, I know that not for a fortune
50   Would you protest or would you importune
        The court to contradict its stern commands
        And remove this writ from out of your hands.

DAMIS   You might get a wholesome beating on the end
        Of your black and gloomy coat, my friend!

55 M. LOYAL   Sir, bid your son be silent and retire.
        I'd hate to have to report his ire
        And his threats of violence and fits of pique.

DORINE [aside]   He says his name is Loyal? I'd say, Sneak.

M. LOYAL   I have a great respect for honesty,
60   And I agreed to serve this writ, you see,
        Just to oblige you and to give you pleasure,
        For others might not execute the seizure

Of your goods with such consideration
As I, who feel for you such admiration.

ORGON   What could be worse, or could be a greater crime   65
Than evicting a man?

M. LOYAL   But, you see, I'm giving you time.
I will suspend till tomorrow, if you need
Some extra time, the service of the deed.
I'll merely come, with a dozen of my men,
To quietly spend the night with you, and then
I'll ask you to deliver to me the keys   70
Of the house before you go to bed, if you please.
Please be assured, we'll not trouble your repose;
It's just a matter of form, you know how it goes.
Tomorrow morning early you'll move out
All your furniture. I've picked some stout   75
And husky fellows; you'll find they're quite discreet,
As well as skilled at moving things out on the street.
No one, I think, could possibly act more fairly,
Nor put the matter before you more sincerely,
And as I'm giving you all this kind assistance   80
I must beg you to offer no resistance.

ORGON [aside]   How happy I would be to give my last
Hundred louis for the chance to blast
This monster of pure impudence and clout
Him violently and squarely on the snout!   85

CLÉANTE   Easy, don't lose your head.

DAMIS   Oh, I insist.
Just one punch. I've got an itching fist.

DORINE   That noble back, monsieur, seems to demand
A good sound beating from a lady's hand.

M. LOYAL   Beware, my dear; the law makes no distinction   90
Regarding sex when it comes to legal action.

CLÉANTE   No more of this, sir; whatever the law allows,
Just give us the writ, and then get out of the house.

M. LOYAL   Au revoir, gentlemen! May God content you! [Exit.]

Scene Five

[ORGON, MADAME PERNELLE, ELMIRE, CLÉANTE, MARIANE, DAMIS, *and* DORINE]

ORGON   May He confound you and the man who sent you! [*to*
  MME. PERNELLE]
  Well, Mother, tell me, was I right
  About this monster who is your delight?

MME. PERNELLE   I'm flabbergasted! I can't believe my ears!

5   DORINE   Well, maybe it's all better than it appears.
  His goal is good; he's doing all he can
  To demonstrate how he loves his fellow-man.
  He knows the soul's corrupted by the love
  Of money, so he'll lovingly remove
10   Temptation from his friends, for their salvation.

ORGON   Oh, shut up! Stop this bickering! Damnation!

CLÉANTE   Let's try to think of the proper course to take.

ELMIRE   Let's tell the world he's a hypocritical fake.
  These despicable tricks he has employed
15   Would render any contract null and void.
  Public opinion, once his deeds are known,
  Will surely rise, and its power will be shown.

Scene Six

[VALÉRE, ORGON, MADAME PERNELLE, ELMIRE, CLÉANTE, MARI-
ANE, DAMIS, *and* DORINE]

VALÉRE   I'm sorry, sir, to cause you any distress,
  But I feel obliged to by the present mess
  You're in; a very old and trusted friend
  Who knows my interest has dared to send
5   Me word of your affairs, in violation
  Of that high secrecy belonging to his station.
  The news he sends is bitter, curt, and tight:
  Your only possible recourse is flight.
  He who has swindled you of everything
10   Has made an accusation to the King,
  And has supported his charges, sad to relate,
  With the strongbox of an outlaw of the state,
  The which he found, he says, in your possession.
  Proof of your most traitorous transgression.

I don't know whether you're innocent or not,   15
But you're ordered to be arrested on the spot,
And Tartuffe himself has been commended
And charged to see that you are apprehended.

CLÉANTE   Thus armed might assists him in his schemes
And helps him realize his evil dreams.   20

ORGON   Oh, that man is wicked past man's thought!

VALÉRE   Any delay will be fatal, so I've brought
My carriage round to whisk you safely away
And a thousand louis to help you on your way.
So don't waste time; this is a fearful blow;   25
Escape is the only answer that I know.
I'll find you a hiding-place with another friend
And I'll stay by your side until the end.

ORGON   I owe so much to your kind consideration,
But that can wait for a happier occasion;   30
I only pray that Heaven gives me the power
To fitly remember your goodness in this hour.
Good-bye, my friends . . .

CLÉANTE   Hurry! No delays! Don't fear,
We'll take care of everything right here.   35

[*Enter* TARTUFFE *and a* POLICE OFFICER. *As* ORGON *starts to exit,*
TARTUFFE *seizes him.*]

Scene Seven

[TARTUFFE, *a* POLICE OFFICER, MADAME PERNELLE, ORGON, EL-
MIRE, CLÉANTE, MARIANE, VALÈRE, DAMIS, *and* DORINE]

TARTUFFE   Here now, good sir! Don't run away so fast!
A lodging's ready for you. No need for haste.
I take you prisoner, in the name of the King.

ORGON   Villain, you are guilty of everything;
You duped me into listening to your counsel   5
So that you might bring about my utter downfall!

TARTUFFE   I will not flinch, although you rave quite wildly.
Heaven has taught me to suffer insults mildly.

CLÉANTE   So these are the lessons your religion has given!

DAMIS   How impudently he plays with the name of Heaven!   10

TARTUFFE   You cannot move me by your enmity;
To do my duty means everything to me.

MARIANE   Much glory you will draw from this affair,
And maybe more honor than even you can bear!

15 TARTUFFE   Glory only accrues unto an action
Blessed and commanded by the royal sanction.

ORGON   Have you forgotten it was my charity
That rescued you from the depths of poverty?

TARTUFFE   True, you helped me with an occasional loan,
20 But my highest duty is to the royal throne.
This sacred and compelling obligation
Extinguishes all small considerations
Of petty gratitude. Upon my life,
I place it ahead of children, family, or wife!

ELMIRE   Impostor!

25 DORINE   This treacherous, sly snake would
Twist and mock all values we hold sacred!

CLÉANTE   But if this noble and religious zeal
Is quite as perfect as you'd have us feel,
How is it that it waited to appear
30 Till you were caught embracing Madame here?
Why did you delay your denunciation
Till you were trapped in that curious situation?
I won't allege, though it might have played a part,
That deed of gift from the goodness of his heart,
35 But why accept the money, then and later,
Of a man whom you denounce now as a traitor?

TARTUFFE [to the POLICE OFFICER]   Deliver me, monsieur, from
attacks like these
And execute your orders, if you please.

OFFICER   Yes, I've delayed too long now, at the best;
40 And, aptly enough, you're the one who makes the request.
So here's the order: kindly follow me
To the prison cell that is your home-to-be.

TARTUFFE   Who, me?

OFFICER   Yes, you.

TARTUFFE   What do you mean? You must be insane!

OFFICER   You're not the one to whom I must explain. [to ORGON]
45 You've had a nasty scare, but, praised be God,
Our present King is an enemy of fraud;
His eyes can penetrate his subjects' hearts
And he's not deluded by a trickster's arts.
His great spirit, mighty, calm, and wise,
50 Watches his kingdom with discerning eyes.

Charlatans and practicers of treason
Cannot delude or shake his sovereign reason.
To worthy men he gives due recompense,
Yet he's not blind to fraud and false pretense.
His love for truth, however, does not eclipse   55
The horror one should feel for hyprocrites.
Tartuffe was not the type who could hoodwink him:
The King is more perceptive than men think him.·
Immediately and subtly he divined
The vile conniving of an evil mind.   60
This man betrayed himself by his accusation
And by a process of due retribution
The King identified him as a thief
With a criminal record almost past belief,
A man of various names, whose numerous crimes   65
Have been recorded a good many times.
In short, His Majesty found so abhorrent
This man's career, that it was ample warrant
For his arrest. This additional crime
Only sealed his fate. That's why I'm   70
With him today. The King commanded me
To accompany him today and see
What impudence he would dare as a last evasion.
Now I shall force him to make you reparation,
Seizing the powers that he might have destroyed;   75
The King declares the contract null and void
Which might have made Tartuffe your legal heir
And he pardons that transgression where
You erred but to protect a friend.
Thus he rewards you, thus does he commend   80
Your past fidelity in the civil wars,
Proving his heart remembers and rewards
A loyal subject; like the King of paradise,
He's mindful more of virtue than of vice.

DORINE   May Heaven be praised!

MME. PERNELLE   Ah, I'm so relieved!   85

ELMIRE   All's well again!

MARIANE   This scarcely can be believed!

ORGON [*to* TARTUFFE]   So now we've got you, villain . . .

[*The* OFFICER *drags* TARTUFFE *away*.]

Scene Eight

[MADAME PERNELLE, ORGON, ELMIRE, MARIANE, CLÉANTE, VA-
LÈRE, DAMIS, *and* DORINE]

CLÉANTE   Please; moderation.
    Don't yield to an unworthy exultation.
    Leave the wretched man to his wretched fate;
    He's already bowed beneath the heavy weight
5   Of his own remorse. Why not hope, rather,
    That his heart may undergo a change, dear brother,
    And by progressing to better from the worse, he
    May move the King to temper justice with mercy,
    The while you kneel before the royal throne
10   To beg that Tartuffe's fate might be like your own.

ORGON   Well said, indeed. So let us, at his feet,
    Thank him for his kindness and entreat
    Mercy for our enemies. This done,
    There's one more crown of joy left to be won,
15   And that's for me to happily declare
    Mariane shall be the bride of Valère.

ON THE NATURE OF THE
DRAMATIC EMOTION

What is the fundamental nature of the dramatic emotion?

The question is not new; Saint-Marc-Girardin long ago placed it. with many others, at the head of his *Cours de Littérature Dramatique;* and now the excellent M. Herckenrath is asking it again in his *Problèmes d'Esthétique et de Morale.* M. Herckenrath is a professor at the Lycée de Groningue and a man of original ideas. He asks, as you may have asked yourselves: "Does not the pleasure which we find in the performance of a tragedy seem at first sight a barbarous enjoyment? We are looking at suffering eagerly, instead of turning away our eyes. Is this pleasure, then, of the same nature as that which certain persons experience in seeing an animal slaughtered, or in witnessing a bloody fight? . . . In short, how can one who is moved by it and who weeps over it, enjoy that sensation?"

I

These are exactly the questions that Saint-Marc-Girardin answered by saying: "The base of the dramatic emotion is the sympathy of man for man." We go to the theatre to be moved by the misfortunes of our fellowmen because we love them; we share their griefs, their pains, their sorrows and their despair, etc.

This is ingenious, but it has never quite convinced me. To *seek out* —note this point, for here's the rub—to seek out the spectacle of human suffering in order to be moved by it, does not seem to me characteristic of an extremely sympathetic and eminently humane soul.

To encounter human misery and to pity it, and particularly to relieve it, and "to relieve it to the point of sharing it" (to recall Mérimée's charming phrase in regard to Nodier), yes, that is to be kind-hearted. But to seek out human suffering with the intention of being moved by it, and with the consoling knowledge that one will not be called upon to relieve it, I don't see wherein that reveals a sympathy of man for man; and I can see, I fear I do see, wherein that indicates the instinct of ferocity, pure and simple, softened, no doubt, by civilization.

And I have a tendency not to be very much irritated by our good M. Herckenrath, who says to us gently: "This real pleasure which we take in seeing suffering, seems to me to be the result of the cruel predispositions engendered in the race by war, formerly a necessary and frequently an habitual condition of tribes and communities. The necessity of inflicting injuries in self-defense has given rise to the pleasure of inflicting them. . . . In most individuals, the ferocious instinct has become weakened; but we must seek vestiges of it in the taste for bloody spectacles, bull-fights, dog-fights, cock-fights, the chase, or recitals of scenes of horror. It finds nourishment daily in the sensational serials, and in the newspaper reports of crimes."

It seems to me that there is some justice in M. Herckenrath's argument, whence it would follow that the base of the dramatic emotion is not exactly the sympathy of man for man, but rather the ferocity of man toward his fellows.

For, after all, we must observe that Saint-Marc-Girardin neglected half the problem in order to simplify it. He based his argument on tragedy, admitting, in the pleasure caused by it, only the pleasure of weeping over great misfortunes; and he left comedy completely out of account.

Now, no one will claim that the pleasure which one experiences at a comedy is founded on the sympathy of man for man. It is too clearly founded on malignity. What we enjoy at a comedy, is laughing at the foibles of beings like ourselves. This is evidently a pleasure founded on ferocity. The gossip, the slanderer, the practical joker, the malicious man, and the man who enjoys comedy, are and must be placed in the same ethical category. They are vicious brutes. I know that very well for I am one of them. They are at bottom, and with differences of degree, vicious brutes.

Well, there is half the drama based on human malignity. Do you believe that the other half is in contrast with it, and is based upon a contrary sentiment?

It might be so, surely; and if someone has made the profound observation that the world is a comedy for the man who thinks, and a tragedy for the man who feels, it may be that the world is also a comedy for the malicious, and a tragedy for the altruistic. However, let us investigate.

In the first place, is there any essential difference between comedy and tragedy? Not at all. There is a difference of degree. The same subjects are comic or tragic. They are comic so long as the passions placed in action and on view before us seem to involve only consequences of small importance; they become tragic when we begin to perceive that they involve and foreshadow consequences which may be terrible.

There is no other difference between comedy and tragedy than the greater or smaller range of the consequences which the passions they depict are supposed to produce.

"Well! but then they are both founded on the same sentiment. At comedy as well as at tragedy we come to see suffering."

"But at comedy we come to see slight suffering, and to laugh at it; at tragedy we come to see horrible suffering, and to weep over it."

"Granted; but in either case, the seeking of this pleasure is not the act of a highly philanthropic soul; and if laughing at human sorrows proves that we come to the comedy from cruelty, weeping over these sorrows does not justify us entirely for having come to the tragedy to enjoy them as a spectacle. You can't get away from this; to happen upon misfortune without having sought it, and then to be moved by it—that is to be tenderhearted; to seek the spectacle of misfortune, even though this be in order to weep over it, evidences depraved liking; it is a dilettantism founded in barbarism."

"I have seen *Phédre*. It is very sad. I wept copiously."

"Did you know what it was?"

"No."

"Did you know what a tragedy is?"

"No."

"*Absolvo te*. You are only to be pitied.

"I have seen *Phèdre*. It is very sad. I wept."

"Did you know what it was?"

"I knew that it was a play in which a woman kills herself from disappointment in love, and where a father kills his son from jealousy."

"And you went to see that? You are not tender-hearted."

"But I wept!"

"That is no excuse for going out and hunting up such a spectacle out of mere curiosity, and paying money for it."

"But I wept!"

"And you found pleasure in weeping."

"Yes."

"That pleasure wipes out even what justification there might have been in your having wept. You went to seek pleasure in the misfortune of others, and you found it. That is all that remains at the bottom of the crucible. You are vicious. Taine would tell you that you are partly cruel gorilla. He claimed, you know, that man is a descendant, only slightly modified, of the cruel and lecherous gorilla. The lecherous gorilla for comedy, and cruel gorilla, for serious drama."

"You are at least cruel yourself, sir."

"I exaggerate a little, that's all. Man is an exaggerating gorilla."

Exaggeration apart, I am within the truth. Man goes to tragedy to seek a pleasure which is derived from the misfortune of man.

Besides, do you ever see on the stage, on any stage, a picture of happiness? Never! Neither in comedy nor in tragedy. Comedy: picture of ludicrous misfortunes. Tragedy: picture of terrifying misfortunes. Picture of happiness, where? Nowhere.

If man, "fond of spectacles" as Bossuet says, "and who makes a spectacle of the depicting of his own errors," enjoyed the spectacle of human happiness, he would have created a dramatic species devoted to the depicting of happiness. But this dramatic species does not exist. The conclusion is obvious.

Some wit once remarked: "Why do all the comedies end with a marriage? Because after that, the tragedy begins."

That is not bad; but it is not complete. We should say that comedy itself is a picture of misfortune. It consists, even when it is not satirical, even when it is sentimental, of the petty troubles of two young people who would like to get married and can't. As soon as they can, it is all over. Oh! drop the curtain! They are going to be happy now; I am going. That has no interest for me any more.

Never has a playwright depicted a honeymoon, except at the moment when it commences to be embittered.

No; the spectacle of happiness does not appeal to us at all, and the lines of Destouches may be applied to any one of us:

Another's happiness gives us chagrin;
Your neighbor's plumpness makes you grow more thin.

And on the other hand the spectacle of misfortune contains for us inexhaustible delights. The theatre, as I have shown, is merely the picture of misfortune, great or small. The novel is the same thing, of course. Women—whom we should always consult to find out what man is, because they are more permanent than we, because their evolution is less, and less rapid, because they are nearer to primitive man, because they constitute an almost unchanging element in the human race—women who go to the circulating library to ask for a book, if they do not know what they want, nearly always ask in the end for "something sad." They like to weep. They meet for that purpose. They come to it very quickly. . . .

For let a woman start to weep, another will begin,
And all the rest who come along will eagerly join in.

The drama, literature, poetry, the conversation of sentimental men and women, all these things are simply the depicting of the misfortunes of humanity.

II

That explains certain constantly recurring tendencies in literature and drama, and conversely, is explained by these tendencies. Periodically the theatre makes an attempt to the point of horror to depict human ills, in obedience to the law of increasing intensity which prevails in the whole field of spectacle. Recently in France the Théâtre-Libre, wishing at the start to make a strong impression on the public imagination with something quite novel, devoted itself to representations of sickness, of violence, and of death. If Saint-Sorlin had been alive, he would have repeated:

Les uns sont pulmoniques,
Les autres catharreux, les autres hydropiques.

That sort of thing does not succeed very long. But what does this indicate? That we do not want the emotion caused in us by the misfortune of others to reach the point of shuddering horror. Do you see? We like to contemplate misfortune so long as it does not affect us. In a word, we like to see suffering without suffering ourselves. And it seems to me that that is not the sympathy of man for man.

An interesting example, cited by M. Herckenrath: "In a little town of Dutch Brabant, a sanguinary drama was being presented. Several murders were committed, one after the other. After viewing two or three in silence, the peaceable townspeople could contain themselves no longer. They crowded on the stage and stopped the performance, crying: 'Enough of this bloodshed!' The incident was related to me by an eyewitness."

These townspeople were, in the first place, very good people; in the second place, people of little learning, that is to say, unversed in the pleasure which it is the function of literature to extract from human suffering; and finally unaccustomed to the theatre and consequently capable, like children, of the dramatic illusion, and believing (almost) that the murders committed on the stage were real.

Therefore, it was too much for them. For man enjoys human suffering up to a certain point. He is not a savage. He is only partly savage. The amount of savagery which remains in the heart of man, the exact amount—that is precisely what the theatre, comic as well as tragic, must know in each generation, and that is also what it registers. We find Molière's comedy somewhat cruel, in *Georges Dandin,* or in the fifth act of the *Misanthrope.* This means that our cruelty is a little less violent than that of our forefathers of the seventeenth century. The melodrama played before the citizens of the little town in Brabant passed the bounds of their blood-thirstiness, as the pathological exhibitions of the early days of the Théâtre-Libre passed the bounds of ours.

But the fundamental fact remains: this is, that the theatre exploits the tendency we have to find pleasure, in one way or another, either with laughter or with tears, in the misfortune of others, without ourselves suffering.

III

But is this all? This is the principal thing. I maintain that. I withdraw nothing of what precedes. However, this is not all. There is something more, something a little more noble, a little more elevated, that enters in, or rather is added to all that I have set forth thus far; something which in some persons is non-existent, in many is more or less developed and which in a few is almost the principal thing, without ever, I think, prevailing entirely.

The misfortune of others makes us laugh, the misfortune of others makes us weep, and in both cases it gives pleasure. To be sure; but also, but furthermore, but at the same time, if you like, it makes us think. Then, along with the cruel pleasure which comedy gives, along with the sad pleasure that tragedy gives, along with these *mala gaudia mentis,* there is mingled or added the pleasure of reflecting on the ills of humanity, of seeing them, not as *res fruenda oculis,* but as matter for thought and meditation; and this is a new point of view. The pleasure which man finds in the theatre, comic as well as tragic, in the representation of the misfortune of others, is in the first place malignity; it is also a desire for truth—and it is further-more a desire to consider human affairs in a serious manner.

It is a desire for truth. Schopenhauer maintained all his life that there is nothing real in the world except misfortune, for the sufficient reason that pain is incontestably real and that pleasure is never anything but the satisfaction of a want, which is suffering, whence it follows that pleasure is negative and that suffering alone is posi-tive.

I am aware of the objections to this view, and I myself consider it incomplete. But there is a good deal of truth in it. It is true in general; it is almost a platitude. Do you realize that after all it leaves out, it misses, only the aesthetic pleasures, which are not the satisfac-tion of a want, which are a joy that needs no suffering to create, which are pleasures not born of pain, and which consequently are not only pure pleasures, but positive pleasures.

As for all the other pleasures, Schopenhauer's theory applies to them perfectly. And if this is the case, this theory may be considered true, in a very general sense.

Now I believe that men, after the age of fifteen and a half, are aware of it. They feel that the one thing which is real in the world is pain; and that the rest is sometimes an illusion and sometimes only a desire satisfied, that is to say a very brief reprieve from suffering. And accordingly, in the domain of art, they do not exactly refuse the representation of happiness, since they know that happiness is still true, in a relative and, so to speak, accidental fashion; they do not refuse the representation of happiness; they are willing to read, and not without pleasure, Lamartine's *Chant d'amour;* they are willing, at the theatre, to listen, and not without pleasure, to an idyllic love episode; but they don't want these things to last too long. These things seem false, or they seem insufficiently true.

Why is it that one need only speak ill of men—perhaps even of women—to have the appearance of knowing them? In the first place that comes of human malignity—and I shall return to this. In the second place, it is because man knows that if it is true that he is good, it is even truer that he is not, and that if unselfishness is true, selfishness is even truer. In the same way, to paint humanity "happy" irritates the reader a little, the same as to paint it "beauti-ful." He does not say: "No!" He does not revolt. He does not enter a categorical denial. But he says: "Let us not exaggerate." To dwell on it provokes a slight suspicion of ingenuousness or of charlatanism.

We must be careful here, because there are many distinctions. Man is irritated also by those who paint misfortune too exclusively and too persistently. He finds that also more or less false, and he is right. And besides, he suspects that this arises from malice, and not merely from the desire for truth: "In God's name, sir, that we are miserable or despicable seems to cause you a good deal of satisfaction!" And again, he likes a little deception, in the direction of optimism, for consolation. "You flatter me; but go on" is a very human attitude; and humanity has always said to its entertainers: "Gild the truth a little, to console me—but not too much."

But in spite of all these reservations, which were necessary, mankind loves truth in art, and that is why it likes art sad—sad in the true sense of the word; and I have shown that comedy is even sadder than tragedy. It likes in art reality forcefully presented; and the most idealistic art is nothing more than a certain reality presented with all the force of a powerful genius.

For these reasons, since mankind comes to the theatre to seek above all a picture of life, an optimistic drama would seem to it false or childish, and we would promptly call it a Sunday school.

Notice that I say "optimistic" and not "noble." Every audience in the world has always been very susceptible to the appeal to admiration. That is another matter. To admire a hero, that is to say a fine specimen of humanity, will always be to readers of novels, to readers of epic poems, to theatergoers, a keen delight. For it isn't there that he finds the unreal. Nothing, though it be rare, is truer. Man knows that he has good instincts. Man knows that he is capable of courage and magnanimity. For example, man knows that he can conquer himself, and that he then experiences an indescribable pleasure, the greatest pleasure that it is granted him to feel here below.

And do you know why? After all, I don't know myself, but I can imagine. Man is a combative animal. It is only by fearful struggles that he has attained, first, his place on the earth, and then civilization. Now that he no longer has such terrible battles to fight (by "now" I mean the historical period), the instinct remains: man still needs to fight. Therefore he fights against himself, against his passions. He experiences infinite pleasure in conquering them, in taming them; and it is still the old tamer of wild beasts who then survives. This pleasure is so keen that sometimes he fights for nothing, without a prize, "for fun," precisely because it is a pleasure. The mania of Corneille in his old age was to show us men exercising their will against themselves, without utility, without any duty to accomplish, and for the mere joy of exercising it; this is an exaggeration, but it is not an absurdity. Such men exist still and are not superhuman;

they are still quite within human nature. The ascetics, for example.

Men accept, then, the noble in drama, but not the optimistic, not the drama which paints humanity as happy, because such a drama is not true. And a good proof, both that this drama would not be true and that men do not desire it, is that it does not exist.

IV

In conclusion I will add that if men accept only a relatively sad drama, it is because that is the only kind that makes them think. Even if it were true, the optimistic drama would be hollow.

Let us suppose that mankind is happy, and that the stage depicts it as it is—but in that case, why depict it? In this world, the thing to think about, and to remedy if possible, is presumably the thing we lack. You have noticed the popular phrase, very French: "There's nothing to say to that." That means: "All goes well." And the fact is there is really "nothing to say" when all goes well. Happy nations have no history. That is why all nations have one. Happiness never needs to be narrated, nor described, nor painted, nor explained. It furnishes no material for the chronicler or dramatist. It is, and it is quite content with merely existing.

Happy people—and there are such and I have seen them—are very interesting to study, and somewhat surprising. They rarely concern themselves with literature, philosophy, ethics, history, or sociology; and they are somewhat surprised that any one else should do so. This is because all those things, at bottom, you may be sure, are only different forms of the search for happiness. Now as they possess this, they are somewhat puzzled that others should be obliged to seek it. Can you imagine literature undertaking to describe and analyze those people?

In the first place we should discover that it would be undertaking a study of the unusual; secondly we should wonder, vaguely, unconsciously, what is the use of depicting those who have found, instead of those who seek, those who have arrived instead of those who are on the way.

—"To show the goal!"

—To be sure, but it is not the goal that needs to be shown; that does no good. It is the way that leads to it which is useful; and the obstacles in the way, which are the most important. The obstacles in the way: our passions, our mistakes, our follies, our illusions, our vices—that is tragedy; our pettinesses, our faults, our absurdities— that is comedy. These are precisely what interest us: these are precisely what give food for reflection; these are precisely what make us think a little; and these are precisely what furnish material for literature and particularly for drama.

We are not clearly aware of it, because we go to the theatre for entertainment. We go only for that. So much is undeniable. But we should make a grave mistake if we thought that on entering the theatre we leave behind the part of us that thinks, which reflects, which is concerned and anxious about the great problems of humanity, and that we have in the orchestra chair only the part of us that wants to be amused. We may think that we have only the latter, but we have at the same time all the companion parts that exist in us.

It is our whole personality that we bring with us; and without our suspecting it, without our intending it, it is our whole personality that the author who is behind the curtain has undertaken to entertain. He will succeed only on condition that he captivate and hold it almost as a whole; and while we laugh at merry jests, or while we weep at pathos, we shall be truly captivated—unconsciously, of course—but we shall be truly captivated only if we are touched deeply, almost entirely, only if we have a vague consciousness that something very serious is in the background of the little story.

It is for no other reason that we are not merely interested, but moved and enthralled when we see *Polyeucte, Athalie, King Lear, Othello, Misanthrope, Maitre Guérin,* the *Visite de Noces,* the *Ami des Femmes;* and for my part, if I place the *Mariage de Figaro* below all these, it is doubtless because in this case I am amused, but I do not feel stirring in me as a spectator the whole man that is myself, or at least the man in me who is interested in the destinies, the happiness or the misfortune, the trials and the hopes and efforts of my fellow man.

Since there is nothing, then, more important in this world than pain, since there is nothing which makes us reflect more deeply than the sight of the things which prevent us from being happy, and of those which cause us to be unhappy, is it surprising that the drama should consist on the one hand of the delineation of our faults, on the other of the representation of our misfortunes, and that thus it is all sad, even when it is apparently gay, sadder still when it is sad because it intends to be?

In a word, it is sad whenever it is not superficial, for the excellent reason given by Mme. de Staël: "Have you never gone to the bottom of everything—that is, to sorrow?"

A little cruelty or malice—a little love of truth—a concern, invincible even when we try to conquer it, with serious things: that is what the spectator always brings to the drama, and that is what forces the drama as a whole, except for brief exceptions, to be the picture of human ills.

It is so in order to be solid, it is so in order to be permanent, it is so in order to exist. Petrarch said:

Null' altro che pianto al mondo dura.
(Nothing endures in the world but sorrow.)

AUGUST STRINDBERG

Miss Julie

Translated by E. M. SPRINCHORN

~~~~~~

AUGUST STRINDBERG

Preface to Miss Julie

Translated by E. M. SPRINCHORN

THE CHARACTERS IN *MISS JULIE*

MISS JULIE, twenty-five years old.

JEAN, valet, thirty years old.

CHRISTINE, the cook, thirty-five years old.

The action of the play takes place in the kitchen of the Count's manor house on Midsummer Eve in Sweden in the 1880's.

MISS JULIE

*The scene is a large kitchen. The walls and ceiling are covered with
draperies and hangings. The rear wall runs obliquely upstage from
the left. On this wall to the left are two shelves with pots and pans
of copper, iron, and pewter. The shelves are decorated with
goffered paper. A little to the right can be seen three-fourths of a
deep arched doorway with two glass doors, and through them can
be seen a fountain with a statue of Cupid, lilac bushes in bloom,
and the tops of some Lombardy poplars. From the left of the stage
the corner of a large, Dutch-tile kitchen stove protrudes with part of
the hood showing. Projecting from the right side of the stage is one
end of the servants' dining table of white pine, with a few chairs
around it. The stove is decorated with branches of birch leaves; the
floor is strewn with juniper twigs. On the end of the table is a large
Japanese spice jar filled with lilacs. An icebox, a sink, a wash basin.
Over the door a big, old-fashioned bell; and to the left of the door
the gaping mouth of a speaking tube.*

CHRISTINE *is standing at the stove, frying something. She is wearing a light-colored cotton dress and an apron.* JEAN *enters, dressed
in livery and carrying a pair of high-top boots with spurs. He sets
them where they are clearly visible.*

JEAN   Tonight she's wild again. Miss Julie's absolutely wild!

CHRISTINE   You took your time getting back!

JEAN   I took the Count down to the station, and on my way back
as I passed the barn I went in for a dance. And there was Miss
Julie leading the dance with the game warden. But then she   5
noticed me. And she came right up and chose me for the ladies'
waltz. And she's been dancing ever since like—like I don't know
what. She's absolutely wild!

CHRISTINE   That's nothing new. But she's been worse then ever
during the last two weeks, ever since her engagement was broken   10
off.

JEAN   Yes, I never did hear all there was to that. He was a good
man, too, even if he wasn't rich. Well, that's a woman for you.
[*He sits down at the end of the table.*]
But, tell me, isn't it strange that a young girl like her—all right,   15
young woman—prefers to stay home here with the servants
rather than go with her father to visit her relatives?

CHRISTINE   I suppose she's ashamed to face them after that fiasco
with her young man.

JEAN   No doubt. He wouldn't take any nonsense from her. Do you   20
know what happened, Christine? I do. I saw the whole thing,
even though I didn't let on.

283

CHRISTINE   Don't tell me you were there?

JEAN   Well, I was. They were in the barnyard one evening—and she was training him, as she called it. Do you know what she was doing? She was making him jump over her riding whip—training
5   him like a dog. He jumped over twice, and she whipped him both times. But the third time, he grabbed the whip from her, broke it in a thousand pieces—and walked off.

CHRISTINE   So that's what happened. Well, what do you know.

JEAN   Yes, that put an end to that affair.—Now have you got
10   something good for me, Christine?

CHRISTINE [*serving him from the frying pan*]   Just a little bit of kidney. I cut it especially for you.

JEAN [*smelling it*]   Wonderful! My special *délice! [feeling the plate]* Hey, you didn't warm the plate!

15   CHRISTINE   You're more fussy than the Count himself when you set your mind to it. [*She rumples his hair gently.*]

JEAN [*irritated*]   Cut it out! Don't muss up my hair. You know I don't like that!

CHRISTINE   Oh, now don't get mad. Can I help it if I like you?

[JEAN *eats.* CHRISTINE *gets out a bottle of beer.*]

20   JEAN   Beer on Midsummer Eve! No thank you! I've got something much better than that. [*He opens a drawer in the table and takes out a bottle of red wine with a gold seal.*] Do you see that? Gold Seal. Now give me a glass.—No, a wine glass of course. I'm drinking it straight.

25   CHRISTINE [*goes back to the stove and puts on a small saucepan*] Lord help the woman who gets you for a husband. You're an old fussbudget!

JEAN   Talk, talk! You'd consider yourself lucky if you got yourself a man as good as me. It hasn't done you any harm to have people
30   think I'm your fiancé. [*He tastes the wine.*] Very good. Excellent. But warmed just a little too little. [*warming the glass in his hands*] We bought this in Dijon. Four francs a liter, unbottled—and the tax on top of that. . . . What on earth are you cooking? It smells awful!

35   CHRISTINE   Some damn mess that Miss Julie wants for her dog.

JEAN   You should watch your language, Christine. . . . Why do you have to stand in front of the stove on a holiday, cooking for that mutt? Is it sick?

CHRISTINE   Oh, she's sick, all right! She sneaked out to the gatekeeper's mongrel and—got herself in a fix. And Miss Julie, you know, can't stand anything like that.

JEAN   She's too stuck-up in some ways and not proud enough in others. Just like her mother. The Countess felt right at home in the kitchen or down in the barn with the cows, but when she went driving, *one* horse wasn't enough for her; she had to have a pair. Her sleeves were always dirty, but her buttons had the royal crown on them. As for Miss Julie, she doesn't seem to care how she looks and acts. I mean, she's not really refined. Just now, down at the barn, she grabbed the game warden away from Anna and asked him to dance. You wouldn't see anybody in our class doing a thing like that. But that's what happens when the gentry try to act like the common people—they become common! . . . But she *is* beautiful! Magnificent! Ah, those shoulders—those——and so forth, and so forth!

CHRISTINE   Oh, don't exaggerate. Clara tells me all about her, and Clara dresses her.

JEAN   Clara, pooh! You women are always jealous of each other. *I've* been out riding with her. . . . And how she can dance!

CHRISTINE   Listen, Jean, you *are* going to dance with me, aren't you, when I am finished here?

JEAN   Certainly! Of course I am.

CHRISTINE   Promise?

JEAN   Promise! Listen if I say I'm going to do a thing, I do it. . . . Christine, I thank you for a delicious meal. [*He shoves the cork back into the bottle.*]

[MISS JULIE *appears in the doorway, talking to someone outside.*]

MISS JULIE   I'll be right back. Don't wait for me.

[JEAN *slips the bottle into the table drawer quickly and rises respectfully.* MISS JULIE *comes in and crosses over to* CHRISTINE, *who is at the mirror.*]

MISS JULIE   Did you get it ready?

[CHRISTINE *signals that* JEAN *is present.*]

JEAN [*polite and charming*]   Are you ladies sharing secrets?

MISS JULIE [*flipping her handkerchief in his face*]   Don't be nosey!

JEAN   Oh, that smells good! Violets.

MISS JULIE [*flirting with him*]   Don't be impudent! And don't tell me you're an expert on perfumes, too. I know you're an expert dancer.—No, don't look! Go away!

JEAN [*inquisitive, but deferential*] What are you cooking? A witch's brew for Midsummer Eve? Something that reveals what
5   the stars have in store for you, so you can see the face of your future husband?

MISS JULIE [*curtly*] You'd have to have good eyes to see that. [*to* CHRISTINE] Pour it into a small bottle, and seal it tight. . . . Jean, come and dance a schottische with me.

10   JEAN [*hesitating*] I hope you don't think I'm being rude, but I've already promised this dance to Christine.

MISS JULIE She can always find someone else. Isn't that so, Christine? You don't mind if I borrow Jean for a minute, do you?

15   CHRISTINE It isn't up to me. If Miss Julie is gracious enough to invite you, it isn't right for you to say no, Jean. You go on, and thank her for the honor.

JEAN Frankly, Miss Julie, I don't want to hurt your feelings, but I wonder if it is wise—I mean for you to dance twice in a row
20   with the same partner. Especially since the people around here are so quick to spread gossip.

MISS JULIE [*bridling*] What do you mean? What kind of gossip? What are you trying to say?

JEAN [*retreating*] If you insist on misunderstanding me, I'll have
25   to speak more plainly. It just doesn't look right for you to prefer one of your servants to the others who are hoping for the same unusual honor.

MISS JULIE Prefer! What an idea! I'm really surprised. I, the mistress of the house, am good enough to come to their dance,
30   and when I feel like dancing, I want to dance with someone who knows how to lead. After all I don't want to look ridiculous.

JEAN As you wish. I am at your orders.

MISS JULIE [*gently*] Don't take it as an order. Tonight we're all just happy people at a party. There's no question of rank. Now
35   give me your arm.—Don't worry, Christine. I won't run off with your boy friend.

[JEAN *gives her his arm and leads her out.*]

PANTOMIME SCENE. *This should be played as if the actress were actually alone. She turns her back on the audience when she feels like it; she does not look out into the auditorium; she does not hurry as if she were afraid the audience would grow impatient.*

CHRISTINE *alone. In the distance the sound of the violins playing the schottische.* CHRISTINE, *humming in time with the music, cleans up after* JEAN, *washes the dishes, dries them, and puts them away in a cupboard. Then she takes off her apron, takes a little mirror from one of the table drawers, and leans it against the jar of lilacs on the table. She lights a tallow candle, heats a curling iron, and curls the bangs on her forehead. Then she goes to the doorway and stands listening to the music. She comes back to the table and finds the handkerchief that* MISS JULIE *left behind. She smells it, spreads it out, and then, as if lost in thought, stretches it, smooths it out, folds it in four, and so on.*

[JEAN *enters alone.*]

JEAN   I told you she was wild! You should have seen the way she was dancing. They were peeking at her from behind the doors and laughing at her. Can you figure her out, Christine?

CHRISTINE   You might know it's her monthlies, Jean. She always acts peculiar then. . . . Well, are you going to dance with me?   5

JEAN   You're not mad at me because I broke my promise?

CHRISTINE   Of course not. Not for a little thing like that, you know that. And I know my place.

JEAN [*grabs her around the waist*]   You're a sensible girl, Christine. You're going to make somebody a good wife——   10

[MISS JULIE, *coming in, sees them together. She is unpleasantly surprised.*]

MISS JULIE [*with forced gaiety*]   Well, aren't you the gallant beau —running away from your partner!

JEAN   On the contrary, Miss Julie. As you can see, I've hurried back to the partner I deserted.

MISS JULIE [*changing tack*]   You know, you're the best dancer   15
I've met.—But why are you wearing livery on a holiday. Take it off at once.

JEAN   I'd have to ask you to leave for a minute. My black coat is hanging right here—[*He moves to the right and points.*]

MISS JULIE   You're not embarrassed because I'm here, are you? Just   20
to change your coat? Go in your room and come right back again. Or else you can stay here and I'll turn my back.

JEAN   If you'll excuse me, Miss Julie. [*He goes off to the right. His arm can be seen as he changes his coat.*]

MISS JULIE [*to* CHRISTINE]   Tell me something, Christine. Is Jean your fiancé? He seems so intimate with you.   25

CHRISTINE   Fiancé? I suppose so. At least that's what we say.

MISS JULIE   What do you mean?

CHRISTINE   Well, Miss Julie, you have had fiancés yourself, and you know—

5   MISS JULIE   But we were properly engaged—!

CHRISTINE   I know, but did anything come of it?

[JEAN *comes back, wearing a cutaway coat and derby.*]

MISS JULIE   *Très gentil, monsieur Jean! Très gentil!*

JEAN   *Vous voulez plaisanter, madame.*

MISS JULIE   *Et vous voulez parler français!* Where did you learn to
10   speak French?

JEAN   In Switzerland. I was *sommelier* in one of the biggest hotels in Lucerne.

MISS JULIE   But you look quite the gentleman in that coat! *Charmant!* [*She sits down at the table.*]

15   JEAN   Flatterer!

MISS JULIE [*stiffening*]   Who said I was flattering you?

JEAN   My natural modesty would not allow me to presume that you were paying sincere compliments to someone like me, and therefore I assumed that you were exaggerating, or, in other
20   words, flattering me.

MISS JULIE   Where on earth did you learn to talk like that? Do you go to the theater often?

JEAN   And other places. I get around.

MISS JULIE   But weren't you born in this district?

25   JEAN   My father worked as a farm hand on the county attorney's estate, next door to yours. I used to see you when you were little. But of course you didn't notice me.

MISS JULIE   Did you really?

JEAN   Yes. I remember one time in particular—. But I can't tell
30   you about that!

MISS JULIE   Of course you can. Oh, come on, tell me. Just this once—for me.

JEAN   No. No, I really couldn't. Not now. Some other time maybe.

35   MISS JULIE   Some other time? That means never. What's the harm in telling me now?

JEAN There's no harm. I just don't feel like it.—Look at her. [*He nods at* CHRISTINE, *who has fallen asleep in a chair by the stove.*]

MISS JULIE Won't she make somebody a pretty wife! I'll bet she snores, too.

JEAN No, she doesn't. But she talks in her sleep. 5

MISS JULIE [*cynically*] Now how would you know she talks in her sleep?

JEAN [*coolly*] I've heard her. . . .

[*Pause. They look at each other.*]

MISS JULIE Why don't you sit down?

JEAN I wouldn't take the liberty in your presence. 10

MISS JULIE But if I were to order you—?

JEAN I'd obey.

MISS JULIE Well then, sit down.—Wait a minute. Could you get me something to drink first?

JEAN I don't know what there is in the icebox. Only beer, I 15 suppose.

MISS JULIE *Only* beer?! I have simple tastes. I prefer beer to wine.

[JEAN *takes a bottle of beer from the icebox and opens it. He looks in the cupboard for a glass and a saucer, and serves her.*]

JEAN At your service.

MISS JULIE Thank you. Don't you want to drink, too? 20

JEAN I'm not much of a beer-drinker, but if it's your wish—

MISS JULIE My wish! I should think a gentleman would want to keep his lady company.

JEAN That's a point well taken! [*He opens another bottle and takes a glass.*]

MISS JULIE Now drink a toast to me! [JEAN *hesitates.*] You're not 25 shy, are you? A big, strong man like you? [*Playfully,* JEAN *kneels and raises his glass in mock gallantry.*]

JEAN To my lady's health!

MISS JULIE Bravo! Now if you would kiss my shoe, you will have hit it off perfectly. [JEAN *hesitates, then boldly grasps her foot and touches it lightly with his lips.*] Superb! You should have 30 been an actor.

JEAN [*rising*] This has got to stop, Miss Julie! Someone might come and see us.

MISS JULIE What difference would that make?

JEAN People would talk, that's what! If you knew how their tongues were wagging out there just a few minutes ago, you wouldn't—

MISS JULIE What sort of things did they say? Tell me. Sit down and tell me.

JEAN [*sitting down*] I don't want to hurt your feelings, but they used expressions that—that hinted at certain—you know what I mean. After all, you're not a child. And when they see a woman drinking, alone with a man—and a servant at that—in the middle of the night—well . . .

MISS JULIE Well what?! Besides, we're not alone. Christine is here.

JEAN Yes, asleep!

MISS JULIE I'll wake her up then. [*She goes over to* CHRISTINE.] Christine! Are you asleep? [CHRISTINE *babbles in her sleep.*] Christine!—How sound she sleeps!

CHRISTINE [*talking in her sleep*] Count's boots are brushed . . . put on the coffee . . . right away, right away, right . . . mm—mm . . . poofff . . .

[MISS JULIE *grabs* CHRISTINE'S *nose.*]

MISS JULIE Wake up, will you!

JEAN [*sternly*] Let her alone!

MISS JULIE [*sharply*] What!

JEAN She's been standing over the stove all day. She's worn out when evening comes. Anyone asleep is entitled to some respect.

MISS JULIE [*changing tack*] That's a very kind thought. It does you credit. Thank you. [*She offers* JEAN *her hand.*] Now come on out and pick some lilacs for me.

[*During the following,* CHRISTINE *wakes up and, drunk with sleep, shuffles off to the right to go to bed.*]

JEAN With you, Miss Julie?

MISS JULIE Yes, with me.

JEAN That's no good. Absolutely not.

MISS JULIE I don't know what you're thinking. Maybe you're letting your imagination run away with you.

JEAN I'm not. The other people are.

MISS JULIE In what way? Imagining that I'm—*verliebt* in a servant?

JEAN I'm not conceited, but it's been known to happen. And to these people nothing's sacred.

MISS JULIE Why, I believe you're an aristocrat!

JEAN Yes, I am.

MISS JULIE I'm climbing down—

JEAN Don't climb down, Miss Julie! Take my advice. No one will ever believe that you climbed down deliberately. They'll say that you fell.

MISS JULIE I think more highly of these people than you do. Let's see who's right! Come on! [*She looks him over, challenging him.*]

JEAN You know, you're very strange.

MISS JULIE Perhaps. But then so are you. . . . Besides, everything is strange. Life, people, everything. It's all scum, drifting and drifting on the water until it sinks—sinks. There's a dream I have every now and then. It's coming back to me now. I'm sitting on top of a pillar that I've climbed up somehow and I don't know how to get back down. When I look down I get dizzy. I have to get down but I don't have the courage to jump. I can't hold on much longer and I want to fall; but I don't fall. I know I won't have any peace until I get down; no rest until I get down, down on the ground. And if I ever got down on the ground, I'd want to go farther down, right down into the earth. . . . Have you ever felt anything like that?

JEAN Never! I used to dream that I'm lying under a tall tree in a dark woods. I want to get up, up to the very top, to look out over the bright landscape with the sun shining on it, to rob the bird's nest up there with the golden eggs in it. I climb and I climb, but the trunk is so thick, and so smooth, and it's such a long way to that first branch. But I know that if I could just reach that first branch, I'd go right to the top as if on a ladder. I've never reached it yet, but some day I will—even if only in my dreams.

MISS JULIE Here I am talking about dreams with you. Come out with me. Only into the park a way. [*She offers him her arm, and they start to go.*]

JEAN Let's sleep on nine midsummer flowers, Miss Julie, and then our dreams will come true!

[MISS JULIE *and* JEAN *suddenly turn around in the doorway.* JEAN *is holding his hand over one eye.*]

MISS JULIE   You've caught something in your eye. Let me see.

JEAN   It's nothing. Just a bit of dust. It'll go away.

MISS JULIE   The sleeve of my dress must have grazed your eye. Sit down and I'll help you. [*She takes him by the arm and sits him down. She takes his head and leans it back. With the corner of her handkerchief she tries to get out the bit of dust.*] Now sit still, absolutely still. [*She slaps his hand.*] Do as you're told. Why, I believe you're trembling—a big, strong man like you.

[*She feels his biceps.*] With such big arms!

JEAN [*warningly*]   Miss Julie!

MISS JULIE   Yes, *Monsieur Jean?*

JEAN   *Attention! Je ne suis qu'un homme!*

MISS JULIE   Sit still, I tell you! . . . There now! It's out. Kiss my hand and thank me!

JEAN [*rising to his feet*]   Listen to me, Miss Julie!—Christine has gone to bed!—Listen to me, I tell you!

MISS JULIE   Kiss my hand first!

JEAN   Listen to me!

MISS JULIE   Kiss my hand first!

JEAN   All right. But you'll have no one to blame but yourself.

MISS JULIE   For what?

JEAN   For what! Are you twenty-five years old and still a child? Don't you know it's dangerous to play with fire?

MISS JULIE   Not for me. I'm insured!

JEAN [*boldly*]   Oh, no you're not! And even if you are, there's inflammable stuff next door.

MISS JULIE   Meaning you?

JEAN   Yes. Not just because it's me, but because I'm a young man—

MISS JULIE   And irresistibly handsome? What incredible conceit! A Don Juan, maybe! Or a Joseph! Yes, bless my soul, that's it: you're a Joseph!

JEAN   You think so?!

MISS JULIE   I'm almost afraid so! [JEAN *boldly steps up to her,*

grabs her around the waist, kisses her. She slaps his face.] None
of that!

JEAN   Are you still playing games or are you serious?

MISS JULIE   I'm serious.

JEAN   Then you must have been serious just a moment ago, too!
You take your games too seriously and that's dangerous. Well,
I'm tired of your games, and if you'll excuse me, I'll return to my
work. The Count will be wanting his boots on time, and it's long
past midnight.

MISS JULIE   Put those boots down.

JEAN   No! This is my job. It's what I'm here for. But I never
undertook to be a playmate for you. That's something I could
never be. I consider myself too good for that.

MISS JULIE   You are proud.

JEAN   In some ways. Not in others.

MISS JULIE   Have you ever been in love?

JEAN   We don't use that word around here. But I've been interested in a lot of girls, if that's what you mean. . . . I even got sick
once because I couldn't have the one I wanted—really sick, like
the princes in the Arabian Nights—who couldn't eat or drink for
love.

MISS JULIE   Who was the girl? [JEAN *does not reply.*] Who was
she?

JEAN   You can't make me tell you that.

MISS JULIE   Even if I ask you as an equal—ask you—as a friend?
. . . Who was she?

JEAN   You.

MISS JULIE [*sitting down*]   How—amusing. . . .

JEAN   Yes, maybe so. Ridiculous . . . . That's why I didn't want to
tell you about it before. But now I'll tell you the whole story.
. . . Have you any idea what the world looks like from below?
Of course you haven't. No more than a hawk or eagle has. You
hardly ever see their backs because they're always soaring above
us. I lived with seven brothers and sisters—and a pig—out on the
waste land where there wasn't even a tree growing. But from
my window I could see the wall of the Count's garden with the
apple trees sticking up over it. That was the Garden of Eden for
me, and there were many angry angels with flaming swords standing guard over it. But in spite of them, I and the other boys found
a way to the Tree of Life. . . . I'll bet you despise me.

Miss Julie   All boys steal apples.

Jean   That's what you say now. But you still despise me. Never mind. One day I went with my mother into this paradise to weed the onion beds. Next to the vegetable garden stood a Turkish pavilion, shaded by jasmine and hung all over with honeysuckle. I couldn't imagine what it was used for. I only knew I had never seen such a beautiful building. People went in, and came out again. And one day the door was left open. I sneaked in. The walls were covered with portraits of kings and emperors, and the windows had red curtains with tassels on them.—You do know what kind of place I'm talking about, don't you? . . . I— [*He breaks off a lilac and holds it under* Miss Julie's *nose.*] I had never been inside a castle, never seen anything besides the church. But this was more beautiful. And no matter what I tried to think about, my thoughts always came back—to that little pavilion. And little by little there arose in me a desire to experience just for once the whole pleasure of . . . *Enfin,* I sneaked in, looked about, and marveled. Then I heard someone coming! There was only one way out—for the upper-class people. But for me there was one more—a lower one. And I had no other choice but to take it. [Miss Julie, *who has taken the lilac from* Jean, *lets it fall to the table.*] Then I began to run like mad, plunging through the raspberry bushes, ploughing through the strawberry patches, and came up on the rose terrace. And there I caught sight of a pink dress and a pair of white stockings. That was you. I crawled under a pile of weeds, under—well, you can imagine what it was like—under thistles that pricked me and wet dirt that stank to high heaven. And all the while I could see you walking among the roses. I said to myself, "If it's true that a thief can enter heaven and be with the angels, isn't it strange that a poor man's child here on God's green earth can't enter the Count's park and play with the Count's daughter."

Miss Julie [*sentimentally*]   Do you think all poor children have felt that way?

Jean [*hesitatingly at first, then with mounting conviction*]   If all poor ch—? Yes—yes, naturally. Of course!

Miss Julie   It must be terrible to be poor.

Jean [*with exaggerated pain and poignancy*]   Oh, Miss Julie! You don't know! A dog can lie on the sofa with its mistress; a horse can have its nose stroked by the hand of a countess; but a servant—! [*Changing his tone*] Of course, now and then you meet somebody with guts enough to work his way up in the world, but how often?—Anyway, you know what I did afterwards? I threw myself into the millstream with all my clothes on. Got fished out and spanked. But the following Sunday, when Pa and everybody else in the house went to visit Grandma, I arranged things so I'd be left behind. Then I washed myself all over with soap and warm water, put on my best clothes, and went off to church— just to see you there once more. I saw you, and then I went home determined to die. But I wanted to die beautifully and comfortably, without pain. I remembered that it was fatal to sleep under an alder bush. And we had a big one that had just blossomed out. I stripped it of every leaf and blossom it had and made a bed of them in a bin of oats. Have you ever noticed how smooth oats are? As smooth to the touch as human skin. . . . So I pulled the lid of the bin shut and closed my eyes—fell asleep. And when they woke me I was really very sick. But I didn't die, as you can see.——What was I trying to prove? I don't know. There was no hope of winning you. But you were a symbol of the absolute hopelessness of my ever getting out of the circle I was born in.

MISS JULIE   You know, you have a real gift for telling stories. Did you go to school?

JEAN   A little. But I've read a lot of novels and gone to the theater. And I've also listened to educated people talk. That's how I've learned the most.

MISS JULIE   You mean to tell me you stand around listening to what we're saying!

JEAN   Certainly! And I've heard an awful lot, I can tell you— sitting on the coachman's seat or rowing the boat. One time I heard you and a girl friend talking——

MISS JULIE   Really? . . . And just what did you hear?

JEAN   Well, now, I don't know if I could repeat it. I can tell you I was a little amazed. I couldn't imagine where you had learned such words. Maybe at bottom there isn't such a big difference as you might think, between people and people.

MISS JULIE   How vulgar! At least people in my class don't behave like you when we're engaged.

JEAN   [*looking her in the eye*]   Are you sure?—Come on now, it's no use playing the innocent with me.

MISS JULIE   He was a beast. The man I offered my love was a beast.

JEAN   That's what you all say—afterwards.

MISS JULIE   All?

JEAN   I'd say so, since I've heard the same expression used several times before in similar circumstances.

MISS JULIE   What kind of circumstances?

JEAN   The kind we're talking about. I remember the last time I—

MISS JULIE [*rising*]   That's enough! I don't want to hear any more.

JEAN   How strange! Neither did she! . . . Well, now if you'll excuse
5   me, I'll go to bed.

MISS JULIE [*softly*]   Go to bed on Midsummer Eve?

JEAN   That's right. Dancing with that crowd up there really doesn't
amuse me.

MISS JULIE   Jean, get the key to the boathouse and row me out
10   on the lake. I want to see the sun come up.

JEAN   Do you think that's wise?

MISS JULIE   You sound as if you were worried about your reputation.

JEAN   Why not? I don't particularly care to be made ridiculous, or
15   to be kicked out without a recommendation just when I'm trying
to establish myself. Besides, I have a certain obligation to Christine.

MISS JULIE   Oh, I see. It's Christine now.

JEAN   Yes, but I'm thinking of you, too. Take my advice, Miss
20   Julie, and go up to your room.

MISS JULIE   When did you start giving me orders?

JEAN   Just this once. For your own sake! Please! It's very late.
You're so tired, you're drunk. You don't know what you're doing.
Go to bed, Miss Julie.——Besides, if my ears aren't deceiving me,
25   they're coming this way, looking for me. If they find us here together, you're done for!

THE CHORUS [*is heard coming nearer, singing*]

> Two ladies came from out the clover,
> Tri-di-ri-di-ralla, tri-di-ri-di-ra.
> And one of them was green all over,
30   > Tri-di-ri-di-ralla-la.
> They told us they had gold aplenty,
> Tri-di-ri-di-ralla, tri-di-ri-di-ra.
> But neither of them owned a penny.
> Tri-di-ri-di-ralla-la.
35   > This wreath for you I may be plaiting,
> Tri-di-ri-di-ralla, tri-di-ri-di-ra.
> But it's for another I am waiting,
> Tri-di-ri-ralla-la!

MISS JULIE   I know these people. I love them just as they love me.
Let them come. You'll find out.

JEAN   No, Miss Julie, they don't love you! They take the food you
give them, but they spit on it as soon as your back is turned. Be-   5
lieve me! Just listen to them. Listen to what they're singing.——
No, you'd better not listen.

MISS JULIE   [*listening*]   What are they singing?

JEAN   A dirty song—about you and me!

MISS JULIE   How disgusting! Oh, what cowardly, sneaking—

JEAN   That's what the mob always is—cowards! You can't fight   10
them; you can only run away.

MISS JULIE   Run away? Where? There's no way out of here. And
we can't go in to Christine.

JEAN   What about my room? What do you say? The rules don't
count in a situation like this. You can trust me. I'm your friend,   15
remember? Your true, devoted, and respectful friend.

MISS JULIE   But suppose—suppose they looked for you there?

JEAN   I'll bolt the door. If they try to break it down, I'll shoot.
Come, Miss Julie! [*On his knees*] Please, Miss Julie!

MISS JULIE   [*meaningfully*]   You promise me that you—?   20

JEAN   I swear to you!

[MISS JULIE *goes out quickly to the right.* JEAN *follows her im-
petuously.*]

[THE BALLET. *The country people enter in festive costumes, with
flowers in their hats. The fiddler is in the lead. A keg of small
beer and a little keg of liquor, decorated with greenery, are set
up on the table. Glasses are brought out. They all drink, after
which they form a circle and sing and dance the round dance,
"Two ladies came from out the clover." At the end of the dance
they all leave singing.*]

[MISS JULIE *comes in alone; looks at the devastated kitchen; clasps
her hands together; then takes out a powder puff and powders
her face.* JEAN *enters. He is in high spirits.*]

JEAN   You see! You heard them, didn't you? You've got to admit
it's impossible to stay here.

MISS JULIE   No, I don't. But even if I did, what could we do?

JEAN   Go away, travel, get away from here!   25

MISS JULIE   Travel? Yes—but where?

JEAN   Switzerland, the Italian lakes. You've never been there?

MISS JULIE   No. Is it beautiful?

JEAN   Eternal summer, oranges, laurel trees, ah . . . !

5   MISS JULIE   But what are we going to do there?

JEAN   I'll set up a hotel—a first-class hotel with a first-class clientele.

MISS JULIE   Hotel?

JEAN   I tell you that's the life! Always new faces, new languages.
10   Not a minute to think about yourself or worry about your nerves.
No looking for something to do. The work keeps you busy. Day
and night the bells ring, the trains whistle, the busses come and
go. And all the while the money comes rolling in. I tell you it's
the life!

15   MISS JULIE   Yes, that's the life. But what about me?

JEAN   The mistress of the whole place, the star of the establishment! With your looks—and your personality—it can't fail. It's
perfect! You'll sit in the office like a queen, setting your slaves in
motion by pressing an electric button. The guests will file before
20   your throne and timidly lay their treasures on your table. You
can't imagine how people tremble when you shove a bill in their
face! I'll salt the bills and you'll sugar them with your prettiest
smile. Come on, let's get away from here—[*He takes a timetable
from his pocket.*]—right away—the next train! We'll be in Malmo
25   at 6:30; Hamburg 8:40 in the morning; Frankfurt to Basle in
one day; and to Como by way of the Gotthard tunnel in—let me
see—three days! Three days!

MISS JULIE   You make it sound so wonderful. But, Jean, you have
to give me strength. Tell me you love me. Come and put your
30   arms around me.

JEAN   [*hesitates*]   I want to . . . but I don't dare. Not any more, not
in this house. I do love you—without a shadow of a doubt. How
can you doubt that, Miss Julie?

MISS JULIE   [*shyly, very becomingly*]   You don't have to be formal
35   with me, Jean. You can call me Julie. There aren't any barriers
between us now. Call me Julie.

JEAN   [*agonized*]   I can't! There are still barriers between us, Miss
Julie, as long as we stay in this house! There's the past, there's
the Count. I've never met anyone I feel so much respect for. I've
40   only got to see his gloves lying on a table and I shrivel up. I
only have to hear that bell ring and I shy like a frightened horse.

I only have to look at his boots standing there so stiff and proud
and I feel my spine bending. [*He kicks the boots.*] Superstitions,
prejudices that they've drilled into us since we were children!
But they can be forgotten just as easily! Just we get to another
country where they have a republic! They'll crawl on their hands   5
and knees when they see my uniform. On their hands and knees,
I tell you! But not me! Oh, no. I'm not made for crawling. I've
got guts, backbone. And once I grab that first branch, you just
watch me climb. I may be a valet now, but next year I'll be own-
ing property; in ten years, I'll be living off my investments. Then   10
I'll go to Rumania, get myself some decorations, and maybe—
notice I only say maybe—end up as a count!

MISS JULIE   How wonderful, wonderful.

JEAN   Listen, in Rumania you can buy titles. You'll be a countess
after all. *My* countess.   15

MISS JULIE   But I'm not interested in that. I'm leaving all that behind. Tell me you love me, Jean, or else—or else what difference
does it make what I am?

JEAN   I'll tell you a thousand times—but later! Not now. And not
here. Above all, let's keep our feelings out of this or we'll make   20
a mess of everything. We have to look at this thing calmly and
coolly, like sensible people. [*He takes out a cigar, clips the end,
and lights it.*] Now you sit there and I'll sit here, and we'll talk
as if nothing had happened.

MISS JULIE [*in anguish*]   My God, what are you? Don't you have   25
any feelings?

JEAN   Feelings? Nobody's got more feelings than I have. But I've
learned how to control them.

MISS JULIE   A few minutes ago you were kissing my shoe—and
now—!   30

JEAN [*harshly*]   That was a few minutes ago. We've got other
things to think about now!

MISS JULIE   Don't speak to me like that, Jean!

JEAN   I'm just trying to be sensible. We've been stupid once; let's
not be stupid again. Your father might be back at any moment,   35
and we've got to decide our future before then.—Now what do
you think about my plans? Do you approve or don't you?

MISS JULIE   I don't see anything wrong with them. Except one
thing. For a big undertaking like that, you'd need a lot of capital.
Have you got it?   40

JEAN [*chewing on his cigar*]   Have I got it? Of course I have. I've
got my knowledge of the business, my vast experience, my

familiarity with languages. That's capital that counts for something, let me tell you.

MISS JULIE   You can't even buy the railway tickets with it.

JEAN   That's true. That's why I need a backer—someone to put up the money.

MISS JULIE   Where can you find him on a moment's notice?

JEAN   You'll find him—if you want to be my partner.

MISS JULIE   I can't. And I don't have a penny to my name.

[Pause]

JEAN   Then you can forget the whole thing.

MISS JULIE   Forget—?

JEAN   And things will stay just the way they are.

MISS JULIE   Do you think I'm going to live under the same roof with you as your mistress? Do you think I'm going to have people sneering at me behind my back? How do you think I'll ever be able to look my father in the face after this? No, no! Take me away from here, Jean—the shame, the humiliation. . . . What have I done? Oh, my God, my God! What have I done? [She bursts into tears.]

JEAN   Now don't start singing that tune. It won't work. What have you done that's so awful? You're not the first.

MISS JULIE [crying hysterically]   Now you despise me!—I'm falling, I'm falling!

JEAN   Fall down to me, and I'll lift you up again!

MISS JULIE   What awful hold did you have over me? What drove me to you? The weak to the strong? The falling to the rising! Or maybe it was love? Love? This? You don't know what love is!

JEAN   Want to bet? Did you think I was a virgin?

MISS JULIE   You're vulgar! The things you say, the things you think!

JEAN   That's the way I was brought up and that's the way I am! Now don't get hysterical and don't play the fine lady with me. We're eating off the same platter now. . . . That's better. Come over here and be a good girl and I'll treat you to something special. [He opens the table drawer and takes out the wine bottle. He pours the wine into two used glasses.]

MISS JULIE   Where did you get that wine?

JEAN   From the wine cellar.

MISS JULIE   My father's burgundy!

JEAN   Should be good enough for his son-in-law.

MISS JULIE   I was drinking beer and you—!

JEAN   That shows that I have better taste than you.   5

MISS JULIE   Thief!

JEAN   You going to squeal on me?

MISS JULIE   Oh, God! Partner in crime with a petty house thief!
I must have been drunk; I must have been walking in my sleep.
Midsummer Night! Night of innocent games—   10

JEAN   Yes, very innocent!

MISS JULIE [*pacing up and down*]   Is there anyone here on earth
as miserable as I am?

JEAN   Why be miserable? After such a conquest! Think of poor
Christine in there. Don't you think she's got any feelings?   15

MISS JULIE   I thought so a while ago, but I don't now. A servant's a servant—

JEAN   And a whore's a whore!

MISS JULIE [*falls to her knees and clasps her hands together*]   Oh,
God in heaven, put an end to my worthless life! Lift me out of   20
this awful filth I'm sinking in! Save me! Save me!

JEAN   I feel sorry for you, I have to admit it. When I was lying
in the onion beds, looking up at you on the rose terrace, I—I'm
telling you the truth now—I had the same dirty thoughts that all
boys have.   25

MISS JULIE   And you said you wanted to die for me!

JEAN   In the oat bin? That was only a story.

MISS JULIE   A lie, you mean.

JEAN [*beginning to get sleepy*]   Practically. I think I read it in a
paper about a chimney sweep who curled up in a wood-bin with   30
some lilacs because they were going to arrest him for nonsupport
of his child.

MISS JULIE   Now I see you for what you are.

JEAN   What did you expect me to do? It's always the fancy talk
that gets the women.   35

MISS JULIE   You dog!

JEAN   You bitch!

MISS JULIE   Well, now you've seen the eagle's back—

JEAN   Wasn't exactly its back—!

MISS JULIE   I was going to be your first branch—!

JEAN   A rotten branch—

5   MISS JULIE   I was going to be the window dressing for your hotel—!

JEAN   And I the hotel—!

MISS JULIE   Sitting at the desk, attracting your customers, padding your bills—!

JEAN   I could manage that myself—!

10   MISS JULIE   How can a human soul be so dirty and filthy?

JEAN   Then why don't you clean it up?

MISS JULIE   You lackey! You shoeshine boy! Stand up when I talk to you!

JEAN   You lackey lover! You bootblack's tramp! Shut your mouth
15   and get out of here! Who do you think you are telling me I'm
coarse? I've never seen anybody in my class behave as crudely as
you did tonight. Have you ever seen any of the girls around here
grab at a man like you did? Do you think any of the girls of my
class would throw themselves at a man like that? I've never seen
20   the like of it except in animals and prostitutes!

MISS JULIE [*crushed*]   That's right! Hit me! Walk all over me! It's
all I deserve. I'm rotten. But help me! Help me to get out of
this—if there is any way out for me!

JEAN [*less harsh*]   I'd be doing myself an injustice if I didn't admit
25   that part of the credit for this seduction belongs to me. But do
you think a person in my position would have dared to look twice
at you if you hadn't asked for it? I'm still amazed—

MISS JULIE   And still proud.

JEAN   Why not? But I've got to confess the victory was a little too
30   easy to give me any real thrill.

MISS JULIE   Go on, hit me more!

JEAN [*standing up*]   No. . . . I'm sorry for what I said. I never hit
a person who's down, especially a woman. I can't deny that, in
one way, it was good to find out that what I saw glittering up
35   above was only fool's gold, to have seen that the eagle's back was
as gray as its belly, that the smooth cheek was just powder, and
that there could be dirt under the manicured nails, that the handkerchief was soiled even though it smelled of perfume. But, in
another way, it hurt me to find that everything I was striving for

wasn't very high above me after all, wasn't even real. It hurts me to see you sink far lower than your own cook. Hurts, like seeing the last flowers cut to pieces by the autumn rains and turned to muck.

MISS JULIE You talk as if you already stood high above me.   5

JEAN Well, don't I? Don't forget I could make you a countess but you can never make me a count.

MISS JULIE But I have a father for a count. You can never have that!

JEAN True. But I might father my own counts—that is, if—   10

MISS JULIE You're a thief! I'm not!

JEAN There are worse things than being a thief. A lot worse. And besides, when I take a position in a house, I consider myself a member of the family—in a way, like a child in the house. It's no crime for a child to steal a few ripe cherries when they're fall-   15
ing off the trees, is it? [*He begins to feel passionate again.*] Miss Julie, you're a beautiful woman, much too good for the likes of me. You got carried away by your emotions and now you want to cover up your mistake by telling yourself that you love me. You don't love me. You might possibly have been attracted by   20
my looks—in which case your kind of love is no better than mine. But I could never be satisfied to be just an animal for you, and I could never make you love me.

MISS JULIE Are you so sure of that?

JEAN You mean there's a chance? I could love you, there's no   25
doubt about that. You're beautiful, you're refined—[*He goes up to her and takes her hand.*]—educated, lovable when you want to be, and once you set a man's heart on fire, I'll bet it burns forever. [*He puts his arm around her waist.*] You're like hot wine with strong spices. One of your kisses is enough to—[*He at-*   30
tempts to lead her out, but she rather reluctantly breaks away from him.]

MISS JULIE Let me go. You don't get me that way.

JEAN Then how? Not by petting you and not with pretty words, not by planning for the future, not by saving you from humilia-   35
tion! Then how, tell me how?

MISS JULIE How? How? I don't know how! I don't know at all!— I hate you like I hate rats, but I can't get away from you.

JEAN Then come away *with* me!   40

MISS JULIE [*pulling herself together*] Away? Yes, we'll go away! ——But I'm so tired. Pour me a glass of wine, will you? [JEAN

pours the wine. MISS JULIE *looks at her watch.*] Let's talk first.
We still have a little time. [*She empties the glass of wine and
holds it out for more.*]

JEAN   Don't overdo it. You'll get drunk.

MISS JULIE   What difference does it make?

5   JEAN   What difference? It looks cheap.——What did you want to
say to me?

MISS JULIE   We're going to run away together, right? But we'll
talk first—that is, I'll talk. So far you've done all the talking.
You've told me your life, now I'll tell you mine. That way we'll
10   know each other through and through before we become traveling companions.

JEAN   Wait a minute. Excuse me, but are you sure you won't regret this afterwards, when you've surrendered your secrets?

MISS JULIE   I thought you were my friend.

15   JEAN   I am—sometimes. But don't count on me.

MISS JULIE   You don't mean that. Anyway, everybody knows my
secrets.—My mother's parents were very ordinary people, just
commoners. She was brought up, according to the theories of her
time, to believe in equality, the independence of women, and all
20   that. And she had a strong aversion to marriage. When my father
proposed to her, she swore she would never become his wife. . . .
But she did anyway. I was born—against my mother's wishes, as
far as. I can make out. My mother decided to bring me up as a
nature child. And on top of that I had to learn everything a boy
25   learns, so I could be living proof that women were just as good
as men. I had to wear boy's clothes, learn to handle horses—but
not to milk the cows. I was made to groom the horses and handle
them, and go out hunting—and even had to try and learn farm-
ing! And on the estate all the men were set to doing the work of
30   women, and the women to doing men's work—with the result that
the whole place threatened to fall to pieces, and we became the
local laughing-stock. Finally my father must have come out of
his trance. He rebelled, and everything was changed according
to his wishes. Then my mother got sick. I don't know what kind
35   of sickness it was, but she often had convulsions, and she would
hide herself in the attic or in the garden, and sometimes she
would stay out all night. Then there occurred that big fire you've
heard about. The house, the stables, the cowsheds, all burned
down—and under very peculiar circumstances that led one to
40   suspect arson. You see, the accident occurred the day after the
insurance expired, and the premiums on the new policy, which
my father had sent in, were delayed through the messenger's

carelessness, and didn't arrive on time. [*She refills her glass and drinks.*]

JEAN   You've had enough.

MISS JULIE   Who cares!——We were left without a penny to our name. We had to sleep in the carriages. My father didn't know   5
where to turn for money to rebuild the house. Then Mother suggested to him that he might try to borrow money from an old friend of hers, who owned a brick factory, not far from here. Father takes out a loan, but there's no interest charged, which surprises him. So the place was rebuilt. [*She drinks some more.*]   10
Do you know who set fire to the place?

JEAN   Your honorable mother!

MISS JULIE   Do you know who the brick manufacturer was?

JEAN   Your mother's lover?

MISS JULIE   Do you know whose money it was?   15

JEAN   Let me think a minute. . . . No, I give up.

MISS JULIE   It was my mother's!

JEAN   The Count's, you mean. Or was there a marriage settlement?

MISS JULIE   There wasn't a settlement. My mother had a little money of her own which she didn't want under my father's con-   20
trol, so she invested it with her—friend.

JEAN   Who grabbed it!

MISS JULIE   Precisely. He appropriated it. Well, my father finds out what happened. But he can't go to court, can't pay his wife's lover, can't prove that it's his wife's money. That was how my   25
mother got her revenge because he had taken control of the house. He was on the verge of shooting himself. There was even a rumor that he tried and failed. But he took a new lease on life and he forced my mother to pay for her mistakes. Can you imagine what those five years were like for me? I felt sorry for   30
my father, but I took my mother's side because I didn't know the whole story. She had taught me to distrust and hate all men— you've heard how she hated men—and I swore to her that I'd never be slave to any man.

JEAN   But you got engaged to the attorney.   35

MISS JULIE   Only to make him slave to me.

JEAN   But he didn't want any of that?

MISS JULIE   Oh, he wanted to well enough, but I didn't give him the chance. I got bored with him.

JEAN Yes, so I noticed—in the barnyard.

MISS JULIE What did you notice?

JEAN I saw what I saw. *He* broke off the engagement.

MISS JULIE That's a lie! It was I who broke it off. Did he tell
5   you that? He's beneath contempt!

JEAN Come on now, he isn't as bad as that. So you hate men,
Miss Julie?

MISS JULIE Yes, I do. . . . Most of the time. But sometimes, when
I can't help myself—oh. . . . [*She shudders in disgust.*]

10 JEAN Then you hate me, too?

MISS JULIE You have no idea how much! I'd like to see you killed
like an animal—

JEAN Like a mad dog, without a moment's hesitation, right?

MISS JULIE Right!

15 JEAN But we don't have anything to shoot him with—and no dog!
What are we going to do?

MISS JULIE Go away from here.

JEAN To torture ourselves to death?

MISS JULIE No. To enjoy ourselves for a day or two, or a week,
20   for as long as we can—and then—to die—

JEAN Die? How stupid! I've got a better idea: start a hotel!

MISS JULIE [*continuing without hearing* JEAN] —on the shores of
Lake Como, where the sun is always shining, where the laurels
bloom at Christmas, and the golden oranges glow on the trees.

25 JEAN Lake Como is a stinking wet hole, and the only oranges I
saw there were on the fruit stands. But it's a good tourist spot
with a lot of villas and cottages that are rented out to lovers.
Now there's a profitable business. You know why? They rent the
villa for the whole season, but they leave after three weeks.

30 MISS JULIE [*innocently*] Why after only three weeks?

JEAN Because they can't stand each other any longer. Why else?
But they still have to pay the rent. Then you rent it out again
to another couple, and so on. There's no shortage of love—even
if it doesn't last very long.

35 MISS JULIE Then you don't want to die with me?

JEAN I don't want to die at all! I enjoy life too much. And moreover, I consider taking your own life a sin against the Providence
that gave us life.

MISS JULIE   You believe in God? You?

JEAN   Yes, certainly I do! I go to church every other Sunday.—
Honestly, I've had enough of this talk. I'm going to bed.

MISS JULIE   Really? You think you're going to get off that easy?
Don't you know that a man owes something to the woman he's   5
dishonored?

JEAN [*takes out his purse and throws a silver coin on the table.*]
There you are. I don't want to owe anybody anything.

MISS JULIE [*ignoring the insult*]   Do you know what the law says—?

JEAN   Aren't you lucky the law says nothing about the women who   10
seduce men!

MISS JULIE   What else can we do but go away from here, get married, and get divorced?

JEAN   Suppose I refuse to enter into this *mésalliance?*

MISS JULIE   *Mésalliance?*   15

JEAN   For me! I've got better ancestors than you. I don't have any
female arsonist in my family.

MISS JULIE   How can you know?

JEAN   You can't prove the opposite because we don't have any
family records—except in the police courts. But I've read the   20
whole history of your family in that book on the drawing-room
table. Do you know who the founder of your family line was?
A miller—who let his wife sleep with the king one night during
the Danish war. I don't have any ancestors like that. I don't have
any ancestors at all! But I can become an ancestor myself.   25

MISS JULIE   This is what I get for baring my heart and soul to
someone too low to understand, for sacrificing the honor of my
family—

JEAN   Dishonor!—I warned you, remember? Drinking makes one
talk, and talking's bad.   30

MISS JULIE   Oh, how sorry I am! . . . If only it had never happened! . . . If only you at least loved me!

JEAN   For the last time—What do you expect of me? Do you want
me to cry? Jump over your whip? Kiss you? Do you want
me to lure you to Lake Como for three weeks and then—? What   35
am I supposed to do? What do you want? I've had more than I can
take. This is what I get for involving myself with women. . . . Miss
Julie, I can see that you're unhappy; I know that you're suffering;
but I simply cannot understand you. My people don't behave like
this. We don't hate each other. We make love for the fun of it, when   40

we can get any time off from our work. But we don't have time
for it all day and all night like you do. If you ask me, you're
sick, Miss Julie. I'm sure that's it, Miss Julie.

MISS JULIE   You can be understanding, Jean. You're talking to me
like a human being now.

JEAN   Well, be human yourself. You spit on me but you don't let
me wipe it off—on you!

MISS JULIE   Help me, Jean. Help me. Tell me what I should do,
that's all—which way to go.

JEAN   For Christ's sake, if only I knew myself!

MISS JULIE   I've been crazy—I've been out of my mind—but does
that mean there's no way out for me?

JEAN   Stay here as if nothing had happened. Nobody knows anything.

MISS JULIE   Impossible! Everybody who works here knows. Christine knows.

JEAN   They don't know a thing. And anyhow they'd never believe
it.

MISS JULIE [*slowly, significantly*]   But . . . it might happen again.

JEAN   That's true!

MISS JULIE   And there might be consequences.

JEAN [*stunned*]   Consequences!! What on earth have I been thinking of! You're right. There's only one thing to do: get away from
here! Immediately! I can't go with you—that would give the whole
game away. You'll have to go by yourself. Somewhere—I don't
care where!

MISS JULIE   By myself? Where?—Oh, no, Jean, I can't. I can't!

JEAN   You've got to! Before the Count comes back. You know as
well as I do what will happen if you stay here. After one mistake, you figure you might as well go on, since the damage is already done. Then you get more and more careless until—finally
you're exposed. I tell you, you've got to get out of the country.
Afterwards you can write to the Count and tell him everything—
leaving me out, of course. He'd never be able to guess it was me.
Anyway, I don't think he'd exactly like to find that out.

MISS JULIE   I'll go—if you'll come with me!

JEAN   Lady, are you out of your mind!? "Miss Julie elopes with
her footman." The day after tomorrow it would be in all the
papers. The Count would never live it down.

MISS JULIE I can't go away. I can't stay. Help me. I'm so tired, so awfully tired. . . . Tell me what to do. Order me. Start me going. I can't think any more, can't move any more. . . .

JEAN Now do you realize how weak you all are? What gives you the right to go strutting around with your noses in the air as if 5 you owned the world? All right, I'll give you your orders. Go up and get dressed. Get some traveling money. And come back down here.

MISS JULIE [almost in a whisper] Come up with me!

JEAN To your room? . . . You're going crazy again! [He hesitates 10 a moment.] No! No! Go! Right now! [He takes her hand and leads her out.]

MISS JULIE [as she is leaving] Don't be so harsh, Jean.

JEAN Orders always sound harsh. You've never had to take them.

[JEAN, left alone, heaves a sigh of relief and sits down at the table. He takes out a notebook and a pencil and begins to calculate, counting aloud now and then. The pantomime continues until CHRISTINE enters, dressed for church, and carrying JEAN's white tie and shirt front in her hand.]

CHRISTINE Lord in Heaven, what a mess! What on earth have 15 you been doing?

JEAN It was Miss Julie. She dragged the whole crowd in here. You must have been sleeping awfully sound if you didn't hear anything.

CHRISTINE I slept like a log. 20

JEAN You already dressed for church?

CHRISTINE Yes, indeed. Don't you remember you promised to go to Communion with me today?

JEAN Oh, yes, of course. I remember. I see you've brought my things. All right. Come on, put it on me. [He sits down, and CHRISTINE 25 starts to put the white tie and shirt front on him. Pause.]

JEAN [yawning] What's the lesson for today?

CHRISTINE The beheading of John the Baptist, I suppose.

JEAN My God, that will go on forever.—Hey, you're choking me! . . . Oh, I'm so sleepy, so sleepy.

CHRISTINE What were you doing up all night? You look green in 30 the face.

JEAN I've been sitting here talking with Miss Julie.

CHRISTINE   That girl! She doesn't know how to behave herself!

[*Pause*]

JEAN   Tell me something, Christine. . . .

CHRISTINE   Well, what?

JEAN   Isn't it strange when you think about it? Her, I mean.

5   CHRISTINE   What's so strange?

JEAN   Everything!

[*Pause.* CHRISTINE *looks at the half-empty glasses on the table.*]

CHRISTINE   Have you been drinking with her?

JEAN   Yes!

CHRISTINE   Shame on you!—Look me in the eyes! You haven't
10   . . . ?

JEAN   Yes!

CHRISTINE   Is it possible? Is it really possible?

JEAN [*after a moment's consideration*]   Yes. It is.

CHRISTINE   Oh, how disgusting! I could never have believed any-
15   thing like this would happen! No. No. This is too much!

JEAN   Don't tell me you're jealous of her?

CHRISTINE   No, not of her. If it had been Clara—or Sophie—I
would have scratched your eyes out! But her—? That's different.
I don't know why. . . . But it's still disgusting!

20   JEAN   Then you're mad at her?

CHRISTINE   No. Mad at you. You were mean and cruel to do a
thing like that, very mean. The poor girl! . . . But let me tell
you, I'm not going to stay in this house a moment longer, not
when I can't have any respect for my employers.

25   JEAN   Why do you want to respect them?

CHRISTINE   Don't try to be smart. You don't want to work for
people who behave immorally, do you? Well, do you? If you ask
me, you'd be lowering yourself by doing that.

JEAN   Oh, I don't know. I think it's rather comforting to find out
30   that they're not one bit better than we are.

CHRISTINE   Well, I don't. If they're not any better, there's no point
in us trying to be like them.—And think of the Count. Think of
all the sorrows he's been through in his time. No, sir, I won't
stay in this house any longer. . . . Imagine! You, of all people! If

it had been the attorney fellow; if it had been somebody respectable—

JEAN   Now just a minute—!

CHRISTINE   Oh, you're all right in your own way. But there's a big difference between one class and another. You can't deny that. ——No, this is something I can never get over. She was so proud, and so sarcastic about men, you'd never believe she'd go and throw herself at one. And at someone like you! And *she* was going to have Diana shot, because the poor thing ran after the gatekeeper's mongrel!—Well, I tell you, I've had enough! I'm not going to stay here any longer. On the twenty-fourth of October, I'm leaving.

JEAN   Then what'll you do?

CHRISTINE   Well, since you brought it up, it's about time that you got yourself a decent place, if we're going to get married.

JEAN   Why should I go looking for another place? I could never get a place like this if I'm married.

CHRISTINE   Well, of course not! But you could get a job as a doorkeeper, or maybe try to get a government job as a caretaker somewhere. The government don't pay much, but they pay regular. And there's a pension for the wife and children.

JEAN   [*wryly*]   Fine, fine! But I'm not the kind of fellow who thinks about dying for his wife and children this early in the game. I hate to say it, but I've got slightly bigger plans than that.

CHRISTINE   Plans! Hah! What about your obligations? You'd better start giving them a little thought!

JEAN   Don't start nagging me about obligations! I know what I have to do without you telling me. [*He hears a sound upstairs.*] Anyhow, we'll have plenty of chance to talk about this later. You just go and get yourself ready, and we'll be off to church.

CHRISTINE   Who is that walking around up there?

JEAN   I don't know. Clara, I suppose. Who else?

CHRISTINE   [*starting to leave*]   It can't be the Count, can it? Could he have come back without anybody hearing him?

JEAN   [*frightened*]   The Count? No, it can't be. He would have rung.

CHRISTINE   [*leaving*]   God help us! I've never heard of the like of this.

[*The sun has now risen and strikes the tops of the trees in the park. The light shifts gradually until it is shining very obliquely*

through the windows. JEAN *goes to the door and signals.* MISS
JULIE *enters, dressed for travel, and carrying a small bird cage,
covered with a towel. She sets the cage down on a chair.*]

MISS JULIE   I'm ready now.

JEAN   Shh! Christine's awake.

MISS JULIE   [*She is extremely tense and nervous during the following.*]   Did she suspect anything?

5   JEAN   She doesn't know a thing.——My God, what happened to
you?

MISS JULIE   What do you mean? Do I look so strange?

JEAN   You're white as a ghost, and you've—excuse me—but
you've got dirt on your face.

10   MISS JULIE   Let me wash it off. [*She goes over to the wash basin
and washes her face and hands.*]   There! Do you have a towel?
. . . Oh, look the sun's coming up!

JEAN   That breaks the magic spell!

MISS JULIE   Yes, we were spellbound last night, weren't we? Mid-
15   summer madness . . . Jean, listen to me! Come with me. I've got
the money!

JEAN   [*suspiciously*]   Enough?

MISS JULIE   Enough for a start. Come with me, Jean. I can't travel
alone today. Midsummer Day on a stifling hot train, packed in
20   with crowds of people, all staring at me—stopping at every station when I want to be flying. I can't, Jean, I can't! . . . And
everything will remind me of the past. Midsummer Day when I
was a child and the church was decorated with leaves—birch
leaves and lilacs . . . the table spread for dinner with friends and
25   relatives . . . and after dinner, dancing in the park, with flowers and
games. Oh, no matter how far you travel, the memories tag right
along in the baggage car . . . and the regrets and the remorse.

JEAN   All right, I'll go with you! But it's got to be now—before
it's too late! This very instant!

30   MISS JULIE   Hurry and get dressed! [*She picks up the bird cage.*]

JEAN   But no baggage! It would give us away.

MISS JULIE   Nothing. Only what we can take to our seats.

JEAN   [*as he gets his hat*]   What in the devil have you got there?
What is that?

35   MISS JULIE   It's only my canary. I can't leave it behind.

JEAN   A canary! My God, do you expect us to carry a bird cage
around with us? You're crazy. Put that cage down!

MISS JULIE   It's the only thing I'm taking with me from my home
—the only living thing who loves me since Diana was unfaithful
to me! Don't be cruel, Jean. Let me take it with me.

JEAN   I told you to put that cage down!——And don't talk so
loud. Christine can hear us.   5

MISS JULIE   No, I won't leave it with a stranger. I won't. I'd rather have you kill it.

JEAN   Let me have the little pest, and I'll wring its neck.

MISS JULIE   Yes, but don't hurt it. Don't—. No, I can't do it!

JEAN   Don't worry, I can. Give it here.   10

[MISS JULIE *takes the bird out of the cage and kisses it.*]

MISS JULIE   Oh, my little Serena, must you die and leave your
mistress?

JEAN   You don't have to make a scene of it. It's a question of your
whole life and future. You're wasting time! [JEAN *grabs the ca-*
nary from her, carries it to the chopping block, and picks up a   15
meat cleaver. MISS JULIE *turns away.*] You should have learned
how to kill chickens instead of shooting revolvers— [*He brings*
the cleaver down.] —then a drop of blood wouldn't make you
faint.

MISS JULIE [*screaming*]   Kill me too! Kill me! You can kill an in-   20
nocent creature without turning a hair—then kill me. Oh, how I
hate you! I loathe you! There's blood between us. I curse the
moment I first laid eyes on you! I curse the moment I was conceived in my mother's womb.

JEAN   What good does your cursing do? Let's get out of here!   25

MISS JULIE [*approaches the chopping block as if drawn to it against*
her will.]   No, I don't want to go yet. I can't.—I have to see.—
Shh! I hear a carriage coming! [*She listens but keeps her eyes*
fastened on the chopping block and cleaver.] You don't think I
can stand the sight of blood, do you? You think I'm so weak! Oh,   30
I'd love to see your blood and your brains on that chopping block.
I'd love to see the whole of your sex swimming in a sea of blood
just like that. I think I could drink out of your skull. I'd like to
bathe my feet in your ribs! I could eat your heart roasted whole!
——You think I'm weak! You think I loved you because my   35
womb hungered for your seed. You think I want to carry your
brood under my heart and nourish it with my blood! Bear your
child and take your name!—Come to think of it, what is your
name anyway? I've never heard your last name. You probably
don't even have one. I'd be Mrs. Doorkeeper or Madame Floor-   40

sweeper. You dog with my name on your collar—you lackey with my initials on your buttons! Do you think I'm going to share you with my cook and fight over you with my maid?! Ohhh!— You think I'm a coward who wants to run away. No, I'm going to stay. Come hell or high water, I don't care! My father comes home—finds his bureau broken into—his money gone. Then he rings—on that bell—two rings for the valet. And then he sends for the sheriff—and I tell him everything. Everything! Oh, it'll be wonderful to have it all over . . . if only it will be over. . . . He'll have a stroke and die. Then there'll be an end to all of us. There'll be peace . . . and quiet . . . forever. . . . His coat of arms will be broken on the coffin; the Count's line dies out. But the valet's line will continue in an orphanage, win triumphs in the gutter, and end in jail!*

[CHRISTINE *enters, dressed for church and with a hymn-book in her hand.* MISS JULIE *rushes over to her and throws herself into her arms as if seeking protection.*]

MISS JULIE Help me, Christine! Help me against this man!

CHRISTINE [*cold and unmoved*] This is a fine way to behave on a holy day! [*She sees the chopping block.*] Just look at the mess you've made there! How do you explain that? And what's all this shouting and screaming about?

MISS JULIE Christine, you're a woman, you're my friend! I warn you, watch out for this—this monster!

JEAN [*ill at ease and a little embarrassed*] If you ladies are going to talk, I think I'll go and shave. [*He slips out to the right.*]

MISS JULIE You've got to understand, Christine! You've got to listen to me!

CHRISTINE No, I don't. I don't understand this kind of shenanigans at all. Where do you think you're going dressed like that? And Jean with his hat on?—Well?—Well?

MISS JULIE Listen to me, Christine! If you'll just listen to me, I'll tell you everything.

CHRISTINE I don't want to know anything.

MISS JULIE You've got to listen to me—!

CHRISTINE What about? About your stupid behavior with Jean? I tell you that doesn't bother me at all, because it's none of my

---

* Most editions of *Miss Julie* have a speech by Jean at this point: "Now there speaks the royal blood! Brava, Miss Julie. Only you mustn't let the cat out of the bag about the miller and his wife." Strindberg wanted this speech expunged as not in keeping with Jean's character.

business. But if you have any silly idea about talking him into skipping out with you, I'll soon put a stop to that.

MISS JULIE [*extremely tense*] Christine, please don't get upset. Listen to me. I can't stay here, and Jean can't stay here. So you see, we have to go away.   5

CHRISTINE Hm, hm, hm.

MISS JULIE [*suddenly brightening up*] Wait! I've got an idea! Why couldn't all three of us go away together?—out of the country— to Switzerland—and start a hotel. I've got the money, you see. Jean and I would be responsible for the whole affair—and Chris-   10 tine, you could run the kitchen, I thought. Doesn't that sound wonderful! Say yes! Say you'll come, Christine, then everything will be settled. Say you will! Please! [*She throws her arms around* CHRISTINE *and pats her.*]

CHRISTINE [*remaining aloof and unmoved*] Hm. Hm.   15

MISS JULIE [*presto tempo*] You've never been traveling, Christine. You have to get out and see the world. You can't imagine how wonderful it is to travel by train—constantly new faces—new countries. We'll go to Hamburg, and stop over to look at the zoo —you'll love that. And we'll go to the theater and the opera.   20 And then when we get to Munich, we'll go to the museums, Christine. They have Rubenses and Raphaels there—those great painters, you know. Of course you've heard about Munich where King Ludwig lived—you know, the king who went mad. And then we can go and see his castles—they're built just like the   25 ones you read about in fairy tales. And from there it's just a short trip to Switzerland—with the Alps. Think of the Alps, Christine, covered with snow in the middle of summer. And oranges grow there, and laurel trees that are green the whole year round.—[JEAN *can be seen in the wings at the right, sharpening his* 30 *straight razor on a strap held between his teeth and his left hand. He listens to* MISS JULIE *with a satisfied expression on his face, now and then nodding approvingly.* MISS JULIE *continues tempo prestissimo.*]—And that's where we'll get a hotel. I'll sit at the desk while Jean stands at the door and receives the guests, goes out   35 shopping, writes the letters. What a life that will be! The train whistle blowing, then the bus arriving, then a bell ringing upstairs, then the bell in the restaurant rings—and I'll be making out the bills—and I know just how much to salt them—you can't imagine how timid tourists are when you shove a bill in their face!—And   40 you, Christine, you'll run the whole kitchen—there'll be no stand- ing at the stove for you—of course not. If you're going to talk to the people, you'll have to dress neatly and elegantly. And with your looks—I'm not trying to flatter you, Christine—you'll run

off with some man one fine day—a rich Englishman, that's who it'll be, they're so easy to—[*slowing down*]—to catch.—Then we'll all be rich.—We'll build a villa on Lake Como.—Maybe it does rain there sometimes, but— [*more and more lifelessly*] —the sun has
5 to shine sometimes, too—even if it looks cloudy.—And—then . . . Or else we can always travel some more—and come back . . . [*pause*] —here . . . or somewhere else. . . .

CHRISTINE Do you really believe a word of that yourself, Miss Julie?

10 MISS JULIE [*completely beaten*] Do I believe a word of it myself?

CHRISTINE Do you?

MISS JULIE [*exhausted*] I don't know. I don't believe anything any more. [*She sinks down on the bench and lays her head between her arms on the table.*] Nothing. Nothing at all.

15 CHRISTINE [*turns to the right and faces* JEAN] So! You were planning to run away, were you?

JEAN [*nonplused, lays his razor down on the table*] We weren't exactly going to run away! Don't exaggerate. You heard Miss Julie's plans. Even if she's tired now after being up all night, her
20 plans are perfectly practical.

CHRISTINE Well, just listen to you! Did you really think you could get me to cook for that little—

JEAN [*sharply*] You keep a respectful tongue in your mouth when you talk to your mistress! Understand?

25 CHRISTINE Mistress!

JEAN Yes, mistress!

CHRISTINE Well of all the—! I don't have to listen—

JEAN Yes, you do! You need to listen more and talk less. Miss Julie is your mistress. Don't forget that! And if you're going to
30 despise her for what she did, you ought to despise yourself for the same reason.

CHRISTINE I've always held myself high enough to—

JEAN High enough to make you look down on others!

CHRISTINE —enough to keep from lowering myself beneath my
35 position. No one can say that the Count's cook has ever had anything to do with the stable groom or the swineherd. No one can say that!

JEAN Yes, aren't you lucky you got involved with a decent man!

CHRISTINE What kind of a decent man is it who sells the oats
40 from the Count's stables?

JEAN   Listen to who's talking! You get a commission on the groceries
and take bribes from the butcher!

CHRISTINE   How can you say a thing like that!

JEAN   And you tell me you can't respect your employers any
more! You! You!   5

CHRISTINE   Are you going to church or aren't you? I should think
you'd need a good sermon after your exploits.

JEAN   No, I'm not going to church! You can go alone and confess
your own sins.

CHRISTINE   Yes, I'll do just that. And I'll come back with enough   10
forgiveness to cover yours, too. Our Redeemer suffered and died
on the cross for all our sins, and if we come to Him in faith
and with a penitent heart, He will take all our sins upon Himself.

JEAN   Grocery sins included?

MISS JULIE   Do you really believe that, Christine?   15

CHRISTINE   With all my heart, as sure as I'm standing here. It was
the faith I was born into, and I've held on to it since I was a
little girl, Miss Julie. Where sin aboundeth, there grace aboundeth also.

MISS JULIE   If I had your faith, Christine, if only—   20

CHRISTINE   But you see, that's something you can't have without
God's special grace. And it is not granted to everyone to receive
it.

MISS JULIE   Then who receives it?

CHRISTINE   That's the secret of the workings of grace, Miss Julie,   25
and God is no respecter of persons. With him the last shall be
the first—

MISS JULIE   In that case, he does have respect for the last, doesn't
he?

CHRISTINE [continuing]   —and it is easier for a camel to go   30
through the eye of a needle than for a rich man to enter the
kingdom of God. That's how things are, Miss Julie. I'm going to
leave now—alone. And on my way out I'm going to tell the
stable boy not to let any horses out, in case anyone has any ideas
about leaving before the Count comes home. Goodbye. [She   35
leaves.]

JEAN   She's a devil in skirts!—And all because of a canary!

MISS JULIE [listlessly]   Never mind the canary. . . . Do you see
any way out of this, any end to it?

JEAN [after thinking for a moment]   No.

MISS JULIE What would you do if you were in my place?

JEAN In your place? Let me think. . . . An aristocrat, a woman, and—fallen. . . . I don't know.——Or maybe I do.

MISS JULIE [*picks up the razor and makes a gesture with it*] Like
5   this?

JEAN Yes. But *I* wouldn't do it, you understand. That's the difference between us.

MISS JULIE Because you're a man and I'm a woman? What difference does that make?

10 JEAN Just the difference that there is—between a man and a woman.

MISS JULIE [*holding the razor in her hand*] I want to! But I can't do it. My father couldn't do it either, that time he should have done it.

15 JEAN No, he was right not to do it. He had to get his revenge first.

MISS JULIE And now my mother is getting her revenge again through me.

JEAN Haven't you ever loved your father, Miss Julie?

MISS JULIE Yes, enormously. But I must have hated him too. I
20   must have hated him without knowing it. It was he who brought me up to despise my own sex, to be half woman and half man. Who's to blame for what has happened? My father, my mother, myself? Myself? I don't have a self that's my own. I don't have a single thought I didn't get from my father, not an emotion I
25   didn't get from my mother. And that last idea—about all people being equal—I got that from him, my betrothed. That's why I say he's beneath contempt. How can it be my own fault? Put the blame on Jesus, like Christine does? I'm too proud to do that— and too intelligent, thanks to what my father taught me. . . . A
30   rich man can't get into heaven? That's a lie. But at least Christine, who's got money in the savings bank, won't get in. . . . Who's to blame? What difference does it make who's to blame? I'm still the one who has to bear the guilt, suffer the consequences—

35 JEAN Yes, but—

[*The bell rings sharply twice.* MISS JULIE *jumps up.* JEAN *changes his coat.*]

JEAN The Count's back! What if Christine—? [*He goes to the speaking tube, taps on it, and listens.*]

MISS JULIE Has he looked in his bureau yet?

JEAN This is Jean, sir! [*Listens. The audience cannot hear what the* COUNT *says.*] Yes, sir! [*Listens.*] Yes, sir! Yes, as soon as I can. [*Listens.*] Yes, at once, sir! [*Listens.*] Very good, sir! In half an hour.

MISS JULIE [*trembling with anxiety*] What did he say? For God's 5 sake, what did he say?

JEAN He ordered his boots and his coffee in half an hour.

MISS JULIE Half an hour then! . . . Oh, I'm so tired. I can't bring myself to do anything. Can't repent, can't run away, can't stay, can't live . . . can't die. Help me, Jean. Command me, and I'll 10 obey like a dog. Do me this last favor. Save my honor, save his name. You know what I ought to do but can't force myself to do. Let me use your will power. You command me and I'll obey.

JEAN I don't know—I can't either, not now. I don't know why. It's as if this coat made me—. I can't give you orders in this. 15 And now, after the Count has spoken to me, I—I can't really explain it—but—I've got the backbone of a damned lackey! If the Count came down here now and ordered me to cut my throat, I'd do it on the spot.

MISS JULIE Pretend that you're him, and that I'm you. You were 20 such a good actor just a while ago, when you were kneeling before me. You were the aristocrat then. Or else—have you ever been to the theater and seen a hypnotist? [JEAN *nods.*] He says to his subject, "Take this broom!" and he takes it. He says, "Now sweep!" and he sweeps. 25

JEAN But the person has to be asleep!

MISS JULIE [*ecstatic*] I'm already asleep. The whole room has turned to smoke. You seem like an iron stove, a stove that looks like a man in black with a high hat. Your eyes are glowing like coals when the fire dies out. Your face is a white smudge, like 30 ashes. [*The sun is now shining in on the floor and falls on* JEAN.] It's so good and warm— [*She rubs her hands together as if warming them at a fire.*] —and so bright—and so peaceful.

JEAN [*takes the razor and puts it in her hand*] There's the broom. Go now, when the sun is up—out into the barn—and— [*He* 35 *whispers in her ear.*]

MISS JULIE [*waking up*] Thanks! I'm going to get my rest. But tell me one thing. Tell me that the first can also receive the gift of grace. Tell me that, even if you don't believe it.

JEAN The first? I can't tell you that.——But wait a moment, Miss 40 Julie. I know what I can tell you. You're no longer among the first. You're among—the last.

MISS JULIE   That's true! I'm among the very last. I am the last!—
Oh!—Now I can't go! Tell me just once more, tell me to go!

JEAN   Now I can't either. I can't!

MISS JULIE   And the first shall be the last. . . .

5   JEAN   Don't think—don't think! You're taking all my strength
away. You're making me a coward. . . . What! I thought I saw
the bell move. No. . . . Let me stuff some paper in it.—Afraid
of a bell! But it isn't just a bell. There's somebody behind it. A
hand that makes it move. And there's something that makes the
10   hand move.——Stop your ears, that's it, stop your ears! But it
only rings louder. Rings louder and louder until you answer it. And
then it's too late. Then the sheriff comes—and then— [*There are
two sharp rings on the bell.* JEAN *gives a start, then straightens
himself up.*] It's horrible! But there's no other way for it to end.
15   —Go! [MISS JULIE *walks resolutely out through the door.*]

THE END

THE AUTHOR'S PREFACE

Like the arts in general, the theater has for a long time seemed to me a *Biblia Pauperum*, a picture Bible for those who cannot read, and the playwright merely a lay preacher who hawks the latest ideas in popular form, so popular that the middle classes—the bulk of the audiences—can grasp them without racking their brains too much. That explains why the theater has always been an elementary school for youngsters and the half-educated, and for women, who still retain a primitive capacity for deceiving themselves and for letting themselves be deceived, that is, for succumbing to illusions and responding hypnotically to the suggestions of the author. Consequently, now that the rudimentary and undeveloped mental processes which take place in the realm of fantasy appear to be evolving to the level of reflection, research, and experimentation, I believe that the theater, like religion, is about to be replaced as a dying institution for whose enjoyment we lack the necessary qualifications. Support for my view is provided by the theater crisis through which all of Europe is now passing, and still more by the fact that in those highly cultured lands which have produced the finest minds of our time—England and Germany— the drama is dead, as for the most part are the other fine arts.

In other countries attempts have indeed been made to create a new drama by filling the old forms with modern ideas. But there has not yet been time enough to popularize the new ideas so that the broad public can grasp them. Moreover, party strife has stirred up the public emotions to such a degree that a pure and dispassionate enjoyment has become an impossibility in the theater, where one is likely to see everything one believes in flouted and scorned, and where a wildly applauding or hissing majority can openly exercise its tyrannical powers to an extent possible nowhere else. And thirdly, the new forms for the new ideas have not been found, and the new wine has burst the old bottles.

In the play which follows I have not tried to accomplish anything new, for that is impossible. I have only tried to modernize the form to satisfy what I believe up-to-date people expect and demand of this art. And with that in mind I have seized upon—or let myself be seized by—a theme which may be said to lie outside current party strife, since the question of climbing up or slipping down the social ladder, of being on the top or on the bottom, better or worse, man or woman, is, has been, and will be of perennial interest. When I took this theme from real life—I heard about it a few years ago and it made a deep impression on me—I thought it would be a suitable subject for a tragedy, for it still strikes us as tragic to see a happily favored individual go down in defeat, even more so to see an entire family line die out. But perhaps a time will come when we shall be so highly developed and so enlightened

321

that we can look with indifference upon the brutal, cynical, and heartless spectacle that life offers us, a time when we shall have laid aside those inferior and unreliable instruments of thought called feelings, which will become superfluous and even harmful as our mental organs develop. The fact that my heroine wins sympathy is due entirely to the fact that we are still too weak to overcome a fear that the same fate might overtake us. The extremely sensitive viewer will of course not be satisfied with expressions of sympathy, and the man who believes in progress will demand that certain positive actions be taken for getting rid of the evil, a kind of program, in other words. But in the first place absolute evil does not exist. The decline of one family is the making of another, which now gets its chance to rise. This alternate rising and falling provides one of life's greatest pleasures, for happiness is, after all, relative. As for the man who has a program for changing the disagreeable circumstance that the eagle eats the dove and that lice eat up the eagle, I should like to ask him why it should be changed? Life is not prearranged with such idiotic mathematical precision that only the larger gets to eat the smaller. Just as frequently the little bee destroys the lion—or at least drives him mad.

If my tragedy makes most people feel sad, that is their fault. When we get to be as strong as the first French Revolutionists were, we shall be perfectly content and happy to watch the forests being cleared of rotting, superannuated trees that have stood too long in the way of others with just as much right to grow and flourish for a while—as content as we are when we see an incurably ill man finally die.

Recently my tragedy *The Father* was criticized for being too unpleasant—as if one wanted amusing tragedies. "The joy of life" is now the slogan of the day. Theater managers send out orders for nothing but farces, as if the joy of life lay in behaving like a clown and in depicting people as if they were afflicted with St. Vitus's dance or congenital idiocy. I find my joy of life in the fierce and ruthless battles of life, and my pleasure comes from learning something, from being taught something. That is why I have chosen for my play an unusual but instructive case, an exception, in other words—but an important exception of the kind that proves the rule—a choice of subject which I know will offend all lovers of the conventional. The next thing that will bother simple minds is that the motivation for the action is not simple and that the point of view is not single. Usually an event in life—and this is a fairly new discovery—is the result of a whole series of more or less deep-seated causes. The spectator, however, generally chooses the one that puts the least strain on his mind or reflects most credit on his insight. Consider a case of suicide. "Business failure," says the middle-class man. "Unhappy love," say the women. "Physical illness," says the sick man. "Lost hopes," says the down-and-out.

But it may be that the reason lay in all of these or in none of them, and that the suicide hid his real reason behind a completely different one that would reflect greater glory on his memory.

I have motivated the tragic fate of Miss Julie with an abundance of circumstances: her mother's basic instincts, her father's improper bringing-up of the girl, her own inborn nature and her fiancé's sway over her weak and degenerate mind. Further and more immediately: the festive atmosphere of Midsummer Eve, her father's absence, her monthly illness, her preoccupation with animals, the erotic excitement of the dance, the long summer twilight, the highly aphrodisiac influence of flowers, and finally chance itself, which drives two people together in an out-of-the-way room, plus the boldness of the aroused man.

As one can see, I have not concerned myself solely with physiological causes, nor confined myself monomaniacally to psychological causes, nor traced everything to an inheritance from her mother, nor put the blame entirely on her monthly indisposition or exclusively on "immorality." Nor have I simply preached a sermon. For lack of a priest, I have let this function devolve on a cook.

I am proud to say that this complicated way of looking at things is in tune with the times. And if others have anticipated me in this, I am proud that I am not alone in my paradoxes, as all new discoveries are called.

As far as the drawing of characters is concerned, I have made the people in my play fairly "characterless" for the following reasons. In the course of time the word *character* has acquired many meanings. Originally it probably meant the dominant and fundamental trait in the soul complex and was confused with temperament. Later the middle class used it to mean an automaton. An individual who once for all had found his own true nature or adapted himself to a certain role in life, who in fact had ceased to grow, was called a man of character, while the man who was constantly developing, who, like a skilled navigator on the currents of life, did not steer a straight course but tacked down wind, was called a man of no character—derogatorily of course, since he was so difficult to keep track of, to pin down and pigeonhole. This middle-class conception of a fixed character was transferred to the stage, where the middle class has always ruled. A character there came to mean an actor who was always one and the same, always drunk, always comic or always melancholy, and who needed to be characterized only by some physical defect such as a club foot, a wooden leg, or a red nose, or by the repetition of some such phrase such as, "That's capital," or "Barkis is willin'." This uncomplicated way of viewing people is still to be found in the great Molière. Harpagon is nothing but a miser, although Harpagon might have been not only a miser but an exceptional financier, a fine father, and a good citizen. Worse still, his "defect" is extremely advantageous to his son-in-law and his daughter who will be his heirs and therefore should not find fault with him, even if they might have to wait a while to jump into bed together. So I do not believe in simple stage characters. And the summary judgments that writers pass on people—he is stupid, this one is brutal, that one is jealous, this one is stingy, and so on—should not pass unchallenged by the naturalists who know how complicated the soul is and who realize that vice has a reverse side very much like virtue.

Since the persons in my play are modern characters, living in a transitional era more hurried and hysterical than the previous one at least, I have depicted them as more unstable, as torn and divided, a mixture of the old and the new. Nor does it seem improbable to me that modern ideas might also have seeped down through newspapers and kitchen talk to the level of the servants.

My souls—or characters—are conglomerations of various stages of culture, past and present. They are pasted together from newspaper clippings and books, pieced up from scraps of human lives, and patched up from old ball gowns that have become rags—just as the human soul is. I have even supplied a little evolutionary history into the bargain by letting the weaker steal and repeat the words of the stronger and by letting these souls pick up each other's ideas—suggestions as they are called in hypnosis.

I say Miss Julie is a modern character not because the man-hating half-woman has not always existed, but because now she has been brought out into the open, has taken the stage and is making a noise for herself. The half-woman is a type that forces itself on others, selling itself for power, medals, recognition, diplomas as formerly it sold itself for money. It represents degeneration. It is not a strong species for it does not maintain itself, but unfortunately it propagates its misery in the following generation. Degenerate men unconsciously select their mates from among these half-women, so that they breed and spread, producing creatures of indeterminate sex to whom life is a torture, but who fortunately are defeated eventually either by hostile reality, or by the uncontrolled breaking loose of their repressed instincts, or else by their disappointment in not being able to compete with the male sex. It is a tragic type, offering us the spectacle of a desperate fight against nature; a tragic legacy of romanticism which is now being dissipated by naturalism—a movement which seeks only happiness, and for that strong and healthy species are required.

But Miss Julie is also a vestige of the old warrior nobility which is now being superseded by a new nobility of nerve and brain. She is a victim of the disorder produced within a family by a mother's "crime," of the mistakes of a whole generation gone wrong, of circumstances, of her own defective constitution—all of which put together is equivalent to the fate or universal law of the ancients. The naturalists have banished guilt along with God, but the consequences of the act—punishment, imprisonment, or the fear of it —cannot be for the simple reason that they remain whether or not the naturalist dismisses the action from his court. Those sitting on the sidelines can easily afford to be lenient; not so, the injured parties. Even if her father were compelled to forgo taking his vengeance, Miss Julie would take vengeance on herself, as she does in the play, because of that inherited or acquired sense of honor which has been transmitted to the upper classes from—well, where does it come from? From the age of barbarism, from the first Aryans, from the chivalry of the Middle Ages. And a very fine code it was, but now inimical to the survival of the race. It is the aristocrat's form of hara-kiri, a law of conscience that bids the Japanese to cut open his stomach when he has lost face. With us, the code which survives in modified form in the duel, a prerogative of the aristocracy. Hence the servant Jean lives on; but not Miss Julie, who cannot live without honor. The advantage that the slave has over his master is that he has not committed himself to this defeatist principle of honor. In all of us Aryans there is enough of the nobleman, or of the Don Quixote, to make us sympathize with the man who takes his own life after having dishonored himself by shameful deeds. And we are all of us aristocrats enough to be distressed at the sight of a great man lying like a dead hulk ready for the scrap pile, even, I would say, if he were to raise himself up again and redeem himself by honorable deeds.

The servant Jean is the beginning of a new species in which noticeable differentiation has already taken place. He began as the child of a poor worker and is now evolving through self-education into a future gentleman of the upper classes. He is quick to learn, has highly developed senses (smell, taste, sight), and a keen appreciation of beauty. He has already come up in the world, for he is strong enough not to hesitate to make use of other people. He is already a stranger to his old friends, whom he despises as reminders of past stages in his development, and whom he fears and avoids because they know his secrets, guess his intentions, and look with envy on his rise and in joyful expectation towards his fall. Hence his character is unformed and divided. He wavers between an admiration of high positions and a hatred of the men who occupy them. He is an aristocrat—he says so himself—familiar with the ins and outs of good society. He is polished on the outside, but coarse underneath. He wears his frock coat with elegance but gives no assurance that he keeps his body clean.

He respects Miss Julie but he is afraid of Christine, for she knows his innermost secrets. Yet he is sufficiently hard-hearted not to let the events of the night upset his plans for the future. Possessing both the coarseness of the slave and the toughmindedness of the born ruler, he can look at blood without fainting, shake off bad luck like water, and take calamity by the horns. Conse-

tly he will escape from the battle unwounded, probably end-
p as proprietor of a hotel. And if he himself does not get to be
a Rumanian count, his son will doubtless go to college and possibly
end up as an official of the state.

Now his observations about life as the lower classes see it, from
below, are well worth listening to—that is, they are whenever he is
telling the truth, which is not too often, because he is more likely
to say what is favorable to him than what is true. When Miss Julie
supposes that everyone in the lower classes must feel greatly oppressed by the weight of the classes above, Jean naturally agrees
with her since he wants to win her sympathy. But he promptly
takes it all back when he finds it advantageous to separate himself
from the mob.

Apart from the fact that Jean is coming up in the world, he is
also superior to Miss Julie in that he is a man. In the sexual sphere,
he is the aristocrat. He has the strength of the male, more highly
developed senses, and the ability to take the initiative. His inferiority
is merely the result of his social environment, which is only temporary and which he will probably slough off along with his livery.

His slave nature expresses itself in his awe of the Count (the
boots) and in his religious superstitions. But he is awed by the
Count mainly because the Count occupies the place he wants most
in life; and this awe is still there even after he has won the daughter
of the house and seen how empty that beautiful shell was.

I do not believe that any love in the "higher" sense can be born
from the union of two such different souls. Therefore I have let
Miss Julie's love be refashioned in her imagination as something
protective and purifying, and I have let Jean imagine that even his
love might have a chance to grow under other social circumstances.
I suppose love is very much like the hyacinth that must strike roots
deep in the dark earth *before* it can produce a vigorous flower.
But here it shoots up, bursts into bloom, and turns to seed all at
once; and that is why it dies so quickly.

Christine—finally to get to her—is a female slave, spineless and
phlegmatic after years spent in front of the kitchen stove, and full
of morality and religion which she uses as cloaks and scapegoats
for her sins. She goes regularly to church where she deftly unloads
onto Jesus her petty household thefts and picks up from Him
another load of innocence. She is only a secondary character, and
I have deliberately done no more than sketch her in—just as I
treated the country doctor and parish priest in *The Father* where I
only wanted everyday people such as most country doctors and
preachers are. That some have found my minor characters one-
dimensional is due to the fact that everyday people while at work
are to a certain extent one-dimensional and do lack an independent
existence, showing only one side of themselves in the performance
of their duties. And as long as the audience does not feel it needs

to see them from different angles, my abstract presentation will pass muster.

Now as far as the dialogue is concerned, I have broken somewhat with tradition in refusing to make my characters into interlocutors who ask stupid questions to elicit witty answers. I have avoided the symmetrical and mathematical design of the artfully constructed French dialogue and have let minds work as irregularly as they do in real life, where no subject is quite drained to the bottom before another mind engages at random some cog in the conversation and regulates it for a while. My dialogue wanders here and there, gathers material in the first scenes which is later picked up, repeated, reworked, developed, and expanded like the theme in a piece of music.

The action of the play poses no problems. Since it really involves only two people, I have limited myself to these two, introducing only one minor character, the cook, and keeping the unhappy spirit of the father brooding over the action as a whole. I have chosen this course because I have noticed that what interests people most nowadays is the psychological action. Our inveterately curious souls are no longer content to see a thing happen; we want to see how it happens. We want to see the strings, look at the machinery, examine the double-bottom drawer, put on the magic ring to find the hidden seam, look in the deck for the marked cards.

In treating the subject this way I have had in mind the case-history novels of the Goncourt brothers, which appeal to me more than anything else in modern literature.

As far as play construction is concerned, I have made a try at getting rid of act divisions. I was afraid that the spectator's declining susceptibility to illusion might not carry him through the intermission, when he would have time to think about what he has seen and to escape the suggestive influence of the author-hypnotist. I figure my play lasts about ninety minutes. Since one can listen to a lecture, a sermon, or a political debate for that long or even longer, I have convinced myself that a play should not exhaust an audience in that length of time. As early as 1872 in one of my first attempts at the drama, *The Outlaw*, I tried out this concentrated form, although with little success. I had finished the work in five acts when I noticed the disjointed and disturbing effect it produced. I burned it, and from the ashes there arose a single, completely reworked act of fifty pages which would run for less than an hour. This play form is not completely new but seems to be my private property and has a good chance of gaining favor with the public when tastes change. (My hope was to get a public so educated that they could sit through a full evening's show in one act. But this needs to be investigated further.) In the meantime, in order to establish resting places for the audience and the actors without destroying the illusion, I have made use of three arts that belong to the drama: the monologue, the pantomime, and the ballet, all of which were part of classic tragedy, the monody having become the monologue and the choral dance, the ballet.

The realists have banished the monologue from the stage as implausible. But if I can motivate it, I make it plausible, and I can then use it to my advantage. Now it is certainly plausible for a speaker to pace the floor and read his speech aloud to himself. It is plausible for an actor to practice his part aloud, for a child to talk to her cat, a mother to babble to her baby, an old lady to chatter to her parrot, and a sleeper to talk in his sleep. And in order to give the actor a chance to work on his own for once and for a moment not be obliged to follow the author's directions, I thought it best not to write out the monologue in detail but simply to outline it. Since it makes very little difference what is said while asleep, or to the parrot or the cat, inasmuch as it does not affect the main action, a gifted player who is in the midst of the situation and mood of the play can probably improvise the monologue better than the author, who cannot estimate ahead of time how much may be said and for how long before the illusion is broken.

Some theaters in Italy have, as we know, returned to the art of improvisation and have thereby trained actors who are truly inventive—without, however, violating the intentions of the author. This seems to be a step in the right direction and possibly the beginning of a new, fertile form of art that will be genuinely productive.

In places where the monologue cannot be properly motivated, I have resorted to pantomime. Here I have given the actor even more freedom to be creative and win honor on his own. Nevertheless, not to try the audience beyond its limits, I have relied on music—well-motivated by the Midsummer Eve dance—to exercise its hypnotic powers during the pantomime scene. I beg the music director to select his tunes with great care, so that associations foreign to the mood of the play will not be produced by reminders of popular operettas or current dance numbers or by folk music of interest only to an ethnographer.

The ballet I introduced could not have been replaced by a so-called crowd scene. Such scenes are always badly acted, with a pack of babbling fools taking advantage of the occasion to "gag it up," thereby destroying the illusion. Inasmuch as country people do not improvise their taunts but make use of material already to hand by giving it a double meaning, I have not composed an original lampoon but have made use of a little known round dance that I noted down in the Stockholm district. The words do not fit the situation exactly, which is what I intended, since the slave in his cunning (i.e., weakness) never attacks directly. At any rate, let us have no comedians in this serious story and no obscene jokes about an affair that nails the lid on a family coffin.

As far as the scenery is concerned, I have borrowed from impressionistic painting the idea of asymmetrical and open composition, and I believe that I have thereby gained something in the way of greater illusion. Because the audience cannot see the whole room and all the furniture, they will have to surmise what's missing; that is, their imagination will be stimulated to fill in the rest of the picture. I have gained something else by this: I have avoided those tiresome exits through doors. Stage doors are made of canvas and rock at the slightest touch. They cannot even be used to indicate the wrath of an angry father who storms out of the house after a bad dinner, slamming the door behind him "so that the whole house shakes." (In the theater it sways.) Furthermore, I have confined the action to one set, both to give the characters a chance to become part and parcel of their environment and to cut down on scenic extravagance. If there is only one set, one has a right to expect it to be as realistic as possible. Yet nothing is more difficult than to make a room look like a room, however easy it may be for the scene painter to create waterfalls and erupting volcanos. I suppose we shall have to put up with walls made of canvas, but isn't it about time that we stopped painting shelves and pots and pans on the canvas? There are so many other conventions in the theater which we are told to accept in good faith that we should be spared the strain of believing in painted saucepans.

I have placed the backdrop and the table at an angle to force the actors to play face to face or in half profile when they are seated opposite each other at the table. In a production of *Aïda* I saw a flat placed at such an angle, which leads the eye out in an unfamiliar perspective. Nor did it look as if it had been set that way simply to be different or to avoid those monotonous right angles.

Another desirable innovation would be the removal of the footlights. I understand that the purpose of lighting from below is to make the actors look more full in the face. But may I ask why all actors should have full faces? Doesn't this kind of lighting wipe out many of the finer features in the lower part of the face, especially around the jaws? Doesn't it distort the shape of nose and throw false shadows above the eyes? If not, it certainly does something else: it hurts the actor's eyes. The footlights hit the retina at an angle from which it is usually shielded (except in sailors who must look at the sunlight reflected in the water), and the result is the loss of any effective play of the eyes. All one ever sees on stage are goggle-eyed glances sideways at the boxes or upwards at the balcony, with only the whites of the eyes being visible in the latter case. And this probably also accounts for that tiresome fluttering of the eyelashes which the female performers are particularly guilty of. If an actor nowadays wants to express something with his eyes, he can only do it looking right at the audience, in which case he makes direct contact with someone outside the proscenium arch—a bad habit known justifiably or not, as "saying hello to friends."*

I should think that the use of sufficiently strong side lights (through the use of reflectors or something like them) would provide the actor with a new asset: an increased range of expression made possible by the play of the eyes, the most expressive part of the face.

I have scarcely any illusions about getting actors to play for the public and not with them, although this should be the goal. Nor do I dream of ever seeing an actor play with his back to the audience through all of an important scene. But is it too much to hope that crucial scenes could be played where the author indicated and not in front of the prompter's box as if they were duets demanding applause? I am not calling for a revolution, only for some small changes. I am well aware that transforming the stage into a real room with the fourth wall missing and with some of the furniture placed with backs to the auditorium would only upset the audience, at least for the present.

If I bring up the subject of makeup, it is not because I dare hope to be heeded by the ladies, who would rather be beautiful than truthful. But the male actor might do well to consider if it is an advantage to paint his face with character lines that remain there like a mask. Let us imagine an actor who pencils in with soot a few lines between his eyes to indicate great anger, and let us suppose that in that permanently enraged state he finds he has to smile on a certain line. Imagine the horrible grimace! And how can the old character actor wrinkle his brows in anger when his false bald pate is as smooth as a billiard ball?

In a modern psychological drama, in which every tremor of the soul should be reflected more by facial expressions than by gestures and noises, it would probably be most sensible to experiment with strong side lighting on a small stage, using actors without any make-up or with a minimum of it.

And then, if we could get rid of the visible orchestra with its disturbing lights and its faces turned toward the public; if the auditorium floor could be raised so that the spectator's eyes are not level with the actor's knees; if we could get rid of the proscenium boxes with their noisy late diners; and if we could have it dark in the auditorium during the performance; and if, above everything else, we could have a *small* stage and a *small* auditorium—then possibly a new drama might arise and at least one theater become a refuge for cultured audiences. While we are waiting for such a theater, we shall have to write for the dramatic stockpile and prepare the repertory that one day shall come.

I have made an attempt at it. If I have failed, there is still time to try again!

AUGUST STRINDBERG

* "Counting the house" would be the equivalent in American theater slang. [Trans.]

ANTON CHEKHOV

Uncle Vanya

Translated by ROBERT W. CORRIGAN

~~~~~~

CHRISTOPHER FRY

Comedy

THE CHARACTERS IN *UNCLE VANYA*

MARINA, an old nurse

MIHAIL LVOVICH ASTROV, a doctor

IVAN PETROVICH VOYNITSKY (UNCLE VANYA)

ALEXANDER VLADIMIROVICH SEREBRYAKOV, a retired professor

YELENA ANDREYEVNA, his wife

SOFYA ALEXANDROVNA (SONYA), his daughter by his first wife

ILYA ILYICH TELYEGIN (WAFFLES), an impoverished landowner

MARYA VASSILYEVNA VOYNITSKAYA, widow of a privy councillor, mother of UNCLE VANYA and of SEREBRYAKOV's first wife

A WORKMAN

A WATCHMAN (YEFIM)

The action takes place on Serebryakov's estate.

UNCLE VANYA

ACT ONE

[*The garden before* SEREBRYAKOV'S *house, on a terrace. A table is set for tea, with a samovar, cups, and the like. Near the table, benches and chairs. A guitar lies on one bench. A hammock is swung near the table. It is three o'clock of a cloudy afternoon.* MARINA, *a small gray-haired woman, sits at the table, knitting. Near her,* ASTROV *is pacing about.*]

MARINA [*pouring a cup of tea*]   Here, my friend, drink a cup of tea.

ASTROV [*reluctantly taking the cup*]   For some reason I don't seem to care for any.

MARINA   Would you rather have some vodka?

ASTROV   No, I don't drink vodka every day. And, besides, the day   5
is too hot and stifling for it. [*A pause.*] Tell me, old nurse, how
long have we known each other?

MARINA [*pondering and thoughtfully*]   Let me see, how long is it?
God only knows. You first came into these parts, let me see—
when was it? Well, Sonya's mother was still alive—she died two   10
years later; that was at least eleven years ago. . . . [*Pondering.*]
Perhaps even longer.

ASTROV   Have I changed much since then?

MARINA   Oh, yes. You were young and handsome then, and now
you seem like an old man. And you drink too.   15

ASTROV   Yes. . . . Ten years have made another man of me. And
why? Because I am overworked. Do you know, nurse, that I am
on my feet from morning till night? I don't know what it is to
rest; at night I hide in bed trembling under the blankets in the
continual fear that I'll be dragged out to visit someone who is   20
sick. Ever since I have known you, I haven't had a single day all
to myself. No wonder I am growing old, how could I help it? And
besides, life is tedious; it is senseless, dirty, stupid, and it just
drags on and on . . . [*Pause*] . . . and finally it swallows you up.
[*Pause*] Every one around here is commonplace, and after you   25
live with them for a couple of years, you, too, become commonplace and queer. It's inevitable. [*Twisting his mustache.*] See what
a long mustache I have. A foolish, long mustache. Yes, I am
just as silly as all the others, nurse, just as trivial, but not as
stupid; no . . . I have not grown stupid. Thank God, my brain   30

333

is not muddled yet, though my feelings have grown dull. There's nothing I want, there's nothing I need, there's no one I love, except, perhaps, you. [*He kisses her head.*] When I was a little boy, I had a nurse just like you.

5 MARINA Don't you want just a little something to eat?

ASTROV No. During the third week of Lent, a typhoid epidemic broke out in the village, and I had to go. The peasants were all stretched out side by side in their huts, and the calves and the pigs were running about among the sick and the dying. How dirty 10 and filthy it was, and the stench of the smoke, ugh, it was unbearable! I slaved among those people all day, and I didn't have a thing to eat. And then when I returned home there was still no rest for me: a switchman was carried in from the railroad; I laid him on the operating table and he died in my arms under the 15 chloroform. And then, my feelings, which should have been deadened, awoke again; my conscience tortured me as if I had murdered the man. I sat down and closed my eyes—like this—and thought: will those who come after us two hundred years from now, those for whom we are breaking the path . . . will they re- 20 member us with grateful hearts? No, nurse, they will forget.

MARINA Man forgets, but God remembers.

ASTROV Thank you for that. You spoke the truth.

[*Enter* VANYA *from the house. He has been asleep after dinner and looks somewhat disheveled. He sits down on the bench and straightens his tie.*]

VANYA H'mm. Yes. [*A pause.*] Yes.

ASTROV Have a good nap?

25 VANYA Yes, very good. [*He yawns.*] Ever since the Professor and his wife came, our daily routine seems to have gone haywire. I sleep at the wrong time, drink too much wine, and I eat the wrong kind of food. It's no good. Sonya and I used to work together and we never had an idle moment. But now she works alone and 30 I . . . I just eat and drink and sleep. Something is wrong.

MARINA [*shaking her head*] Such confusion in the house! The Professor gets up at twelve, the samovar has to be kept boiling all morning, and everything has to wait for him. Before they came we used to have dinner at one o'clock, like everybody else, 35 but now we eat at seven. The Professor sits up all night writing and reading or something, and suddenly, at two o'clock, the bell rings. Heavens, what's that? The Professor wants tea! Wake up the servants, light the samovar! Lord, what disorder!

ASTROV   Will they be here long?

VANYA [*whistling*]   A hundred years! The Professor has decided to stay here for good.

MARINA   Just look at this, for instance! The samovar has been boiling away on the table for two hours now, and they've gone out for a walk!   5

VANYA [*calming her brusquely*]   Here they are—here they are—don't get so excited.

[*Voices are heard.* SEREBRYAKOV, YELENA, SONYA, *and* TELYEGIN *enter from the garden, returning from their walk.*]

SEREBRYAKOV   Superb! Superb! What glorious views!

TELYEGIN   They are lovely, your excellency.   10

SONYA   Tomorrow we shall go to the woods, shall we, father?

VANYA   Ladies and Gentlemen, tea is served.

SEREBRYAKOV   Won't you please send my tea into the library. I have something to do . . . ah, some work to finish.

SONYA   I am sure you will love the woods, father.   15

[YELENA, SEREBRYAKOV, *and* SONYA *go into the house.* TELYEGIN *takes a seat at the table beside* MARINA.]

VANYA   It is hot and humid, but our eminent scholar walks about in his overcoat and galoshes, wearing gloves and carrying an umbrella.

ASTROV   Which means that he takes good care of himself.

VANYA   But how lovely she is! How lovely! I have never see a more beautiful woman.   20

TELYEGIN   Whether I drive through the fields or take a walk under the shady trees in the garden, or look at this table I experience a feeling of indescribable bliss! The weather is enchanting, the birds are singing; we all live in peace and harmony . . .   25 what else do we want? [*Taking a cup of tea.*] Oh, thank you.

VANYA [*dreaming*]   Such eyes—a glorious woman!

ASTROV   Come, Vanya, tell us something.

VANYA [*indolently*]   What shall I tell you?

ASTROV   Haven't you any news for us?   30

VANYA   No, it is all old. I am the same as ever, no . . . worse, for I've become lazy. I do nothing any more but grumble like an old crow. My mother, the old magpie, is still babbling about the emancipation of women, with one eye on her grave and the other on her learned books, in which she is forever rummaging in the hopes of finding the dawn of a new life.

5 ASTROV   And the Professor?

VANYA   The Professor as usual sits in his study reading and writing from morning till night. . . .

> Straining our mind, wrinkling our brow,
> We write, write, write,
> 10 With no respite
> Or hope of praise in the future or now.

Oh, poor unfortunate paper! He ought to write his autobiography; he would make such an excellent subject for a book! Just think, the life of a retired professor, as stale as a piece of mil-15 dewed bread, racked with gout, headaches, and rheumatism, his heart bursting with jealousy and envy, living on the estate of his first wife, although he hates it, because he can't afford to live in town. He is always whining about his hard fate, although, as a matter of fact, he is extraordinarily lucky. [*Nervously.*] He is the 20 son of a common, ordinary parson and has achieved a professor's chair, has become the son-in-law of a senator, is called "your excellency," but forget it! I'll tell you something; he's been writing about art for twenty-five years, and he doesn't know the first thing about it. For twenty-five years he has been hashing over 25 the thoughts of other men on realism, naturalism, and all the other nonsensical "isms"; for twenty-five years he has been reading and writing things that intelligent men have always known and that are stupid and boring to those who don't care; for twenty-five years he has been pouring water from one empty 30 glass into another. Yet . . . consider the man's conceit and pretensions! He has been pensioned off. . . . Not a living soul has ever heard of him. He is totally unknown. He is a nothing. That means that for twenty-five years he has been treating life as if it were a masquerade ball, and all that he has accomplished is to 35 have kept a better man out of a job. But just look at him! He struts across the earth like a demigod!

ASTROV   You know, I believe you envy him.

VANYA   Yes, I do. Look at the success he's had with women! Don Juan himself was no luckier. His first wife, my sister, was beauti-40 ful, gentle, as pure as the blue sky, generous, with more suitors than the number of all his pupils put together and she loved him as only creatures of angelic purity can love those who are as pure and beautiful as they are themselves. My mother adores him to this day, and he still inspires her with a kind of worshipful awe. And now, his second wife is, as you can plainly see, a great beauty, and she is intelligent too; and yet she married him in his old age and surrendered to him all the glory of her beauty and freedom. For what? . . . Why? 5

ASTROV Is she faithful to him?

VANYA Yes, unfortunately she is.

ASTROV Why "unfortunately"?

VANYA Because such fidelity is false and unnatural. Oh, it sounds very good, but there is no rhyme nor reason to it. It is immoral 10 for a woman to deceive and endure an old husband whom she hates. But for her to stifle her pathetic youth, those intense longings within her heart—her feelings . . . that is not immoral!

TELYEGIN [*in a tearful voice*] Vanya, don't talk like that. Really, you know, anyone who is unfaithful to his wife or husband is a 15 disloyal person and will betray his country, too!

VANYA [*crossly*] Oh, Waffles, dry up!

TELYEGIN No, allow me, Vanya. My wife ran away with a lover the day after our wedding, because of my . . . ah . . . rather unprepossessing appearance. Since then I have never failed to do 20 my duty. I love her and am true to her to this day. I help her all I can and I've given my fortune to educate the children she had by her lover. I have lost my happiness, but I have kept my pride. And she? Her youth has fled, her beauty has faded according to the laws of nature, and her lover is dead. What does she have 25 left?

[YELENA *and* SONYA *enter, followed by* MARYA *carrying a book. The latter sits down and begins to read. Someone hands her a cup of tea which she drinks without looking up.*]

SONYA [*hurriedly to the nurse*] Some peasants are waiting inside. Go and see what they want. I'll look after the tea.

[*She pours out several cups.* MARINA *goes out.* YELENA *takes a cup and sits drinking in the swing.*]

ASTROV [*to* YELENA] I came to see your husband. You wrote me saying he is very ill, that he has rheumatism and what not, but he 30 seems fine, as lively as ever.

YELENA He had a fit of depression last night and complained of pains in his legs, but he seems all right again today.

ASTROV And I hurried twenty miles at breakneck speed to get here! But, never mind, it isn't the first time. However, now that I am here, I am going to stay until tomorrow; for the first time in ages I am going to sleep as long as I want.

SONYA   Oh, wonderful! You spend the night with us so seldom. Have you eaten yet?

ASTROV   No.

SONYA   Fine, then you will have dinner with us. We don't eat until seven now. [*Drinks her tea.*] Oh, the tea is cold!

TELYEGIN   Yes, the samovar has gone out.

YELENA   Never mind, Ivan, we'll just have to drink it cold.

TELYEGIN   I beg your pardon, madam, my name is not Ivan, it's Ilya, Ilya Telyegin, or Waffles, as some people call me because of my pock-marked face. I am Sonya's godfather, and his excellency, your husband, knows me very well. I now live here on this estate; perhaps, sometime you will be good enough to notice that I dine with you every day.

SONYA   He is a great help to us—our right-hand man. [*Tenderly.*] Dear godfather, let me pour you some more tea.

MARYA   Oh! Oh!

SONYA   What is it, grandmother?

MARYA   I forgot to tell Alexander—I must be losing my memory—I received a letter today from Paul in Kharkov. He sent me a new pamphlet.

ASTROV   Is it interesting?

MARYA   Yes, but it is so strange. He refutes the very theories he defended seven years ago. Isn't that queer; in fact, it's appalling.

VANYA   Oh, there is nothing so appalling about it. Drink your tea, mother.

MARYA   But I have something to say, I want to talk.

VANYA   But that is all we have been doing for the last fifty years: talk, read a few pamphlets, and talk some more. . . . Talk. Talk. It's time to quit all that nonsense.

MARYA   It seems that you never want to listen to what I have to say. If you will pardon me, Jean, you have changed so much this last year that I hardly know you. You used to be a man of strong convictions and had such an illuminating personality. . . .

VANYA   Oh, yes, to be sure. I had an illuminating personality, I had elevated ideas, which illuminated or elevated no one. [*A pause.*] I had an illuminating personality! You couldn't say anything more cruel. I am forty-seven years old. Until last year I tried, as you still do, to blind my eyes with meaningless pedantry to the truths of life. Yes, I did it on purpose, to avoid seeing life as it really is . . . and I thought I was doing the right thing. But now. . . . Oh, if you only knew! If you knew how I lie awake at night, heartsick and angry, to think how stupidly I wasted my time when I might have been taking from life everything which is now denied me because I am old.

SONYA   Uncle Vanya, how dreary!

MARYA [to her son]   You talk as if your former convictions were somehow to blame, but you yourself, not they, were at fault. You have forgotten that a conviction, in itself, is nothing but a dead letter. You should have done something.

VANYA   Done something! It isn't every man who is capable of being a . . . a writing machine like your dear professor.

MARYA   What do you mean by that?

SONYA [imploringly]   Grandmother! Uncle Vanya! Please!

VANYA   I am silent. I apologize and am silent. [A pause.]

YELENA   What a fine day! Not too hot. [A pause.]

VANYA   Yes, a fine day to hang oneself.

[TELYEGIN tunes his guitar. MARINA appears near the house, calling the chickens.]

MARINA   Here chick, chick, here chick!

SONYA   What did the peasants want, nurse?

MARINA   The same old thing, the same old nonsense. Here chick, chick!

SONYA   Why are you calling the chickens?

MARINA   The speckled hen disappeared with her chicks. I'm afraid the hawks might get them.

[TELYEGIN plays a polka. Everyone listens in silence. A WORKMAN enters.]

WORKMAN   Is the doctor here? [To ASTROV.] Please, Dr. Astrov, I've been sent for you.

ASTROV   Where do you come from?

WORKMAN   The factory.

ASTROV [annoyed]   Thank you. I suppose I shall have to go

whether I want to or not. [*Looking around him for his cap*.] Damn it, this is annoying.

SONYA   Oh, yes, it is too bad. You must come back from the factory for dinner.

5 ASTROV   No, I shan't be able to do that. It will be too late. Now where, where— [*To the* WORKMAN.] Look here, good fellow, get me a glass of vodka, will you? [WORKMAN *goes out*.] Where— where— [*Finds his cap*.] There is a man in one of Ostrovsky's plays with a long mustache and short wits, like me. However,
10 let me bid you good night, ladies and gentlemen. [*To* YELENA.] I should be most delighted if you came to see me some day with Sonya. My place is small, but if you are interested in such things —things like terraced gardens, sapling beds, and nurseries, the likes of which you'll not find within a thousand miles of here—
15 I'd like to show them to you. My estate is surrounded by government forests. But the old forester is always sick and complains so, that I take care of most of the work myself.

YELENA   I have always heard that you were very fond of the woods. Of course you can do a great deal of good by helping to
20 preserve them, but doesn't that work interfere with your real calling? You're a doctor, aren't you?

ASTROV   God alone can know what a man's real work is.

YELENA   And you find it interesting?

ASTROV   Yes, very.

25 VANYA [*sarcastically*]   Oh, extremely.

YELENA   You are still young, I should say certainly not over thirty-six or seven, and I have an idea that the woods do not interest you as much as you claim. I should think that you would find them quite monotonous.

30 SONYA   Dr. Astrov plants new forests every year, and he has been awarded a bronze medal and a diploma. He does his best to prevent the destruction of the forests. If you listen to him you will agree with him entirely. He claims that forests beautify the earth, and so teach man to understand the beautiful, and instill
35 in him a feeling of respect and awe. Forests temper the severity of the climate. In countries where the climate is warmer, less energy is wasted on the struggle with nature and that is why man there is more gentle and loving; the people there are beautiful, supple, and sensitive, their speech is refined and their move-
40 ments graceful. Art and learning flourish among them, their philosophy is not so depressing, and they treat women with refinement and nobility.

VANYA [*laughing*] Bravo, bravo! All this is charming, but not convincing, and so, [*To* ASTROV] I hope you'll permit me, my friend, to go on burning logs in my stove and building my barns with wood.

ASTROV You can burn peat in your stoves and build your barns of stone. Oh, I don't object, of course, to cutting wood when you have to, but why destroy the forests? The woods of Russia are trembling under the blows of the axe. Millions of trees have perished. The homes of the wild animals and the birds have been laid desolate; the rivers are shrinking, and many beautiful landscapes are gone forever. And why? Because men are too lazy and stupid to bend over and pick up their fuel from the ground. [*To* YELENA.] Am I wrong? Who but a senseless savage could burn so much beauty in his stove and destroy what he cannot create himself? Man has reason and creative powers so that he may increase that which has been given to him. Until now, however, he has not created, he has only destroyed. The forests are disappearing, the rivers are drying up, the game is being exterminated, the climate is spoiled, and the earth becomes poorer and more ugly every day. [*To* VANYA.] Oh, I read irony in your eye; you do not take seriously what I am saying; and—and—perhaps I am talking nonsense. But when I cross those pleasant forests which I have saved from the axe, or hear the rustling of the young trees, which I have set out with my own hands, I feel as if I had had some small share in improving the climate, and that if mankind is happy a thousand years from now I shall have been partly responsible in my small way for their happiness. When I plant a young birch tree and see it budding and swaying in the wind, my heart swells with pride and I . . . [*Sees the* WORKMAN, *who is bringing him a glass of vodka on a tray.*] However. . . . [*He drinks.*] . . . I must be off. Probably it is all nonsense, anyhow. Good-bye.

SONYA When are you coming to see us again?

ASTROV I don't know.

SONYA In a month?

[ASTROV *and* SONYA *go into the house.* YELENA *and* VANYA *walk over to the terrace.*]

YELENA Vanya, you have been behaving impossibly again. What sense was there in irritating your mother with all your talk about her pamphlets and the "writing machine." And this morning you quarreled with Alexander, again. How petty and small it all is!

VANYA But suppose I hate him?

YELENA You hate Alexander without reason; he is like everyone else, and no worse than you.

VANYA If you could only see your face, your every movement and gesture! Oh, how tedious your life must be!

5 YELENA Yes, it is tedious, and dreary, too! All of you abuse my husband and look on me with compassion; you think, "Poor woman, she is married to an old man." How well I understand your sympathy and compassion! As Astrov said just now, see how thoughtlessly you destroy the forests, so that soon there will be 10 nothing left on earth. In just the same way you recklessly destroy human beings, and soon, thanks to you, loyalty and purity and self-sacrifice will have vanished along with the woods. Why can't you look with calm indifference at a woman unless she belongs to you? Because . . . the doctor is right. You are all possessed by 15 a devil of destructiveness; you have no feeling, no, not even pity, for either the woods or the birds or women, or for one another.

VANYA Would you mind stopping all this philosophizing; I don't like it.

[*A pause.*]

YELENA That doctor has a sensitive, weary face . . . an inter-20 esting face. Sonya evidently likes him; she is in love with him, and I can understand her feeling. [*Pause.*] This is the third time he has been here since I have come, and I have not had a real talk with him yet or showed him much attention. He thinks I am disagreeable. Do you know, Vanya, why you and I are such 25 friends? I think it is because we are both lonely and tiresome and unsympathetic. [*Pause.*] Yes, unsympathetic. [*Pause.*] Don't look at me that way, I don't like it.

VANYA How can I look at you in any other way since I love you? You are my joy, my life, my youth. I know that my chances of 30 your loving me in return are infinitely small . . . no . . . they are *nil*, nonexistent; there are no chances, but I ask nothing of you, I want nothing. Only let me look at you, listen to you. . . .

YELENA Quiet! Someone may hear you.

VANYA Let me tell you of my love; don't drive me away. I have 35 no other happiness.

YELENA Oh, this is agony!

[*Both go into the house.* TELYEGIN *strums the strings of his guitar and plays a polka.* MARYA *writes something on the leaves of her pamphlet.*]

ACT TWO

[The dining room of SEREBRYAKOV's *house. It is night. The click of the* WATCHMAN's *rattle is heard from the garden.* SEREBRYAKOV *sits dozing in an armchair by an open window and* YELENA, *likewise half asleep, is seated beside him.]*

SEREBRYAKOV *[rousing himself]* Who's there? Is that you, Sonya?

YELENA It is I.

SEREBRYAKOV Oh, it's you, Lenotchka. This pain is unbearable.

YELENA Your blanket has slipped. *[She wraps the blanket around his legs.]* Let me shut the window. 5

SEREBRYAKOV No, leave it open; I am suffocating as it is. *[Pause.]* I just dropped off to sleep . . . and . . . I dreamt that my left leg belonged to someone else, and the pain was so agonizing that I awoke. I don't believe this is gout; it is more like rheumatism. *[Pause.]* What time is it? 10

YELENA Twenty after twelve.

[A pause.]

SEREBRYAKOV I wish you'd look for Batushkov tomorrow morning; we used to have him, I remember. Oh, why do I find it so hard to breathe?

YELENA You're exhausted; this is the second night you've been 15 unable to sleep.

SEREBRYAKOV They say that Turgenev got heart trouble from gout. I'm afraid I'm getting it, too. Oh, damn this terrible, accursed old age! Ever since I've grown old, I have been hateful to myself, and I'm sure, hateful to all of you, too. 20

YELENA You talk as if we were to blame for your old age.

SEREBRYAKOV I am more hateful to you than to all the others.

*[*YELENA *gets up, walks away from him and sits down at a distance.]*

SEREBRYAKOV You are right, of course. I'm no fool; I can understand. You are young and healthy and beautiful. You want and long for life, and I am an old dotard, almost a corpse. Oh, I 25 know it! Certainly, I see that it's foolish for me to go on living for such a long time, but wait! I shall soon set you all free. My life can't drag on too much longer.

YELENA   For God's sake, be quiet! . . . You are exhausting me.

SEREBRYAKOV   It seems that everybody is being exhausted, thanks
to me. Everybody is miserable and depressed; everyone's youth
is wasting away; only I am enjoying life in blissful triumph. Oh,
5   yes, of course!

YELENA   Be quiet! You're torturing me.

SEREBRYAKOV   Why of course, I torture everybody.

YELENA   [*on the verge of tears*]   This is unbearable! Please, just
tell me what you want me to do?

10   SEREBRYAKOV   Nothing.

YELENA   Then please be quiet.

SEREBRYAKOV   It's funny that everybody listens to Vanya and
his old fool of a mother, but the moment I open my mouth, you
all begin to feel abused. You can't even bear the sound of my
15   voice. Suppose I am hateful, suppose I am a selfish and ego-
centric tyrant, haven't I the right to be at my age? Haven't I de-
served it? Haven't I, I ask you, the right to be respected, the right
to be pampered and cared for . . .

YELENA   No one is disputing your rights. [*The window slams in
20   the wind.*] The wind is rising, I must shut the window. [*She shuts
it.*] We shall have rain in a few minutes. [*Pause.*] Your rights
have never been questioned by anybody.

[*The* WATCHMAN *in the garden clicks his rattle.*]

SEREBRYAKOV   I have spent my life working for the cause of
learning. I am accustomed to my study, the library and the lecture
25   hall and to the regard and admiration of my colleagues. And,
now . . . [*Pause*] . . . now, I suddenly find myself in this wilderness, in this vault, condemned to see the same stupid people
from morning till night and to listen to their inane talk. I want
to live; I long for success and fame and the tension of an active
30   world, and here I am in exile! Oh, it's terrible to spend every
moment grieving for a past that is lost, to witness the success of
others and to sit here with nothing to do but fear death. I can't
stand it! It's more than I can endure. And you, you won't even
forgive me for being old!

35   YELENA   Wait; be patient; in four or five years, I shall be old too.

[SONYA *comes in.*]

SONYA   Father, you sent for Dr. Astrov, and now you refuse to
see him. It's not fair to needlessly trouble a busy man.

SEREBRYAKOV   Oh, what do I care about your Astrov? He knows as much about medicine as I do about astronomy.

SONYA   We can't send for famous specialists to come here to cure your gout, can we?

SEREBRYAKOV   I refuse to talk to that madman.   5

SONYA   Do as you wish then. It makes no difference to me. [*She sits down.*]

SEREBRYAKOV   What time is it?

YELENA   One o'clock.

SEREBRYAKOV   It's stifling in here. . . . Sonya, hand me that bottle there on the table.   10

SONYA   [*handing him a bottle of medicine*]   Here you are.

SEREBRYAKOV   [*cross and irritated*]   No, not that one! Don't you ever understand? Can't I ask you to do a single thing?

SONYA   Please don't be cross with me. Some people may enjoy it, but spare me, if you please, because I don't like it. Furthermore,   15
I haven't time for it; we are planning to cut the hay tomorrow and I have to get up early.

[VANYA *enters dressed in a long gown and carrying a candle.*]

VANYA   A thunderstorm is on its way. [*The lightning flashes.*] There it is! Sonya, you and Yelena had better go and get some sleep. I have come to relieve you.   20

SEREBRYAKOV   [*frightened*]   No, no, no! Don't leave me alone with him! Oh please don't. He will begin lecturing me again.

VANYA   But you must let them have a little rest. They haven't slept for two nights now.

SEREBRYAKOV   All right, then let them go to bed, but, please, you   25
go away, too! Thank you. I beg of you, please go away. . . . For the sake of . . . ah . . . our former friendship, don't argue. We'll talk some other time. . . .

VANYA   Our former friendship! Our former. . . .

SONYA   Shh, please be quiet. Uncle Vanya!   30

SEREBRYAKOV   [*to his wife*]   My love, don't leave me alone with him. He will begin his infernal lecturing.

VANYA   This is absurd.

[MARINA *comes in carrying a candle.*]

SONYA   You must go to bed, nurse, it's late.

MARINA   I haven't cleaned up the tea things. I can't go to bed yet.

SEREBRYAKOV   No one can. Everyone is completely worn out. I
5   alone enjoy perfect peace and happiness.

MARINA [*going up to* SEREBRYAKOV *and speaking tenderly*] What's
the matter, little man? Does it hurt? My own legs ache, too, oh,
such pain. [*She arranges the blanket around his legs.*] You've
been sick like this for such a long time. Sonya's mother used to
10   sit up with you night after night, too, and she wore herself out
for you. She loved you dearly. [*A pause.*] Old people like to be
pitied as much as small children, but somehow nobody cares
about them. [*She kisses* SEREBRYAKOV's *shoulder.*] Come to bed,
my little man, let me give you some linden-tea and warm your
15   poor feet. I shall pray to God for you.

SEREBRYAKOV [*moved*]   Let us go, Marina.

MARINA   My own feet ache so badly, too, oh, so badly!

[*She and* SONYA *start leading* SEREBRYAKOV *out.*]

Sonya's mother used to wear herself out with sorrow and weeping
over you. You were still a small and senseless child then, Sonya.
20   Come along now, come along . . .

[SEREBRYAKOV, MARINA, *and* SONYA *go out.*]

YELENA   He so completely exhausts me, that I can hardly stand
up.

VANYA   He has exhausted you and I have exhausted myself. I
haven't had a bit of sleep for three nights now.

25   YELENA   There's something wrong in this house. Your mother
hates everything but her pamphlets and the Professor; the Professor is vexed and irritated, he won't trust me and he fears you;
Sonya is angry with her father and also with me, and she hasn't
spoken to me for two weeks; you hate my husband and openly
30   sneer at your mother. I have reached the limit of my endurance
. . . there is no strength left, why I've nearly burst into tears at
least twenty times today. There is something wrong in this house.

VANYA   Oh, why don't you stop all your speculating.

YELENA   You are a cultured and intelligent man. Vanya. Cer-
35   tainly you must understand that the world is not destroyed by
criminals and fires, but by hate and malice and all this spiteful
gossiping and petty wrangling. Your duty is to make peace; your

work should be to reconcile everyone and not to growl at everything.

VANYA [*seizing her hand*]   My darling! First, help me to make peace with myself.

YELENA   Let go! [*She drags her hand away.*] Go away!

VANYA   The rain will soon be over, and all nature will awake refreshed. Only I am not refreshed by the storm. Night and day I am haunted by the thought that my life has been hopelessly wasted and is lost forever. My past doesn't count, because I frittered it away on trifles, and the present is so grotesque in its senselessness. What shall I do with my life and my love? What is going to become of them? This glorious passion in my heart will be lost as a ray of sunlight is lost in a dark chasm, and my life will be lost with it.

YELENA   It's just as if I were benumbed when you speak to me of your love, and I don't know how to answer you. Forgive me, I have nothing to say to you. [*She tries to leave.*] Good night!

VANYA [*barring her way*]   If you only knew how it tortures me to think that beside me in this house is another life that is being wasted and is lost forever—yours! What are you waiting for? What accursed philosophy, what damn theory, stands in your way? Oh, understand, understand. . . .

YELENA [*looking at him intently*]   Ivan Petrovich, you are drunk.

VANYA   Perhaps . . . perhaps.

YELENA   Where is the doctor?

VANYA   In there. He is going to stay with me tonight. [*Pause.*] Perhaps I am drunk . . . yes, perhaps I am; nothing is impossible.

YELENA   Have you been drinking together? What for?

VANYA   Because in that way at least I experience a semblance of life. Let me do that, Yelena!

YELENA   You never used to drink and you never used to talk so much. Go to bed! You bore me!

VANYA [*falling to his knees before her*]   My darling . . . my precious, beautiful one. . . .

YELENA [*angrily*]   Leave me alone! Really, this has become too disgusting. [*She leaves.*]

VANYA [*alone*]   She is gone! [*A pause.*] It was ten years ago that I first met her at her sister's house. She was seventeen and I thirty-seven. Why didn't I fall in love with her then and propose to her? It would have been so easy . . . then! And if I had, she would now be my wife. Yes, tonight's thunderstorm would have wakened us both. But I would have held her in my arms and whispered: "Don't be afraid! I am here." Oh, bewitching dream, so sweet that I smile when I think of it. [*He laughs.*] But, my God! Why are my thoughts so entangled? Why am I so old? Why won't she understand me? I despise all that rhetoric of hers, that indolent morality, that absurd talk about the destruction of the world. . . . [*A pause.*] Oh, how I have been deceived! For years I have worshiped and slaved for that miserable gout-ridden professor. Sonya and I have milked this estate dry for his sake. We have sold our butter and cheese and wheat like misers, and never kept a bit for ourselves, so that we could scrape together enough pennies to send to him. I was proud of him and his learning; I thought all his words and writings were inspired; he was my life . . . the very breath of my being. And now? My God. . . . Now he has retired, and what is the grand total of his life? A blank! Nothing! He is absolutely unknown, and his fame has burst like a soap-bubble. I have been deceived; I see that now, basely deceived.

[ASTROV *enters. He is wearing his coat but is without waistcoat or collar and is slightly drunk.* TELYEGIN *follows him, carrying a guitar.*]

ASTROV   Play something!

TELYEGIN   But everyone is asleep.

ASTROV   Play!

[TELYEGIN *begins to play softly.*]

ASTROV   Are you alone? No women around? [*Sings with his arms akimbo.*]

> The room is cold, the fire is out.
> How shall the master cure his gout?

The thunderstorm woke me. It was a torrential downpour. What time is it?

VANYA   The devil only knows.

ASTROV   I thought I heard Yelena's voice.

VANYA   She was here a moment ago.

ASTROV   What a beautiful woman! [*Looking at the bottles of medicine.*] Medicine, is it? What an assortment of prescriptions we have! From Moscow, from Kharkov, from Tula! Why, he has

been bothering every city in Russia with his pains! Is he really
sick, or simply pretending?

VANYA He is very ill.

[*Pause.*]

ASTROV What's the matter with you tonight? You seem gloomy
—so melancholic. Is it because you feel sorry for the Professor? 5

VANYA Leave me alone.

ASTROV Or are you in love with the Professor's wife?

VANYA She is my friend.

ASTROV Already?

VANYA What do you mean by "already"? 10

[TELYEGIN *stops playing to listen.*]

ASTROV A woman can be a man's friend only after having first
been his acquaintance and then his mistress . . . then she becomes his friend.

VANYA What coarse philosophy!

ASTROV What do you mean? [*Pause.*] Yes, I'll admit I'm growing 15
vulgar, but then, you see, I'm drunk. Usually I drink like this only
once a month. At such times my courage and boldness know no
bounds. I feel capable of anything. I attempt the most difficult
operations and succeed magnificently. The most brilliant plans
and ideas evolve in my brain. I'm no longer a poor simpleton of 20
a doctor, but mankind's greatest benefactor. I work out my own
system of philosophy and all of the rest of you seem to crawl
insignificantly at my feet like so many worms . . . [*Pause.*] . . .
or microbes. [*To* TELYEGIN.] Play, Waffles!

TELYEGIN My dear fellow, I would be delighted to, especially for 25
you, but listen to reason; everyone in the house is asleep.

ASTROV Play!

[TELYEGIN *plays softly.*]

ASTROV I want a drink. Come, we still have some brandy left.
Then, as soon as morning comes, you'll go home with me. All
right? 30

[SONYA *enters and he catches sight of her.*] I beg your pardon, I
haven't got a tie on.

[*He departs hurriedly, followed by* TELYEGIN.]

SONYA Uncle Vanya, you and the doctor have been drinking again! What a pair you two make! It's all very well for him, he's always been like that. But why must you follow his example? It's wrong at your age.

5 VANYA Age hasn't anything to do with it. When the realities of life are gone, or if you've never had them, then you must create illusions. That is better than nothing.

SONYA All our hay is cut and rotting in these daily rains and here you waste your time living in illusions! You are neglecting the
10 farm completely. I've done all the work myself, until now I'm at the end of my strength . . . [*Frightened.*] Uncle! Your eyes are full of tears!

VANYA Tears? No . . . ah . . . Nonsense, there are no tears in my eyes. [*Pause.*] You looked at me then just as your dead mother
15 used to. Oh my darling child . . . [*He eagerly kisses her face and hands.*] My sister, my dear sister. . . . [*Pause.*] . . . where are you now? [*Pause.*] Oh, if you only knew, if you only knew!

SONYA If she only knew what, Uncle?

VANYA My heart is bursting. Oh it is dreadful . . . so useless.
20 Never mind, though . . . maybe later on. Now, I must go. [*He goes out.*]

SONYA [*knocking at the door*] Mihail! Are you asleep? Please come here for a minute.

ASTROV [*behind the door*] In a moment. [*He appears presently, with his collar and waistcoat on.*] What do you want?

25 SONYA Drink as much as you please, if you don't find it disgusting, but I beg of you, don't let my uncle do it. It's bad for him.

ASTROV All right; we won't drink any more. [*Pause.*] I'm going home at once. That's settled. By the time the horses are harnessed, it will be dawn.

30 SONYA It's still raining; wait until morning.

ASTROV The storm is over. This is only the final blow. I must go. And please don't ask me to visit your father any more. I tell him he has gout, and he insists it is rheumatism. I tell him to lie down and stay in bed, and he sits up and goes about. Today he actually
35 refused to see me.

SONYA He has been spoiled. [*Looking at the sideboard.*] Won't you have something to eat?

ASTROV Yes, I think I will.

SONYA I like to eat at night. I'm sure we shall find something here.

[*Pause.*] They say he has been a great favorite with the ladies all his life and women have spoiled him. Here, have some cheese.

[*They stand eating by the sideboard.*]

ASTROV   I haven't eaten a thing all day. I must drink. [*Pause.*] Your father has a very trying temper. [*Taking a bottle out of the sideboard.*] May I? [*Pouring himself a glass of vodka.*] We are alone here and I can speak frankly. Do you know, I couldn't bear to live in this house—not even for a month! This atmosphere would choke me. There is your father, wholly absorbed in his books and his sickness; there is your uncle Vanya with his melancholy, your grandmother, and finally your stepmother— 5

10

SONYA   What about her?

ASTROV   In a human being, everything ought to be beautiful: face and dress, soul and thoughts. She is very beautiful, there's no denying it, but, after all, all she does is eat, sleep, go for walks, fascinate us by her beauty and—nothing more. She has no duties, 15 other people work for her . . . isn't that so? And an idle life cannot be a pure one. [*Pause.*] And yet, perhaps I'm judging her too harshly. I'm discontented, like your Uncle Vanya, and so both of us are complainers.

SONYA   Aren't you satisfied with life? 20

ASTROV   I like life as life, but I hate and despise it when it means frittering it away in a little Russian village. As far as my personal existence is concerned . . . God! . . . it is absolutely beyond redemption! Haven't you noticed when you cross a dense forest in the middle of night and see a small light shining ahead in the 25 distance, how you forget your weariness and the darkness and the sharp branches that lash your face? I work—as you know— perhaps harder than anyone else around here. Fate pursues me relentlessly; at times I suffer unbearably and I see no light ahead of me in the distance. I have no hope; I do not care for people. 30 And . . . it has been a long time since I have loved any one.

SONYA   You love no one?

ASTROV   No one. . . . At times I feel a kind of tenderness for your old nurse, but that's only for old time's sake. The peasants are all alike; they are stupid, lazy, and dull. And the educated 35 people are difficult to get along with. I am tired of them. All our friends are small in their ideas and small in their feelings. They see no farther than their own noses; or perhaps, more bluntly, they are dull and stupid. The ones who have brains and intelligence are hysterical, morbidly absorbed and consumed in intro- 40 spection and analysis. They whine, they hate, they find fault

everywhere. They crawl up to me secretively, leer at me and say: "That man is crazy, he's neurotic or he is fraudulent." Or, if they don't know what else to call me, if no other label fits, they say I am peculiar. I like the forests; that is peculiar. I don't eat meat;
5   that is peculiar, too. Simple, natural, and genuine relations between man and man or between man and nature have no existence in their eyes. No, none! . . . None!

[*He tries to take a drink;* SONYA *prevents him.*]

SONYA   Please, I beg you, don't drink any more!

ASTROV   Why not?

10 SONYA   It is so debasing. You are so noble, your voice is tender, you are, more than any one I know, beautiful. Why do you wish to be like the common people who drink and play cards? Oh, don't, I beg you! You are always saying people never create anything, but only destroy what God has given them. Why, then, do
15 you insist on destroying yourself? Oh, you must not; don't; I implore you! I entreat you!

ASTROV [*giving her his hand*]   I won't drink any more.

SONYA   Give me your word.

ASTROV   I give you my word of honor.

20 SONYA [*squeezing his hand*]   Thank you!

ASTROV   I'm through with it. You see, I'm perfectly sober again; I've come to my senses, and I shall remain so until the end of my life. [*He looks at his watch.*] But as I was saying, my time is over; there is nothing for me in life; the clock has run its race and has
25 stopped. I am old, tired, unimportant; my feelings are dead. I could never care for any one again. I don't love anyone, and I don't think I shall ever love anyone. The only thing that appeals to me is beauty. I just can't remain indifferent to it. If, for example, Yelena wanted to, she could turn my head in a day. Yet,
30 I know that that isn't love, nor even affection . . . [*He shudders and covers his face with his hands.*]

SONYA   What is the matter?

ASTROV   Nothing. . . . During Lent one of my patients died on the operating table.

SONYA   It is time to forget that. [*Pause.*] Tell me, Mihail, if I had
35 a friend or a younger sister, and if you knew that she, well—that she loved you, what would you do?

ASTROV   I don't know. I don't suppose I'd do anything. I'd make her understand that I could not return her love . . . and anyway,

my mind cannot be bothered with such affairs now. I must start
at once if I am ever to go. Good-bye, my dear girl. At this rate,
we shall stand here talking till daylight. [*Shaking hands with her.*]
If it's all right, I'll go out through the drawing room, because I'm
afraid your uncle might detain me. [*He goes out.*]   5

SONYA [*alone*]   And he really said nothing! His heart and soul are
still hidden from me, and yet for some reason I'm strangely happy.
Why? [*Laughing with pleasure.*] I told him that he was noble and
beautiful and that his voice was tender. Was that wrong? I can
still feel his voice throbbing in the air as it caresses me. [*Wringing*   10
her hands.] Oh, how awful it is that I am not beautiful! How
awful! And I know that I'm not beautiful. I know it, I know. Last
Sunday, as people were coming out of church, I heard them talking about me, and one woman said: "She is so good and generous, what a pity she is not beautiful." Not beautiful. . . .   15

[YELENA *enters and throws open the window.*]

YELENA   The storm has passed! What a refreshing breeze! [*Pause.*]
Where is the doctor?

SONYA   He's gone.

[*Pause.*]

YELENA   Sonya!   20

SONYA   Yes?

YELENA   How much longer are you going to go on brooding? We
have done nothing to hurt each other. Why should we be enemies.
Certainly we should be friends.

SONYA   I feel this too . . . [*Embracing* YELENA.] Oh, let's be   25
friends again!

YELENA   With all my heart.

[*Both are strongly moved. Pause.*]

SONYA   Has father gone to bed?

YELENA   No, he is sitting up in the drawing room. [*Pause.*] You
know, it's strange. . . . I guess only the Lord knows what has
kept us apart all these weeks. [*Seeing the open sideboard.*] Who   30
left the sideboard open?

SONYA   Mihail has just had supper.

YELENA   Here is some wine. Let's drink to our friendship.

SONYA   Yes, let's.

YELENA   Out of one glass. [*Filling a wine glass.*] Now, we are friends, aren't we?

SONYA   Friends.

[*They drink and kiss each other.*]

5   I have wished for us to be friends for so long, but somehow I was ashamed. [*She weeps.*]

YELENA   Why do you weep?

SONYA   I don't know. [*Pause.*] Let's forget it.

YELENA   There, there, don't cry. [*She weeps.*] Silly! Now I am cry-
10   ing, too. [*Pause.*] You're angry with me because you think I married your father for his money, but you must not believe all the gossip you hear. I swear to you I married him for love. I was fascinated by his fame and his learning. I know now that it wasn't real love, although it seemed real enough at the time. I am inno-
15   cent, and yet ever since my marriage your searching suspicious eyes have been accusing me of an imaginary crime.

SONYA   Peace! Come, let's forget the past.

YELENA   You mustn't look at people that way. It isn't right. You must trust and believe in people—[*Pause.*]—or life becomes im-
20   possible.

[*Pause.*]

SONYA   Tell me, truthfully, as a friend, are you happy?

YELENA   Truthfully, no.

SONYA   I knew that. One more question: would you like your husband to be young?

25   YELENA   What a child you are! Of course I would. Go on, ask me something else.

SONYA   Do you like the doctor?

YELENA   Yes, very much indeed.

SONYA [*laughing*]   I have a plain face, haven't I? . . . Yes, I know.
30   He has just left, and his voice still rings in my ears; I can hear the sound of his footsteps; I can see his face in the dark window. Oh, I want so to tell you all that I have in my heart! But I cannot, I am ashamed. Words can never express our feelings. They mean and. . . . Oh, what a silly person you must think I am. [*Pause.*]
35   Please talk to me about him.

YELENA   What do you want me to say?

SONYA He is so wise. He understands everything and he can do anything. He can heal the sick, and plant forests, too.

YELENA It isn't a question of medicine and trees, my dear. He is a man of genius. Do you realize what that means? It means he is a man of great courage, one with deep insights and clear and far-reaching vision. He plants a tree and his mind swings a thousand years into the future and he envisions the happiness of all mankind. Such people are rare and should be loved. What if he does drink and use coarse language at times. In Russia, a man of genius cannot be a saint. Think of his life. There he lives, cut off from the world by frost and storm and trackless muddy roads, surrounded by coarse and savage people who are crushed by poverty and disease. His life is a continuing and endless struggle, from which he shall never rest. How can a man live like that for forty years and remain sober and free from all sin? [*Kissing* SONYA.] With all my heart, I wish you happiness; you deserve it. [*Getting up.*] As for me, I am worthless—an empty and quite pathetic woman. I have always been futile; in music, in love, in my husband's house—in fact, in everything. If I dared even for a moment to consider . . . Oh, Sonya, I am really very, very unhappy. [*Walking excitedly back and forth.*] I can never achieve happiness in this world. Never. Why do you laugh?

SONYA [*laughing and putting her hands over her face*] I am so happy . . . [*Pause.*] . . . so happy!

YELENA How I should like some music at this moment. I believe I could play once more.

SONYA Oh, do, do! [*Embracing her.*] I couldn't possibly go to sleep now. Do play!

YELENA Yes, I will. Your father is still awake. Music annoys him when he is ill, but if he says I may, then I shall play a little. Go . . . go and ask him, Sonya.

SONYA All right. [*She goes out.*]

[*The sound of the* WATCHMAN'S *rattle comes from the back yard.*]

YELENA It's been a long time since I've had the feeling for music. And now, I shall sit and play and cry like a small child. [*Calling out of the window.*] Yefim, is that you out there with your rattle?

VOICE OF WATCHMAN Yes.

YELENA How I should like some music at this moment. I believe

VOICE OF WATCHMAN I'm on my way. [*He whistles a tune as* YELENA *closes the window.*]

SONYA [*returning*] He says "No."

ACT THREE

[*The drawing room of* SEREBRYAKOV's *house. There are doors right, left, and center. It is early afternoon.* VANYA *and* SONYA *are seated.* YELENA *walks back and forth, deep in thought.*]

VANYA His lordship, the Professor, has deigned to express the wish that we all gather in the drawing room at one o'clock. [*Looking at his watch.*] It is now a quarter to one. He has a message of the greatest importance to convey to the world.

5 YELENA It's probably a question of business.

VANYA He never has any business. He writes nonsense, grumbles and eats his heart out with jealousy; that's all he does.

SONYA [*reproachfully*] Uncle!

VANYA Very well. I beg your pardon. [*Pointing to* YELENA.] Look
10 at her. Roaming up and down out of sheer idleness and boredom. A beautiful picture, I must say!

YELENA I'm surprised that it doesn't bore you to play on the same note from morning to night. [*With despair.*] This tedium is killing me. Oh, what am I going to do?

15 SONYA [*shrugging her shoulders*] There is plenty to do if you wish to.

YELENA For instance?

SONYA You could help us run the estate, teach the children, look after the sick . . . isn't that enough? Before you and father came,
20 Uncle Vanya and I used to take the grain to market ourselves.

YELENA I know nothing about such matters, and, besides, I'm not interested in them. It's only in sentimental novels that women go out and teach and look after the sick peasants; furthermore, how could I start in doing it all of a sudden?

25 SONYA I don't know how you can live here and not do it. Be patient and you'll get used to it. [*Embracing her.*] Don't be depressed, my dear friend. [*Laughing.*] You feel out-of-sorts and restless, bored and idle, and unable, somehow, to fit into this life, and your restlessness and idleness is infectious. Look at Uncle
30 Vanya, he does nothing now but follow you about like a shadow, and I have given up my work today to come here and talk with you. I'm getting lazy and losing interest in my work and I can't help it. Dr. Astrov hardly ever came here; it was all we could do to persuade him to visit us once each month, and now he has

356

given up his forestry and forgets his patients, and comes every day. You must be a witch.

VANYA Why should you pine away here in misery and despair? [*Eagerly.*] Come, my darling, my sweet one, be sensible! A mermaid's blood runs in your veins. Why don't you act like one? Let yourself go for once in your life; fall head over heels in love with some other water sprite, and plunge headlong into a bottomless quarry, so that the almighty Professor and all the rest of us might be so amazed that we could escape your charms.

YELENA [*in anger*] Leave me alone! How cruel can you be! [*She tries to leave.*]

VANYA [*preventing her*] There, there, my darling, I apologize. Forgive me. [*He kisses her hand.*] Peace!

YELENA Admit that you would try the patience of a saint.

VANYA As a peace offering and as a symbol of true harmony, I am going to bring you some flowers I picked for you this morning; some autumn roses, exquisite, glorious, melancholy roses. [*He leaves.*]

SONYA Autumn roses, exquisite, glorious, melancholy roses. . . .

[*She and* YELENA *stand at the window looking out.*]

YELENA It's September already! How are we ever going to live through the long winter here? [*Pause.*] Where is the doctor?

SONYA He's writing in Uncle Vanya's room. I'm glad Uncle Vanya left. I must talk to you about something.

YELENA About what?

SONYA About what? [*She puts her head on* YELENA's *breast.*]

YELENA [*caressing her hair*] There, there! Don't, Sonya.

SONYA I am not beautiful!

YELENA You have beautiful hair.

SONYA No! [*Looks round so as to glance at herself in the mirror.*] No! When a woman is not beautiful, she is always told: "You've got beautiful eyes, you've got beautiful hair." For six years now I have loved him; I have loved him more than one can love anyone. Every moment, I seem to hear him by my side. I feel his hand press against mine. I watch the door constantly, imagining that I can hear his footsteps. And—don't you see?—I run to you just to talk about him. He comes here every day now, but he never looks at me, he doesn't even notice that I am here. Yelena, my dear, it is breaking my heart and I have absolutely no hope . . . no hope. [*In despair.*] Oh, God! Give me strength to endure. All

last night I prayed. It has gotten so that I go up to him and speak
to him and look into his eyes. My pride is gone. I no longer have
the strength to control myself. Yesterday I told Uncle Vanya
about my love for him. I couldn't help it. And all the servants
know it, too. Everyone knows that I love him.

YELENA   Does he?

SONYA   No, he never pays any attention to me; it is as if I didn't
exist.

YELENA [*musing*]   He's a strange man. Do you know what? Let
me talk to him. I'll do it carefully. I'll just give him a hint. [*Pause.*]
Now, really, how much longer do you propose to remain in uncertainty? Please! Let me do it!

[SONYA *nods affirmatively.*]

Wonderful! It will be easy to find out whether he loves you or
not. Don't be ashamed, dear one, and don't worry. I shall be
careful; he won't have the least suspicion. We only wish to find
out whether it is yes or no, don't we? [*A pause.*] And if it is no,
then, he must stay away from here, isn't that right?

[SONYA *nods.*]

It would be easier not to see him any more. We won't delay this
another minute. He said he had some maps he wanted to show
me. Go and tell him at once that I wish to see him.

SONYA [*greatly excited*]   Will you tell me the whole truth?

YELENA   Why certainly I will. I'm sure that whatever it is, it will
be easier to endure than this uncertainty. Trust me, my dear.

SONYA   Yes, yes. I shall say that you wish to see his charts. [*She
starts to go, but stops near the door and looks back.*] No, it is
better not to know with certainty . . . one has hope, at least.

YELENA   What did you say?

SONYA   Nothing. [*She leaves.*]

YELENA [*alone*]   There is nothing worse than to know the secret
of another human being, and to realize there's nothing you can do
to help them. [*In deep thought.*] Obviously, he is not in love with
her. But why shouldn't he marry her? To be sure, she is not
beautiful, yet she is good and kind, pure of heart, and so sensible
that she would make an excellent wife for a country doctor of his
age. [*Pause.*] I can understand the poor child's feelings. Here she
lives in the midst of this desperate loneliness with no one about
her except these gray shadows who pass for human beings, who

do nothing but eat, drink, sleep, and talk trivial commonplaces. And, then, who from time to time should appear upon the scene among them but this Dr. Astrov, so unlike the rest—so handsome, interesting, fascinating. . . . It is like seeing the moon rising, rich and full, in the darkness. Oh, to be able to surrender yourself—to 5 forget oneself—body and soul to such a man! Yes, I too, am a little in love with him! Yes, without him I am lonely; when I think of him, I smile. Uncle Vanya says I have a mermaid's blood in my veins: "For once in your life, let yourself go!" Perhaps I should. Oh, to be free as a bird, to fly away from all those drowsy 10 faces and their monotonous mumblings and forget that they have existed at all! Oh, to forget oneself and what one is. . . . But I am a coward; I am afraid, and tortured by my conscience. He comes here every day now. I can guess why, and already my guilt condemns me. I should like to fall on my knees at Sonya's feet and 15 beg her to forgive me and weep . . . But. . . .

[ASTROV *enters carrying a portfolio.*]

ASTROV   Hello, how are you this afternoon? [*Shaking hands with her.*] Sonya tells me that you wish to see my maps.

YELENA   Yes, you promised me yesterday that you'd show me what you had been doing. Have you time now? 20

ASTROV   Of course! [*He lays the portfolio on the table, takes out a sketch and attaches it to the table with thumb tacks.*] Where were you born?

YELENA [*helping him out*]   In Petersburg.

ASTROV   Did you go to school there, too? 25

YELENA   Yes, at the conservatory of music.

ASTROV   I don't imagine you find our way of life very interesting.

YELENA   And why not? It's true I don't know the country very well, but I've read a great deal about it.

ASTROV   I have my own desk there in Vanya's room. When I be- 30 come so completely exhausted that I can no longer go on with my work, I abandon everything and rush over here to forget myself with my maps for an hour or two. Vanya and Sonya rattle away at their counting boards, I feel warm and peaceful, the cricket sings, and I sit near them at my table and paint. However, 35 I usually don't indulge in such a luxury very often, certainly not more than once a month. [*Pointing to the picture.*] Look! This is a survey map of our part of the country as it was fifty years ago. Those areas shaded in green, both light and dark, are forest lands. Half the map, you see, is covered with them. Where the green is 40 stripped with red, the forests were stocked with elk and wild goats. Here on this lake were large flocks of swans, wild geese, and ducks; as the old men used to tell us, there was a "power" of birds of every kind—no end of them. [*Pause.*] Now, they have vanished like thin air. Here, you see, beside the towns and villages, I have jotted down here and there the various settlements, little farms, monasteries, and watermills. This country was rich in cattle and horses, as you can see by this expanse of blue. For instance, see how it deepens in this part; there were great herds here, an average of three horses to every house. [*Pause.*] Now, look below to the second map. This is the country as it was twenty-five years ago. Only a third of the map now is green with forests. The goats have disappeared and only a few elk remain. The green and blue are lighter, and so on and so forth. Now, we come to the third drawing, our district as it is today. Still we see spots of green, but very little. The elk, the swans, the blackcock have also disappeared. In fact, everything is gone. On the whole, it is the picture of a continuous and slow decline which will evidently come to completion in about ten or fifteen years. Perhaps you may object that it is the march of progress, that the old order must give way to the new, and you would be right if roads had been built through these ruined forests, or if factories and schools had taken the place of the monasteries and the watermills. Then the people would have become better educated and healthier and richer, but as it is, and as you can see, we have nothing of the kind. We have the same swamps and mosquitoes; the same disease, poverty, and misery; typhoid, diphtheria, fires. The degradation of our country confronts us, brought on by the human race's fierce struggle for existence. This degeneration is due to inertia and ignorance—to a complete lack of understanding. When a man, cold, hungry and sick, simply to save what little there is left in life that has meaning and importance—to help his children survive—why God only knows, he acts in desperation; he instinctively and unconsciously clutches at anything that will fill his belly and keep him warm. Forced to forget what all this will mean tomorrow, the devil of destruction consumes all the land. And so almost everything has been destroyed and nothing has been created to take its place. [*Coldly.*] But I see by your expression that all this does not interest you.

YELENA   I know so little about such things!

ASTROV   There's nothing to know. It simply doesn't interest you, that's all.

YELENA   Frankly, my thoughts were elsewhere. Forgive me! I must ask you something, but I am embarrassed and I don't know how to begin.

ASTROV Ask me something?

YELENA Yes, a very innocent and probably not too important question. Sit down. [*They both sit.*] It's about a young girl I know. Let's discuss it like honest and mature people, like friends; and then, when we have finished we will forget all about it, shall we? 5

ASTROV All right. Whatever you say!

YELENA What I want to talk to you about is my stepdaughter, Sonya. Do you like her?

ASTROV Yes, I respect her.

YELENA But do you like her as a woman? 10

ASTROV [*not at once*] No.

YELENA Just one thing more and I am finished. Haven't you noticed anything?

ASTROV Nothing.

YELENA [*takes him by the hand*] You don't love her, I can see it 15
from your eyes. She is unhappy. Please understand that and . . . stop coming here.

ASTROV [*gets up*] I'm afraid I'm too old for this sort of thing. And, besides, I haven't the time for it. [*Shrugging his shoulders.*] When indeed could I? [*He is embarrassed.*] 20

YELENA Oh, God! What a disgusting conversation. I am as breathless as if I had been running three miles uphill. Thank heaven, that's over with. Now let us forget everything that has been said. But you must leave at once. You are intelligent and sensible. You do understand, don't you? [*Pause.*] I am actually blushing. 25

ASTROV If you had spoken a month or two ago, perhaps I might have been able to consider it, but now . . . [*Shrugging his shoulders.*] Of course, if she is suffering . . . but wait, there is one thing I can't understand . . . what are your reasons for bringing all this up? [*Searching her face with his eyes and shaking an 30
admonishing finger at her.*] Oh, you're a sly one!

YELENA What do you mean?

ASTROV [*laughing*] A sly one! Suppose Sonya is unhappy. I'm ready to admit it, but what is the real meaning of your interrogation? [*Preventing her from speaking, quickly.*] Please, don't look 35
so surprised, you know perfectly well why I'm here every day. My sweet beast of prey, don't look at me like that, I'm an old hand at this sort of game . . . you can't deceive me.

YELENA [*perplexed*] A beast of prey? I don't understand anything.

ASTROV A beautiful, fluffy weasel. You must have your victims.
Here I've been doing nothing for a whole month, I've dropped
everything, I seek you greedily, and you're awfully pleased about
it, awfully. Well? I'm conquered, and you knew all about it
without your interrogation. [*Folding his arms and bowing his
5   head.*] I submit. Here I am . . . eat me up!

YELENA You've gone crazy!

ASTROV [*laughing ironically*] Oh, you're so shy, aren't you?

YELENA I'm more honorable than you think! I swear it! [*She tries
to leave the room.*]

ASTROV Wait . . . [*Barring her way.*] . . . I'll go away today. I
10   shan't come here any more. But . . . [*Taking her hand and glancing about.*] . . . for the future . . . where are we going to meet?
Tell me quickly, where? Someone may come in. Tell me quickly!
. . . [*Passionately.*] You are so gloriously and wonderfully beautiful! . . . Let me kiss you but once. . . . Oh, if I could kiss your
15   fragrant hair!

YELENA I assure you!

ASTROV Why assure me? You must not! Let's not waste words!
Ah, how lovely you are . . . what hands! [*Kissing her hands.*]

YELENA Stop it! Go away! [*Freeing her hands.*] You're forgetting
20   yourself!

ASTROV Tell me! Tell me! Where will we meet tomorrow? [*Putting
his arms around her.*] Don't you see! We must meet! It is inevitable. [*He kisses her.*]

[VANYA *comes in carrying a bunch of roses, and halts in the doorway.*]

YELENA [*without seeing* VANYA] Have pity! Leave me! [*She lays
25   her head on* ASTROV's *shoulder.*] Don't! [*She tries to break away
from him.*]

ASTROV [*holding her around the waist*] Meet me in the forest
arbor tomorrow at two. Yes! Oh, yes! Will you come?

YELENA [*seeing* VANYA] Let me go! [*Breaking free and going to
the window deeply embarrassed.*] This is horrible!

30 VANYA [*throwing the flowers on a chair, speaking in great excitement and wiping his face with his handkerchief*] Nothing . . .
yes, yes, nothing.

ASTROV [*with bravado*] It's a fine day, my dear Vanya. This
morning, the sky was overcast and it looked like rain, but now the

sun is shining again. After all, we've had a very fine autumn, and the wheat crop looks unusually promising. [*Putting his map back into the portfolio.*] But the days are growing short. [*Goes out.*]

YELENA [*quickly approaching* VANYA] You must do your best; you must use all the power you have to get us away from here today! Do you hear? I say, today! 5

VANYA [*wiping his face*] Oh! Ah! Oh! Very well! Yes, I . . . Yelena, I saw everything!

YELENA [*greatly upset*] Do you hear me? I must leave here today!

[SEREBRYAKOV, SONYA, MARINA, *and* TELYEGIN *enter.*]

TELYEGIN I'm not feeling very well myself, your excellency. I've 10 been lame for two days, and my head. . . .

SEREBRYAKOV Where are the rest? I hate this house. It winds and sprawls like a labyrinth. Everyone is always scattered through its twenty-six rooms. You can never find a soul. [*To* MARINA.] Ask Marya and Yelena to come here! 15

YELENA I am here.

SEREBRYAKOV Please sit down, all of you.

SONYA [*going to* YELENA *and asking anxiously*] What did he say?

YELENA I'll tell you later.

SONYA You are upset. [*Looking swiftly and with inquiry into her* 20 *face.*] I understand; he said he would not come here any more. [*Pause.*] Tell me, did he? . . . Tell me!

[YELENA *nods.*]

SEREBRYAKOV [*to* TELYEGIN] After all, one can become reconciled to being an invalid, but not to this absurd way of life you have here in the country. I feel as if I had been cast off from this earth 25 and dumped onto a strange planet. Please be seated, ladies and gentlemen. Sonya!

[*She does not hear. She stands with her head sadly bent forward.*]

Sonya! [*A pause.*] I guess she does not hear me. [*To* MARINA.] You sit down, too, nurse.

[MARINA *takes a seat and resumes knitting her stocking.*]

I ask your indulgence, ladies and gentlemen; uh . . . check your 30 ears, as it were, on the hat rack of attention. [*He laughs.*]

VANYA [*in agitation*]   Perhaps I'm not needed. . . . May I be excused?

SEREBRYAKOV   No, you are needed now more than anyone else.

VANYA   What do you wish?

5   SEREBRYAKOV   You—but what makes you so angry and out of sorts? If it is anything I have done, I beg your forgiveness.

VANYA   Oh, forget that and your high and mighty tone, too, and come to the point; what do you want?

[MARYA *enters.*]

SEREBRYAKOV   Here is mother. Ladies and gentlemen, let us begin.
10   I have asked you to gather here, my friends, to inform you that the inspector general is coming. [*Laughs.*] All joking aside, however, I wish to discuss a very important matter. I must ask you for your aid and advice, and realizing your unbounded kindness, I believe I can count on both. I am a scholar and bound to my
15   library, and I am not familiar with practical affairs. I am unable, I find, to dispense with the help of well-informed people such as you, Ivan, and you, Ilya, and you, mother. The truth is, *"manet omnes una nox,"* that is to say, our lives rest in the hands of God, and as I am old and ill, I realize that the time has come for me to
20   dispose of my property in the interests of my family. My life is nearly finished, and I am not thinking of myself, but I must consider my young wife and daughter. [*A pause.*] I cannot go on living in the country; we were just not meant for country life. And yet, we cannot afford to live in town on the income from this
25   estate. We might sell the forests, but that would be an expedient to which we could not resort every year. We must work out some method of guaranteeing ourselves a permanent, and . . . ah, more or less fixed annual income. With this object in view, a plan has occurred to me which I now have the honor of proposing to you for
30   your consideration. I shall give you only a rough outline of it, omitting all the bothersome and trivial details. Our estate does not yield, on an average, more than two percent on the investment. I propose to sell it. If then we invest our capital in bonds and other suitable securities, it will bring us four to five percent
35   and we should probably have a surplus of several thousand roubles, with which we could buy a small house in Finland. . . .

VANYA   Wait a minute! Repeat what you said just now; I don't believe I heard you quite right.

SEREBRYAKOV   I said we would invest the money in bonds and
40   with the surplus buy a house in Finland.

VANYA No, not Finland. . . . You said something else.

SEREBRYAKOV I propose to sell this estate.

VANYA Aha! That was it! So you are going to sell the estate? Splendid! That's a fine idea! And what do you propose to do with my old mother and myself and with Sonya, here?   5

SEREBRYAKOV That will be taken care of in due course. After all . . . uh . . . we can't do everything at once, can we?

VANYA Wait! It is clear that up to now I've never had an ounce of sense in my head. I have always been stupid enough to think that the estate belonged to Sonya. My late father bought it as   10 a wedding gift for my sister, and as our laws were made for Russians and not for Turks, I foolishly imagined that my sister's estate would pass on to her child.

SEREBRYAKOV Why, of course, it belongs to Sonya. Has anyone denied it? I don't wish to sell it without Sonya's consent; on the   15 contrary, what I am doing is for Sonya's welfare.

VANYA This is absolutely crazy. Either I have gone insane or . . . or . . .

MARYA Jean, don't contradict Alexander. Trust him; he knows better than we do what is right and what is wrong.   20

VANYA No! Give me some water. [He drinks.] Go on! Say anything you like . . . anything!

SEREBRYAKOV I can't understand why you are so upset. I don't pretend that my plan is ideal, and if you all object to it, I shall not insist.   25

[A pause.]

TELYEGIN [looking embarrassed] I've always had a great reverence for learning, sir, and, if I may say so, my feelings for it have a certain family connection. I mean, sir, that my brother Gregory's wife's brother, Konstantin Lacedaemonov, as you perhaps know, was an M.A. . . .   30

VANYA Wait a minute, Waffles, we're discussing business. Wait a little . . . later . . . [To SEREBRYAKOV.] Here, ask him what he thinks; this estate was purchased from his uncle.

SEREBRYAKOV Ah! Why should I ask questions? What good would it do?   35

VANYA The price was ninety-five thousand roubles. My father paid seventy and left a mortgage of twenty-five. Now listen! This estate could never have been bought if I had not renounced my inheritance in favor of my sister, whom I dearly loved . . . and what is more, I worked like a slave for ten years and paid off the mortgage.

SEREBRYAKOV   I regret that I ever brought the matter up.

5   VANYA   Thanks entirely to my personal efforts, the estate is now free from debt and in good condition; and now . . . as I am getting old, you propose to kick me out!

SEREBRYAKOV   I don't understand what you're talking about.

VANYA   For twenty-five years I have managed this estate. I have
10   sent you the proceeds from it like an honest servant, and you, you have never given me one single word of thanks for my efforts . . . no, not one . . . neither in my youth nor now. You gave me a meager salary of five hundred roubles a year . . . a beggar's pittance, and you have never once thought of adding a rouble to it.

15   SEREBRYAKOV   How should I know about such things, Ivan? I am not a practical man and I don't understand them. You might have helped yourself to all you desired.

VANYA   Yes, why didn't I steal? Don't you all despise me for not stealing? It would have been only fair, and I wouldn't be a poor
20   man now.

MARYA [sternly]   Jean!

TELYEGIN [in agitation]   Vanya, my friend, don't talk like that. Why spoil such a pleasant relationship? Please stop!

VANYA   For twenty-five years I have been sitting here with my
25   mother buried like a mole. Every thought and hope we had was yours and yours alone. All day long we talked with pride of you and your work; and we spoke your name with respect . . . yes, almost with reverence. We wasted our evenings reading your books and articles, which I now detest to the bottom of my heart.

30   TELYEGIN   Don't, Vanya, don't. I can't stand this sort of thing.

SEREBRYAKOV [angrily]   What in God's name do you want, anyhow?

VANYA   We used to consider you a superman, a kind of demigod, but now the scales have fallen from my eyes and I see you as
35   you are! You write about art without knowing a thing about it. Why, those books of yours which I used to think were so wonderful aren't worth a copper kopeck. You are a fake, a fraud, a . . .

SEREBRYAKOV   Can't anyone stop him? I'm leaving here immedi-
40   ately!

YELENA   Ivan Petrovich, I command you to stop this instant! Do you hear me?

SONYA   Please! Uncle Vanya!

VANYA   I refuse!

[SEREBRYAKOV *tries to escape from the room, but* VANYA *bars the door.*]

Wait! I haven't finished yet! You have destroyed my life. I have never really lived. Thanks to you, my best years have gone for nothing. They have been ruined. I hate you!   5

TELYEGIN   I can't stand it; I can't stand it. I'm going. [*He leaves in great excitement.*]

SEREBRYAKOV   What do you want from me? What right do you have to speak to me like that? If the estate is yours, take it! I don't want it.

YELENA   I'm leaving this hell right now! [*Shouts.*] I can't stand it   10
any longer!

VANYA   My life's ruined! I'm gifted, I'm intelligent, I'm courageous. If I'd had a normal life, I might have become a Schopenhauer, a Dostoevsky. I'm talking nonsense. I'm going insane! I'm in despair! Oh, Mother!   15

MARYA   Do as the Professor tells you!

VANYA   Mother, what am I to do? Never mind, don't tell me! I know myself what I must do! [*To* SEREBRYAKOV.] You will remember me! [*Goes out through middle door.*]

[MARYA *goes out after him.*]

SONYA   Oh, nurse, nurse!   20

SEREBRYAKOV   This is too much! Take that madman away! I can't live under the same roof with him! He is always there. [*Points to the middle door.*] Let him move into town or to another house on the grounds, or I will move myself, but I cannot stay in the same house with him.   25

YELENA   [*to her husband*]   We are leaving here today; we must get ready at once.

SEREBRYAKOV   What an utterly insignificant little man.

SONYA   [*on her knees beside the nurse, turning to her father and speaking with emotion*]   You must be merciful, Father. Uncle   30
Vanya and I are both very unhappy! [*Controlling her despair.*] Have mercy on us! Remember how Uncle Vanya and grandmother used to sit up late copying and translating your books for you every night . . . every night. Uncle Vanya has worked without rest; we would never spend a penny on ourselves, but spent   35

it all on you! We earned every mouthful of bread that we ever ate! I am not speaking as I should like to, but you must understand, Father, you must have mercy on us.

YELENA [*to her husband, much excited*] For heaven's sake, Alexander, go and talk to him . . . explain!

SEREBRYAKOV Very well, I shall talk to him. I do not accuse him of anything, and I am not angry, but you must admit that his behavior has been strange, to say the least. Very well, I shall go to him. [*He leaves through the center door.*]

YELENA Be gentle with him. Try to quiet him. [*She follows him out.*]

SONYA [*snuggling nearer to* MARINA] Nurse, oh, nurse!

MARINA It's all right, child. When the geese have cackled they will be silent again. First they cackle and then they stop.

SONYA Nurse!

MARINA [*caressing her hair*] You are trembling all over, as if you had a chill. There, there, my little child, God is merciful. A little linden tea, and it will pass. Don't cry, my sweet. [*Looking angrily at the center door.*] See, the geese have all gone now. The devil take them!

[*A shot is heard.* YELENA *screams behind the scenes.* SONYA *shudders.*]

MARINA What's that?

SEREBRYAKOV [*runs staggering in looking terrified*] Stop him! Stop him! He's gone mad!

[YELENA *and* VANYA *struggle in the doorway.*]

YELENA [*trying to snatch the revolver away from him*] Give it to me! Give it to me, I tell you!

VANYA Let go of me. Let go of me, Yelena! [*Freeing himself, he runs in and looks for* SEREBRYAKOV.] Where is he? Ah, there he is! [*Pointing the revolver at* SEREBRYAKOV.] Bang! [*Pause.*] Missed him! Missed him again! [*Furiously.*] Damn it! Damn! [*Bangs the revolver a few times against the floor and sinks exhausted in a chair.*]

YELENA Take me away from here! Take me away . . . kill me . . . I can't stay here, I can't.

VANYA [*in despair*] What have I done! What have I done!

SONYA [*softly*] Oh, nurse! Nurse!

ACT FOUR

[VANYA'S *bedroom and office. Large table near window; scattered on it are ledgers, scales, and papers. Nearby* ASTROV'S *table with paints and drawing materials. A map, of no use to anyone, of Africa on the wall. A large sofa covered with canvas. A door left to an inner room; door right leads to front hall. It is evening in autumn.* TELYEGIN *and* MARINA *sit facing each other, winding wool.*]

TELYEGIN   Hurry, Marina, or we shall have to go out to say good-bye before we've finished. They have ordered the carriage already.

MARINA   [*trying to wind more rapidly*]   There isn't much left to wind.

TELYEGIN   They are going to live in Kharkov.   5

MARINA   It is wise for them to go.

TELYEGIN   They have been frightened. The Professor's wife refuses to stay here an hour longer. She keeps saying: "If we're going at all, let's hurry. We shall go to Kharkov and look around, and then we can send for our things." They're taking practically noth-   10
ing with them. It seems, Marina, that fate has decreed that they should not live here.

MARINA   And quite rightly. What a storm they raised! It was disgusting!

TELYEGIN   Yes, to be sure! The scene this morning would make a   15
fine story.

MARINA   I wish I'd never laid eyes on them. [*Pause.*] Once more things will be as they used to be; we shall live like normal human beings again: tea at eight, dinner at one, and supper in the evening; everything in order as decent people and Christians like it.   20
[*Sighing.*] It is a long time since I, poor sinner, have eaten noodles.

TELYEGIN   Yes, we haven't had noodles for a great while. [*Pause.*] Not for ages. As I was passing through the village this morning, Marina, one of the storekeepers called after me: "Hi! you hanger-on!" I felt it bitterly.   25

MARINA   Don't pay any attention to them, my friend; we are all dependent upon God. You, Sonya, Uncle Vanya, and myself . . . none of us sits idle; we all must work hard. All! . . . Where is Sonya?

TELYEGIN   In the garden with the Doctor, looking for Vanya.   30

369

They are afraid he may become violent and attempt to kill himself.

MARINA   Where is his gun?

TELYEGIN [*whispering*]   I hid it in the cellar.

5 MARINA [*amused*]   What goings on!

[VANYA *and* ASTROV *enter.*]

VANYA   Let me alone! [*To* MARINA *and* TELYEGIN.] Go away! Get out and leave me to myself. Only for an hour! I won't have you watching me this way!

TELYEGIN [*going out on tiptoe*]   Why, certainly, Vanya.

10 MARINA [*gathering up her wool and leaving*]   The gander is cackling again; ho! ho! ho!

VANYA   Let me alone!

ASTROV   I would, with the greatest pleasure. I should have gone long ago, but I shan't leave you until you have returned what you
15   took from me.

VANYA   I took nothing from you.

ASTROV   I'm not joking, don't delay me, I really have to go.

VANYA   I took nothing of yours.

[*Both sit down.*]

ASTROV   Oh, you didn't? All right, I shall have to stay a while
20   longer, and if you still don't give it up, I will have to resort to force. We shall tie your hands and search you. I warn you, I mean what I say.

VANYA   Do as you please. [*Pause.*] Oh, to think I made such a fool of myself! To shoot twice and miss him both times! I can never
25   forgive myself.

ASTROV   When you first felt the impulse to shoot someone, you would have done better to put a bullet through your own head.

VANYA [*shrugging his shoulders*]   It's strange! I tried to murder a man, and they are not going to arrest me or bring me to trial.
30   That means they think I'm insane. [*Laughing bitterly.*] I! I am insane, and the ones who hide their futility, their stupidity, their harsh cruelty behind a professor's mask, they . . . they are sane! Those who marry old men and then betray them before the eyes of everyone, they are sane! Yes, I saw you kiss her; I saw you in
35   each other's arms!

ASTROV   Yes, I did kiss her; which is more than you can say.

VANYA [*watching the door*]   No, it is the earth that is insane, because it allows us to exist.

ASTROV   That's nonsense.

VANYA   Well? I am a lunatic, aren't I, and therefore irresponsible? Haven't I the right to talk nonsense?   5

ASTROV   This is a farce! You are not insane; you are simply a ridiculous fool. I used to think every fool was out of his senses—abnormal; but now I see that lack of sense is the normal human condition, and you are perfectly normal.   10

VANYA [*covering his face with his hands*]   Oh! If you knew how ashamed I am! There is no pain on earth greater than the bitter sense of shame. [*Agonized.*] I can't endure it! [*Leaning against the table.*] What can I do? What can I do?

ASTROV   Nothing.   15

VANYA   Tell me something! Oh, my God! I am forty-seven. I may live to be sixty; I still have thirteen years ahead of me . . . an eternity! How can I endure life for thirteen years? What shall I do? How can I fill them? Oh, don't you see? [*Pressing* ASTROV's *hand convulsively*.] Don't you see, if I could only live the rest of   20 my life in some new manner! If I could only wake up some still sunny morning and feel that my life had begun all over; that the past was forgotten and had vanished like smoke. [*Weeping.*] Oh, to begin life anew! To start over! Tell me, tell me, how to begin!

ASTROV [*crossly*]   Nonsense! What kind of a new life can we, yes   25 both of us, you and I—look forward to? We have no hope.

VANYA   None?

ASTROV   None. I am convinced of that.

VANYA   Please give me something to live for. [*Putting his hand to his heart.*] I feel such a burning pain here.   30

ASTROV [*shouting angrily*]   Stop! [*More moderately.*] It may be that our posterity, despising us for our blind and stupid lives, will find some road to happiness; but we—you and I—have but one hope, the hope that perhaps, pleasant dreams will haunt us as we rest in our graves. [*Sighing.*] Yes, my friend, in this entire community   35 there were only two decent and intelligent men, you and I. Ten years or so of this life of ours, this wretched life of the commonplace and the trivial, have sucked us under and poisoned us with their destructive vapors, and we have become as contemptible, as petty, and as despicable as the others. [*Resolutely.*] But don't try   40 to put me off! Will you give me what you took from me?

VANYA   I took nothing from you.

ASTROV   You took a bottle of morphine out of my medicine case. [*Pause.*] Listen! If you are positively determined to kill yourself, go into the woods and shoot yourself there. But give me back the morphine, or there will be a great deal of talk and suspicion; people will think I gave it to you. It will be bad enough having to perform your post-mortem. Do you think I shall find it interesting?

[SONYA *enters.*]

VANYA   Leave me alone.

ASTROV [*to* SONYA]   Sonya, your uncle has stolen a bottle of morphine from my medicine case and won't return it to me. Tell him his behavior is—well, unwise. I can't waste any more time, I must be going.

SONYA   Uncle Vanya, did you take the morphine?

[*Pause.*]

ASTROV   Yes, he took it. [*Pause.*] I'm absolutely sure.

SONYA   Give it back! Why do you wish to frighten us? [*Tenderly.*] Give it up, Uncle Vanya! My sorrow is perhaps even greater than yours, but I am not in despair. I endure my grief and shall go on doing so until my life comes to its natural end. You must endure yours, too. [*Pause.*] Give it up! [*Kissing his hands.*] Dear, dear, Uncle Vanya. Give it up! [*Weeping.*] You are so good, I am sure you'll have pity on us and give it back. You must endure your grief with patience, Uncle Vanya; you must endure it.

[VANYA *takes the bottle from the table drawer and gives it to* ASTROV.]

VANYA   There it is! [*To* SONYA.] And now we must get busy at once; we must do something, or else I'll not be able to stand it.

SONYA   Yes, yes, let's work! As soon as we've seen them off, we'll go to work. [*Nervously she straightens out the papers on the table.*] We have neglected everything!

ASTROV [*putting the bottle in the case and closing it*]   Now I can go.

YELENA [*entering*]   Oh, here you are, Vanya. We are leaving soon. Go to Alexander, he wishes to speak to you.

SONYA   Go, Uncle Vanya. [*Taking* VANYA's *arm.*] Come, you and father must make peace; that is absolutely necessary for us.

[SONYA and VANYA *leave.*]

YELENA   I'm leaving. [*Giving* ASTROV *her hand.*] Good-bye.

ASTROV   So soon?

YELENA   The carriage is waiting.

ASTROV   Good-bye.

YELENA   You promised me that today you, too, would go away.   5

ASTROV   I had forgotten. I'll go immediately. [*Pause.*] Were you afraid? [*Taking her by the hand.*] Was it so terrifying?

YELENA   Yes.

ASTROV   Couldn't you stay? Couldn't you? Tomorrow—in the forest arbor—   10

YELENA   No. Everything is settled, and that is why I can look you so squarely in the eyes. Our departure is definite. One thing I must ask of you, however: don't think too harshly of me; I should like you to respect me.

ASTROV   Ah! [*With an impatient gesture.*] Stay, I beg you! Admit   15
there's nothing for you to do in this world. You have no object in life; nothing to occupy your attention. Sooner or later you will give in to your feelings. It is inevitable. But please not in Kharkov or in Kursk, but here, here in the lap of nature. Here, at least, it would be poetic, even beautiful. Here you have forests, Turgenev's   20
half-ruined houses, the autumn roses . . .

YELENA   How absurd you are! I am angry with you and yet I shall always remember you with pleasure. You are an interesting and different kind of man. You and I will never meet again, and so I shall tell you—why conceal it?—that I am in love with you.   25
Come, let's shake hands and part as good friends. Please don't think badly of me.

ASTROV [*pressing her hand*]   Yes, you had better go. [*Thoughtfully.*] You seem sincere and good, and yet there is something strangely restless about your whole personality. The moment you   30
and your husband arrived here, everyone whom you found busy and engaged in active, creative work felt compelled to drop it and give himself up to you and your husband's gout for the entire summer. You and your husband have infected all of us with your idleness. I became infatuated with you and I have done   35
nothing for a whole month, and in the meantime people have been ill and the peasants have been grazing their herds in my newly planted woods . . . so that wherever you and your husband go, you bring destruction everywhere. I am joking, of course, and yet I am strangely convinced that if you had remained here, we   40

should have been overtaken by the most terrible desolation and destruction. I would have perished, and you . . . no good would have come to you either. So go! Our little comedy is over; with a happy ending—Go!

5 YELENA [*snatching a pencil quickly from* ASTROV'S *table*] I shall keep this pencil as a remembrance!

ASTROV How strange it is! We meet, and then all of a sudden it seems that we must part forever. So it is with everything in this world. While we are still alone, before Uncle Vanya comes in
10 with a bouquet—allow me—to kiss you good-bye—May I? [*Kissing her on the cheek.*] There! Wonderful!

YELENA I wish you every happiness. [*Glancing about her.*] For once in my life. . . . [*She kisses him impulsively, and they part quickly.*] I must go.

15 ASTROV Yes, go. Since the carriage is ready, you'd better start at once. [*They stand listening.*] It is finished.

[VANYA, SEREBRYAKOV, MARYA *with her book*, TELYEGIN, *and* SONYA *enter.*]

SEREBRYAKOV [*to* VANYA] Woe be unto him who cannot forgive past offences. I have passed through so much—ah, such experience—in the last few hours that I believe I could write a whole
20 treatise for the benefit of all mankind on the art of living. I accept your apology gladly, and I myself ask your forgiveness. [*He kisses* VANYA *three times.*] Good-bye.

VANYA You will go on receiving your allowance regularly as before. Everything will remain as it was.

[YELENA *embraces* SONYA.]

25 SEREBRYAKOV [*kissing* MARYA'S *hands*] Mother!

MARYA [*kissing him*] Alexander! Have your picture taken again, and send it to me; you know how dearly I love you.

TELYEGIN Good-bye, your excellency. Don't forget us.

SEREBRYAKOV [*kissing* SONYA] Good-bye, good-bye, everyone.
30 [*Shaking hands with* ASTROV.] Many thanks for your pleasant company. I have a deep regard for your opinions, your enthusiasm, and your impulses, but permit an old man to add one last observation—let me give you one piece of advice: do something, my friend! Work! You must work! [*They all bow.*] Good luck to
35 you all.

[*He goes out followed by* MARYA *and* SONYA.]

VANYA [*fervently kissing* YELENA's *hand*]   Good-bye . . . forgive
me. We shall never meet again!

YELENA [*touched*]   Good-bye, my dear Vanya. [*She kisses his head
lightly as he bends over her hand, and then goes out.*]

ASTROV   Tell them to bring my carriage around, too, Waffles.

TELYEGIN   Certainly, my friend. [*He goes out.*]   5

[ASTROV *and* VANYA *alone are left behind.* ASTROV *gathers together
his paints and drawing materials on the table and packs them
away in his bag.*]

ASTROV   Why don't you see them off?

VANYA   Let them go! I—I can't go out there. My heart is so sad-
dened. I must busy myself with something at once. To work! To
work! [*He rummages through his papers on the table.*]

[*Pause. As the horses trot away, the tinkle of bells is heard.*]

ASTROV   They have gone! Somehow I'm sure the professor is glad   10
to go. Nothing will tempt him to return.

MARINA [*entering*]   They have gone. [*She sits down in her arm
chair and resumes her knitting.*]

[SONYA *comes in drying her eyes.*]

SONYA   They have gone. [*Wipes her eyes.*] God be with them. [*To
VANYA.*] And now, Uncle Vanya, let us do something!

VANYA   To work! To work!   15

SONYA   It has been a long, long time since you and I have sat
together at this table. [*Lighting a lamp on the table.*] No ink!
[*Taking the inkstand to the cupboard and filling it from an ink
bottle.*] How sad it is to see them go!

MARYA [*coming in slowly*]   They have gone. [*She sits down and   20
immediately becomes absorbed in her book.*]

[SONYA *sits at the table and looks through an account book.*]

SONYA   First, Uncle Vanya, let us add up the bills. We have
neglected them dreadfully. We received another bill today. Come.
We'll both do them.

VANYA   In account with . . . [*Writing.*] . . . in account with . . .

MARINA [*yawning*]   The sandman is on his way.   25

ASTROV   How silent it is. The pens scratch and the cricket sings;
it is so warm and comfortable. You know, I hate to go.

[*The tinkling of bells is heard.*]

ASTROV   Ah, but my carriage has come. All that remains is to
say good-bye to you, my friends, and to my table here, and then
. . . away! [*He puts the map in the portfolio.*]

MARINA   Why be in such a hurry . . . you can stay a little while
5   longer.

ASTROV   Impossible.

VANYA [*writing*]   And carry forward from the old debt two
seventy-five . . .

[*The* WORKMAN *enters.*]

WORKMAN   Your carriage is waiting, sir.

10   ASTROV   All right. [*He hands the* WORKMAN *his medicine case,
portfolio, and box.*] Be careful, don't crush the portfolio!

WORKMAN   Yes, sir.

SONYA   When shall we see you again?

ASTROV   Probably not before next summer. Certainly not again
15   till winter's over, at any rate. Of course, if anything happens, let
me know, and I'll come at once. [*Shaking hands.*] Thank you for
your hospitality, your kindness . . . for all you've done. [*He goes
to* MARINA *and kisses her head.*] Good-bye, old nurse.

MARINA   Are you going without your tea?

20   ASTROV   I don't care for any, nurse.

MARINA   Won't you have just a little vodka?

ASTROV [*hesitatingly.*]   Yes, I guess I might as well.

[MARINA *goes out.*]

[*After a pause.*] One of my horses has gone lame for some reason.
I noticed it yesterday when Petya was watering him.

25   VANYA   You should have him reshod.

ASTROV   I shall have to stop at the blacksmith's on my way home.
It can't be helped. [*He stands looking up at the map of Africa
on the wall.*] I suppose it is terribly hot in Africa now.

VANYA   Yes, I suppose it is.

[MARINA *comes back carrying a tray with a glass of vodka and a
slice of bread.*]

MARINA   There you are.

[ASTROV *drinks*.]

Your health! [*Bowing deeply*.] Eat your bread with it.

ASTROV   No, I like it this way. And now, good-bye. [*To* MARINA.]
You needn't come out to see me off, nurse. [*He leaves*.]

[SONYA *follows him with a candle to light him to the carriage.*
MARINA *sits in her chair*.]

VANYA [*writing*]   On the second of February, twenty pounds of but-   5
ter; on the sixteenth, twenty pounds of butter again. Buckwheat
flour . . .

[*Pause.   The tinkling of bells is heard*.]

MARINA   He has gone.

[*A pause.*   SONYA *enters and sets the candlestick on the table*.]

SONYA   He has gone.

VANYA [*adding and writing*]   Total, fifteen . . . twenty-five . . .   10

[SONYA *sits down and begins to write*.]

MARINA [*yawning*]   Oh, ho! The Lord have mercy on us.

[TELYEGIN *enters on tiptoe, seats himself near the door, and begins
to tune his guitar*.]

VANYA [*to* SONYA, *caressing her hair*]   My child, I feel so wretched!

SONYA   What can we do? We must go on living. [*Pause*.] Yes, we
shall live, Uncle Vanya. Shall live through the endless procession
of days before us, and through all the long evenings. We shall   15
bear patiently the burdens that fate brings to us. We shall work,
without rest, for others, both now and when we are old. And,
then, when our final hour comes, we shall meet it humbly, and
there beyond the grave, we shall know that we have known suffering and tears . . . that our life was bitter. And God will pity us.   20
Oh, then, dear Uncle, we shall enter into a bright and beautiful
life. We shall rejoice and look back upon our grief here . . . with
tenderness . . . and a smile; [*Pause*.] and we shall have rest. I
have faith, Uncle, fervent, passionate faith. [SONYA *kneels down
in front of her uncle and lays her head in his hands. She speaks*   25
with a weary voice.] We shall have rest.

[TELYEGIN *plays softly on his guitar*.]

We shall have rest. We shall hear the angels sing. We shall see heaven shinging in all its radiant glory. We shall see all the world's evils . . . our every pain, our suffering . . . be engulfed by God's all-pervading mercy that shall enfold the earth. Our life will be peaceful, gentle, and sweet—like a child's caress. Oh, I have faith— [*Wiping away his tears.*] My poor Uncle Vanya, you are crying! [*Through her tears.*] You have never known joy in your life, but wait, Uncle Vanya, wait! You, too, will have rest. [*Embracing him.*] You, too, will rest.

[*The* WATCHMAN'S *rattle is heard from the garden;* TELYEGIN *plays softly;* MARYA *writes on the margin of her pamphlet;* MARINA *is knitting her stocking.*]

We shall rest. . . .

[*The Curtain slowly falls.*]

COMEDY

A friend once told me that when he was under the influence of ether he dreamed he was turning over the pages of a great book, in which he knew he would find, on the last page, the meaning of life. The pages of the book were alternately tragic and comic, and he turned page after page, his excitement growing, not only because he was approaching the answer but because he couldn't know, until he arrived, on which side of the book the final page would be. At last it came: the universe opened up to him in a hundred words: and they were uproariously funny. He came back to consciousness crying with laughter, remembering everything. He opened his lips to speak. It was then that the great and comic answer plunged back out of his reach.

If I had to draw a picture of the person of Comedy it is so I should like to draw it: the tears of laughter running down the face, one hand still lying on the tragic page which so nearly contained the answer, the lips about to frame the great revelation, only to find it had gone as disconcertingly as a chair twitched away when we went to sit down. Comedy is an escape, not from truth but from despair: a narrow escape into faith. It believes in a universal cause for delight, even though knowledge of the cause is always twitched away from under us, which leaves us to rest on our own buoyancy. In tragedy every moment is eternity; in comedy eternity is a moment. In tragedy we suffer pain; in comedy pain is a fool, suffered gladly.

Charles Williams once said to me—indeed it was the last thing he said to me: he died not long after: and it was shouted from the tailboard of a moving bus, over the heads of pedestrians and bicyclists outside the Midland Station, Oxford—"When we're dead we shall have the sensation of having enjoyed life altogether, whatever has happened to us." The distance between us widened, and he leaned out into the space so that his voice should reach me: "Even if we've been murdered, what a pleasure to have been capable of it!"; and, having spoken the words for comedy, away he went like the revelation which almost came out of the ether.

He was not at all saying that everything is for the best in the best of all possible worlds. He was saying—or so it seems to me—that there is an angle of experience where the dark is distilled into light: either here or hereafter, in or out of time: where our tragic fate finds itself with perfect pitch, and goes straight to the key which creation was composed in. And comedy senses and reaches out to this experience. It says, in effect, that, groaning as we may be, we move in the figure of a dance, and, so moving, we trace the outline of the mystery.

Laughter did not come by chance, but how or why it came is beyond comprehension, unless we think of it as a kind of perception. The human animal, beginning to feel his spiritual inches, broke in on to an unfamiliar tension of life, where laughter became inevitable. But how? Could he, in his first unlaughing condition, have contrived a comic view of life and then developed the strange rib-shaking response? Or is it not more likely that when he was able to grasp the tragic nature of time he was of a stature to sense its comic nature also; and, by the experience of tragedy and the intuition of comedy, to make his difficult way? The difference between tragedy and comedy is the difference between experience and intuition. In the experience we strive against every condition of our animal life: against death, against the frustration of ambition, against the instability of human love. In the intuition we trust the arduous eccentricities we're born to, and see the oddness of a creature who has never got acclimatized to being created. Laughter inclines me to know that man is essential spirit; his body, with its functions and accidents and frustrations, is endlessly quaint and remarkable to him; and though comedy accepts our position in time, it barely accepts our posture in space.

The bridge by which we cross from tragedy to comedy and back again is precarious and narrow. We find ourselves in one or the other by the turn of a thought; a turn such as we make when we turn from speaking to listening. I know that when I set about writing a comedy the idea presents itself to me first of all as tragedy. The characters press on to the theme with all their divisions and perplexities heavy about them; they are already entered for the race to doom, and good and evil are an infernal tangle skinning the fingers that try to unravel them. If the characters were not qualified for tragedy there would be no comedy, and to some extent I have to cross the one before I can light on the other. In a century less flayed and quivering we might reach it more directly; but not now, unless every word we write is going to mock us. A bridge has to be crossed, a thought has to be turned. Somehow the characters have to unmortify themselves: to affirm life and assimilate death and preserve in joy. Their hearts must be as determined as the phoenix; what burns must also light and renew: not by a vulnerable optimism but by a hard-won maturity of delight, by the intuition of comedy, an active patience declaring the solvency of good. The Book of Job is the great reservoir of comedy. "But there is a spirit in man . . . Fair weather cometh out of the north . . . The blessing of him that was ready to perish came upon me: And I caused the widow's heart to sing for joy."

I have come, you may think, to the verge of saying that comedy is greater than tragedy. On the verge I stand and go no further. Tragedy's experience hammers against the mystery to make a breach which would admit the whole triumphant answer. Intuition has no such potential. But there are times in the state of man when comedy has a special worth, and the present is one of them: a time when the loudest faith has been faith in a trampling materialism, when literature has been thought unrealistic which did not mark and remark our poverty and doom. Joy (of a kind) has been all on the devil's side, and one of the necessities of our time is to redeem it. If not, we are in poor sort to meet the circumstances, the circumstances being the contention of death with life, which is to say evil with good, which is to say desolation with delight. Laughter may seem to be only like an exhalation of air, but out of that air we came; in the beginning we inhaled it; it is a truth, not a fantasy, a truth voluble of good which comedy stoutly maintains.

OSCAR WILDE

The Importance of Being Earnest

~~~~~~

WILLIAM L. SHARP

A Play: Scenario or Poem

THE CHARACTERS IN *THE IMPORTANCE OF BEING EARNEST*

JOHN WORTHING, J.P.

ALGERNON MONCRIEFF

REV. CANON CHASUBLE, D.D.

MERRIMAN, butler

LANE, manservant

LADY BRACKNELL

HON. GWENDOLEN FAIRFAX

CECILY CARDEW

MISS PRISM, governess

THE IMPORTANCE OF
BEING EARNEST

ACT ONE

Morning-room in Algernon's flat in Half-Moon Street. The room is luxuriously and artistically furnished. The sound of a piano is heard in the adjoining room.

LANE *is arranging afternoon tea on the table, and after the music has ceased,* ALGERNON *enters.*

ALGERNON   Did you hear what I was playing, Lane?

LANE   I didn't think it polite to listen, sir.

ALGERNON   I'm sorry for that, for your sake. I don't play accurately—any one can play accurately—but I play with wonderful expression. As far as the piano is concerned, sentiment is my 5 forte. I keep science for Life.

LANE   Yes, sir.

ALGERNON   And, speaking of the science of Life, have you got the cucumber sandwiches cut for Lady Bracknell?

LANE   Yes, sir. [*Hands them on a salver.*] 10

ALGERNON [*Inspects them, takes two, and sits down on the sofa.*] Oh! . . . by the way, Lane, I see from your book that on Thursday night, when Lord Shoreman and Mr. Worthing were dining with me, eight bottles of champagne are entered as having been consumed. 15

LANE   Yes, sir; eight bottles and a pint.

ALGERNON   Why is it that at a bachelor's establishment the servants invariably drink the champagne? I ask merely for information.

LANE   I attribute it to the superior quality of the wine, sir. I have 20 often observed that in married households the champagne is rarely of a first-rate brand.

ALGERNON   Good heavens! Is marriage so demoralizing as that?

LANE   I believe it *is* a very pleasant state, sir. I have had very little experience of it myself up to the present. I have only been mar- 25 ried once. That was in consequence of a misunderstanding between myself and a young person.

ALGERNON [*languidly*]   I don't know that I am much interested in your family life, Lane.

LANE   No, sir; it is not a very interesting subject. I never think of 30 it myself.

ALGERNON   Very natural, I am sure. That will do, Lane, thank you.

LANE   Thank you, sir.

[LANE *goes out.*]

ALGERNON   Lane's views on marriage seem somewhat lax. Really,
5   if the lower orders don't set us a good example, what on earth is
the use of them? They seem, as a class, to have absolutely no
sense of moral responsibility.

[*Enter* LANE]

LANE   Mr. Ernest Worthing.

[*Enter* JACK. LANE *goes out.*]

ALGERNON   How are you, my dear Ernest? What brings you up to
10   town?

JACK   Oh, pleasure, pleasure! What else should bring one anywhere? Eating as usual, I see, Algy!

ALGERNON [*stiffly*]   I believe it is customary in good society to take
some slight refreshment at five o'clock. Where have you been
15   since last Thursday?

JACK [*sitting down on the sofa*]   In the country.

ALGERNON   What on earth do you do there?

JACK [*pulling off his gloves*]   When one is in town one amuses oneself. When one is in the country one amuses other people. It is
20   excessively boring.

ALGERNON   And who are the people you amuse?

JACK [*airly*]   Oh, neighbours, neighbours.

ALGERNON   Got nice neighbours in your part of Shropshire?

JACK   Perfectly horrid! Never speak to one of them.

25   ALGERNON   How immensely you must amuse them! [*Goes over and
takes sandwich.*] By the way, Shropshire is your county, is it not?

JACK   Eh? Shropshire? Yes, of course. Hallo! Why all these cups?
Why cucumber sandwiches? Why such reckless extravagance in
one so young? Who is coming to tea?

30   ALGERNON   Oh! merely Aunt Augusta and Gwendolen.

JACK   How perfectly delightful!

ALGERNON   Yes, that is all very well; but I am afraid Aunt
Augusta won't quite approve of your being here.

JACK   May I ask why?

ALGERNON   My dear fellow, the way you flirt with Gwendolen is perfectly disgraceful. It is almost as bad as the way Gwendolen flirts with you.

JACK   I am in love with Gwendolen. I have come up to town expressly to propose to her.

ALGERNON   I thought you had come up for pleasure? . . . I call that business.

JACK   How utterly unromantic you are!

ALGERNON   I really don't see anything romantic in proposing. It is very romantic to be in love. But there is nothing romantic about a definite proposal. Why, one may be accepted. One usually is, I believe. Then the excitement is all over. The very essence of romance is uncertainty. If ever I get married, I'll certainly try to forget the fact.

JACK   I have no doubt about that, dear Algy. The Divorce Court was specially invented for people whose memories are so curiously constituted.

ALGERNON   Oh! there is no use speculating on that subject. Divorces are made in Heaven—[JACK *puts out his hand to take a sandwich.* ALGERNON *at once interferes.*] Please don't touch the cucumber sandwiches. They are ordered specially for Aunt Augusta. [*Takes one and eats it.*]

JACK   Well, you have been eating them all the time.

ALGERNON   That is quite a different matter. She is my aunt. [*Takes plate from below.*] Have some bread and butter. The bread and butter is for Gwendolen. Gwendolen is devoted to bread and butter.

JACK   [*advancing to table and helping himself*]   And very good bread and butter it is too.

ALGERNON   Well, my dear fellow, you need not eat as if you were going to eat it all. You behave as if you were married to her already. You are not married to her already, and I don't think you ever will be.

JACK   Why on earth do you say that?

ALGERNON   Well, in the first place, girls never marry the men they flirt with. Girls don't think it right.

JACK   Oh, that is nonsense!

ALGERNON   It isn't. It is a great truth. It accounts for the extraordinary number of bachelors that one sees all over the place. In the second place, I don't give my consent.

JACK Your consent!

ALGERNON My dear fellow, Gwendolen is my first cousin. And before I allow you to marry her, you will have to clear up the whole question of Cecily. [*Rings bell.*]

5 JACK Cecily! What on earth do you mean? What do you mean, Algy, by Cecily? I don't know any one of the name of Cecily.

[*Enter* LANE.]

ALGERNON Bring me that cigarette case Mr. Worthing left in the smoking-room the last time he dined here.

LANE Yes, sir.

[LANE *goes out.*]

10 JACK Do you mean to say you have had my cigarette case all this time? I wish to goodness you had let me know. I have been writing frantic letters to Scotland Yard about it. I was very nearly offering a large reward.

ALGERNON Well, I wish you would offer one. I happen to be
15 more than usually hard up.

JACK There is no good offering a large reward now that the thing is found.

[*Enter* LANE *with the cigarette case on a salver.* ALGERNON *takes it at once.* LANE *goes out.*]

ALGERNON I think that is rather mean of you, Ernest, I must say. [*Opens case and examines it.*] However, it makes no matter,
20 for, now that I look at the inscription inside, I find that the thing isn't yours after all.

JACK Of course it's mine. [*Moving to him.*] You have seen me with it a hundred times, and you have no right whatsoever to read what is written inside. It is a very ungentlemanly thing to
25 read a private cigarette case.

ALGERNON Oh! it is absurd to have a hard and fast rule about what one should read and what one shouldn't. More than half of modern culture depends on what one shouldn't read.

JACK I am quite aware of the fact, and I don't propose to dis-
30 cuss modern culture. It isn't the sort of thing one should talk of in private. I simply want my cigarette case back.

ALGERNON Yes; but this isn't your cigarette case. This cigarette case is a present from someone of the name of Cecily, and you said you didn't know anyone of that name.

JACK Well, if you want to know, Cecily happens to be my aunt.

ALGERNON Your aunt!

JACK Yes. Charming old lady she is, too. Lives at Tunbridge Wells. Just give it back to me, Algy.

ALGERNON [*retreating to back of sofa*] But why does she call 5
herself little Cecily if she is your aunt and lives at Tunbridge Wells. [*Reading.*] "From little Cecily with her fondest love."

JACK [*moving to sofa and kneeling upon it*] My dear fellow, what on earth is there in that? Some aunts are tall, some aunts are not tall. That is a matter that surely an aunt may be allowed 10
to decide for herself. You seem to think that every aunt should be exactly like your aunt! That is absurd. For Heaven's sake give me back my cigarette case. [*Follows* ALGERNON *round the room.*]

ALGERNON Yes. But why does your aunt call you her uncle? 15
"From little Cecily, with her fondest love to her dear Uncle Jack." There is no objection, I admit, to an aunt being a small aunt, but why an aunt, no matter what her size may be, should call her own nephew her uncle, I can't quite make out. Besides, your name isn't Jack at all; it is Ernest. 20

JACK It isn't Ernest; it's Jack.

ALGERNON You have always told me it was Ernest. I have introduced you to every one as Ernest. You answer to the name of Ernest. You look as if your name was Ernest. You are the most earnest-looking person I ever saw in my life. It is perfectly 25
absurd your saying that your name isn't Ernest. It's on your cards. Here is one of them [*taking it from case*]. "Mr. Ernest Worthing, B.4, The Albany." I'll keep this as a proof that your name is Ernest if ever you attempt to deny it to me, or to Gwendolen, or to any one else. [*Puts the card in his pocket.*] 30

JACK Well, my name is Ernest in town and Jack in the country, and the cigarette case was given to me in the country.

ALGERNON Yes, but that does not account for the fact that your small Aunt Cecily, who lives at Tunbridge Wells, calls you her dear uncle. Come, old boy, you had much better have the thing 35
out at once.

JACK My dear Algy, you talk exactly as if you were a dentist. It is very vulgar to talk like a dentist when one isn't a dentist. It produces a false impression.

ALGERNON Well, that is exactly what dentists always do. Now, 40
go on! Tell me the whole thing. I may mention that I have al-

ways suspected you of being a confirmed and secret Bunburyist, and I am quite sure of it now.

JACK Bunburyist? What on earth do you mean by a Bunburyist?

ALGERNON I'll reveal to you the meaning of that incomparable expression as soon as you are kind enough to inform me why you are Ernest in town and Jack in the country.

JACK Well, produce my cigarette case first.

ALGERNON Here it is. [*Hands cigarette case.*] Now produce your explanation, and pray make it improbable. [*Sits on sofa.*]

JACK My dear fellow, there is nothing improbable about my explanation at all. In fact it's perfectly ordinary. Old Mr. Thomas Cardew, who adopted me when I was a little boy, made me in his will guardian to his granddaughter, Miss Cecily Cardew. Cecily, who addresses me as her uncle from motives of respect that you could not possibly appreciate, lives at my place in the country under the charge of her admirable governess, Miss Prism.

ALGERNON Where is that place in the country, by the way?

JACK That is nothing to you, dear boy. You are not going to be invited. . . . I may tell you candidly that the place is not in Shropshire.

ALGERNON I suspected that, my dear fellow! I have Bunburyed all over Shropshire on two separate occasions. Now, go on. Why are you Ernest in town and Jack in the country?

JACK My dear Algy, I don't know whether you will be able to understand my real motives. You are hardly serious enough. When one is placed in the position of guardian, one has to adopt a very high moral tone on all subjects. It's one's duty to do so. And as a high moral tone can hardly be said to conduce very much to either one's health or one's happiness, in order to get up to town I have always pretended to have a younger brother of the name of Ernest, who lives in the Albany, and gets into the most dreadful scrapes. That, my dear Algy, is the whole truth pure and simple.

ALGERNON The truth is rarely pure and never simple. Modern life would be very tedious if it were either, and modern literature a complete impossibility!

JACK That wouldn't be at all a bad thing.

ALGERNON Literary criticism is not your forte, my dear fellow. Don't try it. You should leave that to people who haven't been at a University. They do it so well in the daily papers. What you really are is a Bunburyist. I was quite right in saying you were a Bunburyist. You are one of the most advanced Bunburyists I know.

JACK What on earth do you mean?

ALGERNON You have invented a very useful younger brother called Ernest, in order that you may be able to come up to town as often as you like. I have invented an invaluable permanent invalid called Bunbury, in order that I may be able to go down into the country whenever I choose. Bunbury is perfectly invaluable. If it wasn't for Bunbury's extraordinary bad health, for instance, I wouldn't be able to dine with you at Willis's tonight, for I have been really engaged to Aunt Augusta for more than a week.

JACK I haven't asked you to dine with me anywhere tonight.

ALGERNON I know. You are absurdly careless about sending out invitations. It is very foolish of you. Nothing annoys people so much as not receiving invitations.

JACK You had much better dine with your Aunt Augusta.

ALGERNON I haven't the smallest intention of doing anything of the kind. To begin with, I dined there on Monday, and once a week is quite enough to dine with one's own relations. In the second place, whenever I do dine there I am always treated as a member of the family, and sent down with either no woman at all, or two. In the third place, I know perfectly well whom she will place me next to, tonight. She will place me next to Mary Farquhar, who always flirts with her own husband across the dinner table. That is not very pleasant. Indeed, it is not even decent . . . and that sort of thing is enormously on the increase. The amount of women in London who flirt with their own husbands is perfectly scandalous. It looks so bad. It is simply washing one's clean linen in public. Besides, now that I know you to be a confirmed Bunburyist I naturally want to talk to you about Bunburying. I want to tell you the rules.

JACK I'm not a Bunburyist at all. If Gwendolen accepts me, I am going to kill my brother, indeed I think I'll kill him in any case. Cecily is a little too much interested in him. It is rather a bore. So I am going to get rid of Ernest. And I strongly advise you to do the same with Mr. . . . with your invalid friend who has the absurd name.

ALGERNON Nothing will induce me to part with Bunbury, and if you ever get married, which seems to me extremely problematic, you will be very glad to know Bunbury. A man who marries without knowing Bunbury has a very tedious time of it.

JACK That is nonsense. If I marry a charming girl like Gwendo-

len, and she is the only girl I ever saw in my life that I would
marry, I certainly won't want to know Bunbury.

ALGERNON Then your wife will. You don't seem to realize, that
in married life three is company and two is none.

5   JACK [*sententiously*] That, my dear young friend, is the theory
that the corrupt French Drama has been propounding for the
last fifty years.

ALGERNON Yes! and that the happy English home has proved
in half the time.

10 JACK For heaven's sake, don't try to be cynical. It's perfectly
easy to be cynical.

ALGERNON My dear fellow, it isn't easy to be anything nowadays. There's such a lot of beastly competition about. [*The
sound of an electric bell is heard.*] Ah! that must be Aunt
15 Augusta. Only relatives, or creditors, ever ring in that Wag-
nerian manner. Now, if I get her out of the way for ten minutes, so that you can have an opportunity for proposing to
Gwendolen, may I dine with you tonight at Willis's?

JACK I suppose so, if you want to.

20 ALGERNON Yes, but you must be serious about it. I hate people
who are not serious about meals. It is so shallow of them.

[*Enter* LANE.]

LANE Lady Bracknell and Miss Fairfax.

[ALGERNON *goes forward to meet them. Enter* LADY BRACKNELL
and GWENDOLEN.]

LADY BRACKNELL Good afternoon, dear Algernon, I hope you
are behaving very well.

25 ALGERNON I'm feeling very well, Aunt Augusta.

LADY BRACKNELL That's not quite the same thing. In fact the
two things rarely go together. [*Sees* JACK *and bows to him with
icy coldness.*]

ALGERNON [*to* GWENDOLEN] Dear me, you are smart!

30 GWENDOLEN I am always smart! Am I not, Mr. Worthing?

JACK You're quite perfect, Miss Fairfax.

GWENDOLEN Oh! I hope I am not that. It would leave no room
for developments, and I intend to develop in many directions.
[GWENDOLEN *and* JACK *sit down together in the corner.*]

35 LADY BRACKNELL I'm sorry if we are a little late, Algernon, but
I was obliged to call on dear Lady Harbury. I hadn't been there

since her poor husband's death. I never saw a woman so altered; she looks quite twenty years younger. And now I'll have a cup of tea and one of those nice cucumber sandwiches you promised me.

ALGERNON   Certainly, Aunt Augusta. [*Goes over to tea-table.*]   5

LADY BRACKNELL   Won't you come and sit here, Gwendolen?

GWENDOLEN   Thanks, mamma, I'm quite comfortable where I am.

ALGERNON [*picking up empty plate in horror*]   Good heavens! Lane! Why are there no cucumber sandwiches? I ordered them   10 specially.

LANE [*gravely*]   There were no cucumbers in the market this morning, sir. I went down twice.

ALGERNON   No cucumbers!

LANE   No, sir. Not even for ready money.   15

ALGERNON   That will do, Lane, thank you.

LANE   Thank you, sir. [*Goes out.*]

ALGERNON   I am greatly distressed, Aunt Augusta, about there being no cucumbers, not even for ready money.

LADY BRACKNELL   It really makes no matter, Algernon. I had   20 some crumpets with Lady Harbury, who seems to me to be living entirely for pleasure now.

ALGERNON   I hear her hair has turned quite gold from grief.

LADY BRACKNELL   It certainly has changed its colour. From what cause I, of course, cannot say. [ALGERNON *crosses and hands*   25 *tea.*] Thank you. I've quite a treat for you tonight, Algernon. I am going to send you down with Mary Farquhar. She is such a nice woman, and so attentive to her husband. It's delightful to watch them.

ALGERNON   I am afraid, Aunt Augusta, I shall have to give up   30 the pleasure of dining with you tonight after all.

LADY BRACKNELL [*frowning*]   I hope not, Algernon. It would put my table completely out. Your uncle would have to dine upstairs. Fortunately he is accustomed to that.

ALGERNON   It is a great bore, and, I need hardly say, a terrible   35 disappointment to me, but the fact is I have just had a telegram to say that my poor friend Bunbury is very ill again. [*Exchanges glances with* JACK.] They seem to think I should be with him.

LADY BRACKNELL   It is very strange. This Mr. Bunbury seems to suffer from curiously bad health.   40

ALGERNON   Yes; poor Bunbury is a dreadful invalid.

LADY BRACKNELL   Well, I must say, Algernon, that I think it is
high time that Mr. Bunbury made up his mind whether he was
going to live or to die. This shilly-shallying with the question is
absurd. Nor do I in any way approve of the modern sympathy
with invalids. I consider it morbid. Illness of any kind is hardly
a thing to be encouraged in others. Health is the primary duty
of life. I am always telling that to your poor uncle, but he never
seems to take much notice . . . as far as any improvement in his
ailments goes. I should be much obliged if you would ask Mr.
Bunbury, from me, to be kind enough not to have a relapse on
Saturday, for I rely on you to arrange my music for me. It is
my last reception, and one wants something that will encourage
conversation, particularly at the end of the season when every
one has practically said whatever they had to say, which, in
most cases, was probably not much.

ALGERNON   I'll speak to Bunbury, Aunt Augusta, if he is still
conscious, and I think I can promise you he'll be all right by
Saturday. Of couse the music is a great difficulty. You see, if
one plays good music, people don't listen, and if one plays bad
music, people don't talk. But I'll run over the programme I've
drawn out, if you will kindly come into the next room for a
moment.

LADY BRACKNELL   Thank you, Algernon. It is very thoughtful of
you. [*Rising, and following* ALGERNON.] I'm sure the programme
will be delightful, after a few expurgations. French songs I cannot possibly allow. People always seem to think that they are
improper, and either look shocked, which is vulgar, or laugh,
which is worse. But German sounds a thoroughly respectable
language, and, indeed I believe is so. Gwendolen, you will accompany me.

GWENDOLEN   Certainly, mamma.

[LADY BRACKNELL *and* ALGERNON *go into the music-room;* GWEN-
DOLEN *remains behind.*]

JACK   Charming day it has been, Miss Fairfax.

GWENDOLEN   Pray don't talk to me about the weather, Mr.
Worthing. Whenever people talk to me about the weather, I
always feel quite certain that they mean something else. And
that makes me so nervous.

JACK   I do mean something else.

GWENDOLEN   I thought so. In fact, I am never wrong.

JACK   And I would like to be allowed to take advantage of Lady
Bracknell's temporary absence. . . .

GWENDOLEN   I would certainly advise you to do so. Mamma has a way of coming back suddenly into a room that I have often had to speak to her about.

JACK [*nervously*] Miss Fairfax, ever since I met you I have admired you more than any girl . . . I have ever met since . . . I met you. 5

GWENDOLEN Yes, I am quite aware of the fact. And I often wish that in public, at any rate, you had been more demonstrative. For me you have always had an irresistible fascination. Even before I met you I was far from indifferent to you. [JACK *looks at her in amazement.*] We live, as I hope you know, Mr. Worthing, in an age of ideals. The fact is constantly mentioned in the more expensive monthly magazines, and has reached the provincial pulpits, I am told; and my ideal has always been to love some one of the name of Ernest. There is something in that name that inspires absolute confidence. The moment Algernon first mentioned to me that he had a friend called Ernest, I knew I was destined to love you. 10 15

JACK You really love me, Gwendolen?

GWENDOLEN Passionately!

JACK Darling! You don't know how happy you've made me. 20

GWENDOLEN My own Ernest!

JACK But you don't really mean to say that you couldn't love me if my name wasn't Ernest?

GWENDOLEN But your name is Ernest.

JACK Yes, I know it is. But supposing it was something else? Do 25 you mean to say you couldn't love me then?

GWENDOLEN [*glibly*] Ah! that is clearly a metaphysical speculation, and like most metaphysical speculations has very little reference at all to the actual facts of real life, as we know them.

JACK Personally, darling, to speak quite candidly, I don't much 30 care about the name of Ernest. . . . I don't think the name suits me at all.

GWENDOLEN It suits you perfectly. It is a divine name. It has a music of its own. It produces vibrations.

JACK Well, really, Gwendolen, I must say that I think there are 35 lots of other much nicer names. I think Jack, for instance, a charming name.

GWENDOLEN Jack? . . . No, there is very little music in the name Jack, if any at all, indeed. It does not thrill. It produces absolutely no vibrations. . . . I have known several Jacks, and they all, 40 without exception, were more than usually plain. Besides, Jack is a notorious domesticity for John! And I pity any woman who is married to a man called John. She would probably never be allowed to know the entrancing pleasure of a single moment's solitude. The only really safe name is Ernest.

JACK Gwendolen, I must get christened at once—I mean we must get married at once. There is no time to be lost.

GWENDOLEN Married, Mr. Worthing?

JACK [*astounded*] Well . . . surely. You know that I love you, and you led me to believe, Miss Fairfax, that you were not absolutely indifferent to me.

GWENDOLEN I adore you. But you haven't proposed to me yet. Nothing has been said at all about marriage. The subject has not even been touched on.

JACK Well . . . may I propose to you now?

GWENDOLEN I think it would be an admirable opportunity. And to spare you any possible disappointment, Mr. Worthing, I think it only fair to tell you quite frankly beforehand that I am fully determined to accept you.

JACK Gwendolen!

GWENDOLEN Yes, Mr. Worthing, what have you got to say to me?

JACK You know what I have got to say to you.

GWENDOLEN Yes, but you don't say it.

JACK Gwendolen, will you marry me? [*Goes on his knees.*]

GWENDOLEN Of course I will, darling. How long you have been about it! I am afraid you have had very little experience in how to propose.

JACK My own one, I have never loved any one in the world but you.

GWENDOLEN Yes, but men often propose for practice. I know my brother Gerald does. All my girl-friends tell me so. What wonderfully blue eyes you have, Ernest! They are quite, quite blue. I hope you will always look at me just like that, especially when there are other people present.

[*Enter* LADY BRACKNELL.]

LADY BRACKNELL Mr. Worthing! Rise sir, from this semi-recumbent posture. It is most indecorous.

GWENDOLEN Mamma! [*He tries to rise; she restrains him.*] I must beg you to retire. This is no place for you. Besides, Mr. Worthing has not quite finished yet.

LADY BRACKNELL Finished what, may I ask?

GWENDOLEN I am engaged to Mr. Worthing, mamma. [*They rise together.*]

LADY BRACKNELL Pardon me, you are not engaged to any one. When you do become engaged to some one, I, or your father, should his health permit him, will inform you of the fact. An engagement should come on a young girl as a surprise, pleasant or unpleasant, as the case may be. It is hardly a matter that she could be allowed to arrange for herself. . . . And now I have a few questions to put to you, Mr. Worthing. While I am making these inquiries, you, Gwendolen, will wait for me below in the carriage.

GWENDOLEN [*reproachfully*] Mamma!

LADY BRACKNELL In the carriage, Gwendolen! [GWENDOLEN *goes to the door. She and* JACK *blow kisses to each other behind* LADY BRACKNELL'S *back.* LADY BRACKNELL *looks vaguely about as if she could not understand what the noise was. Finally turns round.*] Gwendolen, the carriage!

GWENDOLEN Yes, mamma. [*Goes out, looking back at* JACK.]

LADY BRACKNELL [*sitting down*] You can take a seat, Mr. Worthing.

[*Looks in her pocket for notebook and pencil.*]

JACK Thank you, Lady Bracknell, I prefer standing.

LADY BRACKNELL [*pencil and notebook in hand*] I feel bound to tell you that you are not down on my list of eligible young men, although I have the same list as the dear Duchess of Bolton has. We work together, in fact. However, I am quite ready to enter your name, should your answers be what a really affectionate mother requires. Do you smoke?

JACK Well, yes, I must admit I smoke.

LADY BRACKNELL I am glad to hear it. A man should always have an occupation of some kind. There are far too many idle men in London as it is. How old are you?

JACK Twenty-nine.

LADY BRACKNELL A very good age to be married at. I have always been of opinion that a man who desires to get married should know either everything or nothing. Which do you know?

JACK [*after some hesitation*] I know nothing, Lady Bracknell.

LADY BRACKNELL I am pleased to hear it. I do not approve of anything that tampers with natural ignorance. Ignorance is like a delicate exotic fruit; touch it and the bloom is gone. The whole

theory of modern education is radically unsound. Fortunately in England, at any rate, education produces no effect whatsoever. If it did, it would prove a serious danger to the upper classes, and probably lead to acts of violence in Grosvenor Square.
5   What is your income?

JACK   Between seven and eight thousand a year.

LADY BRACKNELL [*makes a note in her book*]   In land, or in investments?

JACK   In investments, chiefly.

10   LADY BRACKNELL   That is satisfactory. What between the duties expected of one during one's lifetime, and the duties exacted from one after one's death, land has ceased to be either a profit or a pleasure. It gives one position, and prevents one from keeping it up. That's all that can be said about land.

15   JACK   I have a country house with some land, of course, attached to it, about fifteen hundred acres, I believe; but I don't depend on that for my real income. In fact, as far as I can make out, the poachers are the only people who make anything out of it.

LADY BRACKNELL   A country house! How many bedrooms? Well,
20   that point can be cleared up afterwards. You have a town house, I hope? A girl with a simple, unspoiled nature, like Gwendolen, could hardly be expected to reside in the country.

JACK   Well, I own a house in Belgrave Square, but it is let by the year to Lady Bloxham. Of course, I can get it back whenever
25   I like, at six months' notice.

LADY BRACKNELL   Lady Bloxham? I don't know her.

JACK   Oh, she goes about very little. She is a lady considerably advanced in years.

LADY BRACKNELL   Ah, nowadays that is no guarantee of respecta-
30   bility of character. What number in Belgrave Square?

JACK   149.

LADY BRACKNELL [*shaking her head*]   The unfashionable side. I thought there was something. However, that could easily be altered.

35   JACK   Do you mean the fashion, or the side?

LADY BRACKNELL [*sternly*]   Both, if necessary, I presume. What are your politics?

JACK   Well, I am afraid I really have none. I am a Liberal Unionist.

40   LADY BRACKNELL   Oh, they count as Tories. They dine with us.

Or come in the evening, at any rate. Now to minor matters. Are
your parents living?

JACK I have lost both my parents.

LADY BRACKNELL To lose one parent, Mr. Worthing, may be
regarded as a misfortune; to lose both looks like carelessness. 5
Who was your father? He was evidently a man of some wealth.
Was he born in what the Radical papers call the purple of commerce, or did he rise from the ranks of the aristocracy?

JACK I am afraid I really don't know. The fact is, Lady Bracknell, I said I had lost my parents. It would be nearer the truth 10
to say that my parents seem to have lost me. . . . I don't actually
know who I am by birth. I was . . . well, I was found.

LADY BRACKNELL Found!

JACK The late Mr. Thomas Cardew, an old gentleman of a very
charitable and kindly disposition, found me, and gave me the 15
name of Worthing, because he happened to have a first-class
ticket for Worthing in his pocket at the time. Worthing is a
place in Sussex. It is a seaside resort.

LADY BRACKNELL Where did the charitable gentleman who had
a first-class ticket for this seaside resort find you? 20

JACK [gravely] In a handbag.

LADY BRACKNELL A handbag?

JACK [very seriously] Yes, Lady Bracknell. I was in a handbag—
a somewhat large, black leather handbag, with handles to it—an
ordinary handbag in fact. 25

LADY BRACKNELL In what locality did this Mr. James, or Thomas,
Cardew come across this ordinary handbag?

JACK In the cloakroom at Victoria Station. It was given to him
in mistake for his own.

LADY BRACKNELL The cloakroom at Victoria Station? 30

JACK Yes. The Brighton line.

LADY BRACKNELL The line is immaterial. Mr. Worthing, I confess I feel somewhat bewildered by what you have just told me.
To be born, or at any rate bred, in a handbag, whether it had
handles or not, seems to me to display a contempt for the ordi- 35
nary decencies of family life that reminds one of the worst excesses of the French Revolution. And I presume you know
what that unfortunate movement led to? As for the particular
locality in which the handbag was found, a cloakroom at a railway station might serve to conceal a social indiscretion—has 40
probably, indeed, been used for that purpose before now—but

it could hardly be regarded as an assured basis for a recognized position in good society.

JACK   May I ask you then what you would advise me to do? I need hardly say I would do anything in the world to ensure Gwendolen's happiness.

LADY BRACKNELL   I would strongly advise you, Mr. Worthing, to try and acquire some relations as soon as possible, and to make a definite effort to produce at any rate one parent, of either sex, before the season is quite over.

JACK   Well, I don't see how I could possibly manage to do that. I can produce the handbag at any moment. It is in my dressing-room at home. I really think that should satisfy you, Lady Bracknell.

LADY BRACKNELL   Me, sir! What has it to do with me? You can hardly imagine that I and Lord Bracknell would dream of allowing our only daughter—a girl brought up with the utmost care—to marry into a cloakroom, and form an alliance with a parcel. Good morning, Mr. Worthing!

[LADY BRACKNELL *sweeps out in majestic indignation.*]

JACK   Good morning! [ALGERNON, *from the other room, strikes up the Wedding March.* JACK *looks perfectly furious, and goes to the door.*] For goodness' sake don't play that ghastly tune, Algy! How idiotic you are!

[*The music stops and* ALGERNON *enters cheerily.*]

ALGERNON   Didn't it go off all right, old boy? You don't mean to say Gwendolen refused you? I know it is a way she has. She is always refusing people. I think it is most ill-natured of her.

JACK   Oh, Gwendolen is as right as a trivet. As far as she is concerned, we are engaged. Her mother is perfectly unbearable. Never met such a Gorgon. . . . I don't really know what a Gorgon is like, but I am quite sure that Lady Bracknell is one. In any case, she is a monster, without being a myth, which is rather unfair. . . . I beg your pardon, Algy, I suppose I shouldn't talk about your own aunt in that way before you.

ALGERNON   My dear boy, I love hearing my relations abused. It is the only thing that makes me put up with them at all. Relations are simply a tedious pack of people, who haven't got the remotest knowledge of how to live, nor the smallest instinct about when to die.

JACK   Oh, that is nonsense!

ALGERNON   It isn't!

JACK   Well, I won't argue about the matter. You always want to argue about things.

ALGERNON   That is exactly what things were originally made for.

JACK   Upon my word, if I thought that, I'd shoot myself. . . .   5
[*A pause.*] You don't think there is any chance of Gwendolen becoming like her mother in about a hundred and fifty years, do you, Algy?

ALGERNON   All women become like their mothers. That is their tragedy. No man does. That's his.   10

JACK   Is that clever?

ALGERNON   It is perfectly phrased! and quite as true as any observation in civilized life should be.

JACK   I am sick to death of cleverness. Everybody is clever nowadays. You can't go anywhere without meeting clever people.   15
The thing has become an absolute public nuisance. I wish to goodness we had a few fools left.

ALGERNON   We have.

JACK   I should extremely like to meet them. What do they talk about?   20

ALGERNON   The fools? Oh! about the clever people, of course.

JACK   What fools.

ALGERNON   By the way, did you tell Gwendolen the truth about your being Ernest in town, and Jack in the country?

JACK [*in a very patronizing manner*]   My dear fellow, the truth   25
isn't quite the sort of thing one tells to a nice, sweet, refined girl. What extraordinary ideas you have about the way to behave to a woman!

ALGERNON   The only way to behave to a woman is to make love to her, if she is pretty, and to someone else, if she is plain.   30

JACK   Oh, that is nonsense.

ALGERNON   What about your brother? What about the profligate Ernest?

JACK   Oh, before the end of the week I shall have got rid of him. I'll say he died in Paris of apoplexy. Lots of people die of   35
apoplexy, quite suddenly, don't they?

ALGERNON   Yes, but it's hereditary, my dear fellow. It's a sort of thing that runs in families. You had much better say a severe chill.

JACK   You are sure a severe chill isn't hereditary, or anything of that kind?

ALGERNON   Of course it isn't!

JACK   Very well, then. My poor brother Ernest is carried off suddenly, in Paris, by a severe chill. That gets rid of him.

ALGERNON   But I thought you said that . . . Miss Cardew was a little too much interested in your poor brother Ernest? Won't she feel his loss a good deal?

JACK   Oh, that is all right. Cecily is not a silly romantic girl, I am glad to say. She has got a capital appetite, goes on long walks, and pays no attention at all to her lessons.

ALGERNON   I would rather like to see Cecily.

JACK   I will take very good care you never do. She is excessively pretty, and she is only just eighteen.

ALGERNON   Have you told Gwendolen yet that you have an excessively pretty ward who is only just eighteen?

JACK   Oh! one doesn't blurt these things out to people. Cecily and Gwendolen are perfectly certain to be extremely great friends. I'll bet you anything you like that half an hour after they have met, they will be calling each other sister.

ALGERNON   Women only do that when they have called each other a lot of other things first. Now, my dear boy, if we want to get a good table at Willis's, we really must go and dress. Do you know it is nearly seven?

JACK [*irritably*]   Oh! it always is nearly seven.

ALGERNON   Well, I'm hungry.

JACK   I never knew you when you weren't. . . .

ALGERNON   What shall we do after dinner? Go to a theatre?

JACK   Oh no! I loathe listening.

ALGERNON   Well, let us go to the Club?

JACK   Oh, no! I hate talking.

ALGERNON   Well, we might trot round to the Empire at ten?

JACK   Oh, no! I can't bear looking at things. It is so silly.

ALGERNON   Well, what shall we do?

JACK   Nothing!

ALGERNON   It is awfully hard work doing nothing. However, I don't mind hard work where there is no definite object of any kind.

[*Enter* LANE.]

LANE Miss Fairfax.

[*Enter* GWENDOLEN. LANE *goes out.*]

ALGERNON Gwendolen, upon my word!

GWENDOLEN Algy, kindly turn your back. I have something very particular to say to Mr. Worthing.

ALGERNON Really, Gwendolen, I don't think I can allow this at 5
all.

GWENDOLEN Algy, you always adopt a strictly immoral attitude towards life. You are not quite old enough to do that.

[ALGERNON *retires to the fireplace.*]

JACK My own darling!

GWENDOLEN Ernest, we may never be married. From the expres- 10
sion on mamma's face I fear we never shall. Few parents nowa-days pay any regard to what their children say to them. The old-fashioned respect for the young is fast dying out. Whatever influence I ever had over mamma, I lost at the age of three. But although she may prevent us from becoming man and wife, 15
and I may marry someone else, and marry often, nothing that she can possibly do can alter my eternal devotion to you.

JACK Dear Gwendolen!

GWENDOLEN The story of your romantic origin, as related to me by mamma, with unpleasing comments, has naturally stirred the 20
deeper fibres of my nature. Your Christian name has an irresist-ible fascination. The simplicity of your character makes you ex-quisitely incomprehensible to me. Your town address at the Al-bany I have. What is your address in the country?

JACK The Manor House, Woolton, Hertfordshire. 25

[ALGERNON, *who has been carefully listening, smiles to himself, and writes the address on his shirt-cuff. Then picks up the Railway Guide.*]

GWENDOLEN There is a good postal service, I suppose? It may be necessary to do something desperate. That of course will require serious consideration. I will communicate with you daily.

JACK My own one!

GWENDOLEN How long do you remain in town? 30

JACK Till Monday.

GWENDOLEN Good! Algy, you may turn round now.

ALGERNON Thanks, I've turned round already.

GWENDOLEN   You may also ring the bell.

JACK   You will let me see you to your carriage, my own darling?

GWENDOLEN   Certainly.

JACK [*to* LANE, *who now enters*]   I will see Miss Fairfax out.

5   LANE   Yes, sir. [JACK *and* GWENDOLEN *go off.*]

[LANE *presents several letters on a salver to* ALGERNON. *It is to be surmised that they are bills, as* ALGERNON, *after looking at the envelopes, tears them up.*]

ALGERNON   A glass of sherry, Lane.

LANE   Yes, sir.

ALGERNON   Tomorrow, Lane, I'm going Bunburying.

LANE   Yes, sir.

10   ALGERNON   I shall probably not be back till Monday. You can put up my dress clothes, my smoking jacket, and all the Bunbury suits . . .

LANE   Yes, sir. [*Handing sherry.*]

ALGERNON   I hope tomorrow will be a fine day, Lane.

15   LANE   It never is, sir.

ALGERNON   Lane, you're a perfect pessimist.

LANE   I do my best to give satisfaction, sir.

[*Enter* JACK. LANE *goes off.*]

JACK   There's a sensible, intellectual girl! the only girl I ever cared for in my life. [ALGERNON *is laughing immoderately.*] What on
20   earth are you so amused at?

ALGERNON   Oh, I'm a little anxious about poor Bunbury, that is all.

JACK   If you don't take care, your friend Bunbury will get you into a serious scrape some day.

25   ALGERNON   I love scrapes. They are the only things that are never serious.

JACK   Oh, that's nonsense, Algy. You never talk anything but nonsense.

ALGERNON   Nobody ever does.

[JACK *looks indignantly at him, and leaves the room.* ALGERNON *lights a cigarette, reads his shirt-cuff, and smiles.*]

ACT TWO

Garden at the Manor House. A flight of grey stone steps leads up to the house. The garden, an old-fashioned one, full of roses. Time of year, July. Basket chairs, and a table covered with books, are set under a large yew-tree.

MISS PRISM *discovered seated at the table.* CECILY *is at the back, watering flowers.*

MISS PRISM [*calling*]   Cecily, Cecily! Surely such a utilitarian occupation as the watering of flowers is rather Moulton's duty than yours? Especially at a moment when intellectual pleasures await you. Your German grammar is on the table. Pray open it at page fifteen. We will repeat yesterday's lesson.   5

CECILY [*coming over very slowly*]   But I don't like German. It isn't at all a becoming language. I know perfectly well that I look quite plain after my German lesson.

MISS PRISM   Child, you know how anxious your guardian is that you should improve yourself in every way. He laid particular   10 stress on your German, as he was leaving for town yesterday. Indeed, he always lays stress on your German when he is leaving for town.

CECILY   Dear Uncle Jack is so very serious! Sometimes he is so serious that I think he cannot be quite well.   15

MISS PRISM [*drawing herself up*]   Your guardian enjoys the best of health, and his gravity of demeanor is especially to be commended in one so comparatively young as he is. I know no one who has a higher sense of duty and responsibility.

CECILY   I suppose that is why he often looks a little bored when   20 we three are together.

MISS PRISM   Cecily! I am surprised at you. Mr. Worthing has many troubles in his life. Idle merriment and triviality would be out of place in his conversation. You must remember his constant anxiety about that unfortunate young man his brother.   25

CECILY   I wish Uncle Jack would allow that unfortunate young man, his brother, to come down here sometimes. We might have a good influence over him, Miss Prism. I am sure you certainly would. You know German, and geology, and things of that kind influence a man very much. [CECILY *begins to write in her diary.*]   30

MISS PRISM [*shaking her head*]   I do not think that even I could produce any effect on a character that according to his own brother's admission is irretrievably weak and vacillating. Indeed

405

I am not sure that I would desire to reclaim him. I am not in favor of this modern mania for turning bad people into good people at a moment's notice. As a man sows so let him reap. You must put away your diary, Cecily. I really don't see why you should keep a diary at all.

CECILY   I keep a diary in order to enter the wonderful secrets of my life. If I didn't write them down, I should probably forget all about them.

MISS PRISM   Memory, my dear Cecily, is the diary that we all carry about with us.

CECILY   Yes, but it usually chronicles the things that have never happened, and couldn't possibly have happened. I believe that Memory is responsible for nearly all the three-volume novels that Mudie sends us.

MISS PRISM   Do not speak slightingly of the three-volume novel, Cecily. I wrote one myself in earlier days.

CECILY   Did you really, Miss Prism? How wonderfully clever you are! I hope it did not end happily? I don't like novels that end happily. They depress me so much.

MISS PRISM   The good ended happily, and the bad unhappily. That is what Fiction means.

CECILY   I suppose so. But it seems very unfair. And was your novel ever published?

MISS PRISM   Alas! no. The manuscript unfortunately was abandoned. [CECILY *starts*.] I used the word in the sense of lost or mislaid. To your work, child, these speculations are profitless.

CECILY [*smiling*]   But I see dear Dr. Chasuble coming up through the garden.

MISS PRISM [*rising and advancing*]   Dr. Chasuble! This is indeed a pleasure.

[*Enter* CANON CHASUBLE.]

CHASUBLE   And how are we this morning? Miss Prism, you are, I trust, well?

CECILY   Miss Prism has just been complaining of a slight headache. I think it would do her so much good to have a short stroll with you in the Park, Dr. Chasuble.

MISS PRISM   Cecily, I have not mentioned anything about a headache.

CECILY   No, dear Miss Prism, I know that, but I felt instinctively that you had a headache. Indeed I was thinking about that, and not about my German lesson, when the Rector came in.

CHASUBLE   I hope, Cecily, you are not inattentive.

CECILY   Oh, I am afraid I am.

CHASBULE   That is strange. Were I fortunate enough to be Miss
Prism's pupil, I would hang upon her lips. [MISS PRISM *glares*.]
I spoke metaphorically.—My metaphor was drawn from bees.   5
Ahem! Mr. Worthing, I suppose, has not returned from town
yet?

MISS PRISM   We do not expect him till Monday afternoon.

CHASUBLE   Ah yes, he usually likes to spend his Sunday in London.
He is not one of those whose sole aim is enjoyment, as, by all   10
accounts, that unfortunate young man his brother seems to be.
But I must not disturb Egeria and her pupil any longer.

MISS PRISM   Egeria? My name is Laetitia, Doctor.

CHASUBLE [*bowing*]   A classical allusion merely, drawn from the
Pagan authors. I shall see you both no doubt at Evensong?   15

MISS PRISM   I think, dear Doctor, I will have a stroll with you.
I find I have a headache after all, and a walk might do it good.

CHASUBLE   With pleasure, Miss Prism, with pleasure. We might go
as far as the schools and back.

MISS PRISM   That would be delightful. Cecily, you will read your   20
Political Economy in my absence. The chapter on the Fall of the
Rupee you may omit. It is somewhat too sensational. Even these
metallic problems have their melodramatic side.

[*Goes down the garden with* DR. CHASUBLE.]

CECILY [*picks up books and throws them back on table*]   Horrid
Political Economy! Horrid Geography! Horrid, horrid German!   25

[*Enter* MERRIMAN *with a card on a salver*.]

MERRIMAN   Mr. Ernest Worthing has just driven over from the
station. He has brought his luggage with him.

CECILY [*takes the card and reads it*]   "Mr. Ernest Worthing,
B.4, The Albany, W." Uncle Jack's brother! Did you tell him
Mr. Worthing was in town?   30

MERRIMAN   Yes, Miss. He seemed very much disappointed. I mentioned that you and Miss Prism were in the garden. He said he
was anxious to speak to you privately for a moment.

CECILY   Ask Mr. Ernest Worthing to come here. I suppose you
had better talk to the housekeeper about a room for him.   35

MERRIMAN   Yes, Miss. [MERRIMAN *goes off*.]

CECILY   I have never met any really wicked person before. I feel rather frightened. I am so afraid he will look just like every one else.

[*Enter* ALGERNON, *very gay and debonnaire.*]

He does!

ALGERNON [*raising his hat*]   You are my little cousin Cecily, I'm
5   sure.

CECILY   You are under some strange mistake. I am not little. In
fact, I believe I am more than usually tall for my age. [ALGERNON
is rather taken aback.] But I am your cousin Cecily. You, I see
from your card, are Uncle Jack's brother, my cousin Ernest, my
10   wicked cousin Ernest.

ALGERNON   Oh! I am not really wicked at all, Cousin Cecily. You
mustn't think that I am wicked.

CECILY   If you are not, then you have certainly been deceiving us
all in a very inexcusable manner. I hope you have not been lead-
15   ing a double life, pretending to be wicked and being really good
all the time. That would be hypocrisy.

ALGERNON [*look at her in amazement*]   Oh! Of course I have been
rather reckless.

CECILY   I am glad to hear it.

20   ALGERNON   In fact, now you mention the subject, I have been
very bad in my own small way.

CECILY   I don't think you should be so proud of that, though I am
sure it must have been very pleasant.

ALGERNON   It is much pleasanter being here with you.

25   CECILY   I can't understand how you are here at all. Uncle Jack
won't be back till Monday afternoon.

ALGERNON   That is a great disappointment. I am obliged to go up
by the first train on Monday morning. I have a business appointment that I am anxious . . . to miss!

30   CECILY   Couldn't you miss it anywhere but in London?

ALGERNON   No: the appointment is in London.

CECILY   Well, I know, of course, how important it is not to keep
a business engagement, if one wants to retain any sense of the
beauty of life, but still I think you had better wait till Uncle Jack
35   arrives. I know he wants to speak to you about your emigrating.

ALGERNON   About my what?

CECILY   Your emigrating. He has gone up to buy your outfit.

ALGERNON   I certainly wouldn't let Jack buy my outfit. He has no taste in neckties at all.

CECILY   I don't think you will require neckties. Uncle Jack is sending you to Australia.   5

ALGERNON   Australia! I'd sooner die.

CECILY   Well, he said at dinner on Wednesday night, that you would have to choose between this world, the next world, and Australia.

ALGERNON   Oh, well! The accounts I have received of Australia   10
and the next world are not particularly encouraging. This world is good enough for me, Cousin Cecily.

CECILY   Yes, but are you good enough for it?

ALGERNON   I'm afraid I'm not that. That is why I want you to reform me. You might make that your mission, if you don't mind,   15
cousin Cecily.

CECILY   I'm afraid I've no time, this afternoon.

ALGERNON   Well, would you mind my reforming myself this afternoon?

CECILY   It is rather Quixotic of you. But I think you should try.   20

ALGERNON   I will. I feel better already.

CECILY   You are looking a little worse.

ALGERNON   That is because I am hungry.

CECILY   How thoughtless of me. I should have remembered that when one is going to lead an entirely new life, one requires regu-   25
lar and wholesome meals. Won't you come in?

ALGERNON   Thank you. Might I have a buttonhole first? I never have any appetite unless I have a buttonhole first.

CECILY   A Maréchal Niel? [*Picks up scissors.*]

ALGERNON   No, I'd sooner have a pink rose.   30

CECILY   Why? [*Cuts a flower.*]

ALGERNON   Because you are like a pink rose, Cousin Cecily.

CECILY   I don't think it can be right for you to talk to me like that. Miss Prism never says such things to me.

ALGERNON   Then Miss Prism is a shortsighted old lady. [CECILY   35
puts the rose in his buttonhole.] You are the prettiest girl I ever saw.

CECILY   Miss Prism says that all good looks are a snare.

ALGERNON   They are a snare that every sensible man would like to be caught in.

CECILY   Oh, I don't think I would care to catch a sensible man. I
5   shouldn't know what to talk to him about.

[*They pass into the house.* MISS PRISM *and* DR. CHASUBLE *return.*]

MISS PRISM   You are too much alone, dear Dr. Chasuble. You should get married. A misanthrope I can understand—a woman-thrope, never!

CHASUBLE [*with a scholar's shudder*]   Believe me, I do not deserve
10   so neologistic a phrase. The precept as well as the practice of the Primitive Church was distinctly against matrimony.

MISS PRISM [*sententiously*]   That is obviously the reason why the Primitive Church has not lasted up to the present day. And you do not seem to realize, dear Doctor, that by persistently remain-
15   ing single, a man converts himself into a permanent public temptation. Men should be more careful; this very celibacy leads weaker vessels astray.

CHASUBLE   But is a man not equally attractive when married?

MISS PRISM   No married man is ever attractive except to his wife.

20   CHASUBLE   And often, I've been told, not even to her.

MISS PRISM   That depends on the intellectual sympathies of the woman. Maturity can always be depended on. Ripeness can be trusted. Young women are green. [DR. CHASUBLE *starts.*] I spoke horticulturally. My metaphor was drawn from fruits. But where
25   is Cecily?

CHASUBLE   Perhaps she followed us to the schools.

[*Enter* JACK *slowly from the back of the garden. He is dressed in the deepest mourning, with crepe hatband and black gloves.*]

MISS PRISM   Mr. Worthing!

CHASUBLE   Mr. Worthing?

MISS PRISM   This is indeed a surprise. We did not look for you till
30   Monday afternoon.

JACK [*shakes* MISS PRISM'S *hand in a tragic manner*]   I have re-turned sooner than I expected. Dr. Chasuble, I hope you are well?

CHASUBLE   Dear Mr. Worthing, I trust this garb of woe does not
35   betoken some terrible calamity?

JACK   My brother.

MISS PRISM   More shameful debts and extravagance?

CHASUBLE   Still leading his life of pleasure?

JACK [*shaking his head*]   Dead!

CHASUBLE   Your brother Ernest dead?   5

JACK   Quite dead.

MISS PRISM   What a lesson for him! I trust he will profit by it.

CHASUBLE   Mr. Worthing, I offer you my sincere condolence. You
   have at least the consolation of knowing that you were always
   the most generous and forgiving of brothers.   10

JACK   Poor Ernest! He had many faults, but it is a sad, sad blow.

CHASUBLE   Very sad indeed. Were you with him at the end?

JACK   No. He died abroad; in Paris, in fact. I had a telegram last
   night from the manager of the Grand Hotel.

CHASUBLE   Was the cause of death mentioned?   15

JACK   A severe chill, it seems.

MISS PRISM   As a man sows, so shall he reap.

CHASUBLE [*raising his hand*]   Charity, dear Miss Prism, charity!
   None of us are perfect. I myself am peculiarly susceptible to
   draughts. Will the interment take place here?   20

JACK   No. He seems to have expressed a desire to be buried in
   Paris.

CHASUBLE   In Paris! [*Shakes his head.*] I fear that hardly points
   to any very serious state of mind at the last. You would no doubt
   wish me to make some slight allusion to this tragic domestic   25
   affliction next Sunday. [JACK *presses his hand convulsively.*] My
   sermon on the meaning of the manna in the wilderness can be
   adapted to almost any occasion, joyful, or, as in the present case,
   distressing. [*All sigh.*] I have preached it at harvest celebrations,
   christenings, confirmations, on days of humiliation and festal   30
   days. The last time I delivered it was in the Cathedral, as a
   charity sermon on behalf of the Society for the Prevention of
   Discontent among the Upper Orders. The Bishop, who was present, was much struck by some of the analogies I drew.

JACK   Ah! that reminds me, you mentioned christenings I think,   35
   Dr. Chasuble? I suppose you know how to christen all right?
   [DR. CHASUBLE *looks astounded.*] I mean, of course, you are
   continually christening, aren't you?

MISS PRISM   It is, I regret to say, one of the Rector's most constant duties in this parish. I have often spoken to the poorer classes on the subject. But they don't seem to know what thrift is.

CHASUBLE   But is there any particular infant in whom you are interested, Mr. Worthing? Your brother was, I believe, unmarried, was he not?

JACK   Oh yes.

MISS PRISM [*bitterly*]   People who live entirely for pleasure usually are.

JACK   But it is not for any child, dear Doctor. I am very fond of children. No! the fact is, I would like to be christened myself, this afternoon, if you have nothing better to do.

CHASUBLE   But surely, Mr. Worthing, you have been christened already?

JACK   I don't remember anything about it.

CHASUBLE   But have you any grave doubts on the subject?

JACK   I certainly intend to have. Of course I don't know if the thing would bother you in any way, or if you think I am a little too old now.

CHASUBLE   Not at all. The sprinkling, and, indeed, the immersion of adults is a perfectly canonical practice.

JACK   Immersion!

CHASUBLE   You need have no apprehensions. Sprinkling is all that is necessary, or indeed I think advisable. Our weather is so changeable. At what hour would you wish the ceremony performed?

JACK   Oh, I might trot round about five if that would suit you.

CHASUBLE   Perfectly, perfectly! In fact I have two similar cere-
monies to perform at that time. A case of twins that occurred recently in one of the outlying cottages on your own estate. Poor Jenkins the carter, a most hard-working man.

JACK   Oh! I don't see much fun in being christened along with other babies. It would be childish. Would half-past five do?

CHASUBLE   Admirably! Admirably! [*Takes out watch.*] And now, dear Mr. Worthing, I will not intrude any longer into a house of sorrow. I would merely beg you not to be too much bowed down by grief. What seem to us bitter trials are often blessings in disguise.

MISS PRISM   This seems to me a blessing of an extremely obvious kind.

[*Enter* CECILY *from the house.*]

CECILY   Uncle Jack! Oh, I am pleased to see you back. But what horrid clothes you have got on. Do go and change them.

MISS PRISM   Cecily!

CHASUBLE   My child! My child! [CECILY *goes towards* JACK; *he kisses her brow in a melancholy manner.*]   5

CECILY   What is the matter, Uncle Jack? Do look happy! You look as if you had toothache, and I have got such a surprise for you. Who do you think is in the dining-room? Your brother!

JACK   Who?

CECILY   Your brother Ernest. He arrived about half an hour ago.   10

JACK   What nonsense! I haven't got a brother.

CECILY   Oh, don't say that. However badly he may have behaved to you in the past he is still your brother. You couldn't be so heartless as to disown him. I'll tell him to come out. And you will shake hands with him, won't you, Uncle Jack? [*Runs back   15 into the house.*]

CHASUBLE   These are very joyful tidings.

MISS PRISM   After we had all been resigned to his loss, his sudden return seems to me peculiarly distressing.

JACK   My brother is in the dining-room? I don't know what it all   20 means. I think it is perfectly absurd.

[*Enter* ALGERNON *and* CECILY *hand in hand. They come slowly up to* JACK.]

JACK   Good heavens! [*Motions* ALGERNON *away.*]

ALGERNON   Brother John, I have come down from town to tell you that I am very sorry for all the trouble I have given you, and that I intend to lead a better life in the future. [JACK *glares at him   25 and does not take his hand.*]

CECILY   Uncle Jack, you are not going to refuse your own brother's hand?

JACK   Nothing will induce me to take his hand. I think his coming down here disgraceful. He knows perfectly well why.   30

CECILY   Uncle Jack, do be nice. There is some good in everyone. Ernest has just been telling me about his poor invalid friend Mr. Bunbury whom he goes to visit so often. And surely there must be much good in one who is kind to an invalid, and leaves the pleasures of London to sit by a bed of pain.   35

JACK   Oh! he has been talking about Bunbury, has he?

CECILY   Yes, he has told me all about poor Mr. Bunbury, and his terrible state of health.

JACK   Bunbury! Well, I won't have him talk to you about Bunbury
5   or about anything else. It is enough to drive one perfectly frantic.

ALGERNON   Of course I admit that the faults were all on my side. But I must say that I think that Brother John's coldness to me is peculiarly painful. I expected a more enthusiastic welcome, especially considering it is the first time I have come here.

10   CECILY   Uncle Jack, if you don't shake hands with Ernest I will never forgive you.

JACK   Never forgive me?

CECILY   Never, never, never!

JACK   Well, this is the last time I shall ever do it. [*Shakes hands*
15   *with* ALGERNON *and glares.*]

CHASUBLE   It's pleasant, is it not, to see so perfect a reconciliation? I think we might leave the two brothers together.

MISS PRISM   Cecily, you will come with us.

CECILY   Certainly, Miss Prism. My little task of reconciliation is
20   over.

CHASUBLE   You have done a beautiful action today, dear child.

MISS PRISM   We must not be premature in our judgements.

CECILY   I feel very happy. [*They all go off except* JACK *and* AL-GERNON.]

25   JACK   You young scoundrel, Algy, you must get out of this place as soon as possible. I don't allow any Bunburying here.

[*Enter* MERRIMAN.]

MERRIMAN   I have put Mr. Ernest's things in the room next to yours, sir. I suppose that is all right?

JACK   What?

30   MERRIMAN   Mr. Ernest's luggage, sir. I have unpacked it and put it in the room next to your own.

JACK   His luggage?

MERRIMAN   Yes sir. Three portmanteaus, a dressing-case, two hat-boxes, and a large luncheon-basket.

ALGERNON   I am afraid I can't stay more than a week this time.

35   JACK   Merriman, order the dogcart at once. Mr. Ernest has been suddenly called back to town.

MERRIMAN Yes, sir. [*Goes back into the house.*]

ALGERNON What a fearful liar you are, Jack. I have not been called back to town at all.

JACK Yes, you have.

ALGERNON I haven't heard any one call me.   5

JACK Your duty as a gentleman calls you back.

ALGERNON My duty as a gentleman has never interfered with my pleasures in the smallest degree.

JACK I can quite understand that.

ALGERNON Well, Cecily is a darling.   10

JACK You are not to talk of Miss Cardew like that. I don't like it.

ALGERNON Well, I don't like your clothes. You look perfectly ridiculous in them. Why on earth don't you go up and change? It is perfectly childish to be in deep mourning for a man who is   15 actually staying for a whole week with you in your house as a guest. I call it grotesque.

JACK You are certainly not staying with me for a whole week as a guest or anything else. You have got to leave . . . by the. four-five train.   20

ALGERNON I certainly won't leave you so long as you are in mourning. It would be most unfriendly. If I were in mourning you would stay with me, I suppose. I should think it very unkind if you didn't.

JACK Well, will you go if I change my clothes?   25

ALGERNON Yes, if you are not too long. I never saw anybody take so long to dress, and with such little result.

JACK Well, at any rate, that is better than being always overdressed as you are.

ALGERNON If I am occasionally a little overdressed, I make up for   30 it by being always immensely overeducated.

JACK Your vanity is ridiculous, your conduct an outrage, and your presence in my garden utterly absurd. However, you have got to catch the four-five, and I hope you will have a pleasant journey back to town. This Bunburying, as you call it, has not been a   35 great success for you.

[*Goes into the house.*]

ALGERNON I think it has been a great success. I'm in love with Cecily, and that is everything.

[*Enter* CECILY *at the back of the garden. She picks up the can and begins to water the flowers.*]

But I must see her before I go, and make arrangements for another Bunbury. Ah, there she is.

CECILY   Oh, I merely came back to water the roses. I thought you were with Uncle Jack.

5   ALGERNON   He's gone to order the dogcart for me.

CECILY   Oh, is he going to take you for a nice drive?

ALGERNON   He's going to send me away.

CECILY   Then have we got to part?

ALGERNON   I am afraid so. It's a very painful parting.

10   CECILY   It is always painful to part from people whom one has known for a very brief space of time. The absence of old friends one can endure with equanimity. But even a momentary separation from any one to whom one has just been introduced is almost unbearable.

15   ALGERNON   Thank you.

[*Enter* MERRIMAN.]

MERRIMAN   The dogcart is at the door, sir.

[ALGERNON *looks appealingly at* CECILY.]

CECILY   It can wait, Merriman . . . for . . . five minutes.

MERRIMAN   Yes, miss.

[*Exit* MERRIMAN.]

ALGERNON   I hope, Cecily, I shall not offend you if I state quite
20   frankly and openly that you seem to me to be in every way the visible personification of absolute perfection.

CECILY   I think your frankness does you great credit, Ernest. If you will allow me, I will copy your remarks into my diary. [*Goes over to table and begins writing in diary.*]

25   ALGERNON   Do you really keep a diary? I'd give anything to look at it. May I?

CECILY   Oh no. [*Puts her hand over it.*] You see, it is simply a very young girl's record of her own thoughts and impressions, and consequently meant for publication. When it appears in
30   volume form I hope you will order a copy. But pray, Ernest, don't stop. I delight in taking down from dictation. I have

reached "absolute perfection." You can go on. I am quite ready for more.

ALGERNON [*somewhat taken aback*]   Ahem! Ahem!

CECILY   Oh, don't cough, Ernest. When one is dictating one should speak fluently and not cough. Besides, I don't know how to spell   5
a cough. [*Writes as* ALGERNON *speaks.*]

ALGERNON [*speaking very rapidly*]   Cecily, ever since I first looked upon your wonderful and incomparable beauty, I have dared to love you wildly, passionately, devotedly, hopelessly.

CECILY   I don't think that you should tell me that you love me   10
wildly, passionately, devotedly, hopelessly. Hopelessly doesn't seem to make much sense, does it?

ALGERNON   Cecily.

[*Enter* MERRIMAN]

MERRIMAN   The dogcart is waiting, sir.

ALGERNON   Tell it to come round next week, at the same hour.   15

MERRIMAN [*looks at* CECILY, *who makes no sign*]   Yes, sir.

[MERRIMAN *retires.*]

CECILY   Uncle Jack would be very much annoyed if he knew you were staying on till next week, at the same hour.

ALGERNON   Oh, I don't care about Jack. I don't care for anybody in the whole world but you. I love you, Cecily. You will marry   20
me, won't you?

CECILY   You silly boy! Of course. Why, we have been engaged for the last three months.

ALGERNON   For the last three months?

CECILY   Yes, it will be exactly three months on Thursday.   25

ALGERNON   But how did we become engaged?

CECILY   Well, ever since dear Uncle Jack first confessed to us that he had a younger brother who was very wicked and bad, you of course have formed the chief topic of conversation between myself and Miss Prism. And of course a man who is much talked   30
about is always very attractive. One feels there must be something in him, after all. I daresay it was foolish of me, but I fell in love with you, Ernest.

ALGERNON   Darling. And when was the engagement actually settled?   35

CECILY On the 14th of February last. Worn out by your entire ignorance of my existence, I determined to end the matter one way or the other, and after a long struggle with myself I accepted you under this dear old tree here. The next day I bought this
5   little ring in your name, and this is the little bangle with the true lovers' knot I promised you always to wear.

ALGERNON Did I give you this? It's very pretty, isn't it?

CECILY Yes, you've wonderfully good taste, Ernest. It's the excuse I've always given for your leading such a bad life. And this is
10   the box in which I keep all your dear letters. [*Kneels at table, opens box, and produces letters tied up with blue ribbon.*]

ALGERNON My letters! But, my own sweet Cecily, I have never written you any letters.

CECILY You need hardly remind me of that, Ernest. I remember
15   only too well that I was forced to write your letters for you. I wrote always three times a week, and sometimes oftener.

ALGERNON Oh, do let me read them, Cecily?

CECILY Oh, I couldn't possibly. They would make you far too conceited. [*Replaces box.*] The three you wrote me after I had
20   broken off the engagement are so beautiful, and so badly spelled, that even now I can hardly read them without crying a little.

ALGERNON But was our engagement ever broken off?

CECILY Of course it was. On the 22nd of last March. You can see the entry if you like. [*Shows diary.*] "Today I broke off my
25   engagement with Ernest. I feel it is better to do so. The weather still continues charming."

ALGERNON But why on earth did you break it off? What had I done? I had done nothing at all. Cecily, I am very much hurt indeed to hear you broke it off. Particularly when the weather
30   was so charming.

CECILY It would hardly have been a really serious engagement if it hadn't been broken off at least once. But I forgave you before the week was out.

ALGERNON [*crossing to her, and kneeling*] What a perfect angel
35   you are, Cecily.

CECILY You dear romantic boy [*He kisses her, she puts her fingers through his hair.*] I hope you hair curls naturally, does it?

ALGERNON Yes darling, with a little help from others.

CECILY I am so glad.

40 ALGERNON You'll never break off our engagement again, Cecily?

CECILY I don't think I could break it off now that I have actually met you. Besides, of course, there is the question of your name.

ALGERNON Yes, of course. [*Nervously*.]

CECILY You must not laugh at me, darling, but it had always been a girlish dream of mine to love some one whose name was Ernest. 5 [ALGERNON *rises,* CECILY *also*.] There is something in that name that seems to inspire absolute confidence. I pity any poor married woman whose husband is not called Ernest.

ALGERNON But, my dear child, do you mean to say you could not love me if I had some other name? 10

CECILY But what name?

ALGERNON Oh, any name you like—Algernon—for instance . . .

CECILY But I don't like the name of Algernon.

ALGERNON Well, my own dear, sweet, loving little darling, I really can't see why you should object to the name of Algernon. It is 15 not at all a bad name. In fact, it is rather an aristocratic name. Half of the chaps who get into the Bankruptcy Court are called Algernon. But seriously, Cecily . . . [*moving to her*] if my name was Algy, couldn't you love me?

CECILY [*rising*] I might respect you, Ernest, I might admire your 20 character, but I fear that I should not be able to give you my undivided attention.

ALGERNON Ahem! Cecily! [*Picking up hat*.] Your Rector here is, I suppose, thoroughly experienced in the practice of all the rites and ceremonials of the Church? 25

CECILY Oh, yes. Dr. Chasuble is a most learned man. He has never written a single book, so you can imagine how much he knows.

ALGERNON I must see him at once on a most important christening—I mean on most important business. 30

CECILY Oh!

ALGERNON I shan't be away more than half an hour.

CECILY Considering that we have been engaged since February the 14th, and that I only met you today for the first time, I think it is rather hard that you should leave me for so long a period 35 as half an hour. Couldn't you make it twenty minutes?

ALGERNON I'll be back in no time. [*Kisses her and rushes down the garden*.]

CECILY What an impetuous boy he is! I like his hair so much. I must enter his proposal in my diary. 40

[*Enter* MERRIMAN.]

MERRIMAN   A Miss Fairfax just called to see Mr. Worthing. On very important business, Miss Fairfax states.

CECILY   Isn't Mr. Worthing in his library?

MERRIMAN   Mr. Worthing went over in the direction of the Rec-
5   tory some time ago.

CECILY   Pray ask the lady to come out here; Mr. Worthing is sure to be back soon. And you can bring tea.

MERRIMAN   Yes, Miss.

[*Goes out.*]

CECILY   Miss Fairfax! I suppose one of the many good elderly
10   women who are associated with Uncle Jack in some of his phil-anthropic work in London. I don't quite like women who are in-terested in philanthropic work. I think it is so forward of them.

[*Enter* MERRIMAN.]

MERRIMAN   Miss Fairfax.

[*Enter* GWENDOLEN. *Exit* MERRIMAN.]

CECILY [*advancing to meet her*]   Pray let me introduce myself to
15   you. My name is Cecily Cardew.

GWENDOLEN   Cecily Cardew? [*Moving to her and shaking hands.*] What a very sweet name! Something tells me that we are going to be great friends. I like you already more than I can say. My first impressions of people are never wrong.

CECILY   How nice of you to like me so much after we have known
20   each other such a comparatively short time. Pray sit down.

GWENDOLEN [*still standing up*]   I may call you Cecily, may I not?

CECILY   With pleasure!

GWENDOLEN   And you will always call me Gwendolen, won't you?

CECILY   If you wish.

25   GWENDOLEN   Then that is all quite settled, is it not?

CECILY   I hope so. [*A pause. They both sit down together.*]

GWENDOLEN   Perhaps this might be a favorable opportunity for my mentioning who I am. My father is Lord Bracknell. You have never heard of papa, I suppose?

30   CECILY   I don't think so.

GWENDOLEN   Outside the family circle, papa, I am glad to say is entirely unknown. I think that is quite as it should be. The home seems to me to be the proper sphere for the man. And certainly once a man begins to neglect his domestic duties he becomes painfully effeminate, does he not? And I don't like that. It makes men so very attractive. Cecily, mamma, whose views on education are remarkably strict, has brought me up to be extremely shortsighted; it is part of her system; so do you mind my looking at you through my glasses? 5

CECILY   Oh! not at all, Gwendolen. I am very fond of being looked at. 10

GWENDOLEN [*after examining* CECILY *carefully through a lorgnette*] You are here on a short visit, I suppose.

CECILY   Oh no! I live here.

GWENDOLEN [*severely*]   Really? Your mother, no doubt, or some female relative of advanced years, resides here also? 15

CECILY   Oh no! I have no mother, nor, in fact, any relations.

GWENDOLEN   Indeed?

CECILY   My dear guardian, with the assistance of Miss Prism, has the arduous task of looking after me. 20

GWENDOLEN   Your guardian?

CECILY   Yes, I am Mr. Worthing's ward.

GWENDOLEN   Oh! It is strange he never mentioned to me that he had a ward. How secretive of him! He grows more interesting hourly. I am not sure, however, that the news inspires me with feelings of unmixed delight. [*Rising and going to her.*] I am very fond of you, Cecily; I have liked you ever since I met you! But I am bound to state that now that I know that you are Mr. Worthing's ward, I cannot help expressing a wish you were— well, just a little older than you seem to be—and not quite so very alluring in appearance. In fact, if I may speak candidly— 25 30

CECILY   Pray do! I think that whenever one has anything unpleasant to say, one should always be quite candid.

GWENDOLEN   Well, to speak with perfect candor, Cecily, I wish that you were fully forty-two, and more than usually plain for your age. Ernest has a strong upright nature. He is the very soul of truth and honor. Disloyalty would be as impossible to him as deception. But even men of the noblest possible moral character are extremely susceptible to the influence of the physical charms of others. Modern, no less than Ancient History, supplies us with many most painful examples of what I refer to. If it were not so, indeed, History would be quite unreadable. 35 40

CECILY   I beg your pardon, Gwendolen, did you say Ernest?

GWENDOLEN   Yes.

CECILY   Oh, but it is not Mr. Ernest Worthing who is my guardian. It is his brother—his elder brother.

5   GWENDOLEN [*sitting down again*]   Ernest never mentioned to me that he had a brother.

CECILY   I am sorry to say they have not been on good terms for a long time.

GWENDOLEN   Ah! that accounts for it. And now that I think of it
10   I have never heard any man mention his brother. The subject seems distasteful to most men. Cecily, you have lifted a load from my mind. I was growing almost anxious. It would have been terrible if any cloud had come across a friendship like ours, would it not? Of course you are quite, quite sure that it is not
15   Mr. Ernest Worthing who is your guardian?

CECILY   Quite sure. [*A pause.*] In fact, I am going to be his.

GWENDOLEN [*inquiringly*]   I beg your pardon?

CECILY [*rather shy and confidingly*]   Dearest Gwendolen, there is no reason why I should make a secret of it to you. Our little
20   country newspaper is sure to chronicle the fact next week. Mr. Ernest Worthing and I are engaged to be married.

GWENDOLEN [*quite politely, rising*]   My darling Cecily, I think there must be some slight error. Mr. Ernest Worthing is engaged to me. The announcement will appear in the *Morning Post* on
25   Saturday at the latest.

CECILY [*very politely, rising*]   I am afraid you must be under some misconception. Ernest proposed to me exactly ten minutes ago. [*Shows diary.*]

GWENDOLEN [*examines diary through her lorgnette carefully*]   It
30   is very curious, for he asked me to be his wife yesterday afternoon at 5:30. If you would care to verify the incident, pray do so. [*Produces diary of her own.*] I never travel without my diary. One should always have something sensational to read in the train. I am so sorry, dear Cecily, if it is any disappointment to
35   you, but I am afraid I have the prior claim.

CECILY   It would distress me more than I can tell you, dear Gwendolen, if it caused you any mental or physical anguish, but I feel bound to point out that since Ernest proposed to you he clearly has changed his mind.

40   GWENDOLEN [*meditatively*]   If the poor fellow has been entrapped into any foolish promise I shall consider it my duty to rescue him at once, and with a firm hand.

CECILY [*thoughtfully and sadly*]   Whatever unfortunate entanglement my dear boy may have got into, I will never reproach him with it after we are married.

GWENDOLEN   Do you allude to me, Miss Cardew, as an entanglement? You are presumptuous. On an occasion of this kind it   5
becomes more than a moral duty to speak one's mind. It becomes a pleasure.

CECILY   Do you suggest, Miss Fairfax, that I entrapped Ernest into an engagement? How dare you? This is no time for wearing the shallow mask of manners. When I see a spade I call it a spade.   10

GWENDOLEN [*satirically*]   I am glad to say that I have never seen a spade. It is obvious that our social spheres have been widely different.

[*Enter* MERRIMAN, *followed by the footman. He carries a salver, table cloth, and plate stand.* CECILY *is about to retort. The presence of the servants exercises a restraining influence, under which both girls chafe.*]

MERRIMAN   Shall I lay tea here as usual, Miss?

CECILY [*sternly, in a calm voice*]   Yes, as usual. [MERRIMAN *be-   15
gins to clear table and lay cloth. A long pause.* CECILY *and* GWENDOLEN *glare at each other.*]

GWENDOLEN   Are there many interesting walks in the vicinity, Miss Cardew?

CECILY   Oh! yes! a great many. From the top of one of the hills   20
quite close one can see five counties.

GWENDOLEN   Five counties! I don't think I should like that; I hate crowds.

CECILY [*sweetly*]   I suppose that is why you live in town? [GWEN-
DOLEN *bites her lip, and beats her foot nervously with her para-   25
sol.*]

GWENDOLEN [*Looking round*]   Quite a well-kept garden this is, Miss Cardew.

CECILY   So glad you like it, Miss Fairfax.

GWENDOLEN   I had no idea there were any flowers in the country.   30

CECILY   Oh, flowers are as common here, Miss Fairfax, as people are in London.

GWENDOLEN   Personally I cannot understand how anybody manages to exist in the country, if anybody who is anybody does. The country always bores me to death.   35

CECILY   Ah! This is what the newspapers call agricultural depression, is it not? I believe the aristocracy are suffering very much from it just at present. It is almost an epidemic amongst them, I have been told. May I offer you some tea, Miss Fairfax?

5   GWENDOLEN [*with elaborate politeness*]   Thank you. [*Aside.*] Detestable girl! But I require tea!

CECILY [*sweetly*]   Sugar?

GWENDOLEN [*superciliously*]   No, thank you. Sugar is not fashionable any more. [CECILY *looks angrily at her, takes up the tongs*
10   *and puts four lumps of sugar into the cup.*]

CECILY [*severely*]   Cake or bread and butter?

GWENDOLEN [*in a bored manner*]   Bread and butter, please. Cake is rarely seen at the best houses nowadays.

CECILY [*cuts a very large slice of cake and puts it on the tray*]
15   Hand that to Miss Fairfax.

[MERRIMAN *does so, and goes out with footman.* GWENDOLEN
*drinks the tea and makes a grimace. Puts down cup at once,
reaches out her hand to the bread and butter, looks at it, and
finds it is cake. Rises in indignation.*]

20   GWENDOLEN   You have filled my tea with lumps of sugar, and though I asked most distinctly for bread and butter, you have given me cake. I am known for the gentleness of my disposition, and the extraordinary sweetness of my nature, but I warn you, Miss Cardew, you may go too far.

25   CECILY [*rising*]   To save my poor, innocent, trusting boy from the machinations of any other girl there are no lengths to which I would not go.

GWENDOLEN   From the moment I saw you I distrusted you. I felt that you were false and deceitful. I am never deceived in such
30   matters. My first impressions of people are invariably right.

CECILY   It seems to me, Miss Fairfax, that I am trespassing on your valuable time. No doubt you have many other calls of a similar character to make in the neighbourhood.

[*Enter* JACK.]

GWENDOLEN [*catching sight of him*]   Ernest! My own Ernest!

35   JACK   Gwendolen! Darling! [*Offers to kiss her.*]

GWENDOLEN [*drawing back*]   A moment! May I ask if you are engaged to be married to this young lady? [*Points to* CECILY.]

JACK [*laughing*]   To dear little Cecily! Of course not! What could have put such an idea into your pretty little head?

GWENDOLEN   Thank you. You may! [*Offers her cheek.*]

CECILY [*very sweetly*]   I knew there must be some misunderstanding, Miss Fairfax. The gentleman whose arm is at present round   5
your waist is my dear guardian, Mr. John Worthing.

GWENDOLEN   I beg your pardon?

CECILY   This is Uncle Jack.

GWENDOLEN [*receding*]   Jack! Oh!

[*Enter* ALGERNON.]

CECILY   Here is Ernest.   10

ALGERNON [*goes straight over to* CECILY *without noticing anyone else*]   My own love! [*Offers to kiss her.*]

CECILY [*drawing back*]   A moment, Ernest! May I ask you—are you engaged to be married to this young lady?

ALGERNON [*looking round*]   To what young lady? Good heavens!   15
Gwendolen!

CECILY   Yes: to good heavens, Gwendolen, I mean to Gwendolen.

ALGERNON [*laughing*]   Of course not! What could have put such an idea into your pretty little head?

CECILY   Thank you. [*Presenting her cheek to be kissed.*] You may.   20
[ALGERNON *kisses her.*]

GWENDOLEN   I felt there was some slight error, Miss Cardew. The gentleman who is now embracing you is my cousin, Mr. Algernon Moncrieff.

CECILY [*breaking away from Algernon*]   Algernon Moncrieff! Oh!   25
[*The two girls move towards each other and put their arms round each other's waists as if for protection.*]

CECILY   Are you called Algernon?

ALGERNON   I cannot deny it.

CECILY   Oh!   30

GWENDOLEN   Is your name really John?

JACK [*standing rather proudly*]   I could deny it if I liked. I could deny anything if I liked. But my name certainly is John. It has been John for years.

CECILY [*to* GWENDOLEN]   A gross deception has been practised on   35
both of us.

GWENDOLEN   My poor wounded Cecily!

CECILY   My sweet wronged Gwendolen!

GWENDOLEN [*slowly and seriously*]   You will call me sister, will you not? [*They embrace.* JACK *and* ALGERNON *groan and walk up and down.*]

CECILY [*rather brightly*]   There is just one question I would like to be allowed to ask my guardian.

GWENDOLEN   An admirable idea! Mr. Worthing, there is just one question I would like to be permitted to put to you. Where is your brother Ernest? We are both engaged to be married to your brother Ernest, so it is a matter of some importance to us to know where your brother Ernest is at present.

JACK [*slowly and hesitatingly*]   Gwendolen—Cecily—it is very painful for me to be forced to speak the truth. It is the first time in my life that I have ever been reduced to such a painful position, and I am really quite inexperienced in doing anything of the kind. However, I will tell you quite frankly that I have no brother Ernest. I have no brother at all. I never had a brother in my life, and I certainly have not the smallest intention of ever having one in the future.

CECILY [*surprised*]   No brother at all?

JACK [*cheerily*]   None!

GWENDOLEN [*severely*]   Had you never a brother of any kind?

JACK [*pleasantly*]   Never. Not even of any kind.

GWENDOLEN   I am afraid it is quite clear, Cecily, that neither of us is engaged to be married to anyone.

CECILY   It is not a very pleasant position for a young girl suddenly to find herself in. Is it?

GWENDOLEN   Let us go into the house. They will hardly venture to come after us there.

CECILY   No, men are so cowardly, aren't they?

[*They retire into the house with scornful looks.*]

JACK   This ghastly state of things is what you call Bunburying, I suppose?

ALGERNON   Yes, and a perfectly wonderful Bunbury it is. The most wonderful Bunbury I have ever had in my life.

JACK   Well, you've no right whatsoever to Bunbury here.

ALGERNON   That is absurd. One has a right to Bunbury anywhere one chooses. Every serious Bunburyist knows that.

JACK   Serious Bunburyist? Good heavens!

ALGERNON   Well, one must be serious about something, if one wants to have any amusement in life. I happen to be serious about Bunburying. What on earth you are serious about I haven't got the remotest idea. About everything, I should fancy.   5
You have such an absolutely trivial nature.

JACK   Well, the only small satisfaction I have in the whole of this wretched business is that your friend Bunbury is quite exploded. You won't be able to run down to the country quite so often as you used to do, dear Algy. And a very good thing too.   10

ALGERNON   Your brother is a little off color, isn't he, dear Jack? You won't be able to disappear to London quite so frequently as your wicked custom was. And not a bad thing either.

JACK   As for your conduct towards Miss Cardew, I must say that your taking in a sweet, simple, innocent girl like that is quite   15
inexcusable. To say nothing of the fact that she is my ward.

ALGERNON   I can see no possible defence at all for your deceiving a brilliant, clever, thoroughly experienced young lady like Miss Fairfax. To say nothing of the fact that she is my cousin.

JACK   I wanted to be engaged to Gwendolen, that is all. I love her.   20

ALGERNON   Well, I simply wanted to be engaged to Cecily. I adore her.

JACK   There is certainly no chance of your marrying Miss Cardew.

ALGERNON   I don't think there is much likelihood, Jack, of you and Miss Fairfax being united.   25

JACK   Well, that is no business of yours.

ALGERNON   If it was my business, I wouldn't talk about it. [*Begins to eat muffins.*] It is very vulgar to talk about one's business. Only people like stockbrokers do that, and then merely at dinner parties.   30

JACK   How you can sit there, calmly eating muffins when we are in this horrible trouble, I can't make out. You seem to me to be perfectly heartless.

ALGERNON   Well, I can't eat muffins in an agitated manner. The butter would probably get on my cuffs. One should always eat   35
muffins quite calmly. It is the only way to eat them.

JACK   I say it's perfectly heartless your eating muffins at all, under the circumstances.

ALGERNON   When I am in trouble, eating is the only thing that consoles me. Indeed, when I am in really great trouble, as any   40
one who knows me intimately will tell you, I refuse everything

except food and drink. At the present moment I am eating muffins because I am unhappy. Besides, I am particularly fond of muffins. [*Rising.*]

JACK [*rising*] Well, there is no reason why you should eat them
5 all in that greedy way. [*Takes muffins from* ALGERNON.]

ALGERNON [*offering tea-cake*] I wish you would have tea-cake instead. I don't like tea-cake.

JACK Good heavens! I suppose a man may eat his own muffins in his own garden.

10 ALGERNON But you have just said it was perfectly heartless to eat muffins.

JACK I said it was perfectly heartless of you, under the circumstances. That is a very different thing.

ALGERNON That may be. But the muffins are the same. [*He seizes*
15 *the muffin-dish from* JACK.]

JACK Algy, I wish to goodness you would go.

ALGERNON You can't possibly ask me to go without having some dinner. It's absurd. I never go without my dinner. No one ever does, except vegetarians and people like that. Besides I have just
20 made arrangements with Dr. Chasuble to be christened at a quarter to six under the name of Ernest.

JACK My dear fellow, the sooner you give up that nonsense the better. I made arrangements this morning with Dr. Chasuble to be christened myself at 5:30, and I naturally will take the name
25 of Ernest. Gwendolen would wish it. We can't both be christened Ernest. It's absurd. Besides, I have a perfect right to be christened if I like. There is no evidence at all that I have ever been christened by anybody. I should think it extremely probable I never was, and so does Dr. Chasuble. It is entirely different
30 in your case. You have been christened already.

ALGERNON Yes, but I have not been christened for years.

JACK Yes, but you have been christened. That is the important thing.

ALGERNON Quite so. So I know my constitution can stand it.
35 If you are not quite sure about your ever having been christened, I must say I think it rather dangerous your venturing on it now. It might make you very unwell. You can hardly have forgotten that someone very closely connected with you was very nearly carried off this week in Paris by a severe chill.

40 JACK Yes, but you said yourself that a severe chill was not hereditary.

ALGERNON It usen't to be, I know—but I daresay it is now.
Science is always making wonderful improvements in things.

JACK [*picking up the muffin-dish*] Oh, that is nonsense; you are
always talking nonsense.

ALGERNON Jack, you are at the muffins again! I wish you 5
wouldn't. There are only two left. [*Takes them.*] I told you I
was particularly fond of muffins.

JACK But I hate tea-cake.

ALGERNON Why on earth then do you allow tea-cake to be served
up for your guests? What ideas you have of hospitality! 10

JACK Algernon! I have already told you to go. I don't want you
here. Why don't you go!

ALGERNON I haven't quite finished my tea yet! and there is still
one muffin left. [JACK *groans, and sinks into a chair.* ALGERNON
still continues eating.] 15

ACT THREE

Morning-room at the Manor House. GWENDOLEN *and* CECILY *are at the window, looking out into the garden.*

GWENDOLEN   The fact that they did not follow us at once into the house, as any one else would have done, seems to me to show that they have some sense of shame left.

CECILY   They have been eating muffins. That looks like repent-
5   ance.

GWENDOLEN [*after a pause*]   They don't seem to notice us at all. Couldn't you cough?

CECILY   But I haven't got a cough.

GWENDOLEN   They're looking at us. What effrontery!

10   CECILY   They're approaching. That's very forward of them.

GWENDOLEN   Let us preserve a dignified silence.

CECILY   Certainly. It's the only thing to do now.

[*Enter* JACK *followed by* ALGERNON. *They whistle some dreadful popular air from a British Opera.*]

GWENDOLEN   This dignified silence seems to produce an unpleasant effect.

15   CECILY   A most distasteful one.

GWENDOLEN   But we will not be the first to speak.

CECILY   Certainly not.

GWENDOLEN   Mr. Worthing, I have something very particular to ask you. Much depends on your reply.

20   CECILY   Gwendolen, your common sense is invaluable. Mr. Moncrieff, kindly answer me the following question. Why did you pretend to be my guardian's brother?

ALGERNON   In order that I might have an opportunity of meeting you.

25   CECILY [*to* GWENDOLEN]   That certainly seems a satisfactory explanation, does it not?

GWENDOLEN   Yes, dear, if you can believe him.

CECILY   I don't. But that does not affect the wonderful beauty of his answer.

30   GWENDOLEN   True. In matters of grave importance, style, not sincerity, is the vital thing. Mr. Worthing, what explanation can

430

you offer to me for pretending to have a brother? Was it in order that you might have an opportunity of coming up to town to see me as often as possible?

JACK   Can you doubt it, Miss Fairfax?

GWENDOLEN   I have the gravest doubts upon the subject. But I intend to crush them. This is not the moment for German scepticism. [*Moving to* CECILY.] Their explanations appear to be quite satisfactory, especially Mr. Worthing's. That seems to me to have the stamp of truth upon it.

CECILY   I am more than content with what Mr. Moncrieff said. His voice alone inspires one with absolute credulity.

GWENDOLEN   Then you think we should forgive them?

CECILY   Yes. I mean no.

GWENDOLEN   True! I had forgotten. There are principles at stake that one cannot surrender. Which of us should tell them? The task is not a pleasant one.

CECILY   Could we not both speak at the same time?

GWENDOLEN   An excellent idea! I nearly always speak at the same time as other people. Will you take the time from me?

CECILY   Certainly. [GWENDOLEN *beats time with uplifted finger.*]

GWENDOLEN *and* CECILY [*speaking together*]   Your Christian names are still an insuperable barrier. That is all!

JACK *and* ALGERNON [*speaking together*]   Our Christian names! Is that all? But we are going to be christened this afternoon.

GWENDOLEN [*to* JACK]   For my sake you are prepared to do this terrible thing?

JACK   I am.

CECILY [*to* ALGERNON]   To please me you are ready to face this fearful ordeal?

ALGERNON   I am!

GWENDOLEN   How absurd to talk of the equality of the sexes! Where questions of self-sacrifice are concerned, men are infinitely beyond us.

JACK   We are. [*Clasps hands with* ALGERNON.]

CECILY   They have moments of physical courage of which we women know absolutely nothing.

GWENDOLEN [*to* JACK]   Darling!

ALGERNON [*to* CECILY]   Darling! [*They fall into each other's arms.*]

[*Enter* MERRIMAN. *When he enters he coughs loudly, seeing the situation.*]

MERRIMAN   Ahem! Ahem! Lady Bracknell.

JACK   Good heavens!

[*Enter* LADY BRACKNELL. *The couples separate in alarm. Exit* MERRIMAN.]

LADY BRACKNELL   Gwendolen! What does this mean?

5   GWENDOLEN   Merely that I am engaged to be married to Mr. Worthing, mamma.

LADY BRACKNELL   Come here. Sit down. Sit down immediately. Hesitation of any kind is a sign of mental decay in the young, of physical weakness in the old. [*Turns to* JACK.] Apprised, sir, of my daughter's sudden flight by her trusty maid, whose con-
10   fidence I purchased by means of a small coin, I followed her at once by a luggage train. Her unhappy father is, I am glad to say, under the impression that she is attending a more than usually lengthy lecture by the University Extension Scheme on the Influence of a Permanent Income on Thought. I do not pro-
15   pose to undeceive him. Indeed I have never undeceived him on any question. I would consider it wrong. But of course, you will clearly understand that all communication between yourself and my daughter must cease immediately from this moment. On this point, as indeed on all points, I am firm.

20   JACK   I am engaged to be married to Gwendolen, Lady Bracknell!

LADY BRACKNELL   You are nothing of the kind, sir. And now as regards Algernon! . . . Algernon!

ALGERNON   Yes, Aunt Augusta.

25   LADY BRACKNELL   May I ask if it is in this house that your invalid friend Mr. Bunbury resides?

ALGERNON   [*stammering*]   Oh! No! Bunbury doesn't live here. Bunbury is somewhere else at present. In fact, Bunbury is dead.

LADY BRACKNELL   Dead! When did Mr. Bunbury die? His death
30   must have been extremely sudden.

ALGERNON   [*airily*]   Oh! I killed Bunbury this afternoon. I mean poor Bunbury died this afternoon.

LADY BRACKNELL   What did he die of?

ALGERNON   Bunbury? Oh, he was quite exploded.

35   LADY BRACKNELL   Exploded! Was he the victim of a revolutionary

outrage? I was not aware that Mr. Bunbury was interested in social legislation. If so, he is well punished for his morbidity.

ALGERNON   My dear Aunt Augusta, I mean he was found out! The doctors found out that Bunbury could not live, that is what I mean—so Bunbury died.   5

LADY BRACKNELL   He seems to have had great confidence in the opinion of his physicians. I am glad, however, that he made up his mind at the last to some definite course of action, and acted under proper medical advice. And now that we have finally got rid of this Mr. Bunbury, may I ask, Mr. Worthing, who is that young   10 person whose hand my nephew Algernon is now holding in what seems to me a peculiarly unnecessary manner?

JACK   That lady is Miss Cecily Cardew, my ward. [LADY BRACKNELL *bows coldly to* CECILY.]

ALGERNON   I am engaged to be married to Cecily, Aunt Augusta.   15

LADY BRACKNELL   I beg your pardon?

CECILY   Mr. Moncrieff and I are engaged to be married, Lady Bracknell.

LADY BRACKNELL [*with a shiver, crossing to the sofa and sitting down*]   I do not know whether there is anything peculiarly ex-   20 citing in the air of this particular part of Hertfordshire, but the number of engagements that go on seems to me considerably above the proper average that statistics have laid down for our guidance. I think some preliminary inquiry on my part would not be out of place. Mr. Worthing, is Miss Cardew at all con-   25 nected with any of the larger railway stations in London? I merely desire information. Until yesterday I had no idea that there were any families or persons whose origin was a Terminus. [JACK *looks perfectly furious, but restrains himself.*]

JACK [*in a cold, clear voice*]   Miss Cardew is the granddaughter of   30 the late Mr. Thomas Cardew of 149 Belgrave Square, S.W.; Gervase Park, Dorking, Surrey; and the Sporran, Fifeshire, N.B.

LADY BRACKNELL   That sounds not unsatisfactory. Three addresses always inspire confidence, even in tradesmen. But what proof have I of their authenticity?   35

JACK   I have carefully preserved the Court Guides of the period. They are open to your inspection, Lady Bracknell.

LADY BRACKNELL [*grimly*]   I have known strange errors in that publication.

JACK   Miss Cardew's family solicitors are Messrs. Markby,   40 Markby, and Markby.

LADY BRACKNELL   Markby, Markby, and Markby? A firm of the very highest position in their profession. Indeed I am told that one of the Mr. Markby's is occasionally to be seen at dinner parties. So far I am satisfied.

JACK [*very irritably*]   How extremely kind of you, Lady Bracknell! I have also in my possession, you will be pleased to hear, certificates of Miss Cardew's birth, baptism, whooping cough, registration, vaccination, confirmation, and the measles; both the German and the English variety.

LADY BRACKNELL   Ah! A life crowded with incident, I see; though perhaps somewhat too exciting for a young girl. I am not myself in favor of premature experiences. [*Rises, looks at her watch.*] Gwendolen! the time approaches for our departure. We have not a moment to lose. As a matter of form, Mr. Worthing, I had better ask you if Miss Cardew has any little fortune?

JACK   Oh! about a hundred and thirty thousand pounds in the Funds. That is all. Good-bye, Lady Bracknell. So pleased to have seen you.

LADY BRACKNELL [*sitting down again*]   A moment, Mr. Worthing. A hundred and thirty thousand pounds! And in the Funds! Miss Cardew seems to me a most attractive young lady, now that I look at her. Few girls of the present day have any really solid qualities, any of the qualities that last, and improve with time. We live, I regret to say, in an age of surfaces. [*To* CECILY] Come over here, dear. [CECILY *goes across.*] Pretty child! your dress is sadly simple, and your hair seems almost as Nature might have left it. But we can soon alter all that. A thoroughly experienced French maid produces a really marvellous result in a very brief space of time. I remember recommending one to young Lady Lancing, and after three months her own husband did not know her.

JACK   And after six months nobody knew her.

LADY BRACKNELL [*glares at Jack for a few moments. Then bends, with a practised smile, to* CECILY]   Kindly turn round, sweet child. [CECILY *turns completely round.*] No, the side view is what I want. [CECILY *presents her profile.*] Yes, quite as I expected. There are distinct social possibilities in your profile. The two weak points in our age are its want of principle and its want of profile. The chin a little higher, dear. Style largely depends on the way the chin is worn. They are worn very high, just at present. Algernon!

ALGERNON   Yes, Aunt Augusta!

LADY BRACKNELL   There are distinct social possibilities in Miss Cardew's profile.

ALGERNON   Cecily is the sweetest, dearest, prettiest girl in the whole
world. And I don't care twopence about social possibilities.

LADY BRACKNELL   Never speak disrespectfully of Society, Algernon. Only people who can't get into it do that. [*To Cecily.*]
Dear child, of course you know that Algernon has nothing but   5
his debts to depend upon. But I do not approve of mercenary
marriages. When I married Lord Bracknell I had no fortune of
any kind. But I never dreamed for a moment of allowing that
to stand in my way. Well, I suppose I must give my consent.

ALGERNON   Thank you, Aunt Augusta.   10

LADY BRACKNELL   Cecily, you may kiss me!

CECILY [*kisses her*]   Thank you, Lady Bracknell.

LADY BRACKNELL   You may also address me as Aunt Augusta for
the future.

CECILY   Thank you, Aunt Augusta.   15

LADY BRACKNELL   The marriage, I think, had better take place
quite soon.

ALGERNON   Thank you, Aunt Augusta.

CECILY   Thank you, Aunt Augusta.

LADY BRACKNELL   To speak frankly, I am not in favor of long   20
engagements. They give people the opportunity of finding out
each other's character before marriage, which I think is never advisable.

JACK   I beg your pardon for interrupting you, Lady Bracknell, but
this engagement is quite out of the question. I am Miss Cardew's 25
guardian, and she cannot marry without my consent until she
comes of age. That consent I absolutely decline to give.

LADY BRACKNELL   Upon what grounds, may I ask? Algernon is an
extremely, I may almost say an ostentatiously, eligible young man.
He has nothing, but he looks everything. What more can one   30
desire?

JACK   It pains me very much to have to speak frankly to you, Lady
Bracknell, about your nephew, but the fact is that I do not approve at all of his moral character. I suspect him of being untruthful. [ALGERNON *and* CECILY *look at him in indignant amaze-* 35
ment.]

LADY BRACKNELL   Untruthful! My nephew Algernon? Impossible!
He is an Oxonian.

JACK   I fear there can be no possible doubt about the matter. This
afternoon during my temporary absence in London on an impor-   40
tant question of romance, he obtained admission to my house by
means of the false pretense of being my brother. Under an as-

sumed name he drank, I've just been informed by my butler, an
entire pint bottle of my Perrier-Jouet, Brut, '89; wine I was specially reserving for myself. Continuing his disgraceful deception,
he succeeded in the course of the afternoon in alienating the
5   affections of my only ward. He subsequently stayed to tea, and
devoured every single muffin. And what makes his conduct all the
more heartless is, that he was perfectly well aware from the first
that I have no brother, that I never had a brother, and that I
don't intend to have a brother, not even of any kind. I distinctly
10   told him so myself yesterday afternoon.

LADY BRACKNELL   Ahem! Mr. Worthing, after careful consideration I have decided entirely to overlook my nephew's conduct to
you.

JACK   That is very generous of you, Lady Bracknell. My own de-
15   cision, however, is unalterable. I decline to give my consent.

LADY BRACKNELL [to CECILY]   Come here, sweet child. [CECILY
goes over.] How old are you, dear?

CECILY   Well, I am really only eighteen, but I always admit to
twenty when I go to evening parties.

20   LADY BRACKNELL   You are perfectly right in making some slight
alteration. Indeed, no woman should ever be quite accurate about
her age. It looks so calculating. . . . [In a meditative manner.]
Eighteen, but admitting to twenty at evening parties. Well, it will
not be very long before you are of age and free from the re-
25   straints of tutelage. So I don't think your guardian's consent is,
after all, a matter of any importance.

JACK   Pray excuse me, Lady Bracknell, for interrupting you again,
but it is only fair to tell you that according to the terms of her
grandfather's will Miss Cardew does not come legally of age till
30   she is thirty-five.

LADY BRACKNELL   That does not seem to me to be a grave objection. Thirty-five is a very attractive age. London society is full
of women of the very highest birth who have, of their own free
choice, remained thirty-five for years. Lady Dumbleton is an
35   instance in point. To my own knowledge she has been thirty-five
ever since she arrived at the age of forty, which was many years
ago now. I see no reason why our dear Cecily should not be even
still more attractive at the age you mention than she is at present.
There will be a large accumulation of property.

40   CECILY   Algy, could you wait for me till I was thirty-five?

ALGERNON   Of course I could, Cecily. You know I could.

CECILY   Yes, I felt it instinctively, but I couldn't wait all that
time. I hate waiting even five minutes for anybody. It always

makes me rather cross. I am not punctual myself, I know, but I do like punctuality in others, and waiting, even to be married, is quite out of the question.

ALGERNON   Then what is to be done, Cecily?

CECILY   I don't know, Mr. Moncrieff.   5

LADY BRACKNELL   My dear Mr. Worthing, as Miss Cardew states positively that she cannot wait till she is thirty-five—a remark which I am bound to say seems to me to show a somewhat impatient nature—I would beg of you to reconsider your decision.

JACK   But my dear Lady Bracknell, the matter is entirely in your   10
own hands. The moment you consent to my marriage with Gwendolen, I will most gladly allow your nephew to form an alliance with my ward.

LADY BRACKNELL [rising and drawing herself up]   You must be quite aware that what you propose is out of the question.   15

JACK   Then a passionate celibacy is all that any of us can look forward to.

LADY BRACKNELL   That is not the destiny I propose for Gwendolen. Algernon, of course, can choose for himself. [Pulls out her watch.] Come, dear [GWENDOLEN rises], we have already missed   20
five, if not six, trains. To miss any more might expose us to comment on the platform.

[Enter DR. CHASUBLE.]

CHASUBLE   Everything is quite ready for the christenings.

LADY BRACKNELL   The christenings, sir! Is not that somewhat pre-   25
mature?

CHASUBLE [looking rather puzzled, and pointing to JACK and AL-
GERNON]   Both these gentlemen have expressed a desire for immediate baptism.

LADY BRACKNELL   At their age? The idea is grotesque and irreligious! Algernon, I forbid you to be baptized. I will not hear   30
of such excesses. Lord Bracknell would be highly displeased if he learned that that was the way in which you wasted your time and money.

CHASUBLE   Am I to understand then that there are to be no christenings at all this afternoon?   35

JACK   I don't think that, as things are now, it would be of much practical value to either of us, Dr. Chasuble.

CHASUBLE   I am grieved to hear such sentiments from you, Mr. Worthing. They savour of the heretical views of the Anabaptists, views that I have completely refuted in four of my unpublished sermons. However, as your present mood seems to be one peculiarly secular, I will return to the church at once. Indeed, I have just been informed by the pew-opener that for the last hour and a half Miss Prism has been waiting for me in the vestry.

LADY BRACKNELL [*starting*]   Miss Prism! Did I hear you mention a Miss Prism?

CHASUBLE   Yes, Lady Bracknell. I am on my way to join her.

LADY BRACKNELL   Pray allow me to detain you for a moment. This matter may prove to be one of vital importance to Lord Bracknell and myself. Is this Miss Prism a female of repellent aspect, remotely connected with education?

CHASUBLE [*somewhat indignantly*]   She is the most cultivated of ladies, and the very picture of respectability.

LADY BRACKNELL   It is obviously the same person. May I ask what position she holds in your household?

CHASUBLE [*severely*]   I am a celibate, madam.

JACK [*interposing*]   Miss Prism, Lady Bracknell, has been for the last three years Miss Cardew's esteemed governess and valued companion.

LADY BRACKNELL   In spite of what I hear of her, I must see her at once. Let her be sent for.

CHASUBLE [*looking off*]   She approaches; she is nigh.

[*Enter* MISS PRISM *hurriedly.*]

MISS PRISM   I was told you expected me in the vestry, dear Canon. I have been waiting for you there for an hour and three-quarters. [*Catches sight of* LADY BRACKNELL, *who has fixed her with a stony glare.* MISS PRISM *grows pale and quails. She looks anxiously round as if desirous to escape.*]

LADY BRACKNELL [*in a severe, judicial voice*]   Prism! [MISS PRISM *bows her head in shame.*] Come here, Prism! [MISS PRISM *approaches in a humble manner.*] Prism! Where is that baby? [*General consternation. The* CANON *starts back in horror.* ALGERNON *and* JACK *pretend to be anxious to shield* CECILY *and* GWENDOLEN *from hearing the details of a terrible public scandal.*] Twenty-eight years ago, Prism, you left Lord Bracknell's house, Number 104, Upper Grosvenor Square, in charge of a perambulator that contained a baby of the male sex. You never returned. A few weeks later, through the elaborate investigations of the Metropolitan police, the perambulator was discovered at midnight standing by itself in a remote corner of Bayswater. It contained the manuscript of a three-volume novel of more than usually revolting sentimentality. [MISS PRISM *starts in involuntary indignation.*] But the baby was not there. [*Every one looks at* MISS PRISM.] Prism! Where is that baby? [*A pause.*]

MISS PRISM   Lady Bracknell, I admit with shame that I do not 5 know. I only wish I did. The plain facts of the case are these. On the morning of the day you mention, a day that is for ever branded on my memory, I prepared as usual to take the baby out in its perambulator. I had also with me a somewhat old, but capacious handbag in which I had intended to place the manu- 10 script of a work of fiction that I had written during my few un- occupied hours. In a moment of mental abstraction, for which I can never forgive myself, I deposited the manuscript in the bassinette and placed the baby in the handbag.

JACK [*who has been listening attentively*]   But where did you de- 15 posit the handbag?

MISS PRISM   Do not ask me, Mr. Worthing.

JACK   Miss Prism, this is a matter of no small importance to me. I insist on knowing where you deposited the handbag that con- tained that infant. 20

MISS PRISM   I left it in the cloakroom of one of the larger railway stations in London.

JACK   What railway station?

MISS PRISM [*quite crushed*]   Victoria. The Brighton line. [*Sinks into a chair.*] 25

JACK   I must retire to my room for a moment. Gwendolen, wait here for me.

GWENDOLEN   If you are not too long, I will wait here for you all my life. [*Exit* JACK *in great excitement.*]

CHASUBLE   What do you think this means, Lady Bracknell? 30

LADY BRACKNELL   I dare not even suspect, Dr. Chasuble. I need hardly tell you that in families of high position strange coin- cidences are not supposed to occur. They are hardly considered the thing.

[*Noises heard overhead as if some one was throwing trunks about. Every one looks up.*]

CECILY   Uncle Jack seems strangely agitated. 35

CHASUBLE   Your guardian has a very emotional nature.

LADY BRACKNELL   This noise is extremely unpleasant. It sounds as if he was having an argument. I dislike arguments of any kind. They are always vulgar, and often convincing.

CHASUBLE [*looking up*]   It has stopped now. [*The noise is re-doubled.*]

LADY BRACKNELL   I wish he would arrive at some conclusion.

GWENDOLEN   This suspense is terrible. I hope it will last.

[*Enter* JACK *with a handbag of black leather in his hand.*]

5   JACK [*rushing over to* MISS PRISM]   Is this the handbag, Miss Prism? Examine it carefully before you speak. The happiness of more than one life depends on your answer.

MISS PRISM [*calmly*]   It seems to be mine. Yes, here is the injury it received through the upsetting of a Gower Street omnibus in 10   younger and happier days. Here is the stain on the lining caused by the explosion of a temperance beverage, an incident that oc-curred at Leamington. And here, on the lock, are my initials. I had forgotten that in an extravagant mood I had had them placed there. The bag is undoubtedly mine. I am delighted to have it 15   so unexpectedly restored to me. It has been a great inconvenience being without it all these years.

JACK [*in a pathetic voice*]   Miss Prism, more is restored to you than this handbag. I was the baby you placed in it.

MISS PRISM [*amazed*]   You?

20   JACK [*embracing her*]   Yes . . . mother!

MISS PRISM [*recoiling in indignant astonishment*]   Mr. Worthing, I am unmarried!

JACK   Unmarried! I do not deny that is a serious blow. But after all, who has the right to cast a stone against one who has suf-25   fered? Cannot repentance wipe out an act of folly? Why should there be one law for men, and another for women? Mother, I forgive you. [*Tries to embrace her again.*]

MISS PRISM [*still more indignant*]   Mr. Worthing, there is some error. [*Pointing to* LADY BRACKNELL.] There is the lady who can 30   tell you who you really are.

JACK [*after a pause*]   Lady Bracknell, I hate to seem inquisitive, but would you kindly inform me who I am?

LADY BRACKNELL   I am afraid that the news I have to give you will not altogether please you. You are the son of my poor sister, 35   Mrs. Moncrieff, and consequently Algernon's elder brother.

JACK   Algy's elder brother! Then I have a brother after all. I knew I had a brother! I always said I had a brother! Cecily—how could you have ever doubted that I had a brother? [*Seizes hold of* ALGERNON.] Dr. Chasuble, my unfortunate brother. Miss Prism, my unfortunate brother. Gwendolen, my unfortunate brother. Algy, you young scoundrel, you will have to treat me with more respect in the future. You have never behaved to me like a brother in all your life.

ALGERNON Well, not till today, old boy, I admit. I did my best, however, though I was out of practice.

[*Shakes hands.*]

GWENDOLEN [*to* JACK] My own! But what own are you? What is your Christian name, now that you have become some one else?

JACK Good heavens! . . . I had quite forgotten that point. Your decision on the subject of my name is irrevocable, I suppose?

GWENDOLEN I never change, except in my affections.

CECILY What a noble nature you have, Gwendolen!

JACK Then the question had better be cleared up at once. Aunt Augusta, a moment. At the time when Miss Prism left me in the handbag, had I been christened already?

LADY BRACKNELL Every luxury that money could buy, including christening, had been lavished on you by your fond and doting parents.

JACK Then I was christened! That is settled. Now, what name was I given? Let me know the worst.

LADY BRACKNELL Being the eldest son you were naturally christened after your father.

JACK [*irritably*] Yes, but what was my father's Christian name?

LADY BRACKNELL [*meditatively*] I cannot at the present moment recall what the General's Christian name was. But I have no doubt he had one. He was eccentric, I admit. But only in later years. And that was the result of the Indian climate, and marriage, and indigestion, and other things of that kind.

JACK Algy! Can't you recollect what our father's Christian name was?

ALGERNON My dear boy, we were never even on speaking terms. He died before I was a year old.

JACK His name would appear in the Army Lists of the period, I suppose, Aunt Augusta?

LADY BRACKNELL The General was essentially a man of peace, except in his domestic life. But I have no doubt his name would appear in any military directory.

JACK The Army Lists of the last forty years are here. These de-

lightful records should have been my constant study. [*Rushes to bookcase and tears the books out.*] M. Generals . . . Mallam, Maxbohm, Magley—what ghastly names they have—Markby, Migsby, Mobbs, Moncrieff! Lieutenant 1840, Captain, Lieutenant-
5 Colonel, Colonel, General 1869, Christian names, Ernest John. [*Puts book very quietly down and speaks quite calmly.*] I always told you, Gwendolen, my name was Ernest, didn't I? Well, it is Ernest after all. I mean it naturally is Ernest.

LADY BRACKNELL Yes, I remember now that the General was
10 called Ernest. I knew I had some particular reason for disliking the name.

GWENDOLEN Ernest! My own Ernest! I felt from the first that you could have no other name!

JACK Gwendolen, it is terrible thing for a man to find out sud-
15 denly that all his life he has been speaking nothing but the truth. Can you forgive me?

GWENDOLEN I can. For I feel that you are sure to change.

JACK My own one!

CHASUBLE [*to* MISS PRISM] Laetitia! [*Embraces her.*]

20 MISS PRISM [*enthusiastically*] Frederick! At last!

ALGERNON Cecily! [*Embraces her.*] At last!

JACK Gwendolen! [*Embraces her.*] At last!

LADY BRACKNELL My nephew, you seem to be displaying signs of triviality.

25 JACK On the contrary, Aunt Augusta, I've now realized for the first time in my life the vital Importance of Being Earnest.

THE END

A PLAY: SCENARIO OR POEM

In an article in the *Hudson Review* (Autumn, 1956) entitled "Problems for the Modern Critic of Literature" Mr. Yvor Winters makes some rather startling statements about the drama. He makes some rather startling statements about a good number of other things as well, but his remarks about the dramatic form in general and *Macbeth* in particular ask, I think, for some kind of comment. Mr. Winters is a good critic; the issues he raises here are important issues, issues that should be considered by anyone seriously interested in the dramatic form. And though I think he is wrong, he is wrong in an important way.

The position that Mr. Winters takes in regard to this subject is most clearly stated in the following paragraph.

> Let us suppose that the dramatist is imitating the speech of a character of moderate intelligence in a situation of which the character does not in any serious sense understand the meaning. This presents an almost insoluble problem. If a poet is endeavoring to communicate his own best understanding of a situation, that is one thing. If he is endeavoring to communicate approximately a plausible misunderstanding of a situation on the part of an imaginary character much less intelligent than himself, that is quite another. He can only guess at the correct measure of stupidity which may be proper to such a character in a given situation, whether the character is offered as an imitation or as a plausible imitation of an imitation; and whether he is successful or not, he will still be writing poetry which as poetry will be of an inferior kind. Exactly what is the target? It seems to me that the whole business must in the nature of the case be a rough approximation—and rough approximations are unfortunate affairs in the fine arts.

This insistence on "rough approximations" in drama seems to me, quite simply, not true. On the contrary, if the dramatist is good he is attempting "by his own best understanding of a human situation" to communicate through that complex of attitudes of all of the characters in a play not only what the characters think but what the playwright thinks; and he does this, as does any literary artist, first and foremost with words. Words, to be sure, which are to be spoken by an actor on a stage with all the machinery the stage offers, but words put together in such a fashion that they tell the actor how they are to be spoken and what gestures and mannerisms should accompany them. The words then should guide the actor. If he is a good actor, he allows them to, and the result is a combination of

443

word and gesture that creates the attitude to which we are to respond.

Now since this attitude is originally created and judged by the playwright through the manner in which he puts together the words that create that attitude, that character, he is not imitating "an imaginary character much less intelligent than himself," any more than a lyric poet is imitating a lover much more emotionally involved than himself when he writes a love lyric. I don't know what kind of imitation is going on in the first line of Donne's *Canonization,* but I do feel as I read through the poem that it is an attitude carefully controlled and qualified not by the lover but by the poet.

I suspect that what I would call Mr. Winters' confusion in regard to drama results in part from his concept of character. In the course of his article he spends some time looking at Macbeth's soliloquy, "Is this a dagger which I see before me?" His most extended objections I hope to deal with later, but I would like to look at one comment here. In referring to one part of the soliloquy Mr. Winters says: "It seems unlikely that Macbeth in real life would have spoken anything so elaborate, but had he done so it would doubtless have been violent; and it would certainly have been composed of stereotypes, because at this stage of his development he had only a stereotyped understanding of what he was doing." Now such a view is understandable only if one believes that a playwright is communicating a "plausible misunderstanding of a situation on the part of an imaginary character much less intelligent than himself." If, however, one conceives of a character as a carefully defined series of believably connected attitudes toward a series of events, attitudes furthermore that come out of the real head of Shakespeare rather than the fictional head of Macbeth, there is the possibility, at least, of a very different evaluation of drama and of *Macbeth* than that of Mr. Winters. The problem, of course, is how one is to know which head is talking.

The way to discover the poet's view in a play, at least in a play of Shakespeare, is, it seems to me, very similar to the way one discovers a poet's view in a lyric poem. To be sure the tools in the two genres are not identical. A lyric poet uses language exclusively. A good playwright uses contrasting scenes, contrasting characters, even contrasting actions as well. But he creates his scenes, his actions, and his characters with language. If he is good, with very precise language. One understands a character in a play (and I assume it is clear that by character I mean that complex of attitudes that define one point of view in a play, a point of view called Macbeth, Lady Macbeth, and so on) by examining all of the speeches that create it. And all, here, means not only the speeches of that particular character, but all of those speeches given by other characters that refer to it. All of these speeches create the context in which any single speech must be examined, just as the fourteen lines of a sonnet create the context in which any single line is understood. As a consequence, when Mr. Winters evaluates the "Is this a dagger which I see before me" soliloquy of Macbeth as "not very good poetry," as "an imitation of a second-rate intelligence in a distraught condition," without apparently any sense of the mind of Shakespeare, he is, it seems to me, evaluating badly, if for no other reason than that he is not looking at the whole context of the "poem." To judge a single speech in a play in the same way as one judges a single sonnet is unfair, not because speeches in poetic drama can't be examined on the same terms as a lyric, but because, unless the whole context in which that single speech operates (namely the whole dramatic sequence of events and speeches that have preceded it) is considered, one is not examining that speech on the same terms on which he examines a sonnet. It is more like examining the couplet without reference to the preceding twelve lines.

By the use of scene juxtaposition, previous speeches by a given character, and speeches by other characters both to and about the given one, a dramatist is able to create a point of view, a character, which is not only a part of the experience at which the playwright is looking but is also, in the *way* he is presented, put in some kind of evaluating relation to that experience. This is not to say that any single character or point of view in the play is the same as the playwright's. Obviously it cannot be more than one part of the total attitude expressed in the play, but I do wish to make clear my belief that we should be able to hear what is wrong with Macbeth, whether Macbeth knows it or not, by the way in which he is made to talk. In doing this Shakespeare need no more "guess at the correct measure of stupidity which may be proper to such a character in a given situation" as Mr. Winters would have us believe, than the poet need guess at the particular attitude he takes in any given poem. Macbeth's attitude came out of Shakespeare's head too. In other words, in a good play the dramatist evaluates the experience he examines through the way all of the characters in the play speak about and react to the particular experience (whether it be love or murder) that the playwright is examining, just as surely as the poet evaluates the experience he is looking at in let us say a good sonnet. In both cases the language operates in such a way as to let us know the playwright's and the lyric poet's attitude toward the experience being examined.

Lest all this seem rather vague talk let me look for a moment at two short poems, poems which operate in the way I have been suggesting the drama operates. They are poems which evaluate an experience by creating an attitude toward that experience which looks, on the surface to be that of an "imaginary character," a speaker at any rate, of less intelligence than the poet. Obviously the attitude I am looking at here is the whole attitude, because the poem is the whole work. To make a direct parallel to a play, one would have to examine the whole play, all of the attitudes expressed in it. The method used in both cases, however, is similar.

The first of these speaker-poets I want to consider is Sir Walter Raleigh in his poem *The Lie*. As one reads through this poem, he may feel, as I do, that the tone of voice of the poet (if he hears a tone of voice) is a little too angry, a little too excited in his condemnations, even a little naïve. The series of commands culminating in the next to last verse

> Tell faith it's fled the city;
> Tell how the country erreth;
> Tell, manhood shakes off pity,
> Tell, virtue least preferred:

though saved from preaching by both the rhythm and the rhyme sounds nevertheless a little overstated, and I think consciously so. It is, I think, just this sense of overstatement that allows for the power of "blabbing" in the last verse.

> So when thou hast, as I
> Commanded thee, done blabbing,
> Because to give the lie
> Deserves no less than stabbing
> Stab at thee he that will—
> No stab the soul can kill.

One has heard the over-insistence, the over-annoyance of the speaker at the viciousness of the world around him in these earlier commands, and one is a little suspicious of such zeal, a zeal that almost suggests naïveté, until the sudden appearance of "blabbing" makes clear the knowledge and the sophistication of the speaker. We see clearly, what the carefully controlled rhythm has suggested, that the speaker realizes the kind of overstatement he is making, that he realizes, even though everything he said is true, that one doesn't in some active way *do* anything about it. And the sophistication of the speaker, made evident through the way he says what he says, is what finally determines our own reaction to the poem, our own sense of Raleigh's maturity.

I think much the same process goes on in many lyrics, even such formal structures as sonnets. I mean here not only those sonnets with a directly implied second person like Drayton's *Since there's no help, come let us kiss and part,* but any sonnet, Shakespeare's *When to the sessions of sweet silent thought,* for example. I have heard this poem praised for its beautiful alliteration, for its legal imagery.

At the same time I have heard it damned for its weak couplet. It seems to me that both kinds of comment are legitimate, but I can only really put them altogether as part of a single reading, by referring to the speaker in the poem. One remembers the abundance of *s*'s in the first line, and the *w*'s in the fourth, and occasionally, particularly in that first line, one falls prey to its sweetness, overlooking the fact that as the poem moves on it really gets pretty sloppy and sentimental, not obviously, but surely. There is something a little too self-conscious in drowning an eye "unused to flow," in the repetition of grieve in "grieve at grievances," in those "precious friends" hid in "death's dateless night," and certainly the precious blubbering of "fore-bemoaned moan." This is a grief that one hesitates to take too seriously. The speaker's lace handkerchief almost shows. Even the legal imagery is a little untender, a little conscious. And it seems to me that it is precisely *because* this grief is so self-concious that the couplet (weak as it is to turn the poet from heartfelt grief) is about right *here*. For a really felt grief this thinking-on-thee-dear-friend to end all sorrows is a little easy. If this is all it takes to remove the pain, it couldn't have been much. Yet if we hear those first twelve lines as a nostalgic sigh of pleasureful self-pity, a delight in easy tears, then the change back to normalcy with the ease the couplet suggests seems about right, seems to evaluate the kind of grief here delineated for what it is worth. And one feels the poet, or the speaker here, appreciates this feeling for what it is worth in a way that Shelley, for example, doesn't usually manage.

I mention these poems only to suggest that one of the ways we are able to evaluate and judge the experience the poet presents to us, is by hearing the speaker, by hearing the poet's tone of voice, his particular pose as his choice of words and rhythms define it for us. It may be true that the structural principle in the short poem is logic, as Mr. Winters insists, but we do sometimes get what he calls the "total understanding," "not merely the rational but the emotional as well," by evaluating the speaker and his logic in the poem, by evaluating the particular attitude that the poet adopts in the particular poem under examination. And just as we may hear the poet in a poem *through the speaker the poet creates for us* in that poem, so we hear the dramatist through the characters the dramatist creates for us. To be sure we hear many more speakers in the drama, and we are usually presented with a greater number of experiences, though not unrelated ones. As a consequence the totality of the play may be a good deal more difficult to define than the totality of a single lyric, but not I think, due to an inherent "weakness" in the form.

If, for example, I were to look at that soliloquy that Mr. Winters dismisses so easily as "not very good poetry" in its total context, something Mr. Winters does not do, I think it might even be found to be fairly good, not simply the imitation of a "distraught state of mind" which gives "the actor opportunity to ham it," but a surprisingly precise delineation of both Macbeth's condition at this point in the play and Shakespeare's judgment of that condition. Despite its familiarity I wish to quote it in full so that I can make specific reference.

> Is this a dagger which I see before me,
> The handle toward my hand? Come, let me clutch thee.
> I have thee not, and yet I see thee still.
> Art thou not, fatal vision, sensible
> To feeling as to sight: or art thou but
> A dagger of the mind, a false creation,
> Proceeding from the heat-oppressèd brain?
> I see thee yet, in form as palpable
> As this which now I draw.
> Thou marshal'st me the way that I was going;
> And such an instrument I was to use.
> Mine eyes are made the fools o'the other senses,
> Or else worth all the rest; I see thee still,
> And on thy blade and dudgeon gouts of blood,
> Which was not so before. There's no such thing:
> It is the bloody business which informs
> Thus to mine eyes. Now o'er the one half-world
> Nature seems dead, and wicked dreams abuse
> The curtain'd sleep; witchcraft celebrates
> Pale Hecate's offerings, and wither'd murder,
> Alarum'd by his sentinel, the wolf,
> Whose howl's his watch, thus with his stealthy pace,
> With Tarquin's ravishing strides, toward his design
> Moves like a ghost. Thou sure and firm-set earth,
> Hear not my steps, which way they walk, for fear
> Thy very stones prate of my whereabout,
> And take the present horror from the time,
> Which now suits with it. Whiles I threat, he lives:
> Words to the heat of deeds too cold breath gives.
> I go, and it is done; the bell invites me.
> Hear it not Duncan; for it is a knell
> That summons thee to heaven or to hell.

Mr. Winters seems fairly happy with the first seven lines but finds the next ten redundant and the following five inappropriate to the character speaking them. The last eight lines he conveniently ignores. The repetitions that bother Mr. Winters are obvious enough, the similar phrases in the third, eighth, and thirteenth line and the material following each. In the third line it appears in the last half of that line, "and yet I see thee still"; in the eighth it opens the line

"I see thee yet"; and in the thirteenth it ends the line in the form "I see thee still." This insistence on seeing, on not being able not to see, seems redundant to Mr. Winters. He would be happier, apparently, if the soliloquy moved from the end of the seventh line to the middle of the fifteenth. This is what the lyric poet who "is endeavoring to communicate his own best understanding of a human situation" would have done. Now it's my own belief that if he had done this, he would not have made the same, nor as clear, a judgment of the particular condition being here examined, as Shakespeare does by that repetition.

The emphasis in this soliloquy, particularly in the first fourteen and one-half lines is on sight, and this emphasis is not so that some actor can "ham" it but in order to say something about the importance Macbeth places on what he can see, on what he can determine with his five immediate senses. If he can *see* that dagger here, it must be real, and not a dagger of the mind. If he can convince himself that "there is no such thing," for he would like to persuade himself that *things,* like daggers, have tangible reality or none at all, then he can dismiss this vision as a "wicked dream." One of the major struggles for Macbeth throughout the play is to persuade himself that the immediate, the tangible is worth more than the imagined, that a kingdom on earth will compensate for a possible damnation in hell, that some kind of immediate and tangible protection (no man of woman born, Burnham woods moving) can keep him from a distant and perhaps only imagined hell fire. Hell can't be seen except through an imagination, prompted perhaps by a conscience, but not physically demonstrable. Hell manifests itself in images, in "wicked dreams," and though in the course of the play one is persuaded, as is Macbeth, that those tangible, literal, immediate antidotes to his imagination will not remain on a tangible immediate level, here that answer is still in doubt.

Macbeth would deny his imagination, his conscience if he could, though he knows the difficulty. He had said in the previous scene

> If the assassination
> Could trammel up the consequence, and catch
> With his surcease success; that but this blow
> Might be the be-all and the end-all here,
> But here, upon this bank and shoal of time
> We'd jump the life to come. But in these cases
> We still have judgment here.

The power of that conscience and its instrument, imagined image, has been thoroughly examined by Macbeth, so thoroughly that at the end of the soliloquy he is ready to admit the impossibility of denying it. He doesn't attempt to deny it, until Lady Macbeth's beautiful chop logic lulls his judgment.

> Then you were a man;
> And to be more than what you were, you would
> Be so much more the man.

Logic is not Macbeth's strong point. His judgment operates most surely through his imagination, sub-rationally rather than rationally. When Lady Macbeth appeals in this pseudo-rational fashion Macbeth is swayed, swayed in actuality not by the rationality but by the most universal of female tricks "you don't love me," "you are afraid," and the like. Such arguments convince because the woman that uses them is an immediate tangible desirable presence, a presence that cuts off imagination, Macbeth's surest judge.

The preceding scene (the one that has included both the other soliloquy quoted and the scene with Lady Macbeth) is as necessary in considering both the meaning and judgment implicit in this speech as is the first line or two of a sonnet. The preceding scene in part accounts for the appearance of the dagger at this point in the play. If Lady Macbeth's presence could stifle the imagination, her absence gives it free reign to operate again; and operate it does, to counsel Macbeth against murder. But now Macbeth would fight it, would fight it with his commitment to the present, to the immediate, the tangible. If he can convince himself that this dagger is simply a vision of the mind and not something real, a figment not a fact, then he can reject it; but as long as he can *see* it, as he sees his own very real dagger, that long he can't deny it, that long it is tangible, touchable evidence that is to be trusted, attended to. Only when he sees those "gouts of blood" that Mr. Winters so dislikes can he reject it as imaginative, as something irrational, something not to be attended to—a "wicked dream." It is this last detail that makes it not a real dagger, but a dagger of the mind, that convinces him that his eyes are "made fools o'the other senses" and not "worth all the rest." And the irony of this line is not accidental. Macbeth may judge his eyes as fools because they see what isn't there, but the audience knows they see through Macbeth's imagination what is very much there—a conscience that knows such action as murder cannot be evaluated in the pragmatic terms that Macbeth would like to evaluate it.

Obviously, then, I do not think the lines redundant. The "I see thee" impresses the importance of this aspect of Macbeth's method of evaluating. The deletion of the repetition would give us a much more rationally adequate Macbeth indeed.

Nor is the image of the dagger "abandoned" as Mr. Winters insists, any more than the theme of mid-night horror is "taken up"—as if the poet was tired of the first and looked around haphazardly for the second. Macbeth has fought his vision of the dagger in order to get rid if it, and apparently he has succeeded. It was but one of those "wicked dreams" which "abuse the curtain'd sleep." The tone changes and Macbeth again appears confident—yet he gives himself away, or rather Shakespeare gives him away. These wicked dreams which he would dismiss remind him of "witchcraft" and "Pale Hecate's offerings," and although he may not note the close juxtaposition of those wicked dreams to warning daggers on the one side and the witches in the play on the other, an audience does, Shakespeare did. Nor is it accident that those "wicked dreams" which counseled wisely, when ignored lead on to murder in general, to Tarquin (who also ravished innocence), to Macbeth himself. "Thou sure and firm set earth,/Hear not my steps."

This seems to me good dramatic writing, a speech in which both our understanding of Macbeth and our understanding of Shakespeare's judgment of Macbeth are made quite nicely clear. I understand Mr. Winters' belief, already mentioned, that this last passage is weak because Macbeth would not have spoken them in "real life." But such a position is only possible if one insists on judging dramatic fictions as real persons. Macbeth is not a *real* person. We know no more what he would do in "real life" than we know what the speaker in Shakespeare's sonnet might do in "real life." The series of connected attitudes that we call character in a play come finally out of the playwright's mouth, not that of some real life character whose perceptions are "somewhat sharpened" and whose thoughts are "somewhat accelerated and heightened by the situation." A good playwright doesn't start with real people in a play, he starts with attitudes. One sees these attitudes defined and qualified in the context of an ordered fiction. As one watches or reads a play and hears that point of view called a character he does not constantly, if ever, I think, refer it to some concept of a real Macbeth with a life outside the play. Such business smacks of Morgann's analysis of the youth of Falstaff.

The difference between this speech and the "standard huffing speech" that Mr. Winters would like to make it is precisely Shakespeare's ability to show, through a careful choice both of words and verbal connections, the creation of a conceivable and believable psychological attitude. No simple "huffing speech" ever managed this. The language that Macbeth uses in that *Now o'er the one half-world* section gives away the very rationalization that he thinks will protect him. If the dagger is a bad dream so are the witches that lead to murder. So too the wolf and Tarquin, though they may have incidental meaning to Macbeth, do not to us. If, finally, Macbeth can dismiss the *words* with which he has examined his plight ("Whiles I threat, he lives") as talk, the audience, even the reader, cannot. Those words have given Macbeth away, in a way he may not at this point realize; the audience, however, has no such difficulty.

All of this annoyance with Mr. Winters' easy dismissal of poetic drama, or for that matter all drama, is not simply aimed at Mr. Winters. It comes, in part at least, from the fact that Mr. Winters can and does come off so absolutely unchallenged. His opinion of actors in particular and drama in general is not new, though it is stated more clearly in the article under discussion than anywhere else I know, yet no one interested in drama bothers to attend to him. Perhaps this is because they think his opinions too wrong headed to merit attention. Perhaps, however, it is because they are uncomfortable on his chosen ground, the word. This latter discomfort seems to me unfortunate, even dangerous for a serious dramatic analyst or critic. It suggests that what to me is the most important part of a play, the language, is getting very short shrift. One wonders if there is agreement with Mr. Winters in his final conclusion about drama.

> The play in prose—let us say by Etherege, or Congreve, or Shaw—would seem to offer fewer obstacles as regards performance, for the text is close to normal speech and demands less of the performers. But such a play offers less to the reader, for it enjoys the advantages neither of poetic style on the one hand, nor of the prose analysis of the novel on the other; it comes close to being a mere scenario, dependent for its success upon the mechanical aids of the theatre.

I would hope not. It seems to me that good drama, whether in poetry or prose, defines experience by expressing attitudes toward it just as good lyrics do. Obviously the drama does not do it in precisely the same way lyrics do. It has, certainly, the actors and the scenery to which Mr. Winter refers. But most good drama also has words, and words used with a good deal of precision, enough precision to direct the actor, the setting, and those other "mechanical aids of the theatre." The words in a play, not only by Shakespeare, but by Congreve or Shaw as well, operate precisely and definitively to create those attitudes we call character. In many plays, I think particularly of the flat rhyme in Molière, though it is also true in the careful prose of Congreve, these words define the whole society in which such attitudes exist.

In Congreve, for example, I can hardly see, even in his least successful plays, that the language is particularly "close to normal speech," "demands less of the performers," or is in any way "close to being a scenario." In *The Double Dealer,* one of the funniest and sharpest portraits is that of Lady Pliant, a lady who has a very positive, though altogether unclear, notion of right and wrong. And it is through her speech that this is made clear. Listen to her talk to a would-be seducer: ". . . you are very alluring—And say so many fine Things, and nothing is so moving to me as a fine

Thing." This is not sloppy writing on Congreve's part, but carefully controlled vagueness that allows us to see what kind of a woman she is, at the same time that it makes clear Congreve's judgment of her. The same is true in the apparently careless rhythm and abundant alliteration in her acceptance of that would-be seducer.

> O, you have conquer'd, sweet melting moving sir, you have conquer'd. What heart of marble can refrain to weep, and yield to such sad sayings!

> Oh, I yield myself all up to your uncontrollable embraces! Say, thou dear, dying man, when, where, and how?

Again this is no more careless writing than Shakespeare's "fore-bemoaned moan." We know this woman as we know the speaker in that poem by the way she talks, not so much by what she says as by how she says it; and in both cases it seems to me the writer's judgment is made evident through the way he lets his characters speak.

This is typical in Congreve. Not only in *Love for Love* and *Way of the World* where one might expect it but in such an early and relatively little appreciated work as *The Old Bachelor*. Listen to Sir Joseph Wittol, a naïve country lord, thank Sharper for, as he thinks, saving his life. In point of fact, of course, Sharper has done no such thing. He has been and still is fleecing him of half his living.

> . . . your goodness, like an Inundation will, I hope, totally immerge the recollection of my error, and leave me floating in your sight, upon the full blown bladders of repentence—by the help of which I shall once more swim into your favour.

The stupid fish swimming blandly, if blindly, into the net is Wittol's position entirely. The excited over-enthusiasm in "bladders of repentence" and "Inundation" are part of the flabby insecurity of Sir Joseph. And it is the words and their phrasing that convince us. Character is depicted for the actor, and for the reader, by the *way* he speaks.

The same is true of Shaw. In *Candida,* for example, we could hardly accept the truth of Marchbanks' evaluation of Morell as having "the gift of gab, nothing more and nothing less," of feeding his wife on "sermons, stale perorations, mere rhetoric" unless we had heard some of this ourselves. Without quoting at length listen to one such peroration by Morell spoken to Marchbanks shortly before the above-mentioned outburst.

> You will be one of the makers of the Kingdom of Heaven on earth; and—who knows?—you may be a master builder where I am only a humble journeyman; for don't think, my boy, that I cannot see in you, young as you are, promise of

higher powers than I can ever pretend to. I well know that it is in the poet that the holy spirit of man—the god within him —is most godlike. It should make you tremble to think of that—to think that the heavy burthen and great gift of a poet may be laid upon you.

It is not accidental or careless writing that allows us to hear the public speaker in this speech. The rhetorical building of suspense in the "who knows" which interrupts that first sentence, or the similar interruption of "the god within him" in the second, and the beautifully forced bur*th*en in the last are all carefully controlled verbal patterns to define a certain kind of attitude. Rephrase Morell, let him speak in a truly sincere fashion, and you destroy him.

But why belabor the obvious. Mr. Winters undoubtedly knows better than his generalization suggests. I sometimes think he generalizes in order to annoy, to create opposition. The only pity here is, that in dramatic analysis at least, he doesn't create more. A careful ear in drama, attention to phrasing, has seldom been given less attention than it seems to get today. The popularity of Eugene O'Neill who can't write at all, the verbal pretension of Christopher Fry, and most recently the near destruction of language altogether in the work of Ionesco, attest to the insensitive ear not only of the playwright and his audience, but the dramatic critic as well. So-called "method" actors grunt well because most modern drama doesn't ask them to do anything else. But such inattention on the part of playwrights, actors, audience, and critic alike does not mean that the dramatic form is weak. It only means that full advantage is not being taken of it.

Mr. Winters, I can't help feeling, is very wrong, but until attention, real attention, has been paid to the area in which he condemns drama, his opinion will have more unarguable weight than it deserves, and many plays will be less good in production than they ought to be.

JOHN MILLINGTON SYNGE

Riders to the Sea

~~~~~~~~~~~~~~~~~~~~~~~~~~~~~~~~~~~

KARL JASPERS

Fundamental Interpretations of the Tragic

THE CHARACTERS IN *RIDERS TO THE SEA*

MAURYA, an old woman
BARTLEY, her son
CATHLEEN, her daughter
NORA, a younger daughter
MEN and WOMEN

First performed at the Molesworth Hall, Dublin,
February 25, 1904.

RIDERS TO THE SEA

[*An Island off the West of Ireland. Cottage kitchen, with nets, oil-skins, spinning wheel, some new boards standing by the wall, etc.* CATHLEEN, *a girl of about twenty, finishes kneading cake, and puts it down in the pot-oven by the fire; then wipes her hands, and begins to spin at the wheel.* NORA, *a young girl, puts her head in at the door.*]

NORA [*in a low voice*]   Where is she?

CATHLEEN   She's lying down, God help her, and may be sleeping, if she's able.

[NORA *comes in softly, and takes a bundle from under her shawl.*]

CATHLEEN [*spinning the wheel rapidly*]   What is it you have?

NORA   The young priest is after bringing them. It's a shirt and a   5
plain stocking were got off a drowned man in Donegal.

[CATHLEEN *stops her wheel with a sudden movement, and leans out to listen.*]

NORA   We're to find out if it's Michael's they are, some time her-self will be down looking by the sea.

CATHLEEN   How would they be Michael's, Nora. How would he
go the length of that way to the far north?   10

NORA   The young priest says he's known the like of it. "If it's Michael's they are," says he, "you can tell herself he's got a clean burial by the grace of God, and if they're not his, let no one say a word about them, for she'll be getting her death," says he, "with crying and lamenting."   15

[*The door which* NORA *half closed is blown open by a gust of wind.*]

CATHLEEN [*looking out anxiously*]   Did you ask him would he stop Bartley going this day with the horses to the Galway fair?

NORA   "I won't stop him," says he, "but let you not be afraid. Herself does be saying prayers half through the night, and the Almighty God won't leave her destitute," says he, "with no son   20
living."

CATHLEEN   Is the sea bad by the white rocks, Nora?

NORA   Middling bad, God help us. There's a great roaring in the west, and it's worse it'll be getting when the tide's turned to the wind. [*She goes over to the table with the bundle.*] Shall I open it now?

CATHLEEN   Maybe she'd wake up on us, and come in before we'd done. [*Coming to the table.*] It's a long time we'll be, and the two of us crying.

NORA [*goes to the inner door and listens*]   She's moving about on the bed. She'll be coming in a minute.

CATHLEEN   Give me the ladder, and I'll put them up in the turf-loft, the way she won't know of them at all, and maybe when the tide turns she'll be going down to see would he be floating from the east.

[*They put the ladder against the gable of the chimney; CATHLEEN goes up a few steps and hides the bundle in the turf-loft. MAURYA comes from the inner room.*]

MAURYA [*looking up at CATHLEEN and speaking querulously*]   Isn't it turf enough you have for this day and evening?

CATHLEEN   There's a cake baking at the fire for a short space [*throwing down the turf*] and Bartley will want it when the tide turns if he goes to Connemara.

[*NORA picks up the turf and puts it round the pot-oven.*]

MAURYA [*sitting down on a stool at the fire*]   He won't go this day with the wind rising from the south and west. He won't go this day, for the young priest will stop him surely.

NORA   He'll not stop him, mother, and I heard Eamon Simon and Stephen Pheety and Colum Shawn saying he would go.

MAURYA   Where is he itself?

NORA   He went down to see would there be another boat sailing in the week, and I'm thinking it won't be long till he's here now, for the tide's turning at the green head, and the hooker's tacking from the east.

CATHLEEN   I hear some one passing the big stones.

NORA [*looking out*]   He's coming now, and he in a hurry.

BARTLEY [*comes in and looks round the room. Speaking sadly and quietly*]   Where is the bit of new rope, Cathleen, was bought in Connemara?

CATHLEEN [*coming down*]   Give it to him, Nora; it's on a nail by the white boards. I hung it up this morning, for the pig with the black feet was eating it.

NORA [*giving him a rope*]   Is that it, Bartley?

MAURYA   You'd do right to leave that rope, Bartley, hanging by the boards. [BARTLEY *takes the rope.*] It will be wanting in this place, I'm telling you, if Michael is washed up to-morrow, or the next morning, or any morning in the week, for it's a deep grave we'll make him by the grace of God.   5

BARTLEY [*beginning to work with the rope*]   I've no halter the way I can ride down on the mare, and I must go now quickly. This is the one boat going for two weeks or beyond it, and the fair will be a good fair for horses I heard them saying below.   10

MAURYA   It's a hard thing they'll be saying below if the body is washed up and there's no man in it to make the coffin, and I after giving a big price for the finest white boards you'd find in Connemara. [*She looks round at the boards.*]

BARTLEY   How would it be washed up, and we after looking each   15
day for nine days, and a strong wind blowing a while back from the west and south?

MAURYA   If it wasn't found itself, that wind is raising the sea, and there was a star up against the moon, and it rising in the night. If it was a hundred horses, or a thousand horses you had yourself,   20
what is the price of a thousand horses against a son where there is one son only?

BARTLEY [*working at the halter, to* CATHLEEN]   Let you go down each day, and see the sheep aren't jumping in on the rye, and if the jobber comes you can sell the pig with the black feet if there   25
is a good price going.

MAURYA   How would the like of her get a good price for a pig?

BARTLEY [*to* CATHLEEN]   If the west wind holds with the last bit of the moon let you and Nora get up weed enough for another cock for the kelp. It's hard set we'll be from this day with no   30
one in it but one man to work.

MAURYA   It's hard set we'll be surely the day you're drownd'd with the rest. What way will I live and the girls with me, and I an old woman looking for the grave?

[BARTLEY *lays down the halter, takes off his old coat, and puts on a newer one of the same flannel.*]

BARTLEY [*to* NORA]   Is she coming to the pier?   35

NORA [*looking out*]   She's passing the green head and letting fall her sails.

BARTLEY [*getting his purse and tobacco*]   I'll have half an hour to

·go down, and you'll see me coming again in two days, or in three days, or maybe in four days if the wind is bad.

MAURYA [*turning round to the fire, and putting her shawl over her head.*] Isn't it a hard and cruel man won't hear a word from an old woman, and she holding him from the sea?

CATHLEEN   It's the life of a young man to be going on the sea, and who would listen to an old woman with one thing and she saying it over?

BARTLEY [*taking the halter*]   I must go now quickly. I'll ride down on the red mare, and the gray pony 'll run behind me. . . . The blessing of God on you. [*He goes out.*]

MAURYA [*crying out as he is in the door*]   He's gone now, God spare us, and we'll not see him again. He's gone now, and when the black night is falling I'll have no son left me in the world.

CATHLEEN   Why wouldn't you give him your blessing and he look-ing round in the door? Isn't it sorrow enough is on every one in this house without your sending him out with an unlucky word behind him, and a hard word in his ear?

[MAURYA *takes up the tongs and begins raking the fire aimlessly without looking round.*]

NORA [*turning towards her*]   You're taking away the turf from the cake.

CATHLEEN [*crying out*]   The Son of God forgive us, Nora, we're after forgetting his bit of bread. [*She comes over to the fire.*]

NORA   And it's destroyed he'll be going till dark night, and he after eating nothing since the sun went up.

CATHLEEN [*turning the cake out of the oven*]   It's destroyed he'll be, surely. There's no sense left on any person in a house where an old woman will be talking for ever.

[MAURYA *sways herself on her stool.*]

CATHLEEN [*cutting off some of the bread and rolling it in a cloth; to* MAURYA]   Let you go down now to the spring well and give him this and he passing. You'll see him then and the dark word will be broken, and you can say "God speed you," the way he'll be easy in his mind.

MAURYA [*taking the bread*]   Will I be in it as soon as himself?

CATHLEEN   If you go now quickly.

MAURYA [*standing up unsteadily*]   It's hard set I am to walk.

CATHLEEN [*looking at her anxiously*]   Give her the stick, Nora, or maybe she'll slip on the big stones.

NORA   What stick?

CATHLEEN   The stick Michael brought from Connemara.

MAURYA [*taking a stick* NORA *gives her*]   In the big world the old   5
people do be leaving things after them for their sons and children, but in this place it is the young men do be leaving things behind for them that do be old. [*She goes out slowly.*]

[NORA *goes over to the ladder.*]

CATHLEEN   Wait, Nora, maybe she'd turn back quickly. She's that sorry, God help her, you wouldn't know the thing she'd do.   10

NORA   Is she gone round by the bush?

CATHLEEN [*looking out*]   She's gone now. Throw it down quickly, for the Lord knows when she'll be out of it again.

NORA [*getting the bundle from the loft*]   The young priest said he'd be passing to-morrow, and we might go down and speak to him   15
below if it's Michael's they are surely.

CATHLEEN [*taking the bundle*]   Did he say what way they were found?

NORA [*coming down*]   "There were two men," says he, "and they rowing round with poteen before the cocks crowed, and the oar   20
of one of them caught the body, and they passing the black cliffs of the north."

CATHLEEN [*trying to open the bundle*]   Give me a knife, Nora, the string's perished with the salt water, and there's a black knot on it you wouldn't loosen in a week.   25

NORA [*giving her a knife*]   I've heard tell it was a long way to Donegal.

CATHLEEN [*cutting the string*]   It is surely. There was a man in here a while ago—the man sold us that knife—and he said if you set off walking from the rocks beyond, it would be seven days   30
you'd be in Donegal.

NORA   And what time would a man take, and he floating?

[CATHLEEN *opens the bundle and takes out a bit of a stocking. They look at them eagerly.*]

CATHLEEN [*in a low voice*]   The Lord spare us, Nora! isn't it a queer hard thing to say if it's his they are surely?

NORA   I'll get his shirt off the hook the way we can put the one flannel on the other. [*She looks through some clothes hanging in the corner.*] It's not with them, Cathleen, and where will it be?

CATHLEEN   I'm thinking Bartley put it on him in the morning, for
5   his own shirt was heavy with the salt in it [*pointing to the corner*]. There's a bit of a sleeve was of the same stuff. Give me that and it will do.

[NORA *brings it to her and they compare the flannel.*]

CATHLEEN   It's the same stuff, Nora; but if it is itself aren't there great rolls of it in the shops of Galway, and isn't it many another
10   man may have a shirt of it as well as Michael himself?

NORA [*who has taken up the stocking and counted the stitches, crying out*]   It's Michael, Cathleen, it's Michael; God spare his soul, and what will herself say when she hears this story, and Bartley on the sea?

15   CATHLEEN [*taking the stocking*]   It's a plain stocking.

NORA   It's the second one of the third pair I knitted, and I put up three score stitches, and I dropped four of them.

CATHLEEN [*counts the stitches*]   It's that number is in it [*crying out*]. Ah, Nora, isn't it a bitter thing to think of him floating that
20   way to the far north, and no one to keen him but the black hags that do be flying on the sea?

NORA [*swinging herself round, and throwing out her arms on the clothes*]   And isn't it a pitiful thing when there is nothing left of a man who was a great rower and fisher, but a bit of an old shirt
25   and a plain stocking?

CATHLEEN [*after an instant*]   Tell me is herself coming, Nora? I hear a little sound on the path.

NORA [*looking out*]   She is, Cathleen. She's coming up to the door.

CATHLEEN   Put these things away before she'll come in. Maybe
30   it's easier she'll be after giving her blessing to Bartley, and we won't let on we've heard anything the time he's on the sea.

NORA [*helping CATHLEEN to close the bundle*]   We'll put them here in the corner.

[*They put them into a hole in the chimney corner. CATHLEEN goes back to the spinning-wheel.*]

NORA   Will she see it was crying I was?

35   CATHLEEN   Keep your back to the door the way the light'll not be on you.

[Nora *sits down at the chimney corner, with her back to the door.* Maurya *comes in very slowly, without looking at the girls, and goes over to her stool at the other side of the fire. The cloth with the bread is still in her hand. The girls look at each other, and* Nora *points to the bundle of bread.*]

CATHLEEN [*after spinning for a moment*]   You didn't give him his bit of bread?

[Maurya *begins to keen softly, without turning round.*]

CATHLEEN   Did you see him riding down?

[Maurya *goes on keening.*]

CATHLEEN [*a little impatiently*]   God forgive you; isn't it a better thing to raise your voice and tell what you seen, than to be mak-   5 ing lamentation for a thing that's done? Did you see Bartley, I'm saying to you.

MAURYA [*with a weak voice*]   My heart's broken from this day.

CATHLEEN [*as before*]   Did you see Bartley?

MAURYA   I seen the fearfulest thing.   10

CATHLEEN [*leaves her wheel and looks out*]   God forgive you; he's riding the mare now over the green head, and the gray pony behind him.

MAURYA [*starts, so that her shawl falls back from her head and shows her white tossed hair. With a frightened voice*]   The gray   15 pony behind him.

CATHLEEN [*coming to the fire*]   What is it ails you, at all?

MAURYA [*speaking very slowly*]   I've seen the fearfulest thing any person has seen, since the day Bride Dara seen the dead man with the child in his arms.   20

CATHLEEN *and* NORA   Uah. [*They crouch down in front of the old woman at the fire.*]

NORA   Tell us what is you seen.

MAURYA   I went down to the spring well, and I stood there saying a prayer to myself. Then Bartley came along, and he riding on   25 the red mare with the gray pony behind him. [*She puts up her hands, as if to hide something from her eyes.*] The Son of God spare us, Nora!

CATHLEEN   What is it you seen?

MAURYA   I seen Michael himself.   30

CATHLEEN [*speaking softly*]   You did not, mother. It wasn't Michael you seen, for his body is after being found in the far north, and he's got a clean burial by the grace of God.

MAURYA [*a little defiantly*]   I'm after seeing him this day, and he riding and galloping. Bartley came first on the red mare; and I tried to say "God speed you," but something choked the words in my throat. He went by quickly; and "the blessing of God on you," says he, and I could say nothing. I looked up then, and I crying, at the gray pony, and there was Michael upon it—with fine clothes on him, and new shoes on his feet.

CATHLEEN [*begins to keen*]   It's destroyed we are from this day. It's destroyed, surely.

NORA   Didn't the young priest say the Almighty God wouldn't leave her destitute with no son living?

MAURYA [*in a low voice, but clearly*]   It's little the like of him knows of the sea. . . . Bartley will be lost now, and let you call in Eamon and make me a good coffin out of the white boards, for I won't live after them. I've had a husband, and a husband's father, and six sons in this house—six fine men, though it was a hard birth I had with every one of them and they coming to the world—and some of them were found and some of them were not found, but they're gone now the lot of them. . . . There were Stephen, and Shawn, were lost in the great wind, and found after in the Bay of Gregory of the Golden Mouth, and carried up the two of them on the one plank, and in by that door. [*She pauses for a moment, the girls start as if they heard something through the door that is half open behind them.*]

NORA [*in a whisper*]   Did you hear that, Cathleen? Did you hear a noise in the north-east?

CATHLEEN [*in a whisper*]   There's some one after crying out by the seashore.

MAURYA [*continues without hearing anything*]   There was Sheamus and his father, and his own father again, were lost in a dark night, and not a stick or sign was seen of them when the sun went up. There was Patch after was drowned out of a curagh that turned over. I was sitting here with Bartley, and he a baby, lying on my two knees, and I seen two women, and three women, and four women coming in, and they crossing themselves, and not saying a word. I looked out then, and there were men coming after them, and they holding a thing in the half of a red sail, and water dripping out of it—it was a dry day, Nora—and leaving a track to the door.

[*She pauses again with her hand stretched out towards the door. It opens softly and old* WOMEN *begin to come in, crossing themselves on the threshold, and kneeling down in front of the stage with red petticoats over their heads.*]

MAURYA [*half in a dream, to* CATHLEEN]   Is it Patch, or Michael, or what is it at all?

CATHLEEN   Michael is after being found in the far north, and when he is found there how could he be here in this place?

MAURYA   There does be a power of young men floating round in   5
the sea, and what way would they know if it was Michael they had, or another man like him, for when a man is nine days in the sea, and the wind blowing, it's hard set his own mother would be to say what man was it.

CATHLEEN   It's Michael, God spare him, for they're after sending   10
us a bit of his clothes from the far north.

[*She reaches out and hands* MAURYA *the clothes that belonged to* MICHAEL. MAURYA *stands up slowly and takes them in her hands.* NORA *looks out.*]

NORA   They're carrying a thing among them and there's water dripping out of it and leaving a track by the big stones.

CATHLEEN [*in a whisper to the women who have come in*]   Is it Bartley it is?   15

ONE OF THE WOMEN   It is surely, God rest his soul.

[*Two younger* WOMEN *come in and pull out the table. Then* MEN *carry in the body of* BARTLEY, *laid on a plank, with a bit of a sail over it, and lay it on the table.*]

CATHLEEN [*to the* WOMEN, *as they are doing so*]   What way was he drowned?

ONE OF THE WOMEN   The gray pony knocked him into the sea, and he was washed out where there is a great surf on the white   20
rocks.

[MAURYA *has gone over and knelt down at the head of the table. The* WOMEN *are keening softly and swaying themselves with a slow movement.* CATHLEEN *and* NORA *kneel at the other end of the table. The* MEN *kneel near the door.*]

MAURYA [*raising her head and speaking as if she did not see the people around her*]   They're all gone now, and there isn't anything more the sea can do to me. . . . I'll have no call now to be up crying and praying when the wind breaks from the south, and you can hear the surf is in the east, and the surf is in the west, making a great stir with the two noises, and they hitting one on the other. I'll have no call now to be going down and getting Holy Water in the dark nights after Samhain, and I won't care what way the sea is when the other women will be keening. [*To* NORA.] Give me the Holy Water, Nora, there's a small sup still on the dresser.

[NORA *gives it to her.*]

MAURYA [*drops* MICHAEL'S *clothes across* BARTLEY'S *feet, and sprinkles the Holy Water over him*] It isn't that I haven't prayed for you, Bartley, to the Almighty God. It isn't that I haven't said prayers in the dark night till you wouldn't know what I'ld be saying; but it's a great rest I'll have now, and it's time surely. It's a great rest I'll have now, and great sleeping in the long nights after Samhain, if it's only a bit of wet flour we do have to eat, and maybe a fish that would be stinking. [*She kneels down again, crossing herself, and saying prayers under her breath.*]

CATHLEEN [*to an* OLD MAN] Maybe yourself and Eamon would make a coffin when the sun rises. We have fine white boards her-self bought, God help her, thinking Michael would be found, and I have a new cake you can eat while you'll be working.

THE OLD MAN [*looking at the boards*] Are there nails with them?

CATHLEEN There are not, Colum; we didn't think of the nails.

ANOTHER MAN It's a great wonder she wouldn't think of the nails, and all the coffins she's seen made already.

CATHLEEN It's getting old she is, and broken.

[MAURYA *stands up again very slowly and spreads out the pieces of* MICHAEL'S *clothes beside the body, sprinkling them with the last of the Holy Water.*]

NORA [*in a whisper to* CATHLEEN] She's quiet now and easy; but the day Michael was drowned you could hear her crying out from this to the spring well. It's fonder she was of Michael, and would any one have thought that?

CATHLEEN [*slowly and clearly*] An old woman will be soon tired with anything she will do, and isn't it nine days herself is after crying and keening, and making great sorrow in the house?

MAURYA [*puts the empty cup mouth downwards on the table, and lays her hands together on* BARTLEY'S *feet*] They're all together this time, and the end is come. May the Almighty God have mercy on Bartley's soul, and on Michael's soul, and on the souls of Sheamus and Patch, and Stephen and Shawn [*bending her head*]; and may He have mercy on my soul, Nora, and on the soul of every one is left living in the world.

[*She pauses, and the keen rises a little more loudly from the* WOMEN, *then sinks away:*]

MAURYA [*continuing*]   Michael has a clean burial in the far north,   5
by the grace of the Almighty God. Bartley will have a fine coffin out of the white boards, and a deep grave surely. What more can we want than that? No man at all can be living for ever, and we must be satisfied.

[*She kneels down again and the curtain falls slowly.*]

FUNDAMENTAL INTERPRETATIONS
OF THE TRAGIC

At the edge of doom, the tragic heroes act out the pattern of tragic reality. The poetic work presents this pattern. The heroes put it into words, in general statements about the tragedy of all existence. Knowledge of the tragic becomes itself a basic feature of tragic reality. But the systematic unfolding of a tragic interpretation of the world (a tragic metaphysics) is an intellectual construction that is attempted only in the contemplation of the poetic work, and thus indirectly of reality.

Such reflections of tragic drama upon its own meaning can be systematically arranged and made coherent. Thus they can be made to yield several basic interpretations of tragedy. These can be in terms of myth or of philosophical concepts. . . .

1. *Mythical Interpretation*

Mythical interpretation means thinking in terms of pictures—of pictures taken for realities. Such interpretation dominates Greek tragedy. Tragedy presented with the knowledge of gods and demons as the decisive powers is meaningful only where there is belief in such deities. This puts a certain distance between Greek tragedy and ourselves. We do not sacrifice at the altars of the Greek gods and do not believe in Greek demons. But we can still understand what contents were at work within the forms of ancient tragedy. There is an incomparable fascination in the high seriousness of thoughts, the questions, and the answers embodied in the concrete images of Greek tragic writings.

By contrast, Shakespeare is close to us because his milieu is close to ours. Thanks to this closeness, Shakespeare can speak on the secular stage and in symbolic ciphers rather than in concrete embodiments of the contents of faith. In Shakespeare we find no Eumenides, no Moira, Apollo, or Zeus, but witches, ghosts, and the magic of fairy tales. There is no Prometheus but a Prospero and an Ariel. No cult serves as framework of the dramatic performance. Instead the poet has the noble task of holding the mirror up to the world, of bearing witness to reality, of making the audience feel the background of meaning, order, law, truth, and divinity. Hence any mythical interpretation of Shakespeare's tragedy is invalid.

Above all, mythical interpretation has reference to the ultimate guidance of things:

Man the planner, arrogating to himself this guidance, must make the experience that—despite his planning—he is still subject to something else, something that is both different and more inclusive. The less he knows, the more sensitive his knowledge of the tragic renders him to all that is still veiled: tragic events are guided by a power that is inexorable.

Within the knowledge of the tragic this guidance is thought of as "destiny." But what is held to be the nature of this destiny will appear in the most different mythical forms. It can be an *impersonal* and *anonymous* curse in consequence of some crime perpetuating itself as family curse, from generation to generation. In Aeschylus and Sophocles its agents are demonic beings such as the Erinyes; the gods know of it beforehand; oracles predict it; and one's own actions can promote or impede it. It is by no means human guilt, always or even most of the time. Rather, the hero is justified in saying:

> I have suffered misery, strangers—suffered it through un-
> witting deeds, and of those acts—be Heaven my witness!—no
> part was of mine own choice.

> . . . No wilful sin . . . stainless before the law, void of malice,
> have I come unto this pass!

And summing up:

> . . . how couldst thou justly blame the unknowing deed?

But just as there is curse, there is also *promise*. Promise as unfailing as curse is pitiless (Oedipus, as promised, finds blessed death in the grove sacred to the Eumenides).

The impersonal and anonymous power is, above all, *Moira,* to whom even gods must submit or with whom, as in Aeschylus, Zeus the supreme god is united.

Tyche, Chance, appearing in Euripides, rules arbitrarily without meaning or reference to the gods. In Hellenistic times, Tyche is personified as goddess or demon, and she becomes *Fortuna* to the Romans.

Guidance in Calderon is that *Providence* which as God's inscrutable will leads the soul to its salvation.

Every act of guidance operates through the medium of man's own actions which bring about what man neither contemplates nor desires.

In the mythical view, the world is the arena of forces both divine and demonic. These are interlocked in their anonymous results which appear in persons, actions, and events. If man is to understand all these, he must trace them back to the gods and demons who are their sources.

2. *The Philosophic Interpretations*

Thought seeks to grasp the essential nature of the tragic not in pictures but in concepts. It attempts universal interpretations.

One interpretation locates the tragic in *Being* as such. Whatever exists, exists as self-negation, in the dialectic of Being. Through negation it moves and becomes tragic. God is intrinsically tragic; God suffering the ground of all Being. Such a doctrine of universal tragedy—"pan-tragism"—is a metaphysic of tragedy as universal phenomenon. The tragedy of this world then follows from a fundamental tragic predicament. Being itself has a crack running through it.

To say that the ground of all Being is tragic, however, seems absurd. Instead of actually transcending our world, this narrow pseudo-insight merely absolutizes one of its aspects. Tragedy resides only in the phenomena of this world. For through the tragic, something different speaks to us, something that is no longer tragic.

Another interpretation locates the tragic in the *world*. In that case, world-wide tragedy is the visible manifestation of universal negativity. This negativity is implicit in the finiteness of all things, in the multiplicity of individual variants, in the struggle of all that exists against all else that exists for self-preservation and supremacy; and this negativity is implicit finally in chance. In this sense the course of this world and the universal destruction of all that has arisen are called tragic.

This view is not content to reduce the tragic to the level of all sorts of evil, misery, and suffering. All of these at least presuppose a living agent to experience them. Actually this view would stretch the meaning of the tragic to include negativity in general. Of genuine tragedy, however, one can speak only with reference to man.

Human tragedy can be recognized on two levels:

(a) All human life, activity, achievement, and success are doomed finally to suffer shipwreck. Death, suffering, sickness, and mortality may be veiled from sight, but in the end they engulf all. For life as existence here and now is finite. It is characterized by the multiplicity of elements that mutually exclude and combat one another. Life perishes. To be aware of this is in itself tragic: every particular instance of destruction and every way of suffering that leads to it flow from one basic and all-encompassing reality.

Deeper and truer tragedy arises only where tragic knowledge understands that ruinous conflict is founded in the very nature of truth and goodness, and must inexorably claim its due.

(b) Reality is divided against itself, and so is truth. Truth opposes truth and must defend its own rightful claim not only against injustice, but also against the rightful claims of other truths. Tragedy is real because irreconcilable opposition is real. Mythically, this schism may be reflected in man's obligation to serve many gods, where the service of one impairs or excludes that of another. Or, without such mythical representation, this opposition may be visualized as the battle of every existence against all others. At bottom, all these views agree: human character, mind, and existence are not only linked by common bonds, but also forced into combat by their mutual incompatibility. Every moral imperative is tainted by guilt, for it must destroy others equally moral and equally imperative.

Viewed from this perspective, certain distinctions appear which permit us to point out the very essence of the tragic. Without exception, universal shipwreck is the fundamental characteristic of every existence. This includes accidental misfortune, guilt that is specific and avoidable, and the misery of suffering in vain. We find genuine tragedy, however, only in that destruction which does not prematurely cut short development and success, but which, instead, grows out of success itself. Knowledge that life is at the mercy of blind fate is not yet tragic knowledge. Genuine tragic knowledge sees deeper. It knows that even in his last and innermost strongholds of ostensible success and ostensible security, man is forsaken and abandoned to the bottomless.

Hence there is no trace of tragic knowledge in the mere urge to experience shipwreck and suffering. Such knowledge arises only where man actually accepts danger and that inescapable nexus of guilt and doom implicit in all true action and accomplishment in the real world.

We will not understand the tragic by thinking in the alternatives of "success or failure." We can grasp it only by searching more deeply, by seeing that precisely when we are most highly successful we most truly fail. Apart from this there is that failure whose claim to tragedy is fraudulent, where something merely happened to go wrong, an accidental mishap, or the perverse striving for failure instead of for effectiveness, the striving for a disaster that was not even necessary.

3. *Limits of Interpretation*

What is consummated under the name of tragic knowledge are the original visions of reality. Compared with such visions, all interpretations of the tragic are inadequate. Mythical interpretation itself is just one way of viewing the tragic, confined to Greek tragedy alone. It would therefore be absurd to reduce all these visions to a single concept as their common denominator. For as visions they are forever either more or less than what concepts can express. To seek specific meanings in single strands of tragic knowledge—as in the tragic subjects of literature—is to miss seeing the whole. Interpretations that claim to be one universal interpretation of the tragic do either of two things: they make it narrow, or else they miss it altogether.

We must therefore distinguish, first, tragic reality as such; second, tragic knowledge as the conscious recognition of this reality; third, the philosophy of the tragic. Tragic reality becomes effective only by means of tragic knowledge; this transforms the human personality. The philosophy of the tragic, however—its interpretation—goes one of two ways: either it completely perverts tragic knowledge, or it keeps open the wider awareness derived from its own personal and original vision.

4. *The Distortion of Tragic Knowledge into a Tragic World View*

Every effort to deduce tragedy alone as the dominant law of reality is philosophically unsound. We object to it, as to every metaphysics that would approach Being and Reality deductively and that would make descriptive statements about the nature of Being or God—we object to it because it seeks to make them both absolute and finite. Even those profound dualisms which are postulated as existing at the very base of reality and assumed to account for the origin of tragedy (for instance, that aspect of God which is not Himself) are only code symbols of relative validity within philosophic thought, and no deductive knowledge can be derived from them. Tragic knowledge is open knowledge, well aware of its own ignorance. To freeze it into a pan-tragism of whatever kind is to distort it.

How a tragic philosophy becomes narrow and perverted may be studied in the case of the poet Hebbel. His systematic interpretation becomes absurd, monstrous, and fanatical. The result is poetry contrived by speculation, the loss of all true spiritual depth—poetry reduced on the one hand to nothing but psychology, and on the other to speculatively heightened grandeur. At the same time, as in flashes of lightning, Hebbel achieves some striking insights and perspectives. But his consciousness of tragedy is no more than consciousness of misery decked out in philosophic trimmings.

As a concept of aesthetics, too, the tragic has acquired a coloring which corresponds to this misleading type of tragic philosophy, as when Bahnsen speaks of tragedy as the universal law, or Unamuno of the tragic sense of life.

The most sublime aberration of a tragic world view occurs when the truly tragic is turned into an absolute and made to appear as if it constituted the essence and value of man.

Tragedy is distinct from misfortune, suffering, and destruction, from sickness or death, and from evil. It is so distinct by virtue of the nature of its knowledge; this knowledge is general, not special; it is question, not acceptance—accusation, not lament. Tragic knowledge is further distinct by virtue of the close connection between truth and catastrophe: tragedy grows more intense as the clashing forces increase in scale and as the necessity of their conflict deepens. All misfortune becomes tragic only through the context in which it occurs, or to which we relate it; through the consciousness and knowledge of those who suffer and those who love; through the interpretation, by tragic knowledge, of misfortune as meaningful. But in and for itself misfortune is not tragic; it is simply the burden that all must bear. Tragic knowledge invades and breaks through, but does not master, reality—there is too much it leaves untouched, forgotten, or unexplained. It lures us into an exalting realm of grandeur; and thus, despite all clear-eyed honesty, it obscures the truth.

Tragedy becomes the privilege of the exalted few—all others must be content to be wiped out indifferently in disaster. Tragedy then becomes a characteristic not of man, but of a human aristocracy. As the code of privilege, this philosophy becomes arrogant and unloving; it gives us comfort by pandering to our self-esteem.

Tragic knowledge thus has its limits: it achieves no comprehensive interpretation of the world. It fails to master universal suffering; it fails to grasp the whole terror and insolubility in men's existence. This is clearly shown by the fact that although everyday realities—such as sickness, death, chance, misery, and malice—may well become the media through which tragedy makes its appearance, they are not so considered from the outset simply because they are not in themselves tragic. A tragic philosophy lives in an aura of grandeur; it offers us personal fulfillment, as the fortunate result of an appropriately successful disaster, and thus lifts us high above reality. But in so doing, this philosophy narrows down our awareness. For in so far as men find release in an experience of this kind, they find it only at the price of concealing from themselves the terrifying abysses of reality. Misery—hopeless, meaningless, heartrending, destitute, and helpless misery—cries out for help. But the reality of all this misery without greatness is pushed aside as unworthy of notice by minds that are blind with exaltation. And all the while, man presses for redemption from his terrible realities, which lack the glamor of tragedy.

Together with this unloving blindness, we find a watered-down aesthetic jargon in current phrases about tragedy, a jargon that conveys the essence of tragedy but at the same time distorts its meaning. This jargon untruthfully makes reality appear remote, and all too easily relieves us from having to see the misery of the world as it really is. Thus it is glibly remarked that tragedy reveals the worthlessness of life itself, of all individual finite human life; that the doom of greatness is precisely one of its characteristics; that the world is set up to break and destroy the unusual individual. By such diffuse generalities, so plausible in their vagueness, we cover up the actual ills of reality with a tissue of lies.

In all tragic philosophies the polarity of tragic knowledge has been lost. In the original vision, tragedy and the release from it are linked together. But if we rob tragedy of its opposite pole and isolate it as nothing-but-tragedy, we fall into a bottomless chasm where none of the great tragic compositions have been built.

Whatever total lack of faith seeks to parade as form, it finds the philosophy of nothing-but-tragedy well suited as a camouflage for nothingness. Tragic grandeur is the prop whereby the arrogant nihilist can elevate himself to the pathos of feeling himself a hero. Where seriousness has been lost, an experience of pseudo-seriousness is produced by the violent stimulant of tragedy. The racial past, the sagas, and Greek tragedy are all invoked. Yet what had then been the reality of faith becomes now a deliberate and dishonest substitute for nothingness. The old beliefs are used as phrases to lend a heroic cast to the very unheroic degeneration of one's own existence, or else to lend a cheap aura of heroism to a life lived in comfort and security.

Such perversion of tragic philosophy then sets free the turmoil of dark impulses: the delight in meaningless activity, in torturing and in being tortured, in destruction for its own sake, in the raging hatred against the world and man coupled with the raging hatred against one's own despised existence.

TENNESSEE WILLIAMS

The Rose Tattoo

~~~~~~

TENNESSEE WILLIAMS

The Timeless
World of a Play

AUTHOR'S PRODUCTION NOTES

The locale of the play is a village populated mostly by Sicilians somewhere along the Gulf Coast between New Orleans and Mobile. The time is the present.

As the curtain rises we hear a Sicilian folk-singer with a guitar. He is singing. At each major division of the play this song is resumed and it is completed at the final curtain.

The first lighting is extremely romantic. We see a frame cottage, in a rather poor state of repair, with a palm tree leaning dreamily over one end of it and a flimsy little entrance porch, with spindling pillars, sagging steps and broken rails, at the other end. The setting seems almost tropical, for, in addition to the palm trees, there are tall canes with feathery fronds and a fairly thick growth of pampas grass. These are growing on the slope of an embankment along which runs a highway, which is not visible, but the cars passing on it can occasionally be heard. The house has a rear door which cannot be seen. The facing wall of the cottage is either a transparency that lifts for the interior scenes, or is cut away to reveal the interior.

The romantic first lighting is that of late dusk, the sky a delicate blue with an opalescent shimmer more like water than air. Delicate points of light appear and disappear like lights reflected in a twilight harbor. The curtain rises well above the low tin roof of the cottage.

We see an interior that is as colorful as a booth at a carnival. There are many religious articles and pictures of ruby and gilt, the brass cage of a gaudy parrot, a large bowl of goldfish, cutglass decanters and vases, rose-patterned wallpaper and a rose-colored carpet; everything is exclamatory in its brightness like the projection of a woman's heart passionately in love. There is a small shrine against the wall between the rooms, consisting of a prie-dieu and a little statue of the Madonna in a starry blue robe and gold crown. Before this burns always a vigil light in its ruby glass cup. Our purpose is to show these gaudy, childlike mysteries with sentiment and humor in equal measure, without ridicule and with respect for the religious yearnings they symbolize.

An outdoor sign indicates that SERAFINA, whose home the cottage is, does "SEWING." The interior furnishings give evidence of this vocation. The most salient feature is a collection of dressmaker's dummies. There are at least seven of these life-size mannequins, in various shapes and attitudes. [They will have to be made especially for the play as their purpose is not realistic. They have pliable joints so that their positions can be changed. Their arms terminate at the wrist. In all their attitudes there is an air of drama, somewhat like the

476

poses of declamatory actresses of the old school.] Principal among them are a widow and a bride who face each other in violent attitudes, as though having a shrill argument, in the parlor. The widow's costume is complete from black-veiled hat to black slippers. The bride's featureless head wears a chaplet of orange blossoms from which is depended a flowing veil of white marquisette, and her net gown is trimmed in white satin—lustrous, immaculate.

Most of the dummies and sewing equipment are confined to the dining room which is also SERAFINA'S *work room. In that room there is a tall cupboard on top of which are several dusty bottles of imported Sicilian Spumanti.*

THE CHARACTERS IN
THE ROSE TATTOO

SALVATORE

VIVI

BRUNO

ASSUNTA

ROSA DELLE ROSE

SERAFINA DELLE ROSE

ESTELLE HOHENGARTEN

A LITTLE BOY

THE STREGA

GIUSEPPINA

PEPPINA

VIOLETTA

MARIELLA

TERESA

FATHER DE LEO

A DOCTOR

MISS YORKE

FLORA

BESSIE

JACK HUNTER

THE SALESMAN

ALVARO MANGIACAVALLO

A MAN

ANOTHER MAN

THE ROSE TATTOO

ACT ONE

Scene One

[*It is the hour that the Italians call "prima sera," the beginning of dusk. Between the house and the palm tree burns the female star with an almost emerald lustre. The mothers of the neighborhood are beginning to call their children home to supper, in voices near and distant, urgent and tender, like the variable notes of wind and water. There are three children:* BRUNO, SALVATORE, *and* VIVI, *ranged in front of the house, one with a red paper kite, one with a hoop, and the little girl with a doll dressed as a clown. They are in attitudes of momentary repose, all looking up at something—a bird or a plane passing over—as the mothers' voices call them.*]

BRUNO   The white flags are flying at the Coast Guard station.

SALVATORE   That means fair weather.

VIVI   I love fair weather.

GIUSEPPINA   Vivi! Vieni mangiare![1]

PEPPINA   Salvatore! Come home!   5

VIOLETTA   Bruno! Come home to supper!

[*The calls are repeated tenderly, musically.*]

[*The interior of the house begins to be visible.* SERAFINA DELLE ROSE *is seen on the parlor sofa, waiting for her husband* ROSARIO'S *return. Between the curtains is a table set lovingly for supper; there is wine in a silver icebucket and a great bowl of roses.*]

[SERAFINA *looks like a plump little opera singer in the role of Madame Butterfly. Her black hair is done in a high pompadour that glitters like wet coal. A rose is held in place by glittering jet hairpins. Her voluptuous figure is sheathed in pale rose silk. On her feet are dainty slippers with glittering buckles and French heels. It is apparent from the way she sits, with such plump dignity, that she is wearing a tight girdle. She sits very erect, in an attitude of forced composure, her ankles daintily crossed and her plump little hands holding a yellow paper fan on which is painted*

---

[1] Come and eat!

479

a rose. Jewels gleam on her fingers, her wrists and her ears and about her throat. Expectancy shines in her eyes. For a few moments she seems to be posing for a picture.]

[ROSA DELLE ROSE *appears at the side of the house, near the palm tree.* ROSA, *the daughter of the house, is a young girl of twelve. She is pretty and vivacious, and has about her a particular intensity in her every gesture.*]

SERAFINA   Rosa, where are you?

ROSA   Here, Mama.

SERAFINA   What are you doing, cara?²

ROSA   I've caught twelve lightning bugs.

[*The cracked voice of* ASSUNTA *is heard, approaching.*]

5   SERAFINA   I hear Assunta! Assunta!

[ASSUNTA *appears and goes into the house,* ROSA *following her in,* ASSUNTA *is an old woman in a gray shawl, bearing a basket of herbs, for she is a fattuchiere, a woman who practises a simple sort of medicine. As she enters the children scatter.*]

ASSUNTA   Vengo, vengo. Buona sera. Buona sera.³ There is something wild in the air, no wind but everything's moving.

SERAFINA   I don't see nothing moving and neither do you.

ASSUNTA   Nothing is moving so you can see it moving, but every-
10   thing is moving, and I can hear the star-noises. Hear them? Hear the star-noises?

SERAFINA   Naw, them ain't the star-noises. They're termites, eating the house up. What are you peddling, old woman, in those little white bags?

15   ASSUNTA   Powder, wonderful powder. You drop a pinch of it in your husband's coffee.

SERAFINA   What is it good for?

ASSUNTA   What is a husband good for! I made it out of the dry blood of a goat.

20   SERAFINA   Davero!⁴

ASSUNTA   Wonderful stuff! But be sure you put it in his coffee at supper, not in his breakfast coffee.

² Dear.
³ I'm coming, I'm coming. Good evening. Good evening.
⁴ Really!

SERAFINA My husband don't need no powder!

ASSUNTA Excuse me, Baronessa. Maybe he needs the opposite kind of a powder, I got that, too.

SERAFINA Naw, naw, *no* kind of powder at all, old woman. [*She lifts her head with a proud smile.*]

[*Outside the sound of a truck is heard approaching up on the highway.*]

ROSA [*Joyfully.*] Papa's truck!   5

[*They stand listening for a moment, but the truck goes by without stopping.*]

SERAFINA [*To* ASSUNTA.] That wasn't him. It wasn't no 10-ton truck. It didn't rattle the shutters! Assunta, Assunta, undo a couple of hooks, the dress is tight on me!

ASSUNTA Is it true what I told you?

SERAFINA Yes, it is true, but nobody needed to tell me. Assunta,   10
I'll tell you something which maybe you won't believe.

ASSUNTA It is impossible to tell me anything that I don't believe.

SERAFINA Va bene! Senti, Assunta![5]—I knew that I had conceived on the very night of conception! [*There is a phrase of music as she says this.*]

ASSUNTA Ahhhh?   15

SERAFINA Senti! That night I woke up with a burning pain on me, here, on my left breast! A pain like a needle, quick, quick, hot little stitches. I turned on the light, I uncovered my breast!— On it I saw the rose tattoo of my husband!

ASSUNTA Rosario's tattoo?   20

SERAFINA On me, on my breast, his tattoo! And when I saw it I knew that I had conceived . . .

[SERAFINA *throws her head back, smiling proudly, and opens her paper fan.* ASSUNTA *stares at her gravely, then rises and hands her basket to* SERAFINA.]

ASSUNTA Ecco![6] You sell the powders! [*She starts toward the door.*]

SERAFINA You don't believe that I saw it?   25

ASSUNTA [*Stopping.*] Did Rosario see it?

    [5] All right! Listen, Assunta!
    [6] There!

SERAFINA I screamed. But when he woke up, it was gone. It only lasted a moment. But I *did* see it, and I *did* know, when I seen it, that I had conceived, that in my body another rose was growing!

5 ASSUNTA Did he believe that you saw it?

SERAFINA No. He laughed.—He laughed and I cried . . .

ASSUNTA And he took you into his arms, and you stopped crying!

SERAFINA Si!⁷

ASSUNTA Serafina, for you everything has got to be different. A
10 sign, a miracle, a wonder of some kind. You speak to Our Lady. You say that she answers your questions. She nods or shakes Her head at you. Look, Serafina, underneath Our Lady you have a candle. The wind through the shutters makes the candle flicker. The shadows move. Our Lady seems to be nodding!

15 SERAFINA She gives me signs.

ASSUNTA Only to you? Because you are more important? The wife of a barone? Serafina! In Sicily they called his uncle a baron, but in Sicily everybody's a baron that owns a piece of the land and a separate house for the goats!

20 SERAFINA They said to his uncle, "Voscenza!"⁸ and they kissed their hands to him! [*She kisses the back of her hand repeatedly, with vehemence.*]

ASSUNTA His uncle in Sicily!—So—but *here* what's he do? Drives a truck of bananas?

25 SERAFINA [*Blurting out.*] No! *Not* bananas!

ASSUNTA Not bananas?

SERAFINA Stai zitta [*She makes a warning gesture.*]—No—Vieni qui, Assunta!⁹ [*She beckons her mysteriously.* ASSUNTA *approaches.*]

ASSUNTA Cosa dici?¹⁰

30 SERAFINA On top of the truck is bananas! But underneath—something else!

ASSUNTA Che altre cose?¹¹

SERAFINA Whatever it is that the Brothers Romano want hauled

⁷ Yes.
⁸ "Your Excellency!"
⁹ Keep quiet—No—Come here, Assunta!
¹⁰ What are you saying?
¹¹ What else?

out of the state, he hauls it for them, underneath the bananas! [*She nods her head importantly.*] And money, he gets so much it spills from his pockets! Soon I don't have to make dresses!

ASSUNTA [*Turning away.*]   Soon I think you will have to make a black veil!

SERAFINA   Tonight is the last time he does it! Tomorrow he quits hauling stuff for the Brothers Romano! He pays for the 10-ton truck and works for himself. We live with dignity in America, then! Own truck! Own house! And in the house will be everything electric! Stove—deep-freeze—*tutto!*[12]—But tonight, stay with me . . . I can't swallow my heart!—Not till I hear the truck stop in front of the house and his key in the lock of the door!—When I call him, and him shouting back, *"Si, sono qui!"*[13] In his hair, Assunta, he has—oil of roses. And when I wake up at night —the air, the dark room's—full of—roses . . . Each time is the first time with him. Time doesn't pass . . .

[ASSUNTA *picks up a small clock on the cupboard and holds it to her ear.*]

ASSUNTA   Tick, tick, tick, tick.—You say the clock is a liar.

SERAFINA   No, the clock is a fool. I don't listen to it. My clock is my heart and my heart don't say tick-tick, it says love-love! And now I have two hearts in me, both of them saying love-love!

[*A truck is heard approaching, then passes.* SERAFINA *drops her fan.* ASSUNTA *opens a bottle of Spumanti with a loud pop.* SERAFINA *cries out.*]

ASSUNTA   Stai tranquilla! Calmati![14] [*She pours her a glass of wine.*] Drink this wine and before the glass is empty he'll be in your arms!

SERAFINA   I can't—swallow my heart!

ASSUNTA   A woman must not have a heart that is too big to swallow! [*She crosses to the door.*]

SERAFINA   Stay with me!

ASSUNTA   I have to visit a woman who drank rat poison because of a heart too big for her to swallow.

[ASSUNTA *leaves.* SERAFINA *returns indolently to the sofa. She lifts her hands to her great swelling breasts and murmurs aloud.*]

[12] *Everything!*
[13] Yes, I am here!
[14] Take it easy! Be calm!

SERAFINA Oh, it's so wonderful, having *two* lives in the body, not *one* but two! [*Her hands slide down to her belly, luxuriously.*] I am heavy with life, I am big, big, big with life! [*She picks up a bowl of roses and goes into the back room.*]

[ESTELLE HOHENGARTEN *appears in front of the house. She is a thin blonde woman in a dress of Egyptian design, and her blonde hair has an unnatural gloss in the clear, greenish dusk.* ROSA *appears from behind the house, calling out.*]

5 ROSA Twenty lightning bugs, Mama!

ESTELLE Little girl? Little girl?

ROSA [*Resentfully.*] Are you talking to me?

[*There is a pause.*]

ESTELLE Come here. [*She looks* ROSA *over curiously.*] You're a twig off the old rose-bush.—Is the lady that does the sewing in
10 the house?

ROSA Mama's at home.

ESTELLE I'd like to see her.

ROSA Mama?

SERAFINA Dimi?[15]

15 ROSA There's a lady to see you.

SERAFINA Oh. Tell her to wait in the parlor.

[ESTELLE *enters and stares curiously about. She picks up a small framed picture on the cupboard. She is looking at it as* SERAFINA *enters with a bowl of roses.* SERAFINA *speaks sharply.*]
That is my husband's picture.

ESTELLE Oh!—I thought it was Valentino.—With a mustache.

SERAFINA [*Putting the bowl down on the table.*] You want some-
20 thing?

ESTELLE Yes. I heard you do sewing.

SERAFINA Yes, I do sewing.

ESTELLE How fast can you make a shirt for me?

SERAFINA That all depends. [*She takes the picture from* ESTELLE *and puts it back on the cupboard.*]

25 ESTELLE I got the piece of silk with me. I want it made into a

---

[15] Tell me?

shirt for a man I'm in love with. Tomorrow's the anniversary of the day we met . . . [*She unwraps a piece of rose-colored silk which she holds up like a banner.*]

SERAFINA [*Involuntarily.*]   Che bella stoffa![16] Oh, that would be wonderful stuff for a lady's blouse or for a pair of pyjamas!

ESTELLE   I want a man's shirt made with it.   5

SERAFINA   Silk this color for a shirt for a *man?*

ESTELLE   This man is wild like a Gypsy.

SERAFINA   A woman should not encourage a man to be wild.

ESTELLE   A man that's wild is hard for a woman to hold, huh? But if he was tame—would the woman want to hold him? Huh?   10

SERAFINA   I am a married woman in business. I don't know nothing about wild men and wild women and I don't have much time —so . . .

ESTELLE   I'll pay you twice what you ask me.

[*Outside there is the sound of the goat bleating and the jingle of its harness; then the crash of wood splintering.*]

ROSA [*Suddenly appearing at the door.*]   Mama, the black goat is   15 loose!

[*She runs down the steps and stands watching the goat.* SERAFINA *crosses to the door.*]

THE STREGA [*In the distance.*]   Hyeh, Billy, hyeh, hyeh, Billy!

ESTELLE   I'll pay you three times the price that you ask me for it.

SERAFINA [*Shouting.*]   Watch the goat! Don't let him get in our yard! [*To* ESTELLE.] If I ask you five dollars?   20

ESTELLE   I will pay you fifteen. Make it twenty; money is not the object. But it's got to be ready tomorrow.

SERAFINA   Tomorrow?

ESTELLE   Twenty-five dollars!

[SERAFINA *nods slowly with a stunned look.* ESTELLE *smiles.*]
I've got the measurements with me.   25

SERAFINA   Pin the measurements and your name on the silk and the shirt will be ready tomorrow.

ESTELLE   My name is Estelle Hohengarten.

---

[16] What lovely material!

[*A little* BOY *races excitedly into the yard.*]

THE BOY   Rosa, Rosa the black goat's in your yard!

ROSA [*Calling.*]   Mama, the goat's in the yard!

SERAFINA [*Furiously, forgetting her visitor.*]   Il becco della strega!
—Scusi!¹⁷ [*She runs out onto the porch.*] Catch him, catch him
5   before he gets at the vines!

[ROSA *dances gleefully.* THE STREGA *runs into the yard. She has a
mop of wild grey hair and is holding her black skirts up from her
bare hairy legs. The sound of the goat's bleating and the jingling
of his harness is heard in the windy blue dusk.*]

[SERAFINA *descends the porch steps. The high-heeled slippers, the
tight silk skirt and the dignity of a baronessa make the descent
a little gingerly. Arrived in the yard, she directs the goat-chase
imperiously with her yellow paper fan, pointing this way and
that, exclaiming in Italian. She fans herself rapidly and crosses
back of the house. The goat evidently makes a sudden charge.
Screaming,* SERAFINA *rushes back to the front of the house, all
out of breath, the glittering pompadour beginning to tumble
down over her forehead.*]

SERAFINA   Rosa! you go in the house! Don't look at the Strega!

[*Alone in the parlor,* ESTELLE *takes the picture of* ROSARIO. *Im-
petuously, she thrusts it in her purse and runs from the house,
just as* SERAFINA *returns to the front yard.*]

ROSA [*Refusing to move.*]   Why do you call her a witch?

[SERAFINA *seizes her daughter's arm and propels her into the house.*]

SERAFINA   She has a white eye and every finger is crooked! [*She
pulls* ROSA'S *arm.*]

10   ROSA   She has a cataract, Mama, and her fingers are crooked because she has rheumatism!

SERAFINA   Malocchio—the evil eye—*that's* what she's got! And her
fingers are crooked because she shook hands with the devil. Go
in the house and wash your face with salt water and throw the
15   salt water away! *Go in! Quick!* She's coming!

[THE BOY *utters a cry of triumph.*]

[SERAFINA *crosses abruptly to the porch. At the same moment the*

¹⁷ The goat of the witch! Excuse me!

boy runs triumphantly around the house leading the captured goat by its bell harness. It is a middle-sized black goat with great yellow eyes. THE STREGA *runs behind with the broken rope. As the grotesque little procession runs before her—*THE STREGA, *the goat and the children—*SERAFINA *cries out shrilly. She crouches over and covers her face.* THE STREGA *looks back at her with a derisive cackle.*]

SERAFINA   Malocchio! Malocchio!¹⁸

[*Shielding her face with one hand,* SERAFINA *makes the sign of the horns with the other to ward off the evil eye. And the scene dims out.*]

Scene Two

[*It is just before dawn the next day.* FATHER DE LEO, *a priest, and several black-shawled women, including* ASSUNTA, *are standing outside the house. The interior of the house is very dim.*]

GIUSEPPINA   There is a light in the house.

PEPPINA   I hear the sewing machine!

VIOLETTA   There's Serafina! She's working. She's holding up a piece of rose-colored silk.   5

ASSUNTA   She hears our voices.

VIOLETTA   She's dropped the silk to the floor and she's . . .

GIUSEPPINA   Holding her throat! I think she . . .

PEPPINA   Who's going to tell her?

VIOLETTA   Father De Leo will tell her.   10

FATHER DE LEO   I think a woman should tell her. I think Assunta must tell her that Rosario is dead.

ASSUNTA   It will not be necessary to tell her. She will know when she sees us.

[*It grows lighter inside the house.* SERAFINA *is standing in a frozen attitude with her hand clutching her throat and her eyes staring fearfully toward the sound of voices.*]

ASSUNTA   I think she already knows what we have come to tell her!   15

FATHER DE LEO   Andiamo, Signore!¹ We must go to the door.

¹⁸ Evil eye! Evil eye!
¹ Let's go, ladies.

[*They climb the porch steps.* ASSUNTA *opens the door.*]

SERAFINA [*Gasping.*]   Don't speak!

[*She retreats from the group, stumbling blindly backwards among the dressmaker's dummies. With a gasp she turns and runs out the back door. In a few moments we see her staggering about outside near the palm tree. She comes down in front of the house, and stares blindly off into the distance.*]

SERAFINA [*Wildly.*]   Don't speak!

[*The voices of the women begin keening in the house.* ASSUNTA *comes out and approaches* SERAFINA *with her arms extended.* SERAFINA *slumps to her knees, whispering hoarsely*: "Don't speak!" ASSUNTA *envelopes her in the gray shawl of pity as the scene dims out.*]

Scene Three

[*It is noon of the same day.* ASSUNTA *is removing a funeral wreath on the door of the house. A doctor and* FATHER DE LEO *are on the porch.*]

THE DOCTOR   She's lost the baby.

[ASSUNTA *utters a low moan of pity and crosses herself.*]

Serafina's a very strong woman and that won't kill her. But she is
5   trying not to breathe. She's got to be watched and not allowed out of bed.

[*He removes a hypodermic and a small package from his bag and hands them to* ASSUNTA.]

This is morphia. In the arm with the needle if she screams or struggles to get up again.

ASSUNTA   Capisco![1]

10   FATHER DE LEO   One thing I want to make plain. The body of Rosario must not be burned.

THE DOCTOR   Have you seen the "body of Rosario"?

FATHER DE LEO   Yes, I have seen his body.

THE DOCTOR   Wouldn't you say it was burned?

[1] I understand.

FATHER DE LEO Of course the body was burned. When he was shot at the wheel of the truck, it crashed and caught fire. But deliberate cremation is not the same thing. It's an abomination in the sight of God.

THE DOCTOR Abominations are something I don't know about. 5

FATHER DE LEO The Church has set down certain laws.

THE DOCTOR But the instructions of a widow have to be carried out.

FATHER DE LEO Don't you know why she wants the body cremated? So she can keep the ashes here in the house. 10

THE DOCTOR Well, why not, if that's any comfort to her?

FATHER DE LEO Pagan idolatry is what I call it!

THE DOCTOR Father De Leo, you love your people but you don't understand them. They find God in each other. And when they lose each other, they lose God and they're lost. And it's hard to 15
help them.—Who is that woman?

[ESTELLE HOHENGARTEN *has appeared before the house. She is black-veiled, and bearing a bouquet of roses.*]

ESTELLE I am Estelle Hohengarten.

[*Instantly there is a great hubbub in the house. The women mourners flock out to the porch, whispering and gesticulating excitedly.*]

FATHER DE LEO What have you come here for?

ESTELLE To say good-bye to the body.

FATHER DE LEO The casket is closed; the body cannot be seen. 20
And you must never come here. The widow knows nothing about you. Nothing at all.

GIUSEPPINA *We* know about you!

PEPPINA Va Via! Sporcacciona![2]

VIOLETTA Puttana![3] 25

MARIELLA Assassina![4]

TERESA You sent him to the Romanos.

FATHER DE LEO Shhh!

---

[2] Go away! Dirty pig!
[3] Whore!
[4] Murderer!

[*Suddenly the women swarm dawn the steps like a cloud of attacking birds, all crying out in Sicilian.* ESTELLE *crouches and bows her head defensively before their savage assault. The bouquet of roses is snatched from her black-gloved hands and she is flailed with them about the head and shoulders. The thorns catch her veil and tear it away from her head. She covers her white sobbing face with her hands.*]

FATHER DE LEO   Ferme! Ferme! Signore, fermate vi nel nome di Dio![5]—Have a little respect!

[*The women fall back from* ESTELLE, *who huddles weeping on the walk.*]

ESTELLE   See him, see him, just see him . . .

FATHER DE LEO   The body is crushed and burned. Nobody can
5   see it. Now go away and don't ever come here again, Estelle Hohengarten!

THE WOMEN [*In both languages, wildly.*]   Va via, va via, go away.

[ROSA *comes around the house.* ESTELLE *turns and retreats. One of the mourners spits and kicks at the tangled veil and roses.* FATHER DE LEO *leaves. The others return inside, except* ROSA. *After a few moments the child goes over to the roses. She picks them up and carefully untangles the veil from the thorns. She sits on the sagging steps and puts the black veil over her head. Then for the first time she begins to weep, wildly, histrionically. The little* BOY *appears and gazes at her, momentarily impressed by her performance. Then he picks up a rubber ball and begins to bounce it.* ROSA *is outraged. She jumps up, tears off the veil and runs to the little* BOY, *giving him a sound smack and snatching the ball away from him.*]

ROSA   Go home! My papa is dead!

[*The scene dims out, as the music is heard again.*]

[5] Stop! Stop! Ladies, stop in the name of God!

Scene Four

[*A June day, three years later. It is morning and the light is bright. A group of local mothers are storming* SERAFINA's *house, indignant over her delay in delivering the graduation dresses for their daughters. Most of the women are chattering continually in*

Sicilian, racing about the house and banging the doors and shut-
ters. The scene moves swiftly and violently until the moment when
ROSA *finally comes out in her graduation dress.*]

GIUSEPPINA   Serafina! Serafina Delle Rose!

PEPPINA   Maybe if you call her "Baronessa" she will answer the
door. [*With a mocking laugh.*] Call her "Baronessa" and kiss your
hand to her when she opens the door.

GIUSEPPINA [*Tauntingly.*]   Baronessa! [*She kisses her hand toward*   5
the door.]

VIOLETTA   When did she promise your dress?

PEPPINA   All week she say, "Domani—domani—domani."¹ But
yestiddy I told her . . .

VIOLETTA   Yeah?

PEPPINA   O yeah. I says to her, "Serafina, domani's the high-   10
school graduation. I got to try the dress on my daughter *today.*"
"Domani," she says, "Sicuro! sicuro! sicuro!"² So I start to go
away. Then I hear a voice call, "Signora! Signora!" So I turn
round and I see Serafina's daughter at the window.

VIOLETTA   Rosa?   15

PEPPINA   Yeah, Rosa. An' you know how?

VIOLETTA   How?

PEPPINA   *Naked!* Nuda, nuda! [*She crosses herself and repeats a*
prayer.] In nominis padri et figlio et spiritus sancti.³ Aaahh!

VIOLETTA   What did she do?   20

PEPPINA   Do? She say, "Signora! Please, you call this numero and
ask for Jack and tell Jack my clothes are lock up so I can't
get out from the house." Then Serafina come and she grab-a the
girl by the hair and she pull her way from the window and she
slam the shutters right in my face!   25

GIUSEPPINA   Whatsa the matter the daughter?

VIOLETTA   Who is this boy? Where did she meet him?

PEPPINA   Boy! What boy? He's a sailor.

[*At the word "sailor" the women say "Ahhh!"*]

She met him at the high-school dance and somebody tell Serafina.
That's why she lock up the girl's clothes so she can't leave the   30

¹ "Tomorrow—tomorrow—tomorrow."
² "Surely! surely! surely!"
³ In the name of the Father and of the Son and of the Holy Ghost.

house. She can't even go to the high school to take the examinations. Imagine!

VIOLETTA Peppina, this time *you* go to the door, yeah?

PEPPINA Oh yeah, I go. Now I'm getting nervous.

[*The women all crowd to the door.*]

5   Sera-feee-na!

VIOLETTA Louder, louder.

PEPPINA Apri la porta!⁴ Come on, come on!

THE WOMEN [*Together.*] Yeah, apri la porta! . . . Come on, hurry up! . . . Open up!

10 GIUSEPPINA I go get-a police.

VIOLETTA Whatsa matter? You want more trouble?

GIUSEPPINA Listen, I pay in advance five dollar and get no dress. Now what she wear, my daughter, to graduate in? A couple of towels and a rose in the hair?

[*There is a noise inside: a shout and running footsteps.*]

15 THE WOMEN Something is going on in the house! I hear someone! Don't I? Don't you?

[*A scream and running footsteps are heard. The front door opens and* SERAFINA *staggers out onto the porch. She is wearing a soiled pink slip and her hair is wild.*]

SERAFINA Aiuto! Aiuto!⁵ [*She plunges back into the house.*]

[MISS YORKE, *a spinsterish high-school teacher, walks quickly up to the house. The Sicilian women, now all chattering at once like a cloud of birds, sweep about her as she approaches.*]

MISS YORKE You ladies know I don't understand Italian! So, please . . .

[*She goes directly into the house. There are more outcries inside.* THE STREGA *comes and stands at the edge of the yard, cackling derisively.*]

20 THE STREGA [*Calling back to someone.*] The Wops are at it again! —She got the daughter lock up naked in there all week. Ho, ho,

⁴ Open the door.
⁵ Help! Help!

ho! She lock up all week—naked—shouting out the window tell
people to call a number and give a message to Jack. Ho, ho, ho!
I guess she's in trouble already, and only fifteen!—They ain't
civilized, these Sicilians. In the old country they live in caves in
the hills and the country's run by bandits. Ho, ho, ho! More of   5
them coming over on the boats all the time.

[*The door is thrown open again and* SERAFINA *reappears on the
porch. She is acting wildly, as if demented.*]

SERAFINA [*Gasping in a hoarse whisper.*]   She cut her wrist, my
daughter, she cut her wrist! [*She runs out into the yard.*] Aiii-eeee!
Aiutatemi, aiutatemi! Call the dottore![6] [ASSUNTA *rushes up to*
SERAFINA *and supports her as she is about to fall to her knees in*   10
the yard.] Get the knife away from her! Get the knife, please!
Get the knife away from—she cut her wrist with—Madonna!
Madonna mia . . .

ASSUNTA   Smettila, smettila,[7] Serafina.

MISS YORKE [*Coming out of the back room.*]   Mrs. Delle Rose,   15
your daughter has not cut her wrist. Now come back into the
house.

SERAFINA [*Panting.*]   Che dice, che dice? Che cosa? Che cosa dice?[8]

MISS YORKE   Your daughter's all right. Come back into the house.
And you ladies please go away!   20

ASSUNTA   Vieni, Serafina. Andiamo a casa.[9] [*She supports the
heavy, sagging bulk of* SERAFINA *to the steps. As they climb the
steps one of the Sicilian mothers advances from the whispering
group.*]

GIUSEPPINA [*Boldly.*]   Serafina, we don't go away until we get our   25
dresses.

PEPPINA   The graduation begins and the girls ain't dressed.

[SERAFINA's *reply to this ill-timed request is a long, animal howl of
misery as she is supported into the house.* MISS YORKE *follows
and firmly closes the door upon the women, who then go around
back of the house. The interior of the house is lighted up.*]

MISS YORKE [*To* SERAFINA.]   No, no, no, she's not bleeding. Rosa?

---

[6] Help me, help me! Call the doctor!
[7] Take it away from her, take it away from her.
[8] What are you saying, what are you saying? What is it? What is it
that you're saying?
[9] Come, Serafina. Let's go home.

Rosa, come here and show your mother that you are not bleeding to death.

[ROSA *appears silently and sullenly between the curtains that separate the two rooms. She has a small white handkerchief tied around one wrist.*]

SERAFINA [*Points at the wrist and cries out.*]   Aiieee!

MISS YORKE [*Severely.*]   Now *stop* that, Mrs. Delle Rose!

[SERAFINA *rushes to* ROSA, *who thrusts her roughly away.*]

5   ROSA   Lasciami stare,[10] Mama!—I'm so ashamed I could die. This is the way she goes around all the time. She hasn't put on clothes since my father was killed. For three years she sits at the sewing machine and never puts a dress on or goes out of the house, and now she has locked my clothes up so *I* can't go out. She wants
10   me to be like her, a freak of the neighborhood, the way she is! Next time, next time, I won't cut my wrist but my throat! I don't want to live locked up with a bottle of ashes! [*She points to the shrine.*]

ASSUNTA   Figlia, figlia, figlia, non devi parlare così![11]

15   MISS YORKE   Mrs. Delle Rose, please give me the key to the closet so that your daughter can dress for graduation!

SERAFINA [*Surrendering the key.*]   Ecco la—chiave[12] . . .

[ROSA *snatches the key and runs back through the curtains.*]

MISS YORKE   Now why did you lock her clothes up, Mrs. Delle Rose?

20   SERAFINA   The wrist is still bleeding!

MISS YORKE   No, the wrist is not bleeding. It's just a skin cut, a scratch. But the child is exhausted from all this excitement and hasn't eaten a thing in two or three days.

ROSA [*Running into the dining room.*]   Four days! I only asked her
25   one favor. Not to let me go out but to let Jack come to the house so she could meet him!—Then she locked my clothes up!

MISS YORKE   Your daughter missed her final examinations at the high school, but her grades have been so good that she will be allowed to graduate with her class and take the examinations
30   later.—You understand me, Mrs. Delle Rose!

---

[10] Let me alone.
[11] Daughter, daughter, daughter, you mustn't talk like that.
[12] There's the—key.

[ROSA *goes into the back of the house.*]

SERAFINA [*Standing at the curtains.*]   See the way she looks at me?
   I've got a wild thing in the house, and her wrist is still bleeding!

MISS YORKE   Let's not have any more outbursts of emotion!

SERAFINA   Outburst of—you make me sick! Sick! Sick at my
   stomach you make me! Your school, you make all this trouble!   5
   You give-a this dance where she gets mixed up with a sailor.

MISS YORKE   You are talking about the Hunter girl's brother, a
   sailor named Jack, who attended the dance with his sister?

SERAFINA   "Attended with sister!"—Attended with *sister!*—My
   daughter, she's nobody's sister!   10

[ROSA *comes out of the back room. She is radiantly beautiful in her
   graduation gown.*]

ROSA   Don't listen to her, don't pay any attention to her, Miss
   Yorke.—I'm ready to go to the high school.

SERAFINA [*Stunned by her daughter's beauty, and speaking with a
   wheedling tone and gestures, as she crouches a little.*]   O tesoro,
   tesoro! Vieni qua, Rosa, cara!*13* Come here and kiss Mama one   15
   minute!—Don't go like that now!

ROSA   Lasciami stare!*14*

[*She rushes out on the porch.* SERAFINA *gazes after her with arms
   slowly drooping from their imploring gesture and jaw dropping
   open in a look of almost comic desolation.*]

SERAFINA   Ho solo te, solo te—in questo mondo!*15*

MISS YORKE   Now, now, Mrs. Delle Rose, no more excitement,
   please!   20

SERAFINA [*Suddenly plunging after them in a burst of fury.*]   Senti,
   senti, per favore!*16*

ROSA   Don't you dare come out on the street like that!—*Mama!*

[*She crouches and covers her face in shame, as* SERAFINA *heedlessly
   plunges out into the front yard in her shocking deshabillé, making
   wild gestures.*]

¹³ O treasure, treasure! Come here, dear Rose!
¹⁴ Let me alone!
¹⁵ I have only you, only you—in this world.
¹⁶ Listen, listen, please!

SERAFINA   You give this dance where she gets mixed up with a sailor. What do you think you want to do at this high school?

[*In weeping despair,* ROSA *runs to the porch.*]

How high is this high school? Listen, how high is this high school? Look, look, look, I will show you! It's high as that horse's dirt out there in the street! [SERAFINA *points violently out in front of the house.*] Si! 'Sta fetentissima, scuola! Scuola maledetta![17]

[ROSA *cries out and rushes over to the palm tree, leaning against it, with tears of mortification.*]

MISS YORKE   Mrs. Delle Rose, you are talking and behaving extremely badly. I don't understand how a woman that acts like you could have such a sweet and refined young girl for a daughter!—You don't deserve it!—Really . . . [*She crosses to the palm tree.*]

SERAFINA   Oh, you want me to talk refined to you, do you? Then do me one thing! Stop ruining the girls at the high school! [*As* SERAFINA *paces about, she swings her hips in the exaggeratedly belligerent style of a parading matador.*]

ASSUNTA   Piantala, Serafina! Andiamo a casa![18]

SERAFINA   No, no, I ain't through talking to this here teacher!

ASSUNTA   Serafina, look at yourself, you're not dressed!

SERAFINA   I'm dressed okay; I'm not naked!

[*She glares savagely at the teacher by the palm tree. The Sicilian mothers return to the front yard.*]

ASSUNTA   Serafina, cara? Andiamo a casa, adesso!—Basta! Basta![19]

SERAFINA   Aspetta![20]

ROSA   I'm so ashamed I could die, I'm so ashamed. Oh, you don't know, Miss Yorke, the way that we live. She never puts on a dress; she stays all the time in that dirty old pink slip!—And talks to my father's ashes like he was living.

SERAFINA   Teacher! Teacher, senti![21] What do you think you want to do at this high school? Sentite! per favore![22] You give this-a

[17] Yes! It's the stinkingest, the school! Cursed school!
[18] Stop it, Serafina! Let's go into the house!
[19] Serafina, dear? Let's go into the house, right now!—Enough! Enough!
[20] Wait!
[21] Listen!
[22] Listen, please!

dance! What kind of a spring dance is it? Answer this question, please, for me! What kind of a spring dance is it? She meet this boy there who don't even go to no high school. What kind of a boy? Guardate![23] *A sailor that wears a gold earring!* That kind of a boy is the kind of boy she meets there!—That's why I lock her clothes up so she can't go back to the high school. [*Suddenly to* ASSUNTA.] She cut her wrist! It's still bleeding! [*She strikes her forehead three times with her fist.*]

ROSA Mama, you look disgusting! [*She rushes away.*]

[MISS YORKE *rushes after her.* SERAFINA *shades her eyes with one hand to watch them departing down the street in the brilliant spring light.*]

SERAFINA Did you hear what my daughter said to me?—"You look—disgusting."—She calls me . . .

ASSUNTA Now, Serafina, we must go in the house. [*She leads her gently to the porch of the little house.*]

SERAFINA [*Proudly.*] How pretty she look, my daughter, in the white dress, like a bride! [*To all.*] Excuse me! Excuse me, please! Go away! Get out of my yard!

GIUSEPPINA [*Taking the bull by the horns.*] No, we ain't going to go without the dresses!

ASSUNTA Give the ladies the dresses so the girls can get dressed for the graduation.

SERAFINA That one there she only paid for the goods. I charge for the work.

GIUSEPPINA Ecco![24] I got the money!

THE WOMEN We *got* the money!

SERAFINA The names are pinned on the dresses. Go in and get them. [*She turns to* ASSUNTA.] Did you hear what my daughter called me? She called me "disgusting"!

[SERAFINA *enters the house, slamming the door. After a moment the mothers come out, cradling the white voile dresses tenderly in their arms, murmuring "carino!"[25] and "bellissimo!"[26]*]

[*As they disappear the inside light is brought up and we see* SERA-

[23] Watch out!
[24] There!
[25] "Lovely!"
[26] "Very beautiful!"

FINA *standing before a glazed mirror, looking at herself and re-peating the daughter's word.*]

SERAFINA Disgusting!

[*The music is briefly resumed to mark a division.*]

Scene Five

[*Immediately following.* SERAFINA'S *movements gather momentum. She snatches a long-neglected girdle out of a bureau drawer and holds it experimentally about her waist. She shakes her head doubtfully, drops the girdle and snatches the $8.98 hat off the millinery dummy and plants it on her head. She turns around dis-tractedly, not remembering where the mirror is. She gasps with astonishment when she catches sight of herself, snatches the hat off and hastily restores it to the blank head of the dummy. She makes another confused revolution or two, then gasps with fresh inspiration and snatches a girlish frock off a dummy—an Alice-blue gown with daisies crocheted on it. The dress sticks on the dummy.* SERAFINA *mutters savagely in Sicilian. She finally over-comes this difficulty but in her exasperation she knocks the dummy over. She throws off the robe and steps hopefully into the gown. But she discovers it won't fit over her hips. She seizes the girdle again; then hurls it angrily away. The parrot calls to her; she yells angrily back at the parrot:* "Zitto!"[1]]

[*In the distance the high-school band starts playing.* SERAFINA *gets panicky that she will miss the graduation ceremonies, and ham-mers her forehead with her fist, sobbing a little. She wriggles despairingly out of the blue dress and runs out back in her rayon slip just as* FLORA *and* BESSIE *appear outside the house.* FLORA *and* BESSIE *are two female clowns of middle years and juvenile temperament.* FLORA *is tall and angular;* BESSIE *is rather stubby. They are dressed for a gala.* FLORA *runs up the steps and bangs at the cottage door.*]

BESSIE I fail to understand why it's so important to pick up a polka-dot blouse when it's likely to make us miss the twelve o'clock train.

5 FLORA Serafina! Serafina!

BESSIE We only got fifteen minutes to get to the depot and I'll get faint on the train if I don't have m' coffee . . .

---

[1] Quiet!

FLORA Git a coke on th' train, Bessie.

BESSIE Git nothing on the train if we don't git the train!

[SERAFINA *runs back out of the bedroom, quite breathless, in a purple dress. As she passes the millinery dummy she snatches the hat off again and plants it back on her head.*]

SERAFINA Wrist-watch! Wrist-watch! Where'd I put th' wrist-watch? [*She hears* FLORA *shouting and banging and rushes to the door.*]

BESSIE Try the door if it ain't open.   5

FLORA [*Pushing in.*] Just tell me, is it ready or not?

SERAFINA Oh! You. Don't bother me. I'm late for the graduation of my daughter and now I can't find her graduation present.

FLORA You got plenty of time.

SERAFINA Don't you hear the band playing?   10

FLORA They're just warming up. Now, Serafina, where is my blouse?

SERAFINA Blouse? Not ready! I had to make fourteen graduation dresses!

FLORA A promise is a promise and an excuse is just an excuse!   15

SERAFINA I got to get to the high school!

FLORA I got to get to the depot in that blouse!

BESSIE We're going to the American Legion parade in New Orleans.

FLORA There, there, there, there it is! [*She grabs the blouse from   20
the machine.*] Get started, woman, stitch them bandanas together!
If you don't do it, I'm a-gonna report you to the Chamber of
Commerce and git your license revoked!

SERAFINA [*Anxiously.*] What license you talking about? I got no
license!   25

FLORA You hear that, Bessie? *She hasn't got no license!*

BESSIE *She ain't even got a license?*

SERAFINA [*Crossing quickly to the machine.*] I—I'll stitch them
together! But if you make me late to my daughter's graduation,
I'll make you sorry some way . . .   30

[*She works with furious rapidity. A train whistle is heard.*]

BESSIE [*Wildly and striking at* FLORA *with her purse.*] Train's pullin' out! Oh, God, you made us miss it!

FLORA Bessie, you know there's another at 12:45!

BESSIE It's the selfish—principle of it that makes me sick! [*She walks rapidly up and down.*]

5 FLORA Set down, Bessie. Don't wear out your feet before we git to th' city . . .

BESSIE Molly tole me the town was full of excitement. They're dropping paper sacks full of water out of hotel windows.

FLORA Which hotel are they dropping paper sacks out of?

10 BESSIE What a fool question! The Monteleone Hotel.

FLORA That's an old-fashioned hotel.

BESSIE It might be old-fashioned but you'd be surprised at some of the modern, up-to-date things that go on there.

FLORA I heard, I heard that the Legionnaires caught a girl on
15 Canal Street! They tore the clothes off her and sent her home in a taxi!

BESSIE I double dog dare anybody to try that on me!

FLORA You?! Huh! You never need any assistance gittin' un-dressed!

20 SERAFINA [*Ominously.*] You two ladies watch how you talk in here. This here is a Catholic house. You are sitting in the same room with Our Lady and with the blessed ashes of my husband!

FLORA [*Acidly.*] Well, ex-cuse *me!* [*She whispers maliciously to* BESSIE.] It sure is a pleasant surprise to see you wearing a dress,
25 Serafina, but the surprise would be twice as pleasant if it was more the right size. [*To* BESSIE, *loudly.*] She used to have a sweet figure, a little bit plump but attractive, but setting there at that sewing machine for three years in a kimona and not stepping out of the house has naturally given her hips!

30 SERAFINA If I didn't have hips I would be a very uncomfortable woman when I set down.

[*The parrot squawks.* SERAFINA *imitates its squawk.*]

FLORA Polly want a cracker?

SERAFINA No. He don't want a cracker! What is she doing over there at that window?

35 BESSIE Some Legionnaires are on the highway!

FLORA A Legionnaire? No kidding?

[*She springs up and joins her girl friend at the window. They both laugh fatuously, bobbing their heads out the window.*]

BESSIE He's looking this way; yell something!

FLORA [*Leaning out the window.*]   Mademoiselle from Armentieres, parley-voo!

BESSIE [*Chiming in rapturously.*]   Mademoiselle from Armentieres, parley-voo!   5

A VOICE OUTSIDE [*Gallantly returning the salute.*]   Mademoiselle from Armentieres, hadn't been kissed for forty years!

BOTH GIRLS [*Together; very gaily.*]   Hinky-dinky parley-voooo!

[*They laugh and applaud at the window.   The Legionnaires are heard laughing.   A car horn is heard as the Legionnaires drive away.   SERAFINA springs up and rushes over to the window, jerks them away from it and slams the shutters in their faces.*]

SERAFINA [*Furiously.*]   I told you wimmen that you was not in a honky-tonk! Now take your blouse and git out! Get out on the   10
streets where you kind a wimmen belong.—This is the house of Rosario delle Rose and those are his ashes in that marble urn and I won't have—unproper things going on here or dirty talk, neither!

FLORA Who's talking dirty?   15

BESSIE What a helluva nerve.

FLORA I want you to listen!

SERAFINA You are, you are, dirty talk, all the time men, men, men! You men-crazy things, you!

FLORA Sour grapes—sour grapes is your trouble! You're wild with   20
envy!

BESSIE Isn't she green with jealousy? Huh!

SERAFINA [*Suddenly and religiously.*]   When I think of men I think about my husband. My husband was a Sicilian. We had love together every night of the week, we never skipped one, from the   25
night we was married till the night he was killed in his fruit truck on that road there! [*She catches her breath in a sob.*] And maybe that is the reason I'm not man-crazy and don't like hearing the talk of women that are. But I am interested, now, in the hap-piness of my daughter who's graduating this morning out of high   30
school. And now I'm going to be late, the band is playing! And I have lost her wrist watch!—her graduation present! [*She whirls about distractedly.*]

BESSIE   Flora, let's go!—The hell with that goddam blouse!

FLORA   Oh, no, just wait a minute! I don't accept insults from no one!

5   SERAFINA   Go on, go on to New Orleans, you two man-crazy things, you! And pick up a man on Canal Street but not in my house, at my window, in front of my dead husband's ashes!

[*The high-school band is playing a martial air in the distance. SERAFINA'S chest is heaving violently; she touches her heart and momentarily seems to forget that she must go.*]

10   I am not at all interested, I am not interested in men getting fat and bald in soldier-boy play suits, tearing the clothes off girls on Canal Street and dropping paper sacks out of hotel windows. I'm just not interested in that sort of man-crazy business. I remember my husband with a body like a young boy and hair on his head as thick and black as mine is and skin on him smooth and sweet as a yellow rose petal.

FLORA   Oh, a *rose,* was he?

15   SERAFINA   Yes, yes, a rose, a rose!

FLORA   Yes, a rose of a Wop!—of a gangster!—shot smuggling dope under a load of bananas!

BESSIE   Flora, Flora, let's go!

20   SERAFINA   My folks was peasants, contadini,[2] but he—he came from *land*-owners! *Signorile,*[3] my husband!—At night I sit here and I'm satisfied to remember, because I had the best.—Not the third best and not the second best, but the *first* best, the *only* best!—So now I stay here and am satisfied now to remember . . .

BESSIE   Come on, come out! To the depot!

25   FLORA   Just wait, I wanta hear this, it's too good to miss!

SERAFINA   I count up the nights I held him all night in my arms, and I can tell you how many. Each night for twelve years. Four thousand—three hundred—and eighty. The number of nights I held him all night in my arms. Sometimes I didn't sleep, just held
30   him all night in my arms. And I am satisfied with it. I grieve for him. Yes, my pillow at night's never dry—but I'm satisfied to remember. And I would feel cheap and degraded and not fit to live with my daughter or under the roof with the urn of his blessed ashes, those—ashes of a rose—if after that memory, after
35   knowing that man I went to some other, some middle-aged man,

2 Farmers.
3 Gentlemen.

not young, not full of young passion, but getting a pot belly on him and losing his hair and smelling of sweat and liquor—and trying to fool myself that *that* was love-making! I *know* what love-making was. And I'm satisfied just to remember . . . [*She is panting as though she had run upstairs.*] Go on, you do it, you go on the streets and let them drop their sacks of dirty water on you!— I'm satisfied to remember the love of a man that was mine—*only mine!* Never touched by the hand of *nobody! Nobody* but *me!*—Just me! [*She gasps and runs out to the porch. The sun floods her figure. It seems to astonish her. She finds herself sobbing. She digs in her purse for her handkerchief.*]

FLORA [*Crossing to the open door.*]   Never touched by nobody?

SERAFINA [*With fierce pride.*]   Never nobody but me!

FLORA   *I* know somebody that could a tale unfold! And not so far from here either. Not no further than the Square Roof is, that place on Esplanade!

BESSIE   Estelle Hohengarten!

FLORA   Estelle Hohengarten!—the blackjack dealer from Texas!

BESSIE   Get into your blouse and let's go!

FLORA   Everybody's known it but Serafina. I'm just telling the facts that come out at the inquest while she was in bed with her eyes shut tight and the sheet pulled over her head like a female ostrich! Tie this damn thing on me! It was a romance, not just a fly-by-night thing, but a steady affair that went on for more than a year.

[SERAFINA *has been standing on the porch with the door open behind her. She is in the full glare of the sun. She appears to have been struck senseless by the words shouted inside. She turns slowly about. We see that her dress is unfastened down the back, the pink slip showing. She reaches out gropingly with one hand and finds the porch column which she clings to while the terrible words strike constantly deeper. The high-school band continues as a merciless counterpoint.*]

BESSIE   Leave her in ignorance. Ignorance is bliss.

FLORA   He had a rose tattoo on his chest, the stuck-up thing, and Estelle was so gone on him she went down to Bourbon Street and had one put on her.

[SERAFINA *comes onto the porch and* FLORA *turns to her, viciously.*]

Yeah, a rose tattoo on her chest same as the Wop's!

SERAFINA [*Very softly.*]   Liar . . . [*She comes inside; the word seems to give her strength.*]

BESSIE [*Nervously.*]   Flora, let's go, let's go!

SERAFINA [*In a terrible voice.*]   Liar!— Lie-arrrr! [*She slams the wooden door shut with a violence that shakes the walls.*]

5   BESSIE [*Shocked into terror.*]   Let's get outa here, Flora!

FLORA   Let her howl her head off. I don't care.

[SERAFINA *has snatched up a broom.*]

BESSIE   What's she up to?

FLORA   I don't care what she's up to.

BESSIE   I'm a-scared of these Wops.

10   FLORA   I'm not afraid of nobody!

BESSIE   She's gonna hit you.

FLORA   She'd better not hit me!

[*But both of the clowns are in retreat to the door.* SERAFINA *suddenly rushes at them with the broom. She flails* FLORA *about the hips and shoulders.* BESSIE *gets out. But* FLORA *is trapped in a corner. A table is turned over.* BESSIE, *outside, screams for the police and cries:* "Murder! Murder!" *The high-school band is playing* The Stars and Stripes Forever. FLORA *breaks wildly past the flailing broom and escapes out of the house. She also takes up the cry for help.* SERAFINA *follows them out. She is flailing the brilliant noon air with the broom. The two women run off, screaming.*]

FLORA [*Calling back.*]   I'm going to have her arrested! Police, police! I'm going to have you arrested!

15   SERAFINA   *Have* me arrested, *have* me, you dirt, you devil, you *liar!* Li-i-arrrr! [*She comes back inside the house and leans on the work table for a moment, panting heavily. Then she rushes back to the door, slams it and bolts it. Then she rushes to the window, slams the shutters and fastens them. The house is now dark except for the vigil light in the ruby glass cup before the Madonna, and the delicate beams admitted through the shutter slats.*]

SERAFINA [*In a crazed manner.*]   Have me—have me—arrested— dirty slut—bitch—liar!

[*She moves about helplessly, not knowing what to do, with her big, stricken body. Panting for breath, she repeats the word "liar" monotonously and helplessly as she thrashes about. It is necessary for her, vitally necessary for her, to believe that the woman's story is a malicious invention. But the words of it stick in her mind and she mumbles them aloud as she thrashes crazily around the small confines of the parlor.*]

Woman—Estelle—

[*The sound of band music heard.*]

Band, band, already—started.—Going to miss—graduation. Oh! [*She retreats toward the Madonna.*] Estelle, Estelle Hohengarten?—"A shirt for a man I'm in love with! This man—is—wild like a gypsy."—Oh, oh, Lady—The—rose-colored—silk. [*She   5 starts toward the dining room, then draws back in terror.*] No, no, no, no, no! I don't remember! It wasn't that name, I don't remember the name! [*The band music grows louder.*] High school—graduation—late! I'll be—late for it.—Oh, Lady, give me a—sign! [*She cocks her head toward the statue in a fearful   10 listening attitude.*] Che? Che dice, Signora?[4] *Oh, Lady! Give me a sign!*

[*The scene dims out.*]

Scene Six

[*It is two hours later. The interior of the house is in complete darkness except for the vigil light. With the shutters closed, the interior is so dark that we do not know* SERAFINA *is present. All that we see clearly is the starry blue robe of Our Lady above the flickering candle of the ruby glass cup. After a few moments we hear* SERAFINA'S *voice, very softly, in the weak, breathless tone of a person near death.*]

SERAFINA [*Very softly.*]   Oh, Lady, give me a sign . . .

[*Gay, laughing voices are heard outside the house.* ROSA *and* JACK *appear, bearing roses and gifts. They are shouting back to others in a car.*]

JACK   Where do we go for the picnic?

A GIRL'S VOICE [*From the highway.*]   We're going in three sail-
boats to Diamond Key.   15

A MAN'S VOICE   Be at Municipal Pier in half an hour.

---

⁴ What? What are you saying, Lady?

ROSA Pick us up here. [*She races up the steps.*] Oh, the door's locked! Mama's gone *out!* There's a key in that bird bath.

[JACK *opens the door. The parlor lights up faintly as they enter.*]

JACK It's dark in here.

ROSA Yes, Mama's gone out!

5 JACK How do you know she's out?

ROSA The door was locked and all the shutters are closed! Put down those roses.

JACK Where shall I . . .

ROSA Somewhere, anywhere!—Come here! [*He approaches her*
10 *rather diffidently.*] I want to teach you a little Dago word. The word is "bacio."[1]

JACK What does this word mean?

ROSA This and this and this! [*She rains kisses upon him till he forcibly removes her face from him.*] Just think. A week ago
15 Friday—I didn't know boys existed!—Did you know girls existed before the dance?

JACK Yes, I knew they existed . . .

ROSA [*Holding him.*] Do you remember what you said to me on the dance floor? "Honey, you're dancing too close"?

20 JACK Well, it was—hot in the Gym and the—floor was crowded.

ROSA When my girl friend was teaching me how to dance, I asked her, "How do you know which way the boy's going to move?" And she said, "You've got to feel how he's going to move with your body!" I said, "How do you feel with your body?" And
25 she said, "By pressing up close!"—That's why I pressed up close! I didn't realize that I was—Ha, ha! Now you're blushing! Don't go *away!*—And a few minutes later you said to me, "Gee, you're beautiful!" I said, "Excuse me," and ran to the ladies' room. Do you know why? To look at myself in the mirror! And I saw
30 that I was! For the first time in my life I was beautiful! You'd made me beautiful when you *said* that I was!

JACK [*Humbly.*] You *are* beautiful, Rosa! So much, I . . .

ROSA *You've* changed, *too.* You've stopped laughing and joking. Why have you gotten so old and serious, Jack?

35 JACK Well, honey, you're sort of . . .

ROSA What am I "sort of"?

[1] "Kiss."

JACK [*Finding the right word.*]   *Wild!*

[*She laughs. He seizes the bandaged wrist.*]

I didn't know nothing like this was going to happen.

ROSA   Oh, that, that's nothing! I'll take the handkerchief off and you can forget it.

JACK   How could you do a thing like that over me? I'm—nothing!   5

ROSA   Everybody is nothing until you love them!

JACK   Give me that handkerchief. I want to show it to my ship-mates. I'll say, "This is the blood of a beautiful girl who cut her wrist with a knife because she loved me!"

ROSA   Don't be so pleased with yourself. It's mostly Mercuro-   10
chrome!

SERAFINA [*Violently, from the dark room adjoining.*] Stai zitta!—Cretina![2]

[ROSA *and* JACK *draw abruptly apart.*]

JACK [*Fearfully.*]   I knew somebody was here!

ROSA [*Sweetly and delicately.*]   Mama? Are you in there, Mama?   15

SERAFINA   No, no, no, I'm not, I'm dead and buried!

ROSA   Yes, Mama's in there!

JACK   Well, I—better go and—wait outside for a—while . . .

ROSA   You stay right here!—Mama?—Jack is with me.—Are you dressed up nicely? [*There is no response.*] Why's it so dark in   20
here?—Jack, open the shutters!—I want to introduce you to my mother . . .

JACK   Hadn't I better go and . . .

ROSA   No. Open the shutters!

[*The shutters are opened and* ROSA *draws apart the curtains between the two rooms. Sunlight floods the scene.* SERAFINA *is revealed slumped in a chair at her work table in the dining room near the Singer sewing machine. She is grotesquely surrounded by the dummies, as though she had been holding a silent conference with them. Her appearance, in slovenly deshabillé, is both comic and shocking.*]

ROSA [*Terribly embarrassed.*]   Mama, Mama, you said you were   25
dressed up pretty! Jack, stay out for a minute! What's happened, Mama?

[2] Shut up!—Idiot!

[JACK *remains in the parlor.* ROSA *pulls the curtains, snatches a robe and flings it over* SERAFINA. *She brushes* SERAFINA'S *hair back from her sweat-gleaming face, rubs her face with a handkerchief and dusts it with powder.* SERAFINA *submits to this cosmetic enterprise with a dazed look.*]

ROSA [*Gesturing vertically.*] Su, su, su, su, su, su, su, su, su![3]

[SERAFINA *sits up slightly in her chair, but she is still looking stupefied.* ROSA *returns to the parlor and opens the curtains again.*]

ROSA   Come in, Jack! Mama is ready to meet you!

[ROSA *trembles with eagerness as* JACK *advances nervously from the parlor. But before he enters* SERAFINA *collapses into her slumped position, with a low moan.*]

ROSA [*Violently.*] Mama, Mama, su, Mama!

[SERAFINA *sits half erect.*]

She didn't sleep good last night.—Mama, this is Jack Hunter!

5   JACK   Hello, Mrs. Delle Rose. It sure is a pleasure to meet you.

[*There is a pause.* SERAFINA *stares indifferently at the boy.*]

ROSA   Mama, Mama, say something!

JACK   Maybe your Mama wants me to . . . [*He makes an awkward gesture toward the door.*]

ROSA   No, no, Mama's just tired. Mama makes dresses; she made a whole lot of dresses for the graduation! How many, Mama,
10   how many graduation dresses did you have to make?

SERAFINA [*Dully.*] Fa niente . . .[4]

JACK   I was hoping to see you at the graduation, Mrs. Delle Rose.

ROSA   I guess that Mama was too worn out to go.

SERAFINA   Rosa, shut the front door, shut it and lock it. There was
15   a—policeman . . . [*There is a pause.*] What?—What?

JACK   My sister was graduating. My mother was there and my aunt was there—a whole bunch of cousins—I was hoping that you could—all—get together . . .

ROSA   Jack brought you some flowers.

20   JACK   I hope you are partial to roses as much as I am. [*He hands her the bouquet. She takes them absently.*]

[3] Up, up, up, up, up, up, up, up, up!
[4] It doesn't matter . . .

ROSA   Mama, say something, say something simple like "Thanks."

SERAFINA   Thanks.

ROSA   Jack, tell Mama about the graduation; describe it to her.

JACK   My mother said it was just like fairyland.

ROSA   Tell her what the boys wore!   5

JACK   What did—what did they wear?

ROSA   Oh, you know what they wore. They wore blue coats and white pants and each one had a carnation! And there were three couples that did an old-fashioned dance, a minuet, Mother, to Mendelssohn's *Spring Song!* Wasn't it lovely, Jack? But one girl   10
slipped; she wasn't used to long dresses! She slipped and fell on her—ho, ho! Wasn't it funny, Jack, wasn't it, wasn't it, Jack?

JACK [*Worriedly.*]   I think that your Mama . . .

ROSA   Oh, my prize, my prize, I have forgotten my prize!

JACK   Where is it?   15

ROSA   You set them down by the sewing sign when you looked for the key.

JACK   Aw, excuse me, I'll get them.

[*He goes out through the parlor.* ROSA *runs to her mother and kneels by her chair.*]

ROSA   [*In a terrified whisper.*] Mama, something has happened! What has happened, Mama? Can't you tell me, Mama? Is it be-   20
cause of this morning? Look. I took the bandage off, it was only a scratch! So, Mama, forget it! Think it was just a bad dream that never happened! Oh, Mama! [*She gives her several quick kisses on the forehead.* JACK *returns with two big books tied in white satin ribbon.*]

JACK   Here they are.

ROSA   Look what I got, Mama.   25

SERAFINA [*Dully.*]   What?

ROSA   The Digest of Knowledge!

JACK   Everything's in them, from Abracadabra to Zoo! My sister was jealous. She just got a diploma!

SERAFINA [*Rousing a bit.*]   Diploma, where is it? Didn't you get   30
no diploma?

ROSA   Si, si, Mama! Eccolo! Guarda, guarda![5] [*She holds up the diploma tied in ribbon.*]

[5] Yes, yes, Mama! There it is. Look, look!

SERAFINA   Va bene.⁶—Put it in the drawer with your father's clothes.

JACK   Mrs. Delle Rose, you should be very, very proud of your daughter. She stood in front of the crowd and recited a poem.

5   ROSA   Yes, I did. Oh, I was so excited!

JACK   And Mrs. Delle Rose, your daughter, Rosa, was so pretty when she walked on the stage—that people went "Oooooooooo!" —like that! Y'know what I mean? They all went—"Oooooooooo!" Like a—like a—*wind* had—blown over! Because your daughter,
10   Rosa, was so—*lovely* looking! [*He has crouched over to* SERA-FINA *to deliver this description close to her face. Now he straightens up and smiles proudly at* ROSA.] How does it feel to be the mother of the prettiest girl in the world?

ROSA [*Suddenly bursting into pure delight.*]   Ha, ha, ha, ha, ha, ha! [*She throws her head back in rapture.*]

15   SERAFINA [*Rousing.*]   Hush!

ROSA   Ha, ha, ha, ha, ha, ha, ha, ha, ha, ha! [*She cannot control her ecstatic laughter. She presses her hand to her mouth but the laughter still bubbles out.*]

SERAFINA [*Suddenly rising in anger.*]   Pazza, pazza, pazza! Finiscila!
20   Basta, via!⁷

[ROSA *whirls around to hide her convulsions of joy.*]

[*To* JACK.]   Put the prize books in the parlor, and shut the front door; there was a policeman come here because of—some trouble . . .

[JACK *takes the books.*]

ROSA   Mama, I've never seen you like this! What will Jack think,
25   Mama?

SERAFINA   What do I care what Jack thinks?—You wild, wild crazy thing, you—with the eyes of your—father . . .

JACK [*Returning.*]   Yes, ma'am, Mrs. Delle Rose, you certainly got a right to be very proud of your daughter.

30   SERAFINA [*After a pause.*]   I am proud of the—memory of her—father.—He was a baron . . .

[ROSA *takes* JACK'S *arm.*]

And who are *you*? What are you?—per piacere!⁸

⁶ All right.
⁷ Crazy, crazy, crazy! Stop it! Enough, go away!
⁸ Please.

Rosa Mama, I just introduced him; his name is Jack Hunter.

Serafina Hunt-er?

Jack Yes, ma'am, Hunter, Jack Hunter.

Serafina: What are you hunting?—Jack?

Rosa Mama!   5

Serafina What all of 'em are hunting? To have a good time, and
the Devil cares who pays for it? I'm sick of men, I'm almost as
sick of men as I am of wimmen.—Rosa, get out while I talk to
this boy!

Rosa I didn't bring Jack here to be insulted!   10

Jack Go on, honey, and let your Mama talk to me. I think your
Mama has just got a slight wrong—impression . . .

Serafina [*Ominously.*] Yes, I got an impression!

Rosa I'll get dressed! Oh, Mama, don't spoil it for me!—the happiest day of my life! [*She goes into the back of the house.*]   15

Jack [*After an awkward pause.*] Mrs. Delle Rose . . .

Serafina [*Correcting his pronunciation.*] Delle Rose!

Jack Mrs. Delle Rose, I'm sorry about all this. Believe me, Mrs.
Delle Rose, the last thing I had in mind was getting mixed up in
a family situation. I came home after three months to sea, I   20
docked at New Orleans, and came here to see my folks. My sister
was going to a high-school dance. She took me with her, and there
I met your daughter.

Serafina What did you do?

Jack At the high school dance? We danced! My sister had told me   25
that Rosa had a very strict mother and wasn't allowed to go on
dates with boys so when it was over, I said, "I'm sorry you're not
allowed to go out." And she said, "Oh! What gave you the idea I
wasn't!" So then I thought my sister had made a mistake and I
made a date with her for the next night.   30

Serafina What did you do the next night?

Jack The next night we went to the movies.

Serafina And what did you do—that night?

Jack At the movies? We ate a bag of popcorn and watched the
movie!   35

Serafina She come home at midnight and said she had been with
a girl-friend studying "civics."

Jack Whatever story she told you, it ain't my fault!

Serafina And the night after that?

JACK   Last Tuesday? We went roller skating!

SERAFINA   And afterwards?

JACK   After the skating? We went to a drug store and had an ice cream soda!

5   SERAFINA   Alone?

JACK   At the drug store? No. It was crowded. And the skating rink was full of people skating!

SERAFINA   You mean that you haven't been alone with my Rosa?

JACK   Alone or not alone, what's the point of that question? I still
10   don't see the point of it.

SERAFINA   We are Sicilians. We don't leave the girls with the boys they're not engaged to!

JACK   Mrs. Delle Rose, this is the United States.

SERAFINA   But we are Sicilians, and we are not cold-blooded.—My
15   girl is a *virgin!* She *is*—or she *was*—I would like to know—*which!*

JACK   Mrs. Delle Rose! I got to tell you something. You might not believe it. It is a hard thing to say. But I am—*also a*—*virgin* . . .

SERAFINA   *What? No.* I do not believe it.

20   JACK   Well, it's true, though. This is the first time—I . . .

SERAFINA   First time you *what?*

JACK   The first time I really wanted to . . .

SERAFINA   Wanted to what?

JACK   Make—love . . .

25   SERAFINA   You? A sailor?

JACK   [*Sighing deeply.*]   Yes, ma'am. I had opportunities to!—But I—always thought of my mother . . . I always asked myself, would she or would she not—think—this or that person was—decent!

30   SERAFINA   But with my daughter, my Rosa, your mother tells you *okay?*—go ahead, son!

JACK   Mrs. Delle Rose! [*With embarrassment.*]—Mrs. Delle Rose, I . . .

SERAFINA   Two weeks ago I was slapping her hands for scratching
35   mosquito bites. She rode a bicycle to school. Now all at once— I've got a wild thing in the house. She says she's in love. And you? Do you say *you're* in love?

JACK   [*Solemnly.*]   Yes, ma'am, I do, I'm in love!—very much . . .

SERAFINA   Bambini, tutti due, bambini![9]

[ROSA *comes out, dressed for the picnic.*]

ROSA   I'm ready for Diamond Key!

SERAFINA   Go out on the porch. Diamond Key!

ROSA [*With a sarcastic curtsy.*]   Yes, Mama!

SERAFINA   What are you? Catholic?   5

JACK   Me? Yes, ma'am, Catholic.

SERAFINA   You don't look Catholic to me!

ROSA [*Shouting from the door.*]   Oh, God, Mama, how do Catholics look? How do they look different from anyone else?

SERAFINA   Stay out till I call you!   10

[ROSA *crosses to the bird bath and prays.* SERAFINA *turns to* JACK.]

   Turn around, will you?

JACK   Do what, ma'am?

SERAFINA   I said, *turn around!*

[JACK *awkwardly turns around.*]

   Why do they make them Navy pants so tight?

ROSA [*Listening in the yard.*]   Oh, my God . . .   15

JACK [*Flushing.*]   That's a question you'll have to ask the Navy, Mrs. Delle Rose.

SERAFINA   And that gold earring, what's the gold earring for?

ROSA [*Yelling from the door.*]   For crossing the equator, Mama; he's crossed it three times. He was initiated into the court of   20 Neptune and gets to wear a gold earring! He's a shellback!

[SERAFINA *springs up and crosses to slam the porch door.* ROSA *runs despairingly around the side of the house and leans, exhausted with closed eyes, against the trunk of a palm tree.* THE STREGA *creeps into the yard, listening.*]

SERAFINA   You see what I got. A wild thing in the house!

JACK   Mrs. Delle Rose, I guess that Sicilians are very emotional people . . .

SERAFINA   I want nobody to take advantage of that!   25

JACK   You got the wrong idea about me, Mrs. Delle Rose.

   [9] Children, both of you, children!

SERAFINA   I know what men want—not to eat popcorn with girls or to slide on ice! And boys are the same, only younger.—Come here. Come here!

[ROSA *hears her mother's passionate voice. She rushes from the palm tree to the back door and pounds on it with both fists.*]

ROSA   Mama! Mama! Let me in the door, Jack!

5   JACK   Mrs. Delle Rose, your daughter is calling you.

SERAFINA   Let her call!—Come here. [*She crosses to the shrine of Our Lady.*] *Come here!*

[*Despairing of the back door,* ROSA *rushes around to the front. A few moments later she pushes open the shutters of the window in the wall and climbs half in.* JACK *crosses apprehensively to* SERAFINA *before the Madonna.*]

SERAFINA   You said you're Catholic, ain't you?

JACK   Yes, ma'am.

10   SERAFINA   Then kneel down in front of Our Lady!

JACK   Do—do what, did you say?

SERAFINA   I said to get down on your knees in front of Our Lady!

[ROSA *groans despairingly in the window.* JACK *kneels awkwardly upon the hassock.*]

ROSA   Mama, Mama, *now* what?!

[SERAFINA *rushes to the window, pushes* ROSA *out and slams the shutters.*]

SERAFINA [*Returning to* JACK.]   Now say after me what I say!

15   JACK   Yes, ma'am.

[ROSA *pushes the shutters open again.*]

SERAFINA   I promise the Holy Mother that I will respect the innocence of the daughter of . . .

ROSA [*In anguish.*]   Ma-*maaa!* . . .

SERAFINA   Get back out of that window!—Well? Are you gonna
20   say it?

JACK   Yes, ma'am. What was it, again?

SERAFINA   I promise the Holy Mother . . .

JACK   I promise the Holy Mother . . .

SERAFINA   As I hope to be saved by the Blessed Blood of Jesus . . .

JACK   As I hope to be saved by the . . .

SERAFINA   Blessed Blood of . . .

JACK   Jesus . . .

SERAFINA   That I will respect the innocence of the daughter, Rosa,   5
of Rosario Delle Rose.

JACK   That I will respect the innocence—of—Rosa . . .

SERAFINA   Cross yourself!

[*He crosses himself.*]

Now get up, get up, get up! I am satisfied now . . .

[ROSA *jumps through the window and rushes to* SERAFINA *with arms
outflung and wild cries of joy.*]

SERAFINA   Let me go, let me breathe!   10

[*Outside* THE STREGA *cackles derisively.*]

ROSA   Oh, wonderful Mama, don't breathe! Oh, Jack! *Kiss* Mama!
Kiss Mama! Mama, please kiss Jack!

SERAFINA   Kiss? Me? No, no, no, no!—Kiss my *hand* . . .

[*She offers her hand, shyly, and* JACK *kisses it with a loud smack.*
ROSA *seizes the wine bottle.*]

ROSA   Mama, get some wine glasses!

[SERAFINA *goes for the glasses, and* ROSA *suddenly turns to* JACK.
*Out of her mother's sight, she passionately grabs hold of his hand
and presses it, first to her throat, then to her lips and finally to
her breast.* JACK *snatches his hand away as* SERAFINA *returns with
the glasses. Voices are heard calling from the highway.*]

VOICES OUTSIDE   Ro-osa!—Ro-osa!—Ro-osa!   15

[*A car horn is heard blowing.*]

SERAFINA   Oh, I forgot the graduation present.

[*She crouches down before the bureau and removes a fancily
wrapped package from its bottom drawer. The car horn is honk-
ing, and the voices are calling.*]

ROSA   They're calling for us! *Coming!* Jack! [*She flies out the door,
calling back to her mother.*] G'bye, Mama!

JACK [*Following* ROSA.]   Good-bye, Mrs. Delle Rose!

SERAFINA [*Vaguely.*]   It's a Bulova wrist watch with seventeen jewels in it . . . [*She realizes that she is alone.*] Rosa!

[*She goes to the door, still holding out the present. Outside the car motor roars, and the voices shout as the car goes off.* SERAFINA *stumbles outside, shielding her eyes with one hand, extending the gift with the other.*]

Rosa, Rosa, your present! Regalo, regalo—tesoro![10]

[*But the car has started off, with a medley of voices shouting farewells, which fade quickly out of hearing.* SERAFINA *turns about vaguely in the confusing sunlight and gropes for the door. There is a derisive cackle from* THE STREGA *next door.* SERAFINA *absently opens the package and removes the little gold watch. She winds it and then holds it against her ear. She shakes it and holds it again to her ear. Then she holds it away from her and glares at it fiercely.*]

5   SERAFINA [*Pounding her chest three times.*]   Tick—tick—tick! [*She goes to the Madonna and faces it.*] Speak to me, Lady! Oh, Lady, give me a sign!

[*The scene dims out.*]

[10] A present, a present—my treasure!

ACT TWO

Scene One

[*It is two hours later the same day.* SERAFINA *comes out onto the porch, barefooted, wearing a rayon slip. Great shadows have appeared beneath her eyes; her face and throat gleam with sweat. There are dark stains of wine on the rayon slip. It is difficult for her to stand, yet she cannot sit still. She makes a sick moaning sound in her throat almost continually. A hot wind rattles the cane-brake.* VIVI, *the little girl, comes up to the porch to stare at* SERAFINA *as at a strange beast in a cage.* VIVI *is chewing a licorice stick which stains her mouth and her fingers. She stands chewing and staring.* SERAFINA *evades her stare. She wearily drags a broken grey wicker chair down off the porch, all the way out in front of the house, and sags heavily into it. It sits awry on a broken leg.* VIVI *sneaks toward her.* SERAFINA *lurches about to face her angrily. The child giggles and scampers back to the porch.*]

SERAFINA [*Sinking back into the chair.*]   Oh, Lady, Lady, Lady, give me a—sign . . . [*She looks up at the white glare of the sky.*]

[FATHER DE LEO *approaches the house.* SERAFINA *crouches low in the chair to escape his attention. He knocks at the door. Receiving no answer, he looks out into the yard, sees her, and approaches her chair. He comes close to address her with a gentle severity.*]

FATHER DE LEO   Buon giorno, Serafina.[1]

SERAFINA [*Faintly, with a sort of disgust.*]   Giorno . . .

FATHER DE LEO   I'm surprised to see you sitting outdoors like   5
this. What is that thing you're wearing?—I think it's an undergarment!—It's hanging off one shoulder, and your head, Serafina, looks as if you had stuck it in a bucket of oil. Oh, I see now why the other ladies of the neighborhood aren't taking their afternoon naps! They find it more entertaining to sit on the   10
porches and watch the spectacle you are putting on for them!— Are you listening to me?—I must tell you that the change in your appearance and behavior since Rosario's death is shocking— shocking! A woman can be dignified in her grief but when it's carried too far it becomes a sort of self-indulgence. Oh, I knew   15
this was going to happen when you broke the Church law and had your husband cremated!

[1] Good morning, Serafina.

517

[SERAFINA *lurches up from the chair and shuffles back to the porch.* FATHER DE LEO *follows her.*]

Set up a little idolatrous shrine in your house and give worship to a bottle of ashes.

[*She sinks down upon the steps.*]

—Are you listening to me?

[*Two women have appeared on the embankment and descend toward the house.* SERAFINA *lurches heavily up to meet them, like a weary bull turning to face another attack.*]

SERAFINA   You ladies, what you want? I don't do sewing! Look,
5   I quit doing sewing. [*She pulls down the* "SEWING" *sign and hurls it away.*] Now you got places to go, you ladies, go places! Don't hang around front of my house!

FATHER DE LEO   The ladies want to be friendly.

SERAFINA   Naw, they don't come to be friendly. They think they
10   know something that Serafina don't know; they think I got *these* on my head! [*She holds her fingers like horns at either side of her forehead.*] Well, I ain't got them!

[*She goes padding back out in front of the house.* FATHER DE LEO *follows.*]

FATHER DE LEO   You called me this morning in distress over something.

15   SERAFINA   I called you this morning but now it is afternoon.

FATHER DE LEO   I had to christen the grandson of the Mayor.

SERAFINA   The Mayor's important people, not Serafina!

FATHER DE LEO   You don't come to confession.

SERAFINA [*Starting back toward the porch.*]   No, I don't come, I
20   don't go, I—Ohhh! [*She pulls up one foot and hops on the other.*]

FATHER DE LEO   You stepped on something?

SERAFINA [*Dropping down on the steps.*]   No, no, no, no, no, I don't step on—noth'n . . .

FATHER DE LEO   Come in the house. We'll wash it with antiseptic.

[*She lurches up and limps back toward the house.*]

25   Walking barefooted you will get it infected.

SERAFINA   Fa niente . . .[2]

---

[2] It doesn't matter . . .

[*At the top of the embankment a little* BOY *runs out with a red kite and flourishes it in the air with rigid gestures, as though he were giving a distant signal.* SERAFINA *shades her eyes with a palm to watch the kite, and then, as though its motions conveyed a shocking message, she utters a startled soft cry and staggers back to the porch. She leans against a pillar, running her hand rapidly and repeatedly through her hair.* FATHER DE LEO *approaches her again, somewhat timidly.*]

FATHER DE LEO   Serafina?

SERAFINA   Che, che, che cosa vuole?[3]

FATHER DE LEO   I am thirsty. Will you go in the house and get me some water?

SERAFINA   Go in. Get you some water. The faucet is working.—I   5
can't go in the house.

FATHER DE LEO   Why can't you go in the house?

SERAFINA   The house has a tin roof on it. I got to breathe.

FATHER DE LEO   You can breathe in the house.

SERAFINA   No, I can't breathe in the house. The house has a tin   10
roof on it and I . . .

[THE STREGA *has been creeping through the cane-brake pretending to search for a chicken.*]

THE STREGA   Chick, chick, chick, chick, chick? [*She crouches to peer under the house.*]

SERAFINA   What's that? Is that the . . . ? Yes, the Strega! [*She picks up a flower pot containing a dead plant and crosses the*   15
yard.] Strega! Strega!

[THE STREGA *looks up, retreating a little.*]

Yes, you, I mean you! You ain't look for no chick! Getta hell outa my yard!

[THE STREGA *retreats, viciously muttering, back into the cane-brake.* SERAFINA *makes the protective sign of the horns with her fingers. The goat bleats.*]

FATHER DE LEO   You have no friends, Serafina.

SERAFINA   I don't want friends.   20

___
[3] What, what, what do you want?

FATHER DE LEO You are still a young woman. Eligible for—loving and—bearing again! I remember you dressed in pale blue silk at Mass one Easter morning, yes, like a lady wearing a—piece of the—weather! Oh, how proudly you walked, *too* proudly!—But now you crouch and shuffle about barefooted; you live like a convict, dressed in the rags of a convict. You have no companions; women you don't mix with. You . . .

SERAFINA No, I don't mix with them women. [*Glaring at the women on the embankment.*] The dummies I got in my house. I mix with them better because they don't make up no lies!— What kind of women are them? [*Mimicking fiercely.*] "Eee, Papa, eeee, baby, eee, me, me, me! At thirty years old they got no more use for the letto matrimoniale,⁴ no. The big bed goes to the basement! They get little beds from Sears Roebuck and sleep on their bellies!

FATHER DE LEO Attenzione!⁵

SERAFINA They make the life without glory. Instead of the heart they got the deep-freeze in the house. The men, they don't feel no glory, not in the house with them women; they go to the bars, fight in them, get drunk, get fat, put horns on the women because the women's don't give them the love which is glory.—I did, I give him the glory. To me the big bed was beautiful like a religion. Now I lie on it with dreams, with memories only! But it is still beautiful to me and I don't believe that the man in my heart gave me horns!

[*The women whisper.*]

What, what are they saying? Does ev'rybody know something that I don't know?—No, all I want is a sign, a sign from Our Lady, to tell me the lie is a lie! And then I . . .

[*The women laugh on the embankment.* SERAFINA *starts fiercely toward them. They scatter.*]

Squeak, squeak, squawk, squawk! Hens—like water thrown on them!

[*There is the sound of mocking laughter.*]

FATHER DE LEO People are laughing at you on all the porches.

SERAFINA I'm laughing, too. Listen to me, I'm laughing! [*She breaks into a loud, false laughter, first from the porch, then from*

⁴ Double bed.
⁵ Listen to me!

the foot of the embankment, then crossing in front of the house.]
Ha, ha, ha, ha, ha, ha, ha! Now ev'rybody is laughing. Ha, ha
ha, ha, ha, ha!

FATHER DE LEO Zitta ora!⁶—Think of your daughter.

SERAFINA [*Understanding the word "'daughter.'*"] You, *you* think 5
of my daughter! Today you give out the diplomas, today at the
high school you give out the prizes, diplomas! You give to my
daughter a set of books call the Digest of Knowledge! What does
she know? How to be cheap already?—Oh, yes, that is what to 10
learn, how to be cheap and to cheat!—You know what they do
at this high school? They ruin the girls there! They give the spring
dance because the girls are man-crazy. And there at that dance
my daughter goes with a sailor that has in his ear a gold ring!
And pants so tight that a woman ought not to look at him! This 15
morning, this morning she cuts with a knife her wrist if I don't
let her go!—Now all of them gone to some island, they call it a
picnic, all of them, gone in a—boat!

FATHER DE LEO There *was* a school picnic, chaperoned by the
teachers. 20

SERAFINA Oh, lo so, lo so!⁷ The man-crazy old-maid teachers!—
They all run wild on the island!

FATHER DE LEO Serafina Delle Rose!

[*He picks up the chair by the back and hauls it to the porch when
she starts to resume her seat.*]

—I *command* you to go in the house.

SERAFINA Go in the house? I will. I will go in the house if you 25
will answer one question.—Will you answer one question?

FATHER DE LEO I will if I know the answer.

SERAFINA Aw, you know the answer!—You used to hear the confessions of my husband. [*She turns to face the priest.*]

FATHER DE LEO Yes, I heard his confessions . . . 30

SERAFINA [*With difficulty.*] Did he ever speak to you of a *woman?*

[*A child cries out and races across in front of the house.* FATHER
DE LEO *picks up his panama hat.* SERAFINA *paces slowly toward
him. He starts away from the house.*]

SERAFINA [*Rushing after him.*] Aspettate! Aspettate un momento!⁸

⁶ Quiet now!
⁷ Oh, that, that!
⁸ Wait! Wait a minute!

FATHER DE LEO [*Fearfully, not looking at her.*]   Che volete?[9]

SERAFINA   Rispondetemi![10] [*She strikes her breast.*] Did he speak of a woman to you?

FATHER DE LEO   You know better than to ask me such a question. I don't break the Church laws. The secrets of the confessional are sacred to me. [*He walks away.*]

SERAFINA [*Pursuing and clutching his arm.*]   I got to know. You could tell me.

FATHER DE LEO   Let go of me, Serafina!

SERAFINA   Not till you tell me, Father. Father, you tell me, please tell me! Or I will go mad! [*In a fierce whisper.*] I will go back in the house and smash the urn with the ashes—if you don't tell me! I will go mad with the doubt in my heart and I will smash the urn and scatter the ashes—of my husband's body!

FATHER DE LEO   What could I tell you? If you would not believe the known facts about him . . .

SERAFINA   Known facts, who knows the known facts?

[*The neighbor women have heard the argument and begin to crowd around, muttering in shocked whispers at* SERAFINA'S *lack of respect.*]

FATHER DE LEO [*Frightened.*]   Lasciatemi, lasciatemi stare![11]—Oh, Serafina, I am too old for this—please!—Everbody is . . .

SERAFINA [*In a fierce, hissing whisper.*]   Nobody knew my rose of the world but me and now they can lie because the rose ain't living. They want the marble urn broken; they want me to smash it. They want the rose ashes scattered because I had too much glory. They don't want glory like *that* in nobody's heart. They want—mouse-squeaking!—known facts.—Who knows the known facts? You—padres—wear black because of the fact that the facts are known by nobody!

FATHER DE LEO   Oh, Serafina! There are people watching!

SERAFINA   Let them watch something. That will be a change for them.—It's been a long time I wanted to break out like this and now I . . .

FATHER DE LEO   I am too old a man; I am not strong enough. I am now sixty-seven years old! Must I call for help, now?

[9] What do you want?
[10] Answer me!
[11] Leave me, let me alone!

SERAFINA Yes, call! Call for help, but I won't let you go till you tell me!

FATHER DE LEO You're not a respectable woman.

SERAFINA No, I'm not a respectable; I'm a woman.

FATHER DE LEO No, you are not a woman. You are an animal! 5

SERAFINA Si, si, animale! Sono animale! Animale.[12] Tell them all, shout it all to them, up and down the whole block! The widow Delle Rose is not respectable, she is not even a woman, she is an animal! She is attacking the priest! She will tear the black suit off him unless he tells her the whores in this town are lying to her! 10

[*The neighborhood women have been drawing closer as the argument progresses, and now they come to* FATHER DE LEO'S *rescue and assist him to get away from* SERAFINA, *who is on the point of attacking him bodily. He cries out,* "Officer! Officer!" *but the women drag* SERAFINA *from him and lead him away with comforting murmurs.*]

SERAFINA [*Striking her wrists together.*] Yes, it's me, it's me!! Lock me up, lock me, lock me up! Or I will—*smash!*—the marble . . . [*She throws her head far back and presses her fists to her eyes. Then she rushes crazily to the steps and falls across them.*]

ASSUNTA Serafina! Figlia! Figlia! Andiamo a casa![13] 15

SERAFINA Leave me alone, old woman.

[*She returns slowly to the porch steps and sinks down on them, sitting like a tired man, her knees spread apart and her head cupped in her hands. The* CHILDREN *steal back around the house. A little* BOY *shoots a bean-shooter at her. She starts up with a cry. The* CHILDREN *scatter, shrieking. She sinks down on the steps, then leans back, staring up at the sky, her body rocking.*]

SERAFINA Oh, Lady, Lady, Lady, give me a sign!

[*As if in mocking answer, a novelty* SALESMAN *appears and approaches the porch. He is a fat man in a seersucker suit and a straw hat with a yellow, red and purple band. His face is beet-red and great moons of sweat have soaked through the armpits of his jacket. His shirt is lavender, and his tie, pale blue with great yellow polkadots, is a butterfly bow. His entrance is accompanied by a brief, satiric strain of music.*]

[12] Yes, yes, animal! I am an animal. An animal.
[13] Daughter! Daughter! Come home!

THE SALESMAN   Good afternoon, lady. [*She looks up slowly. The salesman talks sweetly, as if reciting a prayer.*] I got a little novelty here which I am offering to just a few lucky people at what we call an introductory price. Know what I mean? Not a

5   regular price but a price which is less than what it costs to manufacture the article, a price we are making for the sake of introducing the product in the Gulf Coast territory. Lady, this thing here that I'm droppin' right in youah lap is bigger than television; it's going to revolutionize the domestic life of America.—Now I

10   don't do house to house canvassing. I sell directly to merchants but when I stopped over there to have my car serviced, I seen you taking the air on the steps and I thought I would just drop over and . . .

[*There is the sound of a big truck stopping on the highway, and a man's voice, ALVARO's is heard, shouting.*]

ALVARO   Hey! Hey! you road hog!

15   THE SALESMAN [*Taking a sample out of his bag.*]   Now, lady, this little article has a deceptive appearance. First of all, I want you to notice how *compact* it is. It takes up no more space than . . .

[ALVARO *comes down from the embankment. He is about twenty-five years old, dark and very good-looking. He is one of those Mediterranean types that resemble glossy young bulls. He is short in stature, has a massively sculptural torso and bluish-black curls. His face and manner are clownish; he has a charming awkwardness. There is a startling, improvised air about him; he frequently seems surprised at his own speeches and actions, as though he had not at all anticipated them. At the moment when we first hear his voice the sound of a timpani begins, at first very pianissimo, but building up as he approaches, till it reaches a vibrant climax with his appearance to* SERAFINA *beside the house.*]

ALVARO   Hey.

THE SALESMAN [*Without glancing at him.*]   Hay is for horses!—

20   Now, madam, you see what happens when I press this button!

[*The article explodes in* SERAFINA'S *face. She slaps it away with an angry cry. At the same time* ALVARO *advances, trembling with rage, to the porch steps. He is sweating and stammering with pent-up fury at a world of frustrations which are temporarily localized in the gross figure of this salesman.*]

ALVARO   Hey, you! Come here! What the hell's the idea, back there at the curve? You make me drive off the highway!

THE SALESMAN [*To* SERAFINA.] Excuse me for just one minute. [*He wheels menacingly about to face* ALVARO.] Is something giving you gas pains, Maccaroni?

ALVARO My name is not Maccaroni.

THE SALESMAN All right. Spaghetti.   5

ALVARO [*Almost sobbing with passion.*] I am not maccaroni. I am not spaghetti. I am a human being that drives a truck of bananas, I drive a truck of bananas for the Southern Fruit Company for a living, not to play cowboys and Indians on no highway with no rotten road hog. You got a 4-lane highway between Pass Christian   10 and here. I give you the sign to pass me. You tail me and give me the horn. You yell "Wop" at me and "Dago." "Move over, Wop, move over, Dago." Then at the goddam curve, you go pass me and make me drive off the highway and yell back "Son of a bitch of a Dago!" I don't like that, no, no! And I am glad you stop here. Take   15 the cigar from your mouth, take out the cigar!

THE SALESMAN Take it out for me, greaseball.

ALVARO If I take it out I will push it down your throat. I got three dependents! If I fight, I get fired, but I will fight and get fired. Take out the cigar!   20

[*Spectators begin to gather at the edge of the scene.* SERAFINA *stares at* ALVARO, *her eyes like a somnambule's. All at once she utters a low cry and seems about to fall.*]

ALVARO Take out the cigar, take out, take out the cigar!

[*He snatches the cigar from the* SALESMAN'S *mouth and the* SALESMAN *brings his knee up violently into* ALVARO'S *groin. Bending double and retching with pain,* ALVARO *staggers over to the porch.*]

THE SALESMAN [*Shouting, as he goes off.*] I got your license number, Maccaroni! I know your boss!

ALVARO [*Howling.*] Drop dead! [*He suddenly staggers up the steps.*] Lady, lady, I got to go in the house!   25

[*As soon as he enters, he bursts into rending sobs, leaning against a wall and shaking convulsively. The spectators outside laugh as they scatter.* SERAFINA *slowly enters the house. The screen door rasps loudly on its rusty springs as she lets it swing gradually shut behind her, her eyes remaining fixed with a look of stupefied wonder upon the sobbing figure of* ALVARO. *We must understand her profound unconscious response to this sudden contact with distress as acute as her own. There is a long pause as the screen door makes its whining, catlike noise swinging shut by degrees.*]

SERAFINA Somebody's—in my house? [*Finally, in a hoarse, tremulous whisper.*] What are you—doing in here? Why have you—come in my house?

ALVARO Oh, lady—leave me alone!—Please—now!

5 SERAFINA You—got no business—in here . . .

ALVARO I got to cry after a fight. I'm sorry lady. I . . . [*The sobs still shake him. He leans on a dummy.*]

SERAFINA Don't lean on my dummy. Sit down if you can't stand up.—What is the matter with you?

10 ALVARO I always cry after a fight. But I don't want people to see me. It's not like a man.

[*There is a long pause;* SERAFINA'S *attitude seems to warm toward the man.*]

SERAFINA A man is not no different from no one else . . . [*All at once her face puckers up, and for the first time in the play* SERAFINA *begins to weep, at first soundlessly, then audibly. Soon she is sobbing as loudly as* ALVARO. *She speaks between sobs.*]
15 I always cry—when somebody else is crying . . .

ALVARO No, no, lady, *don't* cry! Why should *you* cry? I will stop. I will stop in a minute. This is not like a man. I am ashame of myself. I will stop now; please, lady . . .

[*Still crouching a little with pain, a hand clasped to his abdomen.* ALVARO *turns away from the wall. He blows his nose between two fingers.* SERAFINA *picks up a scrap of white voile and gives it to him to wipe his fingers.*]

SERAFINA Your jacket is torn.

20 ALVARO [*Sobbing.*] My company jacket is torn?

SERAFINA Yes . . .

ALVARO Where is it torn?

SERAFINA [*Sobbing.*] Down the—back.

ALVARO Oh, Dio!¹⁴

25 SERAFINA Take it off. I will sew it up for you. I do—sewing.

ALVARO Oh, Dio! [*Sobbing*] I got three dependents! [*He holds up three fingers and shakes them violently at* SERAFINA.]

SERAFINA Give me—give me your jacket.

ALVARO He took down my license number!

¹⁴Oh, God!

SERAFINA   People are always taking down license numbers and telephone numbers and numbers that don't mean nothing—them numbers . . .

ALVARO   Three, three dependents! Not citizens, even! No relief checks, no nothing!   5

[SERAFINA *sobs.*]

He is going to complain to the boss.

SERAFINA   I wanted to cry all day.

ALVARO   He said he would fire me if I don't stop fighting!

SERAFINA   Stop crying so I can stop crying.

ALVARO   I am a sissy. Excuse me. I am ashame.   10

SERAFINA   Don't be ashame of nothing, the world is too crazy for people to be ashame in it. I'm not ashame and I had two fights on the street and my daughter called me "disgusting." I got to sew this by hand; the machine is broke in a fight with two women.

ALVARO   That's what—they call a cat fight . . . [*He blows his nose.*]   15

SERAFINA   Open the shutters, please, for me. I can't see to work.

[*She has crossed to her work table. He goes over to the window. As he opens the shutters, the light falls across his fine torso, the undershirt clinging wetly to his dark olive skin. SERAFINA is struck and murmurs:*]

"Ohhh. . ."

[*There is the sound of music.*]

ALVARO   What, lady?

SERAFINA [*In a strange voice.*]   The light on the body was like a man that lived here . . .   20

ALVARO   Che dice?[15]

SERAFINA   Niente.—Ma com'è strano!—Lei é Napoletano?[16] [*She is threading a needle.*]

ALVARO   Io sono Siciliano!

[SERAFINA *sticks her finger with her needle and cries out.*]

Che fa?[17]   25

SERAFINA   I—stuck myself with the—needle!—you had—better wash up . . .

[15] What are you saying?
[16] Nothing.—But how strange! Are you Neapolitan?
[17] I'm Sicilian. What are you doing?

ALVARO   Dov'è il gabinetto?[18]

SERAFINA [*Almost inaudibly.*]   Dietro.[19] [*She points vaguely back.*]

ALVARO   Con permesso![20]

[*He moves past her. As he does so, she picks up a pair of broken spectacles on the work table. Holding them by the single remaining side piece, like a lorgnette, she inspects his passing figure with an air of stupefaction. As he goes out, he says:*]
A kick like that can have serious consequences! [*He goes into the back of the house.*]

5   SERAFINA [*After a pause.*]   Madonna Santa![21]—*My husband's body,* with the head of a *clown!* [*She crosses to the Madonna.*] O Lady, O Lady! [*She makes an imploring gesture.*] Speak to me!—What are you saying!—Please, Lady, I can't hear you! Is it a sign? Is it a sign of something? What does it mean? Oh, *speak to me, Lady!*
10   —Everything is too strange!

[*She gives up the useless entreaty to the impassive statue. Then she rushes to the cupboard, clambers up on a chair and seizes a bottle of wine from the top shelf. But she finds it impossible to descend from the chair. Clasping the dusty bottle to her breast, she crouches there helplessly whimpering like a child, as* ALVARO *comes back in.*]

ALVARO   Ciao![22]

SERAFINA   I can't get up.

ALVARO   You mean you can't get down?

SERAFINA   I mean I—can't get down . . .

15   ALVARO   Con permesso,[23] Signora! [*He lifts her down from the chair.*]

SERAFINA   Grazie.[24]

ALVARO   I am ashame of what happen. Crying is not like a man. Did anyone see me?

SERAFINA   Nobody saw you but me. To me it don't matter.

[18] Where's the bathroom?
[19] Back there.
[20] With your permission.
[21] Holy Mother!
[22] So long!
[23] With your permission.
[24] Thanks.

ALVARO   You are simpatica, molto![25]—It was not just the fight that makes me break down. I was like this all today! [*He shakes his clenched fists in the air.*]

SERAFINA   You and—me, too!—What was the trouble today?

ALVARO   My name is Mangiacavallo which means "Eat-a-horse," 5
It's a comical name, I know. Maybe two thousand and seventy years ago one of my grandfathers got so hungry that he ate up a horse! That ain't my fault. Well, today at the Southern Fruit Company I find on the pay envelope not "Mangiacavallo" but "EAT A HORSE" in big print! Ha, ha, ha, very funny!—I open the 10
pay envelope! In it I find a notice.—The wages have been *garnishee!* You know what garnishee is?

[SERAFINA *nods gravely.*]

Garnishee!—Eat a horse!—Road hog!—All in one day is too much! I go crazy, I boil, I cry, and I am ashame but I am not able to help it!—Even a Wop truck driver's a human being! And 15
human beings must cry . . .

SERAFINA   Yes, they must cry. I couldn't cry all day but now I have cried and I am feeling much better.—I will sew up the jacket . . .

ALVARO   [*Licking his lips.*]   What is that in your hand? A bottle 20
of vino?

SERAFINA   This is Spumanti. It comes from the house of the family of my husband. The Delle Rose! A very great family. I was a peasant, but I married a baron!—No, I still don't believe it! I married a baron when I didn't have shoes! 25

ALVARO   Excuse me for asking—but where is the Baron, now?

[SERAFINA *points gravely to the marble urn.*]

Where did you say?

SERAFINA   Them're his ashes in that marble urn.

ALVARO   Ma! Scusatemi! Scusatemi![26] [*Crossing himself.*]—I hope he is resting in peace. 30

SERAFINA   It's him you reminded me of—when you opened the shutters. Not the face but the body.—Please get me some ice from the icebox in the kitchen. I had a—very bad day . . .

ALVARO   Oh, ice! Yes—ice—I'll get some . . .

[25] You are very nice, very!
[26] But! Excuse me! Excuse me!

[*As he goes out, she looks again through the broken spectacles at him.*]

SERAFINA   *Non posso crederlo!*[27]—A clown of a face like that with my husband's body!

[*There is the sound of ice being chopped in the kitchen. She inserts a corkscrew in the bottle but her efforts to open it are clumsily unsuccessful.* ALVARO *returns with a little bowl of ice. He sets it down so hard on the table that a piece flies out. He scrambles after it, retrieves it and wipes it off on his sweaty undershirt.*]

SERAFINA   I think the floor would be cleaner!

ALVARO   Scusatemi!—I wash it again?

5   SERAFINA   Fa niente![28]

ALVARO   I am a—clean!—I . . .

SERAFINA   Fa niente, niente!—The bottle should be in the ice but the next best thing is to pour the wine over the bottle.

ALVARO   You mean over the ice?

10   SERAFINA   I mean over the . . .

ALVARO   Let me open the bottle. Your hands are not used to rough work.

[*She surrenders the bottle to him and regards him through the broken spectacles again.*]

SERAFINA   These little bits of white voile on the floor are not from a snowstorm. I been making voile dresses for high-school gradu-
15   ation.—One for my daughter and for thirteen other girls.—All of the work I'm not sure didn't kill me!

ALVARO   The wine will make you feel better.

[*There is a youthful cry from outside.*]

SERAFINA   There is a wild bunch of boys and girls in this town. In Sicily the boys would dance with the boys because a girl and a
20   boy could not dance together unless they was going to be married. But here they run wild on islands!—boys, girls, man-crazy teachers . . .

ALVARO   Ecco!

[*The cork comes off with a loud pop.* SERAFINA *cries out and staggers against the table. He laughs. She laughs with him, helplessly, unable to stop, unable to catch her breath.*]

[27] *I can't believe it!*
[28] It's nothing!

—I like a woman that laughs with all her heart.

SERAFINA   And a woman that cries with her heart?

ALVARO   I like everything that a woman does with her heart.

[*Both are suddenly embarrassed and their laughter dies out.* SERA-
FINA *smooths down her rayon slip. He hands her a glass of the
sparkling wine with ice in it. She murmurs* "Grazie."]

[*Unconsciously the injured finger is lifted again to her lip and she
wanders away from the table with the glass held shakily*]

ALVARO [*Continuing nervously.*]   I see you had a bad day.

SERAFINA   Sono così—stanca . . .[29]   5

ALVARO [*Suddenly springing to the window and shouting.*]   Hey,
you kids, git down off that truck! Keep your hands off them
bananas!

[*At the words "truck" and "bananas"* SERAFINA *gasps again and
spills some wine on her slip.*]

Little buggers!—Scusatemi . . .

SERAFINA   You haul—you haul bananas?   10

ALVARO   Si, Signora.

SERAFINA   Is it a 10-ton truck?

ALVARO   An 8-ton truck.

SERAFINA   My husband hauled bananas in a 10-ton truck.

ALVARO   Well, he was a baron.   15

SERAFINA   Do you haul just bananas?

ALVARO   Just bananas. What else would I haul?

SERAFINA   My husband hauled bananas, but underneath the bananas was something else. He was—wild like a Gypsy.—"Wild—
like a—Gypsy"? Who said that?—I hate to start to remember, and   20
then not remember . . .

[*The dialogue between them is full of odd hesitations, broken sentences and tentative gestures. Both are nervously exhausted after
their respective ordeals. Their fumbling communication has a
curious intimacy and sweetness, like the meeting of two lonely
children for the first time. It is oddly luxurious to them both,
luxurious as the first cool wind of evening after a scorching day.
SERAFINA idly picks up a little Sicilian souvenir cart from the
table.*]

[29] I'm so—tired . . .

SERAFINA   The priest was against it.

ALVARO   What was the priest against?

SERAFINA   Me keeping the ashes. It was against the Church law. But I had to have something and that was all I could have. [*She sets down the cart.*]

5   ALVARO   I don't see nothing wrong with it.

SERAFINA   You don't?

ALVARO   No! Niente!³⁰—The body would've decayed, but ashes always stay clean.

SERAFINA [*Eagerly.*]   Si, si, bodies decay, but ashes always stay
10   clean! Come here. I show you this picture—my wedding. [*She removes a picture tenderly from the wall.*] Here's me as a bride of fourteen, and this—this—this! [*Drumming the picture with her finger and turning her face to ALVARO with great lustrous eyes.*] My husband!

[*There is a pause. He takes the picture from her hand and holds it first close to his eyes, then far back, then again close with suspirations of appropriate awe.*]

15   Annnh?—Annnnh?—Che dice!³¹

ALVARO [*Slowly, with great emphasis.*]   Che bell' uomo! Che bell' uomo!³²

SERAFINA [*Replacing the picture.*]   A rose of a man. On his chest he had the tattoo of a rose. [*Then, quite suddenly.*]—Do you
20   believe strange things, or do you doubt them?

ALVARO   If strange things didn't happen, I wouldn't be here. You wouldn't be here. We wouldn't be talking together.

SERAFINA   Davvero!³³ I'll tell you something about the tattoo of my husband. My husband, he had this rose tattoo on his chest. One
25   night I woke up with a burning pain on me here. I turn on the light. I look at my naked breast and on it I see the rose tattoo of my husband, on me, on *my* breast, *his* tattoo.

ALVARO   Strano!³⁴

SERAFINA   And that was the night that—I got to speak frankly to
30   tell you . . .

ALVARO   Speak frankly! We're grown-up people.

³⁰ Nothing.
³¹ What are you saying!
³² What a fine man! What a fine man!
³³ It's true.
³⁴ Strange.

SERAFINA That was the night I conceived my son—the little boy that was lost when I lost my husband . . .

ALVARO Che cosa—strana![35]—Would you be willing to show me the rose tattoo?

SERAFINA Oh, it's gone now, it only lasted a moment. But I did 5
see it. I saw it clearly—Do you believe me?

ALVARO Lo credo![36]

SERAFINA I don't know why I told you. But I like what you said. That bodies decay but ashes always stay clean—immacolate![37] —But, you know, there are some people that want to make 10
everything dirty. Two of them kind of people come in the house today and told me a terrible lie in front of the ashes.—So awful a lie that if I thought it was true—I would smash the urn—and throw the ashes away! [*She hurls her glass suddenly to the floor.*] Smash it, *smash it like that!* 15

ALVARO Ma! Baronessa![38]

[SERAFINA *seizes a broom and sweeps the fragments of glass away.*]

SERAFINA And take this broom and sweep them out the back door like so much trash!

ALVARO [*Impressed by her violence and a little awed.*] What lie did they tell you?

SERAFINA No, no, no! I don't want to talk about it! [*She throws* 20
down the broom.] I just want to forget it; it wasn't true, it was false, false, false!—as the hearts of the bitches that told it . . .

ALVARO Yes. I would forget anything that makes you unhappy.

SERAFINA The memory of a love don't make you unhappy unless you believe a lie that makes it dirty. I don't believe in the lie. The 25
ashes are clean. The memory of the rose in my heart is perfect!— Your glass is weeping . . .

ALVARO *Your* glass is weeping too.

[*While she fills his glass, he moves about the room, looking here and there. She follows him. Each time he picks up an article for inspection she gently takes it from him and examines it herself with fresh interest.*]

ALVARO Cozy little homelike place you got here.

[35] What a strange thing!
[36] I believe it!
[37] Uncorrupted!
[38] But!—Baroness!

SERAFINA   Oh, it's—molto modesto.[39]—You got a nice place too?

ALVARO   I got a place with three dependents in it.

SERAFINA   What—dependents?

ALVARO [*Counting them on his fingers.*]   One old maid sister, one
5   feeble-minded grandmother, one lush of a pop that's not worth
the powder it takes to blow him to hell.—They got the parchesi
habit. They play the game of parchesi, morning, night, noon.
Passing a bucket of beer around the table . . .

SERAFINA   They got the beer habit, too?

10   ALVARO   Oh, yes. And the numbers habit. This spring the old maid
sister gets female trouble—mostly mental, I think—she turns the
housekeeping over to the feeble-minded grandmother, a very
sweet old lady who don't think it is necessary to pay the grocery
bill so long as there's money to play the numbers. She plays the
15   numbers. She has a perfect system except it don't ever work. And
the grocery bill goes up, up, up, up, up!—so high you can't
even see it!—Today the Ideal Grocery Company garnishees my
wages . . . There, now! I've told you my life . . . [*The parrot
squawks. He goes over to the cage.*] Hello, Polly, how's tricks?

20   SERAFINA   The name ain't Polly. It ain't a she; it's a he.

ALVARO   How can you tell with all them tail feathers? [*He sticks
his finger in the cage, pokes at the parrot and gets bitten.*] Owww!

SERAFINA [*Vicariously.*]   Ouuu . . . [ALVARO *sticks his injured
finger in his mouth.* SERAFINA *puts her corresponding finger in
her mouth. He crosses to the telephone.*]

I told you watch out.—What are you calling, a doctor?

25   ALVARO   I am calling my boss in Biloxi to explain why I'm late.

SERAFINA   The call to Biloxi is a ten-cent call.

ALVARO   Don't worry about it.

SERAFINA   I'm not worried about it. You will pay it.

ALVARO   You got a sensible attitude toward life . . . Give me the
30   Southern Fruit Company in Biloxi—seven-eight-seven!

SERAFINA   You are a bachelor. With three dependents? [*She
glances below his belt.*]

ALVARO   I'll tell you my hopes and dreams!

SERAFINA   Who? Me?

35   ALVARO   I am hoping to meet some sensible older lady. Maybe a
lady a little bit older than me.—I don't care if she's a little too
plump or not such a stylish dresser!

[39] Very modest.

[SERAFINA *selfconsciously pulls up a dangling strap.*]

The important thing in a lady is understanding. Good sense. And I want her to have a well-furnished house and a profitable little business of some kind . . . [*He looks about him significantly.*]

SERAFINA   And such a lady, with a well-furnished house and business, what does she want with a man with three dependents with the parchesi and the beer habit, playing the numbers! 5

ALVARO   Love and affection!—in a world that is lonely—and cold!

SERAFINA   It might be lonely but I would not say "cold" on this particular day!

ALVARO   Love and affection is what I got to offer on hot or cold 10 days in this lonely old world and is what I am looking for. I got nothing else. Mangiacavallo has nothing. In fact, he is the grandson of the village idiot of Ribera!

SERAFINA [*Uneasily.*]   I see you like to make—jokes!

ALVARO   No, no joke!—Davvero!⁴⁰—He chased my grandmother 15 in a flooded rice field. She slip on a wet rock.—Ecco! Here I am.

SERAFINA   You ought to be more respectful.

ALVARO   What have I got to respect? The rock my grandmother slips on?

SERAFINA   Yourself at least! Don't you work for a living? 20

ALVARO   If I *don't* work for a living I would respect myself *more.* Baronessa, I am a healthy young man, existing without no love life. I look at the magazine pictures. Them girls in the advertisement—you know what I mean? A little bitty thing here? A little bitty thing there? 25

[*He touches two portions of his anatomy. The latter portion embarrasses* SERAFINA, *who quietly announces:*]

SERAFINA   The call is ten cents for three minutes. Is the line busy?

ALVARO   Not the line, but the boss.

SERAFINA   And the charge for the call goes higher. That ain't the phone of a millionaire you're using!

ALVARO   I think you talk a poor mouth. [*He picks up the piggy* 30 *bank and shakes it.*] This pig sounds well-fed to me.

SERAFINA   Dimes and quarters.

ALVARO   Dimes and quarters're better than nickels and dimes.

[SERAFINA *rises severely and removes the piggy bank from his grasp.*]

⁴⁰ It's true.

Ha, ha, ha! You think I'm a bank robber?

SERAFINA   I think you are maleducato![41] Just get your boss on the phone or hang the phone up.

ALVARO   What, what! Mr. Siccardi? How tricks at the Southern
5   Fruit Com'ny this hot afternoon? Ha, ha, ha!—Mangiacavallo!
—What? You got the complaint already? Sentite, per favore![42]
This road hog was—Mr. Siccardi? [*He jiggles the hook; then
slowly hangs up.*] A man with three dependents!—out of a job
. . . [*There is a pause.*]

10   SERAFINA   Well, you better ask the operator the charges.

ALVARO   Oofla! A man with three dependents—out of a job!

SERAFINA   I can't see to work no more. I got a suggestion to make.
Open the bottom drawer of that there bureau and you will find a
shirt in white tissue paper and you can wear that one while I
15   am fixing this. And call for it later.

[*He crosses to the bureau.*]

—It was made for somebody that never called for it.

[*He removes the package.*]

Is there a name pinned to it?

ALVARO   Yes, it's . . .

SERAFINA [*Fiercely, but with no physical movement.*]   Don't tell
20   me the name! Throw it away, out the window!

ALVARO   Perchè?[43]

SERAFINA   Throw it, throw it away!

ALVARO [*Crumpling the paper and throwing it through the window.*]
Ecco fatto.[44] [*There is a distant cry of children as he unwraps the
25   package and holds up the rose silk shirt, exclaiming in Latin delight at the luxury of it.*] Colore di rose! Seta! Seta pura![45]—Oh,
this shirt is too good for Mangiacavallo! Everything here is too
good for Mangiacavallo!

SERAFINA   Nothing's too good for a man if the man is good.

30   ALVARO   The grandson of a village idiot is not that good.

SERAFINA   No matter whose grandson you are, put it on; you are
welcome to wear it.

[41] Bad-mannered!
[42] Listen, please.
[43] Why?
[44] There, I did it!
[45] Rose-colored! Silk! Pure silk!

ALVARO [*Slipping voluptuously into the shirt.*] Sssssss!

SERAFINA How does it feel, the silk, on you?

ALVARO It feels like a girl's hand on me!

[*There is a pause, while he shows the whiteness of his teeth.*]

SERAFINA [*Holding up her broken spectacles.*] It will make you
less trouble.   5

ALVARO There is nothing more beautiful than a gift between people!—Now you are smiling!—You like me a little better?

SERAFINA [*Slowly and tenderly.*] You know what they should of
done when you was a baby? They should of put tape on your
ears to hold them back so when you grow up they wouldn't stick   10
out like the wings of a little kewpie! [*She touches his ear, a very
slight touch, betraying too much of her heart. Both laugh a little
and she turns away, embarrassed.*]

[*Outside the goat bleats and there is the sound of splintering timber.
One of the children races into the front yard, crying out.*]

SALVATORE Mizz' Dell' Rose! The black goat's in your yard!

SERAFINA Il becco della strega![46]

[SERAFINA *dashes to the window, throws the shutters violently open
and leans way out. This time, she almost feels relief in this distraction. The interlude of the goat chase has a quality of crazed
exaltation. Outside is heard the wild bleating of the goat and the
jingling of his harness.*]

SERAFINA Miei pomodori! Guarda i miei pomodori![47]

THE STREGA [*Entering the front yard with a broken length of rope,
calling out.*] Heyeh, Billy! Heyeh, Heyeh, Billy!   15

SERAFINA [*Making the sign of horns with her fingers.*] There is the
Strega! She lets the goat in my yard to eat my tomatoes! [*Backing
from the window.*] She has the eye; she has the malocchio, and so
does the goat! The goat has the evil eye, too. He got in my yard
the night that I lost Rosario and my boy! Madonna, Madonna   20
mia! Get that goat out of my yard! [*She retreats to the Madonna,
making the sign of the horns with her fingers, while the goat
chase continues outside.*]

ALVARO Now take it easy! I will catch the black goat and give
him a kick that he will never forget!

[46] The goat of the witch!
[47] My tomatoes! Watch out for my tomatoes!

[ALVARO *runs out the front door and joins in the chase. The little* BOY *is clapping together a pair of tin pan lids which sound like cymbals. The effect is weird and beautiful with the wild cries of the children and the goat's bleating.* SERAFINA *remains anxiously halfway between the shutters and the protecting Madonna. She gives a furious imitation of the bleating goat, contorting her face with loathing. It is the fury of woman at the desire she suffers. At last the goat is captured.*]

BRUNO   Got him, got him, got him!

ALVARO   Vieni presto, Diavolo![48]

[ALVARO *appears around the side of the house with a tight hold on the broken rope around the goat's neck. The* BOY *follows behind, gleefully clapping the tin lids together, and further back follows* THE STREGA, *holding her broken length of rope, her grey hair hanging into her face and her black skirts caught up in one hand, revealing bare feet and hairy legs.* SERAFINA *comes out on the porch as the grotesque little procession passes before it, and she raises her hand with the fingers making horns as the goat and* THE STREGA *pass her.* ALVARO *turns the goat over to* THE STREGA *and comes panting back to the house.*]

ALVARO   Niente paura![49]—I got to go now.—You have been troppo gentile,[50] Mrs. . . .

5   SERAFINA   I am the widow of Baron Delle Rose.—Excuse the way I'm—not dressed . . . [*He keeps hold of her hand as he stands on the porch steps. She continues very shyly, panting a little.*] I am not always like this.—Sometimes I fix myself up!—When my husband was living, when my husband comes home, when he
10   was living—I had a clean dress on! And sometimes even, I—put a rose in my hair . . .

ALVARO   A rose in your hair would be pretty!

SERAFINA   But for a widow—it ain't the time of roses . . .

[*The sound of music is heard, of a mandolin playing.*]

ALVARO   Naw, you make a mistake! It's always for everybody the
15   time of roses! The rose is the heart of the world like the heart is the—heart of the—body! But you, Baronessa—you know what I think you have done?

SERAFINA   What—what have I—done?

ALVARO   You have put your heart in the marble urn with the ashes.

---

[48] Come quick, devil!
[49] Nothing to be afraid of.
[50] Too kind.

[*Now singing is heard along with the music, which continues to the end of the scene.*]

And if in a storm sometime, or sometime when a 10-ton truck goes down the highway—the marble urn was to *break!* [*He suddenly points up at the sky.*] Look! Look, Baronessa!

SERAFINA [*Startled.*]   Look? Look? I don't see!

ALVARO   I was pointing at your heart, broken out of the urn and away from the ashes!—*Rondinella felice!*[51] [*He makes an airy gesture toward the fading sky.*]

SERAFINA   Oh!

[*He whistles like a bird and makes graceful winglike motions with his hands.*]

Buffone, buffone—piantatela![52] I take you serious—then you make it a joke . . . [*She smiles involuntarily at his antics.*]

ALVARO   When can I bring the shirt back?

SERAFINA   When do you pass by again?

ALVARO   I will pass by tonight for supper. Volete?[53]

SERAFINA   Then look at the window tonight. If the shutters are open and there is a light in the window, you can stop by for your —jacket—but if the shutters are closed, you better not stop because my Rosa will be home. Rosa's my daughter. She has gone to a picnic—may be—home early—but you know how picnics are. They—wait for the moon to—start singing.—Not that there's nothing wrong in two grownup people having a quiet conversation!—but Rosa's fifteen—I got to be careful to set her a perfect example.

ALVARO   I will look at the window.—I will look at the win-dooow! [*He imitates a bird flying off with gay whistles.*]

SERAFINA   Buffone!

ALVARO [*Shouting from outside.*]   Hey, you little buggers, climb down off that truck! Lay offa them bananas!

[*His truck is heard starting and pulling away.* SERAFINA *stands motionless on the porch, searching the sky with her eyes.*]

SERAFINA   Rosario, forgive me! Forgive me for thinking the awful lie could be true!

[*The light in the house dims out. A little* BOY *races into the yard holding triumphantly a great golden bunch of bananas. A little* GIRL *pursues him with shrill cries. He eludes her. They dash around the house. The light fades and the curtain falls.*]

[51] Happy little swallow!
[52] Clown, clown—stop it!
[53] Want me to?

ACT THREE

Scene One

[*It is the evening of the same day. The neighborhood children are playing games around the house. One of them is counting by fives to a hundred, calling out the numbers, as he leans against the palm tree.* SERAFINA *is in the parlor, sitting on the sofa. She is seated stiffly and formally, wearing a gown that she has not worn since the death of her husband, and with a rose in her hair. It becomes obvious from her movements that she is wearing a girdle that constricts her unendurably. There is the sound of a truck approaching up on the highway.* SERAFINA *rises to an odd, crouching position. But the truck passes by without stopping. The girdle is becoming quite intolerable to* SERAFINA *and she decides to take it off, going behind the sofa to do so. With much grunting, she has gotten it down as far as her knees, when there is the sound outside of another truck approaching. This time the truck stops up on the highway, with the sound of screeching brakes. She realizes that* ALVARO *is coming, and her efforts to get out of the girdle, which is now pinioning her legs, become frantic. She hobbles from behind the sofa as* ALVARO *appears in front of the house.*]

ALVARO [*Gaily.*]   Rondinella felice![1] I will look at win-dooooo! Signora Delle Rose!

[SERAFINA'S *response to this salutation is a groan of anguish. She hobbles and totters desperately to the curtains between the rooms and reaches them just in time to hide herself as* ALVARO *comes into the parlor from the porch through the screen door. He is carrying a package and a candy box.*]

ALVARO   C'è nessuno?[2]

SERAFINA [*At first inaudibly.*]   Si, si, sono qui. [*Then loudly and hoarsely, as she finally gets the girdle off her legs.*] Si, si, sono qui![3] [*To cover her embarrassment, she busies herself with fixing wine glasses on a tray.*]

ALVARO   I hear the rattle of glasses! Let me help you! [*He goes eagerly through the curtain but stops short, astonished.*]

SERAFINA   Is—something the matter?

[1] Happy little swallow!
[2] No one here?
[3] Yes, yes, I'm here.

540

ALVARO   I didn't expect to see you looking so pretty! You are a *young* little widow!

SERAFINA   You are—fix yourself up . . .

ALVARO   I been to The Ideal Barber's! I got the whole works!

SERAFINA [*Faintly, retreating from him a little.*]   You got—rose oil   5
—in your hair . . .

ALVARO   Olio di rose! You like the smell of it?

[*Outside there is a wild, distant cry of children, and inside a pause.* SERAFINA *shakes her head slowly with the infinite wound of a recollection.*]

You—*don't*—like—the smell of it? Oh, then I wash the smell *out*, I go and . . .

[*He starts toward the back. She raises her hand to stop him.*]

SERAFINA   No, no, no, fa—niente.—I *like* the smell of it . . .   10

[*A little* BOY *races into the yard, ducks some invisible missile, sticks out his tongue and yells:* "Yahhhhh!" *Then he dashes behind the house.*]

SERAFINA   Shall we—set down in the parlor?

ALVARO   I guess that's better than standing up in the dining room. [*He enters formally.*]—Shall we set down on the sofa?

SERAFINA   You take the sofa. I will set down on this chair.

ALVARO [*Disappointed.*]   You don't like to set on a sofa?   15

SERAFINA   I lean back too far on that sofa. I like a straight back behind me . . .

ALVARO   That chair looks not comfortable to me.

SERAFINA   This chair is a comfortable chair.

ALVARO   But it's more easy to talk with two on a sofa!   20

SERAFINA   I talk just as good on a chair as I talk on a sofa . . .

[*There is a pause.* ALVARO *nervously hitches his shoulder.*]

Why do you hitch your shoulders like that?

ALVARO   Oh, that!—That's a—nervous—habit . . .

SERAFINA   I thought maybe the suit don't fit you good . . .

ALVARO   I bought this suit to get married in four years ago.   25

SERAFINA   But didn't get married?

ALVARO   I give her, the girl, a zircon instead of a diamond. She had it examined. The door was slammed in my face.

SERAFINA   I think that maybe I'd do the same thing myself.

5   ALVARO   Buy the zircon?

SERAFINA   No, slam the door.

ALVARO   Her eyes were not sincere looking. You've got sincere looking eyes. Give me your hand so I can tell your fortune!

[*She pushes her chair back from him.*]

I see two men in your life. One very handsome. One not hand-
10   some. His ears are too big but not as big as his heart! He has three dependents.—In fact he has four dependents! Ha, ha, ha!

SERAFINA   What is the fourth dependent?

ALVARO   The one that every man's got, his biggest expense, worst troublemaker and chief liability! Ha, ha, ha!

15   SERAFINA   I hope you are not talking vulgar. [*She rises and turns her back to him. Then she discovers the candy box.*] What's that fancy red box?

ALVARO   A present I bought for a nervous but nice little lady!

SERAFINA   Chocolates? Grazie! Grazie! But I'm too fat.

20   ALVARO   You are not fat, you are just pleasing and plump. [*He reaches way over to pinch the creamy flesh of her upper arm.*]

SERAFINA   No, please. Don't make me nervous. If I get nervous again I will start to cry . . .

ALVARO   Let's talk about something to take your mind off your troubles. You say you got a young daughter?

25   SERAFINA   [*In a choked voice.*]   Yes. I got a young daughter. Her name is Rosa.

ALVARO   Rosa, Rosa! She's pretty?

SERAFINA   She has the eyes of her father, and his wild, stubborn blood! Today was the day of her graduation from high school.
30   She looked so pretty in a white voile dress with a great big bunch of—roses . . .

ALVARO   Not no prettier than her Mama, I bet—with that rose in your hair!

SERAFINA   She's only fifteen.

35   ALVARO   Fifteen?

SERAFINA [*Smoothing her blue silk lap with a hesitant hand.*]   Yes, only fifteen . . .

ALVARO   But has a boyfriend, does she?

SERAFINA   She met a sailor.

ALVARO   Oh, Dio![4] No wonder you seem to be nervous.   5

SERAFINA   I didn't want to let her go out with this sailor. He had a gold ring in his ear.

ALVARO   Madonna Santa![5]

SERAFINA   This morning she cut her wrist—not much but enough to bleed—with a kitchen knife!   10

ALVARO   Tch, tch! A very wild girl!

SERAFINA   I had to give in and let her bring him to see me. He said he was Catholic. I made him kneel down in front of Our Lady there and give Her his promise that he would respect the inno-cence of my Rosa!—But how do I know he was a Catholic, 15 *really?*

ALVARO [*Taking her hand.*]   Poor little worried lady! But you got to face facts. Sooner or later the innocence of your daughter can-not be respected.—Did he—have a—tattoo?

SERAFINA [*Startled.*]   Did who have—what?   20

ALVARO   The sailor friend of your daughter, did he have a tattoo?

SERAFINA   Why do you ask me that?

ALVARO   Just because most sailors have a tattoo.

SERAFINA   How do I know if he had a tattoo or not!

ALVARO   I got a tattoo!   25

SERAFINA   *You* got a tattoo?

ALVARO   Si, si, veramente![6]

SERAFINA   What kind of tattoo you got?

ALVARO   What kind you think?

SERAFINA   Oh, I think—you have got—a South Sea girl without 30 clothes on . . .

ALVARO   No South Sea girl.

SERAFINA   Well, maybe a big red heart with MAMA written across it.

⁴ Oh, God!
⁵ Holy Mother!
⁶ Yes, yes, truly!

ALVARO   Wrong again, Baronessa.

[*He takes off his tie and slowly unbuttons his shirt, gazing at her with an intensely warm smile. He divides the unbuttoned shirt, turning toward her his bare chest. She utters a gasp and rises.*]

SERAFINA   No, no, no!—*Not a rose!* [*She says it as if she were evading her feelings.*]

ALVARO   Si, si, una rosa!

5   SERAFINA   I—don't feel good! The air is . . .

ALVARO   Che fate, che fate, che dite?⁷

SERAFINA   The house has a tin roof on it!—The air is—I got to go outside the house to breathe? Scu—scusatemi! [*She goes out onto the porch and clings to one of the spindling porch columns for support, breathing hoarsely with a hand to her throat. He comes out slowly.*]

ALVARO [*Gently.*]   I didn't mean to surprise you!—Mi dispiace
10   molto!⁸

SERAFINA [*With enforced calm.*]   Don't—talk about it! Anybody could have a rose tattoo.—It don't mean nothing.—You know how a tin roof is. It catches the heat all day and it don't cool off until—midnight . . .

15   ALVARO   No, no, not until midnight.

[*She makes a faint laughing sound, is quite breathless and leans her forehead against the porch column. He places his fingers delicately against the small of her back.*]

It makes it hot in the bedroom—so that you got to sleep without nothing on you . . .

SERAFINA   No, you—can't stand the covers.

ALVARO   You can't even stand a—*nightgown!* [*His fingers press her back.*]

20   SERAFINA   Please. There is a strega⁹ next door; she's always watching!

ALVARO   It's been so long since I felt the soft touch of a woman!

[*She gasps loudly and turns to the door.*]

Where are you going?

⁷ What are you doing, what are you doing, what are you saying?
⁸ I'm awfully sorry.
⁹ Witch.

SERAFINA I'm going back in the house! [*She enters the parlor again, still with forced calm.*]

ALVARO [*Following her inside.*] Now, now, what is the matter?

SERAFINA I got a feeling like I have—forgotten something.

ALVARO What?

SERAFINA I can't remember.   5

ALVARO It couldn't be nothing important if you can't remember. Let's open the chocolate box and have some candy.

SERAFINA [*Eager for any distraction.*] Yes! Yes, open the box!

[ALVARO *places a chocolate in her hand. She stares at it blankly.*]

ALVARO Eat it, eat the chocolate. If you don't eat it, it will melt in your hand and make your fingers all gooey!   10

SERAFINA Please, I . . .

ALVARO Eat it!

SERAFINA [*Weakly and gagging.*] I can't, I can't. I would choke! Here, you eat it.

ALVARO Put it in my mouth! [*She puts the chocolate in his mouth.*] 15
Now, look. Your fingers are gooey!

SERAFINA Oh!—I better go wash them! [*She rises unsteadily. He seizes her hands and licks her fingers.*]

ALVARO Mmmm! Mmmmm! Good, very good!

SERAFINA Stop that, stop that, stop that! That—ain't—nice . . .   20

ALVARO I'll lick off the chocolate for you.

SERAFINA No, no, no!—I am the mother of a fifteen-year-old girl!

ALVARO You're as old as your arteries, Baronessa. Now set back down. The fingers are now white as snow!

SERAFINA You don't—understand—how *I* feel . . .   25

ALVARO You don't understand how I feel.

SERAFINA [*Doubtfully.*] How do you—feel?

[*In answer, he stretches the palms of his hands out toward her as if she were a fireplace in a freezing-cold room.*]

—What does—*that*—mean?

ALVARO The night is warm but I feel like my hands are freezing!

SERAFINA Bad—circulation . . .   30

ALVARO   No, too *much* circulation! [ALVARO *becomes tremulously pleading, shuffling forward a little, slightly crouched like a beggar.*] Across the room I feel the sweet warmth of a lady!

SERAFINA [*Retreating, doubtfully.*]   Oh, you talk a sweet mouth. I think you talk a sweet mouth to fool a woman.

ALVARO   No, no, I know—I know that's what warms the world, that is what makes it the summer! [*He seizes the hand she holds defensively before her and presses it to his own breast in a crushing grip.*] Without it, the rose—the rose would not grow on the bush; the fruit would not grow on the tree!

SERAFINA   I know, and the truck—the truck would not haul the bananas! But, Mr. Mangiacavallo, that is my hand, not a sponge. I got bones in it. Bones break!

ALVARO   Scusatemi, Baronessa! [*He returns her hand to her with a bow.*] For me it is winter, because I don't have in my life the sweet warmth of a lady. I live with my hands in my pockets! [*He stuffs his hands violently into his pants pockets, then jerks them out again. A small cellophane-wrapped disk falls on the floor, escaping his notice, but not* SERAFINA'S.]—You don't like the poetry!—How can a man talk to you?

SERAFINA [*Ominously.*]   I like the poetry good. Is that a piece of the poetry that you dropped out of your pocket? [*He looks down.*] No, no, right by your foot!

ALVARO [*Aghast as he realizes what it is that she has seen.*]   Oh, that's—that's nothing! [*He kicks it under the sofa.*]

SERAFINA [*Fiercely.*]   You talk a sweet mouth about women. Then drop such a thing from your pocket? Ve via, vigliacco![10]

[*She marches grandly out of the room, pulling the curtains together behind her. He hangs his head despairingly between his hands. Then he approaches the curtains timidly.*]

ALVARO [*In a small voice.*]   Baronessa?

SERAFINA   Pick up what you dropped on the floor and go to the Square Roof with it. Buona notte![11]

ALVARO   Baronessa! [*He parts the curtains and peeks through them.*]

SERAFINA   I told you good night. Here is no casa privata. Io, non sono puttana![12]

[10] Go away, coward!
[11] Good night!
[12] Here is no bawdy house. Me, I'm not a whore!

ALVARO   Understanding is—very—necessary!

SERAFINA   I understand plenty. You think you got a good thing, a thing that is cheap!

ALVARO   You make a mistake, Baronessa! [*He comes in and drops to his knees beside her, pressing his cheek to her flank. He speaks rhapsodically.*] So soft is a lady! So, so, so, so, so soft—is a lady!   5

SERAFINA   Andate via, sporcaccione, andate a casa! Lasciatemi! Lasciatemi stare![13]

[*She springs up and runs into the parlor. He pursues. The chase is grotesquely violent and comic. A floor lamp is overturned. She seizes the chocolate box and threatens to slam it into his face if he continues toward her. He drops to his knees, crouched way over, and pounds the floor with his fists, sobbing.*]

ALVARO   Everything in my life turns out like this!

SERAFINA   Git up, git up, git up!—you village idiot's grandson! There is people watching you through that window, the—strega   10 next door . . .

[*He rises slowly.*]

And where is the shirt that I loaned you?

[*He shuffles abjectly across the room, then hands her a neatly wrapped package.*]

ALVARO   My sister wrapped it up for you.—My sister was very happy I met this *nice* lady!

SERAFINA   Maybe she thinks I will pay the grocery bill while she   15 plays the numbers!

ALVARO   She don't think nothing like that. She is an old maid, my sister. She wants—nephews—nieces . . .

SERAFINA   You tell her for me I don't give nephews and nieces!

[ALVARO *hitches his shoulders violently in his embarrassment and shuffles over to where he had left his hat. He blows the dust off it and rubs the crown on his sleeve.* SERAFINA *presses a knuckle to her lips as she watches his awkward gestures. She is a little abashed by his humility. She speaks next with the great dignity of a widow whose respectability has stood the test.*]

SERAFINA   Now, Mr. Mangiacavallo, please tell me the truth about   20 something. *When* did you get the tattoo put on your chest?

[13] Go away, pig, go home! Leave me! Leave me alone!

ALVARO [*Shyly and sadly, looking down at his hat.*]   I got it tonight
—after supper . . .

SERAFINA   That's what I thought. You had it put on because I told
you about my husband's tattoo.

5   ALVARO   I wanted to be—close to you . . . to make you—happy . . .

SERAFINA   Tell it to the marines!

[*He puts on his hat with an apologetic gesture.*]

You got the tattoo and the chocolate box after supper, and then
you come here to fool me!

ALVARO   I got the chocolate box a long time ago.

10   SERAFINA   How long ago? If that is not too much a personal question!

ALVARO   I got it the night the door was slammed in my face by the
girl that I give—the zircon . . .

SERAFINA   Let that be a lesson. Don't try to fool women. You are
15   not smart enough.—Now take the shirt back. You can keep it.

ALVARO   Huh?

SERAFINA   Keep it. I don't want it back.

ALVARO   You just now said that you did.

SERAFINA   It's a man's shirt, ain't it?

20   ALVARO   You just now accused me of trying to steal it off you.

SERAFINA   Well, you been making me nervous!

ALVARO   Is it my fault you been a widow too long?

SERAFINA   You make a mistake!

ALVARO   *You* make a mistake!

25   SERAFINA   Both of us make a mistake!

[*There is a pause. They both sigh profoundly.*]

ALVARO   We should of have been friends, but I think we meet the
wrong day.—Suppose I go out and come in the door again and
we start all over?

SERAFINA   No, I think it's no use. The day was wrong to begin
30   with, because of two women. Two women, they told me today
that my husband had put on my head the nanny-goat's horns!

ALVARO   How is it possible to put horns on a widow?

SERAFINA   That was before, before! They told me my husband was
having a steady affair with a woman at the Square Roof. What

was the name on the shirt, on the slip of paper? Do you remember the name?

ALVARO   You told me to . . .

SERAFINA   Tell me! Do you remember?

ALVARO   I remember the name because I know the woman. The 5
name was Estelle Hohengarten.

SERAFINA   Take me there! Take me to the Square Roof!—Wait,
wait!

[*She plunges into the dining room, snatches a knife out of the
sideboard drawer and thrusts it in her purse. Then she rushes
back, with the blade of the knife protruding from the purse.*]

ALVARO   [*Noticing the knife.*]   They—got a cover charge there . . .

SERAFINA   I will charge them a cover! Take me there now, this 10
minute!

ALVARO   The fun don't start till midnight.

SERAFINA   I will start the fun sooner.

ALVARO   The floor show commences at midnight.

SERAFINA   I will commence it! [*She rushes to the phone.*] Yellow 15
Cab, please, Yellow Cab. I want to go to the Square Roof out of
my house! Yes, you come to my house and take me to the Square
Roof right this minute! My number is—what is my number? Oh
my God, what is my number?—64 is my number on Front Street!
Subito, subito[14]—quick! 20

[*The goat bleats outside.*]

ALVARO   Baronessa, the knife's sticking out of your purse. [*He
grabs the purse.*] What do you want with this weapon?

SERAFINA   To cut the lying tongue out of a woman's mouth! Saying
she has on her breast the tattoo of my husband because he had put
on me the horns of a goat! I cut the heart out of that woman, she 25
cut the heart out of me!

ALVARO   Nobody's going to cut the heart out of nobody!

[*A car is heard outside, and* SERAFINA *rushes to the porch.*]

SERAFINA   [*Shouting.*]   Hey, Yellow Cab, Yellow Cab, Yellow—
Cab . . .

[*The car passes by without stopping. With a sick moan she wanders
into the yard. He follows her with a glass of wine.*]

[14] At once, at once.

Something hurts—in my heart . . .

ALVARO [*Leading her gently back to the house.*]   Baronessa, drink this wine on the porch and keep your eyes on that star.

[*He leads her to a porch pillar and places the glass in her trembling hand. She is now submissive.*]

You know the name of that star? That star is Venus. She is the
5   only female star in the sky. Who put her up there? Mr. Siccardi, the transportation manager of the Southern Fruit Company? No. She was put there by God. [*He enters the house and removes the knife from her purse.*] And yet there's some people that don't believe in nothing. [*He picks up the telephone.*] Esplanade 9-7-0.

10 SERAFINA   What are you doing?

ALVARO   Drink that wine and I'll settle this whole problem for you. [*On the telephone.*] I want to speak to the blackjack dealer, please, Miss Estelle Hohengarten . . .

SERAFINA   Don't talk to that woman, she'll lie!

15 ALVARO   Not Estelle Hohengarten. She deals a straight game of cards.—Estelle? This is Mangiacavallo. I got a question to ask you which is a personal question. It has to do with a very good-looking truck-driver, not living now but once on a time thought to have been a very well-known character at the Square Roof.
20 His name was . . . [*He turns questioningly to the door where* SERAFINA *is standing.*] What was his name, Baronessa?

SERAFINA [*Hardly breathing.*]   Rosario Delle Rose!

ALVARO   Rosario Delle Rose was the name. [*There is a pause.*]— È vero?—Mah! Che peccato[15] . . .

[SERAFINA *drops her glass and springs into the parlor with a savage outcry. She snatches the phone from* ALVARO *and screams into it.*]

25 SERAFINA [*Wildly.*]   This is the wife that's speaking! What do you know of my husband, what is the lie?

[*A strident voice sounds over the wire.*]

THE VOICE [*Loud and clear.*]   Don't you remember? I brought you the rose-colored silk to make him a shirt. You said, "For a man?" and I said, "Yes, for a man that's wild like a Gypsy!" But if you
30 think I'm a liar, come here and let me show you his rose tattooed on my chest!

[SERAFINA *holds the phone away from her as though it had burst into flame. Then, with a terrible cry, she hurls it to the floor. She*

---

[15] Is it true?—oh! What a shame . . .

staggers dizzily toward the Madonna. ALVARO *seizes her arm and pushes her gently onto the sofa.*]

ALVARO   Piano, piano,[16] Baronessa! This will be gone, this will pass in a moment. [*He puts a pillow behind her, then replaces the telephone.*]

SERAFINA [*Staggering up from the sofa.*] The room's—going round . . .

ALVARO   You ought to stay lying down a little while longer. I know, I know what you need! A towel with some ice in it to put on your forehead—Baronessa.—You stay right there while I fix it. [*He goes into the kitchen, and calls back.*] Torno subito, Baronessa![17]

[*The little* BOY *runs into the yard. He leans against the bending trunk of the palm, counting loudly.*]

THE LITTLE BOY   Five, ten, fifteen, twenty, twenty-five, thirty . . .

[*There is the sound of ice being chopped in the kitchen.*]

SERAFINA   Dove siete, dove siete?[18]

ALVARO   In cucina!—Ghiaccio . . .[19]

SERAFINA   Venite qui![20]

ALVARO   Subito, subito . . .[21]

SERAFINA [*Turning to the shrine, with fists knotted.*] Non voglio, non voglio farlo![22]

[*But she crosses slowly, compulsively toward the shrine, with a trembling arm stretched out.*]

THE LITTLE BOY   Seventy-five, eighty, eighty-five, ninety, ninety-five, one hundred! [*Then, wildly.*] *Ready or not you shall be caught!*

[*At this cry,* SERAFINA *seizes the marble urn and hurls it violently into the furthest corner of the room. Then, instantly, she covers her face. Outside the mothers are heard calling their children home. Their voices are tender as music, fading in and out. The*

---

[16] Easy, easy.
[17] I'll come right back, Baroness.
[18] Where are you, where are you?
[19] In the kitchen!—Ice . . .
[20] Come here!
[21] At once, at once . . .
[22] I don't want to, I don't want to do it!

children appear slowly at the side of the house, exhausted from their wild play.]

GIUSEPPINA Vivi! Vi-vi!

PEPPINA Salvatore!

VIOLETTA Bruno! Come home, come home!

[*The children scatter.* ALVARO *comes in with the ice-pick.*]

ALVARO I broke the point of the ice-pick.

5 SERAFINA [*Removing her hands from her face.*] I don't want ice . . . [*She looks about her, seeming to gather a fierce strength in her body. Her voice is hoarse, her body trembling with violence, eyes narrow and flashing, her fists clenched.*] Now I show you how wild and strong like a man a woman can be! [*She crosses to*
10 *the screen door, opens it and shouts.*] Buona notte,[23] Mr. Mangia-cavallo!

ALVARO You—you make me go *home*, now?

SERAFINA No, no; senti, cretino![24] [*In a strident whisper.*] You make out like you are going. You drive the truck out of sight
15 where the witch can't see it. Then you come back and I leave the back door open for you to come in. Now, tell me good-bye so all the neighbors can hear you! [*She shouts.*] Arrivederci![25]

ALVARO Ha, ha! Capish![26] [*He shouts too.*] Arrivederci! [*He runs to the foot of the embankment steps.*]

20 SERAFINA [*Still more loudly.*] Buona notte!

ALVARO Buona notte, Baronessa!

SERAFINA [*In a choked voice.*] Give them my love; give every-body—my love . . . Arrivederci!

ALVARO Ciao![27]

[ALVARO *scrambles on down the steps and goes off.* SERAFINA *comes down into the yard. The goat bleats. She mutters savagely to herself.*]

25 SERAFINA Sono una bestia, una bestia feroce![28]

[*She crosses quickly around to the back of the house. As she dis-*

---

[23] Good night.
[24] Listen, stupid!
[25] Good-bye!
[26] I understand.
[27] So long!
[28] I'm a beast, a wild beast!

appears, the truck is heard driving off; the lights sweep across the house. SERAFINA *comes in through the back door. She is moving with great violence, gasping and panting. She rushes up to the Madonna and addresses her passionately with explosive gestures, leaning over so that her face is level with the statue's.*]

SERAFINA   Ora, ascolta, Signora![29] You hold in the cup of your hand this little house and you smash it! You break this little house like the shell of a bird in your hand, because you have hate Serafina?—Serafina that *loved* you!—No, no, no, you don't speak! I don't believe in you, Lady! You're just a poor little doll with   5
the paint peeling off, and now I blow out the light and I forget you the way you forget Serafina! [*She blows out the vigil light.*] *Ecco—fatto!*[30]

[*But now she is suddenly frightened; the vehemence and boldness have run out. She gasps a little and backs away from the shrine, her eyes rolling apprehensively this way and that. The parrot squawks at her. The goat bleats. The night is full of sinister noises, harsh bird cries, the sudden flapping of wings in the cane-brake, a distant shriek of Negro laughter.* SERAFINA *retreats to the window and opens the shutters wider to admit the moonlight. She stands panting by the window with a fist pressed to her mouth. In the back of the house a door slams open.* SERAFINA *catches her breath and moves for protection behind the dummy of the bride.* ALVARO *enters through the back door, calling out softly and hoarsely, with great excitement.*]

ALVARO   Dove! Dove sei, cara?[31]

SERAFINA [*Faintly.*]   *Sono qui . . .*[32]   10

ALVARO   You have turn out the light!

SERAFINA   The moon is enough . . .

[*He advances toward her. His white teeth glitter as he grins.* SERAFINA *retreats a few steps from him. She speaks tremulously, making an awkward gesture toward the sofa.*]

Now we can go on with our—conversation . . . [*She catches her breath sharply.*]

[*The curtain comes down.*]

[29] Now listen, Lady!
[30] *There—it's done!*
[31] Where, where are you, dear?
[32] I am here . . .

Scene Two

[*It is just before daybreak of the next day.* ROSA *and* JACK *appear at the top of the embankment steps.*]

ROSA I thought they would never leave. [*She comes down the steps and out in front of the house, then calls back to him.*] Let's go down there.

[*He obeys hesitatingly. Both are very grave. The scene is played as close as possible to the audience. She sits very straight. He stands behind her with his hands on her shoulders.*]

ROSA [*Leaning her head back against him.*] This was the happiest
5   day of my life, and this is the saddest night . . .

[*He crouches in front of her.*]

SERAFINA [*From inside the house.*] Aaaaaahhhhhhhh!

JACK [*Springing up, startled.*] What's that?

ROSA [*Resentfully.*] Oh! That's Mama dreaming about my father.

JACK I—feel like a—*heel!* I feel like a rotten heel!

10   ROSA Why?

JACK That promise I made your mother.

ROSA I hate her for it.

JACK Honey—Rosa, she—wanted to protect you.

[*There is a long-drawn cry from the back of the house: Ohhhh—Rosario!"*]

ROSA She wanted me not to have what she's dreaming about . . .

15   JACK Naw, naw, honey, she—wanted to—protect you . . .

[*The cry from within is repeated softly.*]

ROSA Listen to her making love in her sleep! Is that what she wants *me* to do, just—*dream* about it?

JACK [*Humbly.*] She knows that her Rosa *is* a rose. And wants her rose to have someone—better than *me* . . .

20   ROSA *Better* than—*you!* [*She speaks as if the possibility were too preposterous to think of.*]

JACK You see me through—rose-colored—glasses . . .

ROSA I see you with love!

JACK Yes, but your Mama sees me with—common sense . . .

[SERAFINA *cries out again.*]

I got to be going!

[*She keeps a tight hold on him. A rooster crows.*]

Honey, it's so late the roosters are crowing!

ROSA They're fools, they're fools, it's early!

JACK Honey, on the island I almost forgot my promise. Almost,   5
but not quite. Do you understand, honey?

ROSA Forget the promise!

JACK I made it on my knees in front of Our Lady. I've got to
leave now, honey.

ROSA [*Clasping him fiercely.*] You'd have to break my arms to!   10

JACK Rosa, Rosa! You want to drive me crazy?

ROSA I want you not to remember.

JACK You're a very young girl! Fifteen—fifteen is too young!

ROSA Caro, caro, carissimo![1]

JACK You got to save some of those feelings for when you're   15
grown up!

ROSA Carissimo!

JACK Hold some of it back until you're grown!

ROSA I have been grown for two years!

JACK No, no, that ain't what I . . .   20

ROSA Grown enough to be married, and have a—baby!

JACK [*Springing up.*] Oh, good—Lord! [*He circles around her,
pounding his palm repeatedly with his fist and clamping his teeth
together with a grimace. Suddenly he speaks.*] I got to be going!

ROSA You want me to scream? [*He groans and turns away from*   25
her to resume his desperate circle. ROSA *is blocking the way with
her body.*]—I know, I know! You don't want me! [JACK *groans
through his gritting teeth.*] No, no, you don't want me . . .

JACK Now you listen to me! You almost got into trouble today
on that island! You almost did, but not quite!—But it didn't quite   30
happen and no harm is done and you can just—forget it . . .

ROSA It is the only thing in my life that I want to remember!—
When are you going back to New Orleans?

[1] Dear, dear, dearest!

JACK   Tomorrow.

ROSA   When does your—ship sail?

ROSA   Where to?

JACK   Guatemala.

5   SERAFINA [*From the house.*]   Aahh!

ROSA   Is that a long trip?

JACK   After Guatemala, Buenos Aires. After Buenos Aires, Rio. Then around the Straits of Magellan and back up the west coast of South America, putting in at three ports before we dock at San
10   Francisco.

ROSA   I don't think I will—ever see you again . . .

JACK   The ship won't sink!

ROSA [*Faintly and forlornly.*]   No, but—I think it could just happen once, and if it don't happen that time, it never can—later . . .
15   [*A rooster crows. They face each other sadly and quietly.*] You don't need to be very old to understand how it works out. One time, one time, only once, it could be—God!—to remember.— Other times? Yes—they'd be something.—But only once, God— to remember . . . [*With a little sigh she crosses to pick up his*
20   *white cap and hand it gravely to him.*]—I'm sorry to you it didn't —mean—that much . . .

JACK [*Taking the cap and hurling it to the ground.*]   Look! Look at my knuckles! You see them scabs on my knuckles? You know how them scabs got there? They got there because I banged my
25   knuckles that hard on the deck of the sailboat!

ROSA   Because it—didn't quite happen?

[JACK *jerks his head up and down in grotesquely violent assent to her question.* ROSA *picks up his cap and returns it to him again.*]

—Because of the promise to Mama! I'll never forgive her . . . [*There is a pause.*] What time in the afternoon must you be on the boat?

30   JACK   Why?

ROSA   Just tell me what time.

JACK   Five!—Why?

ROSA   What will you be doing till five?

JACK   Well, I could be a goddam liar and tell you I was going to
35   —pick me a hatful of daisies in—Audubon Park.—Is that what you want me to tell you?

ROSA No, tell me the truth.

JACK All right, I'll tell you the truth. I'm going to check in at some flea-bag hotel on North Rampart Street. Then I'm going to get loaded! And then I'm going to get . . .

[*He doesn't complete the sentence but she understands him. She places the hat more becomingly on his blond head.*]

ROSA Do me a little favor. [*Her hand slides down to his cheek and then to his mouth.*] Before you get loaded and before you— before you— 5

JACK Huh?

ROSA Look in the waiting room at the Greyhound bus station, please. At twelve o'clock, noon! 10

JACK Why?

ROSA You might find me there, waiting for you . . .

JACK What—what good would that do?

ROSA I never been to a hotel but I know they have numbers on doors and sometimes—numbers are—lucky.—Aren't they?— Sometimes?—Lucky? 15

JACK You want to buy me a ten-year stretch in the brig?

ROSA I want you to give me that little gold ring on your ear to put on my finger.—I want to give you my heart to keep forever! And ever! And ever! [*Slowly and with a barely audible sigh she leans her face against him.*] Look for me! I will be there! 20

JACK [*Breathlessly.*] In all of my life, I never felt nothing so sweet as the feel of your little warm body in my arms . . .

[*He breaks away and runs toward the road. From the foot of the steps he glares fiercely back at her like a tiger through the bars of a cage. She clings to the two porch pillars, her body leaning way out.*]

ROSA Look for me! I will be there!

[JACK *runs away from the house.* ROSA *returns inside. Listlessly she removes her dress and falls on the couch in her slip, kicking off her shoes. Then she begins to cry, as one cries only once in a life- time, and the scene dims out.*]

Scene Three

[*The time is three hours later. We see first the exterior view of the small frame building against a night sky which is like the starry blue robe of Our Lady. It is growing slightly paler. The faint light discloses* ROSA *asleep on the couch. The covers are thrown back for it has been a warm night, and on the concave surface of the white cloth, which is like the dimly lustrous hollow of a shell, is the body of the sleeping girl which is clad only in a sheer white slip. A cock crows. A gentle wind stirs the white curtains inward and the tendrils of vine at the windows, and the sky lightens enough to distinguish the purple trumpets of the morning glory against the very dim blue of the sky in which the planet Venus remains still undimmed. In the back of the cottage someone is heard coughing hoarsely and groaning in the way a man does who has drunk very heavily the night before. Bedsprings creak as a heavy figure rises. Light spills dimly through the curtains, now closed, between the two front rooms. There are heavy, padding footsteps and* ALVARO *comes stumbling rapidly into the dining room with the last bottle of Spumanti in the crook of an arm, his eyes barely open, legs rubbery, saying, "Wuh-wuh-wuh-wuh-wuh-wuh . . ." like the breathing of an old dog. The scene should be played with the pantomimic lightness, almost fantasy, of an early Chaplin comedy. He is wearing only his trousers and his chest is bare. As he enters he collides with the widow dummy, staggers back, pats her inflated bosom in a timid, apologetic way, remarking:*]

ALVARO Scusami, Signora,[1] I am the grandson of the village idiot of Ribera!

[ALVARO *backs into the table and is propelled by the impact all the way to the curtained entrance to the parlor. He draws the curtains apart and hangs onto them, peering into the room. Seeing the sleeping girl, he blinks several times, suddenly makes a snoring sound in his nostrils and waves one hand violently in front of his eyes as if to dispel a vision. Outside the goat utters a long "Baaaaaaaaaaa!" As if in response,* ALVARO *whispers, in the same basso key, "Che bella!"[2] The first vowel of "bella" is enormously prolonged like the "baaa" of the goat. On his rubbery legs he shuffles forward a few steps and leans over to peer more intently at the vision. The goat bleats again.* ALVARO *whispers more loudly: "Che bel-la!" He drains the Spumanti, then staggers to his knees, the empty bottle rolling over the floor. He crawls on his*]

---

[1] Pardon me, lady.
[2] How beautiful!

knees to the foot of the bed, then leans against it like a child peering into a candy shop window, repeating: "Che bel-la, che bel-la!" with antiphonal responses from the goat outside. Slowly, with tremendous effort, as if it were the sheer side of a precipice, he clambers upon the couch and crouches over the sleeping girl in a leap-frog position, saying "Che bel-la!" quite loudly, this time, in a tone of innocently joyous surprise. All at once ROSA wakens. She screams, even before she is quite awake, and springs from the couch so violently that ALVARO topples over to the floor.]

[SERAFINA *cries out almost instantly after* ROSA. *She lunges through the dining room in her torn and disordered nightgown. At the sight of the man crouched by the couch a momentary stupefaction turns into a burst of savage fury. She flies at him like a great bird, tearing and clawing at his stupefied figure. With one arm* ALVARO *wards off her blows, plunging to the floor and crawling into the dining room. She seizes a broom with which she flails him about the head, buttocks, and shoulders while he scrambles awkwardly away. The assault is nearly wordless. Each time she strikes at him she hisses: "Sporcaccione!"[3] He continually groans: "Dough, dough, dough!" At last he catches hold of the widow dummy which he holds as a shield before him while he entreats the two women.]*

ALVARO Senti, Baronessa! Signorina![4] I didn't know what I was doin', I was dreamin', I was just dreamin'! I got turn around in the house; I got all twisted! I thought that you was your Mama! —Sono ubriaco! Per favore![5]

ROSA [*Seizing the broom*]   That's enough, Mama!   5

SERAFINA [*Rushing to the phone.*]   Police!

ROSA [*Seizing the phone.*]   No, no, no, no, no, no!—You want everybody to know?

SERAFINA [*Weakly.*]   Know?—Know *what*, cara?[6]

ROSA   Just give him his clothes, now, Mama, and let him get out!   10
[*She is clutching a bedsheet about herself.*]

ALVARO   Signorina—young lady! I swear I was *dreaming!*

SERAFINA   Don't speak to my daughter! [*then, turning to* ROSA]— Who is this man? How did this man get here?

ROSA [*Coldly.*]   Mama, don't say any more. Just give him his clothes in the bedroom so he can get out!   15

---

[3] Dirty pig!
[4] Listen, Baronessa! Young lady!
[5] I'm drunk! Please!
[6] Dear.

ALVARO [*Still crouching.*]   I am so sorry, so sorry! I don't remember a thing but that I was dreaming!

SERAFINA [*Shoving him toward the back of the room with her broom.*]   Go on, go get your clothes on, you—idiot's grandson, you!—Svelto, svelto, più svelto.[7]

[ALVARO *continues his apologetic mumbling in the back room.*]

Don't talk to me, don't say nothing! Or I will kill you!

[*A few moments later* ALVARO *rushes around the side of the house, his clothes half buttoned and his shirt-tails out.*]

ALVARO   But, Baronessa, I *love* you!

[*A tea kettle sails over his head from behind the house. The* STREGA *bursts into laughter. Despairingly* ALVARO *retreats, tucking his shirt-tails in and shaking his head.*]

Baronessa, Baronessa, I love you!

[*As* ALVARO *runs off,* THE STREGA *is heard cackling:*]

THE STREGA'S VOICE   The Wops are at it again. Had a truck-driver in the house all night!

[ROSA *is feverishly dressing. From the bureau she has snatched a shimmering white satin slip, disappearing for a moment behind a screen to put it on as* SERAFINA *comes padding sheepishly back into the room, her nightgown now covered by a black rayon kimono sprinkled with poppies, her voice tremulous with fear, shame, and apology.*]

ROSA [*Behind the screen.*]   Has the man gone?

SERAFINA   That—man?

ROSA   Yes, "that man!"

SERAFINA [*Inventing desperately.*]   I don't know how he got in. Maybe the back door was open.

ROSA   Oh, yes, maybe it was!

SERAFINA   Maybe he—climbed in a window . . .

ROSA   Or fell down the chimney, maybe! [*She comes from behind the screen, wearing the white bridal slip.*]

[7] Quickly, quickly, more quickly!

SERAFINA   Why you put on the white things I save for your wedding?

ROSA   Because I want to. That's a good enough reason. [*She combs her hair savagely.*]

SERAFINA   I want you to understand about that man. That was a   5
man that—that was—that was a man that . . .

ROSA   You can't think of a lie?

SERAFINA   He was a—truck-driver, cara. He got in a fight, he was
chase by—policemen!

ROSA   They chased him into your bedroom?   10

SERAFINA   I took pity on him, I give him first aid, I let him sleep
on the floor. He give me his promise—he . . .

ROSA   Did he kneel in front of Our Lady? Did he promise that he
would respect your innocence?

SERAFINA   Oh, cara, cara! [*Abandoning all pretense*] He was   15
Sicilian; he had rose oil in his hair and the rose tattoo of your
father. In the dark room I couldn't see his clown face. I closed
my eyes and dreamed that he was your father! I closed my eyes!
I dreamed that he was your father . . .

ROSA   Basta, basta, non voglio sentire più niente![8] The only thing   20
worse than a liar is a liar that's also a hypocrite!

SERAFINA   Senti, per favore![9]

[ROSA *wheels about from the mirror and fixes her mother with a
long and withering stare.* SERAFINA *cringes before it.*]

Don't look at me like that with the eyes of your father! [*She
shields her face as from a terrible glare.*]

ROSA   Yes, I am looking at you with the eyes of my father. I see
you the way *he* saw you. [*She runs to the table and seizes the*   25
piggy bank.] Like this, this *pig!*

[SERAFINA *utters a long, shuddering cry like a cry of childbirth.*]

I need five dollars. I'll take it out of this!

[ROSA *smashes the piggy bank to the floor and rakes some coins
into her purse.* SERAFINA *stoops to the floor. There is the sound of
a train whistle.* ROSA *is now fully dressed, but she hesitates, a little
ashamed of her cruelty—but only a little.* SERAFINA *cannot meet
her daughter's eyes. At last the girl speaks.*]

[8] Enough, enough, I don't want to listen any more!
[9] Listen, please!

SERAFINA How beautiful—is my daughter! Go to the boy!

ROSA [*As if she might be about to apologize:*] Mama? He didn't touch me—he just said—"Che bella!"

[SERAFINA *turns slowly, shamefully, to face her. She is like a peasant in the presence of a young princess.* ROSA *stares at her a moment longer, then suddenly catches her breath and runs out of the house. As the girl leaves,* SERAFINA *calls:*]

SERAFINA Rosa, Rosa, the—wrist watch! [SERAFINA *snatches up the little gift box and runs out onto the porch with it. She starts to call her daughter again, holding the gift out toward her, but her breath fails her.*] Rosa, Rosa, the—wrist watch . . . [*Her arms fall to her side. She turns, the gift still ungiven. Senselessly, absently, she holds the watch to her ear again. She shakes it a little, then utters a faint, startled laugh.*]

[ASSUNTA *appears beside the house and walks directly in, as though* SERAFINA *had called her.*]

SERAFINA Assunta, the urn is broken. The ashes are spilt on the floor and I can't touch them.

[ASSUNTA *stoops to pick up the pieces of the shattered urn,* SERAFINA *has crossed to the shrine and relights the candle before the Madonna.*]

ASSUNTA There are no ashes.

SERAFINA Where—where are they? Where have the ashes gone?

ASSUNTA [*Crossing to the shrine.*] The wind has blown them away.

[ASSUNTA *places what remains of the broken urn in* SERAFINA'S *hands.* SERAFINA *turns it tenderly in her hands and then replaces it on the top of the prie-dieu before the Madonna.*]

SERAFINA A man, when he burns, leaves only a handful of ashes. No woman can hold him. The wind must blow him away.

[ALVARO'S *voice is heard, calling from the top of the highway embankment.*]

ALVARO'S VOICE Rondinella felice![10]

[*The neighborhood women hear* ALVARO *calling, and there is a burst of mocking laughter from some of them. Then they all converge*

[10] Happy little swallow!

on the house from different directions and gather before the porch.]

PEPPINA   Serafina Delle Rose!

GIUSEPPINA   Baronessa! Baronessa Delle Rose!

PEPPINA   There is a man on the road without the shirt!

GIUSEPPINA [*With delight.*]   Si, si! Senza'camicia![11]

PEPPINA   All he got on his chest is a rose tattoo! [*to the women*]   5
She lock up his shirt so he can't go to the high school?

[*The women shriek with laughter. In the house* SERAFINA *snatches up the package containing the silk shirt, while* ASSUNTA *closes the shutters of the parlor windows.*]

SERAFINA   Un momento![12] [*She tears the paper off the shirt and rushes out onto the porch, holding the shirt above her head defiantly.*] Ecco la camicia![13]

[*With a soft cry,* SERAFINA *drops the shirt, which is immediately snatched up by* PEPPINA. *At this point the music begins again, with a crash of percussion, and continues to the end of the play.* PEPPINA *flourishes the shirt in the air like a banner and tosses it to* GIUSEPPINA, *who is now on the embankment.* GIUSEPPINA *tosses it on to* MARIELLA, *and she in her turn to* VIOLETTA, *who is above her, so that the brilliantly colored shirt moves in a zigzag course through the pampas grass to the very top of the embankment, like a streak of flame shooting up a dry hill. The women call out as they pass the shirt along:*]

PEPPINA   Guardate questa camicia! Coloro di rose![14]   10

MARIELLA [*Shouting up to* ALVARO.]   Corragio, signor![15]

GIUSEPPINA   Avanti, avanti, signor![16]

VIOLETTA [*At the top of the embankment, giving the shirt a final flourish above her.*] Corragio, corragio![17] The Baronessa is waiting!   15

[*Bursts of laughter are mingled with the cries of the women. Then they sweep away like a flock of screaming birds, and* SERAFINA *is*

[11] Yes, yes, without a shirt!
[12] Just a minute!
[13] Here is the shirt!
[14] Careful of that shirt! Rose color!
[15] Take heart, mister!
[16] Come on, come on, mister!
[17] Take heart, take heart!

*left upon the porch, her eyes closed, a hand clasped to her breast.
In the meanwhile, inside the house,* ASSUNTA *has poured out a
glass of wine. Now she comes to the porch, offering the wine to*
SERAFINA *and murmuring:*]

ASSUNTA   Stai tranquilla.[18]

SERAFINA [*Breathlessly.*]   Assunta, I'll tell you something that maybe
you won't believe.

ASSUNTA [*With tender humor.*]   It is impossible to tell me anything
that I don't believe.

SERAFINA   Just now I felt on my breast the burning again of the
rose. I know what it means. It means that I have conceived! [*She
lifts the glass to her lips for a moment and then returns it to*
ASSUNTA.] Two lives again in the body! Two, two lives again, two!

ALVARO'S VOICE [*Nearer now, and sweetly urgent.*]   Rondinella
felice![19]

[ALVARO *is not visible on the embankment but* SERAFINA *begins to
move slowly toward his voice.*]

ASSUNTA   Dove vai, Serafina?[20]

SERAFINA [*Shouting now, to* ALVARO.]   Vengo, vengo, amore![21]

[*She starts up the embankment toward* ALVARO *and the curtain falls
as the music rises with her in great glissandi of sound.*]

[18] Be calm.
[19] Happy little swallow!
[20] Where are you going, Serafina?
[21] I'm coming, I'm coming, beloved!

THE TIMELESS WORLD OF A PLAY

Carson McCullers concludes one of her lyric poems with the line: "Time, the endless idiot, runs screaming 'round the world." It is this continual rush of time, so violent that it appears to be screaming, that deprives our actual lives of so much dignity and meaning, and it is, perhaps more than anything else, the *arrest of time* which has taken place in a completed work of art that gives to certain plays their feeling of depth and significance. In London notices of *Death of a Salesman* a certain notoriously skeptical critic made the remark that Willy Loman was the sort of man that almost any member of the audience would have kicked out of an office had he applied for a job or detained one for conversation about his troubles. The remark itself possibly holds some truth. But the implication, that Willy Loman is consequently a character with whom we have no reason to concern ourselves in drama, reveals a strikingly false conception of what plays are. Contemplation is something that exists outside of time, and so is the tragic sense. Even in the actual world of commerce, there exists in some persons a sensibility to the unfortunate situations of others, a capacity for concern and compassion, surviving from a more tender period of life outside the present whirling wire-cage of business activity. Facing Willy Loman across an office desk, meeting his nervous glance and hearing his querulous voice, we would be very likely to glance at our wrist watch and our schedule of other appointments. We would certainly *ease* him out with more expedition than Willy had feebly hoped for. But suppose there had been no wrist watch or office clock and suppose there had *not* been the schedule of pressing appointments, and suppose that we were not actually facing Willy across a desk—and facing a person is *not* the best way to *see* him!—suppose, in other words that the meeting with Willy Loman had somehow occurred in a world *outside* of time. Then I think we would receive him with concern and kindness, even with respect. If the world of a play did not offer us this occasion to view its characters under the special condition of a *world without time,* then, indeed, the characters and occurrences of drama would become equally pointless, equally trivial, as corresponding meetings and happenings in life.

The classic tragedies of Greece had tremendous nobility. The actors wore great masks, movements were formal, dance-like, and the speeches had an epic quality which doubtless were as removed from the normal conversation of their contemporary society as they seem today. Yet they did not seem false to the Greek audiences: the magnitude of the events and the passions aroused by them did not seem ridiculously out of proportion to common experience.

565

And I wonder if this was not because the Greek audiences knew, instinctively or by training, that the created world of a play is removed from the element which makes people little and their emotions fairly inconsequential.

Great sculpture often follows the lines of the human body: yet the repose of great sculpture suddenly transmutes those human lines to something that has an absoluteness, a purity, a beauty, which would not be possible in a living mobile form.

A play may be violent, full of motion: yet it has that special kind of repose which allows contemplation and produces the climate in which tragic importance is a possible thing, provided that certain modern conditions are met.

In actual existence the moments of love are succeeded by the moments of satiety and sleep. The sincere remark is followed by a cynical distrust. Truth is fragmentary, at best: we love and betray each other not in quite the same breath but in two breaths that occur in fairly close sequence. But the fact that passion occurred in *passing*, that it then declined into a more familiar sense of indifference, should not be regarded as proof of its inconsequence. And this is the very truth that drama wishes to bring us . . .[1]

Whether or not we admit to ourselves, we are all haunted by a truly awful sense of impermanence. I have always had a particularly keen sense of this at New York cocktail parties, and perhaps that is why I drink martinis almost as fast as I can snatch them from the tray. This sense is the febrile thing that hangs in the air. Horror of insincerity, of *not meaning*, overhangs these affairs like the cloud of cigarette smoke and hectic chatter. This horror is the only thing, almost, that is left unsaid at such functions. All social functions involving a group of people not intimately known to each other are always under this shadow. They are almost always (in an unconscious way) like that last dinner of the condemned: where steak or turkey, whatever the doomed man wants, is served in his cell as a mockingly cruel reminder of what the great-big-little-transitory world has to offer.

In a play, time is arrested in the sense of being confined. By a sort of legerdemain, events are made to remain *events*, rather than being reduced so quickly to mere *occurrences*. The audience can sit back in a comforting dusk to watch a world which is flooded with light and in which emotion and action have a dimension and dignity that they would likewise have in real existence, if only the shattering intrusion of time could be locked out.

About their lives people ought to remember that when they are

---

[1] This punctuation is in the original, as are similar punctuations elsewhere in this essay as printed here. The essay is complete; the punctuation does not indicate omissions.

finished, everything in them will be contained in a marvellous state of repose which is the same as that which they unconsciously admired in drama. The rush is temporary. The great and only possible dignity of man lies in his power deliberately to choose certain moral values by which to live as steadfastly as if he, too, like a character in a play, were immured against the corrupting rush of time. Snatching the eternal out of the desperately fleeing is the great magic trick of human existence. As far as we know, as far as there exists any kind of empiric evidence, there is no way to beat the game of *being* against *non-being,* in which non-being is the predestined victor on realistic levels.

Yet plays in the tragic tradition offer us a view of certain moral values in violent juxtaposition. Because we do not participate, except as spectators, we can view them clearly, within the limits of our emotional equipment. These people on the stage do not return our looks. We do not have to answer their questions nor make any sign of being in company with them, nor do we have to compete with their virtues, nor resist their offenses. All at once, for this reason, we are able to *see* them! Our hearts are wrung by recognition and pity, so that the dusky shell of the auditorium where we are gathered anonymously together is flooded with an almost liquid warmth of unchecked human sympathies, relieved of self-consciousness, allowed to function . . .

Men pity and love each other more deeply than they permit themselves to know. The moment after the phone has been hung up, the hand reaches for a scratch pad and scrawls a notation: "Funeral Tuesday at five, Church of the Holy Redeemer, don't forget flowers." And the same hand is only a little shakier than usual as it reaches, some minutes later, for a highball glass that will pour a stupefaction over the kindled nerves. Fear and evasion are the two little beasts that chase each other's tails in the revolving wire-cage of our nervous world. They distract us from feeling too much about things. Time rushes toward us with its hospital tray of infinitely varied narcotics, even while it is preparing us for its inevitably fatal operation. . . .

So successfully have we disguised from ourselves the intensity of our own feelings, the sensibility of our own hearts, that plays in the tragic tradition have begun to seem untrue. For a couple of hours we may surrender ourselves to a world of fiercely illuminated values in conflict, but when the stage is covered and the auditorium lighted, almost immediately there is a recoil of disbelief. "Well, well!" we say as we shuffle back up the aisle, while the play dwindles behind us with the sudden perspective of an early Chirico painting. By the time we have arrived at Sardi's, if not as soon as we pass beneath the marquee, we have convinced ourselves once more that life has as little resemblance to the curiously stirring and meaningful occurrences on the stage as a jingle has to an elegy of Rilke.

This modern condition of his theater audience is something that an author must know in advance. The diminishing influence of life's destroyer, time, must be somehow worked into the context of his play. Perhaps it is a certain foolery, a certain distortion toward the grotesque, which will solve the problem for him. Perhaps it is only restraint, putting a mute on the strings that would like to break all bounds. But almost surely, unless he contrives in some way to relate the dimensions of his tragedy to the dimensions of a world in which time is *included*—he will be left among his magnificent debris on a dark stage, muttering to himself: "Those fools . . ."

And if they could hear him above the clatter of tongues, glasses, chinaware and silver, they would give him this answer: "But you have shown us a world not ravaged by time. We admire your innocence. But we have seen our photographs, past and present. Yesterday evening we passed our first wife on the street. We smiled as we spoke but we didn't really see her! It's too bad, but we know what is true and not true, and at 3 A.M. your disgrace will be in print!"

EUGÈNE IONESCO

The New Tenant

Translated by DONALD WATSON

〜〜〜〜〜〜〜〜〜〜〜〜〜〜〜〜〜

ROBERT W. CORRIGAN

The Theatre
in Search of a Fix

THE CHARACTERS IN *THE NEW TENANT*

THE GENTLEMAN
THE CARETAKER
THE FIRST FURNITURE MOVER
THE SECOND FURNITURE MOVER

THE NEW TENANT

[*A bare room, without any furniture. In the centre of the back wall, an open window. Double doors on the right and on the left. Light-coloured walls. Like the set and the furniture that will be brought on the stage later, the style of acting must be completely realistic. As the curtain rises, a considerable din is heard off stage: the sounds of voices, and hammers, snatches of song, children shouting, the noise of feet going up and coming down stairs, a barrel-organ, etc. For a moment, as the noise goes on, the stage is empty: then* THE CARETAKER *comes in from the right, crashing the door open and singing in a loud voice; she is holding a bunch of keys.*]

CARETAKER [*as she enters singing*]   La, la, la, tralalala, tralali, tralalalala-a-a! [*And rattling the keys.*] La, la, la, la! [*She interrupts her singing to go and lean out of the open window:*] Bill! Oh, Bill! Bill! Hullo there, George! Go and tell Bill 'e's got to see Mr. Clarence! . . . George . . . [*Silence*] George . . . [*Silence*]   5 Well! If 'e ain't missing too! [*She tries to lean still further out of the window, singing at the top of her voice*] La, la, la, la, la, la, la!

[*While the row continues and* THE CARETAKER *is still craning out of the window,* THE GENTLEMAN *comes silently in from the left: he is middle-aged, with a little black moustache, dressed in dark clothes; he is wearing a bowler hat, black jacket and striped trousers, his shoes are of patent leather; he is carrying gloves, and an overcoat over one arm, and he has a little attaché-case of black leather. He closes the door quietly behind him and walks silently up to* THE CARTAKER, *who does not notice him; he stops beside her and waits for an instant without moving while* THE CARETAKER *suddenly interrupts her singing as she becomes aware of the stranger's presence; but for some moments she does not change her position and turns round only when* THE GENTLEMAN *speaks.*]

GENTLEMAN   Excuse me, are you the caretaker?

CARETAKER [*putting her hand to her heart, she cries out*]   Oh! Oh! Oh! [*And then hiccups.*] I beg pardon, Sir. I've got the hiccups.   10

[THE GENTLEMAN *does not stir.*]

'Ave you only just come in?

GENTLEMAN   Just this moment.

CARETAKER   I was tryin' to see if Bill—or George perhaps—or

someone else anyway, was in the yard . . . It's about going to see
Mr. Clarence. Well! . . . so you've arrived then?

GENTLEMAN   As you can see.

CARETAKER   I wasn't expectin' you, not for today I wasn't . . .
5   I thought you was meant to come tomorrow . . . Pleased to see
you, anyway. Did you 'ave a good journey? Not too tired, I 'ope?
Give me quite a turn, you did! I suppose you got finished sooner
than you expected! That must be it. It's just because it took me
by surprise, like. [*She hiccups.*] It's the hiccups. Shock, you know.
10   It's only what you might expect. Good thing the last lot—the
people what was 'ere before you, you know—moved everything
out in time. I'm not sure as 'ow I know what he used to do, mind.
They said they'd send me some postcards. Worked for the government. Not a bit nervy, 'e wasn't. I suppose you wouldn't be?
15   Would you? Don't know what department 'e worked for. I've
forgot. 'E told me once. Me and them government departments!
And my first 'usband was an office-boy. They was good folks.
Used to tell me everything, they did. I get used to folks' little
secrets, I do. Mum's the word for me! 'Er—the old lady, I mean
20   —she didn't used to work. Never lifted a finger in 'er life. I used
to look after the place for 'em, she used to 'ave someone in to
run errands for 'er and when she didn't used to come, it was me
again! [*She hiccups.*] What a fright you gave me! I wasn't expectin' you till tomorrow. Or the day after. Used to have a little
25   dog, they did, they 'ated cats, but then cats isn't allowed in this
establishment. 'Course it's all the same to me, it's the landlord
what says so! Regular sort of folk they were—no children, of
course—off they'd go to the country every Sunday to some
cousins of theirs, 'olidays in Devonshire, that's where the old
30   gentleman come from, that's where they've gone to live now, but
they didn't used to like the cider they 'ave there—said it used to
go to their heads, lifted a drop of port now and again, just a drop,
of course—*old* they were, even when they were young—well,
there it is we 'aven't all got the same ideas, 'ave we? Take me,
35   for instance. I'm not like that. Still, they was nice folks. And
what about you? In business, are you? Clerk? Got your own
money, perhaps? Pension? Oh, but not yet, you're too young for
that, though you never know, some of them give up early when
they're tired, don't they? And when they've *got* a little money,
40   'course everybody can't, good luck to them that can, that's what
I say. Got any family?

GENTLEMAN   [*laying his case and overcoat on the floor*]   No, I'm
afraid not.

CARETAKER   That's right, put your case down. Nice bit of leather
45   —mustn't 'ave an Irishman's rest! You can put it where you like.

Well I'm blowed! 'iccups 'ave gone! Got over me fright! Why
don't you take your 'at off and make yourself comfortable?

[THE GENTLEMAN *adjusts his hat more firmly on his head*.]

Oh, I shouldn't bother to take your 'at off, Sir. Of course, you're
at 'ome now, aren't you? Last week it wasn't your 'ome yet—
there's always change—it was *their* 'ome—well, can't be helped— 5
you 'ave to get old—it's all a question of age—now this is *your*
'ome, I'm not the one to say it ain't—very nice 'ere it is, a good
'ouse—must be twenty years now—my, that's a good long
stretch . . .

[*Without saying a word*, THE GENTLEMAN *takes a few paces in
the empty room, and looks around carefully, at the walls, the doors,
the ceiling: now he has his hands behind his back*.]

Ooh! they left everything proper, Sir! Clean folks they was, really 10
nice people. Mm? Well, of course they 'ad their faults like you
and me—bit proud they was and not what you might call talkative, not talkative by a long chalk—never said anything much
about anything to me, they didn't—only silly things—'im—the
old 'un. I mean—well, 'e was what you might call all right—but 15
'er, not 'er—threw 'er cat out of the window, she did—'it the
landlord on the 'ead—what a thud!—still, didn't 'urt my flowers.
And as for 'im, 'e didn't 'alf used to beat 'er, if you can believe
it. Sir, in these days—oh, that was their business—didn't go
poking my nose in—when I come up once, 'e was going for 'er 20
with 'is fists, something awful—Screaming she was. 'You brute!
You bleeding bastard!'

[*She bursts out laughing: at this moment* THE GENTLEMAN *is having
a closer look at the state of the walls, still without uttering a
word; he inspects the doors and the locks, moves his hand over
them, shakes his head, etc., while* THE CARETAKER *watches every
movement as she goes on talking; the din outside continues*.]

Oh, I 'ad to laugh, Sir—but there, they're away now, mustn't tell
tales—just as though they was dead, not *just* the same p'raps,
specially as it's all the same really—very nice they was, can't say 25
I 'ad anything to grumble about, except for New Year's Day . . .
Oh, don't you go worrying yourself about the 'ouse, Sir, *that's*
sound enough—this 'ouse wasn't born yesterday, don't make
'em like that nowadays . . . You'll be all right 'ere, that you
will . . . the neighbours are good folk, it's all 'armony 'ere, always 30
nice and quiet—I've never once 'ad to call the police in, 'cept
for the third floor front—Hinspector 'e is, shouts out all the time,
wants to arrest everybody, 'e does . . .

GENTLEMAN [*pointing*]   I beg your pardon, the window! [*In an even, expressionless tone of voice.*]

CARETAKER   Oh, but of course, Sir—I'm only too willing to do for you. I don't ask very much, Sir. Get on fine, you an' me will,
5   you won't 'ave any insurance stamps to worry you . . .

GENTLEMAN [*same gesture, same calm*]   The window, please!

CARETAKER   Oh yes, Sir, I *am* sorry—I was forgettin'. [*As she closes the window, there is a little less noise to be heard.*] . . . You know 'ow it is, Sir, one word leads to the next and don't time fly?

[THE GENTLEMAN *continues his inspection.*]

10   I've closed the window for you, just as you wanted—closes nice and easy.

[THE GENTLEMAN *inspects the window fasteners and the window itself.*]

Of course it looks out on the yard, but it's nice and bright as you can see, that's because it's on the sixth floor . . .

GENTLEMAN   There was nothing available on the ground floor.

15   CARETAKER   Oh! Don't think I don't know what you mean—it's no joke, the sixth floor, not when there's no lift . . .

GENTLEMAN [*rather to himself*]   That's not the point. I'm not at all tired.

CARETAKER   Oh, I see. Then why, Sir? . . . I suppose you don't like
20   the sun? 'Course, it's true it can 'urt your eyes! When you get to a certain age, you can get on quite well without it, burns your skin right off, it does . . .

GENTLEMAN   Not at all.

CARETAKER   Well, not *right* off, of course. You 'aven't anything to
25   sleep on tonight, 'ave you? I can lend you a bed!

[*For some minutes,* THE GENTLEMAN, *still engrossed in his examination of the room, has been deciding where to put the furniture that will be arriving, pointing out to himself the various positions; he takes a tape-measure out of his pocket and starts measuring.*]

I'll 'elp you to arrange the furniture, don't you worry about that, I'll give you some ideas—plenty of them about—won't be the first time, neither—since I'm going to look after you—you won't see it come today, your furniture, at any rate, they won't be
30   bringing it as quick as that, just you see, I know all their little tricks, them tradespeople's all the same . . .

GENTLEMAN Yes, indeed.

CARETAKER *You* think they're going to bring all your things today, do you? No 'arm in *thinking*—suits me all right, I've got no bed to lend you, but mind it'd surprise *me,* 'cause I *know* 'em. My, but I've seen 'em before, this lot's not the first, they won't come, you mark my words, it's a Saturday—no, it ain't, it's a Wednesday —I've got a bed for you . . . since I'm going to do for you . . . [*She goes to open the window.*]

GENTLEMAN If you don't mind!

CARETAKER What's the matter? [*She turns again to open the window.*] I've got to call George to tell 'im to tell Bill to go and see Mr. Clarence . . .

GENTLEMAN Leave the window alone, please.

CARETAKER It's all on account of Mr. Clarence, what wants to know if Mr. Eustace, who's a friend of Bill and George's too, since they're what you might call relations, not exactly, but in a kind of way . . .

GENTLEMAN Please leave the window alone.

CARETAKER All right, all right, I 'eard you, you don't want me to— wouldn't 'ave done no 'arm—you're in your rights of course, it's your window, not mine. I don't want no window—I get you, it's you gives the orders, it's just as *you* like, I won't touch it, you're the boss in your own place—don't pay much for it either —still, no business of mine—the window, that's yours, too, you can buy anything when you've got a spot of money, that's life for you—I don't say nothing, I keeps to myself, it's your affair— 'ave to go down six flights of stairs now to look for Bill, poor old woman like me—Ah, well! Can't 'elp men 'aving their little ways, don't think about nothing they don't—but I'll do just what you like, you know, it's all right with me, that don't worry me, suits me fine that does, I'm going to look after you, be as though I was your servant, like, won't it, Sir?

GENTLEMAN No, I'm afraid it won't.

CARETAKER Beg pardon, Sir?

GENTLEMAN I shan't be needing your services, I'm afraid.

CARETAKER Well, I like that! After all the time you've been asking me to do for you! Bit of bad luck I didn't 'ave no witness, took you at your word, I did, got proper took in . . . Too kind 'earted, that's me . . .

GENTLEMAN I beg your pardon. Please don't get upset about it.

CARETAKER Well, that's all right then.

[*A knock at the door, left.*]

GENTLEMAN   The furniture!

CARETAKER   I'll open the door. Don't you disturb yourself. I'm the one to open the door. Must wait on you, you know. I'm your servant.

[*She goes to open the door, but* THE GENTLEMAN *steps in front of her and stops her.*]

5   GENTLEMAN [*still very calmly*]   Please don't do anything like that!

[*He walks to the door on the left and opens it, while* THE CARE-TAKER, *hands on hips, exclaims:*]

CARETAKER   Well, that's a bit of all right! They make up to you, promise you the 'ole world, and then they go back on their word!

[THE GENTLEMAN *opens the door and the* FIRST FURNITURE MOVER *comes in.*]

FIRST FURNITURE MOVER   'Day to you!

GENTLEMAN   Is the furniture here?

10   FIRST FURNITURE MOVER   Can we bring it up?

GENTLEMAN   Yes, if you like.

FIRST FURNITURE MOVER   Very well, Sir. [*He goes out.*]

CARETAKER   You won't never be able to arrange all that furniture by yourself, Sir.

15   GENTLEMAN That will be all right. I shall have the removal men to help me.

CARETAKER   Well, you 'ardly want *strangers* to do 'it, do you? I don't even know that one, I've never seen 'im before, it's not safe! Your ought to 'ave asked my 'ubby. Ought never to have 20   let 'im come in, don't do to trust no one—you never know, you know, that's just 'ow things 'appen—foolish I call it when there's my old man, my second you know, don't know what 'appened to the first—he's down below, got nothing to do, 'asn't got a job—'e's 'efty enough you know, would 'elp 'im to earn a bit, 25   why give your money away to other people, it don't do no good, 'e could bring it up all right, 'e's tubercular you know, still, got to earn 'is bit, 'asn't 'e?—Them strikers is right, so was my first 'ubby, 'e'd 'ad enough of it, so off 'e went and then everyone's surprised!—Oh well, I'm not a bad sort really, you know, I'll 30   look after you, wouldn't mind looking after you at all . . .

GENTLEMAN I'm afraid I really shan't be needing your services.
I'm extremely sorry. I shall be looking after myself, you see.

CARETAKER [*losing her temper and shouting*] 'e says 'e's sorry, does
'e! Thinks 'e can do what he likes, does 'e!—Oooh! I don't like
these sort of goings on, you can't make no fool out of me! I wish   5
the old couple 'adn't gone, they weren't like that at all. As kind
and ob!iging as you could wish for! They're all alike, one's as bad
as another! Make you waste all your time, as though I 'adn't
got nothing else to do! Tells me to come up, 'e does, and then . . .

[*The noise increases off-stage, especially the sound of hammers.*
THE GENTLEMAN *pulls a wry face;* THE CARETAKER *screams out
into the wings.*]

Don't make so much noise! I can't 'ear myself speak. [*To* THE   10
GENTLEMAN] It's all right, I'm not going to open your window
I don't want to break nobody's window-panes—I'm respectable,
I am, no one never 'ad anything to say about that—So I've been
wasting my time, 'ave I?—and all that washing to do, better for
me if I 'adn't listened to you!   15

[*The door on the left opens noisily and lets the* FIRST FURNITURE
MOVER *appear, carrying two very small stools, while* THE CARE-
TAKER'S *tirade goes on.*]

FIRST FURNITURE MOVER [*to* GENTLEMAN] Here's the first lot
anyway!

CARETAKER [*to the* FIRST FURNITURE MOVER, *who takes no notice*]
Don't you believe a word 'e says, my lad . . .

FIRST FURNITURE MOVER [*to* GENTLEMAN] Where shall I put   20
them?

CARETAKER [*as before*] . . . A pack of lies, you needn't think 'e'll
pay you for it, think they can buy everything with money!

GENTLEMAN [*calmly to the* FIRST FURNITURE MOVER] Would you
mind putting one of them there? And one there! [*He points*   25
either side of the door on the left.]

CARETAKER [*as before*] 'e'll make you sweat, 'e will.

FIRST FURNITURE MOVER [*as before*] Very good, Sir! [*He sets the*
stools down as directed.]

CARETAKER [*as before*] . . . Work yourself to death, that's all life
is for the likes of us . . .   30

[*The* FIRST FURNITURE MOVER *goes out;* THE CARETAKER *turns*
towards THE GENTLEMAN.]

I don't know who you *are*, but I know who *I* am. I know your
sort . . . Mrs. Fairchild, that's me.

GENTLEMAN [*still calm, taking money from his pocket*] Please take
this for your trouble! [*Offering her money.*]

5 CARETAKER Well, I never! Who do you take me for? . . . I'm
no pauper, wasn't my fault if I couldn't 'ave any kids, that's on
account of my old man, they'd be grown up now, they would—
I don't want your money! [*She takes the money and puts it in
her apron-pocket.*] Very good of you, I'm sure, Sir! . . . No! It's
10 no good, you can make as much fuss as you like, you won't
catch me looking after you, not the likes of you, you won't, your
sort's not for me—'e don't need to one, 'e don't, wants to do it
all for 'isself, 'e does—fine thing that is, too, at your time o'
life . . .

[*She rambles on, while* THE GENTLEMAN *walks calmly to the door
on the left, exchanges the position of the two stools and moves
back to judge the effect.*]

15 . . . a bad lot, that's what 'e is, a bad lot in the 'ouse, don't need
nobody 'e don't, not even a blessed dog to keep 'im comp'ny—
that's the sort that prowls round the streets at night—what a time
to live in! Never wanted nobody like that, I didn't, fine state of
affairs, we only 'ave respectable folks in our 'ouse—[*Still louder.*]
20 —that's the sort that frightens folks on purpose when they're
looking out of the window, might have broken my neck and
don't need nothing 'e don't. Only wanted to pass the time o'
day, don't do no one no harm, don't get much fun I don't, 'cept
the pictures now and again and that's about all, don't even know
25 what they want, they don't . . .

[THE GENTLEMAN, *who has finally put the stools back where they
were, moves off again to admire them.*]

. . . don't know much about life, that sort don't, don't do nothing
but kick up a fuss . . .

GENTLEMAN [*inspecting the stools with a satisfied look, but he is too
phlegmatic to show much emotion*] Yes, they're better that way!

[*The* FIRST FURNITURE MOVER *comes in through the left-hand door,
noisily, with a vase in his hand.*]

CARETAKER [*going on in the same way*] Don't 'alf 'ave a fine
30 opinion of themselves either, they do—nothing but a lot of
thieves, louts and good-for-nothings . . .

GENTLEMAN [*to* FIRST FURNITURE MOVER] Here, you may put it
here. [*Points to the left-hand corner of the stage, at the back.*]

FIRST FURNITURE MOVER   There? Very good, Sir! [*Goes to the spot indicated.*]

CARETAKER   Makes all sorts of shameful suggestions to you, they does—for money . . .

GENTLEMAN [*to* FIRST FURNITURE MOVER, *who has not put the object down right in the corner*] No! In the corner, right in the corner, there . . .

CARETAKER   That sort of lark don't cut no ice with me, not with me, it don't!

FIRST FURNITURE MOVER   Here?

GENTLEMAN   Yes, there, it's fine like that . . .

CARETAKER   Oh, no! Money don't buy everything, money don't pervert everyone . . . *I* won't 'ave it any'ow!

FIRST FURNITURE MOVER [*to* THE GENTLEMAN]   But where are you going to put the rest?

GENTLEMAN [*to the* FIRST FURNITURE MOVER]   Oh, please don't trouble about that, I've thought it all out, you'll see, there'll be room . . .

[*The* FIRST FURNITURE MOVER *goes off left.*]

CARETAKER   Not that it's not what I weren't expecting, your sort don't catch me napping, I know 'em, I do, all of the fine gentlemen prowling round the streets, I've got my eyes open, I 'ave, you don't catch me 'aving any, run after anything in a skirt they will, but they don't 'ave me on! I know what you're up to, I know your little game, wanted to make a proper tart out of me, didn't you? Me! Mother of five kids too! Fine cheek you 'ave, come making nasty suggestions to a mother, with five kids too—I'm not so daft as you think I am, I've got my 'ead screwed on all right, good thing for me I 'ave. Listen 'ere, Sir, there's a police hinspector lives right in this very 'ouse, I'll charge you, I will, I'll 'ave you arrested, and then there's my old man too to look after my interests . . . Oh, no! Don't need nobody, 'e don't, eh? We'll see about that!

GENTLEMAN [*who does not look at all menacing, turns towards* THE CARETAKER; *he is extremely calm, does not raise his voice and keeps his dignity perfectly, but he gives a surprising impression of authority*] Please don't upset yourself! Take my advice and accept my apologies; otherwise you will only make yourself ill!

CARETAKER [*somewhat intimidated*]   How dare you talk to me like that! To me! Mother of five children! You won't 'ave me on like that, you won't! Now just you listen to me! You no sooner get 'ere and you 'ave me come upstairs, you takes me on, and then, without not so much as a by-your-leave, you turns me out again! When the old couple were 'ere, 'ere in this very room where you're standing now . . .

5 GENTLEMAN [*without making a gesture—his hands folded behind his back*]   May I suggest you go back to your work? The postman may have called.

[*The* CARETAKER *stops talking as though she were suddenly really frightened;* THE GENTLEMAN, *motionless, stares at her; then he goes back to the vase to admire it; taking advantage of the fact that* THE GENTLEMAN'*s back is turned,* THE CARETAKER *makes a dash for the door on the right, muttering to herself.*]

CARETAKER   The vase is a bit of all right! [*Then, having reached the door, she cries in a louder voice:*] A mother of five kids! You
10 won't 'ave me on a bit of string! I'll go and see the hinspector, I will!

[*As she turns to go out she bumps into the* SECOND FURNITURE MOVER, *who is just coming in.*]

Watch where you're going! [*Then she goes out, still shouting:*] You won't 'ave me on! You won't 'ave me on!

[*While* THE GENTLEMAN *turns to the newcomer.*]

SECOND FURNITURE MOVER   Good-day, Sir. I've come about your
15 furniture, Sir.

GENTLEMAN   Ah, yes! Good morning. Thank you. Your associate is here already. [*He points to the left, over his shoulder.*]

SECOND FURNITURE MOVER   Good, I'll go and help him. [*He crosses the stage towards the door on the left; as he does so he catches
20 sight of the two little stools and the little vase in the corner, which must be about eighteen inches high.*] I see he's already started bringing them up.

GENTLEMAN   Oh, yes! He's already started bringing them up.

SECOND FURNITURE MOVER   Has he been here long?

25 GENTLEMAN   No, only a few minutes.

SECOND FURNITURE MOVER   Is there much left?

GENTLEMAN   Quite a lot, yet.

[*Noise off left.*]

He's coming up now.

FIRST FURNITURE MOVER [*off stage*]   Are you there, Fred? Come and give me a hand, will you?

[*The* SECOND FURNITURE MOVER *goes off left, disappears for a moment and then he can just be seen coming in again backwards and straining hard; meanwhile* THE GENTLEMAN *holds out his arms to indicate different places in the room, pointing to the floor, to the walls, etc., as though it were helping him to imagine the arrangement of the furniture, saying:*]

GENTLEMAN One . . . two . . . three . . . four . . . one . . .

[*The* SECOND FURNITURE MOVER, *coming in backwards, is almost completely visible, though it is still not possible to see what he is carrying with so much difficulty; from the wings can be heard the voice of the—*]

FIRST FURNITURE MOVER [*straining*]   That's it . . . go ahead now!

GENTLEMAN [*as before*]   One . . . two . . . three . . . four . . .   5
one . . .

[*Both* FURNITURE MOVERS *are now visible, struggling to carry between them another empty vase, identical with the first, and obviously extremely light in weight; but their united effort should appear tremendous, so much so that they are in fact stumbling under their burden.*]

FIRST FURNITURE MOVER   Come on now—once more! . . .

SECOND FURNITURE MOVER   Keep a good grip on it, there! . . .

GENTLEMAN [*as before*]   One . . . two . . . three . . .

FIRST FURNITURE MOVER [*to* THE GENTLEMAN]   Where's this one   10
got to go?

GENTLEMAN [*turning towards them*]   Let's see . . . yes, put it there, please! [*He points to a spot to the left of the door on the left, near the footlights.*] That's it!

[*The two* FURNITURE MOVERS *have put the vase down; they straighten up, rubbing their arms and their backs, taking off their caps to wipe their foreheads; meanwhile* THE CARETAKER'S *voice can be heard from time to time raised in conversation and mixed up with other voices, but all the noise will subside gradually.*]

SECOND FURNITURE MOVER   Well, I hope everything's not going to   15
be like that!

GENTLEMAN   Are you tired, gentlemen?

SECOND FURNITURE MOVER   Oh, it's nothing . . . we're used to it, you know . . . [*To his colleague:*] Mustn't waste time! Shall we go? [*They both go out through the door on the left, while—*]

GENTLEMAN [*counting*]   One . . . two . . . three . . . four . . . one
. . . two . . . three . . . [*Then he moves about choosing the places
to put things and sometimes using the tape-measure he is holding
in his hand.*] There, that will be fine . . . and we can put that
there . . . and that can go here . . . That's it . . .

[*The* FIRST FURNITURE MOVER *comes in from the left carrying
another vase, this time by himself but still with difficulty.* THE
GENTLEMAN *points towards the other side of the stage, to the
right-hand corner at the back. The* FIRST FURNITURE MOVER
goes and puts the object down, while THE GENTLEMAN *goes on,
measuring:*]

One . . . two . . . three . . . five . . . one . . . two . . . seven
. . . Good . . . that's it . . . that'll be fine . . .

10   FIRST FURNITURE MOVER   Is that where you want it, Sir?

[*The larger and heavier the articles that the* FURNITURE MOVERS
*bring on, the easier they seem to carry them, until finally it looks
like child's play.*]

GENTLEMAN   Yes, that will do nicely.

[*Then the* FIRST FURNITURE MOVER *goes off left while the* SECOND
FURNITURE MOVER *comes in through the same door, carrying
another vase exactly like the rest.*]

Will you put it there, please? [*He points to the right-hand corner,
near the footlights.*]

SECOND FURNITURE MOVER   Ah, yes!

[*He puts it down and goes off left while the* FIRST FURNITURE
MOVER *comes in through the same door carrying two more tiny
stools, exactly like the first ones, and still with great effort.*]

15   FIRST FURNITURE MOVER   And where are these to go, Sir?

GENTLEMAN [*pointing either side of the door on the right*]   There
and there, of course; then they'll match the two on the other side.

FIRST FURNITURE MOVER   Of course, I should have thought . . .
[*The* FIRST FURNITURE MOVER *sets the objects down in their
place.*] Phew! Is there still any room left? [*He stops for a moment,
with nothing in his hands, in the middle of the room, then he
goes off left.*]

GENTLEMAN   There'll be enough. There's sure to be enough. I have it all worked out. [*To the* SECOND FURNITURE MOVER, *who enters from the left, with a suitcase:*] Put it there please . . . [*He points to the right of the window at the back; as the* SECOND FURNITURE MOVER *moves towards the spot,* THE GENTLEMAN *stops him.*] I'm sorry. Not there. There . . .   5

THE GENTLEMAN *points to the left of the window; the* SECOND FURNITURE MOVER *sets the object down, saying:*]

SECOND FURNITURE MOVER   Right, Sir. It would help if you could be a little more definite, Sir.

GENTLEMAN   Why, yes, of course.

SECOND FURNITURE MOVER   And then we won't tire ourselves out unnecessarily.   10

GENTLEMAN   Of course, I understand.

FIRST FURNITURE MOVER   [*coming in from the left with a pedestal table while the* SECOND FURNITURE MOVER *goes out left*] And this? Where shall I put this?

GENTLEMAN   Ah yes . . . let me see . . . it's not easy to find the right little place for that . . .   15

FIRST FURNITURE MOVER   Here, perhaps, Sir! [*He carries the table to the left of the window.*]

GENTLEMAN   The ideal place! [*These tables are all in different shapes and colours.*]   Ideal!

SECOND FURNITURE MOVER [*coming in left with another pedestal*   20 *table*] And this?

GENTLEMAN [*indicating a place to the left of the first table*]   Here, if you don't mind.

SECOND FURNITURE MOVER [*puts it down*]   But there won't be any room for your plates!

GENTLEMAN   Everything's been accounted for.   25

SECOND FURNITURE MOVER [*looking round the stage*]   I don't quite see . . .

GENTLEMAN   Yes, I assure you.

SECOND FURNITURE MOVER   Well, if you say so. [*He goes off left, while the* FIRST FURNITURE MOVER *arrives, with another table.*]

GENTLEMAN [*to* FIRST FURNITURE MOVER]   Beside the last one.   30

[*Then while the* FIRST FURNITURE MOVER *places the table in position and goes out, and the* SECOND FURNITURE MOVER *comes in, still from the left, with another table,* THE GENTLEMAN *traces a circle on the floor in chalk; then, more carefully, a larger circle*

[*in the middle of the stage;* THE GENTLEMAN *stops and straightens up to show the* SECOND FURNITURE MOVER *where to put his latest pedestal table:*]

There, along by the wall, next to the other!

[*While the* SECOND FURNITURE MOVER *puts it down,* THE GENTLEMAN, *who has finished tracing his circle, straightens up again and says:*]

That will be fine!

[*While the* SECOND FURNITURE MOVER *goes off, still on the left, the* FIRST FURNITURE MOVER *arrives with another pedestal table:*]

Next to the last one!

[*He points out the place, the* FIRST FURNITURE MOVER *puts it down and goes off left.* THE GENTLEMAN, *alone for a moment, counts the pedestal tables.*]

Yes . . . that's it . . . now we shall have to . . .

[*The* SECOND FURNITURE MOVER *comes in from the right with another pedestal table.*]

5   All round the room . . .

[*Then, from the left, the* FIRST FURNITURE MOVER.]

All around . . .

[*Both* FURNITURE MOVERS *go off, the* FIRST *on the left, to come on again from the right, the* SECOND *on the right, to come in again from the left, and they bring on more tables and other objects such as chairs, screens, table-lamps, piles of books, etc., which they set down, one after the other, all round the stage and along the walls, meeting and passing each other as they do so. The movement is carried out in such a way that there is always one* FURNITURE MOVER *on the stage throughout the scene that follows.*]

All around the room, all around . . . all around . . .

[*Then, when the walls are all lined with furniture,* THE GENTLEMAN *says to the* FIRST FURNITURE MOVER, *who comes in, empty-handed, from the left:*]

Now you can bring a step-ladder!

[*The* FIRST FURNITURE MOVER *goes out the way he came in; the* SECOND FURNITURE MOVER *comes on from the right.*]

A step-ladder!

[*The* SECOND FURNITURE MOVER *goes out the way he came in.* THE GENTLEMAN *is looking round the walls and rubbing his hands together:*]

There now! Now it's beginning to take shape. It'll be a very comfortable sort of place. It won't be at all bad.

[*The two* FURNITURE MOVERS *come in from the left and right, each from the side opposite to the one they went out;* THE GENTLEMAN *indicates to the one coming from the left the wall on the right, and vice-versa; he says nothing.*]

FIRST FURNITURE MOVER   Right ho!

SECOND FURNITURE MOVER   Right ho!   5

[*They cross and place their ladders against the walls indicated.*]

GENTLEMAN   Leave the ladders there. You can bring in the pictures now!

[*They come down their ladders and go off right and left. As he moves towards the exit, the* SECOND FURNITURE MOVER *steps on one of the chalk circles, the one in the middle of the stage.*]

Be careful there! Don't spoil my circle.

SECOND FURNITURE MOVER   Oh, yes! We'll try not to.

GENTLEMAN   Be careful!   10

[*The* SECOND FURNITURE MOVER *goes out while the* FIRST FURNITURE MOVER *enters from the opposite side with a large painting representing the head of a hideous old man.*]

Be careful, be careful of my circles. [*This said in a calm and neutral tone.*]

FIRST FURNITURE MOVER   I'll try. It's not easy when you're loaded . . .

GENTLEMAN   Now hang the picture up . . .   15

FIRST FURNITURE MOVER   Yes, Sir.

[*He climbs up the ladder and carefully hangs the picture. The* SECOND FURNITURE MOVER *enters from the side opposite the one*

from which the FIRST FURNITURE MOVER *has just come in, also carrying a large painting representing another hideous old man.*]

GENTLEMAN   My ancestors. [*To the* SECOND FURNITURE MOVER:] Now go up the ladder and hang the picture.

SECOND FURNITURE MOVER [*going up the ladder against the opposite wall, holding the picture*] It's not easy, with all your circles. Especially when we come to the heavy objects. We can't watch out for everything. [*He busies himself hanging the picture.*]

GENTLEMAN   Oh yes, you can, if you really want to.

[THE GENTLEMAN *picks up from amongst the various objects brought on the stage a book or a box or some other still smaller object and takes it to the centre of the stage where he sets it down after having inspected it by raising it above his head; meanwhile, the workmen are busy fixing the paintings carefully on the two walls;* THE GENTLEMAN *could also adjust the position of some of the furniture slightly or retrace his chalk circles again; all this without a word spoken. A slight sound of hammers and the other exterior noises can still be heard, but already transformed into music.* THE GENTLEMAN *contemplates the painting and the room in general with an air of satisfaction. The two workmen have finished, and so has* THE GENTLEMAN: *the work should have lasted some time, acted without words. The* FURNITURE MOVERS *come down from their ladders; they go and put the ladders where there is still a little space, as for example near the two doors; then they join* THE GENTLEMAN, *who studies first one of the pictures, then the other.*]

FIRST FURNITURE MOVER [*pointing to the two pictures, speaking to* THE GENTLEMAN] All right?

GENTLEMAN [*to* FURNITURE MOVER] All right?

SECOND FURNITURE MOVER   Looks all right to me.

GENTLEMAN [*inspecting the pictures*] They're firmly fixed. [*Pause*] Bring in the heavy objects.

SECOND FURNITURE MOVER   It's thirsty work. [*Mops his brow.*]

GENTLEMAN   We must have the sideboard then.

[*Both* FURNITURE MOVERS *go towards the door on the right;* THE GENTLEMAN *turns towards the window.*]

One . . . yes . . . one here . . .

[*Before the two* FURNITURE MOVERS *can reach the door on the right, the two folding doors open of themselves and a sideboard*

*slides onto the stage, propelled by an invisible force; the folding
doors close again and the* FURNITURE MOVERS *seize the sideboard
and glance towards* THE GENTLEMAN, *who with a gesture shows
them where to put it.*]

BOTH FURNITURE MOVERS [*who are now near the centre of the
stage*]   Where?

GENTLEMAN [*his back to the audience, his hands extended towards
the window*]   But there, of course! . . .

FIRST FURNITURE MOVER   You'll shut out all the light.   5

GENTLEMAN   There's electric light, isn't there?

[*The* FIRST FURNITURE MOVER *pushes the sideboard against the
window; it fails to block it up completely; it is not high enough.
The* SECOND FURNITURE MOVER *goes to one of the doors and
switches on the ceiling light; he takes hold of a picture representing a winter landscape, which has glided on to the stage by itself
through the folding doors, and places it on top of the sideboard:
this time the window is completely masked. The* FIRST FURNI-
TURE MOVER *opens the sideboard, takes a bottle out, takes a
swig from it, passes it to the* SECOND FURNITURE MOVER, *who
does the same, and then offers it to* THE GENTLEMAN.]

No, thank you. I never touch it.

[*Then both the* FURNITURE MOVERS *drink in turn out of the bottle,
handing it backwards and forwards, and looking at the blocked-
up window.*]

Much better, like that.

[*The two* FURNITURE MOVERS, *too, still drinking from time to time,
turn to face the window concealed by the sideboard and the canvas representing winter, so that, in this way, all three have their
backs to the audience.*]

FIRST FURNITURE MOVER [*with approval*]   Ah ha!

SECOND FURNITURE MOVER [*with approval*]   Ah ha!   10

GENTLEMAN   It's not quite right [*Indicating the picture.*] I don't
like it . . . Turn it round!

[*The two* FURNITURE MOVERS *turn the picture round while* THE
GENTLEMAN *watches them; only the back of the picture is to be
seen, with its dark frame and hanging cord; then the two* FURNI-
TURE MOVERS *step away a little and again pick up the bottle and
go on drinking; then they go and stand on either side of* THE

GENTLEMAN, *still with their backs to the audience, and again gaze at the sideboard with the picture on top of it in silence for several moments.*]

I like it better like that.

FIRST FURNITURE MOVER   It's much nicer.

GENTLEMAN   Much nicer. More restrained.

SECOND FURNITURE MOVER   Much nicer. More restrained.

5   GENTLEMEN   Ah, yes, it's very much nicer, more restrained.

FIRST FURNITURE MOVER   Ah yes . . .

SECOND FURNITURE MOVER   Ah yes . . .

GENTLEMAN   You can't see anything now.

FIRST FURNITURE MOVER   Well, that's something.

[*Silence*]

10   SECOND FURNITURE MOVER [*after a moment, turning the bottle neck downwards*]   There isn't any more.

FIRST FURNITURE MOVER   The last drop.

SECOND FURNITURE MOVER [*still holding the bottle in the same way, to* THE GENTLEMAN]   There isn't any more.

15   GENTLEMAN   I don't think so either.

[*The* FIRST FURNITURE MOVER *takes the bottle from the* SECOND FURNITURE MOVER *and puts it in the sideboard, which he closes.*]

Won't have any more trouble from the neighbours now.

FIRST FURNITURE MOVER   Better for everybody.

SECOND FURNITURE MOVER   Everybody will be happy.

GENTLEMAN   Everyone will be happy. [*A moment of silence.*] To
20   work. Let's go on. My armchair.

FIRST FURNITURE MOVER   Where can we put it?

SECOND FURNITURE MOVER   Where can we put it?

GENTLEMAN   In the circle. [*He points to the circle in the middle.*]
You won't be able to spoil my circle any more.

25   FIRST FURNITURE MOVER [*to* THE GENTLEMAN]   You'll be able to
see it better.

GENTLEMAN [*to the* FIRST FURNITURE MOVER]   Will you go and
fetch it?

[*The* FIRST FURNITURE MOVER *goes to the door on the right.*]

[*To the* SECOND FURNITURE MOVER:]   Now the heavy furniture in pink wood.

[*The* FIRST FURNITURE MOVER *arrives at the door on the right; the armchair glides on, pushed from behind; he takes hold of it. The* SECOND FURNITURE MOVER *goes to the door on the left; half a wardrobe appears; he seizes hold of it and pulls it towards the centre of the stage; all the movements have slowed down; from now on all the furniture comes on through the two doors alternately, propelled from behind; each item only half appears; the* FURNITURE MOVERS *pull it towards them, and when it has been pulled right into the room, something else slides on, half visible, and so on. The* FIRST FURNITURE MOVER, *then, has hold of the armchair, while the other man is pulling through the other doorway a huge wardrobe lying on its side; the* FIRST FURNITURE MOVER *set the armchair down within the circle.*]

GENTLEMAN [*looking at the pink wardrobe*]   It's a beautiful pink. isn't it?

FIRST FURNITURE MOVER [*after placing the armchair within the* *circle*]   Good armchair.   5

GENTLEMAN [*feeling the upholstery*]   Yes, it's very soft. Well-upholstered. [*To the* FIRST FURNITURE MOVER:] Please don't stop bringing the things in.

[*The* FIRST FURNITURE MOVER *goes to the door on the right, where he finds a second pink wardrobe on its side; the* SECOND FURNITURE MOVER, *still dragging his wardrobe on, glances at* THE GENTLEMAN, *as though asking silently where to put it.*]

There!   10

[*The wardrobes in question—there could be four in all—will be disposed, always according to* THE GENTLEMAN'S *directions, along the three walls, parallel to the other rows of furniture; first one, then the other of the two* FURNITURE MOVERS *will dart a questioning look at* THE GENTLEMAN *each time they have succeeded in dragging the furniture clear of the folding doors and* THE GENTLEMAN *will point and say to them:*]

There! There! There! There!

[*At each 'There!' the* FURNITURE MOVERS *nod their heads affirmatively and bring the furniture in; after the four wardrobes come smaller items—some more tables, settees too, wickerwork baskets, strange furniture never seen before, etc. It is all placed in front of the rest along the three walls, so that* THE GENTLEMAN *is confined*]

[*in an ever-diminishing space in the centre of the stage; the action
is like a ponderous kind of ballet and all the movements are made
very slowly.*]

[*While the* FURNITURE MOVERS *are still bringing on the furniture
and questioning him silently, while the furniture is still sliding on
to the stage, pushed on from behind,* THE GENTLEMAN *is in the
centre, with one hand on the back of the armchair and the other
pointing:*]

There . . . There . . . There . . . There . . . There . . . There . . .
There . . . There . . . There . . . There . . . There . . . There . . .
There . . . There . . . There . . . There . . . There . . .

[*It should be arranged so that this action lasts a long time; in a slow
and broken rhythm. Then, at a certain moment, the* FIRST
FURNITURE MOVER *brings on a radio set from the right; when
his questioning glance alights on* THE GENTLEMAN, *the latter
says, in a voice scarcely louder than before:*]

Oh no! Oh dear me no!

5 FIRST FURNITURE MOVER   It doesn't work.

GENTLEMAN   Well, in that case . . . yes. Here.

[*He indicates a spot near the armchair; the* FIRST FURNITURE
MOVER *deposits the article and moves off towards the right for
more, while the* SECOND FURNITURE MOVER *comes up from the
left, with the same look of interrogation, carrying a chamber-pot;
to the* SECOND FURNITURE MOVER]

Why yes, of course . . . here.

[*He points to the other side of the armchair; the* SECOND FURNITURE
MOVER *lays the chamber-pot down and then they both move off
their own side and come back again with other furniture so that
the space surrounding* THE GENTLEMAN *gets smaller and smaller;
now the action continues without words, in complete silence; little
by little the sounds from outside,* THE CARETAKER'S *voice, etc.,
have died away; the* FURNITURE MOVERS *pad about noiselessly;
the furniture appears on the stage quite silently; each time the*
FURNITURE MOVERS *introduce a new item they still look questioningly at* THE GENTLEMAN *and the latter still indicates by gesture,
without uttering a word, where to put the various articles, which
are slowly but surely closing in on him. This dumb show, with its
broken mechanical movements, should also last a long time, even
longer, perhaps, than the previous scene of* THE GENTLEMAN'S
'There . . . There . . . There . . . There': *finally the* SECOND FURNI-

TURE MOVER *brings on an enormous wall-clock from the left, while the other* FURNITURE MOVER *continues as before; when* THE GENTLEMAN *sees the clock, he shows surprise and uncertainty, then finally makes a sign of refusal; while the* SECOND FURNITURE MOVER *takes the clock away to bring up another piece of furniture the* FIRST FURNITURE MOVER *arrives with a second clock that resembles the first in every respect;* THE GENTLEMAN *dismisses him with a gesture, then changes his mind.*]

GENTLEMAN   But wait . . . after all, why not?

[*The clock is brought up to the armchair, and* THE GENTLEMAN *points to a place near it; next the* SECOND FURNITURE MOVER *comes back with a large and very high screen; as he reaches the armchair the* FIRST FURNITURE MOVER *comes up from his side also carrying a screen of the same height.*]

SECOND FURNITURE MOVER   There'll be no room left!

GENTLEMAN   Oh, yes, there will. [*He sits down in his armchair within the circle.*] Like this there will.

[*The* FURNITURE MOVERS *bring up a second and then a third screen and enclose* THE GENTLEMAN *on three sides, within the circle. Only the side facing the audience remains open.* THE GENTLEMAN *is sitting in the armchair, with his hat on his head, his face turned towards the public; on each side, the two* FURNITURE MOVERS, *their bodies hidden behind the screens, poke their heads round to have a look at* THE GENTLEMAN.]

FIRST FURNITURE MOVER   All right? You comfortable now?

[THE GENTLEMAN *nods his head.*]

It's good to feel at home.

SECOND FURNITURE MOVER   You must have got tired. I should have a little rest.

GENTLEMAN   Don't stop, will you? . . . Is there still much left?

[*Dumb show.* THE GENTLEMAN *is seated, motionless, hat on head, facing the audience; the two* FURNITURE MOVERS *make their way, each to one of the two entrances; the folding doors are wide open; the two openings are completely blocked and one can only see great wooden boards, green on the left, purple on the right, as high as the doors themselves, apparently the backs of tall, wide wardrobes; synchronizing their movements, each man looks at the door in front of him and scratches his head underneath his cap in a puzzled way; they shrug their shoulders and put their*

hands on their hips simultaneously; then, still moving together,
they step back amongst the furniture, each man on his own side
of the stage, and gape at each other. Then:]

FIRST FURNITURE MOVER   What shall we do?

SECOND FURNITURE MOVER   What shall we do?

GENTLEMAN [*without moving*]   Is there still much left? Isn't it
finished yet?

[*The* FIRST FURNITURE MOVER, *without answering* THE GENTLE-
MAN, *makes a meaningful gesture directed at the* SECOND FURNI-
TURE MOVER, *a gesture expressing bewilderment, which the* SEC-
OND FURNITURE MOVER *repeats. Without moving, still very*
calm:]

5   Have you brought up *all* the furniture?

[*Dumb show for a moment. Both* FURNITURE MOVERS, *still standing*
where they were, turn towards their respective doors, and then
towards THE GENTLEMAN, *who can no longer see them.*]

FIRST FURNITURE MOVER   It's really awkward, Sir.

GENTLEMAN   What is?

SECOND FURNITURE MOVER   The rest of the furniture's very big
and the doors aren't.

10   FIRST FURNITURE MOVER   Can't get it in.

GENTLEMAN   What is it that's left?

FIRST FURNITURE MOVER   Wardrobes.

GENTLEMAN   The green and the purple ones?

SECOND FURNITURE MOVER   Yes.

15   FIRST FURNITURE MOVER   And that's not all. There's more to
come.

SECOND FURNITURE MOVER   The staircase is jammed from top to
bottom. Nobody can get up or down.

GENTLEMAN   The yard is cram-full too. So is the street.

20   FIRST FURNITURE MOVER   The traffic's come to a standstill in the
town. Full of furniture.

SECOND FURNITURE MOVER [*to* THE GENTLEMAN]   At least you've
nothing to complain about, Sir. You've got somewhere to sit.

FIRST FURNITURE MOVER   Perhaps the tube's still running.

25   SECOND FURNITURE MOVER   No, it isn't.

GENTLEMAN [*still as before*]   No. All the underground lines are blocked.

SECOND FURNITURE MOVER [*to* THE GENTLEMAN]   Some furniture! It's cluttering up the whole country.

GENTLEMAN   The Thames has stopped flowing, too. Dammed up. 5 No more water.

FIRST FURNITURE MOVER   What can we do then, if we can't get any more in?

GENTLEMAN   It can't be left outside, because of the weather.

[*The* FURNITURE MOVERS *are still speaking from their respective positions.*]

FIRST FURNITURE MOVER   Might be able to get it in through the 10 attic. But then . . . we'd have to break the ceiling in.

SECOND FURNITURE MOVER   Not necessary. Modern house. Sliding ceiling. [*To* THE GENTLEMAN] Did you know?

GENTLEMAN   No.

SECOND FURNITURE MOVER   Well, there you are. It's easy. Just 15 have to clap your hands. [*He makes the gesture.*] The ceiling opens.

GENTLEMAN [*from his armchair*]   No . . . I'm afraid of the rain on the furniture. It's new and easily spoilt.

SECOND FURNITURE MOVER   No fear of that, Sir. I know how it 20 works. The ceiling opens and closes, opens and closes, just as you want.

FIRST FURNITURE MOVER   Come on then, perhaps we can . . .

GENTLEMAN [*from his armchair*]   Providing you close it again at once. No carelessness, mind. 25

FIRST FURNITURE MOVER   We won't forget. *I'm* on the job. [*To the* SECOND FURNITURE MOVER:] Ready?

SECOND FURNITURE MOVER   Yes.

FIRST FURNITURE MOVER [*to* THE GENTLEMAN]   All right?

GENTLEMAN   Right. 30

FIRST FURNITURE MOVER [*to the* SECOND FURNITURE MOVER]   Go ahead.

[*The* SECOND FURNITURE MOVER *claps his hands. From the ceiling huge planks descend at the front of the stage, completely hiding from view* THE GENTLEMAN *in his high-walled enclosure; a few could also come down on to the stage amongst the furniture; the new tenant is thus completely walled-in; clambering over the furniture the* FIRST FURNITURE MOVER, *after knocking three times without response on one of the screens at the side, makes his way, with a ladder, to the place where the planks have completed the enclosure; he holds in one hand a bunch of flowers that he tries to hide from the audience; silently he leans his ladder up against the end plank on the right; when he has reached the top, he looks down into the enclosure and calls out to* THE GENTLEMAN:]

That's it, Sir. Everything in. Are you nice and comfortable? Has the move gone off to your satisfaction?

GENTLEMAN'S VOICE [*just as it has always been; slightly muffled, that's all*]   Ceiling. Close ceiling, please.

5   FIRST FURNITURE MOVER [*from the top of the ladder to his mate*]   He wants you to close the ceiling. You forgot.

SECOND FURNITURE MOVER [*in the same spot*]   Oh, yes. [*He claps for the ceiling to close again.*] There you are.

GENTLEMAN'S VOICE   Thank you.

10   FIRST FURNITURE MOVER [*on the ladder*]   Ah well, you've got a good sheltered spot there, you won't be cold . . . Are you all right?

GENTLEMAN'S VOICE [*after a silence*]   All right.

FIRST FURNITURE MOVER   Hand me your hat, Sir, it might worry you.

[*After a short pause,* THE GENTLEMAN'S *hat can be seen appearing from within the enclosure.*]

15   FIRST FURNITURE MOVER [*taking the hat and throwing· the flowers down inside*]   That's right. You'll be more comfortable like that. Here are some flowers for you. [*To the* SECOND FURNITURE MOVER] Is that all?

SECOND FURNITURE MOVER   That's all.

20   FIRST FURNITURE MOVER   Good. [*To* THE GENTLEMAN] We've brought everything. Sir, you're really at home now. [*He comes down off the ladder.*] We'll be off. [*He leans the ladder against the wall, or perhaps he can prop it up, gently, without making a noise, somewhere amongst the other objects that hem* THE GENTLEMAN
25   *in. To the* SECOND FURNITURE MOVER] Come on.

[*The two* FURNITURE MOVERS, *each still keeping to his own side, make their way, blindly and tentatively, to the back of the stage, towards invisible and problematical exits, Heaven knows where;*

for the window is stopped up and through the open folding doors you can still see the violently coloured wood that blocks the way.]

FIRST FURNITURE MOVER [*at a certain moment, he stops,* THE GENTLEMAN'S *hat in his hand, turns round and directs his words from one end of the stage towards the concealed* GENTLEMAN] Is there anything you want?

[*Silence*]

SECOND FURNITURE MOVER   Is there anything you want?   5

GENTLEMAN'S VOICE [*after a silence; not a movement on the stage*] Put out the light. [*Utter darkness.*] Thank you.

CURTAIN

THE THEATRE IN SEARCH
OF A FIX

One of the most amazing recent phenomena of our theatre is the discovery and gradual acceptance of audiences and critics of the plays of Beckett, Ionesco, Adamov, Genet, and Ghelderode. With a prudishness that is just about par for the course, we have tended to reject these plays and label their authors opprobriously as *avant-garde*. But somehow—in spite of our rejection—these plays keep reasserting themselves; they have a mysterious hold on our sensibilities. We find ourselves going to them, being moved or amused by them, and applauding them—fully aware that we don't always know what they mean or what their authors intend. For all their seeming unintelligibility and simplicity, these plays possess a vitality we have missed, and more important, in their boldly experimental nature they are symptomatic of the unrest which prevails in the contemporary theatre. These playwrights want to "fix" the theatre, and their plays suggest ways that have been taken to revitalize it.

Each of the writers in this movement shares the conviction that the theatre must express the senselessness and irrationality of all human actions. They believe the theatre must confront audiences with that sense of isolation—the sense of man's being encircled in a void—which is an irremediable part of the human condition. In such a universe communication with others is almost impossible, and the language of these plays is symptomatic of their authors' belief in man's inability to communicate and express his basic thoughts and feelings. This has prompted Wallace Fowlie to say that "all of these plays give the impression of being autopsies of our unacknowledged, invisible manias." All that happens in them is beyond rational motivation, happening at random or through the "demented caprice of an unaccountable idiot fate." And so critics, using Ionesco's definition of the "absurd" as "that which has no purpose, or goal, or objective," have come to label the theatre of these playwrights "the Theatre of the Absurd."

But in reducing the human situation to its ultimate absurdity, Beckett, Ionesco, *et al.* realize that the stereotyped dramatic progressions of our determinism-oriented naturalistic theatre will no longer satisfy. They are searching for a new form, new techniques—techniques that are expressive of the central fact of their world: that man's unconscious is no more help to him than his intelligence in solving time's inscrutable ironies.

Now, to revolt against naturalism is not very new; but with the possible exception of Alfred Jarry—and he had so little impact he hardly counts—none of the theatre's revolutionaries beginning with Ibsen and Strindberg have ever resolved so systematically to undermine and destroy not only the superstructure of naturalism, the elaborate settings, the contrived plot, the socially recognizable characters, with their all-too-familiar problems, but the very foundation of the naturalistic vision: the laws of logic.

For the Absurdists, tragedy and comedy are both manifestations of despair, of the act which *exists,* exists alone in its own unmotivated isolation, unmeaningful and absurd. The recognizable hero, the logically motivated heroine, the well-knit plot all give *meaning*— a spurious, illusory, distorting meaning—to the act, and so rob it of its elemental import, which lies in its irreducible absurdity. For the Absurdist playwrights, as for Sartre and Camus, the absurd alone bears the stamp of truth; logic is a pattern imposed by a dishonest philosophy pandering to the comfort of those who dare not face reality.

This attitude toward the so-called natural logic of the universe has had tremendous effects on the dramaturgy of the Absurdist playwrights. The first of these is manifested in their thinking about tragedy and comedy. Tragedy doesn't seem to flourish in the world of the absurd. As early as 1939, Eugene O'Neill sensed the impossibility of his lifelong ambition to write a tragedy, when he remarked:

> It's struck me as time goes on, how something funny, even farcical can suddenly, without apparent reason, break up into something gloomy and tragic. . . . A sort of unfair *non sequitur,* as though events, though life, were manipulated just to confuse us. I think I'm aware of comedy more than I ever was before— a big kind of comedy that doesn't stay funny very long.

When man is forced to admit that the absurd is more than ever inherent in human existence, when he sees his existence as essentially governed by the irrational, the inexplicable, and the nonsensical, he moves into the realm of the comic. For comedy supposes an unformed world, a world being made and turned upside down. In our Punch and Judy world no one is guilty or responsible. As Gautier put it, "comedy is the logic of the absurd," and thus it can admit the disorderly, the absurd, and the improbable into the realm of Art. As Dostoevski, Joyce, and Kafka have so adequately shown in the novel, the fragmentary, schizoid lives that we live are an existential comedy. They suggest that modern man lives in the midst of so many irreconcilable forces that the only way they can be given form is by religious faith or comedy. But it is a special kind of comedy, the "comedy of the grotesque." Our world is similar to the one represented in the apocalyptic paintings of Hieronymus Bosch. The grotesque is a means whereby art can encompass the paradoxical and express the form of the unformed, "the face of a world without a face." However, this grotesque comedy, so aware of the absurdity of experience, is also extremely conscious of its sufferings, struggle, and failure. It is best described as a kind of tragicomedy. It is a vision of life that may be summed up by the closing prayer of Joyce's *Finnegans Wake:*

> Loud, heap miseries upon us yet entwine
> Our arts with laughters low. In the name
> Of the former and of the latter and of
> Their holocaust, All men.

Or as Ionesco put it:

> It all comes to the same thing anyway; comic and tragic are merely two aspects of the same situation, and I have now reached the stage when I find it hard to distinguish one from the other.

The most striking thing about the plays of the *avant-garde* dramatists is that on the surface they seem to be either unintelligible or simple to the point of absurdity. Yet these plays are the result of serious attempts to give dramatic form to all the complexities of our world. Today we must embrace the idea of paradox in our art as well as our foreign policy. As Duerrenmatt has suggested, "Our world seems still to exist only because the atom bomb exists: out of fear of the bomb."

In *Waiting for Godot,* for instance, Beckett has created an image of man searching for relationship—with himself, with his fellow men, and with his God—only to shatter this image by questioning the validity of the quest. Is there, after all, any ultimate and objective truth? How can we know it? Is it possible that we may be wrong? Is it true for all of us? Prove it! Why bother? In short, what's the use of living anyway?

As John R. Moore has pointed out in his essay, "A Farewell to Something," *Waiting for Godot* ends not in a tragic resolution but in a comic impasse. This is what is so new and important about it. Beckett has rejected the heritage of the French (and probably the Western) theatre; Descartes' *cogito, ergo sum* (I think, therefore I am) has become *vomeo, ergo sum* (I retch, therefore I am); the lyric deliberations of Corneille and Racine on the wonder of the human will have been reduced to an emotionally charged shorthand; the Pascalian dialectic of reason and passion has been mocked to absurdity—or as Anouilh put it, *"Waiting for Godot* was the *Pensées* acted out by circus clowns." But Gogo and Didi, two irreducible specimens of humanity, remain comically, tragically, ambiguously alive with the courage of their hallucinations. They affirm that man can still, albeit fearfully, stick his tongue out at the universe. Like Henry James' Bostonian, they have "the ability to dare and endure, to know and not to fear reality, to look the world in the face and take it for what it is."

But for all its concern for man's ontological solitude, the Theatre of the Absurd is not a theatre of ideas. Ionesco makes this point very strongly when he writes:

> The theatre is not the language of ideas. When it tries to become the vehicle of ideologies, it can only become their popularizer. It simplifies them dangerously. . . . Every ideological theatre risks being only a theatre of patronage. What would be, not only its usefulness, but its proper function, if the theatre were condemned to do the work of philosophy, or theology, or politics, or pedagogy? A psychological theatre is insufficiently psychological. It is better to read a treatise on psychology. An ideological theatre is insufficiently philosophical. Instead of going to see the dramatic illustration of such and such a political theory, I prefer to read my usual daily, or listen to a speech by the candidate of my party.

Rather than ideas, then, these playwrights are trying to deal directly with the themes—emptiness, frustration, change, despair, and death —that obsess them. They believe that the theatre of naturalism either does not treat such themes, or if it does, it presents man in a reduced and estranged perspective. "Truth is in our dreams, in the imagination," says Ionesco. This is the clue of his theatre. All of the Absurdists want a theatre "which progresses not through a predetermined subject and plot, but through an increasingly intense and revealing series of emotional states."

But action, which alone can create movement and bring a play to life, is normally provided by the plot. It is the plot that unites ideas, character and language; yet the plot depends upon the close relationship of all three. We are not dealing with a dislocated drama; its traditional elements have been given a violent wrench. So we find that the plot has been twisted into a situation that is to reveal an emotional state. There are many dramatic situations in a plot; here the situation has been stretched to take the place of the plot. This inflation of the *situation* into the source of dramatic action, so that it replaces the plot, is the vital secret of the Theatre of the Absurd. It is the most exciting and the most disturbing aspect of this theatre; disturbing because it has serious limitations. It is no accident that most of Beckett's, Ionesco's, Adamov's, and Ghelderode's plays are written in one act; a plot is capable of endless ramifications largely because character changes circumstances. Once you have fixed your characters, their psychological reactions are no longer of interest. The situation assumes full command.

But if this is so, then what happens to character in the Theatre of the Absurd? None of these playwrights has created a character who can stand alone as a great individual. Traditionally, one of the most successful ways for a dramatist to express a profound truth about life, philosophy, or human nature has been for him to create a great character, a great individual in whom the audience can recognize a universal truth. In the Theatre of the Absurd the characters are types; they have no individuality and often not even names. Sometimes they are interchangeable, as for example in *Godot,* when Pozzo and Lucky change roles; or the same name, in a Kafka-like manner, is used in several plays—as is the case of Berenger in Ionesco's *The Killer* and *Rhinoceros.*

But once you do away with a character's individuality, it is impossible for the dramatist to make individual judgements, for there can be no sequence of acts—no real interaction of character and situation—leading to a judgement. We never feel that the question of whether Gogo and Didi, Hamm and Clov, the Old Man and Woman are good or evil is raised or even pertinent; they are pathetic victims of a nothing which is so much. There are no value judgements or distinctions in values in the world of the Absurd. In Adamov's *Ping-Pong,* the aesthetic, economic, and philosophic implications of pinball machines are discussed with religious fervor. In Ionesco's *Jack or the Submission* the whole action is to convince Jack to accept the family's chief value: "I love potatoes with bacon."

In such a world, human action and self-sacrifice have no meaning. The most horrible aspect of Ionesco's *The Chairs* is the fact that the old couple's immolation at the end of the play is so meaningless. Ionesco presents us with an inverted Messiah and the end of the world is his "salvation." As the Orator signs autographs and the Old Woman sobs, the Old Man begins his final soliloquy:

> Our existence can come to an end in this apotheosis. . . . My mission is accomplished. I will not have lived in vain, since my message will be revealed to the world. . . . Our corpses will fall far from each other, and we will rot in an aquatic solitude. . . .

Confident that their message will save the world, they dive into the sea. The professional orator, who is to deliver their message, takes the podium and turns out to be a deaf-mute; he can only squawk and write two words on a blackboard—"Angelfood" and "Adieu." Ionesco seems to be saying that enriched cake flour is a significant token of farewell for our age; it is the perverted apocalypse of our civilization.

One of the most significant results of the Absurdists' rebellion against the natural laws of logic has been their rejection of the psychologically oriented play. Each of these playwrights is vehement in maintaining that with our almost morbid concern with psychology—particularly here in America—we are denying the theatre's historical nature. For most of this century the remedy that our theatre offered for the mystery of evil was: "change the society!" Since 1945 it has been "Get a doctor!" Now, there is no denying that the increased concern for psychology on the part of our dramatists has had salutary effects on the theatre. But it has gotten to the point where every so-called serious play has become a clinical case history, and this is more detrimental than beneficial.

To begin with, it is a severely limited view of man. When all human actions are explainable in terms of some kind of psychological cause and effect, the possibility of deliberative and moral choice is dissolved. There is an old saw about no man being a hero to his valet. The same is true of his psychoanalyst. And ultimately, the same is true of the dramatic artist. For example, as David Daiches has suggested, Oedipus remains a hero with great stature so long as he is not suffering from an Oedipus complex. But once we learn to explain him in terms of repressed hopes and fears, or traumatic childhood experiences, or a vitamin deficiency in infancy, he may remain interesting—in fact, he will gain a new kind of interest as Cocteau's *The Infernal Machine* attests—but he loses stature. For, to use another old saw, "To understand all, is to forgive all." But when we can do both these things all men are reduced to a common level. Which of us can understand a Hamlet, or a Lear? And which of us can forgive an Othello or a Macbeth? But it is precisely the fact that they are greater than our understanding, that there is a mysterious greatness about them, that makes them the heroes they are. And it is this mystery that makes them great; it is this mysterious quality in men which passeth all understanding that affirms man and his universe.

Maxwell Anderson has written that "from the point of view of the playwright, the essence of a tragedy, or even a serious play, is the spiritual awakening, or regeneration of his hero." But the problem is to know what we mean by the heroic in our time and also what we mean when we speak of spiritual awakening or regeneration. To begin with, it is certainly safe to say that society, as a force for good or evil, plays a larger and more essential role in the modern theatre than in the great plays of earlier periods. Consequently, the typical hero of modern drama will be different. In what ways?

The hero is always best described in terms of those forces which urge him to spiritual redemption. The first important shift in attitude concerning the nature of heroism in the modern drama takes place in *Faust*. When Goethe made Faust settle down to the practical activity of cultivating a strip of land for the purpose of establishing a prosperous (and generalized) society, he created an heroic type whose spiritual state and spiritual concern radically differ from those of Oedipus or Lear. Humanitarianism, no matter how well motivated and beneficent, is not the same thing as the kind of realization that makes Oedipus gouge out his eyes, or makes Lear's flawed heart "Burst smilingly, 'twixt two extremes of passion, joy and grief." As the late Theodore Spencer put it, "Humanitarian devotion is not in itself necessarily a spiritual act." For example, Dr. Stockman in Ibsen's *An Enemy of the People* is not a spiritual figure. Solness in *The Master Builder* is. The discovery Dr. Stockman makes is not of a new dimension inside himself but of an evil in the society outside him. 'Although Stockman fights that evil heroically, it is not a spiritual struggle.

Here we find it necessary to distinguish between moral and spiritual values. In our time, society has come to exert more and more pressure on us as individuals; as a result, we have come to think of society as an agent of Destiny. But when we identify society with Destiny, we feel that Destiny has diminished. Any mind capable of spiritual aspiration must find in the actions of the dramatic hero that which affirms the vitality of the free will in any given situation. Man's free will may be defeated by the forces of Destiny—in fact, the great plays have always testified that the destroying forces of Destiny are as much a part of the hero's character as his free will—it may be paralyzed and thus incapable of action, it may be submerged by the battle in such a way as to become part of that Destiny, it may even turn out to be an illusion; but it must always be an active force if we are to believe that we are partaking in human greatness. Such a Destiny must be greater than an aggregate of human beings or an expression of social patterns.

The playwright who has been influenced by a deterministic view of human nature is certain sooner or later to fail in distinguishing between the hero and the victim, Destiny and society. The consequence in the twentieth century has been a theatre of steadily diminishing stature. This is related to another aspect of psychology which has had even more profound effects on drama. The modern playwright cannot help but have absorbed a great deal that psychology has made known. He knows all about the relationship of infantile frustration and adult neuroses; he has learned about the psychosomatic aspects of illness; and above all he knows that all human actions—even the greatest and most selfless of them—spring from some deep and hidden but nonetheless selfish motivation. Doesn't he feel that there is a danger in passing a moral judgement on individuals? In fact, how can there be a moral pattern to human experience in such a world? For example: A man may commit a murder; but wait, we know that he saw something horrible in the barn when he was a child; we discover that he was brought up on the lower East Side without orange juice and cod-liver oil, and that his mother was a whore. How can we blame him for this murder that he was eventually driven to commit? Oh, yes, we can put him in jail or an asylum; we can even take his life. But this is because he is dangerous to society and does not necessarily involve moral condemnation. If, then, our moral judgements can be dissolved by psychological understanding, how can the dramatist pattern a tragedy or create characters with stature; finally, how can there be drama at all? If there is no possibility for an appraisal of personality as such, why should Hamlet's death be any more significant than that of Rosencrantz or Guildenstern?

The trouble with so much of the modern theatre—particularly in this country—is that the playwright has come to assume that if he explains his characters he has written a play. He has forgotten that a dramatic situation requires not that we should *understand* a character but simply that we should *believe* in him. Dramatic action always leads to a judgement; it requires that something shall happen to and through the characters; something that is embodied in the events of which the characters are a part. Whenever the personality of the character, rather than the action. of which the character should be a part, becomes the playwright's chief concern, the range of the theatre is drastically reduced if not unalterably damaged.

Now, obviously we can't return to the womb of some hypothetical pre-Freudian existence. It will be impossible for us ever again to view man without some degree of psychoanalytic prejudice; but the important issue is whether the theatre will be so dominated by psychology that it is blinded to those older and more valuable insights of a social, moral, and spiritual nature which have been the basis of theatre from the very beginning. The Theatre of the Absurd is revolting against the kind of theatre in which action is conceived in terms of psychological plausibility, a theatre in which actions are dissolved by psychological explanation or by those mists of fantasy which are at one with the spectator's moral evasions.

But more important than the *avant-garde's* concern with man's ontological solitude and its rebellion against psychology is its attitude toward language. Each of these playwrights is revolting against the tyranny of words in the modern theatre. As a result, their plays —at least until very recently—have no "'message"; the dialogue is not a monologue apportioned out to several characters; they are packed with symbols, but these symbols don't mean anything in particular and they suggest many things. Their characters lead their own lives, talk their own thoughts. Their speeches impinge on each other and glance away. There is none of the planted line and heavy-handed cross references we are so accustomed to. There doesn't seem to be any central theme, only many related ideas, to these dramatic St. Vitus' dances. But as the plays draw to a close—they don't end in any Aristotelian sense—each of these ideas is subtly recaptured and made to work for an over-all impact. Finally, and most important, in all of their plays there is an insisting demand that the gestures of pantomime are the theatre's most appropriate and valuable means of expression; the insistence that the mimetic gesture precedes the spoken word and that the gesture is the true expression of what we feel, while words only describe what we feel. In fact, these writers assert that in objectifying the feeling in order to describe it, words kill the very feeling they would describe.

It is no wonder, then, that these playwrights feel a great affinity to the mimes—Étienne Decroux, Marcel Marceau, and Jaques Tati; no wonder that they turn for inspiration to the early films of Charlie Chaplin, Buster Keaton, the Keystone Cops, Laurel and Hardy, and the Marx Brothers; no wonder, finally, that they are all under the influence of Jaques Copeau and Antonin Artaud. It is only with the recent translation into English of Artaud's book *The Theatre and Its Double* (the earlier and the more seminal work of Copeau has not yet been translated) that most of us have been able to discover what the aesthetic of this whole *avant-garde* theatre movement is.

Artaud's basic premise is that it is a mistake in the theatre to assume that "In the beginning was the word." And our theatre does make just that assumption. For most of us, critics as well as play-wrights, the word is everything; there is no possibility of expression without it; the theatre is thought of as a branch of literature, and even if we admit a difference between the text spoken on the stage and the text read by the eyes, we have still not managed to separate it from the idea of a *performed text*. Artaud and the playwrights who have followed him maintain that our modern psychologically oriented theatre denies the theatre's historical nature. For them, as Artaud put it, "the stage is a concrete physical place which must speak its own language—a language that goes deeper than spoken language, a language that speaks directly to our senses rather than primarily to the mind as is the case with the language of words."

This is the most significant thing about the *avant-garde* theatre— it is a theatre of gesture. "In the beginning was the Gesture!" Gesture is not a decorative addition that accompanies words; rather it is the source, cause, and director of language, and insofar as lan-guage is dramatic it is gestural. It is this insistence on restoring the gestural basis to theatre that has resulted in the renascence of panto-mime in such plays as *The Chairs, Waiting for Godot, Ping-Pong, Endgame, The Balcony,* and *Escurial.* But how different this panto-mime is from pantomime as most moderns conceive it! For most of us, pantomime is a series of gestures which represent words or sentences—a game of charades. But this is not the pantomime of history. For the great mimes, as Artaud points out, gestures repre-sent ideas, attitudes of mind, aspects of nature which are realized in an effective, concrete way, by constantly evoking objects or natural details in a manner much like the Oriental language which represents night by a tree on which the bird that has already closed one eye is beginning to close the other.

Now, up to a point this attitude is valid and certainly it is a much needed antidote to the worn-out and expressionless language and structure of most modern plays in the well-made-play tradition of naturalism. However, as is the case with most revolutionaries, the cause is just, but they go too far.

In the first place, for all the noise, the debates, the angry articles, the thumping of the "young Turks," there is nothing really very new in this. Ionesco's essays say nothing that Mallarmé didn't say in his long essay on the theatre seventy years ago. Artaud, the high priest of the Absurdists, says nothing in *The Theatre and Its Double* that Appia, Craig, and Copeau didn't say before him. It is all well and good to say that we should do away with stereotyped plots and concern ourselves with expressing emotional states, but Maeterlinck and the Symbolists were doing this at the turn of the century—and where did Mityl and Tityl get the theatre? It is grand to say that the theatre has a language prior to words, and so Beckett and Ionesco write (is "write" the correct word?) *Acts Without Words;* but how different is this from Jacques Bernard's "Theatre of Silence" of the twenties?

More important—and we tend to forget this—is the fact that it was the desire for more expressive language that caused realistic dialogue to be introduced into the theatre in the first place. Ibsen, Strindberg, and Chekhov didn't write the way they did because they had theories about language; they wrote realistic dialogue partly in reaction to the hollow rhetoric of the romantic play, but chiefly because they had created characters who could best express themselves with this kind of speech.

The Absurdists, in turn, are reacting against the arid language of naturalism. They insist, although I am not sure what they mean by the distinction, that the real content of a play lies in the action and not in the words. As a result, in some of their plays—Beckett's *Act Without Words,* and Ionesco's *The New Tenant*—they have discarded language altogether. However, the answer to the problem doesn't lie in the defiant rejection of language, but rather in the revitalization of it. The big question, then, is how to make the language of the theatre once again dramatic.

The most valuable service the Absurdists have rendered the modern theatre may well be their demand that the language of the theatre be gestural in nature. By insisting that language be gestural, that it be considered as something more than a means of conducting human characters to their external ends, they have forced our playwrights to see beyond the simple distinction that language is made of words and gesture is made of motion, to the reverse distinction: "Words are made of motion, made of action or response; and gesture is made of language—made of the language beneath or beyond or alongside of the language of words." We are becoming aware once again, as R. P. Blackmur has pointed out, that "when the language of words succeeds it *becomes* gesture in its words." It is this quality that must be carried into language whenever the context is imaginative or dramatic. This quality alone makes the language of the stage appear as necessity, as a result of a series of compressions, collisions, scenic frictions, and evolutions. Such language "creates meaning as conscience creates judgment, by feeling the pang, the inner bite, of things forced together," and this is the conflict we call dramatic, the conflict most at home in the theatre.

Now, the basic dramatic gesture of poetry is the metaphor. A metaphor is a *"connector,"* and it links two antagonistic or disparate worlds by finding some similarity between the two which permits the soaring of the poet's imagination toward a clearly conceived picture image. A metaphor then implies an imaginative perception on the part of the poet of similarity, or a common power, which exists between two dissimilar worlds. Furthermore, when a given metaphor is repeated often enough, symbolic image patterns are created, and these metaphoric configurations are used by the playwright to express the meaning of the dramatic action.

This is the kind of "connection" that I think we are going to have to rediscover if we are ever going to "fix" the theatre. But this won't be easy; for apart from the tendency toward artificiality, which characterizes so much of our so-called "poetic drama," there are two other obstacles to overcome. The first is the effect that the movies and TV have had on our audiences. We must face the fact that these two mass media have stepped in between the theatre and the popular imagination. They have seized upon the daydreams of wealth, love, physical beauty, luxury, and adventure that haunt the emotionally starved and financially pinched millions of our civilization. The movies and television, while they appease these longings, at the same time create a whole mythology for them. And this world of fantasy cannot but influence the playwright, since it forms a part of the world picture which confronts the modern sensibility, and since it contributes to the patterns of speech and the reservoir of visual imagination from which the writer draws his metaphors and images. But more important than this is the audience's loss of *imaginative power*, its inclination not so much to share in a dramatic experience as to have it served up as diversion. The consequence of this dulling effect is that more and more of our audiences find it difficult to comprehend anything but the most colloquial and explicit dialogue. They tend to reject anything that demands an active effort or response. One reason for this, I suppose, is that the language of visual images is easier to assimilate but more equivocal than that of words. It allows for the blurring of emotion and situation which is so characteristic of modern plays. We are led up to some psychological climax and then the situation is left inarticulate. We are given some cliché of gesture, a shrug, and a fadeout as a substitute for an artistic solution. One is reminded of *Tea and Sympathy, Dark at the Top of the Stairs, Two for the Seesaw,* and *Look Homeward Angel.*

This leads to the second obstacle: the firmly entrenched convention of inarticulateness in our theatre. The rebels of naturalism were right in rejecting the romantic verse drama with its purple passages, soliloquies, and asides for "real" dramatic speech. But the convention of colloquial speech may be as restricting as any other. The drama is so much more confined in time and space than the novel that it must live by finding short cuts to the imagination. If speech is limited to the flat level of "natural" conversation, the dramatist will find it hard to penetrate any distance below the surface of character and situation, and harder still to "place" his play in relation to the wider universe of thought and experience, which lies behind its physical setting. Finally, the reticence, inarticulateness, and homely idiom of our theatre is no longer a healthy reaction but a lazy abdication, an inarticulateness which is not dramatically significant but is the inarticulateness of characters who have nothing to say.

If we are to "fix" the theatre, we must make the case of articulateness and imagination, for it will be done only by the dramatist who uses metaphor and imagery, whether in verse or prose, to achieve intensity and depth of meaning. We must have plays that are essentially true to human nature, but don't attempt to convince the audience that they are watching a piece of real life. People do not rage in the phrases of Lear or make love in the words of Romeo, though they may wish they could. Dramatic poetry or real dramatic prose is not lifelike; it is larger than life, it employs all the resources of language to illuminate the short hour of experience in which the dramatist has caught his figures and which may bring to a climax the events of a lifetime. In language what the dramatist seeks above all is concentration. Imagery and metaphor, by appealing to our memory or our senses, by relating the concrete to the abstract, are the most highly charged forms of language he can use. And more important, they enable the dramatist to solve the most difficult of his problems: those revelations of the inner life of his characters which may not relate directly to the action of the plot, but are nonetheless significant parts of the play.

It is for this reason that our playwrights need to realize again the basis of their art—the living word. Of all language, that which I've called imaginative is the fullest and most intense, and unless the theatre relates itself to the most vital expression of the modern sensibility it will become as it too often has—superficial. As I have said, such language is not necessarily lifelike, yet it offers the richest and most fully *articulate* expression of human experience; it is the only language which can give the full expression to that balance of human faculties which characterizes the art of the theatre.

In their use of language the Absurdists would deny this, and it is very possible that the theatre they would revive will turn out to be stillborn. I am sure they would counter this by saying that what they write is in accordance with the "facts of life." If the dialogue in their plays consists of meaningless clichés and stereotyped phrases, they would insist that this is the way we talk. If their characters are constantly changing their personalities, these playwrights would point out that no one today is really consistent or truly integrated. If the people in their plays seem to be helpless puppets without any will of their own, the Absurdists would argue that we are all passively at the mercy of blind fate and meaningless circumstance; that their theatre is the true theatre of our time. If that is the case, then: *Hail to the Ultra-Naturalists!*

But if it is true—and I believe it is—that man is a creature of his language, that by his use of it he defines himself, then ours is a civilization that has lost its nerve. It has lost its trust in the possibility of words to communicate meaningfully. I am sure the Absurdists would agree with this, and their plays are persuasive documents of the fact. Whenever an age loses its nerve, more and more it reduces its language to the verb, that verbal expression which denotes action in its simplest and most concrete form. On the other hand, a more confident age uses nouns and adjectives—those verbal forms which express the quality of action. This is the irony and the danger of the *avant-garde* theatre. They would "fix" our theatre by "connecting" it with the vital theatre of former ages; but they forget that the source of vitality of this enduring form of theatre is in that language which they would deny.

By all means let's revitalize the theatre and its language. But we must never forget that the theatre in its most embracing form begins with the play, and if you eliminate the spoken language, the play will not exist. It can be admitted that words are limited in what they can express, but they are finally all we've got. Yes, the language of our stage has become stagnant, but the answer is not to throw it out, but rather—and this I believe is the obligation of all writers —to revitalize language so it can more fully express man's feeling. Only an increased trust in the possibility of words to communicate meaningfully will bring about the renaissance of our theatre.

The Theatre of the Absurd has done us a great service by experimenting with nonverbal techniques. In this it has broken down many of Naturalism's restrictions and in so doing has opened up the theatre. But the final irony is appropriately directed to the playwrights themselves. They are seeking ways to link the contemporary theatre with the traditional theatre, and the traditional theatre is first and foremost a celebration of life, that life which the Absurdists would deny.

The real answer to the despair of the Absurdists, and this is the affirmation of our theatre, is that our playwrights—and I include Beckett, Ionesco, and Adamov—still find human action significant, still find it necessary to *write* plays, and in the very writing attest to the miracle of life that their philosophy would deny. As Yeats put it: "The fiddles are tuning all over the world." For those of us who cannot make such a commitment, these "fiddlers" urge us— and it is important that they do—to maintain as best we can that courtesy of the spirit which accepts the absence of spiritual consolations without complaint and is content to wait in stillness.